www.wadsworth.com

wadsworth.com is the World Wide Web site for Wadsworth and is your direct source to dozens of online resources.

At *wadsworth.com* you can find out about supplements, demonstration software, and student resources. You can also send e-mail to many of our authors and preview new publications and exciting new technologies.

wadsworth.com
Changing the way the world learns®

FROM THE WADSWORTH SERIES IN SPEECH COMMUNICATION

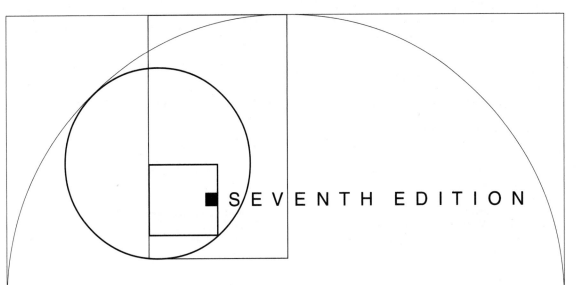

SEVENTH EDITION

THEORIES OF HUMAN COMMUNICATION

Stephen W. Littlejohn

Albuquerque, New Mexico

WADSWORTH

™

THOMSON LEARNING

Australia • Canada • Mexico • Singapore • Spain • United Kingdom • United States

WADSWORTH

★

TM

THOMSON LEARNING

Executive Editor: *Deirdre Cavanaugh*
Assistant Editor: *Nicole George*
Editorial Assistant: *Mele Alusa*
Publisher: *Clark Baxter*
Executive Marketing Manager: *Stacey Purviance*
Project Manager, Editorial Production: *Cathy Linberg*
Print Buyer: *Karen Hunt*
Permissions Editor: *Stephanie Keough-Hedges*
Text Designer: *John Edeen*

Production Service/Compositor: *Anne Draus,*
   Scratchgravel Publishing Services
Copyeditor: *Jennifer Gordon*
Cover Designer: *John Walker*
Cover Image: *Laszlo Moholy-Nagy, "AXXI" © 2001 Artists*
   Rights Society (ARS), New York/VG Bild-Kunst, Bonn.
   Photo © Erich Lessing/Art Resource, NY
Printer: *R. R. Donnelley & Sons, Crawfordsville*

Printed in the United States of America
1   2   3   4   5   6   7   05   04   03   02   01

For permission to use material from this text,
contact us by

Web: http://www.thomsonrights.com
Fax: 1-800-730-2215
Phone: 1-800-730-2214

Wadsworth/Thomson Learning
10 Davis Drive
Belmont, CA 94002-3098
USA

For more information about our products, contact us:
Thomson Learning Academic Resource Center
1-800-423-0563
http://www.wadsworth.com

International Headquarters
Thomson Learning
International Division
290 Harbor Drive, 2nd Floor
Stamford, CT 06902-7477
USA

UK/Europe/Middle East/South Africa
Thomson Learning
Berkshire House
168-173 High Holborn
London WC1V 7AA
United Kingdom

Asia
Thomson Learning
60 Albert Street, #15-01
Albert Complex
Singapore 189969

Canada
Nelson Thomson Learning
1120 Birchmount Road
Toronto, Ontario M1K 5G4
Canada

Library of Congress Cataloging-in-Publication Data

Littlejohn, Stephen W.
   Theories of human communication / Stephen W.
Littlejohn. — 7th ed.
      p.   cm. — (Wadsworth series in speech
communication)
   Includes bibliographical references and index.
   ISBN 0-534-54957-8 (alk. paper)
   1. Communication—Philosophy.   I. Title.   II. Series.
P90 .L48   2001
302.2'01—dc21

                          2001026658

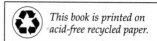

*This book is printed on
acid-free recycled paper.*

BRIEF CONTENTS

DETAILED CONTENTS

P A R T   I I I   CONTEXTUAL THEMES   233

PREFACE

Over the years I have received many comments from professors and students about this book, and I am gratified they continue to appreciate its contribution. I have tried to include in each edition what professors most appreciate—a broad survey of theories that provides a realistic sense of the complexity of our field. I have also tried to maintain what students like—a well-written exposition of theories that is hard to gain from primary sources.

It has been interesting to follow student reactions to this book. I have found repeatedly that students with some background in communication, especially sophisticated upper division and graduate students, appreciate the clarity of the book. Yet students with less academic experience and less background in the field find the same prose difficult. Over the several editions of this book, I have continued to edit the writing to make it as clear and accessible as possible, and I still add new examples in every edition. Yet, without sufficient interest, background, and aptitude, students cannot appreciate and understand theory at this level. I feel that what really matters—the same thing that leads students on to advanced study in communication—is a more-than-superficial interest in the field itself. Once a student becomes fascinated with ideas, and specifically with concepts in communication, he or she will be motivated to press on and will find advanced textbooks both meaningful and interesting. These students are the ones who will develop the background necessary to understand more complex ideas and appreciate the groundwork that books such as this one can provide to their ongoing pursuit. In fact, I have been repeatedly honored by new professors in the field, including many of my own colleagues, who have told me that they found my book helpful in their own studies when they were in school.

Since the second edition, Wadsworth Publishing has been willing to support my desire to serve these more sophisticated students, and the seventh edition maintains this high standard of coverage. It is not written for the introductory student. Although I could have written the text "down" to a more basic level, there is still a need for a good, comprehensive communication theory text at the upper-division and graduate levels. *Theories of Human Communication* continues to provide the kind of material necessary for a student to complete a well-formed undergraduate major and even continue in graduate school.

Eleven reviewers provided assistance in this revision. This group was one of the most constructive and helpful corps of reviewers with whom I have worked. I carefully considered their recommendations and adopted many. The reviewers were especially helpful in suggesting new sources and fresh material. Because I myself am a generalist, I have always had to rely on the intelligence and knowledge of specialists in various aspects of the field, both in their published literature and in manuscript reviews. I want to thank the reviewers for this edition for their very helpful, kind, and constructive criticism and suggestions. These individuals include Walid Afifi, Pennsylvania State University; Dale Brashers, University of Illinois; Bart Collins, University of Louisville; John A. Courtright, University of Delaware; Robert T. Craig, University of Colorado–Boulder; John Greene, Purdue University; Martha J. Haun, University of Houston; Sheena Malhotra, Regis University; Daniel P. Modaff, Ohio University; and Steven R. Wilson, Purdue University.

I also want to thank my research assistant, Yoshitaki Miike, for a six-month labor that allowed me to concentrate on analysis, organization, and composition. Yoshi also brought to my attention several works on Eastern communication theory that allowed me to broaden the context in which the focal Western tradition of this book might be understood.

Stephen W. Littlejohn

An Invaluable Aid to Your Study of Communication Theories

The author has prepared a student guide entitled *Learning and Using Communication Theories.* This insightful guide helps you achieve a better understanding of theory and its application. Designed to be enjoyable, engaging, and helpful, the guide includes chapter maps, word games, Internet challenges, right-brain exercises, action projects, cases, and critical incidents.

THEORIES
OF HUMAN
COMMUNICATION

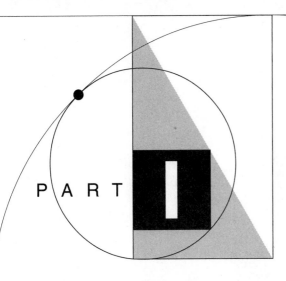

THE NATURE OF INQUIRY AND THEORY

CHAPTER 1

COMMUNICATION THEORY AND SCHOLARSHIP

As long as people have wondered about the world, they have been intrigued by the mysteries of human nature. The most commonplace activities of our lives—the things we take for granted—become great puzzles when we try to understand them. Communication is intertwined with all of human life, and any study of human life must touch on this subject. Some scholars treat communication as central while others see it as more peripheral, but it is always there.

In this book, we treat communication as central to human life. Our guiding question is how scholars from various traditions have described and explained this universal human experience. Although this book does not complete the puzzle of communication, it does show how many of the pieces have been shaped and joined.

WHAT IS COMMUNICATION THEORY?

Any attempt to explain or represent an experience is a theory, an idea of how something happens. Everybody uses theories; we cannot live without them. Our theories guide our understandings and actions. They identify patterns of events so we know what to expect. They draw our attention to important aspects of everyday life. They help us decide what is important and what is not. And they enable us to predict what will happen next.

Although the word *theory* can be used to describe the educated guesswork of ordinary people living their everyday lives, a scholar uses the term more precisely. A scholar's work involves studying a particular kind of experience with a keen eye. As you will see in the next chapter, theory building is not an easy task but requires a great deal of focused observation, hypothesizing, and revision.

The term *communication theory* can refer to a single theory, or it can be used to designate the collective wisdom found in the entire body of theories related to communication. Much disagreement exists about what constitutes an adequate theory of communication. This textbook presents a wide variety of theories, so as you read through the book, make your own judgments about which theories are most helpful and think about why they are helpful.

WHY STUDY COMMUNICATION THEORY?

Communication is one of the most pervasive, important, and complex aspects of human life. Our daily lives are strongly affected by our own communication with others as well as by messages from people we don't even know, people both living and dead, and communicators from near and far. Because communication is so vital to our lives, surely it deserves our careful attention.

Teachers sometimes provide students with a set of recipes for improving communication, but the communication process is too complicated to be approached in this way. Formulas may be useful in particular situations, but they inevitably fail as circumstances become complex. Theories are crucial because they permit us to make our way through what may be a rather difficult thicket.

Everybody tries to make sense of their own experience. We assign meaning to what is going on, both inside us and around us. Sometimes the meaning is shared, and sometimes it is not. Sometimes it is clear and other times vague or contradictory. By developing an understanding

of a variety of theories of communication, we interpret events in more flexible, useful, and discriminating ways.[1]

A colleague of mine used to say that the study of communication theory will help students see things they never saw before. One writer put it this way: "The paradigm observer is not the man who sees and reports what all normal observers see and report, but the man who sees in familiar objects what no one else has seen before."[2] This widening of perception, or unhitching of blinders, helps us transcend habits and become increasingly adaptable and flexible. To borrow some analogies from philosopher Thomas Kuhn, "Looking at a contour map, the student sees lines on paper, the cartographer a picture of a terrain. Looking at a bubble-chamber photograph, the student sees confused and broken lines, the physicist a record of familiar subnuclear events."[3] Theories, then, provide a set of useful tools for seeing new and useful things.

THE ACADEMIC STUDY OF COMMUNICATION

Although communication has been studied since antiquity,[4] it became an especially important topic in the twentieth century. One author describes this development as a "revolutionary discovery," largely caused by the rise of communication technologies such as radio, television, telephone, satellites, and computer networking, along with industrialization, big business, and

---

1   For the importance of the study of diverse theories, see Robert T. Craig, "Communication Theory as a Field," *Communication Theory* 9 (1999):119–161.
2   N. R. Hanson, *Patterns of Discovery* (Cambridge: Cambridge University Press, 1961), p. 30.
3   Thomas S. Kuhn, *The Structure of Scientific Revolutions* (Chicago: University of Chicago Press, 1970), p. 111.
4   See, for example, John Stewart, *Language as Articulate Contact* (Albany: SUNY Press, 1995), pp. 33–101; W. Barnett Pearce and Karen A. Foss, "The Historical Context of Communication as a Science," in *Human Communication: Theory and Research*, eds. G. L. Dahnke and G. W. Clatterbuck (Belmont, CA: Wadsworth, 1990), pp. 1–20; Nancy Harper, *Human Communication Theory: The History of a Paradigm* (Rochelle Park, NJ: Hayden, 1979).

global politics.[5] Clearly, communication has assumed immense importance in our time.

Intense interest in the academic study of communication began after World War I, as advances in technology and literacy made communication a topic of concern.[6] The subject was further promoted by the popular twentieth-century philosophies of progressivism and pragmatism, which stimulated a desire to improve society through widespread social change.

Several developments led to this interest in communication. The political influence of public messages spurred considerable research on propaganda and public opinion. In the early part of this century, researchers began attitude and opinion studies to try to discover the extent to which public opinion could be influenced by the media.

During this same period, the social sciences were developing, and sociology and social psychology emerged as leaders in the study of communication. Much of the research in sociology in the 1930s investigated the ways in which communication affects individuals and communities. Popular research topics in social psychology included the effects of movies on children, propaganda and persuasion, and group dynamics.

Another research tradition in the early part of the century dealt with education. Some areas of special emphasis were the use of radio in education, the teaching of basic communication skills like public speaking and group discussion, and the effects of various kinds of communication in the classroom.

The first half of the twentieth century was also dominated by commercial interests such as advertising. Much of the early research, even in universities, was driven by the desire of people in business to know more about communication for marketing purposes.

After World War II, the social sciences became fully recognized as legitimate disciplines, and the interest in psychological and social processes became intense. Persuasion and decision making in groups were central concerns, not only among researchers but in society in general. After World War II, then, communication studies became quite important.

The approaches to the study of communication, however, took different turns in Europe and the United States.[7] In the United States, researchers tended to study communication quantitatively to try to achieve objectivity. Although the researchers were never in complete agreement on this objective ideal, quantitative methods were the standard for many years. European investigations, on the other hand, were influenced more by historical, cultural, and critical interests and were largely shaped by Marxism. Over the years, tension has grown between these two traditions, although considerable influence has flowed both ways as scientific procedures have developed a toehold in Europe and critical perspectives have been taken seriously in North America.

The study of communication as we understand it in the United States and in Europe is thoroughly Western. Virtually all the theories discussed in this book come from the Western academic tradition. Eastern ways of thinking, however, can also contribute to our understanding of communication. In a valuable and interesting treatment, Lawrence Kincaid contrasts a variety of Western and Eastern perspectives on communication theory.[8]

5   W. Barnett Pearce, *Communication and the Human Condition* (Carbondale: Southern Illinois University Press, 1989).
6   This brief history is based on Jesse G. Delia, "Communication Research: A History," in *Handbook of Communication Science*, eds. C. R. Berger and S. H. Chaffee (Newbury Park, CA: Sage, 1987), pp. 20–98. See also Donald G. Ellis, *Crafting Society: Ethnicity, Class, and Communication Theory* (Mahwah, NJ: Erlbaum, 1999), pp. 16–19; Gustav W. Friedrich and Don M. Boileau, "The Communication Discipline," in *Teaching Communication*, eds. Anita L. Vangelisti, John A. Daly and Gustav Friedrich (Mahwah, NJ: Erlbaum, 1999), pp. 3–13; John Durham Peters, ed., "Tangled Legacies," *Journal of Communication* 46 (1996): 85–147; and Everett M. Rogers, *A History of Communication Study: A Biographical Approach* (New York: Free Press, 1994).
7   This distinction is made by Robert Fortner, "Mediated Communication Theory," in *Building Communication Theories: A Socio/Cultural Approach*, ed. Fred L. Casmir (Hillsdale, NJ: Erlbaum, 1994), pp. 209–240.
8   D. Lawrence Kincaid, *Communication Theory: Eastern and Western Perspectives* (San Diego: Academic, 1987). See also Peter R. Monge, "Communication Theory for a Globalizing World," in *Communication: Views from the Helm for the 21st Century*, ed. Judith S. Trent (Boston: Allyn & Bacon, 1998), pp. 3–7; Wimal Dissanayake, *Communication Theory: The Asian Perspective* (Singapore: Asian Mass Communication Research and Information Center, 1988); Wimal Dissanayake, "The Need for the Study of Asian Approaches to Communication," *Media Asia* 13 (1986): 6–13.

Kincaid notes a number of differences between Asian and Western perspectives.[9] For one, Eastern theories tend to focus on wholeness and unity, whereas Western perspectives are preoccupied with measuring parts and do not integrate these parts into a unified process.

Second, much Western theory is dominated by a vision of individualism. People are considered to be active in achieving personal aims. Most Eastern theories, on the other hand, view communication outcomes as unplanned and natural consequences of events. Even the many Western theories that share the Asian preoccupation with unintended events tend to be individualistic and highly cognitive, whereas most Eastern traditions stress emotional and spiritual convergence as communication outcomes.

A third difference deals with language and thought. Most Western theories are dominated by language. In the East, verbal symbols, especially speech, are downplayed and viewed with skepticism. Western-style thinking is also mistrusted in the Eastern tradition. What counts in many Asian philosophies is intuitive insight gained from direct experience. Such insight can be acquired by not intervening in natural events, which explains why silence is so important in Eastern communication.

Finally, relationships are conceptualized differently in the two traditions. In Western thought, relationships exist between two or more individuals. In many Eastern traditions, relationships are more complicated, evolving out of differences in the social positions of role, status, and power.

Many universities and colleges now have departments of communication, speech communication, or mass communication, but the subject remains largely eclectic and multidisciplinary. The diversity of work in communication theory reflects the complexity of communication itself. Looking for the best theory of communication is not particularly useful because communication is more than one activity.

Each theory looks at the process from a different angle, and each provides insights of its own. Of course, not all theories are equally valid or

useful, and an investigator will find particular theories more useful than others for certain kinds of work. We should therefore welcome rather than avoid a multitheoretical orientation.[10]

Still, the tendency to view communication from the narrow confines of specific academic disciplines is strong. Because fields are somewhat arbitrary, traditional disciplines do not necessarily provide the best method of packaging knowledge. Interdisciplinary cooperation is essential for a useful understanding of this subject.[11] University courses related to communication are found in many departments, just as the theories described in this book represent a wide range of fields. As Dean Barnlund observes, "While many disciplines have undoubtedly benefited from adopting a communication model, it is equally true that they, in turn, have added greatly to our understanding of human interaction."[12] Remember that when people tell you they are communication experts, they are saying little. Their primary interests may be in the sciences or the arts, mathematics or literature, biology or politics.[13]

Researchers in most fields consider communication as a secondary process. For example, psychologists study individual behavior and view communication as a particular kind of behavior. Sociologists focus on society and social process,

9   Kincaid, *Communication Theory*, pp. 331–353.
10   For an excellent case in favor of multiple approaches to communication, see John Waite Bowers and James J. Bradac, "Issues in Communication Theory: A Metatheoretical Analysis," in *Communication Yearbook 5*, ed. M. Burgoon (New Brunswick, NJ: Transaction, 1982), pp. 1–28.
11   For an exploration of the value of treating communication as an interdisciplinary study, see Thomas Streeter, "Introduction: For the Study of Communication and Against the Discipline of Communication," *Communication Theory* 5 (1995): 117–129; and David Sholle, "Resisting Disciplines: Repositioning Media Studies in the University," *Communication Theory* 5 (1995): 130–143.
12   Dean Barnlund, *Interpersonal Communication: Survey and Studies* (New York: Houghton Mifflin, 1968), p. v.
13   The multidisciplinary nature of the study of communication is examined by Craig, "Communication Theory as a Field"; see also Stephen W. Littlejohn, "An Overview of the Contributions to Human Communication Theory from Other Disciplines," in *Human Communication Theory: Comparative Essays*, ed. F. E. X. Dance (New York: Harper & Row, 1982), pp. 243–285; and W. Barnett Pearce, "Scientific Research Methods in Communication Studies and Their Implications for Theory and Research," in *Speech Communication in the 20th Century*, ed. T. W. Benson (Carbondale: Southern Illinois University Press, 1985), pp. 255–281.

seeing communication as one of many social factors. Anthropologists are interested primarily in culture, and if they investigate communication, they treat it as an aspect of a broader theme. Do we conclude that communication is less significant than behavior, society, and culture? No, we do not.

In recent years many scholars have recognized that communication is central to all human experience and have emphasized it above other topics. Some of these scholars were trained in traditional disciplines, and others studied in academic departments of communication, speech communication, or mass communication. Regardless of their original academic homes, however, these scholars have formed the new field called communication.[14] This field is characterized by its focus on communication as the central topic and by its attention to the entire breadth of communication concerns. The work of such organizations as the International Communication Association and the National Communication Association, along with numerous journals devoted to the topic, typify what is happening in the field. Indeed, the young communication field is now producing fresh theories, many of which are covered in this textbook.

DEFINING COMMUNICATION

Communication is difficult to define.[15] Theodore Clevenger has noted that "the continuing problem in defining communication for scholarly or scientific purposes stems from the fact that the verb 'to communicate' is well established in the common lexicon and therefore is not easily captured for scientific use. Indeed, it is one of the most overworked terms in the English language."[16] Scholars have made many attempts to define communication but establishing a single definition has proved impossible and may not be very fruitful.

Frank Dance took a major step toward clarifying this muddy concept by outlining a number of elements used to distinguish communica-

tion.[17] He found three points of "critical conceptual differentiation" that form the basic dimensions of communication. The first dimension is *level of observation*, or abstractness. Some definitions are broad and inclusive; others are restrictive. For example, the definition of communication as "the process that links discontinuous parts of the living world to one another" is general.[18] On the other hand, communication as "the means of sending military messages, orders, etc., as by telephone, telegraph, radio, couriers," is restrictive.[19]

The second distinction is *intentionality.* Some definitions include only purposeful message sending and receiving; others do not impose this limitation. The following is an example of a definition that includes intention: "Those situations in which a source transmits a message to a receiver with conscious intent to affect the latter's behaviors."[20] Here is a definition that does not require intent: "It is a process that makes common to two or several what was the monopoly of one or some."[21]

The third dimension is normative *judgment.* Some definitions include a statement of success or accuracy; other definitions do not contain such implicit judgments. The following definition, for example, presumes that communication is successful: "Communication is the verbal in-

14   For a recent discussion of the status of the communication field, see Tony Atwater, "Communication Theory and Research: The Quest for Credibility in the Social Sciences," in *An Integrated Approach to Communication Theory,* eds. M. B. Salwen and D. W. Stacks (Mahwah, NJ: Erlbaum, 1996), pp. 539–549; and Stanley A. Deetz, "Future of the Discipline: The Challenges, the Research, and the Social Contribution," in *Communication Yearbook 17,* ed. S. A. Deetz (Thousand Oaks, CA: Sage, 1994), pp. 565–600.
15   There are 126 definitions of communication listed in Frank E. X. Dance and Carl E. Larson, *The Functions of Human Communication: A Theoretical Approach* (New York: Holt, Rinehart & Winston, 1976), Appendix A.
16   Theodore Clevenger, Jr., "Can One Not Communicate? A Conflict of Models," *Communication Studies* 42 (1991): 351.
17   Frank E. X. Dance, "The 'Concept' of Communication," *Journal of Communication* 20 (1970): 201–210.
18   Jurgen Ruesch, "Technology and Social Communication," in *Communication Theory and Research,* ed. L. Thayer (Springfield, IL: Thomas, 1957), p. 462.
19   *The American College Dictionary* (New York: Random House, 1964), p. 244.
20   Gerald R. Miller, "On Defining Communication: Another Stab," *Journal of Communication* 16 (1966): 92.
21   Alex Gode, "What Is Communication?" *Journal of Communication* 9 (1959): 5.

RECEIVER BEHAVIOR	SOURCE BEHAVIOR		
	Unintentional Behavior (Symptoms)	**Intentional Behavior**	
		Nonverbal	**Verbal**
Not Received	1A Nonperceived symptomatic behavior	2A Nonperceived nonverbal messages	3A Nonperceived verbal messages
Received Incidentally	1B Incidentally perceived symptoms	2B Incidental nonverbal messages	3B Incidental verbal messages
Attended To	1C Symptoms attended to	2C Nonverbal messages attended to	3C Verbal messages attended to

FIGURE **1.1**

Communication-Related Behaviors

terchange of a thought or idea."[22] The assumption in this definition is that a thought or idea is successfully exchanged. Another definition, on the other hand, does not judge whether the outcome is successful or not: "Communication [is] the transmission of information."[23] Here information is *transmitted*, but it is not necessarily *received* or understood.

Debates on the definition of communication are perennial. Figure 1.1 shows nine behaviors that might be considered to be communication.[24] These nine behaviors hinge on how two questions are answered: (1) Must communication be intentional? (2) Must communication be received? The columns in the figure consist of intentional and unintentional behaviors, and the rows indicate whether the source behaviors were received.

In Figure 1.1, the first column is source behaviors that are unintentional. These are "symptom-

atic" because they could be read as a sign of some state in the communicator such as fatigue, nervousness, or anger. The second column denotes nonverbal behaviors that are intentionally sent to another person, such as waving to a friend or shrugging if you don't know the answer to a

22 John B. Hoben, "English Communication at Colgate Reexamined," *Journal of Communication* 4 (1954): 77.
23 Bernard Berelson and Gary Steiner, *Human Behavior* (New York: Harcourt, Brace, and World, 1964), p. 254.
24 Michael T. Motley, "On Whether One Cannot (Not) Communicate: An Examination Via Traditional Communication Postulates," *Western Journal of Speech Communication* 54 (1990): 1–20; Janet Beavin Bavelas, "Behaving and Communicating: A Reply to Motley," *Western Journal of Speech Communication* 54 (1990): 593–602; Wayne A. Beach, "On (Not) Observing Behavior Interactionally," *Western Journal of Speech Communication* 54 (1990): 613–623; Peter A. Andersen, "When One Cannot Not Communicate: A Challenge to Motley's Traditional Communication Postulates," *Communication Studies* 42 (1991): 309–325; Michael T. Motley, "How One May Not Communicate: A Reply to Andersen," *Communication Studies* 42 (1991): 326–339; Clevenger, "Can One Not Communicate?"

question. The third column includes intentional verbal, or language-oriented, acts, such as writing a letter, having a conversation, or giving a speech.

The three rows in Figure 1.1 represent whether the message is received. The first row is "not received," meaning that no one observes the source's actions or hears the message. How many times have you yawned or maybe even said, "I'm tired," but no one was there to see or hear it? The second consists of incidental reception, in which someone sees something, but it does not register consciously. You might say to a friend, "I'm tired," and your friend would realize that you had looked tired, though she had not paid attention to it at the time. The third row is paying conscious attention to the source's behaviors.

Now we have nine things that might possibly be considered communication:

1A. Nonperceived symptomatic behavior— you yawn, but no one sees it. (Most people agree that this is not communication. At least it is not *interpersonal* communication, but some might call it *intrapersonal* communication.)

1B. Incidentally perceived symptoms—you yawn, and your friend later realizes that you were tired even though she didn't pay any attention to it at the time.

1C. Symptoms attended to—you yawn, and your friend says, "Am I that boring?"

2A. Nonperceived nonverbal messages—you wave at a friend, but he doesn't see you.

2B. Incidental nonverbal messages—your friend later says, "I'm sorry I didn't wave back, but I was thinking about something else and didn't realize you had waved to me until after I turned the corner."

2C. Nonverbal messages attended to—you wave to a friend, and she waves back.

3A. Nonperceived verbal messages—you send a letter to a friend, but it gets lost in the mail.

3B. Incidental verbal messages—you lecture your daughter for having a messy room, and although she knows you are talking to her, she really isn't paying much attention.

3C. Verbal messages attended to—you give a speech to a group that is eager to hear what you have to say.

Which of the above acts are communication and which are not? At least three defensible positions can be taken. The first, espoused by Michael Motley, is that communication should be limited to messages that are intentionally directed at other persons and received by them.[25] Of the nine types of behavior, Motley would limit communication to those cells outlined in Figure 1.2(a). The second position, promoted by Peter Andersen, is that communication should include any behaviors that are meaningful to receivers in any way, whether intended or not.[26] These would include the cells outlined in Figure 1.2(b). Finally, Clevenger agrees with Motley that only intentionally sent messages that are received should count as communication but that intentionality is hard to determine. He suggests that communication behavior should include both intentional sending and receiving, which would include even more cells, as outlined in Figure 1.2(c).[27]

You can see that these three authors—and this is true of virtually all communication scholars— agree that intentional acts that are received do count as communication, but they disagree on what else might be considered communication.

These definitional issues are important, as Andersen reminds us: "While there is not a right or wrong perspective, choices regarding [definitions] are not trivial. These perspectives launch scholars down different theoretical trajectories, predispose them to ask distinct questions, and set them up to conduct different kinds of communication studies."[28] Different definitions have different functions and enable the theorist to do different things. A definition should be evaluated on the basis of how well it helps a scholar to accomplish the purposes of an investigation. Different

---

25 Motley, "On Whether One Cannot (Not) Communicate"; "Communication as Interaction"; "How One May Not Communicate."
26 Andersen, "When One Cannot Not Communicate."
27 Clevenger, "Can One Not Communicate?"
28 Andersen, "When One Cannot Not Communicate," p. 309.

1A	2A	3A
1B	2B	3B
1C	2C	3C

(a) The sender–receiver model

1A	2A	3A
1B	2B	3B
1C	2C	3C

(b) The receiver model

1A	2A	3A
1B	2B	3B
1C	2C	3C

(c) The communication behavior model

FIGURE **1.2**

What Is Communication and What Is Not?

sorts of investigations often require separate, even contradictory, definitions of communication. Definitions, then, are tools that should be used flexibly. In this book we will look at theories that define communication in a variety of ways.

Dance's conclusion is relevant: "We are trying to make the concept of 'communication' do too much work for us."[29] He calls for a family of concepts; collectively, the theories included in the following chapters specify some of the members of this family.

◖ THE PROCESS OF INQUIRY IN COMMUNICATION

Inquiry is the systematic study of experience that leads to understanding and knowledge. People engage in inquiry when they attempt to find out about something in an orderly way. It is not just one process, of course. Many modes can be used, but all are distinguished from common experience.

A Basic Model of Inquiry

All inquiry involves three stages.[30] The first is asking questions. Gerald Miller and Henry Nicholson believe that inquiry is "nothing more . . . than the process of asking interesting, significant questions . . . and providing disciplined, systematic answers to them."[31] Questions of *definition* call for concepts as answers, seeking to clarify what is observed or inferred: What is it? What will we call it? Questions of *fact* ask about properties and relations in what is observed: What does it consist of? How does it relate to other things? Questions of *value* probe aesthetic, pragmatic, and ethical qualities of the observed: Is it beautiful? Is it effective? Is it good?

The second stage of inquiry is *observation.* Here, the scholar looks for an answer. Methods of observation vary significantly from one tradition to another. Some scholars observe by examining records and artifacts, others by personal involvement, others by using instruments and controlled experiment, others by interviewing people. Whatever is used, the investigator employs some planned method for answering the questions.

The third stage of inquiry is *constructing answers.* Here, the scholar attempts to define, to describe and explain, to make judgments. This stage is usually referred to as *theory* and is the focus of this book.

People often think of the stages of inquiry as linear, occurring one step at a time—first questions, then observations, and finally answers. But inquiry does not proceed in this fashion. Each

29   Dance, "The 'Concept' of Communication," p. 210.
30   The process of inquiry is described in Gerald R. Miller and Henry Nicholson, *Communication Inquiry* (Reading, MA: Addison-Wesley, 1976).
31   Miller and Nicholson, *Communication Inquiry,* p. ix. See also Don W. Stacks and Michael B. Salwen, "Integrating Theory and Research: Starting with Questions," in *An Integrated Approach to Communication Theory and Research,* eds. M. B. Salwen and D. W. Stacks (Mahwah, NJ: Erlbaum, 1996), pp. 3–14.

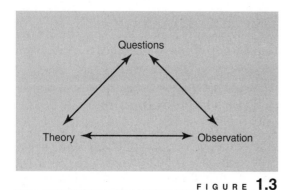

FIGURE **1.3**

The Stages of Inquiry

stage affects and is affected by the others. Observations often stimulate new questions, and theories are challenged by both observations and questions. Theories lead to new questions, and observations are determined in part by theories. Inquiry, then, is more like running around a circle than walking in a straight line. Figure 1.3 illustrates the interaction among the stages of inquiry.

Types of Scholarship

The preceding section outlines the basic elements of inquiry, but it ignores important differences. Different types of inquiry ask different questions, use different methods of observation, and lead to different kinds of theory. Methods of inquiry can be grouped into three broad forms of scholarship: scientific, humanistic, and social scientific.[32] Although these forms of scholarship share the common elements discussed in the previous section, they also have major differences.[33]

Scientific Scholarship. Science often is associated with objectivity. Is science really objective? If by objectivity you mean suspension of values, science definitely is not objective. However, if by objectivity you mean standardization, science is indeed objective, or, more accurately, it aims to be objective. The scientist attempts to look at the world in such a way that all other observers, trained the same way and using the same methods, would see the same thing. Replications of a study should yield identical results.

Standardization and replication are important in science because scientists assume that the world has observable form, and they view their task as seeing the world as it is. The world sits in wait of discovery, and the goal of science is to observe and explain the world as accurately as possible. Because there is no divinely revealed way to know how accurate one's observations are, the scientist must rely on agreement among observers. This is why objectivity and replicability are so important. If all trained observers report the same results, we feel confident that the object has been accurately observed. Because of the emphasis on discovering a knowable world, scientific methods are especially well suited to problems of nature.

Humanistic Scholarship. Whereas science is associated with objectivity, the humanities are associated with subjectivity. Science aims to standardize observation; the humanities seek creative individuality. If the aim of science is to reduce human differences in what is observed, the aim of the humanities is to understand individual subjective response.[34] Most humanists are more interested in individual cases than generalized theory.

Whereas science is an "out there" activity, the humanities stress the "in here." Science focuses on the discovered world; the humanities focus on the discovering person. Science seeks consensus; the humanities seek alternative interpretations. Humanists often are suspicious of the claim that there is an immutable world to be discovered, and they tend not to separate the knower from the known. The classical humanis-

32   An excellent discussion of scholarship can be found in Ernest G. Bormann, *Theory and Research in the Communicative Arts* (New York: Holt, Rinehart & Winston, 1965). See also Nathan Glazer, "The Social Sciences in Liberal Education," in *The Philosophy of the Curriculum*, ed. S. Hook (Buffalo: Prometheus, 1975), pp. 145–158; James L. Jarrett, *The Humanities and Humanistic Education* (Reading, MA: Addison-Wesley, 1973); Gerald Holton, "Science, Science Teaching, and Rationality," in *The Philosophy of the Curriculum*, ed. S. Hook (Buffalo: Prometheus, 1975), pp. 101–108.
33   See, for example, C. P. Snow, *The Two Cultures and a Second Look* (Cambridge: Cambridge University Press, 1964).
34   James A. Diefenbeck, *A Celebration of Subjective Thought* (Carbondale: Southern Illinois University Press, 1984).

tic position is that who one is determines what one sees. Because of its emphasis on the subjective response, humanistic scholarship is especially well suited to problems of art, personal experience, and values.

Science and the humanities are not so far apart that they never come together. Almost any program of research and theory building includes some aspects of both scientific and humanistic scholarship. At times the scientist is a humanist, using intuition, creativity, interpretation, and insight. Ironically, the scientist must be subjective in creating the methods that will eventually lead to objective observation, making research design a creative process. In turn, at times the humanist must be scientific, seeking facts that enable experience to be understood. As we will see in the next section, the point where science leaves off and the humanities begin is not always clear.

The Special Case of the Social Sciences. A third form of scholarship is the social sciences. Although many social scientists see it as an extension of natural science, using methods borrowed from physics, social science is a world apart.[35] Paradoxically, it includes elements of both science and the humanities but is different from both.[36]

In seeking to observe and interpret patterns of human behavior, social scholars make human beings the object of study. To understand human behavior, scholars must observe it. If behavioral patterns do in fact exist, then observation must be as objective as possible. In other words, the social scientist—like the natural scientist—must establish consensus on what is observed. Once the behavioral phenomena are accurately observed, they must be explained or interpreted.

Interpreting may be complicated by the fact that the object of observation, the human subject, is itself an active, knowing being. Unlike objects in the natural world, the human subject is capable of having knowledge, possessing values, making interpretations, and taking action. Can "scientific" explanation of human behavior take place without consideration of the "humanistic" knowledge of the observed person? This question is the central philosophical issue of social science and has provoked considerable concern and debate akin to an identity crisis.[37] In the past, the majority of social scientists believed that scientific methods alone would suffice to uncover the mysteries of human experience, but today many realize that a strong humanistic element is also needed.

Communication as a Social Science. Communication involves understanding how people behave in creating, exchanging, and interpreting messages. Consequently, communication inquiry combines both scientific and humanistic methods.[38] The theories covered in this book, as examples of social science, vary significantly in the extent to which they use scientific or humanistic elements. Traditionally, humanistic theories of communication have been referred to as rhetorical theory and scientific theories as communication theory. This distinction is not particularly useful. All theories we will discuss deal with human communication, and both humanistic and scientific theories are worthy of inclusion in our body of knowledge about human communication.

---

35   See, for example, Charles R. Berger and Steven H. Chaffee (eds.), "The Study of Communication as a Science," in *Handbook of Communication Science* (Newbury Park, CA: Sage, 1987), pp. 15–19. For an interesting discussion of the scientific nature of communication research, see Glenn G. Sparks, W. James Potter, Roger Cooper, and Michel Dupagne, "Is Media Research Prescientific?" *Communication Theory* 5 (1995): 273–289.

36   See, for example, Robert T. Craig, "Why Are There So *Many* Communication Theories?" *Journal of Communication* 43 (1993): 26–33; Hubert M. Blalock, *Basic Dilemmas in the Social Sciences* (Beverly Hills, CA: Sage, 1984), p. 15; Anthony Giddens, *Profiles and Critiques in Social Theory* (Berkeley: University of California Press, 1983), p. 133; Peter Winch, *The Idea of a Social Science and Its Relation to Philosophy* (London: Routledge & Kegan Paul, 1958).

37   See, for example, Klaus Krippendorff, "Conversation or Intellectual Imperialism in Comparing Communication (Theories)," *Communication Theory* 3 (1993): 252–266; Donald W. Fiske and Richard A. Shweder (eds.), "Introduction: Uneasy Social Science," in *Metatheory in Social Science: Pluralisms and Subjectivities* (Chicago: University of Chicago Press, 1986), pp. 1–18; Kenneth J. Gergen, *Toward Transformation in Social Knowledge* (New York: Springer-Verlag, 1982).

38   This position is developed in Thomas B. Farrell, "Beyond Science: Humanities Contributions to Communication Theory," in *Handbook of Communication Science*, eds. C. R. Berger and S. H. Chaffee (Newbury Park, CA: Sage, 1987), pp. 123–139.

COMMUNICATION THEORY AS A FIELD

For many years, communication scholars have grappled with the problem of how to characterize communication theory as a field. This has been a challenge for theorists, teachers, and students because of the number of theories and the complexity of their philosophical and practical differences.[39] In a recent landmark article, Robert T. Craig proposes a vision for communication theory that takes a huge step toward unifying our otherwise disparate field.[40]

Craig argues that our field will never be united by a unified theory or theories. Theories will always reflect the diversity of practical ideas about communication in ordinary life, so we will forever be faced with a multiplicity of approaches. Our goal cannot and should not be to seek a standard model. If this impossible state of affairs were to happen, communication would become "a static field, a dead field."[41]

Instead, we must seek a different kind of coherence based on (1) a common understanding of the similarities and differences, or tension points, among theories and (2) a commitment to manage these tensions through dialogue. Craig writes, "The goal should not be a state in which we have nothing to argue about, but one in which we better understand that we all have something very important to argue about."[42] Here, then, we have two requirements for communication theory as a field.

The first requirement is a common understanding of similarities and differences among theories. More than a list of similarities and differences, we must have a common idea of where and how theories coalesce and clash. We need a *metamodel*. The term *meta* means "above," so a *metamodel* is a "model of models."

The second requirement for coherence in the field is a new definition of *theory*. Rather than viewing a theory as an explanation of a process, it should be seen as a statement or argument in favor of a particular approach. In other words, theories are a form of *discourse*. More precisely,

theories are a discourse about discourse, or *metadiscourse.*

As a student of communication theory, you will find these twin concepts very important because they will help you sort out what this enterprise is all about. If you can find a useful metamodel, you will be able to make connections among theories, and if you see communication theory as metadiscourse, you will begin to understand the value of multiple perspectives in the field. In other words, communication theories will look less like a bunch of rocks laid out on tables in a geology laboratory and more like a dynamic computer model of earth formation in a course on geological history.

As a basic premise for a metamodel, Craig says that communication is the primary process by which human life is experienced; communication *constitutes* reality. How we communicate about our experience itself forms or makes our experience. The many forms of experience are made in many forms of communication. Our meanings change from one group to another, from one setting to another, and from one time period to another, because communication itself is dynamic across situations. Craig describes the importance of this thought to communication as a field:

> Communication . . . is not a secondary phenomenon that can be explained by antecedent psychological, sociological, cultural, or economic factors; rather, communication itself is the primary, constitutive social process that explains all these other factors.[43]

Craig suggests that we move the same principle to another level. Theories are special forms of communication, so theories constitute, or make, an experience of communication. Theories

---

39   For a discussion of genres of communication theory, see previous editions of this book including Stephen W. Littlejohn, *Theories of Human Communication,* 6th ed. (Belmont, CA: Wadsworth, 1999), pp. 12–19.
40   Craig, "Communication Theory as a Field." A similar effort is offered by James A. Anderson, *Communication Theory: Epistemological Foundations* (New York: Guilford, 1996).
41   Craig, "Communication Theory as a Field," p. 123.
42   Craig, "Communication Theory as a Field," p. 124.
43   Craig, "Communication Theory as a Field," p. 126.

communicate about communication, which is exactly what Craig means by metadiscourse. Different theories are different ways of "talking about" communication, each form having its own powers and limits. For unity in the field, then, we need to acknowledge the constitutive power of theories and find a consensual way in which to understand what various theories are designed to address and how they differ in their forms of address.

Craig writes that all communication theories are ultimately practical because every theory is a response to some aspect of communication encountered in everyday life. Every theory attempts to address communication practice in one form or another. So the dialogue within the field can focus on *what* and *how* various theories address the social world in which people live. Craig describes seven traditional standpoints that enter this dialogue: (1) rhetorical, (2) semiotic, (3) phenomenological, (4) cybernetic, (5) sociopsychological, (6) sociocultural, and (7) critical.[44]

The Rhetorical Tradition

Theories in this tradition see communication as a practical art. Communicators such as speakers, media producers, and writers perceive a problem or challenge that needs to be dealt with through

carefully designed messages. In this tradition, then, the communicator develops a strategy, often employing common approaches, to move an audience. Logical and emotional appeals are typically featured in rhetorical theories. This tradition sees the work of the communicator as governed by art and method. It relies on a sense that words are powerful, that information is useful in making judgments, and that communication can be evaluated and improved. Rhetorical theories often challenge those views suggesting that words are not action, that appearance is not reality, that style is not substance, and that opinion is not truth.

The Semiotic Tradition

This tradition, focusing on signs and symbols, treats communication as a bridge between the private worlds of individuals and in which signs elicit meanings that may or may not be shared. It is especially suited to address the problems of gaps, misunderstandings, and subjective responses. It argues in a language that includes terms such as *sign, symbol, meaning, referent, code,* and *understanding*. The power of the semiotic lies in ideas about the need for a common language, its identification of subjectivity as a barrier to understanding, and its engagement with the multiple meanings of signs. Semiotic theories often lie in opposition to theories suggesting that words have correct meanings, that signs stand for objects, or that language is neutral.

The Phenomenological Tradition

The phenomenological tradition concentrates on personal experience, including how individuals experience one another. Communication is seen as a sharing of personal experience through dialogue. Authentic human relationships are honored in this tradition, and it is particularly well adapted theoretically to respond to problems related to the erosion of strong relationships. In this tradition, you will hear a discourse that includes terms such as *experience, self, dialogue, genuine,*

---

44   Many typologies of scholarship have been developed. For a discussion of the problems involved in describing differences, see Stanley Deetz, "Describing Differences in Approaches to Organization Science," *Organization Science* 7 (1996): 191–207. See also Fred R. Dallmayr, *Language and Politics* (Notre Dame, IN: University of Notre Dame Press, 1984); Lawrence Grossberg, "Does Communication Theory Need Intersubjectivity? Toward an Immanent Philosophy of Interpersonal Relations," in *Communication Yearbook 6*, ed. M. Burgoon (Beverly Hills, CA: Sage, 1984), pp. 171–205; and John Stewart, "Speech and Human Being," *Quarterly Journal of Speech* 72 (1986): 55–73; Gibson Winter, *Elements for a Social Ethic: Scientific and Ethical Perspectives on Social Process* (New York: Macmillan, 1966). Winter's scheme was later elaborated by Richard McKeon, "Gibson Winter's Elements for a Social Ethic: A Review," *Journal of Religion* 49 (1969): 77–84; and by Ted J. Smith III, "Diversity and Order in Communication Theory: The Uses of Philosophical Analysis," *Communication Quarterly* 36 (1988): 28–40. See also G. Burrell and G. Morgan, *Sociological Paradigms and Organizational Analysis* (London: Heinemann, 1979). For an elaboration of the Burrell and Morgan model, see Karl Erik Rosengren, "From Field to Frog Ponds," *Journal of Communication* 43 (1993): 6–17; and Karl Erik Rosengren, "Culture, Media, and Society: Agency and Structure, Continuity and Change," in *Media Effects and Beyond,* ed. Karl Erik Rosengren (London: Routledge, 1994), pp. 3–28.

supportiveness, and *openness.* It is appealing as a theoretical approach when it points out the need for human contact, respect, acknowledgement of difference, and common ground. It resists discourses suggesting that communication is a mere skill, that words and things are separate, or that values are separate from facts.

The Cybernetic Tradition

Communication in this tradition is viewed primarily as information processing, and the problems it addresses have mostly to do with noise, overload, and malfunction. It honors a vocabulary of senders and receivers, information, feedback, redundancy, and systems. The cybernetic tradition seems most plausible when issues related to the mind and brain, rationality, and complex systems arise. In general, this tradition challenges arguments that make a distinction between machines and humans or that posit linear cause–effect relationships.

The Sociopsychological Tradition

These theories concentrate primarily on those aspects of communication that include expression, interaction, and influence. They address problems and challenges in which outcomes need to be manipulated. The discourse of this tradition accents behavior, variables, effects, personalities and traits, perception, cognition, attitudes, and interaction. It has been a powerful tradition, especially in situations in which personality seems important, judgments are biased by beliefs and feelings, and people have obvious influence over one another. The sociopsychological tradition stands most in opposition to claims that people are rational, that individuals know what they think, and that perception is a clear route to seeing what is real.

The Sociocultural Tradition

This genre holds social order as its centerpiece and sees communication as the glue of society. The problems and challenges it addresses include conflict, alienation, and the failure to coordinate. It arguing their case, scholars most at home in this tradition will use a language that features such elements as society, structure, rituals, rules, and culture. These scholars typically eschew arguments in favor of individual power and responsibility, unitary self, or separation of human interaction from social structure.

The Critical Tradition

This group of theories tends to see communication as a social arrangement of power and oppression. Critical theories respond to problems of ideology, power, and domination. Critical discourse includes such terms as *ideology, dialectic, oppression, consciousness raising, resistance,* and *emancipation.* It is an appealing approach to theory in situations that include the self-perpetuation of power, the values of freedom and equality, and the importance of informed discussion.

⬤ LEVELS OF COMMUNICATION

It has been interesting to see how the field of communication has organized itself over the years. For good or ill, one very strong pattern has developed—to divide the field along the lines of increasing levels of individual involvement. The usual pattern, with some variation, has been interpersonal, group, organizational, and mass communication. Handbooks, textbooks, and college curricula often are divided into sections corresponding to these levels. In your communication major, for example, you will probably take courses in interpersonal communication, group communication, organizational communication, and mass communication.

Interpersonal communication deals with communication between people, usually in face-to-face, private settings. *Group communication* relates to the interaction of people in small groups, usually in decision-making settings. Group communication necessarily involves interpersonal interaction, and most of the theories of interpersonal communication apply also at the group level. *Organizational communication* occurs in large cooperative networks and includes virtually all aspects of both interpersonal and group communication. It encompasses topics such as the structure and function of organizations, human relations, communication and the process of organizing, and organizational culture. Finally, *mass communication* deals with public communication, usually mediated. Many aspects of interpersonal, group, and organizational communication are involved in the process of mass communication.

Unfortunately, organizing communication in this way reinforces the tendency to think of these communication levels as types that are different from one another, but the levels are really nothing more than a convenient way of organizing content. The division of the field into these levels—especially the division between mass communication and the others—has been contested, and work has been done to bridge these groups.[45]

◖ DEVELOPING CORE COMMUNICATION THEORIES

Many of the theories you will encounter in this book deal with special aspects of communication. As we saw in the previous section, some theories explain particular levels of communication, whereas others focus on general concepts

45   See, for example, Patrick B. O'Sullivan, "Bridging the Mass-Interpersonal Divide," *Human Communication Research* 25 (1999): 569–588; Everett M. Rogers, "Anatomy of the Two Subdisciplines of Communication Study," *Human Communication Research* 25 (1999): 618–631; Jonathan Cohen and Miriam Metzger, "Social Affiliation and the Achievement of Ontological Security Through Interpersonal and Mass Communication," *Critical Studies in Mass Communication* 15 (1998): 41–60; Kathleen K. Reardon and Emmeline G. dePillis, "Multichannel Leadership: Revisiting the False Dichotomy," in *An Integrated Approach to Communication Theory and Research*, eds. M. B. Salwen and D. W. Stacks (Mahwah, NJ: Erlbaum, 1996), pp. 399–407; John Durham Peters, "The Gaps of Which Communication Is Made," *Critical Studies in Mass Communication* 11 (1994): 117–140; Joseph N. Cappella, ed., "Symposium on Mass and Interpersonal Communication," *Human Communication Research* 15 (1988): 236–318; Robert P. Hawkins, John M. Wiemann, and Suzanne Pingree, eds., *Advancing Communication Science* (Newbury Park, CA: Sage, 1988).

and processes common to all communication. We can refer to general treatments as *core communication theory*.

Core theory is especially significant because it helps us understand communication in general. Core theories provide insight into processes that operate whenever communication takes place. The following list illustrates the types of elements included in core communication theories.

First, core theories tell us something about the *development of messages*. How do we create what we write, say, and express to others? What mental processes are involved? To what extent and in what ways are messages created in interaction with others? How does the process of message development differ from culture to culture, and what are the cultural mechanisms that enter into the message development process?

Second, core theories address *interpretation and the generation of meaning*. How do humans understand messages, and how does meaning arise in interaction with other people? How does the mind process information and interpret experience? To what extent and in what ways are meaning and understanding products of culture?

Third, core theories discuss *message structure*, which consists of the elements of messages in writings, the spoken word, and nonverbal forms. How are messages put together, and how are they organized? In what ways does the organization of a message create meaning? How are communicators' messages in a dialogue organized, and how do the participants in a conversation mesh their talk?

The fourth element addressed by core theories is *interactional dynamics*. This involves relationships and interdependency among communicators and the joint creation of discourse and meaning. It addresses the give and take, the production and reception, between parties in a communication transaction, whether those parties are individuals or groups.

Finally, core theories help us understand *institutional and societal dynamics*, or the ways power and resources are distributed in society, the ways culture is produced, and the interaction among segments of society.

No single theory can address all these elements, although when one or more elements are included in a theory, others may be implicated because of the relationship between elements. For example, a theory may focus on interactional dynamics while telling us something indirectly about how messages are organized. This happens because interactional dynamics and message structure are related to each other. Similarly, a theory that discusses message production may also say something about message reception, because they involve similar cognitive mechanisms in processing information.

As you study the various theories in this book, always look for the ways each might contribute to core theory. You will find that many of the theories in Part II address core concepts and processes directly and, as a group, explain a great deal about communication. Other theories in Part II and all those in Part III relate more to particular communication levels, but they too can provide core insights if you examine them closely.

◖ THE INTELLECTUAL STRUCTURE OF THE COMMUNICATION FIELD

In a remarkable attempt to capture both the unity and diversity of the communication field, John Powers has created a model of the intellectual structure of the discipline that accommodates all of the categories discussed earlier in this chapter.[46]

Powers imagines the work of the field in four tiers that can be summarized as follows:

Tier 1—The content and form of messages

Tier 2—Communicators as
(a) Individuals
(b) Participants in social relationships
(c) Members of cultural communities

Tier 3—Levels of communication, including
(a) Public
(b) Small group
(c) Interpersonal

Tier 4—Contexts and situations in which communication occurs, such as health care, courts, organizations, religion, and many others.

This model can be used to organize virtually all of the work of the field, including theory, research, and practical application. For our purposes, it is yet another way—a very useful way—for understanding similarities and differences among theories of communication.

Indeed, the chapters in Parts II and III of this book conform pretty well to Powers's first three tiers. In Part II, Chapters 4 and 5 address message structures, Chapters 6 and 7 cover theories of the individual communicator, Chapters 8 and 9 focus mostly on social concerns, and Chapters 10 and 11 largely address cultural matters. Part III of this text looks at levels of communication similar to those in Powers's third tier. Because the material in the fourth tier is quite specific, it is beyond the scope of this book.

◖ SUMMARY

This chapter is important because it sets the stage for the entire book. Here, you learned about the nature of theory and inquiry and how communication has been studied. Remember that communication theory is not just a mental exercise. Although working with concepts can be rewarding in and of itself, understanding the process of communication by studying theories also provides insights that can make you a better, more adaptive communicator. Communication has assumed great importance in our times, and this is not going to change. Studying communication theory can make you a more informed member of society and can help you understand some of the problems you will face in many areas of your life. Communication theory is also

---

46 John H. Powers, "On the Intellectual Structure of the Human Communication Discipline," *Communication Education* 44 (1995): 191–222.

empowering because it can suggest ideas about how to intervene or institute change.

It does not make sense for you to memorize a list of definitions of communication; you can certainly create enough of your own. But it is important to remember that definitions are created to focus attention on certain observations and experiences that are relevant at the moment. In theory building, definitions are skeletal x-rays of the central concerns of the theory builder. Having a single simple definition of communication would be nice, but in our field, this tidy state of affairs is not possible. The study of communication is too diverse, and multiple definitions are unavoidable, as are multiple theories.

In this chapter and the next, you begin to learn how people think as they create knowledge. This may be the most important learning of the entire book. The content of what we know about communication will change, but the basic approaches to knowledge will not. You will be able to use what you learn about communication for a time, but you will be able to use what you learn about inquiry and critical thinking for the rest of your life. If you go on professionally in communication or some other field in the social sciences, this overview of the theory-building process should be especially valuable.

Remember that there are a variety of ways to create knowledge, and each has its own powers and limits. You will develop preferences based on your own aptitudes and interests in scientific or humanistic methods, and you may even become proficient in moving from one way of knowing to another. Just keep in mind what these tools can and cannot do for you. Remember also that social processes such as communication can never be completely understood from the vantage point of any single way of knowing, and significant contributions have been made by a variety of discovery, interpretive, and critical methods.

One of the most important lessons in this chapter is that a theory is not just a simple exposition of fact or reality. Theories are based on certain assumptions about knowledge, values, and things, and theories therefore differ not only in content but also in form and philosophical perspective. Theoretical categories are useful for understanding similarities and differences among theories, but they are not pure types. Differences abound within each category, and you will even see that theories placed in one category may have some similarities with those placed in another. Theories can also be organized around levels, which can be useful, as long as you keep in mind the substantial overlap among levels.

C H A P T E R **2**

THEORY IN
THE PROCESS
OF INQUIRY

Almost all college and university communication programs include at least one course in communication theory. Why is this topic considered so important? Theories are the academic foundation of every discipline. They are the means by which we codify and organize what we know. They allow scholars, teachers, and students to transform information into knowledge.

We do not see the world in bits of data but organize and synthesize information.[1] We seek patterns and discover connections, and theories are an important way of accomplishing this organizational function. As such, theories can be seen as a form of accumulated knowledge. We do not need to start all over with each investigation. Knowledge is organized into a body of theories, and the investigator begins a study with the organized knowledge of generations of previous scholars.

Besides organizing data, theories also focus our attention on important variables and rela-

tionships. Theories are like maps. From the overall surface, they point out recreation spots, communities, picnic grounds, and shopping centers. Theories are guidebooks for interpreting, explaining, and understanding the complexity of human relations. They help us clarify what is observed, enabling us to understand relationships and interpret events. This makes theories a valuable observational aid, indicating not only *what* to observe but *how* to observe. Many theories also help us make predictions about outcomes and effects in the data. Various communication theories aid this process by helping us substitute well-founded predictions for good guesses.

Theories are indispensable in academic life. Theoretical speculation provides ideas for future research and can guide a series of studies that fill in our gaps of knowledge. This heuristic function of aiding discovery is vital to the growth of knowledge. Theories also help us communicate knowledge. They are like knowledge packages. Most investigators want and need to publish their observations and speculations for other in-

---

1   This function is discussed in some detail by Charles R. Berger, "Evidence? For What?" *Western Journal of Communication* 58 (1994): 11–19.

terested persons.[2] Theory provides a way to do this and provides an open forum for discussion, debate, and criticism. Through the communication of numerous explanations of the things we study, comparison and theory improvement become possible.

Theories enable evaluation as well. They can address values and enable us to judge the effectiveness and propriety of certain behavior. Many theorists now believe that all theory is value laden and control oriented, even when the theory is not explicit about it.[3] Theories also provide a way to challenge existing cultural life and to generate new ways of living. Kenneth Gergen calls this "the capacity to challenge the guiding assumptions of the culture, to raise fundamental questions regarding contemporary social life, to foster reconsideration of that which is 'taken for granted,' and thereby to generate fresh alternatives for social action."[4]

◐ THE NATURE OF THEORY

What is theory? Uses of the term range from Farmer Jones's theory about when his pullets will start laying eggs to Einstein's theory of relativity. Even scientists, writers, and philosophers use the term in a variety of ways. The purpose of this book is to represent a wide range of thought about the communication process. Therefore, I use the term *theory* in its broadest sense as any organized set of concepts and explanations about a phenomenon.[5]

All theories are abstractions. They always reduce experience to a set of categories and as a result always leave something out. A theory focuses on certain things and ignores others. This truism is important because it reveals the basic inadequacy of any theory. No single theory will ever reveal the whole of truth.

Theories are constructions. Theories are created by people, not ordained by God. Theories represent various ways observers see their environments, but theories themselves do not reflect reality.[6] Many readers and theorists forget this

principle, and students often are trapped by the conception that reality can be seen in this or that theory. Abraham Kaplan writes, "The formation of a theory is not just the discovery of a hidden fact; the theory is a way of looking at the facts, of organizing and representing them. . . . A theory must somehow fit God's world, but in an important sense it creates a world of its own."[7]

Stanley Deetz adds that "a theory is a way of seeing and thinking about the world. As such it is better seen as the 'lens' one uses in observation than as a 'mirror' of nature."[8] Two observers using microscopes may see different things in an amoeba, depending on the observers' theoretical points of view. One observer sees a one-celled animal; the other sees an organism without cells. The first viewer stresses the properties of an amoeba that resemble all other cells—the wall, the nucleus, the cytoplasm. The second observer compares the amoeba to other whole animals, which have ingestion of food, excretion, reproduction, and mobility. Neither observer is wrong. Their theoretical frameworks

2 The communicative function is addressed in Klaus Krippendorff, "Conversation or Intellectual Imperialism in Comparing Communication (Theories)," *Communication Theory* 3 (1993): 252–266.
3 For a good recent exploration of normative theory, see Robert T. Craig and Karen Tracy, "Grounded Practical Theory: The Case of Intellectual Discussion," *Communication Theory* 5 (1995): 248–272.
4 Kenneth Gergen, *Toward Transformation in Social Knowledge* (New York: Springer-Verlag, 1982), p. 109.
5 See Steven H. Chaffee, "Thinking About Theory," in *An Integrated Approach to Communication Theory and Research*, eds. M. B. Salwen and D. W. Stacks (Mahwah, NJ: Erlbaum, 1996), pp. 15–32; Stephen W. Littlejohn, "Communication Theory," in *Encyclopedia of Rhetoric and Composition: Communication from Ancient Times to the Information Age*, ed. T. Enos (New York: Garland, 1996), pp. 117–121; Karl Erik Rosengren, "Substantive Theories and Formal Models—Bourdieu Confronted," *European Journal of Communication* 10 (1995): 7–39; Fred L. Casmir, "The Role of Theory and Theory Building," in *Building Communication Theories: A Socio/Cultural Approach*, ed. Fred L. Casmir (Hillsdale, NJ: Erlbaum, 1994), pp. 7–45;
6 This idea is explored by Klaus Krippendorff, "Conversations"; and W. Barnett Pearce, "On Comparing Theories: Treating Theories as Commensurate or Incommensurate," *Communication Theory* 2 (1991): 159–164.
7 Abraham Kaplan, *The Conduct of Inquiry* (San Francisco: Chandler, 1964), p. 309.
8 Stanley A. Deetz, *Democracy in an Age of Corporate Colonization: Developments in Communication and the Politics of Everyday Life* (Albany: SUNY Press, 1992), p. 66. The mirror analogy is developed and critiqued by Richard Rorty, *Philosophy and the Mirror of Nature* (Princeton, NJ: Princeton University Press, 1979).

simply stress different aspects of the observed object.[9] We will see this point again and again in the following chapters. Because theories are constructions, questioning a theory's usefulness is wiser than questioning its truthfulness. Any given truth can be represented in a variety of ways, depending on the theorist's orientation.[10] Here is a simple example:

> The teacher presents four boxes. In each there is a picture—of a tree, cat, dog, and squirrel, respectively. The child is asked which one is different. A child worthy of second grade immediately picks the tree. The child knows not only how to divide plants from animals, but also that the plant/animal distinction is the preferred one to apply . . . [but] the choice is arbitrary and hardly a very interesting way to think about the problem. The squirrel as easily could have been picked if the child had distinguished on the basis of domesticity or things we bought at the store. Or the dog could have been picked because the cat, squirrel, and tree relate in a playful, interactive way. Or the child could have picked the cat since the other three are in the yard.[11]

Theories are intimately tied to action. How we think—our theories—guide how we act; and how we act—our practices—guide how we think. In the world of scholarship, formal theories and intellectual practices are inseparable.[12] James Anderson says that, "Theory . . . contains a set of instructions for reading the world and acting in it. . . . [It] speaks to the singular, overarching question of 'What do I believe to be true in living this scholar's life?' No scholarship has greater importance than the authentic theory."[13]

This book is like an art gallery. As you stroll through the gallery, you will regard some pieces as more artistic, more appealing, or more useful for providing a particular perspective than others. You may question the composition or representativeness of a piece of art, but on some level you can enjoy them all as different creations, each with its own values. If we instead compare theories to paintings in a gallery, we get a fuller and more complete appreciation and understanding of communication.

◖ BASIC ELEMENTS OF THEORY

The most basic element of a theory is its *concepts*, or categories.[14] Things are grouped into conceptual categories according to observed qualities. In our everyday world, some things are considered to be trees, some houses, some cars. Humans are by nature conceptual beings. Thomas Kuhn writes, "Neither scientists nor laymen learn to see the world piecemeal or item by item; . . . both scientists and laymen sort out whole areas together from the flux of experience."[15]

The communication theorist observes many variables in communication and classifies and labels them according to perceived patterns. A goal of theory, then, is to present a set of labeled concepts. Theorists identify concepts by symbols, usually words, and the set of terms becomes an integral part of the theory. Concepts, terms, and definitions tell us what the theorist is looking at and what is considered important.

Some theories stop at the concept level, providing only a list of categories without explaining how they relate to one another. Such theories are known as *taxonomies*, and these theories are primitive because they do not provide an understanding of how things work. Indeed, because taxonomies do not explain, many scholars believe that they are not really theories. The best theories, then, go beyond concepts to provide explanations—statements about how the variables relate to one another—showing how concepts are connected.

9   Examples from N. R. Hanson, *Patterns of Discovery* (Cambridge, MA: Cambridge University Press, 1961), pp. 4–5.
10   This point is made also in Thomas L. Jacobsen, "Theories as Communications," *Communication Theory* 2 (1991): 145–150.
11   Deetz, *Democracy*, pp. 71–72.
12   See James Anderson, *Communication Theory: Epistemological Foundations* (New York: Guilford, 1996), pp. 7–9.
13   Quoted in "Anderson Succeeds Ellis as *Communication Theory* Editor, Invites Papers," *ICA Newsletter* 24-1 (January 1996): 1.
14   For an elaboration of this idea, see John R. Taylor, *Linguistic Categorization: Prototypes in Linguistic Theory* (London: Clarendon Press, 1995).
15   Thomas S. Kuhn, *The Structure of Scientific Revolutions*, 2nd ed. (Chicago: University of Chicago Press, 1970), p. 128.

An *explanation* identifies regularities or patterns in the relationships among variables. In simplest terms, explanation answers the question, Why? An explanation identifies a "logical force" among variables that connect them in some way. A theorist might hypothesize, for example, that if children see a lot of television violence, they will develop violent tendencies. In the social sciences, the connection is rarely taken as total. Instead, we can say that one thing is "often" or "usually" associated with another, that there is a *probable* relationship: If children see a lot of television violence, they will probably develop violent tendencies.

There are many types of explanations, but two of the most common are causal and practical.[16] *Causal explanation* connects events as causal relationships in which one variable is seen as an outcome or result of the other. *Practical explanation* explains actions as goal related in which action is designed to achieve a future state. Causal explanation explains outcomes as responses, whereas practical explanation sees action as controllable and strategic. In causal explanation, the consequent event is determined by some antecedent event. In practical explanation, outcomes are made to happen by actions that are chosen.

To better understand the difference between causal and practical explanation, consider how you might explain to a friend why you failed a test. If you said that you just aren't very good at this subject and had bad teachers in high school, you would be using causal explanation: "My bad grade was caused by things I can't control." On the other hand, if you did well on the test, you would probably use practical necessity: "I needed to increase my grade-point average and studied hard."

◖ THE TRADITIONAL IDEAL OF THEORY

Traditional social science has been dominated by an approach to theory and research modeled on the experimental natural sciences.[17] Such meth-

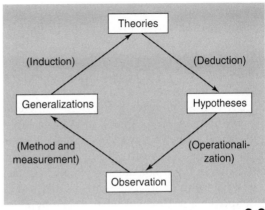

FIGURE **2.2**

The Classical Ideal of Science

Reprinted with permission: Walter L. Wallace (ed.), *Sociological Theory: An Introduction* (New York: Aldine de Gruyter). Copyright © 1969 by Walter L. Wallace.

ods are based on four processes: (1) developing questions, (2) forming hypotheses, (3) testing the hypotheses, and (4) formulating theory. This approach is known as the *hypothetico-deductive method,* and it is based on the assumption that we can best understand complex things in terms of fine analysis of parts, suggesting its alternative name, the *variable-analytic tradition.*

Hypothesis testing is a painstakingly slow process in which theories are fine-tuned by numerous tests. The four processes—questioning, hypothesizing, testing, and theorizing—are repeated in an incremental building-block process. Figure 2.1 illustrates the hypothetico-deductive method.[18] This method is based on five major

---

16   Based on P. Achinstein, *Laws and Explanation* (New York: Oxford University Press, 1971); see also Donald P. Cushman and W. Barnett Pearce, "Generality and Necessity in Three Types of Theory About Human Communication, with Special Attention to Rules Theory," *Human Communication Research* 3 (1977): 344–353. For an excellent discussion of explanation in the social sciences, see Paul F. Secord, ed., *Explaining Human Behavior: Consciousness, Human Action, and Social Structure* (Beverly Hills, CA: Sage, 1982).

17   See, for example, Steven H. Chaffee, "Thinking About Theory"; Michael J. Beatty, "Thinking Quantitatively," in *An Integrated Approach to Communication Theory and Research,* eds. M. B. Salwen and D. W. Stacks (Mahwah, NJ: Erlbaum, 1996), pp. 33–44; Myron W. Lustig, "Theorizing About Human Communication," *Communication Quarterly* 34 (1986): 451–459.

18   Figure 2.1 is adapted from Walter L. Wallace, *Sociological Theory: An Introduction* (Chicago: Aldine, 1969), p. ix.

concepts: hypothesis, operationism, control and manipulation, covering laws, and prediction.

An *hypothesis* is a well-formed guess about a relationship between variables. It is based on intuition, personal experience, or, most desirably, research. Hypotheses should be based on an inductive process of generalizing from numerous observations. An hypothesis must be testable and framed in such a way that potential rejection is possible. In other words, the hypothesis must be falsifiable. If it is not, any test will yield either a positive result or an equivocal one, and it will be impossible to discover whether the hypothesis is wrong. Hypothesis testing, then, is really a process of looking for exceptions.

Suppose, for example, that you think that people do things they find personally rewarding, suggesting an hypothesis: *People are more likely to do what they find rewarding than what they do not find rewarding*. Could you test this hypothesis? You could certainly find instances of people doing things because they liked to do them, but could you find instances of people doing things they did not like? Because virtually anything could be intrinsically rewarding to someone, no action could be ruled out. This hypothesis is poorly stated because you could never disprove it. Some people may even do certain things because, in some perverse way, they find punishment itself rewarding.

Operationism is the principle that all variables in a hypothesis should be stated in ways that explain exactly how to observe them. Operational definitions are the most precise possible definitions because they tell you how the concept is to be observed. One operational definition of *intelligence*, for example, is the Stanford-Binet intelligence test. An operational definition of *dominance* might be a particular set of observer ratings on dominant versus submissive messages.

Return to the intrinsic reward hypothesis stated above. You could improve this hypothesis by specifying more precisely what you mean. Something like the following might work: *A person will repeat an action rated as highly rewarding on an intrinsic rewards test*. Here, intrinsic reward is operationally defined as a rating on an intrinsic

rewards scale. You will notice that this wording makes the hypothesis falsifiable.

As you can see from this example, operationalism relies on *measurement*, or the use of precise, usually numerical, indications. Measurement enables you to detect differences that might otherwise be hard to specify. For example, you might have individuals rate their activities on a 7-point scale, from highly unrewarding to highly rewarding. With this scale you could measure the difference between an activity that is moderately rewarding and one that is only mildly rewarding. You could also measure the difference between one person who found a particular activity highly rewarding and another who found the same activity unrewarding.

Measurement is evaluated in terms of two criteria—validity and reliability. *Validity* is the degree to which an observation measures what it is supposed to measure. How do we know, for example, that the subject's rating really measures reward? Perhaps the rating is influenced by some other hidden factor, or perhaps it reflects nothing in particular. Researchers have methods of estimating whether their measures are valid.

Reliability is the degree to which the construct is measured accurately, and it is most often estimated by consistency. If your bathroom scale gives you a different weight each day, even though you have not gained or lost weight, it is unreliable, just as an intelligence test giving a different result on separate occasions is also unreliable. If all items on a test are designed to measure the same thing, intelligence say, and they prove to be very inconsistent with one another, the test is said to be unreliable.

Returning to your intrinsic rewards study, you must now determine whether your scale actually measures rewards. You might do this, for example, by making sure that it is consistent with other known measures of the same thing. If you can show this, you can argue that the scale is valid. But you would still need to establish its reliability. You might do this by administering the test to the same group of people on two occasions to see that the responses were nearly the same.

The third concept of traditional science is *control and manipulation*. These factors are considered important because they are the only way causality can be ascertained. If one set of variables is held constant (control) and another set is systematically varied (manipulation), the researcher can detect the effect of the manipulated variables without worrying about whether other variables had hidden effects. Control and manipulation can be exercised directly, as in experiments, or through certain kinds of statistics.

Let's return to the intrinsic rewards hypothesis. Assume that you have refined your rewards scale and found it valid and reliable. How would you then test your hypothesis? Would you give a list of activities to a group of subjects and have them rate each in terms of intrinsic rewards? That would tell you how rewarding the subjects found each activity, but it would not tell you whether they would actually do the things they say are rewarding. You might consider having the subjects rate each item twice—once on reward value and once on how frequently they actually do it. That would give you an idea of the correlation between reward and activity, but it would not be sufficient to say that one caused the other.

To really test your hypothesis, you would need to set up an experiment in which you actually tested rewarding activities against unrewarding ones, to see if the former are repeated and the latter not. You might do this by having one group of people do a rewarding set of tasks, such as tasting cookies, and another an unrewarding one, such as tasting raw vegetables, to see if the first group eats more than the second.

The fourth concept is the *covering law*. The covering law is a theoretical statement of cause and effect relevant to a particular set of variables across situations. In traditional science, the covering law is believed to be significant because of its power in explaining events. Covering laws also enable the researcher to make predictions about future events.

Very few social scientists seek covering laws anymore. They realize that absolutely universal statements are unrealistic. Instead, investigators seek statistical relationships among variables,

and their "laws" are probabilistic.[19] Instead of saying that reward leads to action, you would say that reward *usually* leads to action.

Prediction is the final concept of classical social science inquiry. Prediction is an important outcome of inquiry because it gives people power over their environment. If, for example, I can predict that certain behaviors will be repeated if they are rewarding, I may be able to control people's behavior by manipulating the reward value of the desired actions.

This traditional idea most closely approximates what Charles Pavitt now calls *scientific realism*, the philosophy that believes in a real world of real things with true characteristics and causal effects.[20] Theories may not completely and accurately reflect the order of things in the world, but well-worked theories can approximate this reality, and the concepts of a theory can and ultimately should accurately represent objects in the world.

According to Pavitt, if communication theorists are to adopt scientific realism, they must commit to the importance of their concepts, reducing these to an essential set of accurate categories. Theorists should avoid adding new and unnecessary concepts. Furthermore, theorists must use causal explanation and attempt to capture the true causal relations among variables in the real world. Finally, communication theorists must commit to the reliability of meaning and trust that readers will understand terms sufficiently for accurate communication to take place. As we will see in the following section, Pavitt's position is controversial.

◖ AN ALTERNATIVE PARADIGM

The classical approach to research and theory explained above is firmly planted in the scientific tradition of "knowledge as discovery." As

19   Robert Bostrom and Lewis Donohew, "The Case for Empiricism: Clarifying Fundamental Issues in Communication Theory," *Communication Monographs* 59 (1992): 109–129.
20   Charles Pavitt, "The Third Way: Scientific Realism and Communication Theory," *Communication Theory* 9 (1999): 162–188.

Chapter 1 points out, however, the discovery method is often rejected by scholars in other traditions.[21]

In the above section, we imagined that you were trying to test the relationship between action and rewards. Alternative-paradigm theorists would not appreciate your intrinsic rewards hypothesis very much. They might find your idea interesting and even useful, but they would say that this is just one of many ways to understand a person's behavior, and they would find ludicrous your reduction of rewards to a check on a scale. They might also say that your statement that rewards cause behavior is arbitrary and that the link could just as validly be stated in the opposite direction: Action is taken purposely to *create* rewards.

Robyn Penman has outlined five tenets of the alternative paradigm.[22] First, action is voluntary. Persons are in part self-moving, and you cannot predict behavior based on outside variables. If this is true, it would be hard to predict how people would behave based on rewards. For example, some people like raw vegetables better than cookies, or maybe they don't actually like vegetables more but prefer them because vegetables are healthier.

Second, knowledge is created socially. That means that communication theories themselves are created by communication, the very process they are designed to explain. There is no one-to-one relationship between the ideas in a theory and objective reality. So the intrinsic rewards hypothesis is a creation of the theorist, one of many ways of understanding behavior, not a mirror of the "real" reason people do things.

Third, theories are historical. They reflect the settings and times in which they are created, and as times change, so too will theories. Our culture in the United States is materialistic and individualistic. The entire system is predicated on the idea that people are motivated by rewards and punishments. It is no wonder, then, that an intrinsic rewards hypothesis would seem logical. In another era or in another culture, such an idea might not even come up. Stanley Deetz writes:

All current theories will pass in time. It is not as if they are in error, at least little more or less so than those in the past. They were useful in handling different kinds of human problems, problems we might find ill-formed and even silly, as others will ours. What remains is the human attempt to produce theories that are useful in responding to our own issues. We are struggling to find interesting and useful ways of thinking and talking about our current situations and helping us build the future we want.[23]

Fourth, theories affect the reality they are covering. Theorists are not separate from the worlds they create but are part of those worlds. If your intrinsic rewards hypothesis is believed, people will start treating others as reward driven. They will offer rewards when they want something done and withhold them when they do not. Pretty soon people will be operating in an environment created by the ideas of the theorist, and a kind of self-fulfilling prophecy may result.

Fifth, theories are value laden. They are never neutral. An alternative-paradigm critic would say that your hypothesis is rife with values. You chose to look at rewards because your attention was drawn to this particular variable above all other possible ones. You chose to look at individual behavior because you value the person over other possible units of analysis such as the group or culture. This priority is not inherently bad, but it does contain values; and you should recognize your values, according to alternative-paradigm critics.

The tension between the traditional and alternative paradigms is considerable, and it is not trivial. Later in this chapter, we discuss in greater detail the issues that divide these schools of thought.[24]

---

21   See, for example, Robyn Penman, "Good Theory and Good Practice: An Argument in Progress," *Communication Theory* 3 (1992): 234–250; and Krippendorff, "Conversation"; Rom Harré and Paul F. Secord, *The Explanation of Social Behavior* (Totowa, NJ: Littlefield, Adams, 1979), pp. 19–25.
22   Penman, "Good Theory," based on Gergen, *Toward Transformation*; see also James A. Anderson, "Thinking Qualitatively," in *An Integrated Approach to Communication Theory and Research*, eds. M. B. Salwen and D. W. Stacks (Mahwah, NJ: Erlbaum, 1996), pp. 45–59.
23   Deetz, *Democracy*, p. 77.
24   See, for example, the critique of the new paradigm by Bostrom and Donohew, "The Case for Empiricism."

◖ THEORY DEVELOPMENT AND CHANGE

Theories are not just things to be read and learned. They are constantly evolving works. Theories are like arguments in which advocates put forth claims believed worthy of consideration. This kind of work involves several tasks.[25]

At the heart of theory work, of course, is the hard application of acceptable methods, in which the subject matter is "subdued, unmasked, disciplined, and mastered by some superior approach, some set of terms, or a methodology."[26] Anderson describes the significance of this part of the work:

> The achievement of coherent meaning within an analytical frame is a celebratory occasion. This meaning is the medal of honor of the analytic work. It validates the effort. The achievement of this meaning is the evidence of the object and of the superiority of one's analysis over common sense. It is the instrumentality of the analysis, and, in the best of situations, allows an increasing number of others to pursue their goals.[27]

Many other kinds of related work are also necessary in creating theory. One must establish *authority* to make theoretical claims through a complex process of establishing professional credibility over time within the discipline and the highly proficient use of acceptable forms of writing and presentation. One must argue successfully for the *significance* of the work, and one must present the work in a *voice* recognizable within the intellectual community and appropriate to the form of argument being used.

The scholar's work can be presented in a variety of forums, and part of the work of the theorist is to know what these are, where they are, and how to access them. Scholars work hard to develop a presentation appropriate for the forum selected, which means being reviewed by peers, accepting criticism, revising the work, and resubmitting it for publication.

Good theory development is a constant process of testing and formulating. For the traditionalist, this testing is a process of improving hypotheses about the real world. For the alter-

native-paradigm theorist, it is a process of fine-tuning interpretive frameworks for understanding the flow of events.

Theory development therefore always requires research. Research enables the specific investigation of facts considered significant, it allows one to test the theory's predictive power or interpretive utility, and it is a way of developing and articulating the theory further.[28]

Theories may change in several ways. They can be expanded piece by piece, moving from an understanding of one bit of reality to an adjoining bit by adding new concepts to the old. They can also develop an increasingly precise understanding of an individual concept.[29]

In his well-known book on scientific revolutions, Thomas Kuhn states that "normal science" is a process of developing theory with relative consensus among scientists on the basic nature of the things being explained. At some point an extraordinary case is discovered that runs counter to prevailing assumptions of the theory in use. At this point a crisis develops, leading to the development of an entirely new theoretical approach. The new theory (or set of theories) represents a different, competing way of looking at the world.[30]

Gradually, more and more members of the field accept the revolutionary theory, until it becomes the primary theoretical approach in a new normal science. In a scientific revolution, two paradigms are pitted against each other. The old paradigm represents normal science, and the new one represents the revised view. Paradigms are sets of concepts and variables that a group of scholars believe to be important to study, accompanied by a particular opinion of how these things operate. In normal science most scholars agree that certain things are important and should be studied. These scholars also share ideas about how to explain these things.

---

25 Anderson, *Communication Theory*, pp. 127–153.
26 Anderson, *Communication Theory*, p. 141.
27 Anderson, *Communication Theory*, p. 141.
28 Kuhn, *Structure*, pp. 25–27.
29 Kaplan, *Conduct*, p. 305.
30 Kuhn, *Structure*.

In a scientific revolution, the concepts and operations come to be understood in a radically different fashion, requiring redefinition of an entire field of knowledge. Previous areas of study may die, others may be born, and new weddings may occur. "What were ducks in the scientist's world before the revolution are rabbits afterwards. The man who saw the exterior of the box from above later sees its interior from below."[31]

◖ METATHEORY

Theories can differ profoundly from one another. They not only cover different ground, but they are frequently based on different basic assumptions. *Metatheory* is a field that attempts to describe and explain the similarities and differences among theories. We took a brief look at metatheory in the previous chapter. Let's take a closer look here.

Metatheory is a body of speculation on the nature of inquiry that is *above* or *over* the specific content of given theories, addressing such questions as what should be observed, how observation should take place, and what form theory should take. A metatheory is theory about theories. Metatheoretical debates are a natural consequence of uncertainty over the status of knowledge in a field. Since the 1970s, metatheory has dominated the communication field. Communication scholars have come to question their methods and theories, precisely because of the problems of social science summarized in Chapter 1.[32]

Metatheoretical issues are complex but can be grouped into three major themes: epistemology (questions of knowledge), ontology (questions of existence), and axiology (questions of value).

Issues of Epistemology

Epistemology is the branch of philosophy that studies knowledge, or how people know what they claim to know. Any good discussion of inquiry and theory will inevitably come back to epistemological issues. Because of the diversity of disciplines involved in the study of communication and the resulting divergence of thought, epistemological issues are important in this field. The basic issues can be expressed as questions.[33]

To what extent can knowledge exist before experience? Many believe that all knowledge arises from experience. We observe the world and thereby come to know about it. Yet is there something in our basic nature that provides a kind of knowledge even before we experience the world? Many philosophers believe so. This kind of knowledge would consist of inherent mechanisms of thinking and perceiving. For example, strong evidence exists that children do not learn language entirely from hearing it spoken. Rather, they may acquire language by using innate models to test what they hear.

To what extent can knowledge be certain? Is knowledge potentially certain, there for the taking by whoever can discover it? Is truth absolute, or is the knowable relative and changing? The debate over this issue has persisted for hundreds of years. Communication theorists vary in their assumptions about the certainty of truth. Those who take a universal stance will admit to errors in their theories, but they believe that these errors are merely a result of not yet having discovered the complete truth. Relativists would have us believe that knowledge will never be certain because universal reality simply does not exist.

By what process does knowledge arise? This question is extremely complex, and the debate on the

---

31   Kuhn, *Structure*, p. 111.
32   For good discussions of metatheoretical issues, see Pavitt, "The Third Way"; Robert T. Craig, "Communication Theory as a Field," *Communication Theory* 9 (1999): 119–161; John F. Cragan and Donald C. Shields, *Understanding Communication Theory: The Communicative Forces for Human Action* (Boston: Allyn & Bacon, 1998), pp. 1–31; Anderson, *Communication Theory*; Donald W. Fiske and Richard A. Shweder, eds., *Metatheory in Social Science: Pluralisms and Subjectivities* (Chicago: University of Chicago Press, 1986); Mark R. Levy, ed., "The Future of the Field," a special issue of *Journal of Communication* 43 (Summer 1993); Brenda Dervin, Lawrence Grossberg, Barbara O'Keefe, and Ellen Wartella, eds., *Rethinking Communication: Paradigm Issues* (Newbury Park, CA: Sage, 1989).
33   This analysis is from Stephen W. Littlejohn, "Epistemology and the Study of Human Communication" (paper delivered at the Speech Communication Association, New York, November 1980). See also Stephen W. Littlejohn, "An Overview of Contributions to Human Communication Theory from Other Disciplines," in *Human Communication Theory: Comparative Essays*, ed. F. E. X. Dance (New York: Harper & Row, 1982), pp. 247–249. For further discussion, see Pavitt, "The Third Way"; and Anderson, *Communication Theory*, pp. 102–185.

issue lies at the heart of epistemology. To this point, Anatol Rapoport presents the following amusing anecdote about three baseball umpires:

> The first umpire, who was a "realist," remarked, "Some is strikes and some is balls, and I calls them as they is." Another, with less faith in the infallibility of the professional, countered with, "Some is strikes and some is balls, and I calls them as I sees them." But the wisest umpire said, "Some is strikes and some is balls, but they ain't nothing till I calls them."[34]

There are at least four positions on the issue. Mentalism, or *rationalism,* suggests that knowledge arises out of the sheer power of the human mind to know the truth. ("I call 'em as they are.") This position places ultimate faith in human reasoning to ascertain truth. *Empiricism* states that knowledge arises in perception. We experience the world and literally "see" what is going on. ("I call 'em as I see 'em.") *Constructivism* holds that people create knowledge in order to function pragmatically in the world and that they project themselves into what they experience. ("They ain't nothin' till I call 'em.") Constructivists believe that phenomena in the world can be fruitfully understood many different ways and that knowledge is what the person has made of the world. Finally, taking constructivism one step further, *social constructionism* teaches that knowledge is a product of symbolic interaction within social groups. In other words, reality is socially constructed and a product of group and cultural life. (So, our umpires might conclude in the end, "They're what we agree they are.")

Is knowledge best conceived in parts or wholes? Gestaltists teach that true knowledge consists of general, indivisible understandings. They believe that phenomena are highly interrelated and operate as a system. Analysts, on the other hand, believe that knowledge consists of understanding how parts operate separately.

To what extent is knowledge explicit? Many philosophers and scholars believe that you cannot know something unless you can state it. Knowledge is thus seen as explicit. Others claim that much of knowledge is hidden, that people operate on the basis of sensibilities that are not conscious and that they may be unable to express. Such knowledge is said to be *tacit.*[35]

The way scholars conduct inquiry and construct theories depends largely on their epistemological assumptions. Many basic positions arise from the issues just described. Numerous fine distinctions can be made among these positions, but two broad contrasting *worldviews* help crystallize the differences.[36]

Worldview I is based on empiricist and rationalist ideas. It treats reality as distinct from the human being, something that people discover outside themselves. It assumes a physical, knowable reality that is self-evident to the trained observer.[37]

Discovery is important in this position; the world is waiting for the scientist to find it. Because knowledge is viewed as something acquired from outside oneself, Worldview I is often called the *received view.* Objectivity is all important, with investigators being required to define the exact operations to be used in observing events. Most mainstream physical science is Worldview I, and much behavioral and social science follows suit.

Worldview I aims to make lawful statements about phenomena, developing generalizations that hold true across situations and over time.

---

34 Anatol Rapoport, "Strategy and Conscience," in *The Human Dialogue: Perspectives on Communication,* eds. F. Matson and A. Montagu (New York: Free Press, 1967), p. 95.
35 See Michael Polanyi, *Personal Knowledge* (London: Routledge & Kegan Paul, 1958).
36 This analysis is supported in part by several sources. See, for example, C. Arthur Van Lear, "Dialectical Empiricism: Science and Relationship Metaphors," in *Dialectical Approaches to Studying Personal Relationships,* eds. Barbara M. Montgomery and Leslie A. Baxter (Mahwah, NJ: Erlbaum, 1998), pp. 109–136; Anderson, *Communication Theory;* Georg H. von Wright, *Explanation and Understanding* (Ithaca, NY: Cornell University Press, 1971); and Joseph Houna, "Two Ideals of Scientific Theorizing," in *Communication Yearbook 5,* ed. M. Burgoon (New Brunswick, NJ: Transaction, 1982), pp. 29–48. Many other schemes have been devised to classify epistemological approaches. See, for example, Stephen Pepper, *World Hypotheses* (Berkeley: University of California Press, 1942); B. Aubrey Fisher, *Perspectives on Human Communication* (New York: Macmillan, 1978); Kenneth Williams, "Reflections on a Human Science of Communication," *Journal of Communication* 23 (1973): 239–250; Barry Brummett, "Some Implications of 'Process' or 'Intersubjectivity': Postmodern Rhetoric," *Philosophy and Rhetoric* 9 (1976): 21–51; Gerald Miller, "The Current Status of Theory and Research in Interpersonal Communication," *Human Communication Research* 4 (1978): 175.
37 Bostrom and Donohew, "The Case for Empiricism."

Scholars in this tradition try to reveal how things appear and work. In so doing, the scholar is highly analytical, attempting to define each part and subpart of the object of interest. This is therefore the worldview behind the traditional ideal of theory in the social sciences.

Worldview II takes a different turn by relying heavily on constructivism and considering the world in process. In this view people take an active role in creating knowledge.[38] A world of things exists outside the person, but the individual can conceptualize these things in a variety of useful ways. Knowledge therefore arises not out of discovery but from interaction between knower and known. For this reason the perceptual and interpretive processes of individuals are important objects for study.

Worldview II attempts not to uncover universal laws but to describe the rich context in which individuals operate. It is humanistic in that it stresses the individual subjective response. Knowing is interpreting—an activity in which everybody is believed to engage. Many theories of communication take a Worldview II stance, which is based on the assumption that communication itself is a vital vehicle in the social construction of reality.[39] This is the stuff of the alternative paradigm discussed earlier in this chapter.

Issues of Ontology

Ontology is the branch of philosophy that deals with the nature of being, or more narrowly, the nature of the things we seek to know.[40] Actually, epistemology and ontology go hand in hand because our ideas about knowledge depend in part on our ideas about reality. In the social sciences, ontology deals largely with the nature of human existence; in communication, ontology centers on the nature of human social interaction.

Ontological issues are important because the way a theorist conceptualizes communication depends in large measure on how the communicator is viewed. At least four issues are important.[41]

To what extent do humans make real choices? Although all investigators probably would agree that people perceive choice, there is a long-

standing philosophical debate on whether real choice is possible. On one side of the issue are the determinists, who state that behavior is caused by a multitude of prior conditions and that humans are basically reactive and passive. On the other side of the debate are the pragmatists, who claim that people plan their behavior to meet future goals. This group sees people as decision-making, active beings who affect their own destinies. Middle positions also exist, suggesting either that people make choices within a restricted range or that some behavior is determined whereas other behavior is a matter of free will.

Is human behavior best understood in terms of states or traits?[42] States are temporary conditions affecting people. The state view argues that humans change and go through numerous states in the course of a day, year, or lifetime. The state view characterizes humans as dynamic. The trait view believes that people are mostly predictable because they display more or less consistent characteristics. People may change because their traits have changed, but traits do not change easily. Humans are basically static. Many social scientists, of course, believe that both traits and states characterize human behavior.

Is human experience primarily individual or social? Many social scientists view humans as individuals. Although these scholars understand

---

38   Krippendorff, "Conversation"; Penman, "Good Theory." See also Joanna Macy, *Mutual Causality in Buddhism and General System Theory* (Albany: SUNY Press, 1991), pp. 117–137.
39   See, for example, Peter Berger and Thomas Luckmann, *The Social Construction of Reality* (Garden City, NY: Doubleday, 1966); Alfred Schutz, *The Phenomenology of the Social World*, trans. George Walsh and Frederick Lehnert (Evanston, IL: Northwestern University Press, 1967); Kenneth Gergen, "The Social Constructionist Movement in Modern Psychology," *American Psychologist* 40 (March 1985): 266–275; Harré and Secord, *Explanation*.
40   For a discussion of ontology, see Alasdair MacIntyre, "Ontology," in *The Encyclopedia of Philosophy*, vol. 5, ed. P. Edwards (New York: Macmillan, 1967), pp. 542–543. For an excellent recent exploration of ontological issues in communication theory, see Anderson, *Communication Theory*, pp. 13–101.
41   For an ontological discussion of communication theory, see John Waite Bowers and James J. Bradac, "Issues in Communication Theory: A Metatheoretical Analysis," in *Communication Yearbook 5*, ed. Michael Burgoon (New Brunswick, NJ: Transaction, 1982), pp. 1–28.
42   This debate is summarized by Peter A. Andersen, "The Trait Debate: A Critical Examination of the Individual Differences Paradigm in the Communication Sciences," in *Progress in Communication Sciences*, eds. B. Dervin and M. J. Voigt (Norwood, NJ: Ablex, 1986).

that people are not in fact isolated from one another and that interaction is important, they understand behavior as individualistic. Their unit of analysis is the individual human psyche. Many other social scientists, however, focus on social life as the primary unit of analysis. These scholars believe that humans cannot be understood apart from their relationships with others in groups and cultures. This issue is especially important to communication scholars because of our focus on interaction.[43]

To what extent is communication contextual? The question is whether behavior is governed by universal principles or whether it depends on situational factors. Some philosophers believe that human life and action are best understood by looking at universal factors; others believe that behavior is richly contextual and cannot be generalized beyond the immediate situation. The middle ground on this issue is that behavior is affected by both general and situational factors.

Although numerous ontological positions can be seen in communication theory, we can usefully group them into two basic contrasting stands: actional and nonactional. *Actional theory* assumes that individuals create meanings, have intentions, and make real choices. Theorists of the actional tradition are reluctant to seek universal laws because they assume that individual behavior is not governed entirely by prior events. Instead, they assume that people behave differently in different situations because rules change.

Nonactional theory assumes that behavior is basically determined by and responsive to biology and environment. Laws are usually viewed as appropriate in this tradition; active interpretation by the individual is downplayed.

Issues of Axiology

Axiology is the branch of philosophy studying values. For the communication scholar, three axiological issues are especially important.[44]

Can theory be value free? Classical science claims that theories and research are value free; scholarship is neutral, attempting to get the facts as they are. When a scientist's values impinge on his or her work, the result is bad science.[45] But there is a different position on this issue: that scholarship is free of substantive values but embodies such metavalues as the pursuit of truth, the importance of ideas and objectivity, and the value of science itself. Here, the contention is that science is not value free because the researcher's work is guided by an interest in certain ways of conducting inquiry.[46]

Taking yet another view, some contend that theory can never be value free, in method or in substance. Scientists choose what to study, and those choices are affected by personal as well as institutional values. Government and private organizational values determine what research is funded; political and economic ideologies both feed and are fed by particular ways of viewing the world embodied by different forms of theory and research.[47]

A substantial political argument on values in science is occurring. Traditional scientists claim that they are not responsible for the ways scientific knowledge is used, that it can be used for good or ill. Critics object that scientific knowledge by its very nature is instrumentalist and control oriented and that it necessarily promotes power domination in society. Traditional communication knowledge, in this view, is an administrative tool of the power elite. The critics of science do not themselves claim to be above power, but they see themselves as making a choice in favor of a set of values that challenges domination in society rather than perpetuating it. This debate is discussed in more detail in Chapter 11.

To what extent does the practice of inquiry influence that which is studied? This second major value issue centers on the question of whether scholars intrude on and thereby affect the process being studied. The traditional scientific viewpoint is

43   See, for example, Berger and Luckmann, *Social Construction*; Gergen, "Social Constructionist Movement."
44   For a good contemporary discussion of axiology, see Anderson, *Communication Theory*, pp. 186–199.
45   See, for example, Kaplan, *Conduct*, p. 372.
46   For a development of this position, see, for example, Joli Jensen, "The Consequences of Vocabularies," *Journal of Communication* 43 (1993): 67–74.
47   See, for example, Brian Fay, *Social Theory and Political Practice* (London: Allen & Unwin, 1975); Penman, "Good Theory."

that scientists must observe carefully without interference, so that accuracy can be achieved. Critics doubt this is possible. Observation by its very nature distorts that which is being observed. Sometimes the distortion is great, sometimes small, but it is always there.

On a higher level, certain critics maintain that theory and knowledge themselves affect the course of human life.[48] This presents two potential problems. First, the scholar, by virtue of scholarly work, becomes an agent of change. That role must be actively understood and reckoned with. At the very least, the scholar must consider the ethical issues. Second, studying human life changes that life, so that what you believe you know at one time may not be true at another time. This second point has particularly profound epistemological implications.[49]

Finally, *to what extent should scholarship attempt to achieve social change?* Should scholars remain objective, or should they make conscious efforts to help society change in positive ways? Many believe that the proper role of the scholar is to produce knowledge: Let the technicians and politicians do what they will with it. Other scholars vociferously disagree: Responsible scholarship involves an obligation to promote positive change. Obviously, this second view is consistent with the critical approach to the development of knowledge.[50]

Overall then, two general positions reside in these axiological issues. First, *value-conscious scholarship* recognizes the importance of values to research and theory and makes a concerted effort to direct those values in positive ways. What those directions should be, of course, is a matter of debate. Second, *value-neutral scholarship* believes that science is aloof from value issues and that values should not be a great concern.

◖◗ HOW TO EVALUATE A COMMUNICATION THEORY

As you encounter theories of communication, you will need a basis for judging one against another. The following is a list of criteria that can be applied to the evaluation of many theories.[51] Remember that no theory is perfect. All have limitations, and the following criteria are therefore ideals.

Theoretical Scope

A theory's scope is its comprehensiveness or inclusiveness. Theoretical scope relies on the *principle of generality,* or the idea that a theory's explanation must be sufficiently general to cover a range of events beyond a single observation.[52] When an explanation is a mere speculation about a single event, it is not a theoretical explanation. On the other hand, explanations that go beyond a single instance to cover a range of events are theoretical.

The scope of a theory is critical. Stanley Deetz writes that "Few theories are failures in regard to specific situations, and all theories ultimately fail if applied far enough outside of the specific conditions for which they were developed. Theories thus differ more in the sizes of their domains and the realistic nature of their parameters than in correctness."[53]

---

48   See, for example, Fay, *Social Theory;* Gergen, *Toward Transformation,* pp. 21–34; Penman, "Good Theory."

49   This issue is explored by Sheila McNamee, "Research as Social Intervention: A Research Methodology for the New Epistemology" (paper delivered at the Fifth International Conference on Culture and Communication, Philadelphia, October 1988).

50   See, for example, Cees J. Hamelink, "Emancipation or Domestication: Toward a Utopian Science of Communication," *Journal of Communication* 33 (1983): 74–79.

51   Evaluation is discussed in greater depth in Penman, "Good Theory"; B. J. Bross, *Design for Decision* (New York: Macmillan, 1952), pp. 161–177; Karl W. Deutsch, "On Communication Models in the Social Sciences," *Public Opinion Quarterly* 16 (1952): 362–363; Calvin S. Hall and Gardner Lindzey, *Theories of Personality* (New York: Wiley, 1970), chap. 1; Kaplan, *Conduct,* pp. 312–322; Kuhn, *Structure,* pp. 100–101, 152–156. For an excellent illustration of how a critic might use these criteria, see the theoretical critiques of interpersonal deception theory: James B. Stiff, "Theoretical Approaches to the Study of Deceptive Communication: Comments on Interpersonal Deception Theory," *Communication Theory* 6 (1996): 289–296; Bella M. DePaulo, Matthew E. Ansfield, and Kathy L. Bell, "Theories About Deception and Paradigms for Studying It: A Critical Appraisal of Buller and Burgoon's Interpersonal Deception Theory and Research," *Communication Theory* 6 (1996): 297–311.

52   Achinstein, *Laws;* Cushman and Pearce, "Generality." See also Stuart Sigman, "Do Social Approaches to Interpersonal Communication Constitute a Contribution to Communication Theory," *Communication Theory* 2 (1992): 347–356.

53   Deetz, *Democracy,* p. 69.

Two types of generality exist. The first is the coverage of a broad domain. Theories that meet the test of generality in this way deal with many phenomena. A communication theory that meets this test would explain a variety of communication-related behaviors. This has been one of the appeals of system theory (Chapter 3), for example, which explains an incredibly wide spectrum of events.

A theory need not cover a large number of phenomena to be judged as good, however. Indeed, many fine theories are narrow in coverage. Such theories possess the second type of generality: They deal with a narrow range of events, but their explanations of these events apply to a large number of situations. Such theories are said to be powerful. Certain theories of relationship breakups (Chapter 12) illustrate this type of generality. They only cover one topic, but they are powerful because they explain many instances of relationship dissolution.

Appropriateness

Are the theory's epistemological, ontological, and axiological assumptions appropriate for the theoretical questions addressed and the research methods used? In the last chapter, we discussed the fact that different genres of theory allow scholars to do different kinds of things. One criterion by which theories can be evaluated is whether their claims are consistent with their assumptions. If you assume that people make choices and plan actions to accomplish goals, it would be inappropriate to predict behavior on the basis of causal events. If you assume that the most important things affecting behavior are unconscious, it would be inappropriate to report survey data in which subjects were asked why they did certain things. If you believe that theory should be value free, it would be inappropriate to base your definition of communication on some standard of effectiveness.

In a way, then, appropriateness is a kind of logical consistency between theories and assumptions. For example, some writers from the cognitive tradition state that people actively process information and make plans to accomplish personal goals. Yet theories produced by these researchers often make lawlike statements about universal behaviors, which, if true, would leave little room for purposeful action.

Heuristic Value

Will the theory generate new ideas for research and additional theory? Heuristics was discussed in some detail earlier in the chapter, and we mentioned the importance of heuristic value. One example among many is Robert Bales's interaction process theory (Chapter 13), which has spawned much research and further theorizing about group communication. Even Bales's critics find his ideas useful as springboards to develop new concepts.

Validity

Generally speaking, validity is the truth value of a theory. Of course, we must be careful to understand that "truth" is not intended to mean absolute, inerrant fact. Rather, there may be a variety of "truth values" in an experience. Validity as a criterion of theory has at least three meanings.[54]

One kind of validity is that of *value*, or worth. This kind of validity is importance or utility, whether the theory has value. It is the primary form of validity in interpretive and critical theories. Stanley Deetz writes: "The problem with most theories is not that they are wrong or lacking in confirming experiences but that they are irrelevant or misdirect observation, that is, they do not help make the observations that are important to meeting critical goals and needs."[55]

The second kind of validity is that of *correspondence*, or fit. Here the question is whether the concepts and relations specified by the theory can actually be observed. Classical science assumes that one and only one representation will fit, whereas interpretive sciences believe that a

54   This analysis adapted from David Brinberg and Joseph E. McGrath, *Validity and the Research Process* (Beverly Hills, CA: Sage, 1985).
55   Deetz, *Democracy*, p. 67.

number of theories may fit simultaneously. In the latter case, we judge between those theories on the basis of the first kind of validity—utility or value.

The third kind of validity is *generalizability*, which refers to the extent to which the tenets of the theory apply across situations. This is the classical definition of validity and applies almost exclusively to traditional, discovery-oriented, lawlike theories.

Parsimony

The test of parsimony involves *logical simplicity*. If two theories are equally valid, the one with the simplest logical explanation is said to be the best. For example, although classical information theory (Chapter 3) can be faulted on other grounds, it is highly parsimonious. A few core assumptions and premises lead logically to a variety of claims about channels, signals, messages, and transmission.

Openness

Finally, theories can be judged according to their *openness*. This criterion is especially important in the alternative paradigm. It means that a theory is open to other possibilities.[56] It is tentative, contextual, and qualified. The theorist recognizes that his or her construction is a way of looking rather than a reproduction of reality. It admits to diversity and invites dialogue with other perspectives. It acknowledges its own incompleteness.

🄲 SUMMARY

In this chapter you have learned about the study of communication, the nature of theory, and the various forms that theory building can take. You have also learned what theories can do for us and how to evaluate a communication theory.

Theories are constructions: They are created by human interpreters just as all discourse is created. Theories cannot be taken as truth because they are abstractions, and different scholars will see different things in the same observation. Therefore, the constructions employed to understand communication are extremely diverse. They vary not only in what is covered but also in their form and style, and a good deal of disagreement exists about what constitutes a legitimate theory. This forces us to take a rather broad view of theory as any conceptual representation of communication. This broad coverage should be seen as an opportunity, rather than an obstacle, because it will help us explore a wide variety of representations and styles. It will let us see examples of a whole range of ways of depicting knowledge. Although a theory course in certain narrower fields may be like a tour of a Renaissance portrait gallery, ours is like a tour of the full museum with numerous types and forms of art.

Regardless of their differences, however, all theories are basically composed of concepts, or labeled categories, used to classify observations. Many theories also have explanations, which tell us why communication works as it does. Several models of explanation are discussed in this chapter, but what is most important to remember is that all rely on some form of necessity or logical relations among concepts. The logic employed by the theory creates a kind of force that makes one statement follow naturally from another.

Traditionally, you have learned, theory is hypothetical and deductive. In other words, the theory is built on hypotheses and research. A researcher suggests a relationship, tests that relationship, and revises hypotheses on the basis of the research. Theory building in this traditional view is incremental and grows on the basis of repeated hypothesis testing.

Not all theories follow this traditional norm, however, because scholars debate a number of metatheoretical issues affecting the development of communication theory. The assumptions a researcher makes about knowledge, reality, and value determine his or her methods, the form of

---

56   This point is developed in some detail by Penman, "Good Theory."

theoretical statements, and the ways norms and values are treated.

Whatever their form, theories constantly change and develop. Often they grow incrementally, as envisioned in traditional science, by extension from one bit of knowledge to the next. Here, the theory becomes more and more extensive as it grows in coverage. Often, however, theories change in another way, by intension, so that they delve deeper into the subject at hand. More and more detail about the subject is revealed within the theory. The third form of change is revolution, in which the old theory is dumped and a new conceptualization emerges.

As you examine the theories in the following pages, consider the ways in which they meet a variety of functions. How do they organize our knowledge about communication? On what elements of the communication process do they focus our attention? What do they clarify? How do they tell us to observe communication events?

Do they enable us to make any predictions? What new research questions do they suggest, and what holes do they leave unfilled? How have scholars used these theories to communicate with one another about their ideas? And what ideas do these theories generate that can improve social life?

As you look closely at each theory, you will find some that appeal to you and others that do not. You will find some very helpful in your personal quest for understanding, and you will find others that are less so. As you evaluate these theories, think about their scope: How much do they tell us? Think about the appropriateness of their claims: Are they logically consistent? Think about their heuristic value: Do they suggest ideas for further research? And their parsimony: Are they simple but elegant? Finally, how open are the theories you encounter?

Now take a deep breath and plunge in.

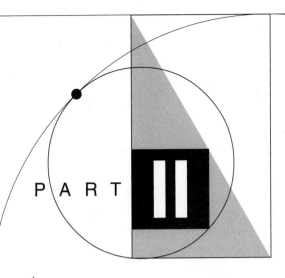

PART II

TOPICS IN COMMUNICATION THEORY

C H A P T E R **3**

SYSTEM THEORY

System theory and two related fields, cybernetics and information theory, offer broad perspectives on how the world operates. System theory deals with the interaction among elements of a larger process, cybernetics deals with control and regulation in systems, and information theory focuses on the measurement and transmission of signals. This group of theories can help us understand a wide variety of physical, biological, social, and behavioral processes, including communication.[1]

The roots of system thinking began at least as far back as the nineteenth century with the theory of Georg Hegel. Hegel viewed the world as being in process and controlled by a tension between opposites. For example, a cold war between two superpowers would be followed historically by an antithesis such as the collapse of one of the superpowers and a new world order. The tension experienced between these opposites—the struggle between the forces of the old and new world orders in our example—would be resolved through a synthesis of the two, such as the creation of a plethora of new nation-states and ethnic strife. The synthesis itself becomes a new po-

sition, only to be thrown off balance again by a new antithesis, beginning the process all over. Hegel explained historical development in terms of this dynamic process, which he called *dialectic*.[2]

Karl Marx quickly applied Hegel's thinking to the distribution of power in society, using it to unite labor in opposition to capitalism (see Chapter 11).[3] Charles Darwin, too, relied on the idea that species evolve and adapt to pressures from outside. However, he explained the process differently than did Hegel and Marx. For Darwin, change is brought about by adaptations and accommodations.[4]

---

1   For excellent discussions of general system theory and other system approaches, see Chang-Gen Bahg, "Major Systems Theories Throughout the World," *Behavioral Science* 35 (1990): 79–107. For an excellent brief history of system theory, see Armand Mattelart and Michèle Mattelart, *Theories of Communication: A Short Introduction* (London: Sage, 1998), pp. 43–55.
2   See, for example, Walter Kaufmann, ed., *Hegel: Texts and Commentary* (Garden City, NY: Anchor, 1966).
3   See, for example, Anthony Giddens, *Profiles and Critiques in Social Theory* (Berkeley: University of California Press, 1982), especially chaps. 8 and 9.
4   Marjorie Grene, *The Knower and the Known* (Berkeley: University of California Press, 1974), chap. 7. For a more detailed treatment of the influence of Darwin on communication study, see Everett M. Rogers, *A History of Communication Study: A Biographical Approach* (New York: Free Press, 1994), pp. 41–64.

Although system theory is a product of Western intellectual history, it has similarities to certain Eastern philosophies as well. As a group, Eastern philosophies stress patterns and wholes, which are the centerpieces of system theory. In addition, system theory and Eastern philosophies avoid simple linear causal reasoning and focus instead on the ways in which many events affect one another.[5]

System theory was used by Ludwig von Bertalanffy, a biologist, as the basis for the field of study known as *general system theory*. GST is a broad, multidisciplinary approach to knowledge.[6] This version of system theory uses system principles to show how things in many different fields are similar to one another.[7] For example, the processes that govern economic growth, biological development, and social movements might be viewed in similar terms.

◖ FUNDAMENTAL SYSTEM PRINCIPLES

What are the qualities that seem to characterize so many different kinds of things? First, let's define a system and then look at the system's qualities.

What Is a System?

Any system can be said to consist of four things.[8] The first is *objects*—the parts, elements, or variables within the system. These may be physical or abstract or both, depending on the nature of the system. Second, a system consists of *attributes*—the qualities or properties of the system and its objects. Third, a system has *internal relationships* among its objects. This characteristic is a crucial aspect, and we will take a closer look at internal relationships throughout this chapter.[9] Fourth, systems exist in an *environment. A system, then, is a set of things that affect one another within an environment and form a larger pattern that is different from any of the parts.*

Closed and open systems are essentially different.[10] A *closed system* has no interchange with its environment. It moves toward internal chaos,

disintegration, and death. The closed system model most often applies to physical systems like stars, which do not have life-sustaining qualities. An *open system* receives matter and energy from its environment and passes matter and energy to its environment. The open system is oriented toward life and growth.

A family is an excellent example of an open system.[11] The members of a family are the "objects," and their characteristics are attributes. The family system is formed by the interaction among the members. Families also exist in a social and cultural environment, and the family and its environment influence each other. Family members are not isolated, and their relationships must be taken into account to fully understand the family as a unit.

System Qualities

Biological, psychological, and sociocultural systems possess certain common characteristics. You will notice that these qualities are not mutually exclusive, but each relates in some way to all the others.[12]

---

5   See, for example, Joanna Macy, *Mutual Causality in Buddhism and General System Theory* (Albany: SUNY Press, 1991); Todd Evan Pressman, "A Synthesis of Systems Inquiry and the Eastern Mode of Inquiry," *System Research* 9 (1992): 46–63; and Wimal Dissanayake, "The Communication Significance of the Buddhist Concept of Dependent Co-origination," *Communication* 8 (1983): 29–45.
6   For a biographical sketch of von Bertalanffy, see "Ludwig von Bertalanffy," *General Systems* 17 (1972): 219–228. For a good general summary of GST, see Macy, *Mutual Causality,* pp. 69–89.
7   For an example of formalized GST, see Masanao Toda and Emir H. Shuford, "Logic of Systems: Introduction to a Formal Theory of Structure," *General Systems* 10 (1965): 3–27.
8   A. D. Hall and R. E. Fagen, "Definition of a System," in *Modern Systems Research for the Behavioral Scientist,* ed. W. Buckley (Chicago: Aldine, 1968), pp. 81–92.
9   Walter Buckley, ed., "Society as a Complex Adaptive System," in *Modern Systems Research for the Behavioral Scientist* (Chicago: Aldine, 1968), pp. 490–513.
10   Hall and Fagen, "Definition"; Anatol Rapoport, "Foreword," in *Modern Systems Research for the Behavioral Scientist,* ed. W. Buckley (Chicago: Aldine, 1968), pp. xiii–xxv. For an excellent short description of open versus closed systems, see Ludwig von Bertalanffy, *General Systems Theory: Foundations, Development, Applications* (New York: Braziller, 1968).
11   Considerable research has been done over the years on family communication. See, for example, Arthur P. Bochner and Eric M. Eisenberg, "Family Process: System Perspectives," in *Handbook of Communication Science,* eds. C. R. Berger and S. H. Chaffee (Newbury Park, CA: Sage, 1987), pp. 540–563.
12   Bahg, "Major System Theories."

Wholeness and Interdependence. A system is a unique whole.[13] It involves a pattern of relationships that is different from any other system. As the saying goes, the whole is more than the sum of its parts. To understand this idea, examine for a moment the opposite view of *physical summativity,* in which a "whole" is merely a collection of parts with no interaction among them, like a box of stones. But a system is the product of the forces or interactions among the parts. A group of people standing in a row at a bus stop is not much of a system, but a group of people sitting around a table having a conversation certainly is a system. Any part of the system, therefore, is always constrained by its dependence on other object parts, and this pattern of interdependence organizes the system itself.[14]

Interdependence is easily illustrated in families. Each member of the family is influenced by the actions of the others. Although each person has some freedom, no one is completely free because of family bonds. The behaviors of a family are patterned and structured, somewhat predictable. What one family member does or says follows from other family behaviors and leads to further behaviors. Because interdependence is the most important characteristic of systems, it is worth exploring in some detail here.

The interdependence among the variables of a system can be expressed as a series of associations, or *correlations.*[15] In a correlation, two or more variables change together. In a family, for example, anger and yelling might be correlated. Some correlations are very strong and others quite weak. In a complex system, many variables interrelate with one another in a web of influences that vary in strength. For example, anger, loudness, frustration, withdrawal, and remorse might be tied together in a family.

One variable sometimes causes change in another. For example, use of power by one family member may cause another to give in. Here, power is directly correlated causally with compliance. Traditionally, causality is considered one way: Variable A affects variable B. In systems, however, causality often runs both ways, such that variable A and variable B influence each other.

Take nagging and withdrawing, for example. As the father nags, the son withdraws, and as the son withdraws, the father nags. Each affects the other. Actual causation in communication is difficult to confirm, although establishing how the participants in a system *perceive* the causes is often useful. For example, the father may perceive that the son's withdrawal causes him to nag, whereas the son perceives that the father's nagging causes him to withdraw.

Variables also may be associated indirectly. In such a relationship, the two variables are correlated but do not cause each other directly; they are both caused by a third variable. For example, school performance and housework could be connected. Children who get their jobs done at home also seem to do well in school, and children who do not do very well at school are also remiss in their household chores. If this correlation were discovered, the researcher might uncover a third variable—perhaps the amount of time parents spend with children. Spending more time with children may bring about greater cooperation at home and school.

A more complex form of relationship occurs in a chain of influence. Variable A causes B, which causes C, which causes D, which causes E, which causes A, in a causal ring.

For example, a father's dominance could cause the mother to withdraw, which causes the child to get depressed, which prevents her from going to school, which creates problems with the teacher. The teacher calls the parents, and the father gets mad. In his domineering style, he tells the mother to get the kid to school, and the mother withdraws.

---

13   Rapoport, "Foreword"; Hall and Fagen, "Definition."
14   For a sophisticated discussion of the various ways in which people can think about interdependence in systems, see Magoroh Maruyama's theory of mindscapes, summarized in *Mindscapes: The Epistemology of Magoroh Maruyama,* eds. Michael T. Caley and Daiyo Sawada (Amsterdam: Gordon and Breach, 1994).
15   Bahg, "Major Systems Theories," p. 104.

Hierarchy. Systems tend to be embedded within one another. In other words, one system is part of a larger system.[16] Arthur Koestler expresses this idea in the following tale:

> There were once two Swiss watchmakers named Bios and Mekhos, who made very fine and expensive watches. Their names may sound a little strange, but their fathers had a smattering of Greek and were fond of riddles. Although their watches were in equal demand, Bios prospered, while Mekhos just struggled along; in the end he had to close his shop and take a job as a mechanic with Bios. The people in the town argued for a long time over the reasons for this development and each had a different theory to offer, until the true explanation leaked out and proved to be both simple and surprising.
>
> The watches they made consisted of about one thousand parts each, but the two rivals had used different methods to put them together. Mekhos had assembled his watches bit by bit—rather like making a mosaic floor out of small coloured stones. Thus each time when he was disturbed in his work and had to put down a partly assembled watch, it fell to pieces and he had to start again from scratch.
>
> Bios, on the other hand, had designed a method of making watches by constructing, for a start, sub-assemblies of about ten components, each of which held together as an independent unit. Ten of these sub-assemblies could then be fitted together into a sub-system of a higher order; and ten of these sub-systems constituted the whole watch. . . .
>
> Now it is easy to show mathematically that if a watch consists of a thousand bits, and if some disturbance occurs at an average of once in every hundred assembling operations—then Mekhos will take four thousand times longer to assemble a watch than Bios. Instead of a single day, it will take him eleven years. And if for mechanical bits, we substitute amino acids, protein molecules, organelles, and so on, the ratio between time-scales becomes astronomical; some calculations indicate that the whole life-time of the earth would be insufficient for producing even an amoeba—unless he [Mekhos] becomes converted to Bios' method and proceeds hierarchically, from simple sub-assemblies to more complex ones.[17]

A system, then, is a series of levels of increasing complexity. The larger system of which a system is a part is called the *suprasystem,* and the smaller system contained within a system is called the *subsystem.* Figure 3.1 illustrates the idea of system hierarchy with a tree model.

Families illustrate hierarchy very well. The suprasystem is the extended family, which itself is part of the larger system of society. Several nuclear family units are part of the extended family, and each family unit may have subsystems such as spouses, children, and parent–child units.

Koestler calls system hierarchy the *Janus effect:*

> The members of a hierarchy, like the Roman god Janus, all have two faces looking in opposite directions: the face turned toward the subordinate levels is that of a self-contained whole; the face turned upward toward the apex, that of a dependent part. One is the face of the master, the other the face of the servant.[18]

Where does a system end and its environment begin? Because systems are part of other systems, boundaries are arbitrary and can only be established by the observer. We can take a very broad view by observing a number of systems that interact with one another in a large suprasystem, or we can take a narrower view by observing a smaller subsystem where the larger system is the environment.

Self-Regulation and Control. Many systems are goal-oriented and regulate their behavior to achieve certain aims. The parts of a system must behave in certain ways and must respond to feedback. Families illustrate this. A family can have a variety of control mechanisms. For example, it may rely on one dominant member for making decisions and providing guidance. This person monitors the family and asserts control as necessary whenever signs (feedback) of deviation from

16   For excellent discussions of hierarchy, see Arthur Koestler, *The Ghost in the Machine* (New York: Macmillan, 1967); W. Ross Ashby, "Principles of the Self-Organizing System," in *Principles of Self-Organization,* eds. H. von Foerster and G. Zopf (New York: Pergamon, 1962), pp. 255–278.
17   Koestler, *Ghost,* pp. 45–47.
18   Koestler, *Ghost,* p. 48.

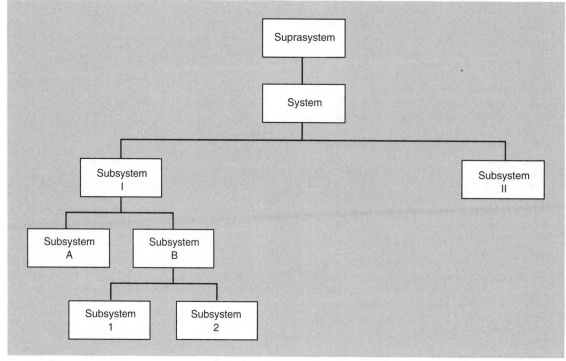

FIGURE **3.1**

System Hierarchy

family standards are detected. Other families may handle control very differently, as is the case for those families with strict role divisions that permit members to exert control over certain kinds of decisions and not others. We'll take a closer look at this aspect of systems in the section on cybernetics.

Interchange with the Environment. Remember that open systems interact with their environment. They take in and let out matter and energy, having *inputs* and *outputs*.[19] For example, parents must adjust constantly to their children's relationships outside the family and deal with influences from friends, teachers, and television.

Balance. Balance, sometimes referred to as *homeostasis*, is a form of self-maintenance.[20] The system must somehow detect when it is off kilter

and make adjustments to get back on track. Deviation and change do occur and can be tolerated by a system, but only for so long. Eventually, the system will fall apart if it does not maintain itself.

The need for balance explains why families seem to struggle so hard to keep things on an even keel. For example, why do parents keep nagging children to behave? Why do couples who are having serious marital difficulties frequently try to get back together? From a system perspective, these efforts are natural attempts to maintain homeostasis. Indeed, many families

19   Gordon W. Allport, "The Open System in Personality Theory," in *Modern Systems Research for the Behavioral Scientist*, ed. W. Buckley (Chicago: Aldine, 1968), pp. 343–350; Hall and Fagen, "Definition."
20   Ashby, "Principles."

have trouble maintaining balance in a complex social environment and do not survive. Often uncomfortable patterns such as anger and blame become part of the family system itself, and these patterns get repeated over and over in the system's attempt to maintain itself. You can see from this example that balance is not necessarily a comfortable state of affairs.

Change and Adaptability. Because it exists in a dynamic environment, a system must be adaptable.[21] Paradoxically, to survive a system must have balance, but it must also change. Complex systems sometimes have to change structurally to adapt to the environment, and that kind of change means getting off balance for a time. Advanced systems actually reorganize themselves to adjust to environmental pressures. The technical term for system change is *morphogenesis.* As members of the family age and develop, as new members come and old members leave, and as the family faces new challenges from the environment, it must adapt.

Equifinality. Finality is the goal achievement or task accomplishment of a system. *Equifinality* means that a particular final state may be accomplished in different ways and from different starting points. The adaptable system can achieve that goal under a variety of environmental conditions. The system is capable of processing inputs in different ways to produce its output.[22] If one pathway fails, another one can take its place. If one process gets cut off, another process steps in. Smart parents, for example, know that children's behavior can be affected by a variety of techniques, that family decision making can occur in more than one way, and that children learn several methods for securing the compliance of the adults in their world.

We have seen in this section that systems are dynamic wholes in which parts relate to one another in complex patterns of interaction. Something happens in a system to make it more than the sum of its parts. What is the currency of system interaction? What is the medium by which

system influences occur? We turn now to a kindred field that attempts to answer these questions—information theory.

INFORMATION THEORY

Information theory, which grew out of the boom in the telecommunications industry after World War II, is the area of study most concerned with communication in systems. *Information theory* involves the quantitative study of signals. It has practical applications in the electronic sciences that design transmitters, receivers, and codes to facilitate efficient handling of information. It has also been used widely in the behavioral and social sciences.[23]

Information theory developed from investigations in physics, engineering, and mathematics. Claude Shannon, a telecommunications engineer at Bell Telephone Laboratories, synthesized the early work in information theory. His book with Warren Weaver, *The Mathematical Theory of Communication,* is now a classic.[24]

Basic Concepts

Information can be understood by starting with entropy, a related concept borrowed from thermodynamics. *Entropy* is randomness, or lack of organization in a situation. A totally entropic situation is unpredictable. Because most of the situations we are confronted with are partially and not completely predictable, entropy is a variable. If dark clouds come over the sky, you

---

21   Hall and Fagen, "Definition"; Buckley, "Adaptive System"; Koestler, *Ghost.*
22   von Bertalanffy, *General Systems Theory,* chap. 3.
23   Several brief histories of the movement are available. See, for example, Rogers, *A History,* pp. 411–444.
24   Claude Shannon and Warren Weaver, *The Mathematical Theory of Communication* (Urbana: University of Illinois Press, 1949). Two sources were particularly helpful in the preparation of this section: Allan R. Broadhurst and Donald K. Darnell, "An Introduction to Cybernetics and Information Theory," *Quarterly Journal of Speech* 51 (1965): 442–453; Klaus Krippendorff, "Information Theory," in *Communication and Behavior,* eds. G. Hanneman and W. McEwen (Reading, MA: Addison-Wesley, 1975), pp. 351–389.

could predict rain, and you might be right or wrong. Because weather is an organized system, predictions are never certain. You cannot predict rain conclusively. The entropy existing in the situation causes some uncertainty. In short, the more entropy, the less organization and predictability. *Information* is a measure of the uncertainty, or entropy, in a situation. The greater the uncertainty, the more the information. When a situation is completely predictable, no information is present. This is a condition known as *negentropy.*

This definition of information is confusing because most people associate information with certainty or knowledge. As used by the information theorist, however, the concept does not refer to meaning but only refers to the quantification of stimuli or signals.

On closer examination, this idea of information is not as nonsensical as it first appears, if you consider information as the number of signals required to reduce completely the uncertainty in the situation. For example, your friend is about to flip a coin. Will it land heads or tails? You are uncertain; you cannot predict. This uncertainty will be eliminated by seeing the result of the flip. Now suppose that you have received a tip that your friend's coin is two-headed. The flip is fixed, resulting in no uncertainty and no information. In other words, you could not receive any more signals that would help you predict any better than you already can. In short, a situation with which you are completely familiar has no new information for you.

Information can be thought of as the number of choices, or alternatives, available to a person in predicting an outcome. In a complex situation with many possible outcomes, more information is available than in a simple situation with few outcomes. In other words, a person would need more facts to predict the outcome of a complex situation than to predict the outcome of a simple one. For example, there is more information in a two-dice toss than in the toss of a single die and more information in a single-die toss than in a coin flip. Because information is a function of the number of alternatives, it reflects the degree of

freedom in making choices within a situation. The more information in a situation, the more choices you can make within that situation.

Language and Information

Many messages consist of a series of stimuli received sequentially, or one at a time. In written language, for example, one letter follows another, and words flow one at a time. Information theory can be applied to this kind of situation. If the letters in a sentence were arranged randomly, you could never predict what letter might follow any other letter. Decoding would be difficult because of the great amount of information in the message. But letters (or sounds in speech) are not organized randomly; there are various predictable patterns. These patterns make decoding easier because there is less information, or greater predictability. For example, in English an adjective has a high probability of being followed by a noun. A *q* is always followed by a *u* in English. Thus, the overall arrangement of a sentence is patterned and partially predictable. This is called *redundancy.*

On the other hand, a sentence does contain some uncertainty because you can never predict with complete accuracy. If you could, there would be no freedom of choice. Once the first letter was written, all the other letters would follow automatically. Language is blessed with moderate redundancy, allowing ease of decoding with freedom of encoding.

Language information is an example of a *Markov process,* in which certain things follow other things in a chain. A Markov process is a series of events, one happening after another in time, such that the occurrence of one element in the chain establishes a probability that another particular element will follow. In addition to language, many other phenomena follow the same pattern; for example, a workday consists of a series of somewhat predictable tasks and driving from one city to another requires following a sequence of turns.

Markov processes like language must be discussed in terms of *average* redundancy because the actual amount varies from point to point in the chain. For example, the average redundancy in English is about 50 percent.

Information Transmission

Information theory is not concerned with the meaning of messages, only their transmission and reception. This is particularly important in electronic communication, where signals are transmitted along a line or through a medium.

The basic model of transmission developed by Shannon and Weaver is one in which a *source* formulates or selects a *message,* consisting of signs to be transmitted.[25] The *transmitter* converts the message into a set of *signals* that are sent over a *channel* to a *receiver.* The receiver converts the signals into a message. This model can be applied to a variety of situations. A television message is a good example in the electronic arena: The producers, directors, and announcers are the source; the message is transmitted by airwaves (channel) to the TV set (receiver), which converts electromagnetic waves back into a visual impression for the viewer.

In interpersonal communication the speaker's brain is the source, the vocal system the transmitter, and the air medium the channel. The listener's ear is the receiver, and the listener's brain the destination. The final element in this model, *noise,* is any disturbance in the channel that distorts or otherwise masks the signal.

Whether the message is coded into regular language, electronic signals, or some other verbal or nonverbal code, the problem of transmission is the same: to reconstruct the message accurately at the destination, as any user of the Internet can testify.

Now you can begin to see the role of redundancy in a message. Redundancy compensates for noise. As noise distorts, masks, or replaces signals, redundancy allows the receiver to correct or fill in missing or distorted data. For example, suppose you receive from a friend a letter

that has been smeared by rain. The first sentences might look like this: "How - - - yo-? I a-fine." Or perhaps because of static, a sentence of radio news comes across as, "The Pres- - - -ed States has - clared. . . ." You can make some sense out of these distorted sentences because of the predictability or redundancy in the language.

Another factor limiting accurate transmission is channel capacity. *Channel capacity* is usually defined in terms of the maximum amount of information that can be transmitted over a channel in a given time period (per millisecond, perhaps). The actual amount of information in the channel is *throughput.* If throughput exceeds channel capacity, distortion will occur or transmission will slow down, as when you set your amplifier too high, beyond the capacity of the speakers.

If you do much Web surfing, you know firsthand the limitations of channel capacity. You may be frustrated downloading a file with a 28.8 modem because you have a channel capacity problem. One answer is to increase the size of the channel by going to a 56.6 or higher modem, or better yet, you can get a cable modem or DSL. On Sunday mornings, even with a modem you can zoom from one site on the Web to another pretty quickly, but by Sunday evening, the Internet is like mud—thick and slow. What's the difference? Not channel capacity, but throughput demand. Hardly anyone is on the Web on Sunday morning, but by evening, everyone wants to get on.

What, then, is necessary for efficient transmission? Efficient transmission involves coding at a maximum rate that will not exceed channel capacity. It also means using a code with sufficient redundancy to compensate for the amount of noise present in the channel. Too much redundancy means transmission will be inefficient; too little means it will be inaccurate.

One way to think about a system is to imagine a bunch of parts with information flowing from one to another. Indeed, the Internet itself is a huge system. What happens in the system to control all of this information flow? This question is the topic of the next subject—cybernetics.

---

25 Shannon and Weaver, *Mathematical Theory,* p. 5.

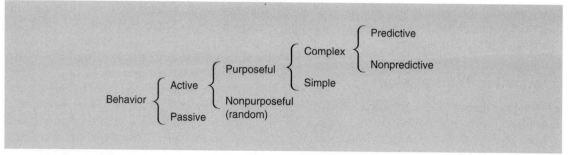

FIGURE **3.2**

Model of Cybernetic Complexity

From *Philosophy of Science*, "Behavior, Purpose, and Teleology," by Arturo Rosenblueth, Norbert Weiner, and Julian Bigelow. Copyright © 1943 by the Williams & Wilkins Co. Reprinted by permission of the publisher.

◖ CYBERNETICS

Cybernetics is the study of regulation and control in systems.[26] Systems are regulated, seek goals, and are purposeful. This is the subject of cybernetics, or the study of feedback.

Feedback Processes

Cybernetics deals with the ways a system gauges its effect and makes necessary adjustments. The simplest cybernetic device consists of a sensor, a comparator, and an activator. The *sensor* provides *feedback* to the *comparator,* which determines whether the machine is deviating from its established norm. The comparator then provides guidance to the *activator,* which produces an output that affects the environment in some way. This fundamental process of output-feedback-adjustment is the basis of cybernetics.

Feedback mechanisms vary in complexity, as Figure 3.2 illustrates.[27] The most basic distinction is between active and passive behavior. *Active behavior* comes from the system itself, whereas *passive behavior* results strictly from outside stimulation. Scratching an itch is passive behavior, but waving to a friend is active. Active behavior can be further divided into purposeless, or random, and purposeful behavior. *Purposeful behavior* is directed toward an objective or aim, whereas *random behavior* is not. Rubbing one's face or

moving a hand may be just a random action, but when done to express an idea or emphasize a point, the action is clearly purposeful.

All purposeful behavior requires feedback, which varies in complexity, as indicated in the model, and purposeful behavior may be further subdivided into complex and simple types.[28] In *simple systems* the organism responds to feedback only by turning on or off. A thermostat is a perfect example of a simple feedback mechanism. *Complex systems,* however, use positive and negative feedback to adjust and adapt during the action itself. Complex systems may be predictive or nonpredictive. *Predictive behavior* is based on anticipated position or response rather than actual position or response. A good quarterback

---

26   Rollo Handy and Paul Kurtz, "A Current Appraisal of the Behavioral Sciences: Information Theory," *American Behavioral Scientist* 7 (6, 1964): 99–104. Supplementary information is found in Gordon Pask, *An Approach to Cybernetics* (New York: Harper & Row, 1961); G. T. Guilbaud, *What Is Cybernetics?* (New York: Grove, 1959). For a historical review, see Norbert Wiener, *Cybernetics or Control and Communication in the Animal and the Machine* (Cambridge, MA: MIT Press, 1961), pp. 1–29. See also Rogers, *A History,* pp. 386–410. For a cybernetic approach to communication, see D. J. Crowley, *Understanding Communication: The Signifying Web* (New York: Gordon and Breach, 1982), especially chap. 1.
27   Arturo Rosenblueth, Norbert Wiener, and Julian Bigelow, "Behavior, Purpose, and Teleology," *Philosophy of Science* 10 (1943): 18–24 [reprinted in *Modern Systems Research for the Behavioral Scientist,* ed. W. Buckley (Chicago: Aldine, 1968), pp. 221–225].
28   I have changed the original nomenclature here to avoid confusion and inconsistency with previous usage in this chapter. The authors' intent is unchanged.

FIGURE **3.3**

A Simple Feedback Model

FIGURE **3.4**

Illustrative Control Models

passes the football to the spot where the receiver will be, not to where the receiver is at the moment. Often, the quarterback even releases the ball before the receiver turns to look for it.

A simple feedback model is represented in Figure 3.3. In the figure, B is an energy source directing outputs to C. A is the control mechanism responding to feedback from C. Depending on the complexity of the system and the nature of the output, the control mechanism itself is restricted in the kind of control it can exert. Figure 3.4 illustrates some possible situations.[29]

The first model in Figure 3.4 demonstrates a situation where the signal itself is modified, in this case amplified, by A. A high-pitched squeal from a loudspeaker is an example. The next model illustrates a simple switch such as a thermostat or circuit breaker. The third model illustrates selection control in which A chooses a channel or position on the basis of criteria. In a guided missile, for example, the guidance system may specify turning in one direction or another, based on feedback from the target.

A regulated system must possess certain control guidelines. The control center must "know" what environmental conditions to respond to and how to do so. It must possess a sensitivity to aspects of the environment that are critical to its goal seeking.[30]

Feedback can be classified as positive or negative, depending on the way the system responds to it. *Negative feedback* is an error message indicating deviation, and the system adjusts by reducing or counteracting the deviation. Negative feedback is important for balance because it maintains a steady state.

A system can also respond by amplifying or maintaining deviation, in which case the feedback is *positive*. This kind of interaction is important in morphogenesis, or system growth such as learning. The inflationary cycle in economics is an example of positive feedback effects. Whether in mechanical or human systems, the response to negative feedback is "cut back, slow down, discontinue." Response to positive feedback is "increase, maintain, keep going."

29   Adapted from Guilbaud, *Cybernetics.*
30   Walter Buckley, *Sociology and Modern Systems Theory* (Englewood Cliffs, NJ: Prentice-Hall, 1967), pp. 52–53.

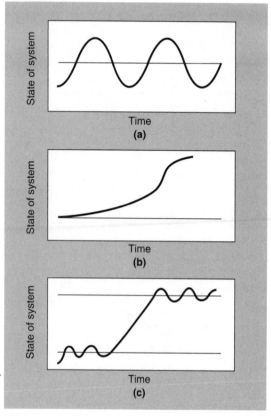

FIGURE **3.5**

Three Feedback States: (a) Steady State, (b) Growth State, and (c) Change State

Figure 3.5 illustrates three system states. The first is a steady state, the second a growth state, and the third a change state. A *steady state* involves the use of negative feedback to keep the system on track. Negative feedback signals deviate from the standard, and the system adjusts in order to return to the line. Notice that the system is always moving; it is constantly changing, but it never gets too far from the desired state because of negative feedback. For example, a manager may want to maintain a supportive relationship with all her subordinates. She continually tries to be supportive, and when employees are feeling unsupported, she detects the dissatisfaction and tries harder to make them feel included.

This manager may waver from time to time but, because of negative feedback, maintains support most of the time.

The second state is *growth*. Here as the system deviates, positive feedback maintains the deviation, and the result is farther and farther movement from the original state. The system accelerates some behavior, and if this continues indefinitely, the system will disintegrate.

Relational spirals are an example. A relational spiral occurs when partners increase the intensity of their responses to each other. Imagine, for example, that a woman goes out with friends without telling her boyfriend, and when he discovers this, he gets irritated. She thinks that his irritation is unjustified and decides to go out with her friends again. Now he gets even more upset, and she goes out again just to make the point that she has the right to do so. In time, she is going out very frequently with her friends, and he is exploding in anger and jealousy. Here, each partner's actions are taken as positive feedback, creating even more deviation from the original state. If the spiral does not stop, the relationship will not survive. Notice that "positive" feedback does not mean "good" feedback; indeed, it may be very bad. And negative feedback is not necessarily bad, because it is needed by the system to maintain balance.

The third state is *change*. Here, the system moves from one state to another state. It requires both negative and positive feedback. Positive feedback gets the system moving in a new direction, but negative feedback comes into play at some level to return the system to balance. The ability of systems to maintain balance and yet continue to adapt and renew themselves is a remarkable feature of both natural and human systems.[31]

Let's return to our example of the supportive manager. As sometimes happens, too much support causes the suppression of productive con-

31   For an excellent discussion of the paradox of stability and change in systems, see Margaret Wheatley, "Change, Stability, and Renewal: The Paradoxes of Self-Organizing Systems," in *Leadership and the New Science: Learning About Organization from an Orderly Universe* (San Francisco: Berrett-Kochler, 1992), pp. 75–99.

flict and the stifling of needed change. Assume that our manager begins to get feedback saying that her department is not productive enough. She responds by criticizing her employees' work habits and in the process becomes less supportive. At some point the workers' productivity increases, and she reduces her criticism. At this point the system has moved to a new state of somewhat less supportiveness and a bit more scrutiny.

Complex Networks

Our discussion of feedback thus far has given the impression that a system responds as a unit to feedback from the outside. This impression is realistic only for the simplest systems such as a heater and thermostat. As a series of hierarchically ordered subsystems, advanced systems are more complex. A subsystem at any moment may be part of the larger system or part of the environment.[32] Further, we know that subsystems respond to one another. As a result we must expand the concept of feedback in complex systems. In a complex system, a series of feedback loops exist within and among subsystems, forming *networks*. At some points the feedback loops are positive, at other points negative. But always, consistent with the basic feedback principle, system output returns as feedback input. No matter how complicated the network, one always comes back to the beginning.

A simple illustration of a system network is the example of urbanization in Figure 3.6.[33] In this figure the pluses (+) represent positive relationships and the minuses (–) negative ones. In a positive relationship, variables increase or decrease together. In a negative relationship, as one increases, the other decreases. For example, as the number of people in the city (P) increases, modernization also increases. With increased modernization comes increased migration, which in turn further increases the population. This relationship is an example of a positive feedback loop. A negative relationship is illustrated by the effect of the number of diseases (D) on population (P).

As our discussion to this point implies, cybernetics is a central process in systems, for it explains such qualities as wholeness (a portion of a system cannot be understood apart from its loops among subsystems), interdependence (subsystems are constrained by mutual feedback), self-regulation (a system maintains balance and changes by responding appropriately to positive and negative feedback), and interchange with the environment (inputs and outputs create feedback loops).

Although these cybernetic concepts originated in the fields of physiology, engineering, and mathematics, they have tremendous implications in the behavioral and social sciences.[34] As Norbert Wiener, the founder of cybernetics, states, "This principle in control applies not merely to the Panama locks, but to states, armies, and individual human beings. . . . This matter of social feedback is of very great sociological and anthropological interest."[35]

Indeed, cybernetics is a way of thinking. Emphasizing circular reasoning, cybernetics challenges the very idea that one thing causes another in a linear fashion. It calls our attention to how things impact one another in a circular way.[36] What goes around comes around. In its more recent forms, cybernetics claims that observers can never see how a system works by standing outside the system itself because the observer is always on some level engaged cybernetically with the system being observed. Let's see how this is so.

---

32   Magoroh Maruyama, "The Second Cybernetics: Deviation-Amplifying Mutual Causal Processes," *American Scientist* 51 (1963): 164–179. See also Caley and Sawada, *Mindscapes,* pp. 99–109.
33   Caley and Sawada, *Mindscapes,* p. 311.
34   See Karl Deutsch, "Toward a Cybernetic Model of Man and Society," in *Modern Systems Research for the Behavioral Scientist,* ed. W. Buckley (Chicago: Aldine, 1968), pp. 387–400.
35   Norbert Wiener, *The Human Use of Human Beings: Cybernetics in Society* (Boston: Houghton Mifflin, 1954), pp. 49–50.
36   See, for example, Klaus Krippendorff, "Cybernetics," in *International Encyclopedia of Communications,* vol. 1, eds. Erik Barnouw et al. (New York: Oxford University Press, 1989), pp. 443–446; Søren Brier, "Forward," *Cybernetics and Human Knowing: A Journal of Second Order Cybernetics and Cyber-Semantics* 1 (1992). *http://www.db.dk/dbaa/sbr/vol1/v1-1for.htm.*

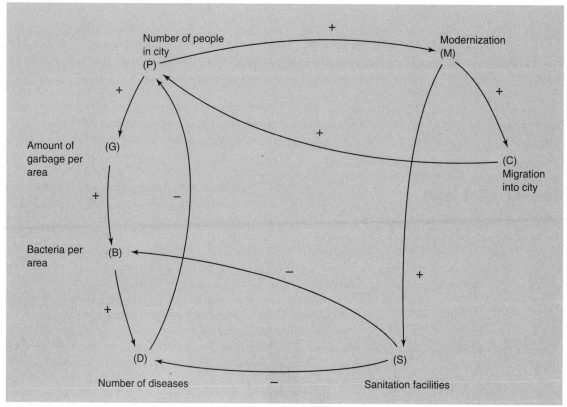

FIGURE **3.6**

A Simplified Feedback Network

From *American Scientist*, "The Second Cybernetics," by Magoroh Maruyama. Copyright © 1963. Reprinted by permission of the publisher.

Second-Order Cybernetics

Whenever you observe a system, you affect and are affected by the system.[37] The term *second-order cybernetics* was coined by Heinz von Foerster to capture this idea. Second-order cybernetics is sometimes called the "cybernetics of the observing system," because it shows how observation itself is a cybernetic mechanism with feedback loops between the observer and observed.

It is also called the "cybernetics of knowing" because it shows that knowledge is a product of feedback loops between the knower and the known.[38] What we observe in a system is determined in part by the categories and methods of observation, which in turn are affected by what is seen. This circle is a cybernetic system, and observers cannot escape it.

The ideas of second-order cybernetics have been developed by a closely knit group of think-

37   Heinz von Foerster, *Observing Systems: Selected Papers of Heinz von Foerster* (Seaside, CA: Intersystems Publications, 1981). For information about von Foerster, his ideas, and his life, see Francisco Varela, "Heinz von Foerster, the Scientist, the Man: Prologue to the Interview," *SEHR* 4(2). *http://shr.stanford.edu/shreview/4-2/text/varela.html*; Stefano Franchi, Güven Güzeldere, and Eric Minch, "Interview: Heinz von Foerster," *SEHR* 4(2). *http://shr. stanford.edu/shreview/4-2/text/interviewconf.html*.
38   Rodney E. Donaldson, "Cybernetics and Human Knowing: One Possible Prolegomenon," *Cybernetics and Human Knowing* 1 (1992): 1–4; Brier, "Forward."

ers, including Heinz von Foerster, Gregory Bateson, Humberto Maturana, and Francisco Varela.[39]

Second-order cybernetics is revolutionary in system theory because it says that objective observation and knowledge are not possible. Traditional system theory and cybernetics treat systems as objectively observable, but in second-order cybernetics, the observed system both affects and is affected by the observer. This idea has powerful implications not only for system theory but for the philosophy of knowing as well (see Chapter 2). Von Foerster puts the matter in these terms:

> One may see this fundamental epistemological change if one considers oneself first to be an independent observer who watches the world go by; or if one considers oneself to be a participant actor in the drama of mutual interaction, of the give and take in the circularity of human relations.[40]

This theory seems strange at first because we human beings feel separate from what we observe. This impression is a result of *autopoiesis,* or the tendency of a living system to distinguish itself from other systems and to act in ways that maintain a sense of autonomy or separateness.[41] Yet the structural relationships within a system limit the distinctions that the system can make. In other words, what we see in another system is very much determined by our own makeup and history, including past interactions with other people.

At the same time, when we observe another system, we are affected by the structure and history of that system. In second-order cybernetics, this is called *structural coupling.* Here two systems can have mutual effects. They coordinate their actions, and they can evolve together. This is true in the natural world as well as in human relations.

The cybernetics of observation becomes interesting when the observed system is the observer's own environment. People make this kind of observation all the time. For example, if you try to explain how brains work, you must account for how your own brain is working right

now as you explain how brains work. Your observation of the system must include an observation of the observation itself! Another example is observing a group of which you are a member. You cannot do this completely if you do not take into account your own behavior (including your observing) as a member of the group.

Family system therapy has made good use of second-order cybernetics and illustrates how it works.[42] Old-style system theorists would say that the therapist can work as an outsider by observing, diagnosing, and prescribing, but second-order cybernetics denies this. When the therapist meets a family, the therapist (herself a system) observes and interacts with the family (another system). The therapist and the family constitute a cybernetic system of feedback loops, in which each affects the other in a new system.

Therefore, the therapist must realize that the therapeutic relationship itself is a system, and the therapist should look at this bigger system too. In other words, the therapist is part of the system being observed. Therapy is a series of *interactions* and is viewed in this tradition as an organic, step-by-step process that can shift from one direction to another. Although the therapist and family hope that the result will be healthier, happier relationships, the precise outcome cannot be predicted or prescribed in advance. The idea is to affect the patterns of interaction in the system in such a way that the family itself comes to discover new ways of changing its system in a positive way.

Human beings always have choices in how they act within a larger cybernetic system. As a part of many systems that have interacted with many other systems, people have a tremendous

---

39   Chief among their works are Gregory Bateson, *Steps to an Ecology of Mind* (New York: Ballantine, 1972); Humberto Maturana and Francisco Varela, *The Tree of Knowledge: The Biological Roots of Human Understanding* (Boston: Shambhala, 1992).
40   Heinz von Foerster, "Ethics and Second-Order Cybernetics," *SEHR* 4(2): 4. *http://shr.stanford.edu/shreview/4-2/text/foerster.html.*
41   Randall Whitaker, "Overview of Autopoietic Theory." *http://www.acm.org/signois/auto/ATReview.html#Background.*
42   For a good discussion of applications of system theory in family therapy, see Janet Yerby, "Family Systems Theory Reconsidered: Integrating Social Construction Theory and Dialectical Process," *Communication Theory* 5 (1995): 339–365.

repertoire of ways to respond to feedback. A fundamental principle of autopoiesis is that the system can act in many ways to maintain its identity as a system.

This means that when you observe another system, you can frame your observations in a variety of ways, and when you respond to what you see, you can act in a variety of creative ways. As an observer, then, you can assume some personal responsibility for how the framework with which you observe may affect the system, how your responses may change the system, and how your observations of the system may change you.

Ecologists use this kind of reasoning. They understand that a redwood forest, say, can be understood in a variety of ways and that how we understand the forest will affect how we act toward it, which in turn will change us and the natural and social environments in which we live.

Because observers never work in isolation and are part of many systems, the second-order cybernetic process can be complex. How we observe a given system, what we see when we observe, and the ways in which we engage a system are produced by a history of interaction with many groups of people over a lifetime. Observation and engagement of any system then is a *social* process. Second-order cybernetics, therefore, is related to theories of *social constructionism* (Chapter 9), with both placing interaction and communication at the center of knowing.[43]

◖ DYNAMIC SOCIAL IMPACT THEORY

System theory has had a major influence on the study of human communication. Although it would be impossible to mention all the lines of work that reflect system influences, several of these appear in the following chapters. In this section, we will look at a very general theory that illustrates clearly how system theory can be applied to communication.

Dynamic social impact theory (DSIT) has been developed by Bibb Latané and his colleagues.[44] The theory imagines society as a giant communication system consisting of numerous cultural subsystems, which include individuals interacting with one another. Because the most basic elements of the system are individuals, let's begin there.

DSIT adopts the widely held axiom that individuals are different in many ways. They have different ideas, beliefs, attitudes, and behaviors. But individuals also share many characteristics with others, and they tend to group together into clusters of like-minded people. Indeed, cultures are large groupings of individuals who share common ideologies and practices. DSIT attempts to explain, in system terms, how these commonalities develop and how cultures form.

Individuals are not isolated. They interact with one another in social spaces. *Social spaces* are the "areas" in which people meet, communicate, and influence one another. Latané has found that social space is largely a physical space, constrained by actual physical distance among individuals. Other things being equal, on average you will be more influenced by people close to you than by individuals far away. Physical distance, however, is not the only aspect of social space. For many reasons, we do not interact equally with everyone in proximity. Various social arrangements, such as race and class, keep people from interacting even though they may live and work close to one another.

Another factor influencing social space are various media of communication that enable people to communicate at a distance, including telephone, email, and mass media. Imagine all of

---

43   Yerby, "Family Systems Theory."
44   Bibb Latané, "Dynamic Social Impact: Robust Predictions from Simple Theory," in *Modelling and Simulation in the Social Sciences from the Philosophy of Science Point of View,* eds. R. Hegselmann, U. Mueller, and K. G. Troitzsch (Dordrecht, Netherlands: Kluwer Theory and Decision Library, 1996), pp. 287–310; see the symposium on DSIT, Edward L. Fink, "Dynamic Social Impact Theory and the Study of Human Communication," *Journal of Communication* 46 (1996): 4–77.

the people you are most likely to communicate with. Most of them live and work close to you, but some may be at a distance. You all occupy a common social space and are likely to influence one another in various ways.

To help understand how dynamic social impact works, imagine your university as a social world. Let's say you are a graduate student in the communication department. With whom are you most likely to communicate? Probably with other members of the communication department and especially those with whom you have regular contact. You are less likely to communicate with medical students or staff members in the grounds maintenance department. You could therefore predict that you will share more attributes with other members of the communication department than with people from other, more distant groups.

In time, as you interact more and more with communication department members, you will begin to influence one another and think alike in certain ways. You will share knowledge, and attitudes will begin to converge. After a while, you might even begin to identify a communication department culture, a way of thinking and doing things common to the department. Even within the department, there will be certain subgroups. For example, a small group of graduate students may get together socially, maybe even going out for drinks every Friday afternoon.

This group clustering phenomenon is caused by mutual influence among individuals who share a common social space. The shared characteristics of a group change dynamically with new contacts and interactions.

Clearly, this grouping phenomenon is not random. Influence among individuals varies along three dimensions. The first is the *strength* of influence of various individuals in the social space. The second is *immediacy,* or the closeness between two persons. The third is the *number* of people in the social space. If you have many people, a large number of whom are influential, drawn together to communicate, the grouping tendency will be very high. If there are fewer

people, few influential people, and little opportunity to talk, grouping will be less likely.

One thing is clear: Individuals in contact with one another will not remain random, unconnected nodes but will organize themselves cybernetically into a dynamic structure of groups with common characteristics. You can see how the organization of the system perpetuates itself: Groups form by proximity in the social space, but those groups in turn give additional structure to the social space, which in a circular way affects the possible patterns of influence within the space itself.

This self-organizing tendency explains the formation of minority groups. Over time the influence of the majority is considerable because of sheer numbers, leading to a preponderance of beliefs being shared by most of the people within the social space. Yet, ironically, continued communication within a minority group bolsters its shared beliefs and practices, shielding it from the majority view. This is a cybernetic mechanism that ensures diversity within the larger system.

Imagine that upon entering the graduate program, you find that the students and faculty differ in their attitudes toward qualitative and quantitative research methods. At first there is no real grouping of individuals into two camps, but over time groups begin to develop. Because of the strong influence of certain members of the department and relatively close relations among some, a majority view favoring quantitative research develops. More and more students come to affiliate with the quantitative group. At the same time, however, a minority qualitative group emerges and reinforces its own view by continual communication among themselves.

An interesting thing happens when groupings like this occur. Once a group is formed, its interaction brings about additional influence and even more convergence on issues that are not logically related to the topics that brought the group together in the first place. For example, suppose that certain members of the quantitative group smoke, and because of their frequent interaction with one another, others start to smoke too. Perhaps the unique interaction patterns in the qualitative group do not lead to this outcome. You would observe, then, that the quantitative group tend to be smokers, whereas the qualitative group are not. Quantitative methods and smoking become correlated, even though there is no logical connection between these variables, and such correlations give further structure to the system.

If the individuals within a social space had equal contact with one another, you would expect that divergent views would slowly converge to the center, making everyone in the social space the same and not extreme in any way. Eventually, you might predict, everyone in the department would come to favor quantitative methods. We know, of course, that this is rarely the case, for the system tends to maintain diversity. This is because interaction is never entirely random, and influence is never entirely linear. Nonlinearity in the system is therefore very important for maintaining system change and diversity. Let's see how.

Especially on important issues, people do not just keep changing incrementally over time. They cling to their ideas and practices for a while until a tipping point is reached and a shift occurs—the straw that broke the camel's back. Once the pressure to change outweighs the pressure to stay the same, a major shift may occur.

The more important the issue and the more involved the individual is with the issue, the less linear change seems to be. In fact, in the face of increasing social pressure, you can actually become more extreme in the views you hold. From our example above, the quantitative and qualitative groups may become polarized, creating even more diversity than before.

You can see positive and negative feedback loops at work here. Negative feedback loops tend to cancel out diversity and lead to convergence, whereas positive feedback loops tend to create diversity and lead to divergence. Imagine society as a huge system of interacting individuals in which many such loops continually bring about both social order and diversity.

◖ COMMENTARY AND CRITIQUE

System theory has been a popular and influential tradition in communication. System theory can be useful for understanding communication in general as well as instances of communication occurring in everyday life.

In the abstract, fundamental system principles may seem esoteric, but when you see them in actual operation, they make sense. The most important system principle is wholeness or interdependence. What really makes a system work is the interaction among its parts. Even system qualities such as self-regulation and interchange with the environment are basically extensions of the interdependence principle.

Interdependence is a cybernetic process, because system parts influence and control one another. Although the simple feedback loop is basic to cybernetics, most complex systems—certainly all human systems—make use of entire networks of influence.

System ideas have been criticized on several fronts, although their supporters remain undaunted.[45] Six major issues have emerged:

1. Does the generality of system theory provide the advantage of integration or the disadvantage of ambiguity?
2. Does the theory's openness provide flexibility in application or confusing equivocality?
3. Is system theory merely a philosophical perspective, or does it provide useful explanations?
4. Has system theory generated useful research?
5. Is the system paradigm an arbitrary convention, or does it reflect reality in nature?
6. Does system theory help to simplify, or does it make things more complicated than they really are?

---

45   For arguments supporting system theory, see especially Ludwig von Bertalanffy, "General Systems Theory: A Critical Review," *General Systems* 7 (1962): 1–20; Buckley, *Sociology*; Peter Monge, "The Systems Perspective as a Theoretical Basis for the Study of Human Communication," *Communication Quarterly* 25 (1977): 19–29; B. Aubrey Fisher, *Perspectives on Human Communication* (New York: Macmillan, 1978).

The first issue clearly relates to theoretical scope. From the beginning, supporters have claimed that system theory provides a common vocabulary to integrate the sciences and that it establishes useful logic that can be fruitfully applied to a broad range of topics. Others, however, claim that system theory merely confuses. If it is everything, it is really nothing. If all phenomena follow the same system principles, we have no basis for understanding how one thing is different from anything else.

Along the same line, some critics point out that system theory cannot have its cake and eat it too. Either it must remain a general framework without explaining real-world events, or it must abandon general integration in favor of making substantive claims. Jesse Delia expresses this concern:

> General System Theory manifests a fundamental ambiguity in that at points it seems to present a substantive perspective making specific theoretical claims and at other points to present a general abstract language devoid of specific theoretical substance for the unification of alternative theoretical views.[46]

The second issue is this: Does the theory's openness provide flexibility of thought or confusing equivocality? Detractors claim that the theory embodies what Delia calls "a fancy form of the fallacy of equivocation." In other words, by permitting a variety of applications in different domains, it cannot prevent inconsistencies among these applications. Two theories using system principles may even contradict each other. Where, then, Delia asks, is the supposed unity brought about by system theory? This problem is exacerbated by the fact that system theories can employ various logics, which are not necessarily consistent with one another.[47]

Chang-Gen Bahg points out that "system theory" as a label is confusing.[48] There are actually a variety of system theories with different names. Bahg discusses twenty-one different system theory traditions. To make matters worse, different system theories sometimes use the same name. "System theory" means different things in different parts of the world.

Particularly confusing among system theories are their different epistemologies, or ways of understanding events. Some are very mechanical and imply a world that works like a machine. Others, like second-order cybernetics, see systems as socially constructed (see Chapter 9).[49]

Supporters answer that openness is one of the main advantages of system theory. It provides not a single tool but a variety of related tools to use in many useful ways. That a set of common ideas such as wholeness and interdependence has been used in so many different ways shows the rich potential of the system enterprise.[50]

Apropos of the third issue, some critics question whether the system approach is a theory at all, claiming that it has no explanatory power. Although it gives us a perspective or way of conceptualizing, it provides little basis for understanding why things occur as they do. B. Aubrey Fisher agrees:

> These principles are quite abstract (that is to say, general). Consequently, they can be applied in numerous ways by differing theorists with equally different results. In fact, system "theory" is probably a misnomer. . . . In short, system theory is a loosely organized and highly abstract set of principles, which serve to direct our thinking but which are subject to numerous interpretations.[51]

System advocates would agree with this assessment of general system theory but point out that any given system theory of communication could itself be highly explanatory. Even if system principles are useful, however, their application to real problems may distract observers from significant problems ignored by system principles. Family system therapy is such a case, according to H. Russell Searight and William Merkel, who

46 Jesse Delia, "Alternative Perspectives for the Study of Human Communication: Critique and Response," *Communication Quarterly* 25 (1977): 51. See also Edgan Taschjan, "The Entropy of Complex Dynamic Systems," *Behavioral Science* 19 (1975): 3.
47 Delia, "Alternative Perspectives," pp. 51–52.
48 Bahg, "Major Systems Theories."
49 Yerby, "Family Systems Theory."
50 See, for example, Bahg, "Major Systems Theories."
51 Fisher, *Perspectives*, p. 196. See also von Bertalanffy, "Critical Review."

write: "By focusing almost solely upon interpersonal interactions as sources of clinical problems, family therapy has neglected intrapersonal factors such as central nervous system dysfunction. This neglect has created unnecessary barriers to treating problems such as attention deficit disorder, learning disabilities, and panic disorder."[52]

Searight and Merkel extend this point further by suggesting that family system theory is culturally inappropriate in the United States. This country is typically an individualistic culture, and problems are understood largely in individualistic terms. There seems to be a split, then, between family system therapy and the culture at large. Searight and Merkel do not reject system therapy, but they judge it as overly closed to other important approaches and hope that future refinements will take into account insights from different theories.

The fourth critical issue questions system theory's heuristic value or its ability to generate research. According to Donald Cushman, "Systems is a perspective which has produced more staunch advocates than theoretical empirical research."[53] Again, critics return to the extreme generality of the approach as the basis of their criticism. They claim that the theory simply does not suggest substantive questions for investigation.

In contrast, advocates claim that the fresh perspective provided by system theory suggests new ways of looking at old problems and thus is highly heuristic. Wayne Beach points out, for example, that a great deal of fruitful research followed Aubrey Fisher and Leonard Hawes's 1971 article on small-group systems.[54] Today a system approach is often assumed in communication theory. It is taken for granted in much of the work of the field without being labeled as such.

The fifth issue relates to the validity of system theory. Critics question whether system theory was developed to reflect what really happens in nature or to represent a useful convention for conceptualizing complex processes. In fact, system advocates themselves take different positions on this issue. Critics place system theory in a dilemma. If the theory attempts to describe phenomena as they really are, it is invalid. It pos-

its similarities among events that are not really there. If, on the other hand, the theory provides merely a useful vocabulary, attributed similarities among events are only semantic and essentially useless for understanding those events. As Delia points out: "[Events] have different referents; they require different explanations; calling them the same thing . . . does not make them the same."[55] Von Bertalanffy calls this objection the "So what?" argument.[56]

The final issue of system theory is parsimony. Adherents claim the world is so complex that a sensible framework such as system theory is necessary to sort out the elements of world processes. Critics generally doubt that events are that complex. They claim that system theory overcomplicates events that are essentially simple. Charles Berger states the case against overcomplication:

> In the behavioral sciences . . . we may be the victims of what I call irrelevant variety. Irrelevant variety is generated by the presence of attributes in a situation which have little to do with the phenomenon we are studying but which give the impression that what we are studying is very complex. . . . Merely because persons differ along a larger number of physical, psychological, and social dimensions, does not mean that all of these differences will make a difference in terms of the phenomena we are studying. . . . It is probably the case that relatively few variables ultimately can account for most of the action.[57]

52 H. Russell Searight and William T. Merkel, "Systems Theory and Its Discontents: Clinical and Ethical Issues," *The American Journal of Family Therapy* 19 (1991): 19–31.
53 Donald Cushman, "The Rules Perspective as a Theoretical Basis for the Study of Human Communication," *Communication Quarterly* 25 (1977): 30–45.
54 B. Aubrey Fisher and Leonard C. Hawes, "An Interact System Model: Generating a Grounded Theory of Small Groups," *Quarterly Journal of Speech* 57 (1971): 444–453. See also Wayne Beach, "Stocktaking Open-Systems Research and Theory: A Critique and Proposals for Action" (paper delivered at the annual conference of the Western Speech Communication Association, Phoenix, November 1977).
55 Delia, "Alternative Perspectives," p. 51.
56 von Bertalanffy, "Critical Review."
57 Charles Berger, "The Covering Law Perspective as a Theoretical Basis for the Study of Human Communication," *Communication Quarterly* 75 (1977): 7–18; see also Gerald R. Miller, "The Pervasiveness and Marvelous Complexity of Human Communication: A Note of Skepticism" (keynote address delivered at the Fourth Annual Conference in Communication, California State University, Fresno, May 1977); see also Beach, "Stocktaking."

And yet, system theory *can* be a parsimonious approach, as dynamic social impact theory so well illustrates.

These six criticisms of general system theory are probably fair. However, actual system theories of communication must be evaluated on their own merit. The many theories of communication that make use of system principles are specific and help us understand concrete experiences, as we can see from the examples earlier in this chapter. You will also notice that these theories tend to be consistent and mutually supportive. Because of system influences, a common vocabulary makes these theories coherent and useful as a group.

The coherence among system theories of communication does not invalidate the criticism that general system theory can be applied in inconsistent ways, but at least in the study of communication, we find instances of consistent application in which system principles clarify rather than obscure. Further, although general system theory is not very explanatory, various applications of system theory can be quite explanatory, as DSIT well illustrates.

No survey of communication is complete without at least touching on information theory. Although this theory has been influential in a variety of ways, these days the concepts of information theory are often considered arcane in human communication studies. The subject is much more relevant to communication technology and engineering. If you are technically minded, enjoy mathematics, and tinker with electronics or broadcasting equipment, you will appreciate information theory and see its relevance. At the same time, however, if you like analogies and looking at human experience by applying physical concepts, you will see the relevance of information theory as a metaphor.

It is not surprising that most students of human communication today find information theory difficult to apply and less relevant than many of the other theories you will encounter in this book. The most directly applicable topic from information theory as presented in this chapter is Shannon and Weaver's model of transmission, which has been immensely popular, although somewhat simplistic, in teaching the basic elements of communication for over half a century.

Although it is indispensable for developing advanced electronic communication devices, some of the original information theorists, system theorists, and other scholars looked to information theory for answers it could not provide. Shannon and Weaver hoped to use the theory as an overarching model for all human and machine communication. However, even Colin Cherry, whose famous 1957 treatise on communication was based largely on information theory, argued later that "the language of physical science is inadequate for discussion of what is essentially human about human communication."[58]

Most criticism of information theory relates to the standard of appropriateness.[59] The philosophical assumptions of the theory are not considered appropriate for understanding many aspects of human communication. Roger Conant captures the essence of the argument:

> When Shannon's theory first appeared it provoked a lot of optimism, not only in the telephone company for which it had clear technical applications, but also among biologists, psychologists, and the like who hoped it would illuminate the ways in which cells, animals, people, and perhaps even societies use information. Although the theory has been put to use in these ways, the results have not been spectacular at all. . . . Shannon's theory provides practically no help in understanding everyday communication.[60]

Many critics have centered on the ill-advised use of the term *information* as a symptom of this problem. Because the usage of the term is at such odds with popular meanings of *information*,

58   Colin Cherry, *On Human Communication*, 3rd ed. (Cambridge, MA: MIT Press, 1978), p. ix.
59   Criticism of information theory can be found in many sources, including the following, on which my summary relies: Anatol Rapoport, "The Promise and Pitfalls of Information Theory," *Behavioral Science* 1 (1956): 303–309 [reprinted in *Modern Systems Research for the Behavioral Scientist*, ed. W. Buckley (Chicago: Aldine, 1968), pp. 137–142]. See also Handy and Kurtz, "Current Appraisal"; Roger C. Conant, "A Vector Theory of Information," in *Communication Yearbook 3*, ed. D. Nimmo (New Brunswick, NJ: Transaction, 1979), pp. 177–196.
60   Conant, "Vector Theory," p. 178.

much confusion has resulted. Ironically, information theory is not at all about information as we commonly understand it. One critic has suggested that the approach be retitled the "theory of signal transmission."[61] Because the term *information* as used by these theorists is so difficult to apply to human communication, other scholars have developed new definitions of the term that have caused even more befuddlement.[62] Of course, terminological confusion is only a symptom of the problems involved in stretching the concept to fit alien domains. Three such problems have been cited frequently in the literature.

The first is that information theory is designed as a measurement tool based on statistical procedures. Human messages in their full complexity are not easily broken down into observable, measurable signals. Although the phonetic structure of language is amenable to analysis, when you add vocal cues, not to mention body

language, information measurement becomes virtually useless. Also, many of the codes used in human communication are continuous, not discrete; that is, they do not consist of off-on signals. Such codes are difficult to fit into the mathematical paradigm.

A second problem of applying information theory to human communication is that the theory downplays meaning. Even if we could predict the amount of information received by a listener, we would know nothing of the degree of shared understanding among the communicators or the impact of the message on them.

Finally, information theory does not deal with the contextual or personal factors affecting an individual's channel capacity. For example, learning, which improves one's ability to comprehend certain types of messages and ultimately one's capacity to receive signals, is left untouched in classical theory.

System theory, cybernetics, and information theory provide an excellent backdrop for many theories of communication. Let us turn our attention now to some of the specific topics of communication theory.

---

61   Yehoshua Bar-Hillel, "Concluding Review," in *Information Theory in Psychology,* ed. H. Quastler (Glencoe, IL: Free Press, 1955), p. 3.
62   See, for example, Krippendorff, "Information Theory."

C H A P T E R **4**

THEORIES OF SIGNS AND LANGUAGE

Many believe that signs are the basis of all communication. In the following two chapters, we will explore the importance of signs and symbols to human life and the often elaborate ways they are used. John Powers, in a wide-ranging integration of the various strands of the communication discipline, suggests that the field can be divided into a series of tiers, the most central of which is *messages*.[1] Messages, according to Powers, have three structural elements—signs and symbols, language, and discourse. The first two of these elements are discussed in Chapter 4, and discourse is the special focus of Chapter 5.

A *sign* designates something other than itself. This basic idea ties together an amazingly broad set of theories dealing with symbols, language, discourse, and nonverbal behaviors. In general, the study of signs is referred to as *semiotics*.[2]

◖ THREE BRANCHES

Charles Morris is a well-known philosopher who wrote for many years about signs and values.[3] His most enduring contribution is the division of

the field into three branches. The first is *semantics*, or the study of how signs relate to things. Here we are interested in what a sign is taken to designate, the relationship between the world of signs and the world of things. The second is *syntactics*, or the study of how signs relate to other signs. This branch examines grammar and structure, pointing to the ways signs are organized into larger sign systems. Finally, in the branch of *pragmatics* we are interested in the actual use of codes in everyday life, including the effects of

---

1   John H. Powers, "On the Intellectual Structure of the Human Communication Discipline," *Communication Education* 4 (1995): 191–222.
2   For a good overview, see Wendy Leeds-Hurwitz, *Semiotics and Communication: Signs, Codes, Cultures* (Hillsdale, NJ: Erlbaum, 1993). See also Kaja Silverman, *The Subject of Semiotics* (New York: Oxford University Press, 1983); Arthur Asa Berger, *Signs in Contemporary Culture: An Introduction to Semiotics* (Salem, WI: Sheffield, 1989); Elizabeth Mertz and Richard J. Parmentier, eds., *Semiotic Mediation: Sociocultural and Psychological Perspectives* (Orlando: Academic, 1985).
3   Morris's classic work on signs is *Signs, Language, and Behavior* (New York: Braziller, 1946). A shorter version can be found in "Foundations of the Theory of Signs," in *International Encyclopedia of Unified Science*, vol. 1, part 1 (Chicago: University of Chicago Press, 1955), p. 84. A unified theory of signs and values is developed in *Signification and Significance* (Cambridge, MA: MIT Press, 1964).

TABLE **4.1**

Summary of Pragmatic and Syntactic Codes

Feature	Pragmatic Code	Syntactic Code
Meaning	In person, assumed	In text
Comprehension	Coherence: Link language to experience	Cohesion: Internal lexical ties
Reasoning	Subjective, organic	Logic
Structure	Implicit	Explicit
Context	High context	Low context
Fragmentation–Integration	Fragmented	Integrated
Involved–Detached	Involved	Detached
Level of Planning	Unplanned	Planned
Oral–Literate	Oral-like	Literate-like

signs on human behavior and the ways people mold signs and meanings in their actual interaction. Organized systems of signs and the use of these systems in everyday life have been referred to as *syntactic and pragmatic codes*.[4]

Because they do not always share common experience, people need to rely on preestablished codes to communicate. *Syntactic codes* consist of a set of features that enable people to communicate in a wide variety of situations, even though they have had no opportunity to negotiate meanings with one another. Syntactic codes need to be relatively complete and formal to make this possible. People understand syntactic codes because they know the rules of the grammar, not because they share a lot of specialized knowledge. Legal writing used for wills and contracts is a good example; it aims to remove ambiguity and leave as little as possible up to the imagination of the communicators. You can read a novel written a hundred years ago in your native language because you share a long-established syntactic code with the author.

In contrast, *pragmatic codes* tend to be used in everyday speech and rely on the practical knowledge of particular groups within given situations. Pragmatic codes can only be understood because of the shared knowledge of those involved in the situation. As an example, you probably have some sense of the meaning of the following terms: *got it done, chop shop, custom stu-*

dio, artist, ink, clean spots, fade, boutique, nice work. You know all of these words, but not in the same way as members of the tattoo subculture. For them, these terms take on special meaning within their pragmatic code. For example, the word *clean* as used by this group is not intended to be the opposite of *dirty* but designates a place on the skin not yet tattooed.

Most talk and writing have both syntactic and pragmatic code features, and differences between messages are generally a matter of degree. Table 4.1 lists the various features of these two aspects of coding.[5]

We address the semantic and syntactic aspects of signs in this chapter and develop the topic of pragmatics in Chapter 5.

◖ CLASSICAL SEMANTIC THEORY

Peirce's Basic Notion of Sign

The first modern theory of signs was developed by the nineteenth-century philosopher and logician Charles Saunders Peirce, founder of modern

---

4   This analysis is based on Donald G. Ellis, "Syntactic and Pragmatic Codes in Communication," *Communication Theory* 2 (1992): 1–23.
5   Ellis, "Syntactic and Pragmatic," adapted from p. 18.

semiotics.[6] Peirce defined *semiosis* as a relationship among a sign, an object, and a meaning.[7] The sign represents the object, or referent, in the mind of an interpreter. Peirce referred to the representation of an object by a sign as the *interpretant*. For example, the word *dog* is associated in your mind with a certain animal. The word is not the animal, but the association you make (the interpretant) links the two. All three elements are required in an irreducible triad in order for signs to operate. This three-part relationship is clearly depicted in a well-known model created by C. K. Ogden and I. A. Richards, shown in Figure 4.1.[8]

An informative illustration of semiosis is the study of generic pronouns by Wendy Martyna.[9] Traditionally in English, the pronoun *he* has been used to designate both males and females when a singular pronoun is required, as in the sentence, "When a teacher returns tests, he usually discusses them with the class." Martyna was interested in finding out what generic pronouns people would actually use in such situations and their meanings for these pronouns. Forty students at Stanford completed a series of sentences requiring the use of a generic pronoun. Some of the sentences referred to people traditionally thought of as male ("Before a judge can give a final ruling, he must weigh the evidence"). Some referred to people traditionally considered female ("After a nurse has completed training, she goes to work"). And some were neutral ("When a person loses money, he is apt to feel bad").

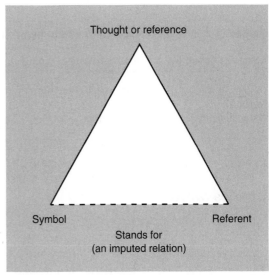

F I G U R E 4.1

Ogden and Richards' Meaning Triangle

From *The Meaning of Meaning*, by C. K. Ogden and I. A. Richards. Copyright © 1923. Reprinted by permission of Harcourt Brace Jovanovich and Routledge & Kegan Paul.

The researcher found that the participants usually used a pronoun that was consistent with sex stereotypes. In the neutral sentences, the masculine was most often used, although some participants deliberately suggested role reversals by switching the pronouns, and others tried to avoid sexism by using a combination, as in *he or she*. Women were less likely to use the masculine generic than men.

After the participants completed the sentences, the researcher asked them what image they had when they completed a sentence. Most often, they imagined a man in male-stereotyped sentences and a woman in female-stereotyped ones. In neutral sentences, the image was almost exclusively male.

This study clearly illustrates that the sign, in this case a pronoun, is connected to its referent through the mind of the user. Meaning thus depends on the image or thought of the person in relation to the sign and the object being signified. Many semiotic theorists have elaborated and expanded this basic idea.

6   Charles Saunders Peirce, *Charles S. Peirce: Selected Writings*, ed. P. O. Wiener (New York: Dover, 1958). See also, for example, John Stewart, *Language as Articulate Contact: Toward a Post-Semiotic Philosophy of Communication* (Albany: SUNY Press, 1995), pp. 76–81; Christopher Hookway, *Peirce* (London: Routledge & Kegan Paul, 1985); Max H. Fisch, *Peirce, Semiotic, and Pragmatism* (Bloomington: Indiana University Press, 1986); Thomas A. Goudge, *The Thought of Peirce* (Toronto: University of Toronto Press, 1950); John R. Lyne, "Rhetoric and Semiotic in C. S. Peirce," *Quarterly Journal of Speech* 66 (1980): 155–168.
7   For a good summary of Peirce's theory, see Richard J. Parmentier, "Signs' Place in Medias Res: Peirce's Concept of Semiotic Mediation," in *Semiotic Mediation: Sociocultural and Psychological Perspectives*, eds. Elizabeth Mertz and Richard Parmentier (Orlando: Academic, 1985), pp. 23–48.
8   C. K. Ogden and I. A. Richards, *The Meaning of Meaning* (London: Kegan, Paul, Trench, Trubner, 1923).
9   Wendy Martyna, "What Does 'He' Mean?" *Journal of Communication* 28 (1978): 131–138.

TABLE **4.2**

Stages of Action in Relation to Dimensions of Signifying and Value

Stages of Action	Dimensions of Signifying	Dimensions of Value
Perceptual	Designative	Detachment
Manipulatory	Prescriptive	Dominance
Consummatory	Appraisive	Dependence

From *Signification and Significance* by Charles Morris (Cambridge, MA: MIT Press, 1964).

Charles Morris

Morris wrote about semiotics for at least thirty years. During this time his theory became increasingly sophisticated. In his later writings, Morris showed that all human action involves signs and meaning in various intriguing ways. Any act consists of three stages—perception, manipulation, and consummation.[10] In *perception* the person becomes aware of a sign. In the *manipulation* stage, the person interprets the sign and decides how to respond to it. Then the act is *consummated* by an actual response.

Signs do different things at each stage. During the perception stage, for example, signs designate—they point, show, or refer to some object or condition. During the manipulation stage, signs tend to prescribe, advise, or tell us what to do. In the consummation stage, they appraise or evaluate. Perception is often a time of detachment, when we objectively view the situation. The manipulation stage is often a time of dominance, when the signs assume some authority. And in the consummation stage, there is often a feeling of dependence as we come to rely on the sign as a way of structuring our response.

As we recall from system theory, a system influences and is influenced by other systems. When one system is being affected by another, it is said to be *dependent* on the other system. When it is affecting another system, it is *dominant* over that other system. A state of *detachment* exists when a system is more or less autonomous. Detachment, then, corresponds to perception and the designative mode of signification. Dominance corresponds to the manipulation and pre-

scriptive factors, and dependence corresponds to consummation and appraisive values. Table 4.2 summarizes these relationships.[11]

Suppose, for example, that you are watching television one evening, and you see a commercial for some product you do not currently use. Viewing the commercial represents the perceptual stage of the act. Here you are detached, simply taking it in. After seeing the commercial, however, you may spend some time thinking about it, considering what was meant by some of the statements in the advertisement, perhaps determining the relevance of the product for yourself. This stage is manipulation. Here you are dominating by thinking over the information and making your decision to buy or not to buy. The third stage would occur in actually purchasing the new product (consummation). Here you allow yourself to become "dependent" on the product, at least temporarily.

At each point in this process, signs are used. In the first stage, the product is identified, and various aspects are designated. In the manipulation stage, you are deciding how to act toward the product (whether or not to buy), thus using primarily prescriptive signs. Finally, in consummation you discover and signify to yourself your like or dislike for the product.

All of our examples so far feature a single individual, but groups can act too. Putting on a party, having a class, arranging a car pool, managing an automobile dealership, and conducting an or-

---

10   George Herbert Mead, *Mind, Self, and Society* (Chicago: University of Chicago Press, 1934). See also Chapter 8.
11   Morris, *Signification*, p. 22.

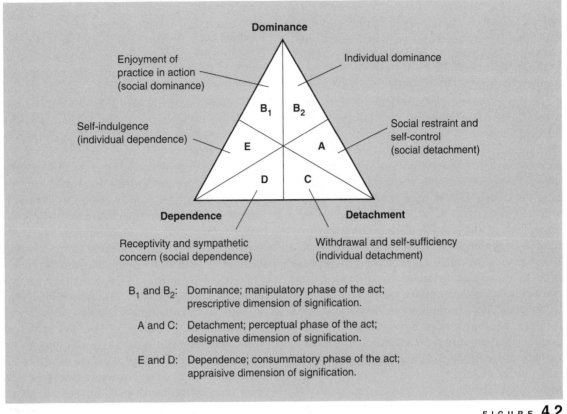

B₁ and B₂: Dominance; manipulatory phase of the act; prescriptive dimension of signification.

A and C: Detachment; perceptual phase of the act; designative dimension of signification.

E and D: Dependence; consummatory phase of the act; appraisive dimension of signification.

F I G U R E **4.2**

Model of the Relation of Values, Signs, and the Act

From *Signification and Significance* by Charles Morris. (Cambridge, MA: MIT Press, 1964).

chestra are just a few examples. When you think about it, very few acts are strictly individual. Group acts, called *social acts*, go through the same stages as individual ones, but in a group you can divide the labor. Because of role specialization, some people may be primarily responsible for perceptual aspects of the act, others for manipulation, and still others for consummation.

In addition, a given individual may show a preference for certain aspects of individual and social acts. This preference—expressed in terms of detachment, dominance, or dependence—represents the person's values.

A value may be individual or social. Social values deal with a person's relationship to others, and individual values deal with his or her personal preferences. Morris identifies five value clusters, including social restraint and self-control, enjoyment of practice in action, withdrawal and self-sufficiency, receptivity and sympathetic concern, and self-indulgence. Figure 4.2 shows the relationship of these factors to the three-point model of the act developed earlier.[12]

Susanne Langer

A prominent and useful theory of language is that of Susanne Langer, whose *Philosophy in a New Key* has received considerable attention by

---

12   Morris, *Signification*, p. 26.

students of symbolism.[13] Langer considers symbolism to be the central concern of philosophy, a topic that underlies all human knowing and understanding. According to Langer, all animal life is dominated by feeling, but human feeling is affected by conception, symbols, and language.

Langer makes a distinction between signs and symbols. She uses the term *sign* in a more restricted sense than Morris to mean a stimulus that signals the presence of something else. A sign corresponds closely to the actual signified object. In this sense clouds may be a sign of rain, laughter a sign of happiness, and a red light a sign of cross traffic. A *symbol* is more complex: "Symbols are not proxy of their objects, but are *vehicles for the conception of objects.*"[14] Symbols allow a person to think about something apart from its immediate presence. In other words a symbol is "an instrument of thought."[15]

Not only do people have a capacity to use symbols, but they possess a basic need for symbols, and symbol-making is a continuous process tantamount to eating and sleeping. Much human behavior can be explained in terms of meeting the symbolic need.

Like Peirce and Morris, Langer sees meaning as the complex relation among the symbol, the object, and the person. As she puts it, "If there is not at least one thing meant and one mind for which it is meant, then there is not a complete meaning."[16] Thus, we have both a logical and psychological sense of meaning—the logical being the relation between the symbol and referent and the psychological the relation between the symbol and the person.

The real significance of language, however, is not in individual words but in *discourse.* Words name things, but "before terms are built into propositions, they assert nothing, preclude nothing . . . say nothing."[17] By tying words together into sentences, people create *propositions,* which are complex symbols that present a picture of something. The word *dog* brings up a conception, but its combination with other words provides a unified picture: The little brown dog is nestled against my foot. Because language possesses this rich potential for combination and organization,

it truly makes us human. Through language we communicate, we think, and we feel.

How, then, do symbols work? Any symbol, including a proposition, communicates a *concept,* a general idea, pattern, or form. The concept is a meaning shared among communicators, but each communicator also will have a private image or meaning that fills in the details of the common picture. This private image is the person's *conception.*

Meaning therefore consists of the individual's private conception and the common concept shared with others. For example, Vincent van Gogh's paintings are filled with symbols with both common and private meanings. The common meanings in these paintings are accessible to anybody who views them; they are the generally recognized images in the scene. The private meanings are those of van Gogh himself and others who have studied the artist.[18]

For instance, his painting *Open Bible* is a view of a large open Bible sitting next to a candle. Next to the Bible is a small copy of a novel, Emile Zola's *The Joy of Living.* For the common viewer, these images are just objects, but for the artist, these images have very particular private meanings. As a whole, the painting symbolizes the life and death of the artist's father. Van Gogh's father, a minister, is symbolized by the open Bible. His death is symbolized by the candle, which casts a light on a passage from Isaiah about the suffering servant. The title of the smaller book symbolizes the elder van Gogh's life. Van Gogh discussed the symbolism of his work in a letter to his brother:

> I want to paint men and women with that something of the eternal which the halo used to

13   Susanne Langer, *Philosophy in a New Key* (Cambridge, MA: Harvard University Press, 1942). See also *Mind: An Essay on Human Feeling,* 3 vols. (Baltimore: Johns Hopkins University Press, 1967, 1972, 1982). A good secondary source is Stewart, *Language as Articulate Contact,* pp. 92–101.
14   Langer, *Philosophy in a New Key,* p. 61.
15   Langer, *Philosophy in a New Key,* p. 63.
16   Langer, *Philosophy in a New Key,* p. 56.
17   Langer, *Philosophy in a New Key,* p. 67.
18   A semiotic analysis of van Gogh's work was done by Mark Roskill, "'Public' and 'Private' Meanings: The Paintings of van Gogh," *Journal of Communication* 29 (1979): 157–169.

symbolize, and which we seek to convey by the actual radiance and vibration of our coloring.

. . . I am always in the hope of being able to express the love of two lovers by a wedding of two complementary colors, their mingling and their opposition, the mysterious vibration of kindred tones. To express the thought of a brow by the radiance of a light tone against a somber background. To express hope by some star, the eagerness of a soul by a sunset radiance.[19]

Langer's vocabulary includes three additional terms: signification, denotation, and connotation. *Signification* is the meaning of a sign, or a simple stimulus announcing the presence of some object. Signification is a simple one-to-one relationship between sign and object, as between a stop sign and cross traffic.

Denotation is the relation of the symbol to its object. For example, the denotation of the symbol *dog* may be your image of a little brown puppy at your feet. This relationship between the word and the puppy occurs only in your mind through your idea of the animal. Even when the puppy is not present, you can think of it because of the relationship between the symbol and idea.

The *connotation* of a symbol is the direct relationship between the symbol and the conception. Connotation includes all of one's personal feelings and associations attached to a symbol. Here you are less concerned with the object (a puppy) associated with the symbol than with your own private orientation to that object—many happy childhood memories, for example.

Langer notes that humans possess a built-in tendency to *abstract*. Abstraction is a process of forming a general idea from a variety of concrete experiences. It is a process of leaving out details in conceiving of objects, events, or situations in ever more general terms. For example, the word *dog* may have a specific connotation, but this conception is incomplete; it always leaves something out. The more abstract the symbol, the sketchier the conception: A *dog* is a *mammal*, which is an *animal*; an animal is a *living thing*, which is an *object*. Each successive term in this series leaves out more details and is therefore more abstract than the previous term.

So far we have emphasized Langer's ideas about language, which she calls *discursive symbolism*. However, she also admits the importance of nondiscursive, or *presentational*, symbols. Some of the most important human experiences are emotional and are best communicated through forms such as worship, art, and music.

◖ LANGUAGE AND THE STUDY OF SYNTACTICS

The study of language has been heavily influenced by semiotics and vice versa.[20] The modern founder of structural linguistics was Ferdinand de Saussure, who, along with figures such as Peirce, Ogden, Morris, and Langer, made substantial contributions to the structural tradition in communication.

Classical Foundations

Saussure taught that signs, including language, are arbitrary.[21] He noted that different languages use different words for the same thing and that there is usually no physical connection between a word and its referent. Therefore, signs are conventions governed by rules. Not only does this assumption support the idea that language is a structure, but it also reinforces the general idea that language and reality are separate. Saussure,

19   Quoted in Roskill, "'Public' and 'Private' Meanings," p. 157.
20   Leeds-Hurwitz, *Semiotics and Communication*, p. 13. For good brief overviews of the study of language, see Donald G. Ellis, *From Language to Communication* (Mahwah, NJ: Erlbaum, 1999); Scott Jacobs, "Language and Interpersonal Communication," in *Handbook of Interpersonal Communication*, eds. Mark L. Knapp and Gerald R. Miller (Thousand Oaks, CA: Sage, 1994), pp. 199–228; Irwin Weiser, "Linguistics," in *Encyclopedia of Rhetoric and Composition*, ed. Theresa Enos (New York: Garland, 1996), pp. 386–391; David Graddol, Jenny Cheshire, and Joan Swann, *Descriptive Language* (Buckingham, England: Open University Press, 1994), pp. 65–101; Adrian Akmajian, Richard A. Demers, Ann K. Farmer, and Robert M. Harnish, *An Introduction to Language and Communication* (Cambridge, MA: MIT Press, 1994), pp. 123–192.
21   Ferdinand de Saussure's primary work on this subject is *Course in General Linguistics* (London: Peter Owen, 1960). Excellent secondary sources include Stewart, *Language as Articulate Contact*, pp. 81–87; Anthony Giddens, *Central Problems in Social Theory: Action, Structure, and Contradiction in Social Analysis* (Berkeley: University of California Press, 1979); and Fred Dallmayr, *Language and Politics* (Notre Dame, IN: University of Notre Dame Press, 1984).

then, saw language as a structured system representing reality. He believed that linguistic researchers must pay attention to language forms, such as speech sounds, words, and grammar. Although language structure is arbitrary, language *use* is not at all arbitrary, because it requires established conventions. You cannot choose any word you wish, nor can you rearrange grammar at a whim.

Language described in structural terms, then, is strictly a system of formal relations without substance. The key to understanding the structure of the system is *difference*. The elements and relations embedded in language are distinguished by their differences. One sound differs from another (like *p* and *b*); one word differs from another (like *pat* and *bat*); one grammatical form differs from another (like *has run* and *will run*). This system of differences constitutes the structure of the language. Both in spoken and written language, distinctions among signified objects in the world are identified by corresponding distinctions among linguistic signs. No linguistic unit has significance in and of itself; only in contrast with other linguistic units does a particular structure acquire meaning.

Saussure believed that all a person knows of the world is determined by language. Unlike other semioticians, then, Saussure does not see signs as referential. Signs do not *designate* objects but *constitute* them. There can be no object apart from the signs used to designate it. In this regard, Saussure's work set the stage for much twentieth-century thought not only in structural linguistics but also interactionist theory (Chapters 8 and 9) and interpretive and critical theories (Chapters 10 and 11).[22]

Saussure made an important distinction between formal language, which he called *langue,* and the actual use of language in communication, which he referred to as *parole*. These two terms correspond to language and speech. Language (langue) is a formal system that can be analyzed apart from its use in everyday life. Speech (parole) is the actual use of language to accomplish purposes. Language is not created by users, but speech is. Indeed, speech makes use of language, but it is less regular and more variable than the formal system of language from which it derives. In other words, when you speak you are using language, but you are also adapting it to enable you to achieve goals.

Linguistics, to Saussure, is the study of langue, not parole: "Taken as a whole, speech [parole] is many-sided and heterogeneous; straddling several areas simultaneously . . . we cannot put it into any category of human facts, for we cannot discover its unity. Language [langue], on the contrary, is a self-contained whole and a principle of classification."[23]

One difference between langue and parole, according to Saussure, is stability. Language is characterized by *synchrony,* meaning that it changes very little over time. Speech, on the other hand, is characterized by *diachrony,* meaning that it changes constantly from situation to situation.

Because of its constant flux, some believe that speech is not particularly suitable for scientific study, which is why linguistics must take a language-oriented, synchronic focus. The point here is not that language never changes but that language form cannot be understood unless a synchronic perspective is adopted.

As we will see in Chapters 8 and 9, however, the distinction between language and speech, and that between synchrony and diachrony, is sharply criticized by theorists from other traditions. We return to the topic of language in Chapter 5 where we explore in more detail theories of how language functions in discourse, or speech.

Structural Linguistics

Let us turn now to a more detailed discussion of language structure itself. Influenced by the work of Saussure, theorists developed the standard model of sentence structure between about 1930

---

22   See Art Berman, *From the New Criticism to Deconstruction* (Urbana: University of Illinois Press, 1988), pp. 114–143.
23   Saussure, *Course,* p. 9.

and 1950.[24] Basically, this model breaks down a sentence into components in hierarchical fashion. Sounds and sound groups combine to form word roots and word parts, which in turn combine to form words, then phrases. Phrases are put together to make clauses or sentences. Thus, language can be analyzed on various levels, roughly corresponding to sounds, words, and phrases.

The first level of analysis involves the study of *phonetics,* or speech sound. A particular speech sound is a *phone.* Phones that sound very similar are grouped into a sound family called *phoneme,* which is the basic building block of any language. Any dialect of a language contains a number of phonemes, which are combined according to rules to produce *morphemes,* the smallest meaningful linguistic unit. Words are combined according to the rules of grammar to form *phrases,* which are linked together into *clauses* and *sentences.*

This structural approach provides an orderly classification of language parts, and segments are sequenced in a sentence-building process. At each level of analysis is a set of classes (for example, phonemes or morphemes) that can be observed in the native language. Sentences are always built up from the bottom of the hierarchy, so that succeeding levels depend on the formation of lower levels. This scheme is known as phrase-structure grammar, a set of rules called *syntax.* Phrase-structure grammar consists of *rewrite rules* that "rewrite" the sentence or other unit into its parts.

For example, a sentence can be broken down according to the following rewrite rule:

sentence = noun phrase (NP) + verb phrase (VP)

The verb phrase can be broken down further according to the following rewrite rule:

VP = verb (V) + noun phrase (NP)

This process continues until all units of the sentence are accounted for. Phrase structures are often illustrated by a tree diagram, as shown in Figure 4.3.

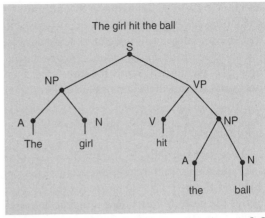

FIGURE **4.3**

A Simple Tree Diagram

Although this approach provides a useful description of the structure of language, it fails to explain how people produce and understand language. This latter question, far more central to communication than language structure, has captured the attention of psycholinguists and sociolinguists since about 1950.

We know that people must possess an intuitive knowledge of their language in order to produce meaningful, grammatical speech. What is the nature of this knowledge? How is it acquired? How is it used? The literature that has emerged from this work is extensive, controversial, and at times highly technical.

Old-fashioned phrase-structure grammar is no longer believed to be adequate by itself to explain the generation of sentences.[25] The primary

24 The major writings of this period include Leonard Bloomfield, *Language* (New York: Holt, Rinehart & Winston, 1933); Charles Fries, *The Structure of English* (New York: Harcourt, Brace & World, 1952); Zellig Harris, *Structural Linguistics* (Chicago: University of Chicago Press, 1951). An excellent summary and critique of this period can be found in J. A. Fodor, T. G. Bever, and M. F. Garrett, *The Psychology of Language: An Introduction to Psycholinguistics and Generative Grammar* (New York: McGraw-Hill, 1974).
25 For an explanation and critique of finite-state and phrase-structure grammar, see Noam Chomsky, "Three Models for the Description of Language," *Transactions on Information Theory* IT-2 (1956): 113–124; and Jerry Fodor, James Jenkins, and Sol Saporta, "Psycholinguistics and Communication Theory," in *Human Communication Theory,* ed. F. E. X. Dance (New York: Holt, Rinehart & Winston, 1967), pp. 160–201.

objection to classical linguistics is that although it is useful as a descriptive tool, it is powerless to explain how language is generated. For example, phrase-structure grammar would analyze the following two sentences exactly the same way, even though their syntactic meanings are different.[26]

John is easy to please.

John is eager to please.

These sentences have entirely different syntactic meanings. In the first sentence, John is the object of the infinitive *to please*. In the second John is the noun phrase of the sentence. Regular phrase structure provides no way to explain these different grammatical meanings by examining the sentences themselves.

Problems like this lead to a series of questions that traditional phrase-structure grammar cannot answer:

- How can a speaker produce an infinite number of novel sentences from just a few rules?
- By what cognitive process are sentences generated and understood?
- How is syntactic ambiguity to be accounted for?
- How is language acquired?

To answer questions such as these, linguists developed generative grammar.[27]

Generative Grammar

Noam Chomsky is the primary force behind generative grammar. As a young linguist in the 1950s, Chomsky parted company with the classical theorists to develop an approach that since has become the mainstay of contemporary linguistics.[28] Like any theoretical tradition, generative grammar now has several positions within it, although the tradition as a whole is built on a cluster of essential ideas.

First, generative grammar rests on the assumption that sentence generation is central to sentence structure. The form of a sentence cannot be separated from the process by which it is generated. Old-style linguistics was powerful in *de-*

scribing the structure of a sentence, but it did not explain how sentences are actually produced by the speaker. Further, there is the suspicion that the surface structure of a sentence may actually mislead us about how sentences are really structured within the mind.

Second, the objective of generative grammar is to isolate a set of rules that explains how any sentence could be generated. Inventing a new rule for each construction is not workable because the brain cannot operate by an infinite set of rules, though people can produce and understand an infinite number. An adequate grammar must explain this paradox. The answer lies in a relatively small number of rules that can be used over and over again to produce novel sentences.

The third essential feature of generative grammar is the transformation. (In fact, generative grammar is also named *transformational grammar*.) At some point the surface structure of a sentence must have been transformed from some other deeper form, and generative grammar seeks to explain this transformation process.

In treating the study of mind as a natural science, Chomsky believes that principles of language and mind are universal and can be discovered by scientists. He is analytical in approach and seeks inherent mechanisms of mind. However, he also sees the individual as creative, so he promotes the idea that knowledge arises from a projection of innate categories onto the world of actual experience.[29] In short, Chomsky is a champion of rationalism, a point of view that until the past decade or two has not been popular in this century.[30]

---

26   Examples from Gilbert Harmon, *On Noam Chomsky: Critical Essays* (Garden City, NY: Anchor, 1974), p. 5.
27   For a brief overview of generative grammar, see Jacobs, "Language and Interpersonal Communication"; Thomas Wasow, "Grammar," in *International Encyclopedia of Communications*, vol. 2, eds. Erik Barnouw et al. (New York: Oxford University Press, 1989), pp. 234–238; and Graddol, Cheshire, and Swann, *Descriptive Language*, pp. 85–89.
28   For a list of Chomsky's works, see the Selected Bibliography.
29   Chomsky discusses features of his epistemology in *Rules and Representations* (New York: Columbia University Press, 1980).
30   The philosopher most associated with rationalism is René Descartes (seventeenth century). See *Meditations on First Philosophy*, trans. Laurence J. LaFleur (Indianapolis: Bobbs-Merrill, 1960).

Generative grammar is highly technical, and we will not cover it in detail here.[31] Language is a fascinating and important subject, but the signs used in communication are certainly not limited to the linguistic. Much of the nuance of meaning is communicated nonverbally.

● THE SEMANTICS AND SYNTACTICS OF NONVERBAL BEHAVIOR

Scholars disagree about what nonverbal communication is, as Randall Harrison points out:

> The term "nonverbal communication" has been applied to a bewildering array of events. Everything from the territoriality of animals to the protocol of diplomats. From facial expression to muscle twitches. From inner, but inexpressible, feelings to outdoor public monuments. From the message of massage to the persuasion of a punch. From dance and drama to music and mime. From the flow of affect to the flow of traffic. From extrasensory perception to the economic policies of international power blocks. From fashion and fad to architecture and analog computer. From the smell of roses to the taste of steak. From Freudian symbol to astrological sign. From the rhetoric of violence to the rhetoric of topless dancers.[32]

As the above quotation shows, there is little agreement on what counts as nonverbal communication. To make this question even more challenging, research on nonverbal behavior is extensive and comes from many fields.[33] For these reasons, classifying and organizing this material is difficult. Various topics relevant to nonverbal communication are covered later in the book; for now, let's concentrate on structural approaches to nonverbal coding.

Burgoon characterizes nonverbal code systems as possessing several structural properties. First, nonverbal codes tend to be *analogic* rather than digital. Whereas digital signals are discrete, like numbers and letters, analogic signals are continuous, forming a spectrum or range, like sound volume and the brightness of light. Therefore, nonverbal signals like facial expression and vocal intonation cannot simply be classed into one category or another—like loud or soft, bright or dim—but are gradations.

A second feature found in some, but not all, nonverbal codes is *iconicity*, or resemblance. Iconic codes resemble the thing being symbolized (like depicting the shape of something with your hands). Third, certain nonverbal codes seem to elicit *universal meaning*. This is especially the case with such signals as threats and emotional displays, which may be biologically determined. Fourth, nonverbal codes enable the *simultaneous transmission* of several messages. With the face, body, voice, and other signals, several different messages can be sent at once. Fifth, nonverbal signals often evoke an *automatic response* without thinking. An example would be stepping on the brake at a red light. Sixth, nonverbal signals are often emitted *spontaneously*, as when you let off nervous energy.

We can use Morris's three dimensions of semantics, syntactics, and pragmatics, defined earlier in the chapter, to characterize nonverbal forms (as well as language). *Semantics* refers to the meanings of a sign. For example, two fingers held up behind someone's head is a way of calling him a "devil." *Syntactics* refers to the ways signs are organized into systems with other signs. One might, for example, hold up two fingers behind someone's head, laugh, and say "Joke's on you!" Here a gesture, a vocal sign (laughing), facial expressions, and language combine to create an overall meaning. *Pragmatics*

---

31   For a brief summary, see previous editions of this book: Stephen W. Littlejohn, *Theories of Human Communication*, 5th ed. (Belmont, CA: Wadsworth, 1996), pp. 75–77; 4th ed. (Belmont, CA: Wadsworth, 1992), pp. 74–77. See also Jacobs, "Language and Interpersonal Communication"; and Wasow, "Grammar."

32   Randall Harrison, *Beyond Words: An Introduction to Nonverbal Communication* (Englewood Cliffs, NJ: Prentice-Hall, 1974), pp. 24–25. Conceptual issues are discussed in Judee K. Burgoon, "Nonverbal Signals," in *Handbook of Interpersonal Communication*, eds. Mark L. Knapp and Gerald R. Miller (Thousand Oaks, CA: Sage, 1994), pp. 229–285; see also Mark Knapp and Judith Hall, *Nonverbal Communication in Human Interaction* (New York: Holt, Rinehart & Winston, 1992).

33   For a broad overview of research, see Burgoon, "Nonverbal Signals."

refers to the effects or behaviors elicited by a sign or group of signs, as when the "devil" sign is taken as a joke rather than an insult.

The meanings attached to both verbal and nonverbal forms are context-bound, or determined in part by the situation in which they are produced. Both language and nonverbal forms allow communicators to combine relatively few signs into an almost limitless variety of complex expressions of meaning.

Nonverbal code systems are often classed according to the type of activity used in the code. Burgoon suggests seven types: kinesics (bodily activity); vocalics or paralanguage (voice); physical appearance; haptics (touch); proxemics (space); chronemics (time); and artifacts (objects).[34] Two of the most well developed of these are kinesics and proxemics.

Birdwhistell on Kinesics

Ray Birdwhistell is considered the originator of kinesics.[35] An anthropologist interested in language, Birdwhistell uses linguistics as a model for his kinesics work. In fact, kinesics is popularly referred to as "body language."

In *Kinesics and Context* Birdwhistell lists seven assumptions on which he bases his theory:[36]

1. All body movements have potential meaning in communicative contexts. Somebody can always assign meaning to any bodily activity.
2. Behavior can be analyzed because it is organized, and this organization can be subjected to systematic analysis.
3. Although bodily activity has biological limitations, the use of bodily motion in interaction is considered to be a part of the social system. Different groups will therefore use gestures differently.
4. People are influenced by the visible bodily activity of others.
5. The ways in which bodily activity functions in communication can be investigated.
6. The meanings discovered in research on kinesics result from the behavior being studied as well as the methods used for research.

7. A person's use of bodily activity will have idiosyncratic features but will also be part of a larger social system shared with others.

Birdwhistell's work is based largely on the perceived similarities between bodily activity and language, which has been called the *linguistic-kinesic analogy.*

> This original study of gestures gave the first indication that kinesic structure is parallel to language structure. By the study of gestures in context, it became clear that the kinesic system has forms which are astonishingly like words in language. The discovery in turn led to the investigation of the components of these forms and to the discovery of the larger complexes of which they were components. . . . It has become clear that there are body behaviors which function like significant sounds, that combine into simple or relatively complex units like words, which are combined into much longer stretches of structured behavior like sentences or even paragraphs.[37]

The similarity of hierarchical structure in kinesics to that of linguistics is striking, and the problem of the kinesicist is similar to that of the linguist: "Kinesics is concerned with abstracting from the continuous muscular shifts which are characteristics of living physiological systems those groupings of movement which are of significance to the communicational process and thus to the interactional systems of particular social groups."[38]

Out of the thousands of perceptible bodily motions produced in a short period of time, certain of these emerge as important in communication. Such movements are called kines. A *kine* is a range of motions or positions seen as a single motion or position. A perceptible movement of the eyelid or a turn of the hand would be an example of a kine. What is defined as a kine in one cultural group may not be in another.

---

34   Burgoon, "Nonverbal Signals," p. 232.
35   Birdwhistell's major works include *Introduction to Kinesics* (Louisville, KY: University of Louisville Press, 1952); *Kinesics and Context* (Philadelphia: University of Pennsylvania Press, 1970).
36   Birdwhistell, *Kinesics and Context*, pp. 183–184.
37   Birdwhistell, *Kinesics and Context*, p. 80.
38   Birdwhistell, *Kinesics and Context*, p. 192.

Kines are further grouped into *kinemes,* elements that have distinct meanings. Like the phoneme in linguistics, the kineme is a group of relatively interchangeable kines. For example, up to twenty-three different positions (kines) of the eyelids can be discerned, but they can be grouped into about four kinemes. Kinemes, like phonemes, occur in context. A complex combination of kinemes throughout the body such as a wink, a smile, and a wave of the hand is called a *kinemorph.*

Ekman and Friesen on Kinesics

For many years Paul Ekman and Wallace Friesen collaborated on research that led to an excellent general model of kinesic behavior, concentrating their work on the face and hands.[39] Their goal was ambitious: "Our aim has been to increase understanding of the individual, his feelings, mood, personality, and attitudes, and to increase understanding of any given interpersonal interaction, the nature of the relationship, the status or quality of communication, what impressions are formed, and what is revealed about interpersonal style or skill."[40]

These authors analyzed nonverbal activity three ways: by origin, by coding, and by usage. *Origin* is the source of an act. A nonverbal behavior may be *innate* (built into the nervous system), *species-constant* (universal behavior required for survival), or *variant* across cultures, groups, and individuals. As examples, one could speculate that eyebrow raising as a sign of surprise is innate, that marking territory is species-constant, and that shaking the head back and forth to indicate no is culture-specific.

Coding is the relationship of the act to its meaning. An act may be *arbitrary,* with no meaning inherent in the sign itself. By convention in our culture, for example, we agree that nodding is an indication of yes, but this coding is purely arbitrary. Other nonverbal signs are *iconic* and resemble the thing being signified. For instance, we often draw pictures in the air or position our hands to illustrate what we are talking about. The third category of coding is *intrinsic.* Intrinsically coded cues contain their meaning within them and are themselves part of what is being signified. Crying is an example of intrinsic coding. Crying is a sign of emotion, but it is also part of the emotion itself.

The third way to analyze a behavior is by *usage.* Usage also includes the degree to which a nonverbal behavior is intended to convey information. A *communicative act* is used deliberately to convey meaning. *Interactive acts* actually influence the behavior of the other participants. An act is both communicative and interactive if it is intentional and influential. For example, if you deliberately wave to a friend as a sign of greeting and the friend waves back, your cue is communicative and interactive. Some behaviors are not intended to be communicative but nevertheless provide information for the perceiver. Such acts are said to be *informative.* On a day when you are feeling less than friendly, you may duck into a hallway to avoid meeting an acquaintance coming your way. If the other person sees the avoidance, your behavior has been informative even though you did not intend to communicate.

All nonverbal behavior is one of five types, depending on origin, coding, and usage. The first type is the *emblem.* Emblems have a verbal translation of a rather precise meaning. They are normally used in a deliberate fashion to communicate a particular message. The victory "V" and the Black power fist are examples. The origin of emblems is cultural learning, and emblems may be either arbitrary or iconic.

Illustrators are the second kind of nonverbal cues. Illustrators are used to depict what is being said verbally. They are intentional, though we may not always be directly aware of them. They include eight types:

39   Ekman and Friesen's major works include "Nonverbal Behavior in Psychotherapy Research," in *Research in Psychotherapy,* vol. 3, ed. J. Shlien (Washington, DC: American Psychological Association, 1968), pp. 179–216; "The Repertoire of Nonverbal Behavior: Categories, Origins, Usage, and Coding," *Semiotica* 1 (1969): 49–98; *Emotion in the Human Face: Guidelines for Research and an Integration of Findings* (New York: Pergamon, 1972); *Unmasking the Face* (Englewood Cliffs, NJ: Prentice-Hall, 1975).
40   Paul Ekman and Wallace Friesen, "Hand Movements," *Journal of Communication* 22 (1972): 353.

Characteristics of Nonverbal Behavior

Behavior	Origin	Coding	Usage
Emblems	Learned	Arbitrary or iconic	Communicative
Illustrators	Learned	Iconic	Informative Communicative Interactive
Adaptors	Innate Species-constant Variant	Iconic or intrinsic	Informative Interactive
Regulators	Learned	Intrinsic or iconic	Interactive
Affect displays	Innate Species-constant Variant	Intrinsic	Informative Interactive

batons—movements that accent or emphasize

ideographs—"sketching" the direction of a thought

deictic movements—pointing

spatial movements—depicting or outlining space

rhythmic movements—pacing motions

kinetographs—depicting physical actions

pictographs—drawing a picture in the air

emblematic movements—illustrating a verbal statement

These types can be combined, since some motions are combinations of types. Illustrators are informative or communicative in use and occasionally may be interactive. They are learned.

The third type of nonverbal behavior is the *adaptor,* which serves to facilitate release of bodily tension. Examples are hand wringing, head scratching, or foot jiggling. *Self-adaptors* are directed to one's own body. They include scratching, stroking, grooming, squeezing. *Alter-adaptors,* like slapping someone on the back, are directed to another's body. *Object-adaptors,* such as twisting a paper clip, are directed at things. In any case, adaptors can be iconic or intrinsic.

Rarely are they intentional, and one is usually not aware of one's own adaptive behaviors. Although they are rarely communicative, they are sometimes interactive and often informative.

Regulators, the fourth type of behavior, are used to control or coordinate interaction. For example, we use eye contact to signal speaking and listening roles in a conversation. Regulators are primarily interactive. They are coded intrinsically or iconically, and their origin is cultural learning.

The final category of behavior is the *affect display.* These behaviors, which may be in part innate, involve the display of feelings and emotions. The face is a particularly rich source for affect display, although other parts of the body also may be involved. Affect displays are intrinsically coded. They are rarely communicative, often interactive, and always informative.[41] These types of nonverbal behaviors are summarized in Table 4.3.

---

41 More recent evidence suggests that affect displays are not necessarily as informative as Ekman and Friesen indicated. Interpretation of affect displays in actual interaction has been found not to be very accurate and may serve more as a nonverbal interjection than a display of emotion. See Michael T. Motley, "Facial Affect and Verbal Context in Conversation," *Human Communication Research,* 20 (1993): 3–40; Michael T. Motley and Carl T. Camden, "Facial Expression of Emotion: A Comparison of Posed Expressions Versus Spontaneous Expressions in an Interpersonal Communication Setting," *Western Journal of Speech Communication* 52 (1988): 1–22.

Hall on Proxemics

Edward Hall shares the view of other communication theorists that communication occurs through multiple channels.[42] Just as language varies from culture to culture, so do nonverbal behaviors. Specifically, *proxemics* refers to the use of space in communication: "the study of how man unconsciously structures microspace—the distance between men in conduct of daily transactions, the organization of space in his houses and buildings, and ultimately the layout of his towns."[43]

According to Hall, the way space is used in interaction is very much a cultural matter. Different senses are important to different cultures. In some countries, such as the United States, sight and hearing predominate; in other places, such as Arab cultures, smell is also important. Some cultures rely on touching more than others. In general, the predominant senses of a culture partially determine the way in which space is used within that culture.

Proxemics also vary because cultural definitions of the self are different. People in most Western cultures learn to identify the self through the skin and clothes. Arabs, however, place the self deeper in the middle of the body. For these reasons, then, the people of a particular culture arrange their space in certain ways.

Hall defines three basic types of space. *Fixed-feature space* consists of unmovable things such as walls and rooms. *Semifixed-feature space* includes movable objects like furniture. *Informal space* is the personal territory around the body that travels with a person, which determines the interpersonal distance between people. Anglo-American culture, for example, uses four discernible distances: intimate (0 to 18 inches), personal (1 to 4 feet), social (4 to 12 feet), and public (over 12 feet).

When people are engaged in conversation, eight factors may be involved in how they use their space:

- *Posture-sex factors*: These include the sex of the participant and the basic position (standing, sitting, lying).
- *Sociofugal-sociopetal axis*: The word *sociofugal* means discouragement of interaction, and *sociopetal* implies encouragement. Axis is the angle of the shoulders relative to the other person. The speakers may be facing each other, may be back to back, or may be positioned toward any other angle in the radius. Thus, some angles, like face to face, encourage interaction, while others, like back to back, discourage it.
- *Kinesthetic factors*: This is the closeness of the individuals in terms of touchability. Individuals may be in physical contact or within close distance, they may be outside body contact distance, or they may be positioned anywhere in between these extremes. This factor also includes the positioning of body parts as well as which parts are touching.
- *Touching behavior*: People may be involved in caressing and holding, feeling, prolonged holding, pressing against, spot touching, accidental brushing, or no contact.
- *Visual code*: This category includes the manner of eye contact ranging from direct (eye to eye) to no contact.
- *Thermal code*: This element involves the perceived heat from the other communicator.
- *Olfactory code*: This factor includes the kind and degree of odor perceived in the conversation.
- *Voice loudness*: The loudness of speech can affect interpersonal space.

COMMENTARY AND CRITIQUE

The study of signs and language is an important core of communication theory. It not only provides a way of looking at communication but also has had a powerful impact on almost all perspectives now employed in communication theory. At the heart of this study is the basic notion of the triad of meaning. Although various

42   Edward Hall's major works include *The Silent Language* (Greenwich, CT: Fawcett, 1959); "A System for the Notation of Proxemic Behavior," *American Anthropologist* 65 (1963): 1003–1026; and *The Hidden Dimension* (New York: Random House, 1966).
43   Hall, "A System for Notation," p. 1003.

theorists have defined the elements of the triad somewhat differently or have stressed different aspects of it, this triad constitutes the heart of semiotic thinking.

Semiotic thinking has gone through a variety of versions. Peirce was primarily responsible for developing the idea of the sign-referent-interpretation unit, and others have built on this basic notion. Saussure applied semiotics to language, whereas Birdwhistell, Hall, and others emphasized nonlanguage forms.

Saussure's idea of difference has been a key concept in our understanding of language, but it applies equally well to all sign systems. Signs do not have a life of their own as independent markers. They assume significance only by virtue of the difference among signs.

Morris's threefold division of semiotics into semantics, syntactics, and pragmatics has been especially useful in clarifying the structural tradition. Many semioticians, including Morris, Langer, and Umberto Eco, have been preoccupied with the semantic dimension, in which the sign brings an idea, feeling, or conception into the mind of the person.

Syntactics, or the relationship among signs, has dominated the study of language and nonverbal communication. Saussure's idea of difference is especially important because it captures that character of signs making organization possible. Individual signs differ, making it possible to distinguish one from another; and organizational patterns differ as well, causing any grammatical structure to imply a meaning different from that implied by other structures.

Pragmatics is the study of how signs make a difference in people's lives. It is the study of the practical effects of signs. In a general sense, many communication theories are pragmatic because they deal with the outcomes or effects of communication. We begin looking at some pragmatic elements in the next chapter, and we will encounter them again at various points in this book.

Classical semiotics, which today may seem self-evident and simplistic to anyone with a modicum of background in language or communication, laid the foundation for more sophisticated linguistic and communication theories in the twentieth century.

Wendy Leeds-Hurwitz shows that because semiotics studies relationships within a complex network of things, it is at the heart of a number of broad communication concerns.[44] The semiotician may begin with individual signs, but the function of a sign can only be known by its connection with other signs in complex codes; and indeed even culture, with all that this broad concept entails, is viewed by some as a system of connected codes. Umberto Eco wrote: "Every act of communication to or between human beings—or any other intelligent biological or mechanical apparatus—presupposes a signification system as its necessary condition."[45] Thomas Sebeok added: "The subject matter of semiotics, it is often credited, is the exchange of any messages whatsoever, in a word, *communication*. . . . Semiotics is therefore classifiable as that pivotal branch of an integrated science of communication."[46]

Most critics agree that language is certainly conventional, but its arbitrariness is more in question. Arbitrariness makes sense only if one accepts that language and speech are separate and that signs are separate from their referents.[47]

Visual signs create special problems in this regard. Most people live constantly in a world of images, and with the electronic media, especially video, imagery becomes increasingly important as central signs in our culture. Yet, visual images do not quite fit the semiotic norm of representation. Surely, images can be understood as representing things, but they are not arbitrary or separate from what is represented. Images resonate with deep levels of actual experience in a way that arbitrary signs do not.[48]

Because visual codes are more open in their potential meanings, their interpretation is ulti-

44   Leeds-Hurwitz, *Semiotics and Communication*, pp. 3–21.
45   Umberto Eco, *A Theory of Semiotics* (Bloomington: Indiana University Press, 1976), p. 9.
46   Thomas Sebeok, "The Doctrine of Sign," in *Frontiers in Semiotics*, eds. J. Deely, B. Williams, and F. E. Kruse (Bloomington: Indiana University Press, 1986), p. 36.
47   For a critique of structuralism, see Giddens, *Central Problems*.
48   Harry Redner, *A New Science of Representation: Towards an Integrated Theory of Representation in Science, Politics, and Art* (Boulder, CO: Westview, 1994).

mately subjective and more connected to the internal perceptual and cognitive processes of the viewer than to conventional restricted representations. This is not to say that a person's meaning for an image is entirely individual. Visual means can and are affected by social learning too, but perceiving visual images is not the same as understanding language. Images require pattern recognition, organization, and discrimination, not just representational connections. Thus the meanings of visual images are a product of both individualized and social perception and knowledge.[49]

In a critique of semiotics, John Stewart challenges five commitments of semiotic theory.[50] The first is the *two worlds* commitment—the idea that signs and objects are separate with one representing the other. The second commitment is *atomism,* or the practice of analyzing sign systems, including language, by breaking them into small parts. The third commitment is *representation*—the belief that signs represent things other than themselves. Next, there is the *system* commitment, which leads to the depiction of signs in objective systems that can be examined and understood from outside. Finally, Stewart critiques the *tool* assumption, or the idea that signs and language are a way of transmitting thoughts and ideas from one place to another.

Stewart does not claim that all language and semiotic scholars explicitly accept these claims. Indeed, as we have seen in this chapter, several make attempts to expand semiotics beyond the simplistic word–thing relationship. Stewart's concern is the baggage that the vocabulary of *sign* and *symbol* bring with it. Once you use these terms, you are led to adopt the five commitments, even if tacitly, which may belie or distort the more complex vision held by the theorist.

Stewart's primary objection to the five commitments is that they just do not work out in practice. When you try to apply them to ongoing social interaction, you run into serious obstacles. Take the words *so, and, about,* and *sure* as examples. What do these represent? Certainly not objects. You might say they represent states of some kind or ideas, but states and ideas can only

be represented by other words. In these cases, meaning is established not by the sign–object relationship, but by the sign–sign relationship; and the latter is determined by how the signs are used by communicators, not by any structural feature of the signs themselves.

Even the task of breaking down sign systems like language into units is problematic. Take a stop sign as an example. What, exactly, is the sign here? Is it the letter *S,* the word *STOP,* the shape of the sign, where it is placed on the road? Or some combination of these? The same difficulty is encountered in trying to analyze language. If you listen to language the way it is actually spoken, phonemes, morphemes, and grammatical rules become distorted and broken. The speech is still understandable but not as neatly analyzed as formal linguistics leads us to believe.

Stewart shares the belief of many critics that the use of signs establishes and constructs the very thing those signs are said to represent. Even Saussure acknowledged that for all practical purposes our knowledge of the world is completely determined by language. These critics also believe that language and communication cannot be separated in the way that Saussure does with his langue–parole distinction because speech and other communicative forms are the mechanisms by which language and signs are created, maintained, and changed.[51] Later semioticians like Eco acknowledge this difficulty. At the same time, certain interactionists and interpretive scholars (Chapters 8, 9, and 10) attack the problem head-on by focusing on the uses of language and nonverbal forms in actual interaction rather than on the structure of the sign system itself.

49   Sandra E. Moriarty, "Abduction: A Theory of Visual Interpretation," *Communication Theory* 6 (1996): 167–187.
50   John Stewart, "The Symbol Model vs. Language as Constitutive Articulate Contact," in *Beyond the Symbol Model: Reflections on the Representational Nature of Language,* ed. John Stewart (Albany: SUNY Press, 1996), pp. 9–63; Stewart, *Language as Articulate Contact.* A similar argument is made by Pierre Bourdieu, *Language and Symbol Power* (Cambridge, MA: Harvard University Press, 1991).
51   This idea is more fully explored in Chapters 8 and 9 of this textbook and is elaborated by Robert Hodge and Gunther Kress, *Social Semiotics* (Ithaca, NY: Cornell University Press, 1988).

As an alternative to semiotics, Stewart proposes that language is "constitutive articulate contact." Language is constitutive because its use *constitutes* or constructs the categories by which we understand the world, and it is *articulate contact* because our social worlds are made by human beings using language when they come into contact with one another. Language is a medium in which things get worked out through dialogue.

Donald Ellis takes a different position on meaning.[52] He would agree with Stewart that signs are not simple representations of real objects, but in order for communication to occur, we must have an assumption of meaning. The system of relations among signs must allow communicators to find real meaning, or communication could not take place. We must share a sense of coherence in messages, or no amount of understanding will be possible, and we must assume that when we make use of the rules of language, large numbers of people who know those rules will be able to understand the meaning we intend.

Following E. D. Hirsch, Ellis finds it helpful to distinguish between *meaning* and *significance*.[53] Because people live in different worlds, they can associate a language with just about anything. These richly different associations constitute the significance of a word or other symbol. At the same time, however, a word or expression must also have a commonly understood referent, which Ellis calls the *meaning* of the term. The stability of meaning may vary from strong to weak, but some correspondence must be present or people will not be able to achieve any order of understanding.

This does not mean that everyone will react the same way to a message or even think the same thoughts. Different people will connect meanings to one another in many different ways, but a basic coherent meaning is still necessary for understanding to occur.

Contemporary philosopher Jean Baudrillard adds another interesting perspective on signs, meaning, and society.[54] Baudrillard is concerned that signs become detached from their referents and take on a life of their own—a process he calls *simulation*. As a social critic, this scholar observes that signs lose their meaning as they become increasingly removed from the objects that would otherwise give them meaning. People come to value signs for their own sake, without grounding in the actual material conditions of life. Kitsch and gizmos are examples of this tendency.

The work on nonverbal communication has been important because it shows that communication consists of many types of signs. At the same time, by emphasizing the nonverbal, most of these theories distract us from the holistic nature of the communication code. Indeed, the analytical nature of both linguistics and nonverbal research belies the complexity of the communication process.[55] This problem is the *fallacy of analysis*. Leeds-Hurwitz describes the problem in these terms: "[Nonverbal codes] are separated only temporarily by analysts in order to make research easier. But we as analysts have gone perhaps too far in our efforts to make research easy, forgetting to ever recombine the separate elements again. To me, the purpose of studying nonverbal communication is to aid the understanding of social interaction as a whole."[56]

Ironically, as nonverbal communication research separates language from other behavior, much of it has relied heavily on a linguistic analogy. In other words, nonverbal codes are believed by some to be organized in essentially the same way as language. This belief is not surprising because of the common semiotic heritage of

---

52   Donald G. Ellis, "Fixing Communicative Meaning: A Coherentist Theory," *Communication Research* 22 (1995): 515–544.

53   E. D. Hirsch, *Validity in Interpretation* (New Haven, CT: Yale University Press, 1967); Donald C. Ellis, *Crafting Society: Ethnicity, Class and Communication Theory* (Mahwah, NJ: Erlbaum, 1999), pp. 74–78.

54   Jean Baudrillard, *The Illusion of the End*, trans. Chris Turner (Cambridge: Polity, 1994). For an overview of Baudrillard's theory, see Sonja K. Foss, Karen A. Foss, and Robert Trapp, *Contemporary Perspectives on Rhetoric*, 3rd ed. (Prospect Heights, IL: Waveland, in press).

55   For a discussion of the limitations of nonverbal communication theories, see Judee Burgoon and Thomas Saine, *The Unspoken Dialogue: An Introduction to Nonverbal Communication* (Boston: Houghton Mifflin, 1978), chap. 2; and Mark Knapp, John Wiemann, and John Daly, "Nonverbal Communication: Issues and Appraisal," *Human Communication Research* 4 (1978): 271–280.

56   Leeds-Hurwitz, *Semiotics and Communication*, p. xvii.

the two lines of research. As the early semioticians so clearly spelled out, the syntax or organization among signs is the most important constituent of meaning. Saussure applied this idea to language, and theorists like Birdwhistell adopted linguistic ideas about syntax to nonlinguistic signs.

This problem is the *fallacy of the linguistic analogy*. Although some superficial similarities may be observed between language and bodily behavior, more differences than similarities exist. Language is presented sequentially and involves discrete signs; nonverbal codes are not presented in a sequential manner and usually do not consist of discrete behaviors. Although language is organized hierarchically, no good evidence shows that nonverbal acts are organized in this way. Language tends to be used consciously, and nonverbal signs are often displayed unconsciously.

One of the limits of most of the theories in this chapter is that they focus on the smallest units of meaning and low-level organizations of signs. The true richness of communication occurs at a higher level, when signs are combined into complex messages. We turn to this concern in Chapter 5 in our discussion of discourse.

C H A P T E R **5**

THEORIES OF
DISCOURSE

In the previous chapter, we discussed language and coding. We saw there that communication can take place with the use of single signs or a combination of signs. Usually communication involves more than simple utterances and actions. Most communication, from the mundane to the elaborate, consists of complex acts that form messages, or *discourse.*

In his study of the intellectual structure of the communication discipline, John Powers identified *messages* as central to the communication process.[1] He noted that messages have three structural properties: (1) relatively independent signs and symbols, (2) language as a formal code, and (3) relatively interconnected discourse structures. This chapter focuses on the third of these.

Discourse analysis enables us to look closely at how messages are organized, used, and understood. The structure of discourse will change depending on what you want to accomplish. The process of discourse analysis enables us to examine the various ways in which accomplishments are achieved through messages.[2]

Although writing and even nonverbal behavior can be considered discourse, most discourse analysis concentrates on naturally occurring talk. There are several strands of discourse analysis, and although various types of methods are used, most discourse analysts would characterize their field as the careful study of the structure of discourse itself.[3]

1   John Powers, "On the Intellectual Structure of the Human Communication Discipline," *Communication Education* 44 (1995): 191–222.
2   For overviews of this subject, see Donald G. Ellis, *From Language to Communication* (Mahwah, NJ: Erlbaum, 1999); Scott Jacobs, "Language and Interpersonal Communication," in *Handbook of Interpersonal Communication,* eds. Mark L. Knapp and Gerald R. Miller (Thousand Oaks, CA: Sage, 1994), pp. 199–228; Donald G. Ellis and William A. Donohue, eds., *Contemporary Issues in Language and Discourse Processes* (Hillsdale, NJ: Erlbaum, 1986).
3   Karen Tracy identifies several strands of discourse analysis in the communication field in "Discourse Analysis in Communication," in *Handbook of Discourse Analysis,* eds. D. Schiffrin, D. Tannen, and H. Hamilton (Oxford, UK: Blackwell), in press. For other approaches, see Glenn F. Stillar, *Analyzing Everyday Texts: Discourse, Rhetoric, and Social Processes* (Thousand Oaks, CA: Sage, 1998); Moira Chimombo and Robert L. Roseberry, *The Power of Discourse: An Introduction to Discourse Analysis* (Mahwah, NJ: Erlbaum, 1998); Jonathan Potter and Margaret Wetherell, *Discourse and Social Psychology: Beyond Attitudes and Behavior* (London: Sage, 1987), pp. 6–7.

Scott Jacobs outlines three types of problems tackled by discourse analysis.[4] The first is the *problem of meaning*. How do people understand messages? What information is embedded in the structure of a statement that enables another person to know that the utterance, "Is Sybil there?" means that you want to talk to her on the telephone, or "You sure are hot" means you think the other person is on a winning streak?

The second challenge of discourse analysis is the *problem of action,* or knowing how to get something done through talk. What kinds of choices do we have when we want to do something like make a request or greet someone? How does a person decide how to say something, and how can he or she know the difference between an appropriate and an inappropriate way of putting something into words?

The *problem of coherence,* the third question of discourse analysis, involves figuring out how to make patterns of talk sensible and logical. In a conversation, for example, there is a back-and-forth flow among participants. How do they string words together rationally? What principles are used to connect one statement with another in a way that everyone understands? If you look at a transcript of a conversation carefully, you often find that it seems disjointed; yet, the communicators made sense of what they were saying as they went along. How did they do this?

Because we understand, act, and have coherent conversations intuitively, these questions may seem mundane; but these questions are challenging when you really try to answer them systematically. Several theories have been proposed to explain meaning and action in discourse.

The idea that people operate by rules in language, discourse, and social action has become widely accepted. Susan Shimanoff summarizes the point:

In order for communication to exist, or continue, two or more interacting individuals must share rules for using symbols. Not only must they have rules for individual symbols, but they must also agree on such matters as how to take turns at speaking, how to be polite or how to insult, to greet, and so forth. If every symbol user manipulated symbols at random, the result would be chaos rather than communication.[5]

Communicators use discourse to accomplish goals, and the way in which they do so is governed by rules. A rather large body of literature has been created to explain the place of rules in discourse.[6] These theories teach that rules govern how discourse can be organized and understood. Rules affect the options available in a given situation, yet because they are situational, rules allow communicators to behave differently at various times and places.

All of the theories in this chapter rely on the rules concept to some extent. For example, we will look at how communicators accomplish their intentions by using rules and how rules are employed for producing and understanding conversation. We begin with the first of these questions—using rule-based discourse to accomplish intentions.

◖ SPEECH-ACT THEORY

Ludwig Wittgenstein, a German philosopher, began a line of thought called *ordinary language philosophy.*[7] He taught that the meaning of language

---

4   Jacobs, "Language and Interpersonal Communication."
5   Susan B. Shimanoff, *Communication Rules: Theory and Research* (Beverly Hills, CA: Sage, 1980), pp. 31–32.
6   Shimanoff, *Communication Rules,* pp. 31–88, lists some of the major scholars who have studied rules as well as a variety of definitions and explanations of rules. See also Donald P. Cushman, "The Rules Perspective as a Theoretical Basis for the Study of Human Communication," *Communication Quarterly* 25 (1977): 30–45; W. Barnett Pearce, "Rules Theories of Communication: Varieties, Limitations, and Potentials" (paper delivered at the meeting of the Speech Communication Association, New York, 1980); Stuart J. Sigman, "On Communication Rules from a Social Perspective," *Human Communication Research* 7 (1980): 37–51; and Donald Cushman, "The Rules Approach to Communication Theory: A Philosophical and Operational Perspective," in *Communication Theory: Eastern and Western Perspectives,* ed. D. L. Kincaid (San Diego: Academic, 1987), pp. 223–234.
7   Wittgenstein's best-known early work was *Tractatus Logico-Philosophicus* (London: Routledge & Kegan Paul, 1922); his later work, which forms the foundation for ordinary language philosophy, is *Philosophical Investigations* (Oxford: Basil Blackwell, 1953). See also the excellent summary by David Silverman and Brian Torode, *The Material Word: Some Theories of Language and Its Limits* (London: Routledge & Kegan Paul, 1980); Richard Buttny, "The Ascription of Meaning: A Wittgensteinian Perspective," *Quarterly Journal of Speech* 72 (1986): 261–273; and Allan Janik and Stephen Toulmin, *Wittgenstein's Vienna* (New York: Simon & Schuster, 1973).

depends on its actual use. Language, as used in ordinary life, is a *language game* because it consists of rules. In other words, people follow rules to do things with language. When you give and obey orders, ask and answer questions, and describe events, you are engaged in language games. Like ordinary games such as chess and poker, each language game has a different set of rules. Later J. L. Austin referred to the practical use of language as speech acts.[8] Speech-act theory, then, is built on the foundation laid by Wittgenstein and Austin.[9]

Today Austin's protégé John Searle is most often associated with the theory. In this theory, the *speech act* is the basic unit of language used to express meaning, an utterance that expresses an intention. Normally, the speech act is a sentence, but it can be a word or phrase as long as it follows the rules necessary to accomplish the intention, or to play the language game.

When one speaks, one performs an act. The act may be stating, questioning, commanding, promising, or a number of other possibilities. Speech, then, is not just used to designate something; it actually does something. That is why it is called speech *act*. Consequently, speech-act theory does not stress the individual referents of symbols but the intent of the act as a whole. If a speech act is successful, the recipient will understand the speaker's intention.

If you make a promise, you are communicating an intention about something you will do in the future, but more important, you are expecting the other communicator to realize from what you have said what your intention is. If you say, "I promise to pay you back," you assume the other person knows the meaning of the words. But knowing the words is not enough; knowing what you intend to accomplish by using the words is vital.

Whenever you make a statement like, "I will pay you back," you are performing at least three and maybe four acts. The first is an *utterance act*, or the simple pronunciation of the words. Second, you are performing a *propositional act* because you are saying something you believe to be true. Third, and most important from a speech-act perspective, you are performing an *illocutionary act* designed to fulfill an intention. (In this example you are making a promise, and it is important to communication that your listener understand this intention.) Finally, you may be performing a *perlocutionary act*, designed to have an actual effect on the other person's behavior. (Maybe you are trying to get him to loan you some money.)

Because the difference between illocution and perlocution is sometimes hard to grasp, let's pursue it a little further. An illocution is an act in which the speaker's primary concern is that the listener understand the intention—to make a promise, a request, or whatever. A perlocution is an act in which the speaker expects the listener not only to understand but to act in a particular way because of that understanding. If I say, "I am thirsty," with the intention of having you understand that I need something to drink, I am performing an illocutionary act. I may also want you to bring me a glass of water. This is called an indirect request, and it is both illocutionary and perlocutionary.

Now let's look at the distinction between propositional acts and illocutionary acts in more detail. The proposition can be understood as one aspect of the content of a statement. It designates some quality or association of an object, situation, or event. "The cake is good," "Salt is harmful to the body," "Her name is Karen" are all examples of propositions. Propositions can be evaluated in terms of their truth value.

8   J. L. Austin, *How to Do Things with Words* (Cambridge, MA: Harvard University Press, 1962); *Philosophy of Language* (Englewood Cliffs, NJ: Prentice-Hall, 1964). For a general summary of Austin's ideas, see also Potter and Wetherell, *Discourse and Social Psychology*, pp. 14–18.
9   John Searle, *Speech Acts: An Essay in the Philosophy of Language* (Cambridge: Cambridge University Press, 1969); "Human Communication Theory and the Philosophy of Language: Some Remarks," in *Human Communication Theory*, ed. F. E. X. Dance (New York: Holt, Rinehart & Winston, 1967), pp. 116–129. Good secondary sources include John Stewart, "Concepts of Language and Meaning: A Comparative Study," *Quarterly Journal of Speech* 58 (1972): 123–133; Paul N. Campbell, "A Rhetorical View of Locutionary, Illocutionary, and Perlocutionary Acts," *Quarterly Journal of Speech* 59 (1973): 284–296; Robert Gaines, "Doing by Saying: Toward a Theory of Perlocution," *Quarterly Journal of Speech* 65 (1979): 207–217.

In speech-act theory, however, truth is not considered central. Rather, the question is what a speaker intends to do by uttering a proposition. Hence, for Searle, propositions must always be viewed as part of a larger context—the illocution. Searle would be interested in acts such as the following: I *ask* whether the cake is good; I *warn* you that salt is harmful to the body; I *state* that her name is Karen. What the speaker is doing with the proposition is the speech act— in these examples, to ask, to warn, and to state.

The meaning of a speech act is its *illocutionary force.* You might, for example, state the proposition "The cake is good" ironically to mean just the opposite: This cake is the worst I ever ate. Here what appears to be a simple proposition has the illocutionary force of an insult.

Searle states fundamentally that "speaking a language is engaging in a rule-governed form of behavior."[10] Two types of rules are important— constitutive and regulative. *Constitutive rules* actually create games; that is, the game is created, or "constituted," by its rules. For example, football as a game exists only by virtue of its rules. The rules make up the game. When you observe people following a certain set of rules, you know the game of football is being played. These rules therefore tell you what to interpret as football, as opposed to baseball or soccer.

In speech acts constitutive rules tell you what to interpret as a promise, as opposed to a request or a command. One's intention is largely understood by another person because of the constitutive rules; they tell others what to count as a particular kind of act.

For example, how do you know a promise when you hear one? Promising involves five basic rules. First, it must include a sentence indicating the speaker will do some future act. Second, the utterance can only be made if the listener would prefer that the speaker do the act rather than not do it. Third, a statement is a promise only when it would not otherwise be obvious to the speaker and hearer that the act would be

done in the normal course of events. Fourth, the speaker must intend to do the act. Finally, a promise involves the establishment of an obligation for the speaker to do the act. These five rules "constitute" a sufficient set of conditions for an act to count as a promise.

Any illocutionary act must have a basic set of constitutive rules. The *propositional content rule* specifies some condition of the referenced object. In a promise, for example, the speaker must state that a future act will be done, to repay a debt perhaps. *Preparatory rules* involve the presumed preconditions in the speaker and hearer necessary for the act to take place. For example, in a promise the utterance has no meaning unless the hearer would rather the future act be done than not be done. In our illustration, the hearer wants to get repaid. The *sincerity rule* requires the speaker to mean what is said. You must truly intend to repay the debt for the statement to count as a promise. The *essential rule* states that the act is indeed taken by the hearer and speaker to represent what it appears to be on the face. In other words the promise establishes a contractual obligation between speaker and hearer.

These constitutive rule types are believed to apply to a wide variety of illocutionary acts, such as requesting, asserting, questioning, thanking, advising, warning, greeting, and congratulating.

The second kind of rule is regulative. *Regulative rules* provide guidelines for acting within a game. The behaviors are known and available before being used in the act, and they tell us how to use speech to accomplish a particular intention. For example, if I want something, I make a request. When I request something of you, you are obligated either to grant the request or to turn it down.

Speech acts are not successful when their illocutionary force is not understood, and they can be evaluated in terms of the degree to which they employ the rules. Whereas propositions are evaluated in terms of truth or *validity*, speech acts, then, are evaluated in terms of *felicity*, or the degree to which the conditions of the act are met. The felicity of a promise is whether the essential rules for executing a promise have been met.

10   Searle, *Speech Acts*, p. 22.

Although many speech acts are direct and involve the use of an explicit statement of intent, other speech acts are indirect. To request his family come to the table, a father might say, "Is anybody hungry?" On the face this appears to be a question, but in actuality it is an indirect request, maybe even a command.

Searle outlines five types of illocutionary acts. The first he calls *assertives*. An assertive is a statement that commits the speaker to advocate the truth of a proposition. It includes such acts as stating, affirming, concluding, and believing. The second are *directives*: illocutions that attempt to get the listener to do something. They are commands, requests, pleadings, prayers, entreaties, invitations, and so forth. *Commissives*, the third type, commit the speaker to a future act. They consist of such things as promising, vowing, pledging, contracting, and guaranteeing. The fourth, *expressives*, are acts that communicate some aspect of the speaker's psychological state, such as thanking, congratulating, apologizing, condoling, and welcoming. Finally, a *declaration* is designed to create a proposition that, by its very assertion, makes it so. Examples include appointing, marrying, firing, and resigning. To illustrate, you are not married until an authorized person actually says the words, "I *pronounce* you husband and wife."

Speech-act theory identifies what it takes to make a successful statement, to have an intention understood. But speech acts are rarely isolated; they are usually part of ongoing conversations. How we organize conversations is a fascinating and important question in communication theory.

◖ CONVERSATION ANALYSIS

One of the most interesting and popular lines of work in communication is conversation analysis.[11] This is part of a branch of sociology called *ethnomethodology*, which is the detailed study of how people organize their everyday lives.[12] It involves a set of methods for looking carefully at

the ways people work together to create social organization.

A conversation, like any aspect of social life, is viewed as a social achievement because it requires that we get certain things done cooperatively through talk.[13] Conversation analysis (CA) attempts to discover in detail exactly what those achievements are.

Conversation analysis is characterized by the careful examination of actual sequences of talk. The analyst looks at a segment of conversation for the kinds of actions that are accomplished within the talk, examining what the speakers seem to be doing as they communicate. They are probably doing many things at once—possibly asking and answering questions, managing turn taking, and protecting face. Most important is *how* these things are done *in language*. What devices and forms are used in the interaction between the parties to accomplish action? Although cognitive theory (Chapters 6 and 7) deals with how people think and behave psychologically, conversation analysis is more concerned with what is going on in the language, in the text, in the discourse. Also CA focuses on interaction in discourse—the back and forth, turn-taking moves that communicators make and how they manage to organize their sequences of talk.[14]

---

11   This section deals with conversation in the discourse analysis tradition, emphasizing the verbal structure of conversational texts. There is also a tradition that studies the management of conversations in a broader sense, including the nonverbal elements. See Joseph N. Cappella, "The Management of Conversations," in *Handbook of Interpersonal Communication*, eds. M. L. Knapp and G. R. Miller (Beverly Hills, CA: Sage, 1985), pp. 393–439.

12   Ethnomethodology is most often associated with its originator, sociologist Harold Garfinkel; see his *Studies in Ethnomethodology* (Englewood Cliffs, NJ: Prentice-Hall, 1967). For a brief description of this tradition, see Potter and Wetherell, *Discourse and Social Psychology*, pp. 18–23. See also Graham Button, ed., *Ethnomethodology and the Human Sciences* (Cambridge: Cambridge University Press, 1991).

13   For detailed discussions of conversation analysis, see George Psathas, *Conversation Analysis: The Study of Talk-in-Interaction* (Thousand Oaks, CA: Sage, 1995); Anna-Brita Stenström, *An Introduction to Spoken Interaction* (London: Longman, 1994); Robert Nofsinger, *Everyday Conversation* (Newbury Park, CA: Sage, 1991).

14   For a good discussion of how the conversation analyst works, see Anita Pomerantz and B. J. Fehr, "Conversation Analysis: An Approach to the Study of Social Action as Sense Making Practices," in *Discourse as Social Interaction*, ed. T. A. van Dijk (Thousand Oaks: Sage, 1997), pp. 64–91. See also Ellis, *From Language to Communication*, pp. 85–89.

Of utmost importance in conversation analysis are the ways in which communicators create stability and organization in their talk. Even when conversations look sloppy on the surface, there is an underlying organization to all coherent talk, and the participants themselves actually create it as they go along. The analyst works inductively by first examining the details of actual conversations—many conversations—and then generalizing possible principles by which the participants themselves organize their own talk.

As an example, consider the simple task of telling a story. When you tell a story, it may appear that you just say it, but your story is really a joint achievement accomplished by you and your listeners. Although you probably take an extended turn, your story is made possible by the cooperation of others in carefully organized turns. First, you have to get the floor by offering to tell a story, and others acknowledge and permit you to do so. During the story itself, listeners may take various types of turns to recognize and reinforce the story, indicate understanding, give you further permission to continue talking, direct or affect the story in some way, or correct or repair something you said. All of this requires work and organization on the part of everyone.[15]

Conversation analysis is concerned with a variety of issues.[16] First, it deals with what speakers need to know to have a conversation—knowing the rules of conversation. The features of a conversation such as turn taking, silences and gaps, and overlaps have been of special interest. Conversation analysis is also concerned with rule violations and the ways people prevent and repair errors in talk.

Certainly the most popular, and perhaps the most significant, aspect of conversation analysis is *conversational coherence*.[17] Simply defined, coherence is connectedness and meaningfulness in conversation. A coherent conversation seems well structured and sensible to the participants. Coherence is normally taken for granted, yet the production of coherence is complex and not altogether understood. A good place to begin the topic of coherence is the theory of H. Paul Grice.

Conversational Maxims

Grice proposed a set of very general assumptions to which all conversationalists must subscribe in order to be perceived as competent.[18] The first and most general is the *cooperative principle*: One's contribution must be appropriate. Cooperation here does not necessarily mean expression of agreement, but it does mean that one is willing to contribute something in line with the purpose of the conversation. For example, if someone asks you a question, you should answer it or respond in some other way that at least acknowledges the question. Otherwise you will be taken as rude. We are bothered when others fail to complete the speech act appropriately because it leads to confusion and the lack of coherence. Cooperation is achieved by following four maxims.

Grice's first is the *quantity maxim*: One's contribution should provide sufficient, but not too much, information. You violate the quantity maxim when your comments don't say enough or say too much. The second is the *quality maxim*: One's contribution should be truthful. You violate the quality maxim when you deliberately lie or communicate in a way that does not reflect an honest intention. The third is the *relevancy maxim*: Comments must be pertinent. You violate this maxim when you make an irrelevant comment. The fourth maxim is the *manner maxim*: Do not be obscure, ambiguous, or disorganized.

You are probably thinking by now that these maxims seem absurdly simple and obvious, but the associated question of how speakers actually use them and how they handle apparent violations is far more complicated and interesting. Of

---

15   Jenny Mandelbaum, "Interpersonal Activities in Conversational Storytelling," *Western Journal of Speech Communication* 53 (1989): 114–126.
16   These issues are outlined in Margaret L. McLaughlin, *Conversation: How Talk Is Organized* (Beverly Hills, CA: Sage, 1984).
17   See Robert T. Craig and Karen Tracy, eds., *Conversational Coherence: Form, Structure, and Strategy* (Beverly Hills, CA: Sage, 1983).
18   H. Paul Grice, "Logic and Conversation," in *Syntax and Semantics*, vol. 3, eds. P. Cole and J. Morgan (New York: Academic, 1975), pp. 41–58.

course, the cooperative principle and maxims are often violated, sometimes on purpose, but what makes them so important is that they are never violated without disrupting the flow of conversation or affecting the perceptions of others in the conversation. In other words, violations are a problem communicators must deal with cooperatively.

When a maxim appears to be violated, communicators wonder what is going on. We manage these violations by making certain interpretations, called *conversational implicatures*, that help us understand what is being implied or implicated by the apparent violation. To assume that the violator is living up to the cooperative principle, the listener must attribute some additional meaning that will make the speaker's contribution seem to conform to the principle. In fact, when you deliberately violate a maxim, you assume that your listener will understand that you really do intend to be cooperative. If, for example, you say, "It is raining cats and dogs," you are technically violating the quality maxim, but others know that you are speaking metaphorically. This is an example of conversational implicature.

Conversational implicature allows you to use all kinds of interesting, indirect statements to achieve your purposes, without being judged incompetent. In fact, competence itself requires the effective use of implicature. Without it our conversations would be dull, predictable, and lifeless.

One of the most common types of violation is to say something indirectly. Indirect communication is important for a variety of social and personal reasons such as politeness. If, for example, someone asks you how much your car cost, you might say, "Oh, quite a bit." Now, on the surface, that violates the maxim of quantity and appears uncooperative, but competent conversationalists will realize that this is really an indirect statement meaning, "It's none of your business."

The study of conversational implicature is really the study of the rules people use to justify violations of other rules; and these implicatures are very important for the overall management of conversations.

Another way that you manage the cooperative principle is to give clues that you are violating a maxim while still intending to be cooperative. Such clues are called *licenses for violations* because they enable you to violate a maxim without objection. For example, you could say, "I might be exaggerating a little, but . . . ." Or you might end a statement by prompting, " . . . if you know what I mean." Using phrases and qualifications such as these is a way of asking for a license to violate one or more of the maxims. Here's a portion of a typical conversation:

Kay: How did you and your husband meet?

Betty: Well, that's a long story.

Kay: Okay, I'm not going anywhere, let's hear it.

When Betty says, "That's a long story," Kay takes this as a request to violate the quantity maxim.[19] There is another possible interpretation, Betty's reply may be a polite way of saying that she does not want to talk about that subject, but Kay misinterprets that request.

Traditional views assume that competent communicators at least intend to cooperate. In an interesting line of work, Steven McCornack and his colleagues question this view. In their *information manipulation theory*, they assert that people often intentionally deceive by violating the maxims.[20] For example, if you wanted to lie, you would violate the quality maxim. If you wanted to obscure, you would violate the quantity maxim. If you wanted to distract, you would violate the relevancy maxim. Scott Jacobs and his colleagues acknowledge that deception may involve either blatant or covert violation of the quality maxim, but these authors point out that covert violations

---

19   Examples of violations are from Susan Swan Mura, "Licensing Violations: Legitimate Violations of Grice's Conversational Principle," in *Conversational Coherence: Form, Structure, and Strategy,* eds. R. T. Craig and K. Tracy (Beverly Hills, CA: Sage, 1983), pp. 101–115.
20   Steven A. McCornack, "Information Manipulation Theory," *Communication Monographs* 59 (1992): 1–17; Steven A. McCornack et. al., "When the Alteration of Information Is Viewed as Deception: An Empirical Test of Information Manipulation Theory," *Communication Monographs* 59 (1992): 17–29.

of the other maxims are deceptive only when they also include false implicatures. In other words, the deceiving communicator violates the maxim while implying that it is a normal, not deceptive, violation.[21] For example, if a co-worker asked if you had finished a certain report, you might reply, "Uh, just running to lunch. Catch you later." This is a clear violation of the relevancy maxim. By getting up and going to the door, you imply that this is a normal violation, when you really are trying to get out of admitting that you did not in fact complete the report.

Conversational Coherence

Coherence involves the question of how communicators create clear meaning. How do you know what is appropriate or inappropriate for keeping a conversation well organized? A variety of theories have been proposed.[22] Some of these use *local* principles, and other theories use *global* ones.

Using Local Principles: The Sequencing Approach. The idea behind the sequencing approach is that a conversation consists of a series of rule-governed speech acts, and coherence is achieved by making sure that each act is an appropriate response to the previous act. For example, the question, "Hi, how are you?" is normally followed by, "Fine, how are you?"

Sequencing approaches focus on the *adjacency pair*, which is two speech acts tied together. The *first-pair part* (FPP) is the first utterance, and the *second-pair part* (SPP) is the second one. The SPP completes the speech act. If I intend to promise something to you and say I will do such and such, you complete my promise by accepting or turning it down. By this approach, a conversation is coherent if proper rules of sequencing are consistently used between the FPP and the SPP.

Perhaps the most influential sequencing model is that of Harvey Sacks, Emanuel Schegloff, and Gail Jefferson.[23] This is basically a turn-taking theory that stipulates that the next turn in a conversation must be a proper response to complete a particular adjacency-pair type. For instance, a question is to be followed by an answer, a greeting by another greeting, an offer by an acceptance, a request by an acceptance or a rejection. A number of adjacency-pair types have been discussed in the literature: assertion-assent/ dissent, question-answer, summons-answer, greeting-greeting, closing-closing, request-grant/ denial, insult-response, apology-acceptance/ refusal, compliment-acceptance/rejection, threat-response, challenge-response, accusation-denial/ confession, and boast-appreciation/derision.

The completion of one speech act signals a turn for another speaker, who is obligated to respond according to appropriate rules. The speaker may designate who the next speaker is to be, or another speaker can appropriately take a turn, as long as a proper response is given. Failing a response, the speaker may continue talking.

Further, adjacency pairs include a *preference for agreement*. In other words, the SPP is normally expected to agree with the FPP. For example, a statement is normally followed by an agreement ("Don't you just love the sun?" "Sure do.") and a request is followed by an acceptance ("Can I borrow your sunscreen?" "Sure."). This does not mean that people always agree, but disagreement calls for special action in the form of an account, excuse, or argument.

Conversation analysts recognize that people do not communicate mechanically in a series of adjacency pairs. In fact, most conversation looks untidy in this regard, so the real challenge of this line of work is to show how conversation partners are able to make sense out of a series of utterances that appear on the surface to be unorganized. In examining actual tape-recorded

21   Scott Jacobs, Edwin J. Dawson, and Dale Brashers, "Information Manipulation Theory: A Replication and Assessment," *Communication Monographs* 63 (1996): 70–82. See also Steven A. McCornack, Timothy R. Levine, Kelly Morrison, and Maria Lapinski, "Speaking of Information Manipulation: A Critical Rejoinder," *Communication Monographs* 63 (1996): 83–92; David B. Buller and Judee K. Burgoon, "Another Look at Information Management: A Rejoinder to McCornack, Levine, Morrison, & Lapinski," *Communication Monographs* 63 (1996): 92–98; Scott Jacobs, Dale Brashers, and Edwin J. Dawson, "Truth and Deception," *Communication Monographs* 63 (1996): 98–103.
22   For a summary of some of the approaches, see Craig and Tracy, *Conversational Coherence.*
23   Harvey Sacks, Emanuel Schegloff, and Gail Jefferson, "A Simplest Systematics for the Organization of Turn Taking for Conversation," *Language* 50 (1974): 696–735.

texts, these researchers are able to show the rules that the communicators are using to assure coherence. Presequence, insertion, and expansion are examples.

A *presequence* is an adjacency pair whose meaning depends on another series of acts that has not yet been uttered. Here, the initial FPP is an invitation for a subsequent one:

FPP: Have you washed your hands?
      (*presequence*)
SPP: No, why?
FPP: 'Cause dinner's ready.
SPP: Okay, I'll do it.

The speaker here intends to make a request, but it cannot be understood as such without including the presequence question.

An *insertion* is an adjacency pair that is between the two parts of another pair and is subordinate to the main pair. Such insertions are necessary to clarify the intention of the initial FPP.

Here is an example:

FPP₁: Would you like to go out sometime?
FPP₂: With you? (*insertion*)
SPP₂: Yeah, me.
SPP₁: Oh, okay.

Such a move is also an example of an *expansion,* which means that a subsequent speaker expands the sequence to include additional or subsidiary intentions. An expansion is involved whenever a segment of talk that could theoretically be accomplished in one turn, like a greeting, compliment, or request, is played out over several turns. This system enables us to parse, or separate, a conversation into parts. Table 5.1 shows an example.

The adjacency-pair idea has been useful and applies to many conversations, but conversation analysts now generally agree that coherence cannot be explained strictly by local rules such as these. It is easy to identify sequences that are ob-

TABLE 5.1

A Conversational Sequence

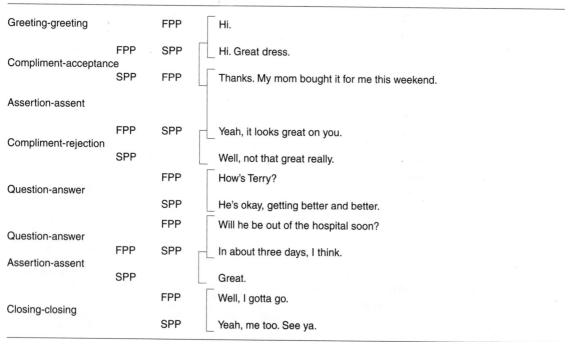

viously clear to the communicators but have adjacent statements that do not make sense out of context. We turn now to how these more complicated situations are handled.

Using Global Principles: The Inferential-Strategic Approach.   The pragmatic, or rational, approach to conversational coherence assumes that conversations are practical acts that achieve goals. Achieving the goal of a conversation requires that the participants reason their way through it. "If I want such and such, I have to do thus and so." Thus the coherence of a conversation depends on the reasoning process of the communicators. They make decisions about what to say and how to achieve their intentions, and coherence is really judged in accordance with this overall reasoning. If the sequence of acts appears rational in relation to agreed-on goals, it is judged coherent.

This theory, most often associated with Sally Jackson and Scott Jacobs, definitely uses a global approach.[24] These scholars use the game analogy to explain how conversation works. The game itself is controlled by a set of rules, which players must know. The players have objectives in the game, and they use the rules of the game to achieve those objectives. The game is coherent because the appropriate use of rules accomplishes rational objectives. So players must have two kinds of knowledge: They must know the rules of the game and what constitutes rational play within the parameters of the rules.

For example, in playing Monopoly you are expected to accumulate properties and cash by purchasing property, houses, and hotels, and you must do this according to rules. In Monopoly your moves are not judged rational or coherent based on whether they are consistent with the moves that came before or after but on

whether they are consistent with the overall objectives of the game.

Conversations can be complicated because, like a game, they are played with other people. One person's moves must mesh with those of other players, and this requires agreement on purpose and some reciprocity of perspective. Utterances have a force that obliges a hearer to understand the speaker's intent, and the speaker must meet certain felicity conditions in order for understanding to occur. Communicators respond not to each individual speech act but to the overall intentions of others. The coherence of a conversation is not judged by adjacency pairs but by the unfolding plan of the game.

Jackson and Jacobs stipulate two kinds of rules necessary for such coherence. *Validity rules* establish the conditions necessary for an act to be judged as a sincere move in a plan to achieve a goal. *Reason rules,* Jackson and Jacob's second type, require the speaker to adjust statements to the beliefs and perspectives of the other participants. This does not mean that speakers say only what listeners want to hear but that they frame their statements in a way that makes logical sense within the perspective of what the other person thinks is going on. For example, if you are talking with a friend about how you did on an exam, you might think it a bit odd if he just blurted out, "I want pizza for dinner." You would wonder what that has to do with anything.

Basically, then, these rules help communicators set up a logical system so that a conversation will feel coherent. Remember that these rules may be violated, and coherence is not always achieved. Communicators may also disagree about whether a sequence meets the required conditions of validity and reason, and such disagreement is often the basis for conflict. Ultimately, because conversations are practical, goal-oriented acts, communicators must constantly judge whether the interaction is leading toward the desired goal and, if it is not, whether and what kinds of adjustments must be made in the conversational moves. This fact makes conversation a dynamic process of back-and-forth practical reasoning.

---

24   Scott Jacobs, "Language," in *Handbook of Interpersonal Communication*, eds. M. L. Knapp and G. R. Miller (Beverly Hills, CA: Sage, 1985), pp. 330–335; also see Scott Jacobs and Sally Jackson, "Speech Act Structure in Conversation: Rational Aspects of Pragmatic Coherence," in *Conversational Coherence: Form, Structure, and Strategy,* eds. R. T. Craig and K. Tracy (Beverly Hills, CA: Sage, 1983), pp. 47–66.

Donald Ellis proposes a *coherentist theory of meaning* to explain this process further.[25] Understanding discourse is a pragmatic act in which communicators use shared meanings to achieve coherence. Communication is possible only because communicators possess shared meanings. Three characteristics of discourse make understanding possible.

The first characteristic is *intelligibility*. Discourse is intelligible if it contains or points to evidence that enables communicators to make inferences about its meaning. A father may ask his son, "Is that your coat on the floor?" The son correctly reasons that this is a request or command for him to pick up the coat. Both father and son have experience in similar situations that make it possible for them to share this meaning. The coat on the floor, the timing of the father's question, and the use of similar questions in the past are evidence that the boy can use to draw this conclusion.

The second characteristic is *organization*. Statements are part of larger organized systems of linguistic structures. You cannot assign any meaning you want to a sentence; a statement's meaning is limited, and competent communicators know what the possible range of meanings are. This quality of discourse makes rational talk possible.

Jackson and Jacobs's analogy of the game is useful here. The rules of the game tell us what moves mean and how to respond rationally within the system of permissible moves. In the game of making requests, communicators know that questions can be taken as a form of request, so the father's question may be understood as a statement about what his son should do. Indeed, within this situation, it probably should be understood in this way.

And this fact leads to Ellis's third characteristic of discourse—*verification*. In the stream of a conversation, one's statements can verify, or confirm, the meaning of other statements. When the son in our example replies, "Yeah, I'll pick it up." He is verifying the command issued by the father. Thus, participants use the give-and-take of their conversation to test meaning and reason their way to an agreed-upon conclusion.

Using global principles does not negate the value of local principles. Indeed, adjacency-pair coherence is a special case of a rational action. The FPP invites the listener to join into a kind of microplan for achieving a goal, and the SPP is coherent if it joins into that plan. A greeting invites the listener to make contact, and a returned greeting fulfills a kind of greeting contract. Responses to an FPP may simply and directly cooperate, indirectly cooperate, approximate agreement, or attempt to extend, change, or refuse the goal set up by the first utterance. Over a sequence of utterances, communicators actually negotiate a goal-achievement plan. Jackson and Jacobs call this *the transformation of belief/want contexts.* Communicators ask themselves mentally, What do we want to accomplish here, and what logical moves are required by each of us to accomplish this? The conversation will be coherent if agreement is achieved and the actions seem appropriate for achieving the goals.

To see more concretely how these ideas can be applied, let's look at Jackson and Jacobs's applications of their theory to requests.[26] Actually, requests are among the most studied of all speech acts, and their theory provides an excellent extension and modification of a whole line of research.

You can handle requests in a variety of ways. Your actions can range from very direct to indirect to irrelevant. The clearer and more direct a request and the clearer and more direct the response, the more coherent the request sequence. This is because directness supports clarity and relevance. Therefore, if I say, "Please pass the butter," my goal is clear and your response, "Sure," is obviously relevant. On the other hand, if I say, "My toast is dry," my goal of getting you to pass the butter is less clear, and your response, "You should turn the toaster down a little," just frustrates me.

25   Donald G. Ellis, "Fixing Communicative Meaning: A Coherentist Theory," *Communication Research* 22 (1995): 515–544.
26   Scott Jacobs and Sally Jackson, "Strategy and Structure in Conversational Influence Attempts," *Communication Monographs* 50 (1983): 285–304; Sally Jackson and Scott Jacobs, "Conversational Relevance: Three Experiments on Pragmatic Connectedness in Conversation," in *Communication Yearbook 10*, ed. M. McLaughlin (Newbury Park, CA: Sage, 1987), pp. 323–347.

Jackson and Jacobs provide a list of utterance types that may be taken as a request, ranging from direct to irrelevant. "Please pass the butter" is an absolutely direct request. An indirect request would be less clear: "My toast is dry." A hint is even less direct: "Some people at this table have something I sure would like."

There are also utterances commonly found in conversations that function as prerequests. These set up the listener for a request in the future. An example is, "Could I interrupt to ask for something?"

Once a request or prerequest is made, a listener can respond in a variety of direct or indirect ways. If the communicator recognizes the intent of a request, he or she can clarify things by responding directly. An example would be an *anticipatory move*, in which the listener recognizes the hidden or indirect request and grants it immediately ("My toast is sure dry." "Here, have some butter."). Such moves provide coherence because they are oriented to the apparent goals of the other communicator. Responses that misinterpret the speaker's statement are less coherent, as in the case of someone who takes an innocent statement to be a request that was never intended as such.

A fruitful line of theory that illustrates the inferential-strategic approach is conversational argument, the topic of the following section.

Conversational Argument

The study of conversational argument is another major application of the rational-pragmatic model explained above, and it illustrates that model very well.[27] This area of study treats arguments as conversations, showing how they follow rational coherence rules. Specifically, conversational argument allows people to manage disagreement. Managing disagreement, like any of the structural features of talk, is a rule-governed, cooperative achievement.

There can be a number of levels of disagreement in conversation. In the typical case, both parties openly disagree and state reasons for their positions. More typically, however, the dis-

agreement is less open. Because of the preference for agreement, the goal of conversational argument is to achieve agreement. Each turn must be a rational move toward bringing agreement about, and the coherence of an argument is largely judged in terms of the rationality of moves in achieving this objective. Thus, conversational argument is a method of managing disagreement so that it is minimized and so that agreement is achieved as quickly as possible.

There are basically two kinds of arguments. *Argument₁* involves *making* an argument, or stating a case by giving reasons. One makes an argument by presenting a case or supporting one's position with reasons, as in "Mary is arguing that smoking is bad for her son's health." *Argument₂* is *having* an argument, or exchanging objections, as in "Mary and her son are arguing about smoking." People can make an argument without having one, but they cannot easily have an argument without making one.[28] Here is an example of a typical argument:

George: Well, I better get this grass cut.
Harry: Yeah, me too.
George: Can I borrow your mower?
Harry: Well, I really need it myself.
George: I'll return it right away.
Harry: Last time you kept it two weeks.
George: No, I'll return it.
Harry: Last spring you kept it a month.
George: Gosh, Harry, I really will get it back to you today.

Here, George makes a request and a promise. The argument (argument₂) ensues because Harry does not grant the request as would normally be

27 The best recent statement of the theory of conversational argument is Frans H. van Eemeren, Rob Grootendorst, Sally Jackson, and Scott Jacobs, *Reconstructing Argumentative Discourse* (Tuscaloosa: University of Alabama Press, 1993). See also Frans H. van Eemeren and Rob Grootendorst, *Argumentation, Communication, and Fallacies: A Pragma-Dialectical Perspective* (Hillsdale, NJ: Erlbaum, 1992); Douglas N. Walton, *Plausible Argument in Everyday Conversation* (Albany: SUNY Press, 1992); Scott Jacobs and Sally Jackson, "Building a Model of Conversational Argument," in *Rethinking Communication: Paradigm Exemplars*, vol. 2, eds. B. Dervin, L. Grossberg, B. J. O'Keefe, and E. Wartella (Newbury Park, CA: Sage, 1989), pp. 153–171.
28 This distinction was originally made by Daniel J. O'Keefe, "Two Concepts of Argument," *Journal of the American Forensic Association* 13 (1977): 121–128.

expected, and he challenges George's promise. In objecting, Harry makes an argument (argument₁) by saying that George has not been reliable in the past, and George comes back by supporting his intent to return the item.

Like all conversations, arguments have a certain order and rationality that may or may not be apparent on the surface. For the participants the argument will probably seem coherent because of the cooperative principle, which, in the case of arguments, requires the communicators to cooperate in creating a dispute-resolving episode.

This is ironic because arguments do not sound very cooperative, but you cannot have an argument unless both parties cooperate in doing so. Notice that the following somewhat comical conversation is not a very coherent argument because one party refuses to cooperate:

Katie: You never turn your reports in on time, Sara.
Sara: I know, I really like taking my time on things.
Katie: But this infuriates me!
Sara: Just what I really like, a good emotional reaction.
Katie: Stop it. I want to know why you are falling down on the job.
Sara: I sure do enjoy being the center of attention. This is great!

Arguers are essentially agreeing to use certain kinds of speech acts and to meet certain goals, and in the above conversation, Sara refuses to participate in the game.

Just as promises and requests have their own requirements, so do arguments. To have an argument, you must put forth an opinion that you do not expect the other person initially to accept. In conversational argument theory this is called a *standpoint*. You have to support the standpoint with certain assertions that you expect will not be immediately apparent to the other person. And, of course, you are not cooperating in "having an argument" if you do not at least initially believe your own standpoints and assertions.

There are many forms an argument can take, but there is one idealized form that most argu-

ments approximate. This consists of four stages necessary for a complete argument to take place—confrontation, opening, argumentation, and concluding. These should not be considered the "steps" of an argument because they rarely occur in this order. Instead, you should think of these as aspects or parts of an argument. When they are all present, the communicators are said to be participating in a *critical discussion*.

The *confrontation stage* identifies the disagreement. The *opening stage* establishes agreement on how the dispute will be handled. The *argumentation stage* includes an exchange of competing positions. The *concluding stage* establishes resolution or continued disagreement.

These stages are characterized by certain kinds of speech acts, as outlined in Table 5.2.[29] In general the idealized model is like a code of conduct for having an argument. People will come as close to it as they can within the constraints of the situation. The idealized model is a measuring stick by which actual arguments can be compared and evaluated.

COMMENTARY AND CRITIQUE

No discussion of language or communication is complete without addressing discourse, or message units larger than sentences that are part of ongoing communication, including talk, written texts, and even nonverbal forms. Although language and other symbol systems are the building blocks of communication, discourse is the material of communication itself.

Karen Tracy agrees with this assessment and shows how the study of discourse has become central to the communication field.[30] In the field of communication, discourse analysts have made a special contribution. She characterizes the focus as one in which (1) talk is given preference over written texts, (2) discourse is seen as strate-

---

29   Van Eemeren, Grootendorst, Jackson, and Jacobs, *Reconstructing*, p. 31.
30   Tracy, "Discourse Analysis in Communication."

TABLE **5.2**

Distribution of Speech-Act Types Across Functional Stages in Discussion

Stage in Discussion	Speech-Act Type
Confrontation	
1.1	expressing standpoint (assertive)
1.2	accepting or not accepting standpoint (commissive)
Opening	
2.1	challenging to defend standpoint (directive)
2.2	accepting challenge to defend standpoint (commissive)
2.3	deciding to start discussion; agreeing on discussion rules (commissive)
Argumentation	
3.1	advancing argumentation (assertive)
3.2	accepting or not accepting argumentation (commissive)
3.3	requesting further argumentation (directive)
3.4	advancing further argumentation (assertive)
Concluding	
4.1	establishing the result (assertive)
4.2	accepting or withholding acceptance of standpoint (commissive)
4.3	upholding or retracting standpoint (assertive)
(Any stage)	
5.1	requesting usage declarative (directive)
5.2	defining, precizating [sic], amplifying, and so on (usage declarative)

gic and audience-centered, (3) problems in discourse are emphasized over obvious patterns, (4) debatable issues are tackled in an argumentative style, and (5) talk is considered the process by which human beings accomplish practical tasks and assert moral action.

Discourse as a part of everyday life is governed by rules, and much has been written about this topic. Rules are guidelines for action, and they say how language is used at every level—semantic, syntactic, and pragmatic. In other words, communicators use rules to determine how a sentence should be uttered, what words mean, and how to use language in ongoing communication. In this chapter we have seen how rules are used in the production of speech acts and in conversations.

The rule concept has been popular in communication studies because it acknowledges that people can make choices while still behaving somewhat predictably. Still, rule theory has had its share of critics. Criticism of rule theory has centered around two issues: conceptual coherence and explanatory power. Even its adherents admit that the rule tradition lacks unity and coherence. Jesse Delia verbalizes this objection in strong terms:

> The terrain covered by notions of "rules," then, is broad, grossly diffuse, and imprecisely articulated. And the real problem for any position purporting to be a general rules perspective is that the meaning of "rule" does not remain constant either within or across these domains. The "rules" territory taken as a whole is, in fact, little short of chaotic. At the least, it is clear that there is no unifying conception of the rule construct, of the domain of phenomena to which the construct has reference, of whether rules have generative power in producing and directing behavior . . . or of the proper way to give an account of some domain of phenomena utilizing the construct. The idea of "rules" as a general construct represents only a diffuse notion devoid of specific theoretical substance.[31]

The theories we have covered illustrate this lack of coherence. Linguistic rules are bound to an inherent structure of language and as such pretty much determine how sentences are generated and understood. As described by Searle, speech acts also are regulated by strict rules. Wittgenstein, on the other hand, considers the

---

31   Jesse Delia, "Alternative Perspectives for the Study of Human Communication: Critique and Response," *Communication Quarterly* 25 (1977): 54.

rules of language games to be malleable and changeable, much as in the rule-using tradition. The original conversation-analysis work, especially that governed by adjacency sequencing, used rules in the narrower, more restrictive sense; but Jackson and Jacobs in their global, rational approach see rules as something that communicators negotiate in the conversation itself.

The second issue related to rule theory involves its explanatory power. Critics generally believe that rule approaches cannot be explanatory as long as they fail to develop general principles that cut across contexts. To identify the rules in operation within a particular context is not sufficient to explain communication. Charles Berger believes that "at some point one must go beyond the description of 'what the rules are' and ask why some rules are selected over others . . . [and] what social forces produced the kinds of conventions and appropriate modes of behavior we now observe."[32] Berger's view is that a covering law approach is necessary to explain events, and rule theories are nothing more than covering laws in disguise.

Most rule advocates do not go along with this argument. Shimanoff points out that most rule explanations, in contrast to law explanations, are practical, or reason giving. Behaviors are explained in terms of their practical impact on creating desired outcomes. Although universal explanations are not desirable, and perhaps not even possible, rule theories should seek reason-giving explanations that cover relatively broad classes of situations, even to the point of allowing for prediction.[33]

The appropriate question here is not whether rule theories are explanatory but what kind of explanation the critic believes is necessary. Clearly, Berger and Shimanoff disagree on the level of generality necessary for adequate explanation. We must also keep in mind that different rule theories possess different levels of explanatory power.[34]

An important application of rule theory has been ordinary language philosophy and speech-act theory, which are among the most productive and useful creations of contemporary philosophy and social science. The power of these theories is in their use of intent to explain discourse. When we communicate we not only convey content, referential meaning, or our own version of truth but also an intent to do something with the words we use. This idea expresses so clearly how people use language to act or to accomplish objectives.

Still, speech-act theory has influenced a number of other theoretical lines of work, including conversation analysis. As researchers have worked with the concept of speech acts and applied it to various contexts, they have brought a number of weaknesses to light.

Critics generally agree that intentions are an important aspect of meaning, that speech constitutes a form of action, and that speech acts are governed by rules, but they argue that the conceptual categories of speech-act theory are vague or meaningless. Austin's threefold distinction among locutionary, illocutionary, and perlocutionary acts has been severely criticized from this standpoint, prompting one critic to state: "And now Austin has, in my judgment, erected a structure that is in imminent danger of collapse."[35]

Critics question the utility of locution as a concept, if the utterance of a locution automatically constitutes an illocution, as Austin claims it does. The distinction between illocutionary and perlocutionary acts is equally unclear to many readers, who point out that even if one could observe the difference between these concepts, it is doubtful that they constitute a useful distinction for guiding our understanding of speech acts. It would perhaps be more fruitful to recognize that any given speech act may be fulfilling a variety of intents and may be taken in a variety of different ways by different listeners.[36]

32 Charles R. Berger, "The Covering Law Perspective as a Theoretical Basis for the Study of Human Communication," *Communication Quarterly* 25 (1977): 12.
33 Shimanoff, *Communication Rules*, pp. 217–234.
34 Pearce, "Rules Theories."
35 Campbell, "A Rhetorical View," p. 287.
36 This point is made by John Lyne, "Speech Acts in a Semiotic Frame," *Communication Quarterly* 29 (1981): 202–208; and by Robert Trapp, "The Role of Disagreement in Interactional Argument," *Journal of the American Forensic Association* 23 (1986): 23–41.

The distinction between regulative and constitutive rules is equally fuzzy.[37] The problem here is that once any act becomes standardized, as in the case of almost all illocutionary acts, rules no longer are constitutive in the sense of creating new acts. Rules that regulate can be taken as constitutive, and rules that constitute an act also regulate.

Another application of rule theory, and one also heavily influenced by speech acts, is conversation analysis, the ethnomethodological study of ways actors cooperate in organizing interaction. It involves the careful examination of the details of actual conversations in an attempt to discover how people accomplish tasks and solve problems together.

Basically, conversation is a cooperative endeavor. People must play the game by the same rules or they would never know what was going on. For cooperation to occur, participants make certain assumptions about the other person, that he or she is conversing in good faith with the intent to speak in accordance with the rules. Even blatant violations of conversational rules are interpreted through implicature as being cooperative. Indeed, the combination of basic rules of cooperation—such as appropriate quantity of talk, truthfulness, relevance, and organization with the flexibility permitted by conversational implicature—makes it possible for humans to enact an infinite number of often creative expansions of talk to meet a whole array of intentions.

Perhaps the most important aspect of conversation analysis is the discovery of ways conversations are made coherent. This is also one of the most problematic aspects of the field. Originally, conversation analysts explained coherence strictly in terms of local rules, or the ways adjacent pairs of turns were consistent with one another. Most analysts now agree, however, that strictly local adjacency explanations are inadequate.[38]

This weakness has given rise to more global explanations of coherence. Perhaps the most interesting of these is the rational model of Jackson and Jacobs. In this more humanistic explanation, communicators understand what is going on within a broader context than the simple sequence of acts at a given moment. They use conversation to negotiate plans, and the overall conversation itself comes to be rational. Acts that appear unrelated to one another when examined locally become consistent when you understand the broader context in which they appear.

A significant application of the rational approach is Jackson and Jacobs's work on conversational argument, which looks at the ways communicators manage disagreements in conversations. It examines the ways speakers and listeners have an argument and the ways they make arguments in conversations. The distinction between *making* an argument and *having* one is important and captures two dimensions of conversations—the individual speech act and the organization of interactions.

One major objection to conversation analysis is that it works entirely within the confines of the discourse itself. The researcher makes observations and inferences entirely on the basis of the text, without reference to outside factors or even the opinions of the participants themselves. The researcher relies solely on his or her intuitions as a member of the culture in analyzing the discourse.[39] Although this procedure has merits, it is insensitive to the problem of possible multiple interpretations of speech acts. The participants in a conversation may not understand what is going on in the same way as the researcher thinks they do. Kathy Kellermann and Carra Sleight have written that coherence is not in the text but is in the cognitive system of the perceiver.[40] Although cues may be presented in the discourse, the actual coherence itself results from the application of a knowledge structure in the mind of the communicator to the discourse.

A similar argument is made by Barbara O'Keefe and Bruce Lambert, who address the

37 Shimanoff, *Communication Rules*, pp. 84–85. For additional critique, see McLaughlin, *Conversation*, pp. 63–68.
38 Jacobs, "Language."
39 This process is discussed in some depth by Wayne Beach, "Orienting to the Phenomenon," in *Communication Yearbook 13*, ed. James Anderson (Newbury Park, CA: Sage, 1990), pp. 216–244.
40 Kathy Kellermann and Carra Sleight, "Coherence: A Meaningful Adhesive for Discourse," in *Communication Yearbook 12*, ed. James Anderson (Newbury Park, CA: Sage, 1989), pp. 95–129.

inadequacies of global theories from the perspective of cognition. These theorists argue that from a cognitive perspective, messages are designed locally based on knowledge and assessment of what is happening right in the immediate situation.[41]

An even broader view connecting cognition, meaning, and social structure is provided by Teun A. van Dijk, who suggests that cognition and societal power structures are linked through discourse.[42] Certain ideologies of domination and control are expressed through discourse and thereby come to affect the thinking of both the oppressor and oppressed in society. In turn, these thoughts, held in cognition, affect how we talk, or discourse, which in turn reproduces societal power arrangements and oppression. For van Dijk, you cannot separate societal structures, discourse structures, and cognitive structures.

A related issue is whether conversational organization is correlated without other outside factors such as characteristics of the communicators or social situation. Without going outside the discourse itself, the researcher cannot know whether such associations exist. Most conversation analysts agree that they are not concerned with these kinds of issues and leave such questions to others who do not use conversation-analysis methods.

A natural tension exists between discourse analysis and poststructural approaches to texts. Discourse analysts of every variety assume that the meaning and function of talk can be uncovered by careful examination of the structure of the text. Poststructuralists deny this assumption out of hand.

Poststructural theorists do not see discourse as a strategic method of accomplishing individual objectives. Poststructuralism is most generally understood as a reaction against structural theories of language and discourse, including most of the theories discussed in Chapters 4 and 5.

Most poststructuralists reject the idea that discourse is primarily a tool of communication. It may be considered so by communicators, but in fact it functions in far more profound ways that defy the traditional methods of discourse analysis discussed in this chapter. The three best-known poststructuralists are Jacques Derrida, Jacques Lacan, and Michel Foucault. Their ideas differ substantially from one another, and, in fact, calling poststructuralism theoretical at all is stretching the truth. If anything, it is probably antitheoretical because of its rejection of the truth claims of discourse, including theories themselves.[43]

Jacques Derrida rejects absolutely the idea that language means anything definite.[44] He believes that there are always alternative meanings in a text and that any proposed meaning is only one alternative. Derrida's method of *deconstruction* is designed to take meaning apart and show that texts cannot be understood as expressions of particular meanings or truths.

Jacques Lacan, a student of Freud, deals with the effects of discourse on the self.[45] He shows how, at an early age, when the child is beginning to see the self as a unified being, language shapes some ideas about the self and represses others. The self is thus nothing in and of itself but is a product of discourse.

Foucault takes a somewhat different approach and denies that communicators create and use

---

41   Barbara J. O'Keefe and Bruce L. Lambert, "Managing the Flow of Ideas: A Local Management Approach to Message Design," in *Communication Yearbook 18*, ed. Brant R. Burleson (Thousand Oaks, CA: Sage, 1995), pp. 54–82.
42   Teun A. van Dijk, "Discourse Semantics and Ideology," *Discourse and Society* 6 (1995): 243–289; "Principles of Critical Discourse Analysis," *Discourse and Society* 4 (1993): 249–283; *Communicating Racism: Ethnic Prejudice in Thought and Talk* (Newbury Park, CA: Sage, 1987).
43   For an excellent discussion of poststructuralism, see Art Berman, *From the New Criticism to Deconstruction: The Reception of Structuralism and Post-Structuralism* (Urbana: University of Illinois Press, 1988). A briefer treatment is Robert Young, ed., "Post-Structuralism: An Introduction," in *Untying the Text: A Post-Structuralist Reader* (Boston: Routledge & Kegan Paul, 1981), pp. 1–28.
44   Derrida's chief work is *Of Grammatology*, trans. G. Spivak (Baltimore: Johns Hopkins University Press, 1976). For a brief overview, see the third edition of this book, *Theories of Human Communication* (Belmont, CA: Wadsworth, 1989), pp. 58–60. A more thorough treatment is that of Berman, *From the New Criticism*, pp. 199–222. See also Anthony Giddens, *Central Problems in Social Theory: Action, Structure, and Contradiction in Social Analysis* (Berkeley: University of California Press, 1979), pp. 28–48.
45   See Jacques Lacan, *The Four Fundamental Concepts of Psycho-Analysis*, trans. A. Sheridan (New York: Norton, 1981). See also Berman, *From the New Criticism*, pp. 185–194.

discourse to meet their goals.[46] The structure of discourse and how it is used are determined not by communicators, but by historical and social processes in which certain forms of discourse are made necessary by power structures prevalent during the period. In Foucault's theory, discourse forms the very structure of knowledge in an era. The rules embedded in discourse dictate how we do what we do, and speakers are merely taking roles established in the discursive formation. For Foucault, as one poststructuralist, the text precedes the talk in the sense that language has both knowledge and action embedded in it and predetermines how actors will respond in their use of speech.

Donald Ellis, a defender of language and discourse theory, attacks poststructuralism head-on:

Little could be more contrary to a theory of communication than principles that emerge from poststructuralism and the critical theory that it spawns. Human beings are language-using and message-producing animals, and theories of human communication engage us in understanding how messages are interpreted, evaluated, understood, and produced. A theory

of communication must position itself away from poststructuralists who "de-form" language, and move closer to a theory of communication based on intentionality where meaning is "in-formed" by how language is directed toward objects and processes in the world.[47]

In the next two chapters, we move to a set of theories that deal with communicators apart from discourse. We will examine the cognitive structures and processes that affect discourse production and processing.

---

46   Foucault's primary works on this subject include *The Archaeology of Knowledge,* trans. A. M. Sheridan Smith (New York: Pantheon, 1972); *The Order of Things: An Archaeology of the Human Sciences* (New York: Pantheon, 1970); and *Power/Knowledge: Selected Interviews and Other Writings 1927–1977,* trans. Colin Gordon and others, ed. Colin Gordon (New York: Pantheon, 1980). For an excellent short summary, see Sonja K. Foss, Karen A. Foss, and Robert Trapp, *Contemporary Perspectives on Rhetoric* (Prospect Heights, IL: Waveland, 1991). See also Carole Blair, "The Statement: Foundation of Foucault's Historical Criticism," *Western Journal of Speech Communication* 51 (1987): 364–383; Sonja K. Foss and Ann Gill, "Michel Foucault's Theory of Rhetoric as Epistemic," *Western Journal of Speech Communication* 51 (1987): 384–402; Nancy Fraser, *Unruly Practices: Power, Discourse, and Gender in Contemporary Social Theory* (Minneapolis: University of Minnesota Press, 1989), pp. 17–68.
47   Donald G. Ellis, "Post-Structuralism and Language: Non-Sense," *Communication Monographs* 58 (1991): 213–224.

6

THEORIES OF MESSAGE PRODUCTION

Communication can be viewed as an information-based, message-centered process, and many communication theories address these concerns. Consistent with this approach, this chapter and the next present theories of message production and reception. Although they acknowledge the social nature of communication, the theories in Chapters 6 and 7 tend not use social explanations. Rather, these theories view message production and reception as psychological matters, focusing on individual characteristics and processes.[1]

These theories tend to be of three types. The first involves *trait explanations*, which focus on relatively static characteristics of individuals and the ways these characteristics are associated with other variables. They predict that when you have a certain personality trait, you will tend to communicate in certain ways or produce certain kinds of messages.

The second type of theory of message production and reception rely on *behavioral explanations*. These tend to focus on types of behavior, how that behavior develops, and how certain behaviors are associated with other behaviors, feelings, thoughts, and traits.

The third approach involves *cognitive explanations*, which attempt to capture the mechanisms of the mind. These theories focus on the ways information is acquired and organized, how memory is used, how persons decide how to act, how messages are designed to accomplish goals, and a host of other similar concerns.

TRAITS AND BEHAVIORS

Traits and behaviors are often associated, so it makes sense organizationally to include trait and behavior theories in the same section in this book. Perhaps the most commonly held belief among psychology researchers today is that your

---

1 For a discussion of the significance of this line of theory, see the special edition of *Communication Theory* 10 (2000): 135–250; John O. Greene, ed., *Message Production: Advances in Communication Theory* (Mahwah, NJ: Erlbaum, 1997); John H. Powers, "On the Intellectual Structure of the Human Communication Discipline," *Communication Education* 44 (1995): 191–222.

behavior is determined by a combination of traits and situational factors. How you communicate at any given moment depends on your traits as an individual and the situation in which you find yourself.[2]

Three Examples of Traits

Numerous traits have been studied in communication research, and we cannot cover them all here.[3] As examples, we feature three interesting and well-developed traits.

Conversational Narcissism.   Narcissism—loosely, self-love—has been discussed in psychology for many years. Applying this concept to communication, Anita Vangelisti, Mark Knapp, and John Daly have identified a communication trait that they call *conversational narcissism*, or the tendency to be self-absorbed in conversation.[4] Conversational narcissists tend to inflate their self-importance by such behaviors as "one-upping" or boasting. They tend to want to control the flow of conversation, especially to provide opportunities for them to talk about themselves. They are known to use nonverbal, exhibitionist behaviors such as exaggerated gestures, and they tend to be insensitive or nonresponsive to others.

Argumentativeness.   This is the tendency to engage in conversations about controversial topics, to support your own point of view, and to refute opposing beliefs.[5] Dominic Infante and his colleagues, who have been primarily responsible for developing this concept, believe that argumentativeness can improve learning, help people see others' points of view, enhance credibility, and build communication skill. Argumentative individuals are by definition assertive, although not all assertive people are argumentative. These authors distinguish between argumentativeness, which is a positive trait, and verbal aggressiveness and hostility, which are negative ones. Indeed, knowing how to argue properly may be a solution to otherwise hurtful aggressive tendencies.

As a case in point, Infante and two colleagues studied husbands and wives in violent relationships and discovered that violent marriages are characterized by higher verbal aggressiveness and lower argumentativeness than are nonviolent ones.[6] It seems that many nonviolent spouses deal with their problems by arguing constructively, whereas violent spouses may be unable to solve their differences in this way.

Social and Communicative Anxiety.   Many people are afraid of communication, and there has been much research on this problem. Within the communication field, the best-known work is that of James McCroskey and his colleagues on *communication apprehension*.[7] Although everyone has occasional stage fright, *trait CA* is an enduring tendency to be apprehensive about communication in a variety of settings. Normal apprehension is not a problem, but pathological CA, in which an individual suffers persistent and extreme fear of communication, certainly is. Abnormally high CA creates serious personal problems, including extreme discomfort and avoidance of communication to the point of preventing productive and happy participation in society.

---

2   For a discussion of situational factors in communication, see Lynn C. Miller, Michael J. Cody, and Margaret L. McLaughlin, "Situations and Goals as Fundamental Constructs in Interpersonal Communication Research," in *Handbook of Interpersonal Communication*, 2nd ed., eds. Mark L. Knapp and Gerald R. Miller (Thousand Oaks, CA: Sage, 1994), pp. 162–197.
3   For an overview of several traits studied by communication researchers, see Howard Giles and Richard L. Street, Jr., "Communicator Characteristics and Behavior," in *Handbook of Interpersonal Communication*, 2nd ed., eds. Mark L. Knapp and Gerald R. Miller (Thousand Oaks, CA: Sage, 1994), pp. 103–161.
4   Anita L. Vangelisti, Mark L. Knapp, and John A. Daly, "Conversational Narcissism," *Communication Monographs* 57 (1990): 251–274.
5   For a summary of this work, see Dominic A. Infante and Andrew S. Rancer, "Argumentativeness and Verbal Aggressiveness: A Review of Recent Theory and Research," in *Communication Yearbook 19*, ed. Brant R. Burleson (Thousand Oaks, CA: Sage, 1996), pp. 319–352; Dominic A. Infante, Andrew S. Rancer, and Deanna F. Womack, *Building Communication Theory* (Prospect Heights, IL: Waveland, 1993), pp. 162–168.
6   Dominic A. Infante, Teresa A. Chandler, and Jill E. Rudd, "Test of an Argumentative Skill Deficiency Model of Interspousal Violence," *Communication Monographs* 56 (1989): 163–177.
7   This work is summarized in James C. McCroskey, "The Communication Apprehension Perspective," in *Avoiding Communication: Shyness, Reticence, and Communication Apprehension*, eds. J. A. Daly and J. C. McCroskey (Beverly Hills, CA: Sage, 1984), pp. 13–38.

Communication apprehension is part of a family of concepts including, for example, social avoidance, social anxiety, interaction anxiety, and shyness. As a group these have been called "social and communicative anxiety." In a huge survey of literature and analysis of this literature, Miles Patterson and Vicki Ritts outlined several parameters.[8]

In general, social and communicative anxiety has *physiological* aspects such as heart rate and blushing, *behavioral* manifestations such as avoidance and self-protection, and *cognitive* dimensions such as self-focus and negative thoughts. Interestingly, these researchers found that the cognitive correlates are the strongest of the three, which may mean that social and communicative anxiety has mostly to do with how we think about ourselves in regard to communication situations. Negative thinking can lead to anxious self-preoccupation that keeps a person from considering all of the information and cues in the environment, disrupts normal information processing, and leads to reinforcing behaviors such as withdrawal.

Traits, Temperament, and Biology

For a number of years, psychologists have been exploring the biological bases of human behavior, and traits have been increasingly explained in terms of genetic predisposition. Recently, James McCroskey and Michael Beatty have brought this line of work into the communication field.[9] Generally, this work is predicated on the idea that traits are predispositions of temperament rooted in genetically determined neurobiological structures, or brain activity. This is very important because brain functioning lies behind all psychological processes, including how we think, feel, and behave. How we experience the world, then, is very much a matter of what is happening in our brain, and that in turn is largely genetically determined. The impact of the environment, or learning, is not very large, so we can expect that individual differences in how people communicate can be explained biologically. McCroskey and Beatty point to work in

psychology suggesting that all traits can be reduced to just a few dimensions that are about 80 percent determined by genetics.[10]

McCroskey and Beatty apply the *communibiological paradigm* to their own work in communication apprehension, calling this trait a form of "neurotic introversion," which is a particular type of temperament. After years of exploring an explanation for this trait, they are now convinced that the cause of high trait CA is biological. This is a retreat from the generally accepted thesis held by many researchers, including McCroskey himself at an earlier time, that fear of communication is learned. From a biological perspective, temperamentally based traits are caused by activity deep in the brain.

The *limbic system* of the brain controls emotion, and our emotional differences often relate to these brain differences. The more sensitive your limbic system, the more anxiety you may experience. Stimuli in the environment are processed through a part of your brain known as the *behavioral inhibition system* (BIS). Negative stimuli cause an arousal of the BIS, which in turn activates your limbic system. When your BIS is stimulated, you tend to pay more attention to threats. Thus, people who have an overactive BIS will be more prone to anxiety and fear than individuals with a less activated one.

In communication apprehension, something has to happen to cause communication to be viewed as a very aversive stimulus. This involves yet another part of your brain, the *behavioral activation system* (BAS). Because it is associated with rewards, this system seems to stimulate motivation and bring about action. Even apprehensive persons are at least occasionally motivated to

---

8   Miles L. Patterson and Vicki Ritts, "Social and Communicative Anxiety: A Review and Meta-Analysis," in *Communication Yearbook 20* (Thousand Oaks, CA: Sage, 1997), pp. 263–303.
9   Michael J. Beatty, James C. McCroskey, and Alan D. Heisel, "Communication Apprehension as Temperamental Expression: A Communibiological Paradigm," *Communication Monographs* 65 (1998): 197–219. See also James C. McCroskey, ed., *Personality and Communication: Trait Perspectives* (New York: Hampton Press, 1998).
10   H. J. Eysenck. "Biological Dimensions of Personality," in *Handbook of Personality*, ed. L. A. Pervin (New York: Guilford, 1991), pp. 244–276.

communicate because of perceived rewards. For example, you might go ahead and give a presentation in a speech class because you want a high grade. In this case the BAS would enable you to do something potentially fearful.

The problem for highly apprehensive individuals is that they will experience extreme fear in the process of giving the speech, making the overall experience unpleasant. They will remember this and continue to associate the communication experience with negative stimuli.

The biological approach is relatively new in communication studies, and it will be interesting to see the course of this direction in the future.

Accommodation and Adaptation

If you observe interaction closely, you will notice that speakers frequently adjust their behaviors to one another. For example, two speakers may adjust their accents to sound more alike, may begin to speak at the same speed, or may use mirror-like gestures. Sometimes speakers do just the opposite and actually exaggerate their differences. Researchers have also noticed these behaviors and have studied them in a variety of ways. Here we look at two landmark projects that address this issue.

Accommodation Theory.   One of the most influential behavioral theories of communication, *accommodation theory,* was formulated by Howard Giles and his colleagues to explain this pattern of behavior.[11] Giles and his colleagues have confirmed the common observation that communicators often seem to mimic one another's behavior. This they call *convergence,* or coming together. The opposite, *divergence,* or moving apart, happens when speakers begin to

exaggerate their differences. Accommodation in both of these forms has been seen in almost all imaginable communication behaviors, including accent, rate, loudness, vocabulary, grammar, voice, gestures, and other features. Convergence or divergence can be *mutual,* in which case both communicators come together or go apart, or it can be *nonmutual,* in which one person converges to or diverges from the other. Convergence can also be *partial* or *complete.* For example, you might speak somewhat faster so that you are a little closer to another person's speech rate, or you might go all the way and speak just as fast as this person does.

Although accommodation is sometimes done consciously, the speaker is usually unaware of doing it. The use of accommodation is similar to any number of other functional but subconscious processes that are scripted, or enacted without having to attend to all the details of each behavior. You are probably more aware of divergence than convergence.

Accommodation researchers have found that accommodation can be important in communication. It can lead to social identity and bonding or disapproval and distance. For instance, convergence often happens in situations in which you seek the approval of others. This can occur in groups that are already alike in certain ways because such groups consist of similar individuals who can coordinate their actions. The result of convergence can be increased attractiveness, predictability, intelligibility, and mutual involvement.

When you converge, you rely on your perception of the other person's speech qualities. Often you are correct in this perception, but sometimes you can be wrong, which will lead to negative results. For example, people sometimes converge not with the other person's actual speech but with a stereotype, such as when a nurse speaks to an elderly patient using baby talk or when someone speaks loudly and slowly to a blind person.

Observing how people evaluate the convergence of others is interesting. Typically, some convergence is appreciated. You tend to respond

11   See Howard Giles, Justine Coupland, and Nikolas Coupland, "Accommodation Theory: Communication, Context, and Consequence," in *Contexts of Accommodation: Developments in Applied Sociolinguistics,* eds. Howard Giles, Justine Coupland, and Nikolas Coupland (Cambridge: Cambridge University Press, 1991), pp. 1–68. See also Howard Giles, Anthony Mulac, James J. Bradac, and Patricia Johnson, "Speech Accommodation Theory: The First Decade and Beyond," in *Communication Yearbook 10,* ed. M. L. McLaughlin (Newbury Park, CA: Sage, 1987), pp. 13–48.

favorably to someone who makes an attempt to speak in your style. But you will probably dislike too much convergence, especially if you think it is inappropriate. People tend to appreciate convergence from others that is accurate, well intended, and appropriate in the situation.

How you evaluate convergence depends in part on why you think others are copying you, or their motive. Studies have shown that when listeners perceive that the speaker is intentionally speaking in a style close to their own, they will tend to like it, but when convergence is seen as out of the speaker's control, it may be distasteful to the other party. Almost certainly, any convergence move that is seen as inappropriate in the situation or done out of ill will will be evaluated negatively. This includes, for example, mocking, teasing, insensitivity to social norms, or inflexibility.

Of course, you do not always match the behavior of others in order to seek their approval. Often higher-status speakers will slow their speech or use simpler vocabulary when talking with a person who has lower status to increase understanding. In contrast, lower-status communicators will sometimes upgrade their speech to match the higher-status person because they want that person's approval.

Accommodation often seems to be associated with power. For example, in New York City where Blacks are viewed as having more power than Puerto Ricans, the latter converge more to the accent of the former. In organizations, subordinates have been observed to converge with superiors more often than the reverse.

Although the rewards of speech convergence can be substantial, so are the costs. Convergence requires effort, and it may mean the loss of personal identity. Sometimes it is even viewed as abnormal and may be frowned on.

Instead of converging, you sometimes maintain your own style or actually move in the opposite direction. You may work to maintain your own style when you want to reinforce your identity. This would be the case, for example, among members of an ethnic group with a strong accent, who work to perpetuate the accent in the face of threats from homogenizing influences of a dominant culture. Divergence often functions to accentuate in-group identity vis-à-vis members of an out-group.

Sometimes members of a group will accentuate their speech characteristics in a strange community to elicit sympathy from the host group. This is a kind of self-handicapping method that frees speakers from responsibility for violation of certain social norms with which they may not be familiar. Sometimes, too, speakers will diverge from the style of other speakers in order to affect the others' behavior in some way. Teachers may deliberately talk over the heads of students in order to challenge the students to learn. You might speak extra slowly when talking with a very fast speaker in order to get him or her to slow down.

Interaction Adaptation Theory. Accommodation theory lays the basic groundwork for identifying various types of accommodation and their correlates, but this phenomenon is actually part of a much more complex process of adaptation in interaction: the topic of the interaction adaptation theory of Judee Burgoon and her associates.[12]

These researchers noticed that communicators have a kind of *interactional synchrony*, a coordinated back-and-forth pattern. If you were to videotape a conversation with a friend, you would probably notice this effect. At some moments you might see the two of you behaving in a similar way, mirroring or converging in a *reciprocal* pattern. At other moments, you might see yourselves sort of backing away or diverging in a pattern of *compensation*. Using the lens of interaction adaptation theory, you would begin to notice that you and your friend's behavior are influenc-

---

12   Judee K. Burgoon, "It Takes Two to Tango: Interpersonal Adaptation and Implications for Relational Communication," in *Communication from the Helm for the 21st Century*, ed. Judith S. Trent (Boston: Allyn & Bacon, 1998), pp. 53–59; Judee K. Burgoon and Cindy H. White, "Researching Nonverbal Message Production: A View from Interaction Adaptation Theory," in *Message Production: Advances in Communication Theory*, ed. John O. Greene (Mahwah, NJ: Erlbaum, 1997), pp. 279–312; Judee K. Burgoon, Lesa A. Stern, and Leesa Dillman, *Interpersonal Adaptation: Dyadic Interaction Patterns* (New York: Cambridge University Press, 1995); Judee K. Burgoon, Leesa Dillman, and Lesa A. Stern, "Adaptation in Dyadic Interaction: Defining and Operationalizing Patterns of Reciprocity and Compensation," *Communication Theory* 3 (1993): 295–316.

ing each other, creating the pattern. This theory attempts to explain what is happening.

When you begin communicating with another person, you have a rough idea about what will happen. This is your *interaction position*, the place where you will begin. It is determined by a combination of factors that the theorists cleverly named RED, which stands for requirements, expectations, and desires. Your *requirements* are the things you really need in the interaction. These may be biological as in a request for food, or they may be social in terms of needed affiliation, continued friendship, or even managing a smooth interaction. Your *expectations* are the patterns you predict will happen. If you are not that familiar with the other person, you will rely on social norms of politeness and aspects of the situation such as the purpose of the meeting. If you know the other person well, your expectations will probably be based largely on past experience. Your *desires* are what you want to accomplish, what you hope will happen.

Your initial behaviors in the interaction consist of a combination of verbal and nonverbal behaviors that reflect your interaction position, as well as environmental factors and skill level. However, in most interactions, your behavior will change—and so will that of your partner—as you experience mutual influence. The effect of mutual influence is considerable and in most situations probably far greater than any preplanning you have done. Normally, you will reciprocate your partner's behavior as a kind of default response. A hug, for example, will be reciprocated. Humans seem to need organized patterning, which reciprocation can help achieve. This tendency to reciprocate may be caused by a combination of biological and socially conditioned factors. This does not mean that we always reciprocate, however. Sometimes the reciprocal pattern is disrupted or disabled, leading to a second kind of response—compensation.

If you like your partner's behavior more than you thought you would, you will probably reciprocate, or converge, making your behavior more like that of your partner. If it turns out that your partner's behavior is more negative than you thought it would be, you will probably engage in a pattern of compensation, maintaining your own style and maybe even exaggerating what you would have initially done. Let's say, for example, that you feel very close to your friend and would like to get a hug, but you don't really expect to. Surprisingly, however, he comes up and puts his hand on your shoulder, so you reciprocate by putting your arm around his waist. That's an example of positive evaluation and reciprocation.

On the other hand, assume that you hope to get a hug but are disappointed when your partner fails to touch you. In this situation, you would probably compensate by walking over and giving him a hug. On the other hand, if you expected a hug but didn't want one, his failure to touch you would be a good thing, and you would reciprocate that by backing off or maintaining some distance yourself. Human interaction is complex and involves a mix of motives and patterns. You can actually reciprocate some behaviors and compensate others at the same time.

The adaptation explanation of interaction behavior is based on the expectancy violations hypothesis: the idea that you make judgments about violations of expectations, which in turn affect your subsequent behavior. Burgoon and her colleagues have developed this idea in some detail, and we will revisit this theory in Chapter 7.

Accommodation and adaptation theories describe one way that behaviors are organized in an interaction. In the following section, we move to theories that help us understand how people actually formulate messages. These theories are in the cognitive tradition.

☾ COGNITIVE THEORIES

The *cognitive tradition* concentrates on the mental processes that mediate between inputs and outputs, between stimulus and response.[13] Cognitive theories assume you have purposes and

---

13 For an introduction to cognitive process, see Patricia G. Devine, David L. Hamilton, and Thomas M. Ostrom, *Social Cognition: Impact on Social Psychology* (San Diego: Academic, 1994), pp. 2–13; John O. Greene, "Evaluating Cognitive Explanations of Communicative Phenomena," *Quarterly Journal of Speech* 70 (1984): 241–254.

make choices, and these theories deal with the mental processes that make your actions possible. Cognitive theories focus on the content, structure, and process of your mind.

The content of the cognitive system consists of the information—thoughts, attitudes, and concepts—that you use to understand your experiences and plan your actions. The structure of the system reflects how you organize the content of your thoughts within your memory banks as well as the procedures, or operations, you use to manage this content—how you actually change it and use it on a daily basis.

Unlike trait theories, cognitive approaches attempt to explain the mechanism by which communicators produce messages, or as we will see in the following chapter, how they process information in the reception of messages. Cognition helps us organize knowledge in order to act appropriately in given situations.

This section is organized into three areas—theories of planning and action, theories of message selection, and theories of message design.

Theories of Planning and Action

Action Assembly Theory.   We begin this section with a general cognitive theory that explains what you actually go through to produce communicative action. Developed by John Greene, action assembly theory examines the ways you organize your knowledge and use it in communication.[14]

According to this theory, you possess both *content knowledge* and *procedural knowledge.* You know *about* things, and you know *how to do* things. In action assembly theory, procedural knowledge takes center stage. To get an idea of what your procedural knowledge looks like,

imagine that your memory is full of connected elements. Each element of memory is a *node*, and the nodes are connected to one another, much like Web sites are linked in the Internet. Specifically, procedural knowledge consists of associated nodes related to behavior, consequences, and situations. For example, you probably smile when you greet someone and say something like, "Hi, how are you?" Then, the other person smiles back and says, "Fine. How are you?" You hold this in your memory as a set of associated nodes in which links are made between the situation of greeting someone, smiling, using certain words, and the result of having the greeting returned.

Although the above example is very simple, your actual network of associated nodes is a constantly changing, complex system. However, it is not an unorganized system. At any given time, the associations that have been most frequently or most recently activated are stronger, so that certain nodes tend to cluster together into modules, which Greene calls *procedural records.* The smiling-greeting ritual described above is a simple example of a procedural record. However, procedural records are not distinct with firm boundaries. Because the elements—smiling, greeting, asking about health, and so on—are also associated with other things, procedural records are imprecise.

A procedural record, then, is a set of links among nodes in a network of action. Some of these are just automatic associations. Because you have done certain things together over and over, they have become associated, like removing one foot from the gas and pushing in the clutch with your other foot. Other records actually contain information, or meaning—like knowing that the foot routine with the gas and clutch are a part of changing gears, necessary for driving a car with a stick shift.

Whenever you act, you must "assemble" appropriate procedures, or behaviors. Out of all the actions in your procedural memory, you must select the most appropriate ones within the situation to accomplish the consequences you wish. You do this by selecting an action sequence. The

14   John O. Greene and Deanna Geddes, "An Action Assembly Perspective on Social Skill," *Communication Theory* 3 (1993): 26–49; John O. Greene, "Action Assembly Theory: Metatheoretical Commitments, Theoretical Propositions, and Empirical Applications," in *Rethinking Communication: Paradigm Exemplars*, eds. B. Dervin, L. Grossberg, B. J. O'Keefe, and E. Wartella (Newbury Park, CA: Sage, 1989), pp. 117–128; "A Cognitive Approach to Human Communication: An Action Assembly Theory," *Communication Monographs* 51 (1984): 289–306.

word *selecting*, however, belies the complexity of what is really happening—often unconsciously—behind the scenes within your mind. According to the theory, whenever you act, you must assemble associated behaviors from appropriate procedural records.

Some sets of assembled action are so strongly entrenched and so frequently used that you rely on them commonly as preformed or programmed actions. Called *unitized assemblies*, these are highly efficient routines that require little effort. You don't have to think much about what to do because the whole sequence is already there in your memory. Greeting rituals are a good example of unitized assemblies.

Often, however, situations require you to do some cognitive work. A number of outcomes may be desired, including achieving an objective with another person, expressing information, managing conversations, producing intelligible speech, and other results. When introducing yourself, for example, you may want to meet the other person, make yourself look good, and have a good time, all in one set of actions. You essentially assemble the procedures necessary to accomplish these objectives, and the result is a mental representation for a coordinated set of actions. This mental model is called *output representation*; it is the "plan" your mind holds about what you will do within the situation you face.

Let's say, for example, that you see a friend walking toward you. You are suddenly filled with dread because you know that your friend's mother has just died, and you will need to say and do something appropriate. How will your mind handle this difficult situation?

First, the situation will trigger, or activate, a host of nodes on such topics as death, friend, greeting, feeling, speaking, gesturing, and so on. Each of these activated nodes is part of a variety of procedural records. These coalesce into what Greene calls a *coalition*. So at the moment you see your friend, your mind will pull together a coalition of possible procedural records, but you cannot use them all. From the coalition, your mind will quickly and simultaneously piece together a set of actions ranging from very low level (such

as uttering words) to high level (such as accomplishing a goal). This is the *output representation*: everything you need to remember in order to act in an appropriate and coordinated way. All of the actions—from remembering how to pronounce certain words to how to express sympathy—are tightly associated at this moment. At that instance, other associations that are part of less relevant procedural records fade away in a process called *decay*, leaving a fairly coherent output representation for this particular situation.

It is clear, then, that no single action can stand by itself. Every action implicates other actions in one way or another. To introduce yourself, you have to use a variety of actions from moving your vocal chords to using certain words and gestures. To write a paragraph, you must combine a variety of actions from coordinating knowledge to using language to writing or typing. Actions, then, are integrated into a network of knowledge. Each piece of knowledge in the overall routine is a representation of something that needs to be done. Higher-order goals (such as making an introduction) and lower-level routines (such as smiling) are integrated into an output representation that guides your communication actions.

There is a special class of action that enables you to guide, monitor, adapt, and change. These are the *executive processes*. Although they help to make actions more conscious and careful, they are still composed of procedural records, just as any other aspect of action. Executive processes not only help you to guide your actions but also enable you to identify goals, plan, and begin action-assembly protocols.

The action assembly process is complex and not always successful. To do something well requires not only knowledge and motivation but also the ability to retrieve and organize the necessary actions efficiently and quickly. If you make a mistake or have trouble doing something, even when you have the correct knowledge and motivation, it means you are not able to put together the best routine for any number of reasons. For example, you may not be practiced in doing it, you may be unable to pay attention to important aspects of the situation, you may be relying too much on unitized routines, or you may experience other problems in the action-assembly process.

Action assembly takes time and effort. Thinking is work. The more complex the assembly task, the more time and effort it takes. Introducing yourself is usually not as difficult as expressing sympathy in a surprise situation. Even though communicators seem to respond to a situation immediately without effort, research shows that every response does take time, if only a fraction of a second, and that more complex tasks take more time than simple ones. You know from your own experience that you think through and struggle with communicating in unfamiliar situations. This difficulty in processing information in communication can be seen in people's pausing and dysfluency patterns. When people take a long time to say something, pause and stutter, or generally seem confused, they may be having difficulty in integrating procedural knowledge and formulating an action. When people respond quickly and fluently, they are demonstrating that the task is relatively easy for them in this situation.

Action assembly theory is what we might call a microcognitive theory because it deals with very specific cognitive operations. In contrast, the following theory is a macrocognitive theory since it deals with general processes of planning at a higher order.

Planning Theory.   A well-known theory of planning in the communication field was produced by Charles Berger to explain the process that individuals go through in planning their communication behavior.[15] The study of planning is a centerpiece of cognitive science, and psychologists have given the subject considerable thought and research. Linking cognitive planning with communication behavior, however, has not received as much attention, and Berger hopes to close this gap by his own research and theory.

Berger writes that plans are "hierarchical cognitive representations of goal-directed action sequences."[16] In other words, plans are mental images of the steps one will go through to meet a goal. They are hierarchical because certain actions are necessary to set things up so that other actions will work. Planning, then, is the process of thinking up these action plans.

Because communication is so important in achieving goals, planning messages is a critical concern. If you want to do well in a class, you probably talk to other students, friends, and even the professor to find out what might be done. Your assignments will be carefully crafted to meet requirements, and you will think consciously about what to do and how to do it.

Among the many goals we try to achieve every day, from planning meals to getting where we want to go, *social goals* are especially important. Because we are social creatures, other people are important in our lives, and we aim to influence them in a variety of ways. We can achieve many types of goals by communicating in particular ways, but communication is absolutely central in meeting social goals. Understanding something about how we plan to meet such goals, then, is an important research aim.

Studying goal behavior is no easy task. For one thing, goals tend to be complex. Goals seem to be arranged in hierarchies, and achieving certain goals first makes it possible to achieve other ones later. For example, you may find another person attractive and want to get to know this person, but you will probably have to accomplish quite a few subgoals first, such as finding a way to start a conversation with this person.

Many of our goals are actually part of the planning process itself. These *metagoals* guide the plans we make. For example, we usually want to do planning in the easiest way possible, making efficiency an important metagoal. (That's why we don't reinvent the wheel every time we take a drive.) We want to behave in socially appropriate ways, so social appropriateness is another

---

15   Charles R. Berger, *Planning Strategic Interaction: Attaining Goals Through Communicative Action* (Mahwah, NJ: Erlbaum, 1997).
16   Berger, *Planning Strategic Interaction*, p. 25.

metagoal. Another metagoal is politeness, for whatever else we might want to accomplish in our communication, we often aim to be polite.

Because we want our planning to be efficient, we often rely on *canned plans* we have used before. These are stored in *long-term memory,* and we rely on them whenever possible. Because you have started so many conversations in your life, you know how to do it without thinking, and you rely on the same methods you have used over and over again.

Often canned plans don't work or are foiled in some way. Or the goal is new and complicated and requires fresh thinking. Let's say you need a substantial loan and think you can get the money from a close relative—say, your aunt. You have never done this before and don't know exactly how to approach it. Here you must put a new plan together in your *working memory.* The working memory is a place where you can use parts of old plans, knowledge, and creative thinking to come up with a way to approach the problem.

The strength of the goal seems to influence how complex our plans tend to be. If you want something very badly, you will probably work pretty hard and come up with a fairly elaborate plan. If you really need the loan, you will probably work out the plan carefully. Of course, the complexity of your plan will also depend on how much knowledge you have about loans and about your aunt as well as your knowledge about persuasion. Berger refers to information about the topic (for example, loans and relatives) as *specific domain knowledge* and information about how to communicate (for example, persuading people) as *general domain knowledge.* The theory predicts that the more you know (specific and general), the more complex your plan will be. Obviously, then, if you have a lot of motivation and knowledge, you will create more complex plans, and if your motivation and knowledge are low, your plan will probably be underdeveloped.

Naturally, however, there are limits on how complicated a plan can be. In interpersonal com-

munication, this is especially so because of the metagoals of efficiency and social appropriateness. You can't do just anything you want because of the effort it would take and because some actions are not socially appropriate. For example, you probably would not make up a 100-point plan to get money from your aunt because that would take too much effort, and you certainly would not include the socially unacceptable strategy of insulting her to secure the loan.

What happens if your attempt to achieve a goal is thwarted? If the goal is important, you will probably persist, but it is unlikely that you will continue to use the same strategy over and over. There are two things you might consider. One course of action is to try different specific actions, which Berger calls *low-level plan hierarchy alterations,* or you could adjust more general actions (*abstract alterations*).

People tend to make lower-level adjustments first. For example, say you decide to broach the subject of the loan by just mentioning that your tuition is due. Suppose that your aunt replies, "Boy, I bet you're glad you had such a high-paying job last summer!" You don't get the reaction you expected, and you will probably try a different message, something like, "Right, and that did help, but my books were so expensive and my apartment rent is out of sight." This is an example of a low-level alteration.

Sometimes, though, the situation calls for alteration of a higher level of strategy. For example, if your aunt were to say, "Yes, money can sure be a problem. My assets are all tied up in a big investment deal right now, and I am also having a little cash flow problem myself," you would probably reconsider what you were trying to accomplish. Instead of asking for the loan now, you might change your goal a little and decide to wait a few weeks.

Berger's theory suggests that whether you make low- or high-level adjustments depends largely on how motivated you are to achieve the goal. If the goal is very important, you will tend to make higher-level adjustments, and you will do so sooner than if your motivation is low.

Planning and goal achievement are very much tied into our emotions.[17] We are not robots, and if our goals are thwarted, we tend to react negatively. On the other hand, if our plans go well, we often feel uplifted. The negative feelings we experience when we fail to meet a goal depend on how important the goal is. They also are determined in part by how hard we have worked to achieve the goal and how close to the goal we actually got. If you worked really hard to get the loan from your aunt, and she led you on so you were pretty optimistic about getting it, you would be really upset if the final answer was, "Sorry, but no."

Berger has said that social appropriateness is an important metagoal. We normally act in socially appropriate ways, but there are exceptions. Because of the negative emotions we often feel when goals are thwarted, we often act in socially unacceptable ways when this happens. This is especially true if our goals are repeatedly thwarted and if the thwarted goals are important to us. Something else will happen at times like this too: We keep trying to get to the goal, but out of desperation, we tend to use simpler and simpler plans.

Even if we try to maintain a complex plan, we may falter and have trouble invoking it. The ease with which we follow a plan is called *action fluidity*, and people find that they sometimes have great fluidity and sometimes not. The more complex a plan and the more emotional we get, the less fluid our actions become.

For example, in an experiment conducted by Berger and his colleagues, subjects were asked to present arguments to another person supporting their position on a controversial campus issue.[18] Some of the subjects were given no time to plan their arguments, others were given some planning time, and others were given planning time and invited to prepare contingency plans as well. The person to whom the subjects gave their argument was actually a confederate of the experimenter instructed to resist their arguments and thereby frustrate the subjects. The experimenters then counted the number of disruptions in the subjects' speech as a measure of fluidity.

The subjects who were given an opportunity to develop alternative plans were less fluid in general than those who were not. This result was probably caused by the fact that this group had more complex plans.

There may be many variables affecting how easily one can put a plan into effect. One of these is the degree of complexity that an individual can handle in his or her thinking.

Theories of Message Selection

Focusing on persuasion, Steven Wilson proposed two generations of work within the cognitive tradition—*strategy selection* and *goal pursuit*.[19] Strategy selection deals with the issue of what types of messages are available to communicators and the processes involved in selecting strategies. Goal pursuit concentrates on how people actively create or design messages based on their goals.[20] Barbara O'Keefe used a similar analysis and expanded it to message production in general.[21] She terms these the *strategy choice* and *message design* models. In this section we will explore two theories of the first group—strategy selection.

---

17   The role of emotions in message production has attracted the attention of cognitive researchers in recent years. See, for example, Brant R. Burleson and Sally Planalp, "Producing Emotion(al) Messages," *Communication Theory* 10 (2000): 221–250; Ross Buck, "From DNA to MTV: The Spontaneous Communication of Emotional Messages," in *Message Production: Advances in Communication Theory*, ed. John O. Greene (Mahwah, NJ: Erlbaum, 1997), pp. 313–340.

18   Charles R. Berger, Susan H. Karol, and Jerry M. Jordan, "When a Lot of Knowledge Is a Dangerous Thing: The Debilitating Effects of Plan Complexity on Verbal Fluency," *Human Communication Research* 16 (1989): 91–119.

19   Steven R. Wilson, "Developing Theories of Persuasive Message Production: The Next Generation," in *Message Production: Advances in Communication Theory*, ed. John O. Greene (Mahwah, NJ: Erlbaum, 1997), pp. 15–46.

20   For a discussion of the importance of goals in cognitive research, see Charles R. Berger, "Goal Detection and Efficiency: Neglected Aspects of Message Production," *Communication Theory* 10 (2000): 156–166; and James Price Dillard, "Explicating the Goal Construct: Tools for Theorists," in *Message Production: Advances in Communication Theory*, ed. John O. Greene (Mahwah, NJ: Erlbaum, 1997), pp. 47–70; Janet R. Meyer, "Cognitive Influences on the Ability to Address Interaction Goals," in *Message Production: Advances in Communication Theory*, ed. John O. Greene (Mahwah, NJ: Erlbaum, 1997), pp. 71–90.

21   Barbara J. O'Keefe, "Variation, Adaptation, and Functional Explanation in the Study of Message Design," in *Developing Communication Theories*, ed. Gerry Philipsen (Albany: SUNY Press, 1997), pp. 85–118.

Compliance Gaining. Gaining the compliance of another person is one of the most common communication goals. It involves trying to get other people to do what you want them to do, or to stop doing something you don't like. Compliance-gaining messages are among the most researched areas in the field.[22] The prolific research program on compliance-gaining strategies in the communication field received its impetus from the groundbreaking studies of Gerald Marwell and David Schmitt.[23]

These researchers isolated sixteen strategies commonly used in gaining the compliance of other people, as outlined in Table 6.1. Marwell and Schmitt use an exchange-theory approach: Compliance is an exchange for something else supplied by the compliance seeker. If you do what I want, I will give you something in return—esteem, approval, money, relief from obligations, good feelings, and other things. The exchange approach, which is frequently used in social theory, rests on the assumption that people basically act to gain something from others in exchange for something else. This model is inherently power-oriented. In other words, you can gain the compliance of others if you have sufficient resources to provide or withhold something they want.

One of the most important theoretical questions about compliance-gaining tactics has been how to reduce the list of all possible tactics to a manageable set of general strategies or dimensions. A long list of how people persuade others does not tell you much more than you already know. A shorter list would crystallize the tactics into essential qualities, functions, goals, or some

TABLE **6.1**

Marwell and Schmitt's Compliance-Gaining Strategies

1. *Promising* Promising a reward for compliance
2. *Threatening* Indicating that punishment will be applied for noncompliance
3. *Showing expertise about positive outcomes* Showing how good things will happen to those who comply
4. *Showing expertise about negative outcomes* Showing how bad things will happen to those who do not comply
5. *Liking* Displaying friendliness
6. *Pregiving* Giving a reward before asking for compliance
7. *Applying aversive stimulation* Applying punishment until compliance is received
8. *Calling in a debt* Saying the person owes something for past favors
9. *Making moral appeals* Describing compliance as the morally right thing to do
10. *Attributing positive feelings* Telling the other person how good he or she will feel if there is compliance
11. *Attributing negative feelings* Telling the other person how bad he or she will feel if there is non-compliance
12. *Positive altercasting* Associating compliance with people with good qualities
13. *Negative altercasting* Associating noncompliance with people with bad qualities
14. *Seeking altruistic compliance* Seeking compliance simply as a favor
15. *Showing positive esteem* Saying that the person will be liked by others more if he or she complies
16. *Showing negative esteem* Saying that the person will be liked less by others if he or she does not comply

other set of dimensions that would help explain what people are actually accomplishing when they try to persuade other people.

In an attempt to create such a set of principles, Marwell and Schmitt asked subjects to apply the sixteen items to various compliance-gaining situations, and from these data the items were analyzed. Five general strategies, or clusters of tactics, emerged. These included *rewarding* (for example, promising), *punishing* (for instance, threatening), *expertise* (as in displaying knowledge of rewards), *impersonal commitments*

---

22   For some reviews of this work, see James B. Stiff, *Persuasive Communication* (New York: Guilford, 1994), pp. 199–211; David R. Seibold, James G. Cantrill, and Renee A. Meyers, "Communication and Interpersonal Influence," in *Handbook of Interpersonal Communication*, 2nd ed., eds. Mark L. Knapp and Gerald R. Miller (Thousand Oaks, CA: Sage, 1994), pp. 542–588; Michael G. Garko, "Perspectives on and Conceptualizations of Compliance and Compliance-Gaining," *Communication Quarterly* 38 (1990): 138–157; Gerald R. Miller, "Persuasion," in *Handbook of Communication Science*, eds. C. R. Berger and S. H. Chaffee (Newbury Park, CA: Sage, 1987), pp. 446–483.
23   Gerald Marwell and David R. Schmitt, "Dimensions of Compliance-Gaining Strategies: A Dimensional Analysis," *Sociometry* 30 (1967): 350–364.

(examples would include moral appeals), and *personal commitments* (such as debts).

One of the most comprehensive analyses of the compliance-gaining literature is that of Lawrence Wheeless, Robert Barraclough, and Robert Stewart, who review and integrate the variety of compliance-gaining schemes.[24] These researchers believe that compliance-gaining messages are best classified according to the kinds of power employed by communicators when attempting to gain the compliance of another individual. Power is access to influential resources. It is a result of interpersonal perception, since people have as much power as others perceive that they have.

The Wheeless group isolated three general types of power. The first is the perceived ability *to manipulate the consequences* of a certain course of action. Parents often use this kind of power when punishing and rewarding their children. If you tell your children that you will buy them new boots if they stay indoors out of the rain, you are using this source of power.

The second kind of power is the perceived ability to determine one's *relational position* with the other person. Here the powerful person can identify certain elements of the relationship that will bring about compliance. For example, if your boyfriend or girlfriend thinks you are not all that committed to the relationship, you may be able to get a lot of cooperation because he or she may be afraid you will want to leave the relationship.

The third type of power involves the perceived ability to *define values* or *obligations* or both. Here one person has the credibility to tell the other what norms of behavior are accepted or necessary. Returning a favor is a good example of this. Behaving kindly is another. Being sensitive to others' needs is still another example. In each case, one communicator defines what is right and good, and the other person complies by behaving in accordance with this standard.

In a compliance-gaining situation, then, one assesses his or her power and chooses tactics that invoke that power. Wheeless lists a number of tactics associated with the three classes of power.

For example, the ability to affect another person's expectations and consequences may lead you to use tactics like promises, threats, and warnings. The ability to manipulate the relationship may lead you to choose such tactics as saying you like the other person, attributing positive or negative esteem, making emotional appeals, flattering, and so on. The third category of power—defining values and obligations—may lead you to use moral appeals, debt, guilt, and other similar techniques.

The compliance-gaining literature is dominated by lists of possible strategies that people can use, but most of these studies do little to help us understand the basis for strategy choice. The following theory steps in to fill this void.

Constructivism. Constructivism, a theory developed by Jesse Delia and his colleagues, has had immense impact on the field of communication.[25] The theory says that individuals interpret and act according to conceptual categories of the mind. Reality does not present itself in raw form but must be filtered through the person's own way of seeing things.

Constructivism is based partially on George Kelly's theory of personal constructs, which proposes that persons understand experience by grouping events according to similarities and

24 Lawrence R. Wheeless, Robert Barraclough, and Robert Stewart, "Compliance-Gaining and Power in Persuasion," in *Communication Yearbook 7*, ed. R. N. Bostrom (Beverly Hills, CA: Sage, 1983), pp. 105–145.
25 For a summary of the theory and its various tributaries and applications, see Anne Maydan Nicotera, "The Constructivist Theory of Delia, Clark, and Associates," in *Watershed Research Traditions in Human Communication Theory*, eds. Donald P. Cushman and Branislav Kovačić (Albany: SUNY Press, 1995), pp. 45–66; John Gastil, "An Appraisal and Revision of the Constructivist Research Program," in *Communication Yearbook 18*, ed. Brant Burleson (Thousand Oaks, CA: Sage, 1995), pp. 83–104. See also Brant R. Burleson, "The Constructivist Approach to Person-Centered Communication: Analysis of a Research Exemplar," in *Rethinking Communication: Paradigm Exemplars*, eds. B. Dervin, L. Grossberg, B. J. O'Keefe, and E. Wartella (Newbury Park, CA: Sage, 1989), pp. 29–46; Jesse G. Delia, "Interpersonal Cognition, Message Goals, and Organization of Communication: Recent Constructivist Research," in *Communication Theory: Eastern and Western Perspectives*, ed. D. L. Kincaid (San Diego: Academic, 1987), pp. 255–274; Jesse G. Delia, Barbara J. O'Keefe, and Daniel J. O'Keefe, "The Constructivist Approach to Communication," in *Human Communication Theory: Comparative Essays*, ed. F. E. X. Dance (New York: Harper & Row, 1982), pp. 147–191.

distinguishing between things by their differences.[26] Perceived differences are not natural, but determined sets of opposites within the individual's cognitive system. Opposite pairs like tall-short, hot-cold, and black-white, used to understand events and things, are called *personal constructs.* Hence the name of Kelly's theory—personal construct theory.

An individual's cognitive system consists of numerous such distinctions. By classifying an experience into categories, the individual gives it meaning. So, for example, you might see your mother as tall and your father as short, coffee as hot and milk as cold, your favorite jacket as black and a favorite hat as white.

Constructs are organized into interpretive schemes, which identify something and place the object in a category. With interpretive schemes, we make sense out of an event by placing it in a larger category. Interpretive schemes develop as you mature, according to the *orthogenetic principle,* by moving from relative simplicity and generality to relative complexity and specificity.[27] Thus, very young children have simple construct systems, while most adults have much more sophisticated ones. When you were young, for example, you might have placed all people into two types: big and little. Now, on the other hand, you have an immense number of constructs with which to distinguish among different people.

Constructivism recognizes that constructs have social origins and are learned through interaction with other people. Consequently, culture seems especially significant in determining the meanings of events. Culture can influence the way communication goals are defined, how goals should be achieved, as well as the types of constructs employed in the cognitive schema.[28] Although it acknowledges the impact of social interaction and culture on the cognitive system, constructivism deals primarily with individual differences in construct complexity and strategies used in communication.

Individuals with highly developed interpretive schemes make more discriminations than those who see the world simplistically. Although the construct system develops throughout childhood and adolescence, even adults differ widely in their cognitive complexity. Also, different parts of your construct system differ in complexity, so that you might have elaborate thoughts about music but simple ideas about international relations.

Because cognitive complexity plays an important role in communication, this concept is a mainstay of constructivism.[29] Complexity or simplicity in the system is a function of the relative number of constructs and the degree of distinctions you can make. You do not have a consistent level of cognitive complexity, but think at different levels of sophistication on different topics. The number of constructs you use on a particular topic is called *cognitive differentiation.* Cognitively sophisticated people can make more distinctions than cognitively uncomplicated people. That is why many of us go to a tax accountant every year.

Delia and his colleagues have shown that messages vary according to complexity. Simple messages attack only one goal, more complex messages separate goals and deal with each in turn, and the most sophisticated messages actually integrate several goals in one message.[30] We often attempt to accomplish more than one thing by a single action, and our messages vary in the extent to which they can achieve multiple, sometimes conflicting, objectives simultaneously.

26   George Kelly, *The Psychology of Personal Constructs* (New York: North, 1955).
27   H. Werner, "The Concept of Development from a Comparative and Organismic Point of View," in *The Concept of Development,* ed. D. B. Harris (Minneapolis: University of Minnesota Press, 1957).
28   For a discussion of the effects of culture on the cognitive system, see James L. Applegate and Howard E. Sypher, "A Constructivist Theory of Communication and Culture," in *Theories in Intercultural Communication,* eds. Y. Y. Kim and W. B. Gudykunst (Newbury Park, CA: Sage, 1988), pp. 41–65.
29   The idea of cognitive complexity was originally developed by Walter H. Crockett, "Cognitive Complexity and Impression Formation," in *Progress in Experimental Personality Research,* vol. 2, ed. B. A. Maher (New York: Academic, 1965), pp. 47–90.
30   Multiple goal achievement is developed in detail by Barbara J. O'Keefe and Gregory J. Shepherd, "The Pursuit of Multiple Objectives in Face-to-Face Persuasive Interactions: Effects of Construct Differentiation on Message Organization," *Communication Monographs* 54 (1987): 396–419.

Cognitive differentiation thus affects how complex messages can be.

Further, the simplest persuasive messages only address your own goals without considering the other person's needs, whereas more adaptive, complex persuasive messages are designed to meet your needs and the needs of the other person.

For example, if you want to get a person to change his or her behavior, to stop smoking perhaps, you might want to do it in a way that would help the other person save face. This would require you to achieve at least two objectives in the same message: deliver a nonsmoking message and protect the other person's ego. Simple messages cannot do this, but more complex messages can be employed precisely for this purpose. Constructivists have found that one's tendency to help the other person save face is directly related to his or her cognitive complexity.

Interpersonal constructs are especially important because they guide how we understand other people. Individuals differ in the complexity with which they view others. If you are cognitively simple, you will tend to stereotype other people, whereas if you have more cognitive differentiation, you will make subtler and more sensitive distinctions.

The research on this topic has shown that cognitive complexity generally leads to greater understanding of others' perspectives and better ability to frame messages in terms understandable to other people. This ability, called *perspective taking*, seems to lead to more sophisticated arguments and appeals.[31] Adjusting one's communication to others is referred to as *person-centered communication*, and people vary in their use of person-centered messages.

Compliance gaining is one of several types of communication that have been studied from a person-centered perspective.[32] Persuasive messages range from the least to the most person-centered. On the simplest level, for example, one could attempt to achieve the single objective of compliance by commanding or threatening. On a more complex level, one might also try to help a person understand why compliance is

necessary by offering reasons for complying. On an even higher level of complexity, a communicator could try to elicit sympathy by building empathy or insight into the situation. As one's messages become more complex, they necessarily involve more goals and are more person-centered.

Comforting messages have also been studied from a constructivist perspective. People try to provide social support to others in a variety of ways, and some of these methods are more sophisticated than others. Research on comforting messages generally supports the view that cognitively complex individuals produce more sophisticated messages than less complex individuals, that sophisticated messages are more person-centered than less sophisticated ones, and that more sophisticated messages are more effective in eliciting comfort than less sophisticated ones.[33]

As an example of person-centered communication, consider the study of Susan Kline and Janet Ceropski on doctor–patient communication.[34] This study involved forty-six medical students who completed a variety of tests, participated in videotaped interviews with patients, and wrote statements on what they thought the purpose of medical interviews to be.

The interviews were carefully examined by the researchers and classified according to how person-centered they were. The person-centered messages used by the medical students were

---

31 This literature is reviewed by Claudia Hale, "Cognitive Complexity-Simplicity as a Determinant of Communication Effectiveness," *Communication Monographs* 47 (1980): 304–311.
32 See, for example, Jesse G. Delia, Susan L. Kline, and Brant R. Burleson, "The Development of Persuasive Communication Strategies in Kindergartners Through Twelfth-Graders," *Communication Monographs* 46 (1979): 241–256; James L. Applegate, "The Impact of Construct System Development on Communication and Impression Formation in Persuasive Messages," *Communication Monographs* 49 (1982): 277–289.
33 Brant R. Burleson, "Comforting Messages: Significance, Approaches, and Effects," in *Communication of Social Support: Messages, Interactions, Relationships, and Community,* eds. Brant R. Burleson, Terrance L. Albrecht, and Irwin G. Sarason (Thousand Oaks, CA: Sage, 1994), pp. 3–28.
34 Susan L. Kline and Janet M. Ceropski, "Person-Centered Communication in Medical Practice," in *Emergent Issues in Human Decision Making,* eds. G. M. Phillips and J. T. Wood (Carbondale: Southern Illinois University Press, 1984), pp. 120–141.

found to be more complex than messages that were not person-centered. The researchers found that about 40 percent of the medical students were person-centered in persuading patients. These individuals explained why compliance was necessary and took patients' feelings into consideration. About 50 percent of the subjects used person-centered communication in dealing with distress by acknowledging rather than denying patients' feelings, helping patients understand their discomfort, and giving advice on how to relieve the distress. Finally, about 70 percent of those studied used person-centered communication in gathering information. Their questions were more detailed, and they gave patients more leeway in telling their story.

This research confirms that those who use person-centered strategies have more complex cognitive schemas for understanding other people and are better able to take the perspective of others and to have empathy for others.

As sophisticated as it is, constructivism is still basically a strategy-choice theory. Constructivist research procedures usually asked subjects to select different message types and classified these in terms of strategy categories. Recognizing the potential weakness of strategy-choice theories, researchers have developed a new generation of work to look at the design processes that communicators employ.

Theories of Message Design

As we saw in the previous section, theories of message selection imagine that communicators choose abstract strategies for accomplishing their communication goals. In contrast to selection models, theories of message design imagine a more complex scenario in which communicators actually design messages that are in line with their intentions within the situations they face. The difference is the same as between selecting a home from five different floor plans versus designing a house to meet your family's particular needs. Like the specially designed house, the form of the message matches its function. Here we look at two theories of this tradition.

Politeness. When we communicate we most often try to accomplish several things at once, and politeness, or protecting the face of the other person, is often one of the goals we aim to achieve. The best-known theoretical treatment of politeness and face is that of Penelope Brown and Stephen Levinson.[35] This theory states that in everyday life we design messages that protect face and achieve other goals as well.

Brown and Levinson believe that politeness is often a goal because it is a culturally universal value. Different cultures have different levels of required politeness and different ways of being polite, but all people have the need to be appreciated and protected, which these researchers call *face needs*. *Positive face* is the desire to be appreciated and approved, to be liked and honored, and *positive politeness* is designed to meet these desires. Showing concern, complimenting, and using respectful forms of address are examples. *Negative face* is the desire to be free from imposition or intrusion, and *negative politeness* is designed to protect the other person when negative face needs are threatened. Acknowledging the imposition when making a request is a common example.

Politeness is especially important whenever we must threaten another person's face, which happens frequently in our relations with others. We commit *face-threatening acts* (FTAs) whenever we behave in a way that could potentially fail to meet positive or negative face needs. Face threatening is normal and not itself a problem, but it must be handled in certain ways to mitigate potential problems that could result. There are a wide range of ways to handle FTAs, and we do not always do it the same way. Whether we deliver an FTA, how we do so, and what forms of politeness are used depend on a variety of things.

35   Penelope Brown and Stephen Levinson, *Politeness: Some Universals in Language Usage* (Cambridge: Cambridge University Press, 1987). See also Roger Brown, "Politeness Theory: Exemplar and Exemplary," in *The Legacy of Solomon Asch: Essays in Cognition and Social Psychology*, ed. Irvin Rock (Hillsdale, NJ: Erlbaum, 1990), pp. 23–38. For a discussion of politeness as a factor in social support, see Daena J. Goldsmith, "The Role of Facework in Supportive Communication," in *Communication of Social Support*, eds. Brant R. Burleson, Terrance L. Albrecht, and Irwin G. Sarason (Thousand Oaks, CA: Sage, 1994), pp. 29–49.

When an FTA is possible, there are five approaches we can use. We can (1) deliver the FTA baldly, without polite action; (2) deliver the FTA along with some form of positive politeness; (3) deliver the FTA along with some form of negative politeness; (4) deliver the FTA indirectly, off the record; or (5) not deliver the FTA at all. These five choices are arranged in order from the most to the least face threatening.

Suppose that you would like to ask your professor to reconsider an exam grade. This is a face issue for the professor because he or she has already declared what your grade is and could be made to feel inadequate by the request. How would you do it? One approach would be to deliver the bald FTA: "I would like you to reconsider my grade," period. You probably would not choose this approach because it would not be very polite.

A slightly less threatening method would be to combine the request with positive politeness, something like this: "I would appreciate it if you could look at my grade again. Other students have said you're really nice about that." Here we have a request (FTA) combined with a compliment.

Even less threatening would be to combine the FTA with negative politeness: "I'm really sorry. I know you're very busy, but could I have a moment of your time? If you're not too busy, I would really appreciate it if you could look at my grade again." Notice that this message meets negative face needs by acknowledging and apologizing for the imposition.

Number 4 is particularly interesting and complex. An "off-record" FTA is one that is indirect and ambiguous, which enables you to deny having meant the statement as an FTA. For example, you might ask to borrow your friend's car by saying, "I wonder how I will get to town this afternoon to pick up my laundry." You hope your friend will get the hint and say, "Oh, why don't you use my car," but if he says, "Well, you can't use *my* car," you can always reply, "Oh, I wasn't asking for it."

In requesting your professor to reconsider your grade, you might say something like, "Gosh, I didn't think I had done this badly on the exam." You hope she will reply, "Well, why don't I read it again?"—but if she looks at you funny, you can always deny that you were requesting a reconsideration.

Now, what determines which of these strategies you use? Brown and Levinson say that your strategy depends on a simple formula:

$$W_x = D(S,H) + P(H,S) + R_x$$

This formula means that the amount of work (W) one puts into being polite depends on the social distance (D) between the speaker (S) and the hearer (H), plus the power (P) of the hearer over the speaker, plus the risk (R) of hurting the other person.

Let's consider two examples. Imagine that you want to ask your brother for a simple, nonthreatening favor—to drop you off at the mall, let's say. You and your brother have the same status, he does not have any special power over you, and the request is not threatening. You will probably put little work into being polite.

On the other hand, suppose you want to get a loan from your parents. Assuming that you consider your parents somewhat higher in status than you, that they have considerable power over your finances, and that a request for money is considerably more serious than asking for a candy bar, you will probably be quite polite in your request. Of course, these assumptions may not hold in your particular case, but you can probably think of other examples that would require considerable face-saving work on your part.

There are, of course, a variety of levels of politeness between these two extremes. One variable can counteract another. For example, there may be little social distance, but quite a bit of power disparity. Or perhaps the distance and power don't matter much because the FTA is so minor.

The theory of Brown and Levinson is considered foundational in the message design field. It suggests one area—politeness—in which considerable message design is necessary.

Message Design Logic.   Barbara O'Keefe began her work as a constructivist, but has expanded the theoretical orientation to incorporate a message design model. Her thesis is that people think differently about communication and messages, and they employ different logics in deciding what to say to another person in a given situation. She uses the term *message design logic* to describe the thought processes behind messages.[36]

O'Keefe outlines three possible message design logics that range from least person-centered to most person-centered. The *expressive logic* sees communication as a mode of self-expression for communicating feelings and thoughts. Its messages are open and reactive in nature, with little attention given to the needs or desires of others. An example of a message resulting from this logic would be an angry response to a friend who forgot to get tickets to a concert:

> Now we are not going to get our tickets. I was counting on getting to go to this concert. This is my favorite group and I really really wanted to hear them. I have been thinking about this for weeks. Nothing I really want to do ever works out. I am going to be mad at you for a long time about this.[37]

The *conventional logic* sees communication as a game to be played by rules. Here communication is a means of self-expression that proceeds according to accepted rules and norms including the rights and responsibilities of each person involved. This logic aims to design messages that are polite, appropriate, and based on rules that everyone is supposed to know. A response to the ticket situation using conventional logic might go like this:

> It was your responsibility to pick up the tickets. Everyone decided what job they would do in organizing this evening, and that was the job you picked. So you will just have to figure out some way to get them yourself, even if you have to pay a taxi to deliver them.[38]

The *rhetorical logic* views communication as a way of changing the rules through negotiation. Messages designed with this logic tend to be flexible, insightful, and person-centered. They tend to reframe the situation so that various goals—including persuasion and politeness—are integrated into a seamless whole. Following is an

example of how the ticket situation might be handled by someone who uses the rhetorical logic:

> Gee, I'm sorry you have been so pressed. This really has put us in a pickle. I know what you can do. Bob has to go right by the ticket office on his way home from work. Call the ticket office and charge the tickets on your MasterCard. Then call Bob and see if he can stop and pick up the tickets. Or maybe he could just pick you up and run you by the ticket office.[39]

O'Keefe has noticed that in certain situations, messages are pretty much the same, but in other situations, they are different. For example, if you asked ten friends to describe their apartments, they would do so in essentially the same way. On the other hand, if you asked them to evaluate your work on a team project, they probably would do so in rather different ways. This example illustrates *message diversity*. In some situations, there is little diversity, and in others there is a great deal. If the goals of the communication are fairly simple and face is not much of an issue, each design logic will lead to the same message form. On the other hand, if goals are numerous and complex and face is an issue, they will lead to different message forms. In these more complex situations, you can really see the quality of one's thinking process at work.

◖◗ COMMENTARY AND CRITIQUE

Cognitive approaches have been very popular in the United States. Some of these theories focus on the traits of individuals and how they are correlated with various message behaviors, others deal with the effects of the situation on message behavior, and still others concentrate on the actual processes of producing messages.

---

36 Barbara J. O'Keefe, "Variation, Adaptation, and Functional Explanation"; Barbara J. O'Keefe, "The Logic of Message Design: Individual Differences in Reasoning About Communication," *Communication Monographs* 55 (1988): 80–103.
37 O'Keefe, "Logic," p. 100.
38 O'Keefe, "Logic," p. 102.
39 O'Keefe, "Logic," p. 103.

Although these theories have many differences, they share a common concern for behavior and the generative mechanisms that produce it. These concerns are not new. Indeed, the individualistic and cognitive traditions have dominated the human sciences throughout the twentieth century.

The individualistic approach is common in the study of communication and in the behavioral and social sciences at large. This is understandable within our cultural milieu.[40] Western thought since the eighteenth-century Enlightenment has been dominated by the individual. The autonomous person is the primary unit of analysis in much Western thinking.[41] The psychological view sees persons as entities with characteristics that lead them to behave in independent ways. It views the single human mind as the locus for processing and understanding information and generating messages. It is hardly surprising, then, that psychological explanations have been so appealing to many communication scholars.

Yet the individualistic approach is not the only way to understand communication. Ironically, the defining feature of communication is that it happens between people, so communication cannot be explained solely from the perspective of the individual mind.[42] Even certain researchers in the cognitive tradition are now acknowledging this difficulty. Vincent Waldron and Donald J. Cegala wrote:

> Although cognition is typically treated as an individual-level variable in communication research, a systems perspective suggests extending our views about cognition beyond the individual. For example, conversation, particularly between friends or intimates, both reflects and creates the cognitive interdependence of the partners.[43]

Vernon Cronen is one of the harshest critics of individualism in communication theory.[44] Calling it a "wreck," Cronen outlines several intellectual problems: Individualistic approaches fail to depict meaning as emergent and social, they detach the person from social process, they ignore interactional patterns, and they fail to take con-

joint production into account. Cronen seems even more concerned with the social and cultural impacts of individualism, worrying that it threatens human values, cultural difference, and institutional change. Individualistic approaches also muddy ethical questions of responsibility and connection with lived experience.

Psychological theorists respond to this type of criticism in three ways. One is to acknowledge the social nature of communication but to argue that social explanations by themselves are also inadequate. Communication in this view is both social and individual. The individual is involved in the process and must be studied. Focusing on the individual does not negate the value of social theories, but it does provide a vital link in our overall understanding of communication.[45]

The second answer to the criticism is to refute it directly. Although communication involves people acting together in some fashion, everything that happens in this process is filtered through and generated by the separate minds of the individuals involved. Although the outcome of communication may be social in nature, its ultimate genesis is individual, making psychological explanations crucial.[46]

---

40   John W. Lannamann, "Deconstructing the Person and Changing the Subject of Interpersonal Studies," *Communication Theory* 2 (1992): 139–148; "Interpersonal Communication Research as Ideological Practice," *Communication Theory* 1 (1991): 179–203.

41   See, for example, Robert N. Bellah and others, *Habits of the Heart* (Berkeley: University of California Press, 1985); Alistair MacIntyre, *After Virtue* (Notre Dame, IN: University of Notre Dame Press, 1984); Floyd W. Matson, *The Idea of Man* (New York: Delacorte, 1976). A critique of the assumptions of the individual mind is presented in Rom Harré, "Language Games and Texts of Identity," in *Texts of Identity*, eds. J. Shotter and K. Gergen (London: Sage, 1989), pp. 20–35.

42   John Shotter and Kenneth J. Gergen, "Social Construction: Knowledge, Self, Others, and Continuing the Conversation," in *Communication Yearbook 17*, ed. Stanley Deetz (Thousand Oaks, CA: Sage, 1994), pp. 3–33; Giles and Street, "Communicator Characteristics."

43   Vincent R. Waldron and Donald J. Cegala, "Assessing Conversational Cognition: Levels of Cognitive Theory and Associated Methodological Requirements," *Human Communication Research* 18 (1992): 606.

44   Vernon E. Cronen, "Communication Theory for the Twenty-First Century: Cleaning Up the Wreckage of the Psychology Project," in *Communication: Views from the Helm for the 21st Century*, ed. Judith S. Trent (Boston: Allyn & Bacon, 1998), pp. 18–38.

45   For an example of this response, see Dean E. Hewes and Sally Planalp, "The Individual's Place in Communication Science," in *Handbook of Communication Science*, eds. C. R. Berger and S. H. Chaffee (Newbury Park, CA: Sage, 1987), pp. 146–183.

The third answer is to expand cognitive process research to include interdependence. In discussing her research plans, Sally Planalp has written that "the first line of research that I plan to pursue deals with mutual knowledge in interpersonal communication. Mutual knowledge is knowledge that conversation partners share, know they share, and rely on in communicating with one another."[47]

Cognitive researchers such as Planalp do acknowledge areas for future development and ways to strengthen their theories.[48] John Greene suggests that cognitive research has been oriented too much to verbal communication, prepositional content, and mentalistic explanations.[49] For him, this line of theory must aim to capture more complex processes and explain these in dynamic, multidimensional terms that help us understand the lack of coherence in thought and action as well as coherent messages.

The simplest contributions to the message-production literature are trait theories. Communication traits abound.[50] Not only have "communication traits" been developed, but much research has made use of other related traits such as self-monitoring, self-esteem, and dogmatism. Here, we only present a few of the more prominent trait theories.

Most of these theories have proved interesting and useful, but like most theories that concentrate on traits, they do not go far enough in explaining the link between traits and actions. Dean Hewes and Sally Planalp make this point in strong terms:

Predispositions do not explain much. Whenever trait theorists have been pressed to explain why a trait works, they have been forced to look for the mechanisms *behind* that trait, mechanisms outside the realm of predispositions that almost always involve processes of interpretation and production of behavior or adaptation. Trait approaches, when successful, *do* warn us that something about individuals is the locus of causality for social action, but by oversimplifying explanations of individuals' capabilities they do not take us far enough. They tell us *that* individuals are important in the study of human communication but not *how* or *why*.[51]

Trait theories, although they do not ignore the situation, certainly downplay it. If a trait is stable across contexts, then by definition it will usually override situational factors. The entire idea of testing for a trait is predicated on this assumption. And yet much research shows that people do behave differently in different situations. A natural theoretical tension exists between trait explanations and situational ones. A challenge for both trait and situational theories is to deal with this tension more directly.[52]

One answer to this dilemma is to combine trait and situational explanations, suggesting that a certain amount of variation is caused by situational factors and another portion of variation by traits. This solution is inherently problematic, however, because of the assumption of stability in trait measurement. Trait instruments are designed and tested to capture stability, and correlating such a measure with other measures of situational difference is methodologically and conceptually inconsistent.

Trait theories are designed to identify qualities in persons. This is a semantic process, for the theorist must label the qualities believed to exist. Thus, like all theoretical concepts, traits are constructed by the theorist. Indeed, some sophisticated data analysis will be required to verify the fit of the hypothesized trait to research subjects' actual behaviors and perceptions, but ultimately a name is attached and an abstraction is reified.

---

46   For an example of this point of view, see Greene, "Action Assembly Theory."
47   Sally Planalp, "Communication, Cognition, and Emotion," *Communication Monographs* 60 (1993): 3–4.
48   See, for example, the special issue of *Communication Theory* 10 (May 2000); and Greene, *Message Production*.
49   John O. Greene, "Evanescent Mentation: An Ameliorative Conceptual Foundation for Research and Theory on Message Production," *Communication Theory* 10 (2000): 139–155.
50   For a discussion and critique of the trait tradition, see Gün R. Semin, "Everyday Assumptions, Language, and Personality," in *Everyday Understanding: Social and Scientific Implications*, eds. Gün R. Semin and Kenneth J. Gergen (London: Sage, 1990), pp. 151–175.
51   Hewes and Planalp, "Individual's Place."
52   These issues are explored by Peter A. Andersen, "The Trait Debate: A Critical Examination of the Individual Differences Paradigm in the Communication Sciences," in *Progress in Communication Sciences*, eds. B. Dervin and M. J. Voigt (Norwood, NJ: Ablex, 1986).

This process of construction can lead to problems. One is clarity and distinctiveness of traits. For example, what is the difference between communication apprehension, shyness, reticence, neuroticism, introversion, and avoidance? Are these the same trait or similar ones, or are they conceptually different? Among communication apprehension researchers, little agreement exists on the overall dimensions that bind this cluster of variables.[53] Even more confusion results from the advent of the biological approach to CA, which correlates this trait with very basic brain functions, leading to the conclusions that such traits as communication apprehension may be no different from any fear-based reaction.

Confusion can easily result from labeling. For instance, Infante divides aggression into four categories of traits—assertiveness, argumentativeness, hostility, and verbal aggressiveness. Here, the general term *aggression* is used to label both positive and negative traits, but *verbal aggressiveness* labels only a negative trait. How, then, can assertive and argumentative behaviors, which are largely verbal, be positive? This may sound like a word game, but it illustrates the kinds of semantic difficulties that trait labeling can involve.

A second problem created by trait construction is the endless number of traits that can be and are "discovered." Virtually any tendency can be defined as a trait. According to trait theory, a person is not only a bundle of traits but a very large bundle at that. How can we say in any given situation which traits predominate over others, and, indeed, how can any trait predominate over another if traits are stable across contexts?

The key question for evaluating trait theories, then, is not whether the traits actually exist but how useful they are in communication scholarship, teaching, and intervention. What are the limits of the utility of trait definition? We know, for example, that communication apprehension has been a useful concept for communication teachers who must deal with a practical difficulty that many students face in communication classes.

The third problem resulting from the constructed nature of traits is their value orientation. Trait theories often originate in an attempt to identify individuals who have particular positive or negative communication qualities. This is certainly the case with the three traits discussed in this chapter—argumentativeness, narcissism, and social anxiety. Such trait definitions are often value laden, making such theories normative, or prescriptive, in orientation. For example, we learn from the theories in this chapter that it is better to be low in communication apprehension than to be high; it is better to be argumentative than hostile; and it is better to be nonnarcissistic than the opposite.

A potential problem occurs when one confuses the researcher's value concept with an objective trait. The way traits are described and measured will often lead the reader to believe that something in the person is being discovered objectively, when in fact the researcher has carefully designed a test to find instances of thoughts, behaviors, and feelings that exemplify the theorist's own positive and negative values.

This state of affairs can create theoretical difficulties. What, for example, do we do with people who display a negative trait? Because traits are defined as stable predispositions, maybe even biologically determined, do we merely condemn and avoid these individuals, or do we reform them? If people can change their traits—and most trait theorists would at least entertain the possibility—perhaps the trait is merely a state. Then the important theoretical questions deal with how, when, and under what conditions people behave one way as opposed to another.

Min-Sun Kim looks critically from a cultural perspective at those trait approaches concentrating on the motivation to communicate.[54] These

---

53   A critique of this line of work can be found in Gerald R. Miller, "Some (Moderately) Apprehensive Thoughts on Avoiding Communication," in *Avoiding Communication: Shyness, Reticence, and Communication Apprehension*, eds. J. A. Daly and J. C. McCroskey (Beverly Hills, CA: Sage, 1984), pp. 237–246.

54   Min-Sun Kim, "Cross-Cultural Perspectives on Motivations of Verbal Communication: Review, Critique, and a Theoretical Framework," in *Communication Yearbook 22*, ed. Michael E. Roloff (Thousand Oaks, CA: Sage, 1999), pp. 51–89.

would include, for example, communication apprehension and argumentativeness. The assumptions of these theories tend to be that the willingness to communicate in certain ways is a positive trait. Kim shows that these theories are based on assumptions that do not hold in all cultures, especially collectivist ones. Indeed, the meaning of "avoidance" is quite different in individualist and collectivist cultures. What may look like avoidance in a Western setting may actually be a very active strategy of promoting the interests of the community over the individual in a frame in which the self is viewed as *inter*dependent rather than independent.

Cognitive theories are designed in part to overcome many of the problems encountered by trait theories. Three kinds of cognitive theories are encountered in this chapter. One type of theory in this category attempts to explain the cognitive mechanism that generates actions. Action assembly theory is an example. This kind of problem is difficult to study. The behaviorists were correct in asserting that cognitive processes cannot be observed directly. Indeed, one reason why so much trait research has been done is that it is relatively easy in comparison to cognitive process research.

All cognitive research involves indirect observation and a great deal of inference. The theorist posits certain cognitive mechanisms and looks for evidence in actual behavior. Action-assembly research, for example, looks for differences in the amount of time it takes to process information in difficult versus simple tasks. Because the action-assembly process takes time, these differences are taken as evidence of the existence of the proposed mechanism. The problem is that such evidence indicates only that the proposed model *could be* operating, not that it *is* operating. Many other cognitive models might lead to the same behavioral differences.[55]

A second approach, illustrated by compliance-gaining research, attempts to deduce the implicit strategic choices people are making on the basis of an analysis of message types. By inferring strategic choice from behavior, these theories are "cognitive" in a weak sense. The

problem here is that you can never be sure, based on an external analysis of behavior, what actual cognitive mechanisms are in operation. Just because someone makes a promise, for example, does not mean that the individual has strategically chosen to be direct, to use sanctions, and to maintain control over the consequences of interaction. In fact, some entirely different set of dimensions may have been operating in the person's mind.

Classifying message strategies is especially problematic, as the work on compliance-gaining strategies illustrates. In a severe critique of this work, Kathy Kellermann and Tim Cole point out that the classification schemes used in this research have been entirely inadequate, that they are incomplete, unclear, and even invalid.[56] Daniel O'Keefe is sufficiently concerned about this problem that he calls for the abandonment of the strategy concept altogether.[57] Instead, he believes, we should look at the features of compliance-gaining discourse, without trying to attribute strategy.

David Seibold and his colleagues believe that the difficulty of compliance-gaining research is overreliance on the *strategic choice model.* They suggest instead a *goal limitation model,* in which a communicator's choices are constrained by his or her goals within the situation.[58] Under the former model, communicators were viewed as strategy machines that defined an influence goal and made a decision about how to achieve it. Under the more recent model, communicators do have goals, but they may be multiple and vague. The actual strategic choices people make rely on some combination of programmed habit and situational constraints. People will vary in

55   Confirming cognitive processes by research is difficult. This problem is discussed in some detail by Waldron and Cegala, "Assessing Conversational Cognition."
56   Kathy Kellermann and Tim Cole, "Classifying Compliance Gaining Messages: Taxonomic Disorder and Strategic Confusion," *Communication Theory* 4 (1994): 3–60. See also the entire special issue of *Communication Theory* 4, no. 1 (February 1994). See also Charles R. Berger, *Planning Strategic Interaction,* pp. 3–6.
57   Daniel J. O'Keefe, "From Strategy-Based to Feature-Based Analyses of Compliance Gaining Message Classification and Production," *Communication Theory* 4 (1994): 61–69.
58   Seibold, Cantrill, and Meyers, "Communication and Interpersonal Influence."

what they believe to be effective and appropriate and the logics they use in constructing messages. Rather than listing strategies, then, these authors suggest that our time would be better spent understanding the cognitive and situational constraints on message design.

Both strategy choice and message design models give individual communicators quite a bit of power in preplanning their messages. This is probably not a very good representation of how communication actually takes place. Although the cognitive processes that occur before interaction takes place are important, Burgoon and her colleagues have consistently found in their research that the actual behavior encountered in interaction has far more power to influence what a communicator does than any preplanning.[59] Most of the cognitive work of interaction is probably done moment to moment as communicators adjust and adapt to one another. This is certainly a view supported by a long tradition of research in conversation analysis and interaction studies (see Chapter 5). Indeed, Barbara O'Keefe, who is probably the leader of the message-design movement, now believes that conversation management is primarily a local, rather than global, activity.[60]

Constructivism does posit a cognitive structure behind message selection. People make distinctions by applying cognitive constructs to what is perceived. As differentiation becomes increasingly complex, more differences can be seen, and more sophisticated messages can be constructed. In a critique of this representation, John Gastil points out that the actual cognitive process by which distinctions are made, goals established, and messages constructed is fuzzy.[61] How is information actually processed in this

system? What is the nature of memory, and how are cognitive constructs held and retrieved from memory? Finally, how are strategic choices actually made?

Clearly, cognitive-process theory is difficult. It is hard enough to substantiate the existence and nature of a single process, but communication is probably driven by multiple simultaneous processes. Many researchers are becoming aware that current process theories are inadequate, as Austin Babrow points out: "Emerging views are sensitizing researchers to issues that have often been glossed over: (a) Communication involves multiple, substantively distinct processes; (b) these processes may be redundant, complementary, or contradictory; and (c) processes may mediate or moderate other processes."[62]

The coverage of this chapter is admittedly limited. This chapter is the first in a two-chapter set on theories of message production, reception, and processing. As such, it tells only part of the story of how people process information to generate and understand messages. Although it is necessary to divide this material in some way in order to study it, these chapters should be read in concert with each other. Together, they present a variety of interrelated theories on the role of the individual in communication. To complete the picture, we turn now to theories of message processing and communication outcomes.

59   This work is summarized by Burgoon and White, "Researching Nonverbal Message Production."
60   Barbara J. O'Keefe and Bruce L. Lambert, "Managing the Flow of Ideas: A Local Management Approach to Message Design," in *Communication Yearbook 18*, Brant R. Burleson, ed. (Thousand Oaks, CA: Sage, 1995), pp. 54–82.
61   Gastil, "An Appraisal."
62   Austin Babrow, "The Advent of Multiple-Process Theories of Communication," *Journal of Communication* 43 (1993): 110.

C H A P T E R **7**

THEORIES OF MESSAGE RECEPTION AND PROCESSING

This is the second chapter in a two-part series on theories of message production and processing. In Chapter 6 we dealt with theories explaining how messages are produced. Here we concentrate on how they are received. The main question of the theories in this chapter is how human beings come to understand, organize, and use the information contained in messages. The amount of theorizing on this topic is vast, and we can only touch on it here.[1] This chapter includes some classic treatments of the subject of message processing as well as some recent extensions.

Most of the theories in this chapter are firmly in the cognitive tradition, which was described in Chapter 1. Briefly, cognition is the study of thinking, or information processing. In an excellent review, Thomas Ostrom and his colleagues outline three broad dimensions of the cognitive system—codes, structures, and processes.[2]

Cognitive codes are the basic elements of information that are kept in memory and manipulated in various ways when we think. The precise nature of these codes is in dispute; we likely have several types of codes operating at the same time. Some coding possibilities include linguistic

propositions, visual images, event memories, action sequences, and emotions.

The second dimension is *cognitive structures*, or ways of organizing codes. It is clear that single things such as words, sentences, or images are not independent units. We organize them in some way. Again, cognitive psychologists disagree about exactly how this is done, but several theories have been proposed. One common explanation, for example, is that codes are grouped into categories that differ from one another. For example, "trees" would probably be in a different category from "fish." Another approach is that the elements of cognition are linked to one another by associative pathways or links in complex networks. For example, you might associate "trees" with the color "green." A more elaborate

---

1   For a brief summary of the message tradition in communication studies, see Klaus Krippendorff, "The Past of Communication's Hoped-For Future," *Journal of Communication* 43 (1993): 34–44.
2   Thomas M. Ostrom, John J. Skowronski, and Andrezej Nowak, "The Cognitive Foundation of Attitudes: It's a Wonderful Construct," in *Social Cognition: Impact on Social Psychology,* eds. Patricia G. Devine, David L. Hamilton, and Thomas M. Ostrom (San Diego: Academic, 1994), pp. 196–258.

version of this theory is the structured network approach, in which associative networks are embedded in larger networks in a hierarchical fashion, something like the hypertext of the World Wide Web.

The third dimension of cognition is *cognitive processes,* or operations. What do we do with information? Again, various theories have been proposed. One is the spreading-activation approach, which suggests that something in the environment activates or stimulates a node in the cognitive network, and this activation spreads out and excites other nodes that then come into play. An example is action assembly, discussed in Chapter 6, which states that people assemble "instructions" from memory in hierarchical fashion to accomplish a task.

The chapter is divided into three interrelated segments. The first deals with processes of *interpretation,* or understanding and meaning. The theories summarized here define meaning and show how it develops, how the content of messages and intentions of communicators are understood, and how the causes of behavior are assessed.

The second section deals with *information organization.* These theories tell us how information is integrated into the cognitive system and how it affects attitudes, how we think about information that relates to our attitudes, and how consistency is used as an organizing principle.

The third section of the chapter relates to the process of *making judgments.* These theories deal with how information is compared to what we already know and expect, deviations from expectations, and how the value of information is assessed. As you probably already suspect, this is a rather technical and complicated body of theory. Let's get started.

C MESSAGE INTERPRETATION

Interpretation is one term for how we understand our experience. Chapter 10 presents a number of theories of interpretation from a textual and philosophical perspective, but in this chapter we approach the subject psychologically.

Osgood on Meaning

Charles Osgood, a well-known researcher of the 1960s, developed one of the most influential theories of meaning. In those days, psychology was dominated by behaviorism, but cognitive approaches were just beginning to get popular, and his theory actually has a foot in both traditions. Osgood's theory, then, deals with the ways in which meanings are learned and how they relate to thinking and behavior.[3] This theory was immensely influential and is now considered a classic. Although it is not as popular today, it is still useful and a good place to begin thinking about the topics of this chapter. Let's begin with a simple example and see how Osgood would work with it.

What associations do you have for the word *flight?* Perhaps you see flight as a gentle, floating, pleasant experience, or maybe you see it as rough, dangerous, and frightening. Whatever your associations, these are your *connotations* for the term. Osgood's theory attempts to explain what these connotations consist of and where they come from.

The learning theory used by Osgood begins with the assumption that individuals respond to stimuli in the environment, forming a stimulus–response relationship. He believes that this basic S–R association is responsible for the establishment of meaning, which is an internal, mental response to a stimulus. When you see an airplane, for example, an internal association will appear in your mind, and this association constitutes your meanings for the concepts of airplanes and flight.

Your actual association between the stimulus and response is somewhat more complicated than the above example implies. Outwardly, you see a physical stimulus (the plane), and you have a behavioral response (not to board). This response is mediated by internal representations in your mind, which is your meaning lying between the outward stimulus (airplane) and your response (not getting on). The outward stimulus

3   Charles Osgood, "On Understanding and Creating Sentences," *American Psychologist* 18 (1963): 735–751.

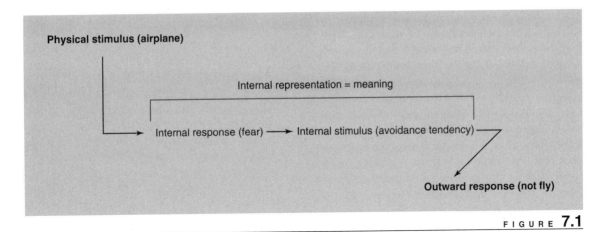

Physical stimulus (airplane)

Internal representation = meaning

Internal response (fear) ⟶ Internal stimulus (avoidance tendency)

Outward response (not fly)

FIGURE **7.1**

Meaning as Internal Representation

leads to an internal meaning, which leads to an outward response.

The internal meaning itself can be broken down into two parts: an internal response and an internal stimulus. The whole chain, then, consists of the following: (1) physical stimulus → (2) internal response → (3) internal stimulus → (4) outward response. A person who is afraid of flying, for example, has an internal response (fear) to the airplane, and this fear leads to an avoidance tendency, which is an internal stimulus for the outward response of not boarding the plane. Figure 7.1 illustrates this.

In addition to physical objects, we also have meanings for the signs of those objects, such as words and gestures. In other words, when the sign is paired with the meaning, that sign comes to elicit the same or a similar response. This is why the mere mention of flying frightens some people. Even if they are not actually scared at the mention of an airplane, they will tell you that they would prefer not to fly because they know what their actual response would be.

Meaning, because it is internal and unique to the person's own experience with the natural stimulus, is said to be *connotative*. If you are afraid of spiders, a spider elicits an escape response. When the word *spider* is associated with the object as it might have been when you were a small child, a portion of your response (fear) becomes associated with the word itself. This internal meaning mediates your response to the word, even when the actual object is not present.[4]

Most meanings are not learned as a result of direct experience with the natural stimulus but are learned by an association between one sign and another, a process that can occur in the abstract out of physical contact with the original stimulus. Here the meaning of one concept "rubs off" by association with another. To continue our example, imagine that as a child you had already established internal responses to the words *spider, big,* and *hairy.* Let's say you listened to a story about a tarantula, characterized as a "big, hairy spider." Through association you would now have a meaning for the new word *tarantula,* which may also carry some mixture of the connotations earlier attached to the other words because of its association with these words. If you associated *spider* with *fear, big* with *dangerous,* and *hairy* with feeling *creepy,* then you might well react to a real or imagined tarantula by running away. The examples of the fear of flying and the fear of spiders are negative, but all meanings—including positive and neutral ones—are learned the same way.

4   Charles Osgood, "The Nature of Measurement of Meaning," in *The Semantic Differential Technique,* eds. J. Snider and C. Osgood (Chicago: Aldine, 1969), pp. 9–10.

One of Osgood's major contributions is his work on the measurement of meaning. This method of measuring meaning, the *semantic differential*, assumes that one's meanings can be expressed by the use of adjectives.[5] The method begins by finding a set of adjectives that could be used to express your connotations for any stimulus, including a sign. These adjectives are set against one another as opposites, such as good-bad, high-low, slow-fast. You are given a topic, word, or other sign and are asked to indicate on a 7-point scale how you associate the sign with the adjective pairs. A scale looks like this:

good __:__:__:__:__:__:__ bad

The subject places a check mark on any space between these adjectives to indicate the degree of good or bad associated with the stimulus. The subject may fill out as many as fifty such scales for each stimulus, each with a different set of bipolar adjectives (fast-slow, active-inactive, and so on). You might be presented with a word like *airplane* or *spider* and asked to fill out this set of scales.

Osgood then uses a statistical technique called *factor analysis* to find your basic dimensions of meaning. His findings in this research have led to the theory of *semantic space*.[6] Your meaning for any sign is said to be located in a metaphorical space of three major dimensions: evaluation, activity, and potency. A given sign, perhaps a word or concept, elicits a reaction in the person, consisting of a sense of *evaluation* (good or bad), *activity* (active or inactive), and *potency* (strong or weak). Your connotative meaning will lie somewhere in this hypothetical space, depending on your responses on the three factors. Figure 7.2 illustrates the semantic space.

Airplane, for example, might be viewed as good, active, and strong. Or it might be seen as bad, active, and strong. A *spider* might be perceived as bad, passive, and strong, or perhaps good, active, and weak.

Osgood and others have done semantic differential research on a variety of types of concepts, including words, music, art, and even sonar sounds.[7] In addition, they have done research

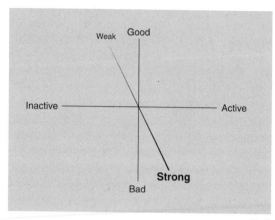

FIGURE **7.2**

Three-Dimensional Semantic Space

across a wide range of cultures. Osgood believes that the three factors of meaning—evaluation, activity, and potency—apply across all people and all concepts.[8] If these dimensions are universal as Osgood believes they are, he has significantly advanced our understanding of meaning. This claim is controversial, however, and we examine it more carefully in the concluding section of this chapter.

Attribution Theory

Attribution theory deals with the ways people infer the causes of behavior. Unlike scientific psychology, which attempts to ascertain the actual causes of behavior, "naive psychology," as attribution theory is sometimes called, centers on the *perceived* causes of behavior by ordinary people in everyday life. It explains the processes

5   Osgood, "Nature."
6   Osgood has hypothesized that bipolarity is the basic factor in all language and human thought. See Charles Osgood and Meredith Richards, "From *Yang* and *Yin* to *and* or *but*," *Language* 49 (1973): 380–412.
7   A sampling of studies illustrating the applications can be found in James Snider and Charles Osgood, eds., *The Semantic Differential Technique* (Chicago: Aldine, 1969). This work also includes an atlas of approximately 550 concepts and their semantic profiles.
8   This point of view is expressed in Charles Osgood, "Semantic Differential Technique in the Comparative Study of Cultures," in *The Semantic Differential Technique*, eds. J. Snider and C. Osgood (Chicago: Aldine, 1969), pp. 303–323; and *Cross Cultural Universals of Affective Meaning* (Urbana: University of Illinois Press, 1975).

by which you come to understand your own behavior and that of others.

Fritz Heider, founder of attribution theory, outlines several kinds of causal attributions that people commonly make.[9] These include situational causes (being affected by the environment), personal effects (influencing things personally), ability (being able to do something), effort (trying to do something), desire (wanting to do it), sentiment (feeling like it), belonging (going along with something), obligation (feeling you ought to), and permission (being permitted to).

There is not a one-to-one relationship between the observed behavior and the cause. A variety of behaviors may be perceived as stemming from a single cause, or, conversely, one behavior may be thought to arise from several causes. When you are communicating, then, you often need to resolve such ambiguities.

For example, let's say you are the supervisor in a small company. You notice that one of your employees seems particularly industrious all of a sudden. You will probably want to figure out why. You might think that this person is being forced to work hard, which would be an attribution to the environment. Or you might think that he is angling for a raise. Or maybe he is ingratiating himself to you. Or maybe he is bored and needs to keep himself busy.

Naturally, people make use of this context to help them determine the cause of the behavior. So in assessing your employee's hard work, you also can get additional information by observing him at work repeatedly over time. And you can observe when he works hard and when he does not.

Causal perception is mediated variables in your own psychological makeup. One of these is your meanings. You always assign meaning to what you observe, and these are crucial to what you "see." Meanings help you integrate your perceptions and organize your observations into patterns that help you make sense of the world. Because of a need for consistency, you define things in such a way that helps you make sense

of them, so that your attributions become integrated and consistent. For example, if you think that you have a great company, you may have a tendency to attribute your employee's hard work to loyalty.

The way you resolve ambiguities and establish a consistent pattern may be different from the way other people do so. Heider calls individual patterns of perception *perceptual styles*. He recognizes that any state of affairs may give rise to a number of interpretations, each of which seems true to the person involved.

One of the most interesting attributions occurs when you perceive that someone did something on purpose. If you think that someone did something on purpose, you are recognizing two underlying attributes: ability and motivation. Suppose, for example, that an associate of yours fails to show up for a meeting. You figure that she could not make it or didn't try. If she wasn't able, something might have been wrong with her (such as illness), or something else might have prevented her appearance (for example, a flat tire). If she did not try, she either didn't want to (an attribution of intent) or was too lazy (an attribution of exertion).

Now you can see what happens in interpersonal perception. In this instance you will infer the causes of your associate's behavior according to your overall experience, your meanings, the situational factors, and your own perceptual style.

Another interesting kind of attribution happens when you think that you "ought" to do something. An obligation is seen as an impersonal, objective demand. It can have a tremendous sense of validity because most people would agree with it. For example, you might say, "You ought to go to the dentist," or "I ought to report the theft." But "oughts" do not necessarily correspond with values. Perhaps you dread going to the dentist even though you think you should. Because people want to be consistent, they will balance their obligations and values:

> There exists a tendency to be in harmony with the requirements of the objective order. Thus the situation is balanced if one likes to do what

9   Fritz Heider, *The Psychology of Interpersonal Relations* (New York: Wiley, 1958).

one ought to do, if one likes and enjoys the entities one believes are valuable, if happiness and goodness go together, if p [perceiver] admires the person he likes and likes the person with whom he shares values, if what ought to be conforms with what really is, etc.[10]

Heider's theory was highly influential. We will not take the space here to discuss the many other attribution theories, but let's look at an extended example of how attribution works in everyday life. Brant Burleson tape-recorded a conversation between two teaching assistants about a student.[11] In this conversation one teacher, Don, complains to his colleague, Bob, that one of his students failed an exam three times. Don is very concerned and explores the reasons for the student's failure.

Don and Bob first explore the possibility that the test was too hard, but Don says that the test was not changed and that no one else failed it. They also establish that the student's behavior was consistent over time. Thus, they were able to rule out test difficulty as a cause. They then conclude that the failure must be something about the student herself. Either she did not have the ability or she wasn't trying. She completed all assignments and took the test three times, so she appeared to be trying. By deduction, then, they conclude that she just did not have the ability to pass the test. In the end Don says that he will ask her to drop the class because he doesn't think she can pass the course.

In this example, it looks like Don and Bob are being very logical and systematic in trying to determine the student's problem, but one of the most common research findings is that people are often illogical and biased in their attributions. People are not always objective when making causal inferences about themselves and other people. Rather than weighing all factors, people seem to make quick judgments based on available cues and emotional factors. Research also shows that people's prior judgments are hard to dislodge, no matter how compelling the evidence. Thus, once you make an attribution, you are apt to stick with it.

Yet there is a persistent assumption in attribution theory that people are logical and systematic. How do we reconcile these research findings? Several researchers have adopted the position that people can process information in both logical and illogical ways, depending on the circumstances such as motivation. If motivation to promote the self is high, as when we need to save face, there is probably a tendency to be biased in favor of self-serving, situational attributions. If you were late for a date, for example, you would probably make an excuse. On the other hand, when a person is motivated to control the situation, there will probably be a bias toward attributions of personal responsibility. So if you boss gave you a compliment about your work, you would probably think that you were personally responsible for doing so well.

One of the most persistent findings in attribution research is the *fundamental attribution error*. This is the tendency to attribute the cause of events to personal qualities. It is a feeling that people are personally responsible for what happens to them. In general, we seem to be insensitive to many circumstantial factors that cause events, overlooking things that may not be the person's fault.

This tendency, however, is reduced when we are evaluating our own responsibility. In other words, we tend to blame other people for what happens to them but blame the situation for what happens to us. If your roommate fails a test, you are apt to claim that he did not study hard enough, but if you fail the test, you will probably say that the test was too hard.

The literature on attribution theory is vast.[12] We do not have the space here to summarize all

---

10   Heider, *Psychology*, p. 233.

11   Brant R. Burleson, "Attribution Schemes and Causal Inference in Natural Conversations," in *Contemporary Issues in Language and Discourse Processes*, eds. D. G. Ellis and W. A. Donohue (Hillsdale, NJ: Erlbaum, 1986), pp. 63–86.

12   For a recent summary, see Eliot R. Smith, "Social Cognition Contributions to Attribution Theory and Research," in *Social Cognition: Impact on Social Psychology*, eds. Patricia G. Devine, David L. Hamilton, and Thomas M. Ostrom (San Diego: Academic, 1994), pp. 77–108. See also David R. Seibold and Brian H. Spitzberg, "Attribution Theory and Research: Formalization, Review, and Implications for Communication," in *Progress in Communication Sciences*, vol. 3, eds. B. Dervin and M. J. Voigt (Norwood, NJ: Ablex, 1981), pp. 85–125; Alan L. Sillars, "Attribution and Communication," in *Social Cognition and Communication*, eds. M. E. Roloff and C. R. Berger (Beverly Hills, CA: Sage, 1982), pp. 73–106.

of this, but let's look at one illustrative study. Alan Sillars conducted a landmark study on the effects of attribution in conflict resolution among college roommates. This research shows how attribution can affect communication in everyday life.[13] Sillars conducted two studies. In the first, he asked college students to write about a conflict they had had with their roommates, and in the second study, he actually videotaped roommates discussing problems such as irritability, boyfriend or girlfriend problems, and disagreements about music. He then looked for three types of conflict strategies, including passive methods such as avoidance or submission; competitive strategies such as requests, demands, and threats; and cooperative strategies such as problem solving. He found that the roommates' attributions very much affected the kinds of strategies they employed in managing their conflicts.

If, for example, the students saw their roommates as cooperative, they were more likely to use a cooperative strategy. Attributing self-blame led to the use of cooperative strategies, whereas attributing blame to the other person led to competitive ones. The attribution of certain negative personality traits to the other person also seemed to prevent the use of cooperation. In addition, Sillars found that, because of the fundamental attribution error, both partners tended to blame the other for the conflict and saw themselves as merely responding to it.

Interpretation is an important aspect of message receiving. Once a message is understood, its information must be organized in some way. Let's turn to this issue next.

◖ INFORMATION ORGANIZATION

In this section we will deal with the ways you organize and manage information and how information affects your cognitive system. Several of the theories in this chapter deal with *attitudes*. Attitude and attitude change have been popular subjects in communication research and theory for fifty years.[14] Originally, attitudes were stud-

ied as a kind of "mental" behavior that is learned and shaped largely as other behaviors are. In more recent years, however, attitude theory has taken a distinct cognitive turn. Attitudes are viewed as elements of the cognitive system that you hold in your memory and access when you respond to various situations.[15]

Information-Integration Theory

The information-integration approach centers on the ways people accumulate and organize information about some person, object, situation, or idea and form attitudes. An *attitude* is a predisposition to act in a positive or negative way toward some object. The information-integration approach is one of the most popular models of the nature of attitudes and attitude change.[16]

According to this theory, all information has the potential of affecting your attitudes, but two variables are important in how attitudes are changed. The first is valence, or direction. *Valence* refers to whether information supports your beliefs or refutes them. When information supports your beliefs and attitudes, it has "positive" valence. When it does not, it has "negative" valence. If you favor school vouchers, a statement opposing school vouchers would be negative and one supporting them would be positive.

The second variable that affects the impact of information is the *weight* you assign to the

13   Alan L. Sillars, "Attributions and Communication in Roommate Conflicts," *Communication Monographs* 47 (1980): 180–200; "The Sequential and Distributional Structure of Conflict Interaction as a Function of Attributions Concerning the Locus of Responsibility and Stability of Conflict," in *Communication Yearbook 4,* ed. D. Nimmo (New Brunswick, NJ: Transaction, 1980), pp. 217–236.
14   For a good discussion of attitude theory and its importance, see Ostrom, Skowronski, and Nowak, "The Cognitive Foundation of Attitudes"; James Price Dillard, "Persuasion Past and Present: Attitudes Aren't What They Used to Be," *Communication Monographs* 60 (1993): 90–97.
15   David R. Roskos-Ewoldsen, "Attitude Accessibility and Persuasion: Review and a Transactive Model," in *Communication Yearbook 20,* ed. Brant Burleson (Thousand Oaks, CA: Sage, 1997), pp. 185–225; Ostrom, Skowronski, and Nowak, "The Cognitive Foundation of Attitudes."
16   Contributors include Norman H. Anderson, "Integration Theory and Attitude Change," *Psychological Review* 78 (1971): 171–206; Martin Fishbein and Icek Ajzen, *Belief, Attitude, Intention, and Behavior* (Reading, MA: Addison-Wesley, 1975); Robert S. Wyer, *Cognitive Organization and Change* (Hillsdale, NJ: Erlbaum, 1974).

information. Weight is a function of credibility. If you think the information is probably true, you will assign a higher weight to it; if not, you will assign a lower weight.

So valence affects *how* information influences your attitudes, and weight affects *how much* it does so. When the weight of information is low, the information will have little effect, no matter what its valence. Suppose that you have two friends—one who strongly favors legalized euthanasia and another who strongly opposes it. Suppose that a television documentary airs a report that legalized mercy killing has been badly abused in other countries. How will this information affect your friends' attitudes toward the issue?

Let's begin with your friend who favors euthanasia. If he assigns little weight to the news report, this information will not affect his attitude much one way or the other. On the other hand, if he decides that the information is true, he will assign a high weight to it, and it will affect his attitude. The combination of a high weight and a negative valence will change his attitude to be less in favor.

Now let's look at your friend who opposes legalized euthanasia. Again, if she assigns low weight to the information, it will have little effect, but if she believes this information and assigns high weight to it, it will make her even more opposed to legalization than she originally was. Why? Because the combination of high weight and positive valence reinforces her opinion.

An attitude is considered to be an accumulation of information about an object, person, situation, or experience. Attitude change occurs because new information adds to the attitude or because it changes one's judgments about the weight or valence of other information. Any one piece of information usually does not have too much influence on an attitude because the attitude consists of a number of things that could counteract the new information.

You would not expect your friends to completely reverse their attitudes because they have other beliefs that enter the picture. Your friend who favors legalized euthanasia does so for a

number of reasons, and he may not be very worried about abuse. Even though the television program persuades him that mercy killing has been abused in certain other countries, he might say that abuse can be prevented by good regulations. Let's now look at extensions on this theory that help explain why attitudes do not change easily.

Expectancy-Value Theory. One of the best-known and respected information-integration theorists is Martin Fishbein.[17] Fishbein highlights the complex nature of attitudes in what is known as *expectancy-value theory.*

According to Fishbein, there are two kinds of belief. The first is *belief in* a thing. When you believe in something, you would say that this thing exists. The second kind of belief, *belief about,* is your sense of the probability that a particular relationship exists between two things. For example, you might *believe in* the existence of pain and suffering late in life. You may also have a *belief about* pain and suffering, that people want to die so that they can avoid it.

Attitudes differ from beliefs because they are evaluative. Attitudes are correlated with beliefs and lead you to behave a certain way toward the attitude object. So the two beliefs mentioned above would probably lead you to vote in favor of a ballot proposition that would legalize euthanasia.

Fishbein sees attitudes as organized, so that general attitudes are predicted from specific ones in a summative fashion. So a general positive attitude toward euthanasia would consist of other attitudes—about life, death, individual rights, and pain and suffering. The relationship between beliefs and attitudes is represented algebraically as follows:[18]

17 Fishbein has published several articles on this topic. See the Selected Bibliography. For an excellent secondary source, see David T. Burhans, "The Attitude-Behavior Discrepancy Problem: Revisited," *Quarterly Journal of Speech* 57 (1971): 418–428. For more recent treatments, see Fishbein and Ajzen, *Belief*; Daniel J. O'Keefe, *Persuasion: Theory and Research* (Newbury Park, CA: Sage, 1990), pp. 45–60.
18 Martin Fishbein, ed., "A Behavior Theory Approach to the Relations Between Beliefs About an Object and the Attitude Toward the Object," in *Readings in Attitude Theory and Measurement* (New York: Wiley, 1967), p. 394.

TABLE **7.1**

A Simplified Example of an Attitude Hierarchy According to the Fishbein Model

Attitude object (o) → jogging	$N = 6$ (number of beliefs in system)	
Associated concepts (x_i)	Probability of association (B_i)	Evaluation (a_i)
x_1 Cardiovascular health	B_1 Jogging promotes cardiovascular vigor.	a_1 Cardiovascular vigor is good.
x_2 Disease	B_2 Jogging reduces the chance of disease.	a_2 Disease is bad.
x_3 Obesity	B_3 Jogging reduces weight.	a_3 Being overweight is bad.
x_4 Mental health	B_4 Jogging promotes peace of mind.	a_4 Letting off mental tensions is good.
x_5 Friendship	B_5 Jogging introduces a person to new friends.	a_5 Friendship is important.
x_6 Physique	B_6 Jogging builds better bodies.	a_6 A beautiful body is appealing.

$$A_o = \sum_i^N B_i a_i$$

where

A_o = attitude toward object o

B_i = strength of belief i about o; that is, the probability or improbability that o is associated with some other concept x

a_i = evaluative aspect of B; that is, the evaluation of x

N = number of beliefs about o

Thus, an attitude toward an object equals the sum of each belief about that object times its evaluation.

The distinctive feature of Fishbein's formula is its proposition that attitudes are a function of a complex combination of beliefs and evaluations. The example in Table 7.1 helps clarify this model. This table describes a hypothetical attitude toward jogging. Here, jogging is associated with beliefs about six concepts—cardiovascular health, disease, obesity, mental health, friendship, and physique. Each of these concepts is associated with a belief, and each belief has either positive or negative valence. In this example, when you add up all the beliefs times the evaluations, you end up with a very positive attitude about jogging.

According to this theory, attitude change can occur from three sources. First, information can

alter the believability, or weight, of particular beliefs. The two friends mentioned above might learn, for example, that the report on the abuse of euthanasia is erroneous. Second, information can change the valence of a belief. For instance, your friends might learn that these "abuses" were technical and legal and not self-serving in any way, making the information seem positive rather than negative. Finally, information can add new beliefs to the attitude structure. So, for example, your friends might learn that euthanasia was actually requested in the vast majority of cases.

This theory suggests some of the ways information affects the cognitive system, but how do the resultant attitudes affect behavior? This is a more complicated issue.

Theory of Reasoned Action. Adding to this theory, Icek Ajzen and Martin Fishbein argue that behavior results in part from intentions, a complex outcome of attitudes.[19] Specifically, your intention to behave in a certain way is determined by your attitude toward the behavior and a set of beliefs about how other people would like you to behave. Consider your progress in college as an example. Do you plan to

---

19   Fishbein and Ajzen, *Belief;* Icek Ajzen and Martin Fishbein, *Understanding Attitudes and Predicting Social Behavior* (Englewood Cliffs, NJ: Prentice-Hall, 1980). See also James B. Stiff, *Persuasive Communication* (New York: Guilford, 1994), pp. 51–57.

continue until you get your degree or drop out for a while? The answer to this question depends on your attitude toward school and what you think other people want you to do. Each factor—your attitude and others' opinions—is weighted according to its importance. Sometimes your attitude is most important, sometimes others' opinions are most important, and sometimes they are more or less equal in weight. The formula is as follows:

$$BI = A_B w_1 + (SN)w_2$$

where

BI = behavioral intention
A_B = attitude toward the behavior
SN = subjective norm (what others think)
w_1 = weight of attitude
w_2 = weight of subjective norm

So your intention to do something equals your attitude toward the behavior times the strength of that attitude plus what others think times the strength of their opinion.

Now let us return to the example of your intention regarding college. If you have developed a poor attitude toward school and your friends are encouraging you to drop out for a semester to work, that is probably what you will do. On the other hand, if your friends are encouraging you to stick it out and their opinions are very important to you, you will probably stay despite your negative attitude. If your friends' opinions don't matter that much, your attitude will win out, and your intention will be to get a job.

The preceding formula predicts your behavioral *intention,* but it does not necessarily predict the *actual behavior.* This is because you do not always behave in accordance with your intentions. We know that people are notorious for going against their own best intentions. Sometimes, for example, people cannot do what they want because they are not able to. Smokers may want to stop smoking but cannot because they are addicted. You might want to drop out of school, but your parents' threat to cut off your support might prevent you from doing so.

One of the most powerful factors in how you organize information is consistency. Let us turn now to some theories that address the principle of consistency.

Consistency Theories

Undoubtedly, one of the largest bodies of work related to attitude, attitude change, and persuasion is consistency theory. All consistency theories begin with the same premise: People are more comfortable with consistency than inconsistency. Consistency, then, is a primary organizing principle in cognitive processing, and attitude change can result from information that disrupts this balance.

Although the vocabulary and concepts of these theories differ, the basic assumption of consistency is present in all of them. In system language (Chapter 3), people seek homeostasis; as open systems, people aim to achieve self-maintenance and balance.

In the remainder of this section, two theories of cognitive consistency are summarized. These were chosen because of their prominence in the field and their relatively complete explanations. The first is Leon Festinger's theory of cognitive dissonance and the second is Milton Rokeach's theory of attitudes, beliefs, and values.

The Theory of Cognitive Dissonance.   Leon Festinger's theory of cognitive dissonance is one of the most important theories in the history of social psychology. Over the years it has produced a prodigious quantity of research and volumes of criticism, interpretation, and extrapolation.[20]

Festinger teaches that any two cognitive elements, including attitudes, perceptions, knowledge, and behaviors, will have one of three kinds of relationships. The first of these is null, or *irrelevant;* the second is consistent, or *consonant;* and

---

20   Leon Festinger, *A Theory of Cognitive Dissonance* (Stanford, CA: Stanford University Press, 1957). Many short reviews of dissonance theory are available. See, for example, Stiff, *Persuasive Communication,* pp. 68–75; O'Keefe, *Persuasion.*

the third is inconsistent, or *dissonant*. Dissonance occurs when one element would not be expected to follow from the other. If you think that saturated fats are harmful to your health, you would probably reduce the amount of meat in your diet. What is consonant or dissonant for one person, however, may not be for another, so we must always ask what is consistent or inconsistent within a person's own psychological system. You might think, for example, that meat provides valuable protein that mitigates the need to reduce dietary meats.

Two overriding premises govern dissonance theory. The first is that dissonance produces tension or stress that creates pressure to change. Second, when dissonance is present, the individual will not only attempt to reduce it but will also avoid situations in which additional dissonance might be produced. The greater the dissonance, the greater the need to reduce it. For example, the more inconsistent your diet is with your knowledge about cholesterol, the greater the pressure you will feel.

Dissonance itself is a result of two other variables—the importance of the cognitive elements and the number of elements involved in the dissonant relation. In other words, if you have several things that are inconsistent and if they are important to you, you will experience greater dissonance. If health is not important to you, knowledge that certain fats are bad for your health is probably not going to affect your actual eating habits.

How do you deal with your cognitive dissonance? Festinger imagined a number of methods. First, you might change one or more of the cognitive elements, a behavior or an attitude perhaps. For example, you might become a vegetarian, or you might start believing that fats are less important than genetics. Second, new elements might be added to one side of the tension or the other. For instance, you might switch to using olive oil exclusively. Third, you might come to see the elements as less important than they used to be. For example, you might decide that health isn't as important as state of mind. Fourth, you

might seek consonant information such as evidence for the benefits of meat by reading new studies on the topic. Fifth, you might reduce dissonance by distorting or misinterpreting the information involved. This could happen if you decided that although a lot of meat poses a health risk, meat is not as harmful as the loss of important nutritional ingredients like iron and protein. No matter which of these methods you employed, it would reduce your dissonance and make you feel better about your attitudes, beliefs, and actions.

Much of the theory and research on cognitive dissonance has centered around the various situations in which dissonance is likely to result. These include such situations as decision making, forced compliance, initiation, social support, and effort.

Decision making has received a great deal of research attention. Salespeople label the dissonance that occurs after buying something "buyer's remorse." In 1970 an interesting study was published about automobile buying.[21] Often, while waiting for delivery of a car, a customer will cancel the purchase because of *postdecisional dissonance*, or buyer's remorse. In this study, a group of automobile customers were called twice during the period between signing the contract and actual delivery to reassure them about their purchase. Members of a control group were not called. As expected, significantly more of those who were not called canceled the order (about twice as many).

The amount of dissonance one experiences as a result of a decision depends on four variables, the first of which is the importance of the decision. Certain decisions, such as that to skip breakfast, may be unimportant and produce little dissonance, but buying a car can result in a great deal of dissonance.

The second variable is the attractiveness of the chosen alternative. Other things being equal,

---

21   J. H. Donnelly and J. M. Ivancevich, "Post-Purchase Reinforcement and Back-Out Behavior," *Journal of Marketing Research* 7 (1970): 399–400.

the less attractive the chosen alternative, the greater the dissonance. You will probably suffer more dissonance from buying an ugly car than a pretty one.

Third, the greater the perceived attractiveness of the unchosen alternative, the more dissonance you will feel. If you wish you had saved your money to go to Europe instead of buying a car, you will suffer dissonance.

Finally, the greater the degree of similarity or overlap between the alternatives, the less the dissonance. If you are debating between two similar cars, making a decision in favor of one will not result in much dissonance, but if you are deciding between buying a car and going to Europe, you might have quite a bit.

Another situation in which dissonance is apt to result is forced compliance, or being induced to do or say something contrary to your beliefs or values. This situation usually occurs when a reward is involved for complying or a punishment for not complying. This could happen at work, for example, when your boss asks you to do something you would rather not do. Dissonance theory predicts that the less the pressure to conform, the greater the dissonance. If you were asked to do something you didn't like doing but were offered a handsome bonus for doing so, you would feel more justified than if you were offered a company mug.

In a well-known experiment, after completing a boring task, some students were "bribed" to tell other students that the task would be fun.[22] Some of these participants were paid $1 to lie, and the others were paid $20. As expected, because they experienced more dissonance, the $1 liars tended to change their opinion of the task to actually believe it was fun, whereas the $20 liars tended to maintain their belief that the task was dull but justified the lie on the basis that they could pocket a considerable piece of cash (in 1959 dollars).

The less external justification (such as reward or punishment), the more you must focus on the internal inconsistency within yourself. This is why, according to the dissonance theorist, "soft" social pressures can be so powerful by causing a

great deal of dissonance. It also explains why you might stay in a high-paying job you dislike. The high pay can be used as a justification for doing so.

Dissonance theory also makes several other predictions. The theory predicts, for example, that the more difficult one's initiation into a group, the greater commitment one will develop. The more social support one receives from friends on an idea or action, the greater the pressure to believe in that idea or action. The greater the amount of effort one puts into a task, the more one will rationalize the value of that task. Have you ever put a lot of work into an assignment you hadn't looked forward to, only to discover after completing it that you liked it after all?

Rokeach: Beliefs, Attitudes, and Values. Although there are many consistency theories, one of the most comprehensive is that of Milton Rokeach. He has developed an extensive explanation of human behavior based on beliefs, attitudes, and values.[23] His theory builds on earlier work and provides some interesting and valuable extensions.

Rokeach believes that each person has a highly organized system of beliefs, attitudes, and values, which guides behavior. *Beliefs* are the hundreds of thousands of statements that we make about self and the world. Beliefs can be general or specific, and they are arranged within the system in terms of their centrality or importance to the ego. At the center of the belief system are those well-established, relatively unchangeable beliefs that form the core of the belief system. At the periphery of the system lie numerous insignificant beliefs that can change easily. Believing that your parents have a good marriage is probably pretty central, since it impacts a lot of other things you assume to be true. Believing that you need a haircut, on the other hand, is peripheral.

22   Leon Festinger and James M. Carlsmith, "Cognitive Consequences of Forced Compliance," *Journal of Abnormal and Social Psychology* 58 (1959): 203–210.
23   Milton Rokeach, *Beliefs, Attitudes, and Values: A Theory of Organization and Change* (San Francisco: Jossey-Bass, 1969); *The Nature of Human Values* (New York: Free Press, 1973).

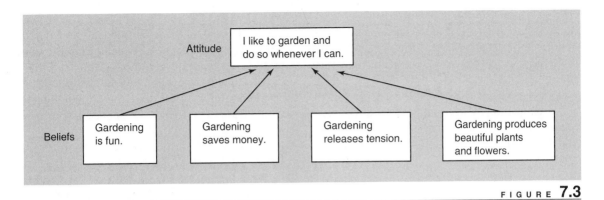

FIGURE **7.3**

A Simple Example of the Belief Structure of an Attitude

The more central a belief, the more resistant it is to change and the more impact such change will have on the overall system. In other words, if one of your central beliefs changes, expect rather profound changes in how you think about many things. This is why children are often shaken when parents get a divorce.

Attitudes are groups of beliefs that are organized around a focal object and predispose a person to behave in a particular way toward that object. You have hundreds of thousands of beliefs and probably thousands of attitudes, each consisting of a number of beliefs about the attitude object. Figure 7.3 illustrates, in overly simple form, the organization of an attitude.

Rokeach believes attitudes are of two important kinds that must always be viewed together. These are *attitude toward object* and *attitude toward situation.* One's behavior in a particular situation is a function of these two in combination. If you do not behave in a given situation consistently with your attitudes toward certain things, it is probably because your attitude toward the situation prevents it. An example of this kind of inconsistency is eating foods you do not like when they are served to you as a guest. The point here is that behavior is a complex function of a variety of sets of attitudes, and the system consists of many beliefs ranging in their centrality.

Rokeach believes that of the three concepts in explaining human behavior, values are the most important. *Values* are specific types of beliefs that are central in the system and act as life guides. Values are of two kinds. *Instrumental values—*such as hard work and loyalty—are guidelines for living on which we base our daily behavior. *Terminal values* are the ultimate aims of life toward which we work; examples include wealth and happiness.

Another component in the belief-attitude-value system that assumes great overall importance is your *self-concept,* your beliefs about yourself. It is your answer to the question, Who am I? Self-concept is particularly important to the system because self-regard is a primary motivation supported by all other elements of the cognitive system. Thus, while beliefs, attitudes, and values comprise the components of your system, self-concept provides its guiding goal or purpose.

Rokeach is basically a consistency theorist. He concludes in the end that people are guided by a need for consistency and that inconsistency creates pressure to change. However, his approach to consistency is more systemic and more cognitive than any of the other consistency theories. Taking the total system into consideration, he sees consistency as extremely complex. For this reason, Rokeach calls his work a *comprehensive theory of change.*

Rokeach believes that the most important inconsistencies in a person's psychological system are those involving cognitions about the self. Only when inconsistencies involve the self-conception will there be significant, lasting change. The reason for this is that such contradictions increase self-dissatisfaction. Because maintenance of self-regard is the overall aim of the psychological system, it is natural that this should be so.

Thus far we have discussed the interpretation and organization of information. One of the outcomes of information processing is judgment. The theories in the following section address this point.

◉ JUDGMENT PROCESSES

The theories in this section deal with the ways individuals make judgments in communication—judgments of arguments, nonverbal behavior, belief claims, and attitudes.

Social Judgment Theory

We begin this section with social judgment theory because it is a classical theory of judgment and is a foundation for much of the other theorizing in this area. The work of psychologist Muzafer Sherif and his associates, this theory deals with the way people make judgments about messages.[24] The theory is based on early psychophysical research, in which people were tested on their ability to judge physical stimuli such as the weight of an object or the brightness of a light. Using this work as an analogy, Sherif investigated the ways individuals judge messages, and he learned that many principles of psychophysics hold for social judgment as well.

Research shows that people make judgments on the basis of anchors, or reference points. Suppose that you were asked to judge the relative weight of five objects. On what would you base your judgment? If the experimenter handed you a weight and told you it was 10 pounds, you would first feel the reference weight and then judge the weight of the other objects based on the feeling of the first one. The known weight would act as an "anchor," influencing your perception of the others.

To demonstrate this idea of anchors, try a simple experiment. Take three bowls. Fill the first with hot water, the second with cold water, the third with tepid water. Put one hand in the hot water and the other in the cold water. After a few moments, place both hands in the third bowl. Your perceptions of the temperature of this water will be different for each hand because each hand had a different anchor or reference.

Sherif reasons that similar processes operate in judging communication messages. In social perception anchors are internal and based on past experience. The internal anchor, or reference point, is always present and influences the way a person responds to messages. The more important the issue is to one's ego, the more strongly the anchor will influence what is understood.

In a social judgment experiment, you would be given a large number of statements about some issue. You then would be asked to sort them into groups according to their similarity. You could use as many groups as you wished. Then you would put the piles in order from positive to negative. Next you would indicate which piles of statements are acceptable to you personally, which are not acceptable, and which are neutral. (This is called a Q-sort.)

The first group forms your *latitude of acceptance*, the statements you can agree with; the second your *latitude of rejection*, those you cannot agree with; and the third your *latitude of noncommitment*. This research procedure is just a systematic way of simulating what happens in everyday life. On any issue, there will usually be a range of statements, pro or con, that you are willing to tolerate, and there will also be a range that you reject totally.

A person's latitudes of acceptance and rejection are influenced by a key variable—ego in-

24   The first major work in this area was Muzafer Sherif and Carl I. Hovland, *Social Judgment* (New Haven, CT: Yale University Press, 1961). See also Muzafer Sherif, Carolyn Sherif, and Roger Nebergall, *Attitude and Attitude Change: The Social Judgment-Involvement Approach* (Philadelphia: Saunders, 1965). For a brief overview of the theory, see Muzafer Sherif, *Social Interaction—Process and Products* (Chicago: Aldine, 1967), chaps. 16–18. Several secondary sources are also available; see, for example, Stiff, *Persuasive Communication*, pp. 138–142; Leonard Martin and Abraham Tesser, eds., *The Construction of Social Judgments* (Hillsdale, NJ: Erlbaum, 1992); O'Keefe, *Persuasion*, pp. 29–44.

volvement. *Ego involvement* is the degree of personal relevance of an issue. It is the degree to which one's attitude toward something affects the self-concept, or the importance assigned to the issue.

For example, you may have read much about the depletion of the ozone layer and have come to believe that this is a serious problem. If you have not yet experienced any personal difficulties because of this problem, it may be unimportant to you, because your ego involvement is low. On the other hand, if you have already been treated for skin cancer, the issue would be considerably more ego involving.

Ego involvement makes a great deal of difference in how you respond to messages related to a topic. Although you probably have a more extreme opinion on those topics with which you are ego-involved, this is not always the case. You could have a moderate opinion and still be ego-involved.

What does social judgment say about communication? First, we know from Sherif's work that individuals judge the favorability of a message based on their own internal anchors and ego involvement. However, this judgment process can involve distortion. On a given issue, such as the ozone hole, a person may distort the message by contrast or assimilation. The *contrast effect* occurs when individuals judge a message to be farther from their own point of view than it actually is, and the *assimilation effect* occurs when people judge the message to be closer to their own point of view than it actually is.

Basically, when a message is relatively close to one's own position, that message will be assimilated, whereas more distant messages will be contrasted. These assimilation and contrast effects are heightened by ego involvement. So, for example, if you believe strongly that industry should be regulated to stop chlorofluorocarbon (CFC) emissions, a moderately favorable statement might seem like a strong positive statement because of the assimilation effect, whereas a slightly unfavorable statement might be perceived to be strongly opposed to regulation because of the contrast effect. If you were highly ego-involved in the issue, this effect would be even greater.

The second area in which social judgment theory aids our understanding of communication is attitude change. Social judgment theory makes the following predictions:

First, messages falling within the latitude of acceptance facilitate attitude change. An argument in favor of a position within the range of acceptance will be somewhat more persuasive than an argument outside of this range. If you think that no CFC emissions should be allowed, you might be persuaded by a message advocating that some CFC emissions be permitted, provided this position is within your latitude of acceptance.

Second, if you judge a message to lie within the latitude of rejection, attitude change will be reduced or nonexistent. In fact, a *boomerang effect* may occur in which the discrepant message actually increases your position on the issue. Thus your positive attitude toward CFC regulation would probably not be changed by a message advocating no regulation, assuming it was in your latitude of rejection. In fact, such a message might even make you more firmly favor regulation.

Third, within the latitude of acceptance and noncommitment, the more discrepant the message from your own stand, the greater the expected attitude change. However, once the message hits the latitude of rejection, change will not be expected. A statement farther from your own attitude will probably bring about more change than one that is not very far from your position.

Finally, the greater your ego involvement in the issue, the larger the latitude of rejection, the smaller the latitude of noncommitment, and thus the less the expected attitude change. Highly ego-involved persons are hard to persuade. They tend to reject a wider range of statements than people who are not highly ego-involved, and rejected messages are not effective. So if you were highly ego-involved in the ozone-depletion problem, you would have a large latitude of rejection and would be persuaded by very few statements divergent from your own.

To illustrate how social judgment works, consider an interesting experiment done by a group of researchers shortly after Oklahoma passed a prohibition law in the 1950s.[25] The researchers recruited a number of people who were deeply involved in the issue on one side or the other and several who were moderate and not very involved in the issue. They found that those who were highly ego-involved and extreme in their opinions had much wider latitudes of rejection than did moderates, and the moderate subjects had much wider latitudes of noncommitment than did those who held extreme opinions. Interestingly, when presented with the same moderate message, the extreme "drys" judged it to be much more toward the nonprohibition side than did other subjects, and the "wets" judged it to be much more toward the prohibition side than the other subjects. In other words, both extreme groups had a contrast effect. Generally, the attitude change experienced by the moderates after hearing a message on the issue was about twice as much as the attitude change experienced by those who were highly involved in the issue.

Clearly, ego involvement is a central concept of social judgment theory. We move now to a theory that picks up on involvement and relates it to critical thinking processes.

Elaboration Likelihood Theory

Social psychologists Richard Petty and John Cacioppo developed elaboration likelihood theory as a general summation of insights from many other attitude-change theories.[26] It has become one of the most popular persuasion theories today.

According to this theory, you evaluate information in various ways. Sometimes you evaluate

messages in an elaborate way, using critical thinking, and sometimes you do so in a simpler, less critical manner. Sometimes you are thoughtful about arguments, and other times you are not.

Elaboration likelihood is the probability of critical evaluation of arguments, and it can range from little to great. The likelihood of elaboration depends on the way a person processes the message. There are two: the central and peripheral routes. Elaboration, or critical thinking, occurs in the *central route* and nonelaboration, or the lack of critical thinking, in the *peripheral* one. Thus, when you process information through the central route, you actively think about and weigh it against what you already know. When you process information through the peripheral route, you are much less critical.

When you use the central route, you consider arguments carefully, and if your attitude changes, it is apt to be relatively enduring and will probably affect how you actually behave. On the other hand, if you use the peripheral route, any resulting change is probably temporary and may have less effect on how you act. Keep in mind, however, that because elaboration likelihood is a variable, you will probably use both routes somewhat, depending on the degree of personal relevance.

Your critical thinking depends on two general factors—motivation and ability. When you are highly motivated, you are likely to use central processing, and when motivation is low, peripheral processing is more likely. For example, if you are a typical college student, you would probably pay more attention to the campus newspaper's arguments for and against fee increases than you would to its arguments for and against installing new roofing on the student center (unless your family owned the roofing business!).

Motivation consists of at least three things. The first is involvement, or the personal relevance of the topic. The more important the topic, the more likely that you will think critically about the issues involved. The second factor in motivation is diversity of argument. You will tend to think more about arguments that

---

25   Carl I. Hovland, O. J. Harvey, and Muzafer Sherif, "Assimilation and Contrast Effects in Reactions to Communication and Attitude Change," *Journal of Abnormal and Social Psychology* 55 (1957): 244–252.
26   Richard E. Petty and John T. Cacioppo, *Communication and Persuasion: Central and Peripheral Routes to Attitude Change* (New York: Springer-Verlag, 1986). For brief summaries, see Stiff, *Persuasive Communication,* pp. 179–191; and O'Keefe, *Persuasion,* pp. 95–116. For an additional explanation and refutation of critiques, see Richard E. Petty and others, "Conceptual and Methodological Issues in the Elaboration Likelihood Model of Persuasion: A Reply to the Michigan State Critics," *Communication Theory* 3 (1993): 336–362.

come from a variety of sources. The reason for this is that when you hear several people talking about an issue, you cannot make snap judgments very easily. Other things being equal, then, where multiple sources and multiple arguments are involved, receivers tend to process the information centrally.

The third factor in motivation is one's personal tendency to enjoy critical thinking. People who enjoy mulling over arguments will probably use more central processing than those who do not.

No matter how motivated you are, however, you cannot use central processing unless you have the ability to do so. Most students would be more critical of a speech on fashion trends than one on quarks and electrons.

Figure 7.4 illustrates the central and peripheral processing.[27] According to this figure, if you are not motivated and do not have the ability to process the message, you will be monitoring peripheral cues. If you are motivated and can process the message, you will compare the information in the message with what you already know. If that knowledge is insufficient to make these kinds of judgments, you'll go the peripheral route.

When processing information in the central route, you will carefully consider the arguments. What might persuade you under these conditions? Certainly the degree to which the message matches your previous attitude would have an effect here. Messages that are more favorable to your view would probably be evaluated more positively than those that are not. On the other hand, the strength of the argument certainly plays a role because in central processing you are thinking critically. You identify good and bad arguments, and you tend to be influenced more by good ones.

In peripheral processing, you do not look closely at the strength of the argument. Indeed, you make judgments quickly about whether to believe what you hear or read on the basis of simple cues. For example, when source credibility is high, the message may be believed. Also, you tend to believe people you like. The number of arguments can also be a cue in that you may

rely on the sheer number of arguments to determine whether to accept a message. In most peripheral processing, many types of cues are used.

The following experiment is an example of how central and peripheral processing work. In the experiment, 145 students were asked to evaluate audiotaped arguments in favor of instituting comprehensive examinations for seniors at their college.[28] Two versions were used, one with strong arguments and the other with weak ones. Half of the students were told that the examination could go into effect the following year, but the other half were led to believe that the change would not occur for ten years. Obviously, the first group would find the message more personally relevant than the second group and would therefore be more motivated to scrutinize the arguments carefully. It was expected that these students would be less susceptible to peripheral cues.

To test this hypothesis, the researchers told half of the high-relevance group and half of the low-relevance group that the tape was based on a report from a high school class, and the other half of these groups was told that it was based on a report of the Carnegie Commission. Thus, the first group was presented with a low-source credibility cue, whereas the other group was presented with a high-credibility cue.

As expected, the students who heard the highly relevant message were motivated to pay careful attention to the quality of the arguments and were more influenced by the arguments than were the students who heard the less relevant message. Those students who heard the less relevant message were more influenced by credibility as a peripheral cue than were the other students. Petty, Cacioppo, and their colleagues have done a number of similar studies with the same results.

The lesson from this theory might seem to be that you should always be critical in evaluating

27   Petty and Cacioppo, *Communication*, p. 4.
28   Richard E. Petty, John T. Cacioppo, and R. Goldman, "Personal Involvement as a Determinant of Argument-Based Persuasion," *Journal of Personality and Social Psychology* 41 (1981): 847–855.

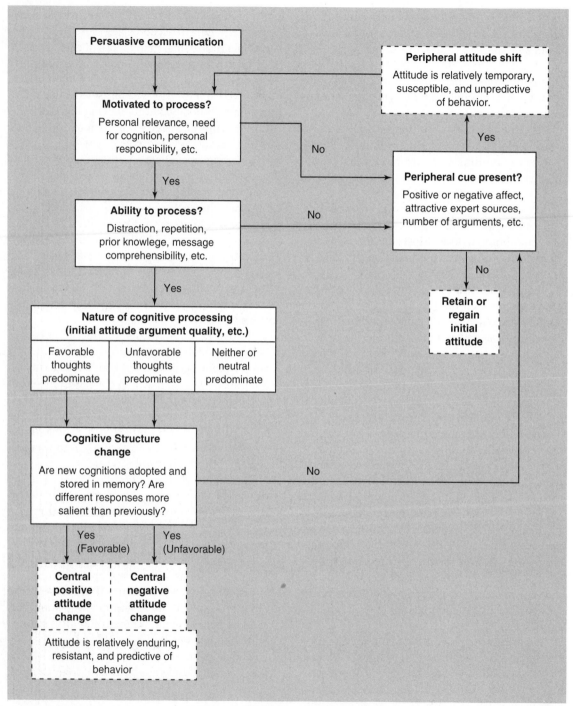

FIGURE 7.4

Schematic Depiction of the Two Routes to Persuasion

From *Communication and Persuasion: Central and Peripheral Routes to Attitude Change* by Richard E. Petty and John T. Cacioppo. © 1986 by Springer-Verlag. Reprinted by permission of the publisher.

messages, but, practically speaking, you cannot always attend carefully to every message. Some combination of central and peripheral processing is always to be expected. Most of the time, you are influenced by both. Even when motivation and ability are low, you might still be influenced somewhat by strong arguments, and even when you are processing in the central route, other less critical factors can also affect your attitudes.

Expectancy Violations Theory

As we saw in the Chapter 6, Judee Burgoon and her colleagues have been developing an intriguing theory of interaction based on the idea that communicators adapt and adjust their behaviors to one another. Although the theorists' ideas have been presented in parts as subtheories, they are really part of the larger master theory of interaction presented in Chapter 6. In that chapter, we summarized the basic ideas of the "big" theory under the title "interaction adaptation theory."[29] In this section we look at applications of this theory in the areas of the violation of expectations and deception. First we turn to expectancy violations theory.

How do you respond when people violate your expectations? This interesting question has been the subject of much attention, and Burgoon's theory is a leader in this tradition.[30] According to this theory, we have expectations about the behavior of another person based on social norms as well as our previous experience with the other person and the situation in which the behavior occurs. These expectations can involve virtually any nonverbal behavior, including, for example, eye contact, distance, and body angle. (Actually, we probably have expectations for verbal behavior as well, but this theory does not address this subject.)

The common assumption is that when expectancies are met, the other person's behaviors are judged as positive, and when they are violated, the behaviors are judged as negative; however, Burgoon has found that this is not always the case. Violations are often judged favorably.

Whether judged as good or bad, violations cause the perceiver to be aroused. If someone stands too close to you or too far away, if another person's eye contact is abnormal, or if an individual violates some other set of expectations, you will feel differently. This arousal is not necessarily negative. In fact, in some cases it might feel pleasant, especially when the other person seems to like you. Sometimes, however, violations can make you feel uncomfortable. Apparently, we learn to have expectations and to detect violations early in life, even in infancy.

What seems to happen is that your attention is drawn to behavior that would otherwise go unnoticed. When your expectations are met, you don't notice the behavior, but when they are violated, you become distracted by it. This distraction can certainly get your attention and lead you to evaluate the other person's behavior.

Imagine, for example, that you have just been introduced to an attractive person. In getting to know each other, you talk about everything from the weather to family. Suddenly you become aware that this person is standing unusually

29   Judee K. Burgoon and Cindy H. White, "Researching Nonverbal Message Production: A View from Interaction Adaptation Theory," in *Message Production: Advances in Communication Theory*, ed. John O. Greene (Mahwah, NJ: Erlbaum, 1997), pp. 279–312; Judee K. Burgoon, Lesa A. Stern, and Leesa Dillman, *Interpersonal Adaptation: Dyadic Interaction Patterns* (New York: Cambridge University Press, 1995); Judee K. Burgoon, Leesa Dillman, and Lesa A. Stern, "Adaptation in Dyadic Interaction: Defining and Operationalizing Patterns of Reciprocity and Compensation," *Communication Theory* 3 (1993): 295–316.
30   Judee K. Burgoon and Jerold L. Hale, "Nonverbal Expectancy Violations: Model Elaboration and Application," *Communication Monographs* 55 (1988): 58–79. For brief summaries see also Beth A. LePoire, "Two Contrasting Explanations of Involvement Violations: Expectancy Violations Theory Versus Discrepancy Arousal Theory," *Human Communication Research* 20 (1994): 560–591; Judee K. Burgoon, "Nonverbal Signals," in *Handbook of Interpersonal Communication*, eds. Mark L. Knapp and Gerald R. Miller (Thousand Oaks, CA: Sage, 1994), pp. 253–255. For other approaches to expectancy violations, see Joseph N. Cappella, "The Management of Conversational Interaction in Adults and Infants," in *Handbook of Interpersonal Communication*, eds. Mark L. Knapp and Gerald R. Miller (Thousand Oaks, CA: Sage, 1994), pp. 406–407; Peter A. Andersen, "Nonverbal Immediacy in Interpersonal Communication," in *Multichannel Integrations of Nonverbal Behavior*, eds. A. W. Siegman and S. Feldstein (Hillsdale, NJ: Erlbaum, 1985), pp. 1–36; Joseph N. Cappella and John O. Greene, "A Discrepancy-Arousal Explanation of Mutual Influence in Expressive Behavior for Adult-Adult and Infant-Adult Interaction," *Communication Monographs* 49 (1982): 89–114; M. L. Patterson, *Nonverbal Behavior: A Functional Perspective* (New York: Springer-Verlag, 1983).

close to you. You try to back off, but the other person continues to move in. Your first tendency will be to interpret this behavior, then evaluate it. You might interpret the behavior as a "come on." If you like this person, this will be good, but if you don't, it will be bad.

As this example shows, an important variable in the evaluation process is *reward valence,* or the degree to which you find the interaction rewarding. A conversation might be rewarding, for example, because it will lead to a positive outcome. On the other hand, valence might be negative because it entails more costs than benefits. One of the reasons sexual harassment can be such a problem is that it is a negative behavior in what may be an otherwise rewarding setting, such as a job situation.

Figure 7.5 illustrates the violation–evaluation process. The figure shows that expectations arise from one's perception of the communicator's characteristics, the state of the relationship, and the context in which the behavior occurs.

Violations accentuate the judgments made in this process. Here the reward valence of the other communicator is especially strong: Violations cause arousal, which in turn accentuate evaluation of communication with the other person and the meaning of the message. If the exchange is valued and the behavior has a positive meaning, a positive outcome will result.

Figure 7.5 includes other possibilities as well. The meaning of the behavior may be ambiguous, and one is not sure what to make of it. This theory predicts that ambiguous behavior by a valued communicator will be taken as positive, but such behavior by an unrewarding communicator will be taken as negative. Again, this effect will be accentuated in cases of a violation.

An interesting study of eye gaze shows how violations can affect judgments of behavior and communication outcomes.[31] The researchers trained four confederates to manipulate their eye behavior to effect seemingly natural violations in

an interview. About 150 students in an organizational communication course volunteered to participate in the study as part of an interviewing assignment. They took the role of an employment interviewer, and each interviewed one of the confederates. In preparation for half of the interviews, the subjects were given a high-status résumé, and the other half were given a low-status one. The first group was set up to find the interview rewarding, whereas the other would obviously find it less so. Some interviewers got a confederate who gave them normal eye contact, some got a person who gave them no eye contact, and some got a confederate who gave above-normal eye contact.

The experiment aimed to test the effects of eye-gaze violations in high- and low-reward interactions. After the interview, each subject completed a set of scales related to the credibility of the applicant, how likely they would be to hire this individual, how attracted they were to this person, and other aspects of the relationship that developed between them in the interview.

The results of this experiment showed that the failure to have eye contact with the interviewer definitely hurt the applicants' images whether they were high or low status. A higher-than-normal level of eye gaze was also found to be a violation, but it was interpreted somewhat differently between the two conditions. High-status applicants with nearly constant eye contact were judged more favorably than were low-status applicants with constant eye contact.

One of the most interesting judgments we make about the behavior of others is their honesty. Over the past twenty years or so, there has been a great deal of research on deception and deception detection. As a natural extension of their work on expectancy violations, David Buller and Judee Burgoon have pulled much of this work together in a newly developing theory of interpersonal deception.

Interpersonal Deception Theory

Buller and Burgoon see deception and its detection as part of an ongoing interaction between

---

31   Judee K. Burgoon, "Communicative Effects of Gaze Behavior: A Test of Two Contrasting Explanations," *Human Communication Research* 12 (1986): 495–524.

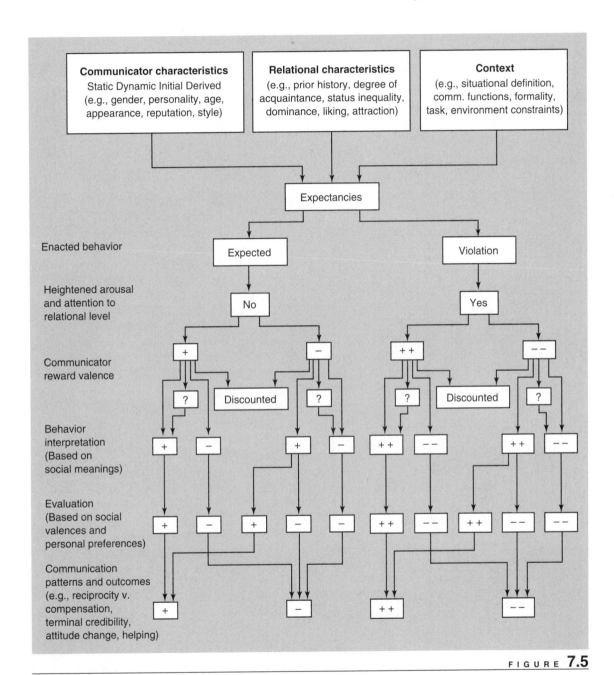

FIGURE **7.5**

Nonverbal Expectancy Violation Model

NOTE: For simplicity, communicator reward valence, behavior interpretation, and behavior evaluation valence have been dichotomized into positive and negative but should be understood to represent continua. Double pluses and minuses denote greater magnitude of effect.

From Judee K. Burgoon and Jerold L. Hale, "Nonverbal Expectancy Violations: Model Elaboration and Application," *Communication Monographs* 55 (1988): 64. Reprinted by permission of Speech Communication Association and the authors.

communicators involving a back-and-forth process.[32] Deception involves the deliberate manipulation of information, behavior, and image in order to lead another person to a false belief or conclusion. Typically, when a speaker deceives, that person engages in *strategic behavior* that distorts the truthfulness of the information or is incomplete, irrelevant, unclear, or indirect. Speakers may even disassociate themselves from the deceptive information. Listeners often detect the use of these strategies and can become suspicious that they are being deceived.

The deceiver may experience a certain amount of apprehension about being detected, and the receiver may experience a certain amount of suspicion about being deceived. These "internal" thoughts can often be seen in "outward" behavior. This being so, receivers look for signs of lying, and liars look for signs of suspicion. Over time, in this back-and-forth process, the sender may come to perceive that the deception was successful or not, and the receiver may come to see that the suspicion was warranted or not.

Deception apprehension and suspicion can come out in strategically controlled behaviors, but they are more apt to show up in nonstrategic behaviors, or the behaviors not being manipulated. This is a process called *leakage*. You might be suspicious that you are being lied to because of behaviors that the other person is not aware of, and if you are trying to deceive another person, you may experience apprehension based on the fact that the receiver could detect it through some behavior you are not controlling. For example, you might have perfect control of your voice and face, but your feet and hands give you away.

As we learned above, communicators' expectations are significant anchors with which to judge behavior. So expectations play a definite role in deception situations. When receivers' expectations are violated, their suspicions may be aroused. Likewise, when senders' expectations

are violated, their deception apprehension may also be aroused.

Many factors affect this ongoing process—for example, the degree to which the communicators can actually interact fully. This variable is called *interactivity*. Talking face to face is more interactive than talking on the telephone, which in turn is more interactive than communicating by email or letter. Interactivity can increase immediacy, or the degree of psychological closeness between the communicators. When we have high immediacy, we pay close attention to a variety of live cues. We may stand closer, look more attentively at what is going on, and generally avail ourselves of a richer set of actions. You might predict that the more access communicators have to one another's behavior, the more cognitive data they have to assess one another's intentions or suspicions, and sometimes this may be true. Yet research seems to indicate that the opposite can also happen. Immediacy and relational closeness can cause you to feel more engaged with others and less suspicious.

Also when we are relationally close, we have a degree of familiarity between us. When we are familiar with one another, we have certain biases or expectations about what we are going to see. A *truth bias* makes us less inclined to see deception. In a positive relationship, communicators more or less assume that they are telling one another the truth. Under these conditions, we will not be very suspicious about lying and may not pay close attention to behavioral deception cues. On the other hand, a *lie bias* may accentuate our suspicions and lead us to think people are lying when they may not be.

Our ability to deceive or detect deception is also affected by *conversational demand*, or the amount of stuff we have to do when we are communicating. If several things are going on at once or if the communication is complex and involves numerous goals, we cannot pay as close attention to everything as we would if the situational demands were light.

Familiarity also increases the amount of information we have about one another—both our histories and ways of behaving. So in some situ-

32   David B. Buller and Judee K. Burgoon, "Interpersonal Deception Theory," *Communication Theory* 6 (1996): 203–242; Judee K. Burgoon et al., "Interpersonal Deception: XII. Information Management Dimensions Underlying Deceptive and Truthful Messages," *Communication Monographs* 63 (1996): 50–69.

ations, familiarity may make it harder to lie and easier to detect lying.

Two other factors that affect the deception-detection process are the level of motivation to lie or to detect lying and the skill in deception and deception detection. Where motivation is high, our desire to deceive may override our apprehension about being caught. At the same time, if the receiver knows that our motivation is high, his or her suspicions will be increased. Some people are more skilled at deceiving than others because they have a larger range of behaviors they can perform. This could be counteracted, however, by the other person's ability to detect deception.

Remember, however, that communicators engage in both strategic and nonstrategic behaviors. When we lie, we typically exert a great deal of control over how we manage information, behavior, and image (all strategic behaviors); but at the same time, some of our behavior that is not being controlled (nonstrategic) is sometimes detected by others, depending on their motivation and skill. In highly interactive situations—those in which we are fully engaged with one another—we often dampen our use of nonstrategic behaviors, which in some situations could make it harder to detect the deception.

The purpose of deception also seems to enter the formula. Senders deceiving for personal gain may have a harder time hiding it than senders who deceive for more altruistic purposes. Of course, the results of deceptive behavior depend in part on how motivated the receiver is to detect it. If the receiver is suspicious and the lying matters, he or she will probably put considerable effort into detecting the lie.

◖ COMMENTARY AND CRITIQUE

The theories discussed in this chapter explain how people process information. For the most part, these are receiver-oriented theories, which is not to suggest that they are divorced from message production. Indeed, message produc-

tion and reception are two sides of the same coin and cannot be separated in actual practice, as interaction adaptation theory illustrates.

Still, these theories show us that communication depends on how messages are understood and judged. All these theories tell us in one form or another what message receivers do and how they do it. As a group, the theories address three interrelated accomplishments—interpreting, organizing, and judging.

The first of these accomplishments is interpretation. We assign meaning to concepts, we try to figure out intentions, and we attribute causes. The second accomplishment is organization, in which new information is integrated into a system of existing beliefs and attitudes. Finally, people constantly make judgments on the basis of information. We sometimes evaluate arguments carefully, and sometimes we attend to less central aspects of the message or source. As part of the judgment process, we evaluate nonverbal behaviors, argument claims, and attitude statements.

Although the theories in this chapter are organized around these three elements of information processing, each tells us something about all three accomplishments outlined above. Indeed, interpretation, organization, and judgment are basically different aspects of the same process, and they definitely relate to one another.

The theories in this chapter share a number of ideas about how people process information. Four general processes are suggested by the theories in this chapter. The first is *assigning meaning.* Osgood's theory of meaning shows us how individual concepts are interpreted on the basis of evaluation, potency, and activity. Relevance theory states that relevance is the key to interpreting intentions, and attribution theory addresses the causal nature of meaning. Even the nonverbal expectancy violations model shows that interpretation is a vital part of how nonverbal behaviors are judged.

Another mechanism that permits information processing is *reasoning,* or inference making. Reasoning enters into interpretation, organization, and judgment in a variety of ways. Several theories in this chapter address this concern. For example, the theory of reasoned action shows how communicators weigh information, and attribution theory also reveals the reasoning process that people use to assess causes.

Several of the theories in this chapter also address the process of *comparing ideas.* This is the central idea of social judgment theory, and a number of other theories also provide insights into this process. Consistency theory and information-integration theory are examples. Consistency theories show us how new information is compared with the other elements of cognition and how inconsistency is handled. Information-integration theory shows us that various pieces of information are weighed in terms of their overall effects within the cognitive system.

Finally, several of these theories deal with processes of *change.* Information-integration theory shows how change occurs as a result of newly integrated information. Consistency theory shows how imbalance leads to change. Social judgment theory shows how change results from the perception of attitude statements. Elaboration likelihood theory shows the relative effects of central and peripheral processing on attitude change.

If we take a cognitive approach to persuasion, however, change becomes more complex and interesting. Many traditional attitude theories are somewhat linear, suggesting that certain source, message, situation, and receiver variables in combination will lead to change. David Roskos-Ewoldsen challenges this view.[33] He takes seriously the proposition that attitudes are embedded in a highly connected and complex cognitive system. As such they may not be readily accessible to a person at every moment. He criticizes traditional attitude theory for assuming that messages act directly on attitudes. Instead, he believes that memory plays an important role and that persuasion can function indirectly by making attitudes more accessible, which in turn will have a circular effect on the cognitive system, leading to eventual change.

Virtually all theories in the chapter follow the rational person model to some extent. As a group these theories share the idea that people think through problems and situations rationally and

objectively. There are exceptions, of course. For example, some adherents to attribution theory have made the point that people are often inaccurate and irrational in their judgments. Social judgment theory indicates that people often distort information, and elaboration likelihood theory says that people weigh evidence and evaluate arguments only part of the time. Virtually all theorists in this chapter, however, admit to the possibility of rational decision making, and few would deny that people try to be rational and objective.

Actually, there has been quite a bit of research and theory-making in communication and psychology on emotional responses to messages. Cognitive theorists are realizing increasingly that emotion is an important part of the communication process. One of the most useful theories in this field is *appraisal theory,* which suggests that when receivers perceive change in their environment, they evaluate it, which can lead to a positive or negative emotional response.[34]

The rational person model makes a clear assumption about the nature of human thought. Humans are conceived as independent, rational, choice-making beings. This view is deeply embedded in Western philosophy and is part of many Western cultural views. Many other cultures, however, would find this description of people strange. Like all theory, then, these approaches are definitely products of a particular worldview.[35]

This is a worldview that explains human experience in terms of individual cognition. It is a view that assumes a universal cognitive mechanism behind most action. The point of the experiments, measurements, hypotheses, and theories of message processing is to discover these underlying mechanisms. Many theories in this chapter exemplify this type of thinking directly; others

33   Roskos-Ewoldsen, "Attitude Accessibility."
34   For a summary of this work, see James Price Dillard, Terry A. Kinney, and Michael G. Cruz, "Influence, Appraisals, and Emotions in Close Relationships," *Communication Monographs* 63 (1996): 105–131.
35   John W. Lannamann, "Deconstructing the Person and Changing the Subject of Interpersonal Studies," *Communication Theory* 2 (1992): 139–148; "Interpersonal Communication: Research as Ideological Practice," *Communication Theory* 1 (1991): 179–203.

are more specific in explaining certain types of behaviors.

Most of these theories posit certain principles, operations, or mechanisms that drive human thought and action. Other theories such as expectancy violations and attribution address particular types of thought and action. Given their overall aim, then, the chief strengths of all these theories are their parsimony and intuitive appeal. Most explain a great deal with only a few key variables. Osgood narrows all of connotative meaning down to three dimensions. Fishbein and Ajzen show how a vast array of thought and behavior can be explained by a simple integrative mechanism. Festinger and even Rokeach reduce cognitive organization to a single principle of consistency. And so it goes. These theories are appealing because they truly help us understand rather esoteric processes normally baffling to the average person. One of the reasons cognitive explanations are so popular is the common "aha" response they produce.

Cognitive consistency theories are a good example of this strength. These theories have had a major impact on our thinking about attitude and attitude change. A mainstay of social psychology for many years, cognitive consistency is appealing because of its parsimony and heuristic value. For a twenty-year period, it stimulated a great deal of research. The popularity of consistency theory is understandable, given the goal of this field to discover a few important variables that would predict social behavior. Consistency theories do just that. They isolate certain elements of cognition and show how manipulations among these variables can predict a person's feelings, thoughts, or actions. They also appeal to the scientist's sense of logic, providing an explanation for behavior that makes intuitive sense. At one time consistency theories were so well accepted that debates centered not on whether people respond to dissonance but on ways to improve the precision of predictions based on these theories.

At the same time, however, there are serious hazards in this kind of theorizing. Two concerns are relevant here. First, there is the nagging question of universality: Are cognitive processes really universal, and if not, how wide a scope do

these processes cover? Osgood's three "universal" dimensions of meaning offer a good example of the problem. Although many cognitive researchers admit the usefulness of semantic differential technique for measuring connotative meaning, they question the view that the factors of meaning—evaluation, potency, and activity— are invariant and universal across situations, concepts, and cultures. Although these factors have shown up in an amazingly diverse set of studies, they do not always appear; to suggest that they are universal is an overgeneralization. What appears as universal may in fact not be so.

Another problem in trying to discover cognitive universals is the mistaken idea that if one's hypothesized mechanism fits the data, it alone can explain the data, when any number of hypothesized mechanisms may explain what is going on. How, then, do we choose from among competing explanations? This is a difficult problem. The theory of cognitive dissonance, as an example, has been criticized for precisely this problem.[36]

The second concern related to the reduction of complex processes to a parsimonious set of predictors is oversimplification. The elaboration likelihood model (ELM), for example, has been criticized for leaving out important variables. Its predictions have not always been verified by research, and some believe that a more elaborate theory is necessary to explain the discrepancy.[37] Some researchers have reached a similar conclusion about expectancy-value theory.[38]

Michael Slater has put forth an interesting argument that casts light on ELM, social judgment

36 Natalia P. Chapanis and Alphonse Chapanis, "Cognitive Dissonance: Five Years Later," *Psychological Bulletin* 61 (1964): 21.

37 For a set of detailed critiques of elaboration likelihood theory, see Mark A. Hamilton, John E. Hunter, and Franklin J. Boster, "The Elaboration Likelihood Model as a Theory of Attitude Formation: A Mathematical Analysis," *Communication Theory* 8 (1993): 50–64; Paul Mongeau and James B. Stiff, "Specifying Causal Relationships in the Elaboration Likelihood Model," *Communication Theory* 8 (1993): 65–72; Mike Allen and Rodney Reynolds, "The Elaboration Likelihood Model and the Sleeper Effect: An Assessment of Attitude Change over Time," *Communication Theory* 8 (1993): 73–82.

38 Michael Burgoon, Deborah A. Newton, and Thomas S. Birk, "A Theory of Belief, Attitude, Intention, and Behavior Extended to the Domain of Corrective Advertising," in *Communication Yearbook 15*, ed. Stanley A. Deetz (Newbury Park, CA: Sage, 1992), pp. 263–286.

theory, and other approaches that use involvement as a central concept.[39] He argues that receiver involvement depends largely on receiver goals, and theories to date have not taken this complicating factor into account. Slater suggests that theories of persuasion need to be expanded to include such receiver goals as entertainment, information gain, surveillance, self-assessment, and value defense or reinforcement. He maintains that receivers' information processing will be different depending upon their goals.

Of course, virtually all the theories in this chapter could be criticized for oversimplification. Most, for example, suggest that information is integrated or organized in a relatively consistent, rational fashion when we all know from our own experience that information processing is often problematic.

This point is the theme of Austin Babrow's emerging theory of *problematic integration,* which deals with the ways communication creates inconsistent, contradictory cognitions.[40] In opposition to consistency theory, which says that information is used to reduce inconsistency, Babrow shows how it often increases it. Ironically, we also use communication to cope with these sorts of problems, and the more we do so, the more difficult integration can become. Communication can make what we want inconsistent with what we expect, it can cause ambiguity, it can bring about ambivalence, and it can even make what we want or expect impossible. And reducing or eliminating these discrepancies is rarely easy and often impossible.

Cognitive processes do not present themselves in self-defined form. Despite the scientific leanings of many researchers, cognitive processes do not lie in wait of discovery, but must be defined by the theorist. Inquiry into information processing involves inferring underlying processes from observed behavior and naming the variables believed to be operating. As we have seen in the history of the social sciences, there is no end to the number of constructs that can be created and named. Theoretical definitions are abstract and partial, which always leaves room for additional constructing, naming, and defin-

ing. This state of affairs leads to the natural question of whether real structures of mind can ever be "discovered."[41]

In this chapter we have encountered a wide variety of constructs, which have been given a host of interesting names: dissonance, elaboration, attitude, expectancy, relevance, attribution, ego involvement, and more. The mere fact that these concepts vie for our attention as competing explanations of thought and action demonstrates the challenge of explaining cognition and action.

There are a variety of responses to this state of affairs. One is competition: Which theory will win? This response is problematic because of the impossibility of falsifying all but one explanation.[42] Another response is integration: How can the theories be combined? This response is appealing because it recognizes the utility of all theories, but it is a pretext, resulting in a loss of parsimony and failure to discover cognitive universals. A third response is flexibility: How can each theory be used appropriately for certain purposes without denying the utility of the others? This approach has the benefit of enabling us to see more than could be viewed from the confines of a single theory, but it can only be done after abandoning the attempt to find a parsimonious, central mechanism of thought and action.

The creation and definition of constructs can lead to a self-fulfilling prophecy on the part of the theorist. Once a set of constructs is found to fit, even if only partially, there is a strong tendency to see the same things no matter where you look. Osgood always "saw" evaluation, potency, and activity in his factor-analysis results.

---

39   Michael D. Slater, "Persuasion Processes Across Receiver Goals and Message Genres," *Communication Theory* 7 (1997): 125–148.

40   Austin Babrow, "Communication and Problematic Integration: Understanding Diverging Probability and Value, Ambiguity, Ambivalence, and Impossibility," *Communication Theory* 2 (1992): 95–130.

41   This point is explored in some detail by Kenneth J. Gergen and Gün R. Semin, "Everyday Understanding in Science and Daily Life," in *Everyday Understanding: Social and Scientific Implications,* eds. Gün R. Semin and Kenneth J. Gergen (London: Sage, 1990), pp. 1–18.

42   See, for example, Peter A. Andersen, Laura K. Guerrero, David Buller, and Peter F. Jorgensen, "An Empirical Comparison of Three Theories of Nonverbal Immediacy Exchange," *Human Communication Research* 24 (1998): 501–535.

Social judgment theory is a good example of how researcher biases affect the interpretation of results. In many of their experiments, researchers compared individuals who were highly ego-involved with people less involved and concluded that the differences were due to their level of involvement. Actually, these groups of people could have been different for other reasons as well, which would invalidate the interpretation offered by social judgment theory.[43]

Like the interpretation of any research results, social judgment theorists had to make certain assumptions in their interpretations. The theory assumes, for example, that there is a sequential, causal mechanism whereby judgment as a cognitive activity precedes attitude change, and social judgment research was unable to prove this assumption.

Looked at objectively, the results of many experiments on cognitive processes are less clear than the author believes them to be. For instance, most of the negative criticism of information-integration theory relates to the validity of measurement. Although the idea that attitudes consist of accumulated and weighted beliefs is generally accepted, much doubt exists that one can measure the overall accumulated weight and value of a belief system with any degree of validity. In the natural setting, a researcher would first have to isolate beliefs contributing to an attitude, measure them accurately, and factor out the influence of other elements of the system. Because this process is difficult or impossible to do, most research in this tradition is artificial, hypothetical, and controlled. This problem thus casts doubt on the external validity of the claims. A related problem is that disagreement exists about the way one accumulates information to form an attitude. The research evidence is equivocal on this point and casts doubt on the validity of the approach.[44] Research on ELM has also been criticized for lack of validity.[45]

The basic standard for any predictive theory is that it should be stated in such a way that contra-

dictory evidence could prove the theory wrong in its predictions. In other words, the theory must be falsifiable. A chief complaint about dissonance theory, for example, is that it can be used to explain various, contradictory results and cannot be proved wrong, which creates a situation wherein the dissonance theorist wins no matter how an experiment comes out. If attitude change results from the manipulations, one can argue that the change was caused by dissonance; if attitude change does not occur, one can say that dissonance did not exist.

Furthermore, dissonance is such a general concept that it can take any number of forms. Thus, the experimenter can claim that a particular result was caused by one kind of dissonance but that an entirely different result was produced by another kind of dissonance. This circular reasoning results because dissonance researchers do not measure dissonance per se but infer dissonance from behavior. Indeed, there is some question about whether dissonance is directly observable at all. This is the case with virtually all cognitive processes.

All these objections to theories of message processing are "easy punches." They belie the intelligence and hard work that have gone into the development of these theories. In Chapter 2 we noted that no theory has a direct line to truth. Theories are based on guess, inference, and creativity, and that is the best we can do. Whether or not you believe in universal processes of mind, the theories presented in this chapter and others like them provide insights that are intriguing and useful in our attempt to understand communication.

43   This point is made by O'Keefe, *Persuasion*. For a thorough critique of social judgment theory, see Martin and Tesser, *Construction*.
44   For a review of the issues in this dispute, see Mary John Smith, *Persuasion and Human Action: A Review and Critique of Social Influence Theories* (Belmont, CA: Wadsworth, 1982), pp. 245–248; and O'Keefe, *Persuasion*, pp. 55–59.
45   Hamilton, Hunter, and Boster, "The Elaboration Likelihood Model."

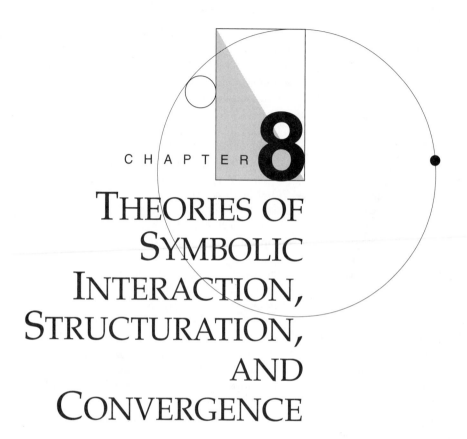

THEORIES OF SYMBOLIC INTERACTION, STRUCTURATION, AND CONVERGENCE

The theories discussed in Chapters 8 and 9 take quite a turn from the cognitive theories discussed in the previous two chapters. For the scholars in the interactional tradition, communication and meaning are unabashedly social, and cognitive explanations are seen as secondary at best.[1] For these theorists, meaning is created and sustained by interaction in the social group. Interaction establishes, maintains, and changes certain conventions—roles, norms, rules, and meanings—within a social group or culture, and these conventions in turn define the reality of the culture itself. Language assumes special importance in these theories, as language is the container within which reality resides.

We discuss this group of theories in two chapters. This chapter covers the foundational literature in symbolic interactionism and related ideas on structuration and convergence. Chapter 9 examines theories of the social construction of reality, rules, and culture.

● SYMBOLIC INTERACTIONISM

Symbolic interactionism is a movement located primarily in sociology characterized by certain ideas about communication and society. It is

---

1   For an overview of social approaches, see Wendy Leeds-Hurwitz, ed., *Social Approaches to Communication* (New York: Guilford, 1995). See also the forum on social approaches in *Communication Theory*, vol. 2 (May 1992): 131–177; and vol. 2 (November 1992): 329–356.

based on the idea that social structures and meanings are created and maintained in social interaction. Barbara Ballis Lal summarizes the premises of this movement:[2]

- People make decisions and act in accordance with their subjective understandings of the situations in which they find themselves.
- Social life consists of interaction processes rather than structures and is therefore constantly changing.
- People understand their experience through the meanings found in the symbols of their primary groups, and language is an essential part of social life.
- The world is made up of social objects that are named and have socially determined meanings.
- People's actions are based on their interpretations, in which the relevant objects and actions in the situation are taken into account and defined.
- One's self is a significant object and like all social objects is defined through social interaction with others.

Early interactionism was divided into two schools.[3] The Chicago School, led primarily by Herbert Blumer, continued the work of George Herbert Mead. Blumer believed above all that the study of humans could not be conducted in the same manner as the study of things. Researchers should try to empathize with the subject, enter his or her experience, and attempt to understand the value of each person. Blumer and his followers avoided quantitative and scientific approaches and stressed life histories, autobiographies, case studies, diaries, letters, and nondirective interviews. Blumer particularly emphasized the importance of participant observation in the study of communication. Further, the Chicago tradition saw people as creative, innovative, and free to define each situation in unpredictable ways. Self and society were viewed as process, not structure; to freeze the process would be to lose the essence of social relationships.

The second tradition, the Iowa School, took a more scientific approach. Manford Kuhn and Carl Couch, its leaders, believed that interactionist concepts could be operationalized. Although Kuhn accepted the basic tenets of symbolic interactionism, he argued that objective methods are more fruitful than the "soft" methods employed by Blumer. As we will see later in the chapter, Kuhn was responsible for a well-known measurement technique called the Twenty Statements Test.[4]

The basic ideas of these early schools of interaction live on today and have been adopted by many social scientists. Yet symbolic interactionism has changed significantly since its early years, as Gary Fine suggests.[5] It has expanded by adopting insights from other theoretical areas and has increasingly contributed to the work of other areas of social science.

Today, according to Fine, symbolic interactionism has incorporated the study of how groups coordinate their actions, how emotions are understood and controlled, how reality is constructed, how self is created, how large social structures get established, and how public policy can be influenced.

In this chapter we concentrate on classical symbolic interactionism, the basic ideas of the movement, and the theoretical extensions most recognized in the communication field.

The Chicago School

George Herbert Mead is usually viewed as the primary originator of the movement, and his work certainly forms the core of the Chicago

---

2   Barbara Ballis Lal, "Symbolic Interaction Theories," *American Behavioral Scientist* 38 (1995): 421–441. See also Joel M. Charon, *Symbolic Interactionism: An Introduction, an Interpretation, an Integration* (Englewood Cliffs, NJ: Prentice-Hall, 1992); Larry T. Reynolds, Interactionism: Exposition and Critique (Dix Hills, NY: General Hall, 1990); Jerome G. Manis and Bernard N. Meltzer, eds., *Symbolic Interaction* (Boston: Allyn & Bacon, 1978). For continuing coverage of SI, see the ongoing editions of the journal *Studies in Symbolic Interaction*.
3   Bernard N. Meltzer and John W. Petras, "The Chicago and Iowa Schools of Symbolic Interactionism," in *Human Nature and Collective Behavior*, ed. T. Shibutani (Englewood Cliffs, NJ: Prentice-Hall, 1970).
4   Meltzer and Petras, "Chicago and Iowa Schools."
5   Gary Alan Fine, "The Sad Demise, Mysterious Disappearance, and Glorious Triumph of Symbolic Interactionism," *Annual Review of Sociology* 19 (1993): 61–87.

School.[6] Herbert Blumer, Mead's foremost apostle, invented the term *symbolic interactionism,* an expression Mead himself never used. Blumer refers to this label as "a somewhat barbaric neologism that I coined in an offhand way. . . . The term somehow caught on."[7]

The three cardinal concepts in Mead's theory, captured in the title of his best-known work, are society, self, and mind. These categories are different aspects of the same general process, the *social act.* The social act is an umbrella concept under which nearly all other psychological and social processes fall. The act is a complete unit of conduct that cannot be analyzed into specific subparts. An act may be short and simple, such as tying a shoe, or it may be long and complicated, like the fulfillment of a life plan. Acts relate to one another and are built up throughout a lifetime. Acts begin with an impulse; they involve perception and assignment of meaning, mental rehearsal, weighing of alternatives, and consummation.

In its most basic form, a social act involves a three-part relationship: an initial gesture from one individual, a response to that gesture by another, and a result. The result is the communicators' meaning for the act. Meaning does not reside solely in any one of these things but in the triadic relationship of all three.[8]

In a holdup, for example, the robber indicates to the victim what is intended. The victim responds by giving money or belongings, and in the initial gesture and response, the defined result (a holdup) has occurred. Even individual acts, such as a solitary walk, are interactional because they are based on gestures and responses that occurred many times in the past and continue in the mind of the individual. One never takes a walk by oneself without relying on meanings and actions learned in social interaction with others.

The *joint action* of a group of people, such as marriage, trade, war, or church worship, consists of an *interlinkage* of smaller interactions. Blumer notes that in an advanced society the largest portion of group action consists of highly recurrent, stable patterns that possess common and estab-

lished meanings for their participants. Because of the frequency of such patterns and the stability of their meanings, scholars have tended to treat them as structures, forgetting their origins in interaction. Blumer warns us not to forget that new situations present problems requiring adjustment and redefinition. In a recent treatment, Donald Ellis writes, "that macrotopics of sociology (e.g., ethnicity) are never actually seen but exist in and through the activities of individuals in microsituations."[9]

Even in highly repetitious group patterns, nothing is permanent. Each case must begin anew with individual action. No matter how solid a group action appears to be, it is still rooted in individual human choices: "It is the social process in group life that creates and upholds the rules, not the rules that create and uphold group life."[10]

Interlinkages may be pervasive, extended, and connected through complicated networks. Distant actors may be interlinked ultimately in diverse ways, but contrary to popular thinking, "a network or an institution does not function automatically because of some inner dynamics or system requirements: it functions because people at different points do something, and what they do is a result of how they define the situation in which they are called on to act."[11]

---

6   Mead's primary work in symbolic interactionism is *Mind, Self, and Society* (Chicago: University of Chicago Press, 1934). For a general discussion of the history, influence, and methods of the Chicago School, see Jesse G. Delia, "Communication Research: A History," in *Handbook of Communication Science,* eds. C. R. Berger and S. H. Chaffee (Newbury Park, CA: Sage, 1987), pp. 30–37. For outstanding secondary sources on Mead and the Chicago School, see Everett M. Rogers, *A History of Communication Study: A Biographical Approach* (New York: Free Press, 1994), pp. 137–202; Bernard N. Meltzer, "Mead's Social Psychology," in *Symbolic Interaction,* eds. J. G. Manis and B. N. Meltzer (Boston: Allyn & Bacon, 1972), pp. 4–22; Charles Morris, "George H. Mead as Social Psychologist and Social Philosopher" (Introduction), in *Mind, Self, and Society;* and C. David Johnson and J. Stephen Picou, "The Foundations of Symbolic Interactionism Reconsidered," in *Micro-Sociological Theory: Perspectives on Sociological Theory,* vol. 2, eds. H. J. Helle and S. N. Eisenstadt (Beverly Hills, CA: Sage, 1985), pp. 54–70.
7   Herbert Blumer, *Symbolic Interactionism: Perspective and Method* (Englewood Cliffs: NJ: Prentice-Hall, 1969), p. 1.
8   Wayne Woodward, "Triadic Communication as Transactional Participation," *Critical Studies in Mass Communication* 13 (1996): 155–174.
9   Donald G. Ellis, *Crafting Society: Ethnicity, Class, and Communication Theory* (Mahwah, NJ: Erlbaum, 1999), p. xii.
10   Blumer, *Symbolic Interactionism,* p. 19.
11   Blumer, *Symbolic Interactionism,* p. 19.

With this idea of social acts in mind, then, let us look more closely at the first facet of Meadian analysis—society.

Society, or group life, consists of the cooperative behaviors of society's members. Human cooperation requires that we understand others' intentions, which also entails figuring out what you and others will do in the future. Thus, cooperation consists of "reading" other people's actions and intentions and responding in an appropriate way.

Meaning is an important outcome of communication. Your meanings are the result of interaction with others. So, for example, although you may never have heard of a "toilet telephone," prison inmates know it well; they have learned that they can communicate by listening to voices traveling through the sewer pipes in the prison.

We use meanings to interpret the happenings around us. Interpretation is like an internal conversation: "The actor selects, checks, suspends, regroups, and transforms the meanings in light of the situation in which he is placed and the direction of his actions."[12] Clearly, we could not communicate without sharing the meaning of the symbols we use. Mead calls a gesture with shared meaning a *significant symbol.* Society is made possible by significant symbols. Because of the ability to vocalize symbols, we literally can hear ourselves and thus can respond to the self as others respond to us. We can imagine what it is like to receive our own messages, and we can empathize with the listener and take the listener's role, mentally completing the other's response. Society, then, consists of a network of social interactions in which participants assign meaning to their own and others' actions by the use of symbols.[13] Even the various institutions of society are built up by the interactions of people involved in those institutions.

Consider the court system in the United States as an example. The courts are nothing more than the interactions among judges, juries, attorneys, witnesses, clerks, reporters, and others who use language to interact with one another. *Court* has no meaning apart from the interpretations of the actions of those involved in it. The same can be said for school, church, government, industry, and any other segment of society. This interplay between responding to others and responding to self is an important concept in Mead's theory, and it provides a good transition to his second concept—the *self.*[14]

You have a self because you can respond to yourself as an object. You sometimes react favorably to yourself and feel pride, happiness, and encouragement. You sometimes become angry or disgusted with yourself. The primary way you come to see yourself as others see you is through *role taking* or assuming the perspective of others, and this is what leads you to have a self-concept.

Another term for self-concept is *generalized other,* a kind of composite perspective from which you see yourself. The generalized other is your overall perception of the way others see you. You have learned this self-picture from years of symbolic interaction with other people in your life. *Significant others,* the people closest to you, are especially important because their reactions have been very influential in your life.

Consider, for example, the self-image of adolescents. As a result of their interactions with significant others such as parents, siblings, and peers, teenagers come to view themselves as they think others have viewed them. They come to take on the persona that has been reflected to them in their many interactions with other people. As they behave in ways that affirm this image, it is strengthened, and others respond accordingly in a cyclical fashion. So, for example, if a young person feels socially inept, he or she may withdraw, further reinforcing the image of being inadequate.

The self has two facets, each serving an essential function. The *I* is the impulsive, unorganized, undirected, unpredictable part of you. The *me* is

12   Blumer, *Symbolic Interactionism,* p. 5.
13   For a thoughtful discussion of the social nature of symbols, see Wendy Leeds-Hurwitz, "A Social Account of Symbols," in *Beyond the Symbol Model: Reflections on the Representational Nature of Language,* ed. John Stewart (Albany: SUNY Press, 1996), pp. 257–278.
14   For a probing discussion of self within this tradition, see Norbert Wiley, *The Semiotic Self* (Chicago: University of Chicago Press, 1994).

the generalized other, made up of the organized and consistent patterns shared with others. Every act begins with an impulse from the *I* and quickly becomes controlled by the *me*. The *I* is the driving force in action, whereas the *me* provides direction and guidance. Mead used the concept of *me* to explain your socially acceptable and adaptive behavior and the *I* to explain your creative, unpredictable impulses.

For example, many people will deliberately change their life's situation in order to alter their own self-concept. Here, the *I* moves the person to change in ways that the *me* would not permit. Such a change might have occurred, for example, when you went to college. Many high school students decide that they will use college to establish a new *me* by associating with a new group of significant others and by establishing a new generalized other. This is what people mean when they say that they got a new start.

Your ability to use significant symbols to respond to yourself makes thinking possible. Thinking is Mead's third concept, which he calls *mind*. The mind is not a thing, but a process. It is nothing more than interacting with yourself. This ability, which develops along with the self, is crucial to human life, for it is part of every act. *Minding* involves hesitating (postponing overt action) while you interpret the situation. Here you think through the situation and plan future actions. You imagine various outcomes and select and test possible alternatives.

People possess significant symbols that allow them to name objects. You always define an object in terms of how you might act toward it. A seascape is a seascape when you value looking at it. A glass of lemonade is a drink when you conceive of drinking it (or not drinking it). Objects become the objects they are through the individual's symbolic minding process; when the individual envisions new or different actions toward an object, the object is changed.

For Blumer, objects are of three types—physical (things), social (people), and abstract (ideas). People define objects differently, depending on how they act toward those objects. A police officer may mean one thing to the residents of an inner-city ghetto and something else to the inhabitants of a posh residential area; the different interactions among the residents of these two vastly different communities will determine different meanings.

A fascinating study of marijuana use by Howard Becker illustrates the concept of social object very well.[15] Becker found that users learn at least three things through interaction with other users. The first is to smoke the drug properly. Virtually everyone Becker talked to said that they had trouble getting high at first until others showed them how to do it. Second, smokers must learn to define the sensation produced by the drug as a "high." In other words, the individual learns to discriminate the effects of marijuana and to associate these with smoking. Becker claims that this association does not happen automatically and must be learned through social interaction with other users. In fact, some experienced users reported that novices were absolutely stoned and didn't know it until they were taught to identify the feeling. Finally, users must learn to define the effects as pleasant and desirable. Again, this is not automatic; many beginners do not find the effects pleasant at all until they are told that they should consider them so.

Here, we see that marijuana is a social object. Its meanings are created in the process of interaction. How people think about the drug (mind) is determined by those meanings, and the assumptions of the group (society) are also a product of interaction. Although Becker does not report information about self-concept specifically, it is easy to see that part of the self may also be defined in terms of interactions in the marijuana-smoking community.

The Iowa School

Manford Kuhn and his students, although maintaining basic interactionist principles, take two new steps not previously seen in the old-line

---

15   Howard Becker, "Becoming a Marihuana User," *American Journal of Sociology* 59 (1953): 235–242.

theory. The first is to make the concept of self more concrete; the second, which makes the first possible, is the use of quantitative research. In this latter area, the Iowa and Chicago schools part company. Blumer strongly criticizes the trend in the behavioral sciences to operationalize; Kuhn makes a point to do just that! As a result Kuhn's work moves more toward microscopic analysis than does the traditional Chicago approach.[16]

Kuhn's theoretical premises are consistent with Mead's thought. Kuhn conceives of the basis of all action as symbolic interaction. The child is socialized through interaction with others in the society into which he or she is born. The person has meaning for and thereby deals with objects in the environment through social interaction. To Kuhn, the naming of an object is important, for naming is a way of conveying the object's meaning. Kuhn agrees with his Chicago colleagues that the individual is not a passive reactor but an active planner. He reinforces the view that individuals undertake self-conversations as part of the process of acting. Kuhn also stresses the importance of language in thinking and communicating.

Like Mead and Blumer, Kuhn discusses the importance of objects in the actor's world. The *object* can be any aspect of the person's reality: a thing, a quality, an event, or a state of affairs. The only requirement for something to become an object is that the person name it, represent it symbolically. Reality for people is the totality of their social objects, which are always socially defined.

A second concept important to Kuhn is the *plan of action,* a person's total behavior pattern toward a given object. *Attitudes,* or verbal statements that indicate the values toward which action will be directed, guide the plan. Because attitudes are verbal statements, they too can be observed and measured. Going to college in-

volves a plan of action, actually a host of plans, guided by a set of attitudes about what you want to get out of college. You might be guided, for example, by positive attitudes toward money, career, and personal success.

A third concept important to Kuhn is the *orientational other,* someone who has been particularly influential in a person's life. This term is essentially synonymous with *significant other,* as used by Mead. These individuals possess four qualities. First, they are people to whom the individual is emotionally and psychologically committed. Second, they are the ones who provide the person with general vocabulary, central concepts, and categories. Third, they provide the individual with the basic distinction between self and others, including one's perceived role differentiation. Fourth, the orientational others' communications continually sustain the individual's self-concept. Orientational others may be in the present or past; they may be present or absent. The important idea behind the concept is that the individual comes to see the world through interaction with particular others who have touched one's life in important ways.

Finally, we come to Kuhn's most important concept—the *self.* Kuhn's theory and method revolve around self, and it is in this area that Kuhn most dramatically extends symbolic interactionist thinking. The self-conception, the individual's plans of action toward the self, consists of one's identities, interests and aversions, goals, ideologies, and self-evaluations. Such self-conceptions are anchoring attitudes, for they act as one's most common frame of reference for judging other objects. All subsequent plans of action stem primarily from the self-concept.

Kuhn is responsible for a technique known as the *Twenty Statements Self-Attitudes Test* (TST) for measuring various aspects of the self. If you were to take the TST, you would be confronted with twenty blank spaces preceded by the following simple instructions:

---

16   Like many of the interactionists, Kuhn never published a truly unified work. The closest may be C. A. Hickman and Manford Kuhn, *Individuals, Groups, and Economic Behavior* (New York: Holt, Rinehart & Winston, 1956). See also Charles Tucker, "Some Methodological Problems of Kuhn's Self Theory," *Sociological Quarterly* 7 (1966): 345–358.

There are twenty numbered blanks on the page below. Please write twenty answers to the simple question, "Who am I?" in the blanks. Just give twenty different answers to this question. Answer as if you were giving the answers to yourself, not to somebody else. Write the answers in the order that they occur to you. Don't worry about logic or "importance." Go along fairly fast, for time is limited.[17]

There are a number of ways to analyze the responses from this test, each tapping a different aspect of the self. Two of these are the ordering variable and the locus variable. The *ordering variable* is the relative salience of identifications the individual possesses. It is observable in the order of statements listed on the form. For example, if the person lists "Baptist" a great deal higher than "father," the researcher may conclude that the person identifies more readily with religious affiliation than with family affiliation. The *locus variable* is the extent to which the subject in a general way tends to identify with consensual groupings such as "American" rather than idiosyncratic, subjective qualities such as "strong."

In scoring the self-attitude test, you can place statements in one of two categories. A statement is *consensual* if it consists of a discrete group or class identification, such as student, woman, husband, Baptist, from Chicago, premed student, daughter, oldest child, engineering student. Other statements are not descriptions of commonly agreed-on categories. Examples of *subconsensual* responses are happy, bored, pretty, good student, too heavy, good wife, interesting. The number of statements in the consensual group is the individual's locus score.

Symbolic interactionism has certainly been an influential force in social theories of communication. We turn now to several related theories.

Extending Interactionism: Erving Goffman

Erving Goffman is one of the best-known sociologists of the twentieth century.[18] He is well known for using a theatrical metaphor, in which the ordinary setting is a stage and people are actors who use performances to make an impression on the audience.

Goffman begins with the assumption that the person must somehow make sense of events en-

countered in everyday life.[19] Your interpretation of a situation is your *definition of the situation*. In any typical situation, people tend to ask the mental question, What is going on here? Their answer constitutes a definition of the situation. Often the first definition is not adequate and a rereading may be necessary, as in the case of a practical joke, a mistake, or a misunderstanding. Rereading is important because we are often deceptive with one another.

One's definition of a situation can be divided into strips and frames. A *strip* is a sequence of activity such as opening the refrigerator door, removing the milk, pouring it into a glass, drinking it, and putting the glass into the dishwasher. A *frame* is a basic organizational pattern used to define the strip. The strip of activities listed above, for example, would probably be framed as "getting a drink."

Frame analysis thus consists of examining the ways experience is organized for the individual. The frame allows the person to identify and understand otherwise meaningless events, giving meaning to the ongoing activities of life. A natural framework is an unguided event of nature with which the individual must cope such as a windstorm. A social framework, on the other hand, is seen as controllable, guided by some intelligence, such as planning a meal. These two types of frameworks relate to each other because social beings act on and are in turn influenced by the natural order.

Frameworks, then, are the models we use to understand our experience, the ways we see things as fitting together into some coherent

---

17 Tucker, "Some Methodological Problems," p. 308.
18 See the Selected Bibliography for a listing of Goffman's works.
19 Erving Goffman, *Frame Analysis: An Essay on the Organization of Experience* (Cambridge, MA: Harvard University Press, 1974). See also Jef Verhoeven, "Goffman's Frame Analysis and Modern Micro-Sociological Paradigms," in *Micro-Sociological Theory: Perspectives on Sociological Theory*, vol. 2, eds. H. J. Helle and S. N. Eisenstadt (Beverly Hills, CA: Sage, 1985), pp. 71–100; Stuart J. Sigman, *A Perspective on Social Communication* (Lexington, MA: Lexington, 1987), pp. 41–56; Spencer Cahill, "Erving Goffman," in *Symbolic Interactionism: An Introduction, an Interpretation, an Integration*, ed. Joel M. Charon (Englewood Cliffs, NJ: Prentice-Hall, 1992), pp. 185–200.

whole. A *primary framework* is a basic organizational unit such as conversing, eating, and dressing, but primary frames can be transformed or altered into *secondary frameworks*. Here the basic organizational principles of a primary frame are used to meet different ends. A game, for example, is a secondary framework modeled after the primary framework of a fight or competition. A large portion of our frameworks are not primary at all, though they are modeled after primary ones. Examples include plays, deceptions, experiments, and other fabrications. Ordinary life is filled with secondary frameworks.

Communication activities, like all activities, are viewed in the context of frame analysis. A *face engagement*, or *encounter*, occurs when people interact with one another in a focused way.[20] In a face engagement, you have a single focus of attention and a perceived mutual activity. In unfocused interaction in a public place, you acknowledge the presence of another person without paying much attention. This happens, for example, when you are standing in line at a bus stop. In such an unfocused situation, you may be accessible for an encounter that could begin when another passenger strikes up a conversation. Once an engagement begins, a mutual contract exists to continue the engagement to some kind of termination. Face engagements are both verbal and nonverbal, and the cues exhibited are important in signifying the nature of the relationship as well as a mutual definition of the situation.

People in face engagements take turns presenting dramas to one another. Storytelling, or recounting past events, impresses the listener by dramatic portrayal:

I am suggesting that often what talkers undertake to do is not to provide information to a recipient but to present dramas to an audience. Indeed, it seems that we spend most of our time not engaged in giving information but in giving shows. And observe, this theatricality is not based on mere displays of feelings or faked exhibitions of spontaneity or anything else by way of the huffing and puffing we might derogate by calling theatrical. The parallel between stage and conversation is much, much deeper than that. The point is that ordinarily when an

individual says something, he is not saying it as a bold statement of fact on his own behalf. He is recounting. He is running through a strip of already determined events for the engagement of his listeners.[21]

In engaging others, you present a particular character to the audience. Like a stage actor, you present a character in a particular role, and your audience normally accepts the characterization.[22] Goffman believes that the self is literally determined by these dramatizations. Here is how he explains the self:

A correctly staged and performed scene leads the audience to impute a self to a performed character, but this imputation—this self—is a product of a scene that comes off, and is not a cause of it. The self, then, as a performed character, is not an organic thing that has a specific location, whose fundamental fate is to be born, to mature, and to die; it is a dramatic effect arising diffusely from a scene that is presented, and the characteristic issue, the crucial concern, is whether it will be credited or discredited.[23]

You have only to think about the many situations in which you project a certain image of yourself. It is doubtful that you behave the same way with your best friend as you do with your parents, and it is unlikely that the self you present to a professor is the same one you present at a party. In most of the situations in which you participate, you decide on a role and enact it.

In attempting to define a situation, you go through a two-part process—first, you get information about the other people in the situation, and then you give information about yourself. This process of exchanging information enables people to know what is expected of them. Usually, this exchange occurs indirectly through observing the behavior of others and structuring

---

20   On the nature of face-to-face interaction, see Erving Goffman, *Encounters: Two Studies in the Sociology of Interaction* (Indianapolis: Bobbs-Merrill, 1961); *Behavior in Public Places* (New York: Free Press, 1963); *Interaction Ritual: Essays on Face-to-Face Behavior* (Garden City, NY: Doubleday, 1967); and *Relations in Public* (New York: Basic, 1971).
21   Goffman, *Frame*, p. 508.
22   The best sources on self-presentation are Erving Goffman, *The Presentation of Self in Everyday Life* (Garden City, NY: Doubleday, 1959); and *Relations in Public*.
23   Goffman, *Presentation*, pp. 252–253.

your own behavior to elicit impressions in others. *Self-presentation* is very much a matter of *impression management:*

> He may wish them to think highly of him, or to think that he thinks highly of them, or to perceive how in fact he feels toward them or to obtain no clear-cut impression; he may wish to insure sufficient harmony so that the interaction can be sustained, or to defraud, get rid of, confuse, mislead, antagonize, or insult them.[24]

Predicaments are especially interesting. Suppose you get blamed for something. You can respond in a number of ways—you can give excuses, justifications, apologies, and more. For example, in making an excuse, you might say that you didn't mean to do it, that you did not realize what would happen, or that you couldn't help it. Justifications include appeals to a higher authority, self-defense, loyalty, or some other set of values.[25]

Because all participants in a situation project images, an overall definition of the situation emerges. This general definition is normally unified. Once the definition is set, moral pressure is created to maintain it by suppressing contradictions and doubts. A person may add to the projections but never contradict the image initially set. The very organization of society is based on this principle.

STRUCTURATION THEORY

In general, symbolic interactionism concentrates on microprocesses, or the actual interactions that occur between persons at the lowest possible level. They make the case that these microprocesses create macrostructures in society, but they do not elaborate this idea very well, nor, in general, do they acknowledge the opposite effect—the influence of macrostructure on microprocess. Structuration theory was designed as a more complete explanation of the micro–macro relationship.

Structuration theory, the brainchild of sociologist Anthony Giddens and his followers, is a general theory of social action.[26] This theory

states that human action is a process of producing and reproducing various social systems. Communicators act strategically according to rules to achieve their goals and thereby create structures that come back to affect future actions. Structures like relational expectations, group roles and norms, communication networks, and societal institutions both affect and are affected by social action. These structures provide individuals with rules that guide their actions, but their actions in turn create new rules and reproduce old ones. Ellis calls interaction and social structure "braided entities."[27]

Giddens overcomes the debate between those who hold that human action is caused by outside forces and those who advocate the intentionality of human action. He claims that both sides in this dispute are right because social life is a two-sided coin. We do act deliberately to accomplish our intentions; at the same time, our actions have the *unintended consequences* of establishing structures that affect our future actions. When we do certain things to attain our goals, we are unaware of many of the outcomes of action and their consequent structures.

Consider how this might work in a group. Someone will do something in order to accomplish certain objectives. Because this member acts a certain way, other group members come to see this person as one who has particular ideas and who can do special kinds of things. In time, a role is created. This role, which was very much an unintended consequence of action, will become a kind of structure that constrains that individual's future behavior in the group.

---

24 Goffman, *Presentation,* p. 3.
25 For a well-developed discussion of impression management in predicaments, see J. T. Tedeschi and M. Reiss, "Verbal Strategies in Impression Management," in *The Psychology of Ordinary Explanations of Social Behavior,* ed. C. Antaki (New York: Academic, 1981), pp. 271–309.
26 See, for example, Anthony Giddens, *New Rules of Sociological Method* (New York: Basic, 1976); *Studies in Social and Political Theory* (New York: Basic, 1977). For a brief summary of the theory, see *Profiles and Critiques in Social Theory* (Berkeley: University of California Press, 1982), pp. 8–11. See also Stephen P. Banks and Patricia Riley, "Structuration Theory as an Ontology for Communication Research," *Communication Yearbook 16,* ed. Stanley Deetz (Newbury Park, CA: Sage, 1993), pp. 167–196.
27 Ellis, *Crafting Society,* p. 123.

For example, let's say you hate clutter and want to make sure that your group's meeting room is always tidy. You take the responsibility of picking things up before each meeting. Before long, the other members will expect you to do this, and you will have created the role of "custodian." Even when you don't feel like it, you may still straighten up the committee room because that is your role. Giddens believes that this kind of "structuration" saturates all social life, in ways far more profound than getting a room cleaned.

As an example, Donald Ellis shows how ethnicity is entailed in structuration.[28] We create ethnic difference by interactional patterns within and between groups. Ethnicity is a structural arrangement created over history through many local practices throughout the world. It is a creation of interaction in much the same way as symbolic interactionists would imagine. Yet once created, ethnicity has a life of its own and constrains future action, so that it becomes almost impossible not to see and act into ethnic experience in some way or another. Well-intentioned people acting normally in their everyday lives to solve problems and achieve goals create unintended categories of social structure, which limit what they can do in the future interaction. These structures are not necessarily bad, but they do include power arrangements in which one group may dominate another. There have been grand social experiments designed to change macrostructures by changing microstructures, but in the end new unintended structures are produced that contain their own powers and limits.

Giddens believes that structuration always involves three major modalities, or dimensions. These are (1) an interpretation or understanding, (2) a sense of morality or proper conduct, and (3) a sense of power in action. The rules we use to guide our actions, in other words, tell us how something should be understood (interpretation), what should be done (morality), and how to get things accomplished (power). In turn, our actions reinforce those very structures of interpretation, morality, and power.

Imagine a group that has created a structure in which everybody is expected to speak up on every topic. Like all structuration, this was not planned but emerged as an unintended consequence of the well-intentioned actions of group members over time. In this scenario, a norm of *interpreting* emerges, in which the group is understood as egalitarian. It is considered *proper* for everyone to address every issue and not remain quiet on any subject. And *power* is granted to speech, as individuals use language to persuade one another.

In actual practice your behavior is rarely affected by a single structure such as the "cleaning-up" role or "talking-up" norm used as examples above. Rather, your acts are affected by and affect several different structural elements at the same time. Two things can happen. First, one structure can *mediate* another. In other words, the production of one structure is accomplished by producing another. For example, the group may produce a communication network, but it does so by establishing individual roles. Here, the role structure mediates the communication network.

The second way structures relate to one another is through *contradiction*. Here, the production of a structure requires the establishment of another structure that undermines the first one. This is the stuff of classical paradox. Contradictions lead to conflict, and through a dialectic or tension between the contradictory elements, system change results.

The old problem of task and relationship work in groups is a good example of contradictory structure. To accomplish a task, the group has to work on its interpersonal relationships, but working on relationships detracts from accomplishing the task. Concentrating too much on task does not leave enough time to mend fences and work on relationships, which must be done for high-quality task accomplishment.

A profound contradiction has emerged in the United States on the issues of equal opportunity and affirmative action. In the U.S. Constitution, citizens are considered theoretically equal and should receive equal treatment and opportunity. This is ideal has actually been written into federal

28   Ellis, *Crafting Society.*

law, and various enforcement mechanisms are in place. It is against the law to discriminate in employment, education, sports, housing, and so forth. At the same time, it was recognized that compensatory action must be taken to level the playing field. Prohibiting discrimination was not considered enough, and affirmative action to bring underrepresented groups into parity was added to the legislation. Equal opportunity and affirmative action laws sit side by side as an attempt to change microinteractional processes in order to eliminate oppressive macrostructures in society.

What an organization faces, then, is the prohibition against discrimination, but the requirement of giving special treatment to certain protected groups. Notice the profound contradiction between equal opportunity and affirmative action. This has led to a great deal of conflict in the United States on both macro and micro levels. The issue is currently being debated, and continual changes will occur as a result. This is an excellent example of how contradiction in structuration can lead to social change in micro and macro social structures.

● SYMBOLIC PROCESSES IN CONVERGENCE

If, as symbolic interactionists claim, people are drawn together by common meanings in language, and if, as structurationists claim, there is a tight connection between interaction and social structure, then it makes sense to look at how people can use language to create structures that enhance influence through convergence. In this section we look at two well-known theories of this type.

Kenneth Burke and Identification

Kenneth Burke has written widely in many areas, including creative writing, literary and rhetorical criticism, social psychology, and linguistic analysis. Burke's concepts are not derived directly from the work of Mead and the other early sociologists, but his work is highly consistent with the other approaches presented in this chapter.

Burke is no doubt a giant among symbol theorists.[29] He wrote over a period of fifty years, and his theory is one of the most comprehensive of all symbol theories. One follower wrote, "It may be said without exaggeration that anyone writing today on communication, however 'original' he may be, is echoing something said by Burke."[30] Burke published a number of books, from 1931 to 1989.[31] A number of scholars have provided written interpretations of Burke's ideas.[32] In surveying Burke's communication theory, we will begin with a summary of his concept of action; then we will turn to his central ideas on symbols, language, and communication; and finally we will sketch Burke's method.

Burke sees the act as the basic concept in dramatism, that of distinguishing between action and motion. *Action* consists of purposeful, voluntary behaviors; *motions* are nonpurposeful, nonmeaningful ones. Objects and animals possess motion, but only human beings have action.

Burke views the individual as a biological and neurological being, distinguished by symbol-using behavior, the ability to act. People are symbol-creating, symbol-using, and symbol-misusing animals. They create symbols to name things and situations; they use symbols for communication; and they often abuse symbols by misusing them to their disadvantage.

29   See, for example, Bernard L. Brock, "Evolution of Kenneth Burke's Criticism and Philosophy of Language," in *Kenneth Burke and Contemporary European Thought: Rhetoric in Transition*, ed. Bernard L. Brock (Tuscaloosa: University of Alabama Press, 1995), pp. 1–33; Herbert W. Simons and Trevor Melia, eds., *The Legacy of Kenneth Burke* (Madison: University of Wisconsin Press, 1989). Although in the communication field Burke is most often considered a symbol theorist, he is also a major social critic. For a discussion of this aspect of his work, see Omar Swartz, *Conducting Socially Responsible Research* (Thousand Oaks, CA: Sage, 1997), pp. 68–90.
30   Hugh Duncan, "Communication in Society," *Arts in Society* 3 (1964): 105.
31   For a list of Burke's works, see the Selected Bibliography.
32   For a comprehensive overview on Kenneth Burke, see William Rueckert, ed., *Critical Responses to Kenneth Burke* (Minneapolis: University of Minnesota Press, 1969). For brief summaries, see Brock, "Evolution"; John F. Cragan and Donald C. Shields, *Symbolic Theories in Applied Communication Research: Bormann, Burke, and Fisher* (Cresskill, NJ: Hampton, 1995), pp. 61–81; Sonja K. Foss, Karen A. Foss, and Robert Trapp, *Contemporary Perspectives on Rhetoric* (Prospect Heights, IL: Waveland, 1991), pp. 169–208.

Burke's view of symbols is broad, including an array of linguistic and nonverbal elements as well. Especially intriguing for Burke is the notion that a person can symbolize symbols. One can talk about speech and can write about words. History itself is a process of writing about what people have already spoken and written in the course of events.

People filter reality through a symbolic screen. Reality is mediated through symbols. Burke agrees with Mead that language functions as the vehicle for action. Because of the social need for people to cooperate in their actions, language shapes behavior.

Language, as seen by Burke, is always emotionally loaded. No word can be neutral. As a result, your attitudes, judgments, and feelings invariably appear in the language you use. Language is by nature selective and abstract, focusing attention on particular aspects of reality at the expense of other aspects. Language is economical, but it is also ambiguous.

An overriding consideration for all of Burke's work is his concept of guilt. The term *guilt* is Burke's all-purpose word for any feeling of tension within a person—anxiety, embarrassment, self-hatred, disgust, and so forth. For Burke, guilt is a condition caused by symbol use. He identifies three related sources of guilt, the first of which is the *negative*. Through language people moralize. They construct myriad rules and proscriptions. These rules are never entirely consistent, and in following one rule, you necessarily are breaking another, creating guilt. Religions, professions, organizations, families, and communities all have implicit rules about how to behave. We learn these throughout life and therefore judge almost any action as good or bad.

The second reason for guilt is the *principle of perfection*. People are sensitive to their failings. Humans can imagine (through language) a state of perfection. Then, by their very nature, they spend their lives striving for whatever degree of this perfection they set for themselves. Guilt arises as a result of the discrepancy between the real and the ideal. Many peace activists are motivated by this kind of guilt. For example, a speaker at a rally may say that war is a barbaric and inappropriate method of resolving conflict in the twenty-first century. This speaker can imagine a world without war and is motivated to speak out because of the principle of perfection.

A third reason for guilt is the *principle of hierarchy*. In seeking order, people structure society in social pyramids or hierarchies (social ratings, social orderings), which is done with symbols. Competitions and divisions result among classes and groups in the hierarchy, and guilt results. Ethnic strife is a perfect example.

For Burke, guilt is the primary motive behind all action and communication. We communicate to purge our guilt. In describing communication, Burke uses several nearly synonymous terms: *consubstantiality, identification, persuasion, communication,* and *rhetoric*. Let us see how these concepts are integrated in his theory.

First, *consubstantiality:* Any object has an essence, or substance. *Substance* is the general nature, or essence, of a thing. People have substance too, and each person has a separate substance; however, the substances of any two people always overlap to some extent. The overlap is never total, making perfect communication impossible. Whatever communication occurs between individuals is a direct function of their shared, or common, substance, called consubstantiality.

When you and a friend are relaxing next to the swimming pool on a warm summer morning, you communicate with each other in a free and easy manner because you share meanings for the language in use. You are, so to speak, consubstantial. On the other hand, when you ask a question of a harried busboy in a Swiss restaurant, you may feel frustration because of your lack of shared meaning with this individual. To combine Mead and Burke, a significant symbol is one that allows for shared meaning through consubstantiality.

Another important term in Burke's theory is *identification*. As generally conceived, identification is similar to consubstantiality. The opposite of identification is *division,* or separateness. Division and the guilt it produces are the primary motives for communication. Through communication, identification is increased. In a spiraling fashion as identification increases, shared meaning increases, thereby improving understanding. Identification thus can be a means to persuasion and effective communication, or it can be an end in itself. Identification can be conscious or unconscious, planned or accidental.

Three overlapping sources of identification exist among people. *Material identification* results from goods, possessions, and things, like owning the same kind of car or having similar tastes in clothes. *Idealistic identification* results from shared ideas, attitudes, feelings, and values, such as being a member of the same church or political party. *Formal identification* results from the arrangement, form, or organization of an event in which both parties participate. If two people who are introduced shake hands, the conventional form of handshaking causes some identification to take place.

Identification is not an either/or occurrence but a matter of degree. Some consubstantiality will always be present merely by virtue of the shared humanness of any two people. Identification can be great or small, and it can be increased or decreased by the actions of the communicators. Second, although any two persons will always experience some identification and some division, communication is more successful when identification is greater than division.

People of lower strata in a hierarchy often identify with people at the top of the hierarchy, despite tremendous apparent division. This kind of identification can be seen, for example, in the mass following of a charismatic leader. Why does this happen? First, individuals perceive in others an embodiment of the perfection for which they themselves strive. Second, the mystery surrounding the charismatic person simultaneously tends to hide the division that exists. This phenomenon can be called *identification through mystification*.

Because it is so important to successful communication, people adopt certain *strategies* of identification when they interact with others. Since identification can occur in an almost un-limited number of ways, Burke does not attempt to outline all available strategies but suggests that in analyzing a rhetorical event, you should try to figure out what strategies the communicators are using.

Burke's most basic method for analyzing events is the *dramatistic pentad*. Pentad, meaning a group of five, is an analytical framework for the most efficient study of any act. The first part of the pentad is the *act*, what is done by the actor. It is a view of what the actor played, what was accomplished. The second part is the *scene*, the situation or setting in which the act was accomplished. It includes a view of the physical setting and the cultural and social milieu in which the act was carried out. The third component is the *agent*, the actor, including all that is known about the individual. The agent's substance reaches all aspects of his or her being, history, personality, demeanor, and any other contributing factors. The *agency*, the fourth component, is the means, or vehicle, the agent uses in carrying out the act. Agency may include channels of communication, devices, institutions, strategies, or messages. Fifth, the *purpose* is the reason for the act—the rhetorical goal, the hoped-for effect or result of the act.

For example, in writing a paper for your communication theory course, you, the agent, gather information and present it to the instructor (the act). Your course, your university, your library, your desk and room, the social atmosphere of your school constitute the scene; the format of the paper itself is the agency. You have a variety of purposes, including, in all likelihood, getting a good grade.

David Ling shows how Burke's pentad can be used to understand a communication event.[33] In 1969 Edward Kennedy, a senator from Massachusetts, was involved in an automobile accident with an aide, Mary Jo Kopechne, in which he accidentally drove a car off a bridge into a pond. Kennedy escaped, but Kopechne drowned. In a

---

33   David A. Ling, "A Pentadic Analysis of Senator Edward Kennedy's Address to the People of Massachusetts, July 25, 1969," *Central States Speech Journal* 21 (1970): 81–86.

remarkable address to the people of Massachusetts about a week later, he explained what happened and attempted to regain the support of the people. Ling writes that Kennedy wanted to achieve two things: to minimize his own responsibility for the accident and to make the people of Massachusetts responsible for whether or not he would continue in office.

Kennedy's appeal on the first point describes himself (agent) as a helpless victim of the events leading to the death of the young woman (scene). He explains his own failure to report the accident (act) as a consequence of his confusion and injuries. Kennedy's depiction makes him out to be a victim of a tragic situation. Later in his speech, Kennedy essentially offered to resign if the citizens wanted him to. Here, the scene shifted to the public reaction to the accident, the agent became the people of Massachusetts, the act was their decision as to whether he should resign, the agency would be a statement of resignation, and the purpose would be to remove him from office. Ling believes this was a very effective speech. The reaction was overwhelmingly positive, and Kennedy continued in office.

Burke places strong emphasis on the role of language and symbols in bringing people together or driving them apart. He shows that we can develop strategies for doing either. In the following theory, we see how the deep structure of narrative can accomplish group consciousness in much the same way.

Symbolic Convergence Theory

Symbolic convergence theory, often known as *fantasy-theme analysis*, is a well-developed theory by Ernest Bormann, John Cragan, and Donald Shields dealing with the use of narrative in communication.[34] The theory imagines that individuals' images of reality are guided by stories reflecting how things are believed to be. These stories are created in symbolic interaction within small groups, and they are chained out from person to person and group to group.

Fantasy themes are part of larger dramas that are longer, more complicated stories called rhe-

torical visions. A *rhetorical vision* is essentially a view of how things have been, are, or will be. Rhetorical visions structure our sense of reality in areas that we cannot experience directly but can only know by symbolic reproduction. Consequently, such visions give us an image of things in the past, in the future, or in faraway places; in large measure these visions form the assumptions on which a group's knowledge is based.

In the corporate world, for example, plans are almost always designed to generate profit. In a limited marketplace, not all competitors will be profitable, so you would expect corporate planners to live in a world filled with competition-oriented rhetorical visions, and they would tell stories that express this vision.

Fantasy themes, and even the larger rhetorical visions, consist of characters, plot line, scenes, and sanctioning agent. The *characters* can be heroes, villains, and other supporting players. The *plot line* is the action or development of the story. The *scene* is the setting, including location, properties, and sociocultural milieu. Finally, the *sanctioning agent* is a source that legitimizes the story. This source may be an authority who lends credibility to the story or authorizes its telling, a common belief in God or another sanctioning ideal like justice or democracy, or a situation or event that makes telling the story seem appropriate.

Imagine a group of executives gathering for a high-level meeting. Just before the meeting starts, at the beginning, and at various points during the meeting, members will share experiences and stories—fantasy themes—that bring the group

---

34   See, for example, John F. Cragan and Donald Shields, *Understanding Communication Theory: The Communicative Forces for Human Action* (Boston: Allyn & Bacon, 1998), pp. 93–121; Bormann's major works on fantasy-theme analysis are *Communication Theory* (New York: Holt, Rinehart & Winston, 1980), pp. 184–190; *The Force of Fantasy: Restoring the American Dream* (Carbondale: Southern Illinois University Press, 1985); "Fantasy and Rhetorical Vision: The Rhetorical Criticism of Social Reality," *Quarterly Journal of Speech* 58 (1972): 396–407; and "Fantasy and Rhetorical Vision: Ten Years Later," *Quarterly Journal of Speech* 68 (1982): 288–305; Ernest G. Bormann, John F. Cragan, and Donald C. Shields, "An Expansion of the Rhetorical Vision Component of the Symbolic Convergence Theory: The Cold War Paradigm Case," *Communication Monographs* 63 (1996): 1–28. See also John F. Cragan and Donald C. Shields, *Applied Communication Research: A Dramatistic Approach* (Prospect Heights, IL: Waveland, 1981); John F. Cragan and Donald C. Shields, *Symbolic Theories*, pp. 29–48.

together. Some of these will be stories heard again and again. Each will have a cast of characters, a plot, a scene, and sanctioning agents. In many cases the sanctioning agent will be the company itself.

Rhetorical visions are never told in their entirety but are built up piecemeal by sharing associated fantasy themes. To grasp the entire vision, one must attend to the fantasy themes because these comprise the content of conversation in groups of people when the vision is being created and chained out. You can recognize a fantasy theme because it is repeated again and again. In fact, some themes are so frequently discussed and so well known within a particular group or community that the members no longer tell the whole episode, but abbreviate it by presenting just a "trigger" or *symbolic cue.* This is precisely what happens with an inside joke. An executive might say, for example, "Yeah, that's just like the *Frasier* episode!" and everyone will laugh, knowing just what she is referring to. Fantasy themes that develop to this point of familiarity are known as *fantasy types*—stock situations told over and over within a group. Often these retold stories relate to personal, group, or community achievements and take on the form of a *saga.* You probably have sagas within your family and your work organization, and you have certainly heard many national and societal sagas such as Washington and the Revolutionary War, the Declaration of Independence, and even the story of Bill Gates.

As people come to share fantasy themes, the resulting rhetorical vision pulls them together and gives them a sense of identification with a shared reality. In this process, people converge or come to hold a common image as they share their fantasy themes. In fact, shared rhetorical visions—and especially the use of fantasy types—can be taken as evidence that convergence has occurred.

As rhetorical visions get established through the sharing of fantasy themes within a limited group, they fulfill a consciousness-creating function. They make people more aware of a certain way of seeing things. This happens because the elements of rhetorical visions at this stage are novel and have explanatory power, and yet they can also attract attention and build consciousness because they imitate former ways of seeing things that look familiar. In other words, they build or maintain a group or community's *shared consciousness.*

Once consciousness is created among early adherents to a rhetorical vision, the consciousness can be disseminated, as more and more people are converted through *consciousness-raising* communication. There seems to be a critical mass of adherence at which widespread dissemination of the rhetorical vision takes place. After this happens, the rhetorical vision begins to fulfill a *consciousness-sustaining* function. Here the fantasy themes serve to maintain commitment.

Rhetorical visions are not just narrative stories but have a deep structure that reflects and influences our sense of reality. The Bill Gates story, for example—depending upon which version you hear—has a deep structure of individual ingenuity, hard work, and success. The underlying stories are master analogues that compete for our attention and vie for truth. *Righteous analogues* attempt to tell us how to live our lives morally, what is right and good. *Social analogues* tell us how we should relate to other people. And *pragmatic analogues* tell us how to do things, offering practical, efficient solutions.

Clearly, fantasy themes are an important ingredient in persuasion. Public communicators—in speeches, articles, books, films, and other media—often tap into the audience's predominant fantasy themes. Public communication can also add to or modify the rhetorical vision by amplifying, changing, or adding fantasy themes. One way to evaluate the use of fantasy themes, then, is to look at their effectiveness. If you listened to a speaker draw in an audience effectively with the use of shared fantasy themes, you might say that the speech was effective.

But use of fantasy themes goes well beyond the world of persuasion. It is a social bonding agent, a way in which we create narrative structures that give meaning to our lives and a sense of community. Perhaps a better way to evaluate fantasy themes, then, is in its *artistry*—the creativity, novelty, and wisdom with which they are used, combined, and formed into visions. If you look beyond the surface of a highly rated movie, for example, you may notice that it taps into an underlying current of reality in the culture, and it does so in a very artistic way. This is what the theorists mean by fantasy-theme artistry.

Karen Foss and Stephen Littlejohn's critique of *The Day After*—a television movie about a nuclear war that played in 1983 at the height of public concern over the nuclear arms buildup—shows how artistry works.[35] These researchers asked about eighty people to write descriptions of what they thought a nuclear war would be like. They then compared these personal statements with the fantasy themes in the film and discovered a close association between the two.

The film was watched by a huge television audience, and it appears that it was effective in using a rhetorical vision shared with that audience. Foss and Littlejohn believe that the deep structure of the vision is irony, which consists primarily of the inconsistency of being both a detached observer and an involved participant in the nuclear-attack drama. This kind of irony is typical of the visions presented by films because films draw you in as a participant, but they also rely on you to be an observing and detached audience.

◖ COMMENTARY AND CRITIQUE

The theories in this chapter see communication as the thread with which the fabric of society is held together. A culture's reality is defined in terms of its meanings, which arise from interaction within social groups. Individuals' meanings for words and symbols, objects, stories, and roles are determined by the ways symbols are used to define objects and people in actual communication situations. Action, then, is a product of the meanings that arise from interaction. Figure 8.1 summarizes the basic interactional process.[36]

Social institutions are nothing more than grand networks of interaction in which common meanings are generated. The self as an object is especially important; the self, too, is defined in terms of symbols and meanings derived from one's interaction with other people.

As people interact in society, they perform in ways that make social life much like a drama. They act within scenes, make presentations, represent characters, and tell stories. These communication activities create, sustain, and change the very nature of reality in a group or culture.

Although many specific objections have been raised against symbolic interactionism, most can be combined into four major criticisms.[37] First, symbolic interactionism is said to be nonempirical. That is, one cannot readily translate its concepts into observable, researchable units. Second, it is said to be overly restrictive in the variables it takes into account. Critics have charged that it ignores crucial psychological variables on one end and societal variables on the other. Third, it uses concepts in an inexact, inconsistent way. Fourth, it takes a naively cooperative view of meaning. Let us look at each of these objections more closely.

The first major criticism of symbolic interactionism has broad implications. Despite Blumer's protests to the contrary, critics maintain that in actual practice the researcher does not know what to look for in observing interactionist concepts in real life. This problem seems to stem from the vague, intuitive claims of early interactionists. What is mind, for example? How can this concept be observed? We already have noted Kuhn's failure to operationalize interactionist

35   Karen A. Foss and Stephen W. Littlejohn, "*The Day After*: Rhetorical Vision in an Ironic Frame," *Critical Studies in Mass Communication* 3 (1986): 317–336.
36   Charon, *Symbolic Interactionism*, p. 49.
37   For reviews of specific objections to symbolic interactionism, see Michael A. Katovich and William A. Reese III, "Postmodern Thought in Symbolic Interaction: Reconstructing Social Inquiry in Light of Late-Modern Concerns," *The Sociological Quarterly* 34 (1993): 391–411; Gil Richards Musolf, "Structure, Institutions, Power, and Ideology: New Directions Within Symbolic Interactionism," *The Sociological Quarterly* 33 (1992): 171–189; Jerome G. Manis and Bernard N. Meltzer, eds., "Appraisals of Symbolic Interactionism," *Symbolic Interaction* (Boston: Allyn & Bacon, 1978), pp. 393–440; Bernard N. Meltzer, John Petras, and Larry Reynolds, *Symbolic Interactionism: Genesis, Varieties, and Criticism* (London: Routledge & Kegan Paul, 1975); Reynolds, *Interactionism*, pp. 129–180.

FIGURE **8.1**

Interaction to Action

concepts without giving up his assumptions about the process nature of behavior. Most basically, this criticism questions the appropriateness of symbolic interactionism to lead to a more complete understanding of everyday behavior. As such, critics believe it to be more social philosophy than theory.

John Lofland's criticism is especially biting. He claims that interactionists participate in three main activities: "doctrinaire reiteration of the master's teachings, . . . [making] slightly more specific the general imagery, . . . [and connecting] descriptive case studies and interactionism."[38] As a result of this alleged failure, symbolic interactionism is not thought to be adequately heuristic, generating few testable hypotheses and little research.

Carl Couch, a leading proponent (and house critic) of the movement, points out that interactionists do engage in research but that their observations do not cast light on the theory's key concepts, making revision and elaboration difficult. Couch believes this circumstance need not be so, and his newer Iowa tradition has emerged out of a need for interactionists to do "serious sociological work."[39] Given some of the more recent work done in the area, this criticism, once

valid, no longer holds. It is probably a more valid critique of early interactionism.

The second major criticism is that interactionism has either ignored or downplayed important explanatory variables. Critics say it leaves out the emotions of the individual on one end and societal organization on the other. These arguments as a whole make the case that interactionism is overly restrictive in scope. To cover as much of social life as it believes it does, interactionism must take into account social structures as well as individual feelings. Again, however, if we turn to the many theories associated with interactionist thinking, whether they go by the name symbolic interactionism or not, we find that a much wider range of concepts is included. In Chapter 9, for example, we will encounter the work of theorists who deal with such concerns as the social construction of emotions, values, and morality. We will look at the process of making accounts and enacting social life. All these topics

38   John Lofland, "Interactionist Imagery and Analytic Interruptus," in *Human Nature and Collective Behavior*, ed. T. Shibutani (Englewood Cliffs, NJ: Prentice-Hall, 1970), p. 37.
39   Carl Couch, "Symbolic Interaction and Generic Sociological Principles" (paper delivered at the Symposium on Symbolic Interaction, Boston, 1979).

have been well researched and are included in the interactionist tradition broadly conceived.[40]

The alleged failure of symbolic interactionism to deal with social organization is a major concern. Social organization or structure removes individual prerogative, a highly valued idea in old-style interactionism. Social structure is normally a matter of power, since some groups seem to have more influence in defining a situation than others, but interactionists have been loath to admit this power inequality. However, the concept of power can be investigated from an interactionist perspective, and several research programs have begun to look at power.[41] Again, current interactionists have taken this criticism seriously and have done a great deal of work to show the relevance of symbolic interactionism (SI) to social structure and the production of power. Much of this work has been done by merging SI with cultural studies, a critical research tradition discussed in Chapter 11.[42]

Of course, Gidden's structuration theory takes a major step in handling this concern. Although Giddens would not consider himself a symbolic interactionist, he would certain acknowledge that his work incorporates SI concepts and adds to these in a way that advances our thinking about social organization.

The third general criticism of symbolic interactionism is that its concepts are not used consistently. As a result such concepts as *I, me, self, role,* and *others* are vague. However, we must keep in mind that symbolic interactionism is not a unified theory. Rather, it is a general framework, and as we have seen, it has different versions. Therefore, although this is a valid criticism of early interactionism, it is not a fair picture of the movement today.

One inconsistency that persists in most versions of symbolic interactionism involves the problem of determinism. Most mainstream interactionists clearly teach that individuals and groups have the capacity to seek goals, to define situations in new ways, and to change. Yet the idea of the social genesis of meaning creates a kind of determinism. In other words, if the group creates meaning through interaction, the individual has little choice but to see the world in predetermined ways. Mead tried to handle this difficulty with the concept of the *I*, but this is a vague, mystical, and ill-defined concept.

The question that plagues interactionism today is how people can act in accord with personal goals yet be affected by meanings that have been established through a history of interaction. Structuration theory is perhaps the most serious and credible answer to this problem, as it shows how action results in unintended consequences that return to constrain future action.[43] Many believe that Giddens has successfully reconciled structural, deterministic approaches with interactionist ones in a unified theory of social life.

The fourth objection to symbolic interactionism is its naive reliance on a basically cooperative view of meaning and self.[44] The problem here is that in classical symbolic interactionism, meanings, including the concept of the self, just sort of emerge effortlessly from interaction, and social life is essentially a cooperative endeavor. Yet critical theorists show that powerful groups often reflect views of certain persons in ways that are harmful and demeaning. How we see ourselves is not always defined by these negative views, and in fact, people often define themselves by opposing what others say about them. In other words, our conceptions of self often emerge from conflict and manipulation, not cooperation.

Indeed, theorists like Goffman say that people often manipulate situations in a variety of ways

---

40   Actually, much has been done in this area. See, for example, Thomas J. Scheff, *Microsociology: Discourse, Emotion, and Social Structure* (Chicago: University of Chicago Press, 1990); for a summary of work on emotion, see Bernard N. Meltzer and Nancy J. Herman, "Epilogue: Human Emotions, Social Structure, and Symbolic Interactionism," in *Interactionism: Exposition and Critique,* ed. Larry T. Reynolds (Dix Hills, NY: General Hall, 1990), pp. 181–225.
41   This line of work is discussed in Peter M. Hall, "Structuring Symbolic Interaction: Communication and Power," in *Communication Yearbook 4,* ed. D. Nimmo (New Brunswick, NJ: Transaction, 1980), pp. 49–60.
42   For a summary of this work, see Musolf, "Structure, Institutions, Power, and Ideology"; and Norman K. Denzin, *Symbolic Interactionism and Cultural Studies: The Politics of Interpretation* (Oxford: Blackwell, 1992); Michal M. McCall and Howard S. Becker, *Symbolic Interaction and Cultural Studies* (Chicago: University of Chicago Press, 1990); Meltzer and Herman, "Epilogue."
43   See, for example, Giddens, *New Rules.*
44   This view is explored in some depth by Katovich and Reese, "Postmodern Thought."

to present views of self that may be in opposition to customary ways of seeing things. This is possible because no one image of self emerges from a lifetime of interaction. Because we can define the self in so many ways, we can define ourselves in a variety of antithetical ways.

This view has not been lost on interactionists. In fact, interactionists themselves have done much to broaden the view of self, meaning, and action in social life.

Burke's theory has captured worldwide attention over the years. Some believe that it has opened vistas of great import; others believe that Burke's lack of focus has led to interminable confusion, if not exhaustion. For example, John Stewart addresses Burke's apparent confusion in regard to the symbol model.[45]

Stewart's thesis is that we cannot separate symbols from things, but that reality itself may by the use of language in everyday communication. According to Stewart, Burke is ambivalent on this issue. He seems to acknowledge the importance of language in the construction of reality, yet his works are filled with the idea that symbols somehow represent a world apart. This is an interesting point because Burke has been so often identified with symbolic interactionism, which itself opposes the very symbol model that Stewart finds indefensible.

As another recent example, James Chesebro has argued that Burke's system is overly limited and needs revision to remain fresh in today's multicultural thinking.[46] Specifically, he worries that Burke offers a rather single-minded model for viewing human knowledge, a model that is inappropriately reliant on language and inappropriate for many cultures.

Of the several theories covered in this chapter, Goffman's ideas are perhaps least theoretical in that they are scattered and hard to assemble into a single rubric. His numerous writings are in-

sightful and interesting but hard to integrate. He rarely uses the same vocabulary twice and, until the end of his career, seemed more interested in pointing out idiosyncratic observations than in making a general statement. Fortunately, his final work, *Frame Analysis,* provides an overall scheme that can be used to integrate a lifetime of work.

Bormann's theory, too, has received both praise and blame. Bormann and his associates also put a good deal of work into clarifying and elaborating the vocabulary of fantasy-theme analysis. This work has been very useful. Indeed, telling stories and sharing rhetorical visions is a common, perhaps universal, human activity. The function of stories in communication and persuasion is therefore a significant area of study. Considerable controversy still exists about the place of narrative in communication. Critiques of symbolic convergence theory, for example, have been wide ranging. The theory has been criticized for its failure to clarify basic assumptions; its inappropriate application of a small-group phenomenon to public, mass audiences; its overreliance on the subjective observations of the researcher rather than the categories of the theory; and its lack of a fresh perspective. These objections, of course, have not gone unanswered, and Bormann and his colleagues have responded that much of this criticism is polemical and unsubstantiated.[47]

In the following chapter, we extend this discussion by pursuing the social construction of reality and cultural variations of meaning.

---

45   John Stewart, *Language as Articulate Contact* (Albany: SUNY Press, 1995), pp. 197–228.
46   James W. Chesebro, "Extending the Burkeian System: A Response to Tompkins and Cheney," *Quarterly Journal of Speech* 80 (1994): 83–90.
47   Ernest G. Bormann, John F. Cragan, and Donald C. Shields, "In Defense of Symbolic Convergence Theory: A Look at the Theory and Its Criticisms After Two Decades," *Communication Theory* 4 (1994): 259–294.

CHAPTER 9

THEORIES OF
SOCIAL AND
CULTURAL
REALITY

Interactionist approaches to communication theory address the ways our understandings, meanings, norms, roles, and rules are worked out interactively in communication.[1] In the previous chapter, we looked at some foundational work in this area. We continue this discussion here by exploring the interactional worlds in which people live. This work as a group can be called the social approach to communication.[2] We begin our tour of this material with theories of the *social construction of reality*, an important intellectual base for this line of work.

THE SOCIAL CONSTRUCTION OF REALITY

The theories in this movement rest on the idea that reality is not an objective set of arrangements outside ourselves, but is constructed through a process of interaction in groups, communities, and cultures. Although symbolic interactionism (Chapter 8) set the stage for this line of work, it

was given impetus by Peter Berger and Thomas Luckmann in their treatise *The Social Construction of Reality* and Alfred Schutz, *The Phenomenology of the Social World*.[3] Kenneth Gergen has labeled this the *social constructionist movement*.[4]

---

1   Much of this theory is based on the work of American pragmatism, especially the work of Dewey and Mead. For a philosophical discussion, see Vernon Cronen and Peter Lang, "Language and Action: Wittgenstein and Dewey in the Practice of Therapy and Consultation," *Human Systems: The Journal of Systemic Consultation and Management* 5 (1994): 5–43. For a discussion of the ideas of Wittgenstein in regard to the social construction of meaning, see John Shotter, "Before Theory and After Representationalism: Understanding Meaning 'From Within' a Dialogue Process," in *Beyond the Symbol Model: Reflections on the Representational Nature of Language,* ed. John Stewart (Albany: SUNY Press, 1996), pp. 103–134.
2   For a good general discussion of this school of thought, see Wendy Leeds-Hurwitz, ed., *Social Approaches to Communication* (New York: Guilford, 1995). See also the forum "Social Approaches to Interpersonal Communication," *Communication Theory* 2 (1992): 131–172, 329–359.
3   Peter L. Berger and Thomas Luckmann, *The Social Construction of Reality: A Treatise in the Sociology of Knowledge* (New York: Doubleday, 1966); Alfred Schutz, *The Phenomenology of the Social World,* trans. G. Walsh and F. Lehnert (Evanston, IL: Northwestern University Press, 1967).
4   Kenneth J. Gergen, "The Social Constructionist Movement in Modern Psychology," *American Psychologist* 40 (1985): 266–275; see also *Toward Transformation in Social Knowledge* (New York: Springer-Verlag, 1982). See also the special section on social constructionism in Stanley Deetz, ed., *Communication Yearbook 17* (Thousand Oaks, CA: Sage, 1994), pp. 3–300; Vivien Burr, *Introduction to Social Constructionism* (London: Routledge, 1995).

The basic idea of social construction can be illustrated in an interesting classroom exercise. Each student produces an object. The objects are put on a table in front of the class, and someone is then asked to sort them. This is easy to do. One might, for example, put wooden articles in one group, metal ones in another, cloth in another, and plastic in a fourth pile. Another student is then asked to sort the objects again. Someone else is asked to do it a third time. The objects are sorted again and again, each time in a different way. They might be sorted by size, use, color, number of parts, things you would or would not give a child, or things that could be used as a weapon and things that could not.

There is a seemingly endless number of ways to understand each object. You can see that our language gives us labels that we use to distinguish objects in our world.[5] How we understand objects and how we behave toward them depend in large measure on the social reality in force, the arrangements we have worked out through interaction.

Like all movements, social constructionism is not entirely consistent and has various versions.[6] Most, however, share a set of assumptions. Robyn Penman summarizes these as follows:[7]

1. *Communicative action is voluntary.* Like the symbolic interactionists, most constructionists see that communicators make choices. This does not mean that people have free choice. Indeed, the social environment does constrain what can be and is done. Within a social group, people have the latitude to act in a variety of ways, but they are also prevented by meanings, moral orders, roles, and rules from unbridled action.
2. *Knowledge is a social product.* Knowledge is not something that is discovered objectively but is "achieved" through interaction with others in particular times and places. Language and how it is used are particularly powerful in determining meanings and influencing action.
3. *Knowledge is contextual.* Our meanings for events derive from interaction in particular times and places, in a particular social milieu.

Our understandings of events change as times change, and each of us understands our experience in a variety of ways, depending on the context in which we are working.
4. *Theories create worlds.* Theories, and scholarly and research activity in general, are not objective tools for the discovery of truth, but contribute to the creation of knowledge. Scholarship, which itself is a social activity, has an effect on what is being observed and how experience is understood.
5. *Scholarship is value laden.* What we see in an investigation, or what we explain in a theory of communication, is always affected by the values embedded in the approach used.

Traditionally, communication has been treated as a category different from other categories. Some things were considered to be communication, and some things were not. *Communication* is not the same thing as *houses, horses,* and *hoops.* It is different from *eating, earning,* and *eloping.* Indeed, the field of communication is usually seen as distinct from other disciplines like physics, forestry, and geography.

With the advent of social constructionism, however, we can view communication differently—as a "perspective" rather than a "subject matter."[8] Because communication is the process

---

5   For a thorough discussion of the role of language in the construction of reality, see John Stewart, *Language as Articulate Contact: Toward a Post-Semiotic Philosophy of Communication* (Albany: SUNY Press, 1995). For a brief version, see John Stewart, "The Symbol Model vs. Language as Constitutive Articulate Contact," in *Beyond the Symbol Model: Reflections on the Representational Nature of Language,* ed. John Stewart (Albany: SUNY Press, 1996), pp. 9–68.
6   For a good description of the intellectual traditions and various versions of constructionism, see W. Barnett Pearce, "A Sailing Guide for Social Constructionists," in *Social Approaches to Communication,* ed. Wendy Leeds-Hurwitz (New York: Guilford, 1995), pp. 88–113; Klaus Krippendorff, "The Past of Communication's Hoped-For Future," *Journal of Communication* 43 (1993): 34–44; W. Barnett Pearce, "A 'Camper's Guide' to Constructionisms," *Human Systems: The Journal of Systemic Consultation and Management* 3 (1992): 139–161.
7   Robyn Penman, "Good Theory and Good Practice: An Argument in Progress," *Communication Theory* 2 (1992): 234–250. For another account, see John Shotter and Kenneth J. Gergen, "Social Construction: Knowledge, Self, Others, and Continuing the Conversation," in *Communication Yearbook 17,* ed. Stanley Deetz (Thousand Oaks, CA: Sage, 1994), pp. 3–33.
8   Stanley Deetz, "Future of the Discipline: The Challenges, the Research, and the Social Contribution," in *Communication Yearbook 17,* ed. Stanley Deetz (Thousand Oaks, CA: Sage, 1994), pp. 565–600.

by which all reality is constructed, it is involved in all things and separate from none. If we view communication as a perspective, we can no longer make the distinction between "communication" and "noncommunication," though we might distinguish between "the communication perspective" and "other perspectives."

What then is the *communication perspective?* W. Barnett Pearce has developed this idea in some depth in his book *Communication and the Human Condition.*[9] According to Pearce, a perspective is a way of looking at or thinking about something, and he sets out to establish *how* one would look at or think about things from the communication perspective.

In brief, whenever you look at something in terms of how it is constructed in interaction among people, you are taking a communication perspective. For example, architecture is a form of expression in which designers, builders, and users make a certain social world. The cultures of the world differ substantially in how they express their values and beliefs through the kinds of buildings and homes they make. Clothing is another example. We use clothing to "say" things about ourselves. Even something as mundane as the lowly sidewalk makes a statement. Is the sidewalk wide and spacious, narrow and crowded, or cluttered with market carts and booths? How do people use sidewalks, and how do they evolve within a city?

Virtually any aspect of human experience can be viewed from the perspective of how it is made and used in the social construction of reality. Our *resources* consist of all of the building blocks we work with in life. Resources include ideas, values, stories, symbols, meanings, institutions, and anything else used to build a reality. These are shared with others and constructed jointly through interaction in society. *Practices* consist of what is done or performed, including behaviors, actions, and forms of expression. Resources and practices are tightly connected and cannot really be separated. Resources are constructed in practice, and practices are shaped by resources. This is the recursive loop of resources and practices.

The communication perspective, then, is a way of thinking about experience in which this resource–practice loop is observed, studied, and taken into account. You can illustrate this idea to yourself by thinking of any experience that is important to you. Let's say, for example, that you love skiing. How would you look at this sport from the communication perspective?

Skiing is a social world, a world of places, times of the year, equipment, abilities, habits, terms, attitudes, skills, and methods. People approach skiing with a host of resources, including ideas about what it is, views about the best equipment to use and places to go, how to get there, and how to organize the ski day. But these are not isolated pieces of knowledge; they are constantly reinforced by action. What you "know" about skiing and what you "do" about it are tightly connected. And it is always social, affected by interaction with others. When you realize this and begin to take it seriously, you are using the communication perspective.

Even the hard sciences can be understood from the communication perspective. Any object in the natural world, from atoms to elk, is always understood from within a social world. Scientists jointly invent ways of looking at natural objects; together they create a vocabulary or set of terms to use: They attend conferences and share ideas; they write articles and books read by others; they share and debate the values of studying certain things and set priorities about what is most important to study; they debate the validity of one another's findings; and they appeal to outside agencies and the general public for support. All of these social practices shape the scientists' way of understanding the objects of their study. So even rocks, rockets, and red tides can be viewed from the communication perspective.

Persons are also socially constructed. How you see the self as a manifestation of being a person is, like skiing and all the rest, a product of social construction.

---

9   W. Barnett Pearce, *Communication and the Human Condition* (Carbondale: Southern Illinois University Press, 1989).

Some Examples of
Social Construction

The Self.   Among contemporary social scientists who have made constructionist assumptions central to their work is Rom Harré. Recognizing that self is both individual and social, Harré emphasizes the ways individuals account for and explain their own behavior in particular episodes.

Harré and his colleague Paul Secord are responsible for *ethogeny*—the study of how people understand their actions within a predictable sequence of acts, called *episodes*.[10] An episode is an event with a beginning and an end that all participants would identify as such. Having dinner, making a speech, holding a commencement ceremony, having an argument, driving to work, and negotiating an agreement are episodes. Ethogeny is the study of how people understand episodes. The ordinary language that people use to describe and explain episodes such as these reflects their meanings for these episodes.

Two people who say they are "in love" have a theory of what love is and how it should be acted out—a theory that is probably widely shared with many other people. When people talk about "being in love," they use their theory to describe, explain, or account for this common experience. This is true of all realms of life. Through interaction, people create theories of life to explain their experience of reality.[11] A group's theory characterizes an episode and predicts the logical outcome of actions within it. These "theories" are *structured templates* of the course of action anticipated in the episode. For example, the meanings attached to the events of an episode give rise to rules that guide the participants' actions within the episode. Participants know how to act because of the rules in force at a particular moment. For instance, our hypothetical couple may engage in the episode of "making love," which consists of a series of acts with a beginning and an end, which have meaning and an anticipated course. The episode of making love will be different for other couples, who have their own definitions of what it means to make love and the action sequence required.

The concept of *self*, which is so important in symbolic interactionism (Chapter 8), has been the chief concern of Harré in most of his theoretical work.[12] Harré says that like any other experience, the self is structured by a personal theory. That is, you learn to understand yourself by employing a theory that defines it. This may seem odd, but there is an important difference between a "self" and a "person."

For Harré, the *person* is a publicly visible being that is characterized by certain attributes and characteristics established within a culture or social group. For example, people in most European American cultures are viewed as autonomous beings that make choices to achieve goals. Not all cultures view people in this way.

The *self*, in contrast to the person, is your private notion of your own unity as a person. Personhood is *public*, whereas the self, though you may share it with others, is ultimately *private*. The character of persons is governed by your culture's theory of personhood; your self is governed by your theory of your own being as one member of the culture.

Personal being is thus two-sided, consisting of a social being (person) and a personal being (self). For example, many traditional cultures conceptualize the person as the embodiment of a role (such as mother, father, priest, worker). People in general are seen as manifestations of these roles. A single person, on the other hand, will assign a particular nature, feeling, and character to the self, as an individual within a role: "I am the father of Zuk and a field-worker. I am a good father and worker."

Your self theory is learned through a history of interaction with other people. All our thoughts, intentions, and emotions are cast in terms learned through social interaction. The range of possible "selves" is highly variable from one cul-

10   Rom Harré and Paul Secord, *The Explanation of Social Behavior* (Totowa, NJ: Littlefield, Adams, 1972).
11   Rom Harré, *Social Being: A Theory for Social Psychology* (Totowa, NJ: Rowman & Littlefield, 1979).
12   Harré, *Social Being*; see also *Personal Being: A Theory for Individual Psychology* (Cambridge, MA: Harvard University Press, 1984).

ture to another because the social realities of cultures are different from one to another. For instance, most Western industrialized cultures stress theories of self that emphasize whole, undivided, and independent persons. The Javanese, in contrast, see themselves as being two independent parts—an inside of feelings and an outside of observed behaviors. Moroccans have yet another theory of self, as embodiments of places and situations, and their identities are always tied to these situations.[13]

The self consists of a set of elements that can be viewed spatially along three dimensions. The first dimension is *display*—whether an aspect of the self is displayed publicly or remains private. For example, you might define "emotions" as private and "personality" as public. In other cultures, "emotions" might be defined as quite public.

The second dimension is *realization*, or source—the degree to which some feature of the self is believed to come from within the individual or a group. Elements of a self that are believed to come from the person are *individually realized*, whereas those elements believed to derive from the person's relationship to the group are *collectively realized*. For instance, a self theory might treat "purpose" as individually realized because it seems to be something that individuals have on their own. On the other hand, "cooperation" may be collectively realized because it seems to be something that one can only do as a member of a group.

The third dimension—*agency*—is the degree of active power attributed to the self. *Active* elements (like "speaking" or "driving") are contrasted with *passive* elements (like "listening" or "riding"). One person's self may differ from another's because the various aspects of self such as emotion, personality, purpose, and cooperation are defined differently within the three-dimensional scheme. For example, people of Anglo-Saxon descent tend to treat emotions as privately displayed, individually realized, and passive. In other words, they feel that emotions just happen to them and are within them. Many southern Europeans, on the other hand, see emo-

tions as public, collective, and active. In other words, they believe that emotions are something they create as a group and display together.

All self theories have three elements in common. First, they all contain a sense of *self-consciousness*. This means that one thinks of oneself as an object. When you think about yourself or talk about yourself, you are displaying consciousness of yourself. There are, then, two senses of the word *I*—the self that "knows" and the self that is "known about." Consider the following statement: "I_1 know that I_2 am afraid." I_1 reflects the sense of being aware, and I_2 reflects the sense of being the object of fear.

An important part of our conception of self is the consistency with which we define and practice I_1 and I_2. Harré calls this the *double singularity principle*.[14] A group's idea of self must treat each *I* as a consistent unity. You must possess a continual awareness of yourself as a unified being, and if you don't, you will be judged abnormal or mentally ill. In other words, you must always see yourself as you. You must also have a sense of coherence or consistency among your various self attributions, making coherent sense out of your experience. The failure to do so will create a problem for you and others. Hypocrisy, for example, is seen as an incoherent and immoral state of saying one thing and doing another.

The first aspect of self, then, is self-consciousness. The other two aspects are *agency* and *autobiography*. The self is always seen as having certain powers to do things. People see themselves as agents, capable of having intentions and actions. *Autobiography* is a sense of having a history and a future. Your agency is evident whenever you plan something, and your autobiography is apparent whenever you tell someone about yourself.

Harré uses the Eskimo as an example of the construction of self.[15] The Eskimo self is viewed

---

13 Clifford Geertz, *Local Knowledge: Further Essays in Interpretive Anthropology* (New York: Basic, 1983), p. 60.
14 Rom Harré, "Is There Still a Problem About the Self?" in *Communication Yearbook 17*, ed. Stanley Deetz (Thousand Oaks, CA: Sage, 1994), pp. 55–73.
15 Harré, *Personal Being*, p. 87.

in a network of relations with others. An Eskimo may have private feelings, but these are generally considered unimportant. Instead, the self is usually defined in terms of relationships with others. In English we would say, "I hear him." The Eskimo equivalent would be something like, "He is making a sound with reference to me." Both positive and negative emotions are considered public displays rather than private feelings.

Visitors sometimes observe that Eskimos tend to display emotions as a group. For example, they all laugh together or they all cry together. Most Eskimo virtues are social in that they are necessary for the preservation of the community as a whole. Eskimo art illustrates this quality as well. Eskimos do not have a concept for individual creativity but believe they are merely releasing something already present in the material. When they carve a log, for example, the resulting figure is seen as being revealed by the log and not something created by the carver.

The idea of the self as a socially constructed "object" is profound and important in the constructionist movement. Emotions are an important part of self, and they too are socially constructed.

Emotion.   We usually do not think of emotions as "constructed," yet they can be considered so. Harré suggests that emotions are constructed concepts, like any other aspect of human experience, because they are determined by the local language and moral orders of the culture or social group.[16]

One of the scholars best known for work on the social construction of emotions is James Averill.[17] According to Averill, emotions are belief systems that guide one's definition of the situation. As such, emotions consist of internalized social norms and rules governing feelings. These norms and rules tell us how to define and respond to emotions. Emotions do have a physiological component, but identifying and labeling bodily feelings are learned socially within a culture. In other words, the ability to make sense of emotions is socially constructed.

Averill calls emotions *syndromes*, which are clusters or sets of responses that go together. No single response is sufficient by itself to define an emotion, but all must be viewed together. Emotional syndromes are socially constructed because people learn through interaction what particular clusters of behavior should be taken to mean and how to perform a particular emotion. Emotions are acted out in specific ways, and we learn these roles from communication. What does grief look like? It looks different in various societies. People must learn how to recognize and carry out the role of the grieving person, or the angry person, or the jealous person.

Each experience of an emotion has an *object*, which is where the emotion is directed, and each emotion has a limited range of possible objects. When you are angry, you are angry at someone. When you are envious, you have envy about some achievement or possession. When you grieve, you grieve some loss. As Averill points out, you cannot be proud of the stars because pride is something reserved for accomplishment. You may say that you "love" your new car, but you cannot really be "in love" with it. Nor can you say that someone's angry attack on you makes you feel jealous.

How an emotion is labeled, what it is called, is instrumental in how the emotion is experienced. You may have very different meanings for the same physiological response depending on whether you call it "anger" or "fear." You experience an emotion one way when you call it "jealousy" and quite another when you call it "loneliness." We have rules for what anger, fear, jealousy, and loneliness are, and we have rules for how to respond to these feelings, rules constructed in social interaction throughout a lifetime.

Four kinds of rules govern emotions. *Rules of appraisal* tell you what an emotion is, where it is

---

16   Rom Harré, ed., "An Outline of the Social Constructionist Viewpoint," in *The Social Construction of Emotions* (New York: Blackwell, 1986), pp. 2–14.
17   Among Averill's most pertinent writings in this line of work are "A Constructivist View of Emotion," in *Theories of Emotion*, eds. K. Plutchik and H. Kellerman (New York: Academic, 1980), pp. 305–339; "On the Paucity of Positive Emotions," in *Assessment and Modification of Emotional Behavior*, eds. K. R. Blankstein, P. Pliner, and J. Polivy (New York: Plenum, 1980), pp. 7–45; *Anger and Aggression: An Essay on Emotion* (New York: Springer-Verlag, 1982); "The Acquisition of Emotions During Adulthood," in *The Social Construction of Emotions*, ed. Rom Harré (New York: Blackwell, 1986), pp. 98–119.

directed, and whether it is positive or negative. *Rules of behavior* tell you how to respond to the feeling—whether to hide it, to express it in private, or to vent it publicly. *Rules of prognosis* define the progression and course of the emotion. How long should it last, what are its different stages, how does it begin, and how does it end? *Rules of attribution* dictate how an emotion should be explained or justified. What do you tell others about it? How do you express it publicly?

If you were angry at another person, your rules of appraisal would tell you what you were feeling and who the target of the feeling was. These rules would also define whether that anger was positive (like righteous indignation) or negative (rage). Behavior rules would guide your behavior, including how to express the anger, whether to lash out or remain quiet, whether to aggress or retreat. Prognosis rules would guide how long the anger episode should last and the different phases through which it might pass. Finally, the rules of attribution would help you explain the anger ("She was acting like a jerk and made me mad").

Thus, emotions are not just things in themselves. They are defined and handled according to what has been learned in social interaction with other people. We learn emotional rules in childhood and throughout life. Averill is clear that people can and do change emotionally. When you enter a new life situation, you are exposed to new ways of understanding emotion, and your feelings, their expression, and the ways you manage those emotions change.

Averill conducted an interesting study in which he isolated over five hundred terms for various emotions, a list that was representative of emotional terms in the English language.[18] His subjects then rated these terms on a number of dimensions, including evaluation (for example, pleasant-unpleasant). He found that far more emotional terms were evaluated as negative (such as anger, jealousy) than positive (for instance, joy, happiness). This is an interesting puzzle: Why do negative emotions outweigh positive ones by about two to one?

The answer is that emotions do not come prepackaged as positive or negative, but we define

them that way based on our social constructions. In Averill's sample, positive outcomes tend to be action oriented, whereas negative results tend to be seen as beyond one's control. So, for example, courage is the result of one's brave actions, whereas jealousy is the consequence of an unfortunate situation.

Further, emotions in general tend to be viewed in our society as beyond control, something that just happens to us. So it is logical that positive outcomes are defined less as emotions and more as actions, whereas negative outcomes are more often seen as emotions, which leads to the idea that emotional terms are more often negative than positive. In other cultures the outcome might be quite different.

For example, the Ifaluk of Micronesia experience several forms of anger, including that which accompanies sickness, that which builds up slowly from several bothersome irritations, that which is experienced when relatives do not live up to expectations, and that which is caused by personal misfortune.[19] Clearly, in this culture, anger is not just anger; the various types are sharply distinguished

Justifiable anger, called *song*, occurs in a highly predictable pattern among the Ifaluk. A rule must be violated, and someone must point out that this occurred. The person who witnessed the violation must condemn the act, and the one who did it must react to this condemnation with fear, promising not to do it again.

Accounts. One of the ways people construct social realities is by making accounts, or explaining and justifying their behavior.[20] For example,

18 Averill, "On the Paucity of Positive Emotions."
19 Catherine Lutz, "Morality, Domination, and Understandings of 'Justifiable Anger' Among the Ifaluk," in *Everyday Understanding: Social and Scientific Implications*, eds. Gün R. Semin and Kenneth J. Gergen (London: Sage, 1990), pp. 204–226.
20 For a classification of accounts, see Margaret L. McLaughlin, Michael J. Cody, and Nancy E. Rosenstein, "Account Sequences in Conversations Between Strangers," *Communication Monographs* 50 (1983): 102–125; Margaret L. McLaughlin, Michael J. Cody, and H. Dan O'Hair, "The Management of Failure Events: Some Contextual Determinants of Accounting Behavior," *Human Communication Research* 9 (1983): 208–224. For a longer, more diverse treatment, see Margaret L. McLaughlin, Michael J. Cody, and Stephen Read, eds., *Explaining One's Self to Others: Reason-Giving in a Social Context* (Hillsdale, NJ: Erlbaum, 1992).

if you forgot your mother's birthday, you would have some explaining to do. You might say that you were busy at school and forgot, which reinforces the idea that being productive is good; or that you lost your calendar, which suggests that record keeping is important; or that you have no excuse and are sorry, which says that family relationships should not be ignored. No matter what you say, you are reconstructing some aspect of the social reality in force at the time you make the account.

John Shotter provides a useful extension of constructionist thinking into the subjects of responsibility and morality.[21] Shotter believes that human experience cannot be separated from communication. Our speech both reflects and creates our experience of reality. Central to this link between communication and experience is the process of making accounts.

In everyday conversation the "I" cannot be separated from the "you," because the speaker (I) and the listener (you) go back and forth. So in a conversation, people are making demands on one another. They are telling others how to behave and what to think, and the morality of everyday life is constructed in this process.[22]

Communicators believe they have the power to act, yet they may feel somewhat constrained by rules of action. Rules may be followed or broken, but people are at least expected to explain their actions on the basis of rules or exceptions to those rules. Because of the presence of rules and our personal powers to follow or break them, we must think through and plan our actions, and these plans are largely framed in light of what we would have to say to explain what we did. Think about it: When you undertake an action, you often consider ahead of time what you would say if you had to explain that action to others. In other words, potential accounts actually help shape your actions before they occur.

Like other constructionists, Shotter believes that people are constantly assigning meaning to and making sense of their experiences. The meanings assigned to an event are closely tied to the language used to account for the event in communication among participants. Richard

Buttny suggests that in any kind of failure event the participants have an interest in controlling the meaning for that event.[23] Accounts serve precisely this function. They are a way of accomplishing goals, such as saving face and preserving relationships. Buttny says that accounts essentially reframe events by creating a context in which to interpret those events.

Buttny presents the example of a student–teacher conference about a speech assignment.[24] The teacher confronts the student on a poor performance, and the student offers an excuse: "It was a bad day, I just, ah, blew a math test before it, so I didn't really feel like speaking." Here, the student is trying to create the context of a bad day, in which it is okay to do poorly. By giving an account, the student attempts to control the meaning of the situation.

Shotter shows that the relationship between communication (talking and making accounts) and the experience of reality constitutes a loop: Communication determines how reality is experienced, and the experience of reality affects communication. Figure 9.1 illustrates this relationship.[25]

Let's return to the birthday example. Birthdays are an ordinary activity in most Western cultures, and we have a number of forms of talk relevant to this event, including certain kinds of accounts. The standard birthday card that apologizes in an amusing way for forgetting a birthday or being late is a good example of institutionalized accounting. These forms of talk in turn contribute to certain ideas we have about the importance of individuals and their lives. They also address our cultural theories of personal responsibility and interpersonal relations. (You better remember Mom's birthday, or she will think you

---

21   John Shotter, *Social Accountability and Selfhood* (Oxford: Blackwell, 1984).
22   This argument is developed in John Shotter, "Social Accountability and the Social Construction of 'You,'" in *Texts of Identity*, eds. J. Shotter and K. J. Gergen (London: Sage, 1989), pp. 133–151.
23   Richard Buttny, "Accounts as a Reconstruction of an Event's Context," *Communication Monographs* 52 (1985): 57–77. See also "Sequence and Structure in Accounts Episodes," *Communication Quarterly* 35 (1987): 67–83.
24   Buttny, "Accounts."
25   Shotter, *Social Accountability*, p. 140.

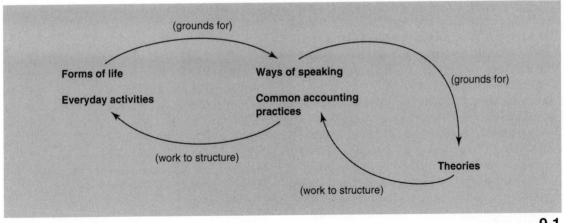

FIGURE 9.1

Communication–Experience Loop

Adapted from *Social Accountability and Selfhood* by John Shotter. Copyright © 1984 by Basil Blackwell Publishers. Reprinted by permission of the publisher.

don't care about her.) When you acknowledge a person's birthday, you are reinforcing the idea that individuals are important in our society, which is certainly an important part of our culture's theory of personhood. Those theories in turn affect how we talk, including the forms of speech used in birthday celebrations.

Much like Harré, Shotter believes that the individual and the society are inseparable. Persons are not independent: "Attention is not concentrated upon the supposed relation between people's 'outer' behavior and their 'inner' workings, for it is not focused upon individuals at all, but upon the relations between people."[26] The overall milieu is essentially a moral world of rights, duties, privileges, and obligations. The moral framework of human experience is expressed in and through communication: "To preserve their autonomy, people must be able to account, not only for their actions, but also for themselves, i.e. who and what they are."[27]

Coordinated Management of Meaning

The theory of the coordinated management of meaning (CMM), developed by Barnett Pearce, Vernon Cronen, and their colleagues, is the most

comprehensive and codified theory of social construction.[28] Actually, the theory integrates work from several fields, including system theory (Chapter 3), symbolic interactionism (Chapter 8), social construction (Chapter 9), speech acts (Chapter 5), and relational communication (Chapter 12).

As a rule theory, CMM states that people interpret and act on the basis of rules. Individuals

26   Shotter, *Social Accountability,* p. 94.
27   Shotter, *Social Accountability,* p. 152.
28   For a recent summary of the theory, see Gerry Philipsen, "The Coordinated Management of Meaning Theory of Pearce, Cronen, and Associates," in *Watershed Research Traditions in Human Communication Theory,* eds. Donald P. Cushman and Branislav Kovačić (Albany: SUNY Press, 1995), pp. 13–43. For some primary sources, see W. Barnett Pearce and Vernon Cronen, *Communication, Action, and Meaning* (New York: Praeger, 1980); W. Barnett Pearce and Kimberly A. Pearce, "Extending the Theory of the Coordinated Management of Meaning (CMM) Through a Community Dialogue Process," *Communication Theory* 10 (2000): 405–423; Vernon Cronen, Victoria Chen, and W. Barnett Pearce, "Coordinated Management of Meaning: A Critical Theory," in *Theories in Intercultural Communication* (Newbury Park, CA: Sage, 1988), pp. 66–98; Vernon Cronen, W. Barnett Pearce, and Linda Harris, "The Coordinated Management of Meaning," in *Comparative Human Communication Theory,* ed. F. E. X. Dance (New York: Harper & Row, 1982); W. Barnett Pearce, "The Coordinated Management of Meaning: A Rules Based Theory of Interpersonal Communication," in *Explorations in Interpersonal Communication,* ed. G. R. Miller (Beverly Hills, CA: Sage, 1976), pp. 17–36; Vernon Cronen, W. Barnett Pearce, and Linda Harris, "The Logic of the Coordinated Management of Meaning," *Communication Education* 28 (1979): 22–38.

within any social situation first want to understand what is going on and apply rules to figure things out. They then act on the basis of their understandings, employing rules to decide what kind of action is appropriate.

There are two types of rules. *Constitutive rules* are essentially *rules of meaning,* used by communicators to interpret or understand an event or message. *Regulative rules* are essentially *rules of action,* used to determine how to respond or behave.

For example, if a friend says something to you, you decipher the meaning of the message. You interpret it; you figure out what it means. Usually this is a simple and almost unconscious experience because your interpretation rules are immediately available and simple. Sometimes, however, interpretation is more difficult, and you may have to dig for appropriate rules of understanding. Once you feel you know what was said, action rules help you decide how to respond.

Rules of meaning and action always operate within a *context,* or frame of reference for interpreting and acting. One context is always embedded within another so that each context is itself part of a bigger one. Figure 9.2 illustrates this idea.

Here, four typical contexts are depicted. The *relationship context* includes mutual expectations among members of a group. The *episode context* is an event. The *self-concept context* is one's sense of personal definition. Finally, the *archetype context* is an image of general truth. As an example, you might interpret your daughter's snippy remark as an insult within the context of your negative relationship. The relationship, in turn, might be judged as negative in terms of the episode of an argument, which you view as typical given your self-concept as a headstrong person.

The order of contexts shown in Figure 9.2 is not universal and often shifts. Sometimes, for example, self is understood within the context of the relationship, but on other occasions the relationship is understood in reference to the self. Also, although the contexts listed in Figure 9.2 are representative and common, they by no means exhaust the possible contexts within

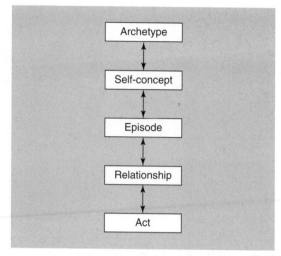

F I G U R E **9.2**

Hierarchy of Contexts

Adapted from *Communication, Action, and Meaning* by W. Barnett Pearce and Vernon Cronen. Copyright © 1980 by Praeger Publishers. Reprinted by permission of the authors.

which interpretations and actions are made. Humans have the ability to create numerous contexts for interpretation and action.

Any event or action being interpreted is known as a *text.* In the example above, the snippy comment is the "text," and your relationship is the "context." Often text and context form a loop (Figure 9.3), such that each is used from time to time to interpret the other.[29] This situation is called *reflexivity* because each context reflects the other. Reflexivity always enters the context hierarchy at some point because the hierarchy cannot keep going up forever. At some point the ladder of contexts must come to an end and start coming down again. In other words, at some point, the context must become the text.

29   Loops are discussed in Vernon E. Cronen, Kenneth M. Johnson, and John W. Lannamann, "Paradoxes, Double Binds, and Reflexive Loops: An Alternative Theoretical Perspective," *Family Process* 20 (1982): 91–112; and Robert J. Branham and W. Barnett Pearce, "Between Text and Context: Toward a Rhetoric of Contextual Reconstruction," *Quarterly Journal of Speech* 71 (1985): 19–36. For an interesting recent extrapolation and extension of this idea, see James R. Taylor, Francois Cooren, Nicole Giroux, and Daniel Robichaud, "The Communicational Basis of Organization: Between the Conversation and the Text," *Communication Theory* 6 (1996): 1–39.

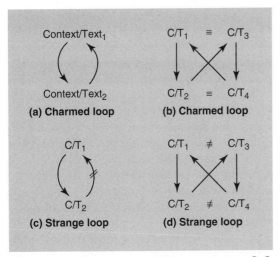

FIGURE **9.3**

Text-Context Loop Patterns

Adapted from "Between Text and Context: Toward a Rhetoric of Contextual Reconstruction" by Robert J. Branham and W. Barnett Pearce, in *Quarterly Journal of Speech* 71 (1985): 23, 25. Reprinted by permission of the authors and publisher.

When the rules of meaning are consistent throughout the loop, the loop is said to be *charmed*, or self-confirming. The example of the link between your daughter's insult and relationship is a charmed loop; each confirms the other. Often, however, the rules of interpretation change from one point in the loop to another, causing a paradox, or *strange loop*, in which each context disconfirms the other. This would happen, for example, if you felt that you had a good relationship, but it included lots of insulting

comments. Here the relationship would not confirm the insults, and the insults would not confirm the relationship. The result would be confusion.

The strange loop of the alcoholic is illustrated in Figure 9.4. Notice here the alcoholic is confused about control. Within the context of the self as a controlled drinker, drinking is accepted as okay, but within the context of the episode of drinking, the self is defined as out of control, making drinking not okay. If you follow the loop in Figure 9.4, you see what many alcoholics go through. First, they drink and come to see themselves as out of control. Then they stop drinking, now believing they are in control, so that they can begin drinking again.

Pearce and Cronen use a set of symbols to demonstrate how rules operate. Figure 9.5 shows how to depict rules graphically.

Rules give us a sense of what is logical or appropriate in a given situation. This is called *logical force*. Because people behave in a manner consistent with their rules, rules provide a logical force for acting in certain ways. Four types of logical force operate in communication.

The first type of logical force is *prefigurative*, or *causal force*, an antecedent-to-act linkage in which you perceive that you are being pressured to behave in certain ways because of prior conditions. If you think that you are being caused to do something, prefigurative force is at play. For example, you might tell someone that you are in school because your parents made you go.

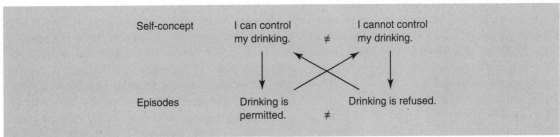

FIGURE **9.4**

The Alcoholic's Paradox

Adapted from "Between Text and Context: Toward a Rhetoric of Contextual Reconstruction" by Robert J. Branham and W. Barnett Pearce, in *Quarterly Journal of Speech* 71 (1985): 26. Reprinted by permission of the authors and publisher.

= in the context of
= counts as
⊃ = if, then

play
insult ⟶ joke

In the context of play, an insult is to be taken as a joke. *Meaning rule:* An insult counts as a joke.

conflict
insult ⟶ put-down

In the context of conflict, an insult is to be taken as a put-down. *Meaning rule:* An insult counts as a put-down.

argument
husband insults wife's family ⊃ wife cries

In the context of an argument, when the husband insults the wife's family, she cries. *Action rule:* An insult leads to crying.

playful banter
husband insults wife's family ⊃ wife playfully hits husband ⟶ fun

In play it is considered fun for the wife to "hit" the husband after he insults her family. *Action rule:* Wife should respond to husband's insult by "hitting" him. *Meaning rule:* This sequence is taken as fun.

FIGURE **9.5**

Logical Rules

Practical force is an act-to-consequent linkage in which you behave in a certain way to achieve a future condition. So, for example, you might believe you are in college because you want to get a better job than you could get with only a high school education.

The third type of logical force is contextual. *Contextual force* is a pressure from the context. Here, you believe that the action or interpretation is a natural part of the context. Within the context of your self-concept, for example, you might feel that going to college is just necessary, just part of who you are.

Finally, *implicative force* is a pressure to transform or change the context in some way. Here, you act to create a new context or to change an existing one. Implicative force might come into play, for example, if your family did not value college and never encouraged its children to go on to school. You might take it on yourself to change this situation, to create a new family definition, to make the family proud of one of its members for getting a degree. In this kind of situation, you would actually be trying to change the context of family expectations.

In modern society a person is part of many systems, each with its own set of meaning and action rules. The rules are learned through interaction in social groups. Over time, individuals internalize many of these rules and draw on them to guide their actions. The basic problem of communication is that when an individual enters an interaction, that person has no way of knowing precisely what rules the other participants will be using. The primary task in all communication, then, is to achieve and then sustain some form of coordination.

Coordination involves meshing one's actions with those of another to the point of feeling that the sequence of actions is logical or appropriate. The communicators in an exchange need not interpret the events the same way, but each must feel, from within his or her own system of rules, that what is happening makes sense.

Figure 9.6 shows how coordination operates.[30] Person A acts in a certain way, and person B takes this as a message. Person B uses meaning rules to interpret the message. Person A's act thus becomes an antecedent event to which person B responds, based on B's action rules. B's act is in turn interpreted by A as a message from the standpoint of A's meaning rules, and B's act becomes the consequent to A's initial move. If A and B are operating with substantially different rule structures, they will quickly discover that one person's behavior does not represent the consequent intended, and they will readjust their rules until some level of coordination is achieved.

30 Pearce and Cronen, *Communication*, p. 174.

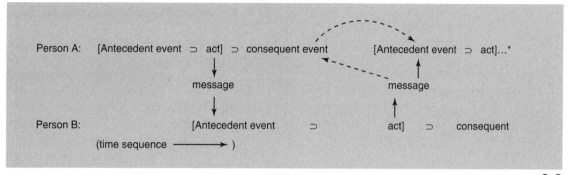

FIGURE **9.6**

Coordination Process

*Solid arrows denote constitutive rules. Broken arrows denote the coorientational state of comparing the subsequent message to the anticipated consequent event in anticipation of the next act. From *Communication, Action, and Meaning* by W. Barnett Pearce and Vernon Cronen. Copyright © 1980 by Praeger Publishers. Reprinted by permission of the authors.

Consider the simple example of a child trying to get back a ball after accidentally throwing it through a neighbor's window.[31] The adult begins with the following rule structure:

- *Meaning rule:* If I say, "Is this ball yours?" in a stern fashion, this act will be taken as anger, a demand for a confession, and a threat.
- *Action rule:* My act, taken as anger, will elicit crying and apologies. I, in turn, will become less angry and will give back the ball.

The child, on the other hand, has a different set of rules:

- *Meaning rule:* When the neighbor says, "Is this your ball?" he is asking for information. My statement, "Give it back," will be taken as a request.
- *Action rule:* When the neighbor requests information, I will respond with a factual answer, "Yes, it is." I will say, "Give it back," and he will give it back.

Now observe the actual conversation:

Neighbor: Is this your ball?
Child: Yes, it is. Give it back.

31   This example is adapted from Pearce and Cronen, *Communication*, pp. 162–164. Originally, the example was developed in K. T. Alvy, "The Development of Listener-Adapted Communication in Grade-School Children from Different Social Class Backgrounds," *Genetic Psychology Monographs* 87 (1973): 33–104.

Obviously, the neighbor did not get the expected response and will interpret the child's remark as impudence rather than the simple request intended by the child. At this point the interaction is not coordinated. Now the neighbor must adjust the action rule by trying a different approach:

Neighbor: Give it back? This ball went through my window. Do you know that?

If the child has a sufficiently complex rule structure to provide options, he may adjust so that a successful outcome can be achieved. If not, coordination may not be achieved. Consider:

Unsatisfactory outcome:
Child: Give my ball back. I'll tell Daddy if you don't give it back.
Neighbor: Get out of my yard, kid!

Successful outcome (coordination achieved):
Child: I'm sorry. I didn't mean to do it, and I will be careful in the future.
Neighbor: Okay. Here's your ball.

An important contribution of CMM is the idea that people can have perfectly satisfactory coordination without understanding one another. In other words, communicators can organize their actions in ways that seem logical to all parties, yet they understand what is going on in a variety of different ways. For example, a speaker and audience may coordinate very well. The speaker is dynamic and effusive, and the audience responds enthusiastically. The speaker thinks she is educating and persuading the audience, but the audience is merely entertained and forgets the point of the message within hours. Here, both sides are satisfied, and each thinks what happened was appropriate; yet what the speaker thought was happening did not happen.

As an example of coordination without understanding, Uma Narula and Barnett Pearce studied the communication patterns of development, or economic improvement, in India.[32] The Indian government has had such a program for many years, with legislation, direct action, and communication as its cornerstone. The communication aspect of the program was designed to make the people more aware of their problems and get them involved in local improvement projects. The result was that they became very aware of problems and the potential for improvement, but they did not become involved in their own development. This is a case of coordination without understanding.

The rules used by the population to interpret and respond to the development campaigns were different from those of the government. The government intended to have the people become directly involved in development projects of their own. The people saw the direct action of the government as the answer and expected the government to do it all. This led to a pattern of "passive involvement," in which the population became increasingly critical of the government for not solving their problems for them. The government thought its communication program had been a failure, when in fact it had been very successful. The government did not realize that its own direct action was also taken by the population as a message—that problems could be solved by the government alone.

Clearly, language is important in CMM, as it is in social constructionism generally. We turn now to theories relating language to culture.

Ⓒ LANGUAGE AND CULTURE

So far in this chapter, it should be apparent that language and culture are vital aspects of social life. In the final section of this chapter, we examine some prominent theories of culture and language and their link to one another.[33] In addition to the theories presented in this section, this subject is also taken up in Chapter 10.

The study of language and culture is known as *sociolinguistics,* a broad term covering any study of language that makes significant use of social data or any study of social life that makes use of linguistic data. Sociolinguistics contrasts sharply with the structural approaches covered in Chapter 4, which view language as separate from communication. Today, most students of language believe that language is affected by both structural and social properties.[34]

We turn now to two important classic theoretical contributions to language and culture.

Linguistic Relativity

The *Sapir-Whorf hypothesis,* otherwise known as the theory of linguistic relativity, is based on the work of Edward Sapir and his protégé Benjamin Lee Whorf.[35] Whorf is best known for his fieldwork in linguistics, and his analysis of the Hopi language is particularly well known. In his research Whorf discovered that fundamental syntactic differences are present among language groups. The Whorfian hypothesis of linguistic

32   Uma Narula and W. Barnett Pearce, *Development as Communication: A Perspective on India* (Carbondale: Southern Illinois University Press, 1986).
33   For a discussion of the role of culture in the communication field, see John H. Powers, "On the Intellectual Structure of the Human Communication Discipline," *Communication Education* 44 (1995): 191–222.
34   Gillian Sankoff, *The Social Life of Language* (Philadelphia: University of Pennsylvania Press, 1980), p. xvii.
35   Edward Sapir, *Language: An Introduction to the Study of Speech* (New York: Harcourt, Brace & World, 1921); Benjamin L. Whorf, *Language, Thought, and Reality,* ed. John. B. Carroll (New York: Wiley, 1956). In the Whorf book, the following articles are most helpful: John B. Carroll, "Introduction," pp. 1–34; "The Relation of Habitual Thought and Behavior to Language," pp. 134–159; "Language, Mind, and Reality," pp. 246–270.

relativity simply states that the structure of a culture's language determines the behavior and habits of thinking in that culture. In the words of Sapir,

> Human beings do not live in the objective world alone, nor alone in the world of social activity as ordinarily understood, but are very much at the mercy of the particular language which has become the medium of expression for their society. . . . The fact of the matter is that the "real world" is to a large extent unconsciously built up on the language habits of the group. . . . We see and hear and otherwise experience very largely as we do because the language habits of our community predispose certain choices of interpretation.[36]

This hypothesis suggests that our thought processes and the way we see the world are shaped by the grammatical structure of the language. As one writer reacted, "All one's life one has been tricked . . . by the structure of language into a certain way of perceiving reality."[37]

Whorf spent much of his life investigating the relationship of language and behavior. His work with the Hopi illustrates the relativity hypothesis. Like all cultural groups, the Hopi possess a reality, which represents their view of the world at large. One area of Whorf's extensive analysis of Hopi thought is the analysis of time. Whereas many cultures refer to points in time (such as seasons) as nouns, the Hopi conceive of time as a passage or process. Thus, the Hopi language never objectifies time. The Hopi would not refer to summer as "in the summer." Instead, the Hopi would refer to the passing or coming of a phase that is never here and now but always moving, accumulating. In our culture three tenses indicate locations or places in a spatial analogy: past, present, and future. Hopi verbs have no tense in the same sense. Instead, their verb forms relate to duration and order. In the Standard Average European (SAE) languages, including English, we visualize time as a line. The Hopi conception is more complex, as illustrated in the following example.[38]

Suppose a speaker reports that a man is running: "He is running." The Hopi would use the word *wari,* which is a statement of *running as a fact.* The same word would be used for a report of past running: "He ran." For the Hopi, the statement of fact is what is important, not whether the event is presently occurring or happened in the past. If, however, the Hopi speaker wishes to report *running from memory* (the hearer did not actually see it), a different form would be used, *era wari.* The English sentence "He will run" would translate *warikni,* which communicates *running as expectation.* Again, it is not the location in past, present, or future that is important to the Hopi but whether it is observed fact, recalled fact, or expectation. Another English form, "He runs [on the track team]," would translate *warikngwe.* This latter Hopi form again refers to *running as a condition.*

As a result of these linguistic differences, Hopi and SAE cultures will think about, perceive, and behave toward time differently. For example, the Hopi tend to engage in lengthy preparing activities. Experiences (getting prepared) tend to accumulate as time "gets later." The emphasis is on the accumulated experience during the course of time, not on time as a point or location. In SAE cultures, with their spatial treatment of time, experiences are not accumulated in the same sense. Elaborate and lengthy preparations are not often found. The custom in SAE cultures is to record events such that what happened in the past is objectified. Whorf summarizes this view: "Concepts of 'time' and 'matter' are not given in substantially the same form by experience to all men but depend upon the nature of the language or languages through the use of which they have been developed."[39]

Notice that the theory of linguistic relativity is different from the social constructionist theories discussed earlier in the chapter. In social constructionism people are believed to create their realities in the process of interaction, whereas

36   Quoted in Whorf, *Language, Thought, and Reality,* p. 134.
37   Carroll (in Whorf's *Language, Thought, and Reality*), "Introduction," p. 27.
38   Adapted from Whorf, *Language, Thought, and Reality,* p. 213.
39   Whorf, *Language, Thought, and Reality,* p. 158.

Whorf and Sapir teach that reality is already embedded in the language and therefore comes preformed. Both theories deal with cultural reality, but they approach the topic in opposite ways.

Elaborated and Restricted Codes

One of the most important sociolinguistic theories is that of Basil Bernstein on elaborated and restricted codes.[40] This theory shows how the structure of the language employed in everyday talk reflects and shapes the assumptions of a social group. Bernstein is especially interested in social class and the ways the class system creates different types of language and is maintained by language.

The basic assumption of this theory is that the relationships established in a social group affect the type of speech used by the group. At the same time, the structure of the speech used by a group makes different things relevant or significant. This happens because different groups have different priorities, and language emerges from what is required to maintain relationships within the group. In other words, people learn their place in the world by virtue of the language codes they employ.

For example, in one family where a strict authoritarian control system is used, children learn that they must respond to simple commands. In this kind of family, persuasive appeals would be not only irrelevant but counterproductive. For Bernstein, role and language go hand in hand. The kinds of roles that children learn are reinforced by the kind of language employed in the community, especially the family. The term *code* refers to a set of organizing principles behind the language employed by members of a social group. Two children who both speak English might employ very different codes because their talk is different.

Bernstein's theory centers on two codes— elaborated and restricted. *Elaborated codes* pro-

vide a wide range of different ways to say something. These allow speakers to make their ideas and intentions explicit. Because they are more complex, elaborated codes require more planning, explaining why speakers may pause more and appear to be thinking as they talk. *Restricted codes* have a narrower range of options, and it is easier to predict what form they will take. These codes do not allow speakers to expand on or elaborate very much on what they mean.

Restricted codes are appropriate in groups in which there is a strongly shared set of assumptions and little need to elaborate on what is meant. Elaborated codes are appropriate in groups in which perspectives are not shared. Here, people are required to expand on what they mean. Restricted codes are oriented toward social categories, for which everybody has the same meaning, whereas elaborated codes are oriented toward individualized categories that others might not share.

For example, in some groups everybody knows the difference between masculine and feminine, and people are clearly identified in a male or female role. Everybody knows the place of a woman and a man, a girl and a boy. You can assume what people think and feel based on their gender identification, and there is little need to explore individual differences. In other groups, however, gender is not as useful because there is not a common understanding of what masculine and feminine mean. You can see that it would take more words to explore what is appropriate behavior for the individual child than it would to tell a girl to go to the kitchen and help her mother.

Thus, elaborated codes are used by speakers who value individuality above group identification. Because the intent of the speakers cannot be inferred from their role, they have to be able to express themselves individually in some detail. Bernstein offers the example of a couple that has just come out of a movie and stops by to visit with friends. There, they discuss the film at some length. The other couple has not seen it but can understand their friends' ideas about the film anyway:

40   Basil Bernstein, *Class, Codes, and Control: Theoretical Studies Toward a Sociology of Language* (London: Routledge & Kegan Paul, 1971).

An hour is spent in the complex moral, political, aesthetic subtleties of the film and its place in the contemporary scene. . . . The meanings now have to be made public to others who have not seen the film. The speech shows careful editing, at both the grammatical and lexical levels. It is no longer contextualized. The meanings are explicit, elaborated and individualized. . . . The experience of the listeners cannot be taken for granted. Thus each member of the group is on his own as he offers his interpretation.[41]

A primary difference between the types of groups that use these two codes is their degree of openness. A *closed-role system* is one that reduces the number of alternatives for the participants. Roles are set, and people are viewed in terms of those roles. This understanding of who people are and how they should behave forms the basis of a common knowledge within the group. Because of this shared meaning in the group, an elaborated language is not necessary and therefore not cultured or learned.

An *open-role system* is one that expands the number of alternatives for individuals in the group. Roles are not categorical and simple; they are individualized and negotiated; they are fluid and change. Thus, there may be little shared understanding of a person's identity within an open system, and an elaborated code is necessary for communication to take place in this system.

Two major factors contribute to the development of an elaborated or restricted code within a system. The first is the nature of the major socializing agencies within the system, including the family, peer group, school, and work. Where the structure of these groups is well defined in terms of fixed roles, a restricted code is likely to develop. Where the structure of these groups is less well defined and has fluid roles, an elaborated code is more likely to be created.

The second major factor is values. Pluralistic societies that value individuality promote elaborated codes, whereas narrower societies promote restricted ones.

You can now see how codes are so strongly associated with social class. Bernstein says that members of the middle class use both types of

systems. They may, for example, be exposed to rather open roles at home but somewhat closed ones in the workplace. Or peer groups may use closed roles, whereas the school employs open ones.

Members of the working class, however, are less likely to use elaborated codes. For working-class individuals, both the values and the role systems reinforce restricted codes, which leads Bernstein to write,

> Without a shadow of a doubt the most formative influence upon the procedures of socialization, from a sociological viewpoint, is social class. The class structure influences work and educational roles and brings families into a special relationship with each other and deeply penetrates the structure of life experiences within the family. . . . I shall go on to argue that the deep structure of communication itself is affected, but not in any final or irrevocable way.[42]

In a well-known study, Bernstein tape-recorded young men from the working class and the middle class in England talking about capital punishment.[43] He analyzed samples of this speech and found interesting class differences. Even when the data were controlled for intelligence, the working-class speakers used longer phrases, shorter words, and less pausing than middle-class speakers. With an elaborated code, the middle-class boys needed more planning time, which explains their shorter phrases and longer pauses.

Many other differences found in this study illustrate elaborated and restricted codes. For example, middle-class speakers used "I think" significantly more than did working-class speakers. Working-class speakers made greater use of short phrases at the end of sentences to confirm the other person's common understanding; these included expressions like "isn't it?" "you know," and "wouldn't he?" Middle-class speakers had longer, more complex verb phrases, more passive verbs, more uncommon adverbs and adjectives.

---

41   Bernstein, *Class, Codes, and Control*, p. 177.
42   Bernstein, *Class, Codes, and Control*, p. 175.
43   Bernstein, *Class, Codes, and Control*, pp. 76–117.

And middle-class speakers made more use of the personal pronoun *I*.

Elaborated codes are empowering because they enable speakers to adapt to a wide range of audiences and appeal to widely different types of persons. On the other hand, elaborated codes can be alienating because, as Bernstein writes, they separate "feeling from thought, self from other, private belief from role obligation."[44]

Although he acknowledges the limitations of restricted talk, Bernstein does not devalue it: "Let it be said immediately that a restricted code gives access to a vast potential of meanings, of delicacy, subtlety and diversity of cultural forms, to a unique aesthetic the basis of which in condensed symbols may influence the form of the imagining."[45] However, Bernstein also notes that those in power in society often do devalue this type of speech, which further perpetuates the class system.

The family is especially important in the development of code. Two types of families correspond to the two types of codes. *Position families* have a clear and formally determined role structure. They often have a closed communication system and use restricted codes. Such families tend to have sharp boundaries in their use of space and in their conception of objects and persons. They define objects and people in terms of their position.

Person-centered families determine roles on the basis of individuals' personal orientations rather than formally defined divisions. They tend to use open communication and elaborated codes. Roles and relations within these families tend to be unstable and constantly in negotiation. These families do not maintain sharp boundaries in their use of space or in their ideas about people and things.

Although a family may have a variety of means of exerting control and regulating behavior, there seems to be a predominant or preferred method employed, depending on the type of family. Some families prefer an *imperative mode* of regulation, which is based on command and authority. In this type of family, when Dad says, "Shut up," you do. This is preferred in hierarchical families in which certain members are defined as in control according to the role structure. This kind of control is delivered with a restricted code.

Other families prefer *positional appeals,* based on role-related norms. Here, control is exerted by relying on commonly understood norms associated with each role. Examples of this kind of appeal are "You are old enough to know better," or "Boys don't play with dolls." This kind of control can be expressed with restricted or elaborated codes, depending on the degree of differentiation in the system.

Finally, *personal appeals* are based on individualized characteristics and individualized rules, and these appeals often consist of giving reasons for why a person should or should not do something. Again, the code employed can be restricted or elaborated, depending on the degree of shared understanding in the family.

COMMENTARY AND CRITIQUE

For the most part, this chapter fills in the blanks left by symbolic interactionism in Chapter 8. We see here the many ways in which people construct reality through communication. The idea of social constructionism has won widespread favor because of its intuitive appeal. All theories in this chapter see a close relationship between language and reality. All show that the language used in a culture shapes the reality in which that culture lives.

We see from these theories that all aspects of reality are socially constructed, including, for example, the self and emotions. We have looked at the ways common forms of talk such as accounts contribute to the construction of reality within a social group or culture. Rules are an important part of a social reality, and they provide guidance for the communication that affects our sense of reality.

44   Bernstein, *Class, Codes, and Control*, p. 186.
45   Bernstein, *Class, Codes, and Control*, p. 186.

An important question deals with the role of interaction in this reality-constructing system. Symbolic interactionism assumes that language is an outcome of interaction. The social constructionists use the same assumption as the basis for the idea that reality is constructed through communication.

Sapir and Whorf, on the other hand, assume that language precedes interaction and that our interaction patterns are a result, not a cause, of language structure. In a remarkable review of the literatures on language learning, language differences, bilingualism, and sensori-neuroscience, Thomas Steinfatt concluded that although the Whorfian hypothesis cannot be tested, the evidence for it is weak.[46]

One can, of course, take a stand in the middle and suggest that both the language-thought and thought-language connections are true. Interaction does shape language, but language in turn shapes interaction.[47] Most constructionists today would probably agree with this position.

Bernstein's work illustrates this idea very well. The type of interaction in the family and other socializing institutions determines the sort of language learned, but language in turn reinforces the interaction patterns that led to it in the first place. We will return to the issue of the primacy of language versus interaction in Chapter 10 in our examination of phenomenology and textual interpretation.

Although the social constructionist thesis is appealing, there is also strong resistance to this idea from some quarters. Social constructionism remains controversial because it conflicts with the commonsense notion that reality is objective and independent, an idea deeply rooted in Western thought. Many social researchers and philosophers of science strongly believe that we use language to communicate about the objects in the world and that those objects exist in a particular form prior to any communication about them.

Although it seems patently obvious to constructionists that human experience is formed largely in and through culture, many sociobehavioral scientists have not adopted this assumption at all. Much social science still rests on the assumption that the human experience is largely universal, owing to a common biological inheritance and common cognitive structure. Noam Chomsky (Chapter 4), for example, has taught that language structures are universal and that cultural differences in languages are merely superficial. Further, he believes that certain language universals are innate and that language is acquired by an interaction between experience and wired-in structures. Charles Osgood (Chapter 7) has come to the conclusion that the dimensions of meaning are universal, which is antithetical to social constructionism.

If these structuralists are right, cultural relativists are barking up the wrong tree. We should not be looking for richly different language and meaning experiences; instead, we should discover the common universals that provide an explanatory basis for human behavior across the board. This is a debate that will not die, and we encounter it again at other points throughout this text.

Donald Ellis recently posed a series of thoughtful challenges to social constructionism.[48] Ellis believes that communication cannot proceed without assuming that we live in a world of *a priori* realism. We must assume that we are all talking about the same thing, or communication cannot take place. This argument is based on two principles—semantic realism and coherentism.

Semantic realism is the idea that words have standard meanings. When you say something to someone, you assume that this person will share your meanings. You essentially enter a contract with your listener that says, "We agree to use a standard set of meanings." Further, these meanings are very stable. Although it is true that

46   Thomas M. Steinfatt, "Linguistic Relativity," in *Language, Communication, and Culture: Current Directions*, eds. Stella Ting-Toomey and Felipe Korzenny (Newbury Park, CA: Sage, 1989), pp. 35–75.

47   This intermediate position is given weight by the influential theory of structuration, attributed most notably to Anthony Giddens. See, for example, *Profiles and Critiques in Social Theory* (Berkeley: University of California Press, 1982), chaps. 1–3.

48   Donald G. Ellis, "Fixing Communicative Meaning: A Coherentist Theory," *Communication Research* 22 (1995): 515–544. See also, Donald G. Ellis, *Crafting Society: Ethnicity, Class, and Communication Theory* (Mahwah, NJ: Erlbaum, 1999).

meanings change, communication could not oc-cur if meaning did not remain essentially the same. Otherwise you could not read a nine-teenth-century novel and understand it.

Semantic realism is not the same thing as sci-entific realism. The latter assumes that the struc-ture of reality exists apart from humans' under-standings of it, a proposition thoroughly rejected by constructionists. Semantic realism, on the other hand, says that meaning itself is real. These two—semantic and scientific reality—are related because we can only assume real meaning if we can also assume objective reality too. We need the structure of the world to give structure to meaning. This leads to Ellis's second principle.

The *coherentist principle* states that from a strictly pragmatic perspective meanings must be verifiable in experience. We can only assume se-mantic realism by relating it to our perceptual experience. A table is a table because we can see and touch it. This does not mean that the table "really exists," only that we can assume it does because of a common experience of "tableness." There may be no giant map in heaven to verify reality, but we can trust our own experience to verify that what we say relates to something be-yond what we say.

Ellis is not implying here that everyone al-ways understands one another perfectly or that errors do not occur. But we have an ideal and clear sense of reality that gives us confidence that we can at least aim for understanding and ratio-nality in our communications with others.

Social constructionists do not deny the facticity of objects in the world. If you are stand-ing in the way of a locomotive, do not deny that it is real![49] The issue is not whether the locomo-tive exists apart from human construction but how it is seen, what it is, and how it relates to other objects in the person's experience. A loco-motive is not in and of itself a locomotive but is created by human beings within a vast and rich context of social meanings, and the oncoming lo-comotive can never be viewed as meaningful apart from social interaction. The same is true of the death and dismemberment that might occur if you did stand in front of the train. The mean-ing of injury and death as a result of an accident

involving machinery would have vastly different meanings from one culture to another.

A serious question, however, remains: If real-ity is indeed socially constructed, how can we produce generalizable knowledge? If communi-cation is context-bound, how is theory pos-sible?[50] Acknowledging the attractiveness of so-cial approaches, Joseph Cappella expresses the pragmatic difficulty of this kind of scholarship in this question: "In short, when competing knowl-edge claims are generated, how will they be ad-judicated?"[51] The answer to this critique is to fall back on the basic position of the movement. Good communication theory should not attempt to achieve a standard set of criteria. Instead, it should be judged in terms of its utility and its potential for enriching human experience.[52]

A related set of theories in this chapter are rule theories, which further add to our understanding of social and cultural reality. The rule concept is appealing because it explains a mechanism by which people understand reality. As pointed out in Chapter 5, however, the rule concept is not par-ticularly coherent because different theories use different definitions of rules. This lack of consis-tency in the use of rules has led to some confu-sion. For instance, in criticizing CMM David Brenders relies on ideas from the rule-following tradition to show that Pearce and Cronen have blurred distinctions about meaning that Austin, Searle, and others (Chapter 5) thought impor-tant.[53] In their response, Cronen, Pearce, and Xi

49   The locomotive example is used by Richard A. Cherwitz and James W. Hikins, *Communication and Knowledge: An Investigation of Rhetorical Epistemology* (Columbia: University of South Carolina Press, 1986), p. 19. Cherwitz and Hikins advance an argument against constructionism similar to that of Ellis.

50   See, for example, Robert Bostrom and Lewis Donohew, "The Case for Empiricism: Clarifying Fundamental Issues in Communi-cation Theory," *Communication Monographs* 59 (1992): 109–129; Stuart J. Sigman, "Do Social Approaches to Interpersonal Commu-nication Constitute a Contribution to Communication Theory?" *Communication Theory* 2 (1992): 347–356.

51   Joseph Cappella, "Remaking Communication Inquiry," in *Rethinking Communication: Paradigm Issues,* eds. Brenda Dervin, Lawrence Grossberg, Barbara O'Keefe, and Ellen Wartella (Newbury Park, CA: Sage, 1989), p. 142.

52   Penman, "Good Theory."

53   David A. Brenders, "Fallacies in the Coordinated Manage-ment of Meaning: A Philosophy of Language Critique of the Hier-archical Organization of Coherent Conversation and Related Theory," *Quarterly Journal of Speech* 73 (1987): 329–348.

Changsheng argue that the ideas about meaning implied by this tradition are not appropriate for understanding communication as the process by which people shape their very experience.[54] If communication is used as a tool to relay meanings, as Brenders suggests, the rules are followed to accomplish this task. If, on the other hand, communication is the process by which meaning itself is constructed, as Pearce and Cronen assert, rules themselves are part of the socially constructed reality, and rule-following approaches are not very useful.

Brenders' critique and the CMM response take us full circle back to the basic issue surrounding social constructionism: Is communication a tool for communicating accurately about the world, or is it the means by which the world itself is determined? I do not expect this controversy to be settled anytime soon.[55]

----

54   Vernon E. Cronen, W. Barnett Pearce, and Xi Changsheng, "The Meaning of 'Meaning' in the CMM Analysis of Communication: A Comparison of Two Traditions," *Research on Language and Social Interaction* 23 (1989–1990): 1–40.
55   This issue is discussed by Sigman, "Social Approaches."

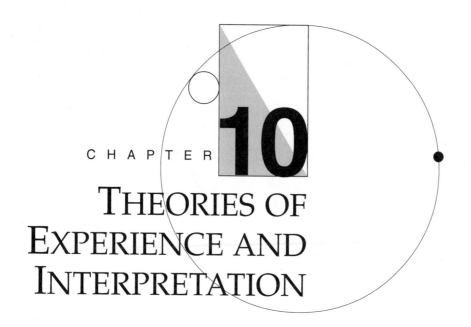

C H A P T E R **10**

THEORIES OF EXPERIENCE AND INTERPRETATION

The field of communication explores a variety of human experiences. The theories in this chapter tell us about the nature of conscious experience and the role of communication in it. Specifically, we will explore two traditions: phenomenology and hermeneutics.[1]

The central assumption of most theories in this chapter is that people actively interpret their experience by assigning meaning to what they see. As you read this book, for example, you attend to it consciously, you interpret it, and what you are reading means something.

Interpretation, sometimes known by the German term *Verstehen* (understanding), is the active process of assigning meaning to something you observe, like a text, an act, or a situation—any experience, really. Because a message or other act could mean a variety of things, meaning cannot be simply "discovered." Interpretation, by definition, is an active, disciplined process of the mind, a creative act of searching for possible meanings.

◖ PHENOMENOLOGY

Phenomenology is the study of the knowledge that comes from consciousness, or the way you come to understand objects and events by consciously experiencing them. It looks at objects and events from your perspective. A *phenomenon* is the appearance of an object, event, or condition in your perception. Maurice Merleau-Ponty, a theorist of this tradition, expresses this point of view as follows: "All my knowledge of the world, even my scientific knowledge, is gained from my own particular point of view, or from some experience of the world without which the symbols of science would be meaningless."[2]

---

1   For a good recent overview of these areas, see James A. Anderson, *Communication Theory: Epistemological Foundations* (New York: Guilford, 1996).
2   Maurice Merleau-Ponty, *The Phenomenology of Perception*, trans. C. Smith (London: Routledge & Kegan Paul, 1974), p. viii. For an excellent general discussion of phenomenology, see also Michael J. Hyde, "Transcendental Philosophy and Human Communication," in *Interpersonal Communication*, ed. J. J. Pilotta (Wash-

This approach is a striking departure from scientific methods that assume the existence of a reality that people cannot know in their ordinary experience. Phenomenology makes actual lived experience the basic data of reality. All you can know, it claims, is what you experience. "Phenomenology means letting things become manifest as what they are, without forcing our own categories on them."[3] An "objective" scientist hypothesizes a particular structure and then looks to see if it is there; a phenomenologist never hypothesizes but carefully examines actual lived experience to see what it looks like. If you want to know what love is, you would not ask the psychologists; you would tap into your own experience of love.

Stanley Deetz summarizes three basic principles of phenomenology.[4] First, knowledge is conscious. Knowledge is not inferred from experience but is found directly in conscious experience. Second, the meaning of a thing consists of the potential of that thing in one's life. In other words, how you relate to an object determines its meaning for you. A set of keys, for example, becomes a paperweight when you see that it could be used that way. The third assumption is that language is the vehicle of meaning. We experience the world through the language used to define and express that world. We know keys because of their associated labels: "lock," "open," "metal," "weight," and so forth.

Edmund Husserl is usually considered the founder of modern phenomenology.[5] Husserl, who wrote during the first half of the twentieth century, attempted to develop a method for ascertaining truth through focused consciousness. For Husserl, no conceptual scheme outside of actual direct experience is adequate for uncovering truth; rather, the conscious experience of the individual must be the route for discovering reality. Only through conscious attention can truth be known. In other words, we can know the things of the world by carefully examining them in an unbiased way.

Husserl is no longer in favor among most phenomenologists today because of his rather

radical subject-object distinction. In other words, he felt that the person was separate from objects but that they could come to know the object by carefully eliminating biases. Most phenomenologists today would say that experience is subjective, not objective, and that we need to value subjectivity as an important kind of knowledge in its own sake. Maurice Merleau-Ponty takes this latter view.

Merleau-Ponty was greatly influenced by Husserl, but he strongly rejected Husserl's idealism.[6] For Merleau-Ponty, the human being is a unified physical and mental being that creates meaning in the world. As a subject or knower, a person has a relationship to things in the world: Human life is both affected by the world and in turn defines and assigns meaning to the world. Merleau-Ponty is opposed to realism because things do not exist in and of themselves. People give meaning to the things in the world, but there is no human experience outside the world. Thus, the world of things and events exist in a give-and-take, or dialogic, relationship, each affecting the other.

Communication is the vehicle by which you assign meaning to experience. Your thoughts result from speech because meaning itself is created by your speech. When you communicate,

ington, DC: Center for Advanced Research in Phenomenology, 1982), pp. 15–34.
3   Richard E. Palmer, *Hermeneutics: Interpretation Theory in Schleiermacher, Dilthey, Heidegger, and Gadamer* (Evanston, IL: Northwestern University Press, 1969), p. 128.
4   Stanley Deetz, "Words Without Things: Toward a Social Phenomenology of Language," *Quarterly Journal of Speech* 59 (1973): 40–51.
5   Edmund Husserl, *Ideas: General Introduction to Pure Phenomenology,* trans. W. R. B. Gibson (New York: Collier, 1962); *Phenomenology and the Crisis of Philosophy,* trans. Q. Lauer (New York: Harper & Row, 1965). For a brief summary of Husserl's ideas, see Zygmunt Bauman, *Hermeneutics and Social Science* (New York: Columbia University Press, 1978).
6   Merleau-Ponty's most important work is *Phenomenology of Perception* (New York: Humanities, 1962), original published in 1945 in Paris. See also Richard L. Lanigan, *Phenomenology of Communication: Merleau-Ponty's Thematics in Communicology and Semiology* (Pittsburgh: Duquesne University Press, 1988); Remy C. Kwant, *The Phenomenological Philosophy of Merleau-Ponty* (Pittsburgh: Duquesne University Press, 1963); Samuel B. Mallin, *Merleau-Ponty's Philosophy* (New Haven, CT: Yale University Press, 1979); Wayne Froman, *Merleau-Ponty: Language and the Act of Speech* (Lewisburg, PA: Bucknell University Press, 1982). Many other secondary sources are available.

you work out new ways of seeing the world. At the same time, we have access to a whole range of understandings as part of the language, or "spoken word," available to us in everyday life.

Knowledge is very much bound up with language and communication. The language you use at a particular time attaches certain meanings to the object of your experience, but those meanings are temporary and can change. For Merleau-Ponty, reduction to the "essence" is impossible. People who share a language also share meanings.

A contemporary of Merleau-Ponty is Alfred Schutz.[7] Schutz further applies phenomenology to social life, investigating events from the perspective of those actually participating in them. In everyday life you make three fundamental assumptions, according to Schutz. First, you assume that reality is constant—that the world will remain as it appears. Second, you assume that your own experience of the world is valid. Ultimately, you will believe that what you see is accurate. Third, you see yourself as having the power to act and accomplish things, to affect the world.

Our world depends on what we learn from others in our social and cultural communities. This knowledge is always part of a historical situation, and people in various times and places experience the world differently. Reality is socially constructed within the group, which is why no universal reality can be found. As one commentator puts it, "The world, when filtered through my biographical situation, becomes 'my' world."[8]

What is real for us depends on the categories employed within our culture. These categories are generalizations, which Schutz calls *typifications*. They are typical trees, typical children, typical love, typical greetings, ad infinitum; and trees, children, love, greetings, and everything else will vary from one social situation to another. Within a given social group, then, you understand other people and objects by placing them within a generalized category that typifies them.

Language and other signs consist of typifying categories. You interpret signs on the basis of the categories you share with others, and your communication can only be successful to the extent that you have shared meanings within social groups and communities.

Of course, typifications differ from group to group, from culture to culture, and from time to time. How, then, can we study social life at all? What can ever be known? Schutz's solution is to explore only the typifications of particular cultures and groups, not universal categories. General truths about human experience cannot be found, but specific truths of individual historical groups can be discovered.

For Schutz, social knowledge consists of formulas or *social recipes*—typical, well-understood ways of doing things in particular situations. They enable you to classify things according to some kind of mutually understood logic, to solve problems, to take roles, to communicate, and to behave properly in different situations. Conducting negotiations, getting married, worshipping, raising children, selling goods, and most other social activities proceed according to these recipes.

Perhaps the most well-known phenomenologist today is Martin Heidegger, known primarily for his work in *hermeneutic phenomenology*, or *philosophical hermeneutics*.[9] Most important for Heidegger is the natural experience that inevitably occurs by merely existing in the world. His

7   Alfred Schutz, *The Phenomenology of the Social World*, trans. G. Walsh and F. Lehnert (Evanston, IL: Northwestern University Press, 1967); original published in 1932. For a clear summary of Schutz's ideas, see Robert A. Gorman, *The Dual Vision: Alfred Schutz and the Myth of Phenomenological Social Science* (London: Routledge & Kegan Paul, 1977). See also Richard Lanigan, "A Treasure House of Preconstituted Types: Alfred Schutz on Communicology," in *Phenomenology of Communication*, pp. 203–222.
8   Gorman, *Vision*, p. 38.
9   Martin Heidegger, *Being and Time*, trans. J. Macquarrie and E. Robinson (New York: Harper & Row, 1962); *On the Way to Language*, trans. P. Hertz (New York: Harper & Row, 1971); *An Introduction to Metaphysics*, trans. R. Manheim (New Haven, CT: Yale University Press, 1959). For secondary treatments, see Bauman, *Hermeneutics*, pp. 148–171; Palmer, *Hermeneutics*, pp. 124–161; Deetz, "Words"; John Stewart, "One Philosophical Dimension of Social Approaches to Interpersonal Communication," *Communication Theory* 2 (1992): 337–347.

philosophy has been called the *hermeneutic of Dasein,* which means "interpretation of being."

For Heidegger, the reality of something is not known by careful analysis or reduction but by natural experience, which is created by the use of language in everyday life. What is real is what is experienced through the natural use of language in context: "Words and language are not wrappings in which things are packed for the commerce of those who write and speak. It is in words and language that things first come into being and are."[10]

This tradition of phenomenology—linking experience with language and social interaction—is closely associated with hermeneutics, the topic to which we now turn.

◖ TEXT HERMENEUTICS

Hermeneutics is the study of understanding, especially that of interpreting action and text. There are several branches of hermeneutics, including interpretation of scripture (exegesis), interpretation of literary texts (philology), and interpretation of human personal and social actions (social hermeneutics).[11]

Modern hermeneutics began in the early nineteenth century with Friedrich Schleiermacher.[12] Schleiermacher attempted to establish a system for discovering what authors meant in their writings. He used a scientific approach to text analysis, which he believed would be the key to authors' original meanings and feelings. Later in the century, Schleiermacher's biographer, Wilhelm Dilthey, was strongly influenced by these ideas.[13] For Dilthey, however, hermeneutics is the key to all of the humanities and social sciences; he believed that we come to understand all aspects of human life, not by scientific method, but through subjective interpretation. For Dilthey, the human world is social and historical and requires understanding in terms of the community in which human actors live and work. Human works are not fixed and cannot be known objectively. Dilthey therefore promoted a

kind of historical relativism common in the social sciences today.

Just about any interpretive activity can be labeled "hermeneutic." This means understanding another person's feelings and meanings, understanding the meaning of an episode or event, translating the actions of a group into terms understandable to outsiders, or uncovering the meaning of a written text.

For our purposes, hermeneutic scholars fall into two general groups: those who use hermeneutics to understand texts and those who use hermeneutics as a tool for interpreting actions. The first type is perhaps best termed *text hermeneutics* and the second *social or cultural hermeneutics.*[14] In this chapter, we cover text hermeneutics in this section and cultural hermeneutics in the following one.

Generally speaking, *texts* are any artifacts that can be examined and interpreted.[15] Text hermeneutics, although usually applied to the written word, is not limited to it. Any kind of action can be recorded. A text is essentially a recording, whether written, electronic, photographic, or preserved by some other means. Even actions can be viewed as texts, but more often, the term designates written documents and other records.[16] The problem remains the same: How do we interpret a message that is no longer part of an actual live event?

---

10   Heidegger, *Introduction,* p. 13.
11   For an analysis of different approaches to hermeneutics, see Bauman, *Hermeneutics.* See also David Tracy, "Interpretation (Hermeneutics)," in *International Encyclopedia of Communications,* ed. E. Barnouw (New York: Oxford University Press, 1989), pp. 343–348.
12   Friedrich Schleiermacher, *Hermeneutik,* ed. H. Kimmerle (Heidelberg, Germany: Carl Winter, Universitaetsverlag, 1959).
13   Wilhelm Dilthey, "The Rise of Hermeneutics," trans. F. Jameson, *New Literary History* 3 (1972): 229–244.
14   For an analysis of the different approaches to hermeneutics, see Bauman, *Hermeneutics.*
15   For a good discussion of the various senses of the term *text,* see George Cheney and Phillip K. Tompkins, "On the Facts of the Text as the Basis of Human Communication Research," in *Communication Yearbook 11,* ed. J. A. Anderson (Newbury Park, CA: Sage, 1988), pp. 455–481, and attendant commentaries (pp. 482–501).
16   Actually, the concept of *text* is complex and should not be read simply as an object, action, or writing. For an excellent brief exposition of the concept, see Cheney and Tompkins, "Facts of the Text."

Although little agreement exists on specific techniques of interpretation, almost all schools of thought rely on a common notion of its general process. This process is called the *hermeneutic circle.* You interpret something by going from general to specific and from specific to general. You look at a specific text in terms of a general idea of what that text may mean, then modify the general idea based on the examination of the specifics of the text. Your interpretation is ongoing, as you move back and forth between specific and general. You can look at the composite meaning of a text and then examine the specific linguistic structures of that text. Then you might return to the overall meaning, only to go back to the specifics again.

Within the circle, you always relate what is seen in the object to what you already know. You then alternate between a familiar set of concepts and the unfamiliar until the two merge in a tentative interpretation. In interpreting the actions of a foreign culture, for example, an anthropologist first tries to understand what is happening with familiar concepts; later the anthropologist discovers how the natives understand their experiences in their own way and uses this information to modify the categories initially employed. This back-and-forth process is exactly what is used in textual interpretation as well.

Consider the Bible as an example. The interpreter begins by relating the text to what he or she already understands, looks for strange or unaccounted-for details in the scripture, modifies the original interpretation, reexamines the text, and so on. You can see that this is really a dialogue between the meanings in the text and one's own present-day assumptions.

The interpretation of texts has long been the central problem of hermeneutics. Hermeneutics arose as a way to understand ancient texts such as the Bible that can no longer be explained by the author. The Supreme Court uses hermeneutics to interpret the Constitution. Today, virtually any text is open for interpretation, and whether the author is alive to explain what he or she meant is not considered relevant. The text itself speaks to us; it has meanings of its own apart from what any author, speaker, or audience member might mean by it. The challenge of textual hermeneutics, then, is to ascertain the meanings of the text.

There are many prominent writers on text interpretation. Two of the best known, Paul Ricoeur and Stanley Fish, represent very different approaches to the text-interpretation problem.

Paul Ricoeur

Ricoeur is a major interpretive theorist who relies heavily on both the phenomenological and hermeneutic traditions.[17] Although he recognizes the importance of actual speech, most important for Ricoeur is text. Once speech is recorded, it becomes divorced from the actual speaker and situation in which it was produced. Texts cannot be interpreted in the same fashion as live discourse because they exist in a permanent form. Speech is ephemeral, but texts live on. Textual interpretation is especially important when speakers and authors are not available, as is the case with historical documents. However, it need not be limited to these situations. Indeed, the text itself always speaks to us, and the job of the interpreter is to figure out what it is saying.

The separation of text from situation is *distanciation.* The text has meaning irrespective of the author's original intention. In other words, you can read a message and understand it despite the fact that you were not part of the original speech event. Thus, the author's intent does not prescribe what the text can subsequently be taken to mean, nor does any reader's peculiar understanding limit what the text itself says. Once written, the text can be consumed by anybody who can read, providing a multitude of possibilities—and multiple readings (meanings) are definitely possible. For these reasons the interpretation of textual material is for Ricoeur

---

17   Paul Ricoeur, *Interpretation Theory: Discourse and the Surplus of Meaning* (Fort Worth: Texas University Press, 1976); *Hermeneutics and the Human Sciences: Essays on Language, Action, and Interpretation,* trans. and ed. J. B. Thompson (Cambridge: Cambridge University Press, 1981); Don Ihde, ed., *The Conflict of Interpretations: Essays in Hermeneutics* [by Paul Ricoeur] (Evanston, IL: Northwestern University Press, 1974).

more complex and more interesting than that of spoken discourse.

The problem is like interpreting a musical score.[18] You may not know exactly what mood and feeling Mozart had in composing and conducting the Jupiter Symphony. If you are an experienced music lover, you might be able to produce a number of believable interpretations of your own, but those interpretations are not unlimited; they are constrained by the musical notation. A conductor carefully studies the elements of the text to determine what meanings are embedded in it and then proceeds to produce a musical interpretation. Orchestral versions will differ substantially in the interpretation performed, but you will always recognize the piece as the Jupiter Symphony.

Like a musical interpretation, the meaning of a text is always a pattern of the whole, never just a composite of individual elements. To account for this, Ricoeur's version of the hermeneutic circle consists of explanation and understanding. *Explanation* is empirical and analytical: It accounts for events in terms of observed patterns among parts. In studying a book of the Bible, for example, you would carefully examine the individual words of each verse and note the ways they form patterns of meaning. In the analysis of a text, an interpreter might look for recurring words and phrases, narrative themes, and theme variations. Ricoeur himself is interested in particular words that have metaphorical value, words that point to meanings hidden below the surface of the writing. None of these structural elements is meaningful in and of itself; they must be put together into a whole pattern in the understanding phase of interpretation.

Understanding is synthetic, accounting for events in terms of overall interpretation. So in continuing your study of the Bible, you would also look for a holistic, or general, meaning of the passage under consideration. In hermeneutics, one goes through both processes, breaking down a text into its parts and looking for patterns, then stepping back and judging subjectively the meaning of the whole. You move from understanding to explaining and back to understand-

ing again in a continuing circle. Explanation and understanding, then, are not separate but are two poles in an interpretive spectrum.

Ricoeur agrees that an intimate interaction exists between text and interpreter. The text can speak to and change the interpreter. Ricoeur refers to the act of being open to the meanings of a text as *appropriation.* If you are open to the message of a text, you appropriate it, or make it your own. Thus, interpretation begins with distanciation but ends with appropriation. To interpret the sections of the Bible, you would remove your own interests from your study of the intrinsic meanings in the text, but then you would apply those meanings to your own situation.

An example of a Ricoeurian interpretation is Barbara Warnick's study of the Gettysburg Address.[19] In a careful examination of the text, Warnick looks at expressions of agent, place, and time. *Agents* include "our fathers," "those who have given their lives," "we," and the people of the future. *Place* references include our nation "upon this continent" and "a great battle-field." *Time* references include the far past ("four score and seven years"), the near past, a frozen present, and a possible future. The text can transcend the immediacy of the present situation by cycling back and forth from the present to other times, from immediate agents to other agents in past and future, and from this place to other places. In so doing, the text tells a story of birth, adversity, recognition of values, rebirth, and perpetuation of the treasured values.

In an example of appropriation, Warnick notes that this story parallels that of the Christian narrative, which appeals to people so deeply in our society. Other values of American culture are deeply embedded in the text as well. Warnick shows how the details of the text and the overall understanding of it as a projection of the American ideal go hand in hand. Warnick's overall understanding of the speech, then, is

18 The musical analogy of textual hermeneutics can be found in Ricoeur, *Interpretation Theory,* p. 75.
19 Barbara Warnick, "A Ricoeurian Approach to Rhetorical Criticism," *Western Journal of Speech Communication* 51 (1987): 227–244.

that it expresses values that are part of but transcend the immediate situation, and for this reason, the text is relevant to generation after generation of Americans.

Stanley Fish

Fish is a literary critic known mostly in the fields of English and literary studies. With a keen interest in literature, much of his work centers around text interpretation and the question of where meaning resides. Taking a distinctly different turn from Riceour, Fish denies that any meaning can be found in text. For him, meaning lies strictly in the reader, which leads to the name most associated with Fish's work—*reader-response theory*.[20] The proper question is not, "What does a text mean?" but "What does a text do?"

Clearly, texts do stimulate active readership, but the readers themselves provide the meaning, not the text. If you have ever taken a nineteenth-century American literature course, you probably spent some time talking about the meaning of *Moby Dick*. You may have discovered that different students saw different things in the text. Perhaps you spent time trying to figure out what the true meaning of the text is, and you probably used hermeneutics to do it. Fish would say that *Moby Dick* as a text means nothing, but readers will take it to mean many things.

Fish is clear, however, that assigning meaning is not an individual matter. You do not arbitrarily decide what meaning to assign to a text, nor is your meaning idiosyncratic. Following a social constructionist approach (Chapter 9), Fish teaches that readers are members of *interpretive communities,* groups that interact with one another, construct common realities and meanings, and employ these in their readings. So meaning really resides in the interpretive community of readers.

In your literature class, then, you may come to share a common reading of *Moby Dick*. This will happen because of your common identity as English students, discussions in class, sharing a common textbook, completing the same assignments, taking the same tests, and having the same professor. It is likely that the class will become an interpretive community with very similar meanings for the novel. Indeed, your class will become linked with other classes, in prior and future semesters, and because your professor reads the same journals as professors in other universities and attends conferences on nineteenth-century literature, it is very possible that you will become a member of a huge interpretive community of the American novel.

Of course, if you subscribe to Fish's theory, you will not search for a single meaning. There is no correct reading of a text. The matter is entirely dependent on the audience's interpretation. Meaning, then, is not objective, so don't look for it in the features of the text. Needless to say, this is a highly controversial idea in literary studies. Much of literary criticism looks at the intention of the author and how the author communicates that in the way the text is written.

On this point, however, Ricoeur and Fish would agree: Don't look to the author for meaning. Where they very much disagree is in the role of the text. Both Ricoeur and Fish use the hermeneutic circle, but they emphasize somewhat different things in doing so. For Ricoeur, the reader is always testing his or her interpretation by looking at features of the text so as to find the meaning that lies there. For Fish, the reader always projects his or her own meaning into features of the text and only comes up with the reader's meaning in the end. For Ricoeur, the text is like a template; for Fish it is like a Rorschach test.

Distanciation, the principle that is so important to Ricoeur, is senseless to Fish because readers can never be distanced from the text; they are always embedding their own meanings into it.

Reader-response theory has had a major impact on media studies. If literary texts always get their meaning from the reader, media depictions must also derive meaning from the interpretive community. We will take a closer look at this idea later in the chapter.

20   Stanley Fish, *Is There a Text in This Class?* (Cambridge, MA: Harvard University Press, 1980). For a brief, clear secondary source, see Chris Lang, "A Brief History of Literary Theory III" *http://www.xenos.org/essays/litthry4.htm*; "A Brief History of Literary Theory VII" *http://www.xenos.org/essays/litthry8.htm.*

Hans-Georg Gadamer

Hans-Georg Gadamer, a protégé of Heidegger, teaches that individuals do not stand apart from things in order to analyze and interpret them; instead, we interpret naturally as part of our everyday existence.[21] We cannot be human without interpreting. That means that our experience and the world we interpret are so closely intertwined that they are virtually the same thing.

The central tenet of Gadamer's theory is that one always understands experience from the perspective of presuppositions, or assumptions. Our tradition gives us a way of understanding things, and we cannot divorce ourselves from that tradition. Observation, reason, and understanding are never objectively pure; they are colored by history and our experience with other people.

Further, history is not to be separated from the present. We are always simultaneously part of the past, in the present, and anticipating the future. In other words, the past operates on us now in the present and affects our conceptions of what is yet to come. At the same time, our present notions of reality affect how we view the past.

These ideas do not deny change. Over time we become distanced from the events of the past. Our way of seeing things in the present time creates a temporal distance from an object of the past such that artifacts have both a strangeness and a familiarity. If you look at your grandmother's old dress from a dusty trunk in the attic, it will look somewhat familiar, but strange at the same time.

We understand an artifact because of what we have learned from history, which is a residue of highly relevant, but essential, meaning. For example, you recognize your grandmother's dress because of its "dressness" learned by viewing old pictures and reading and hearing about old-time fashion. Even though the dress might be very old, you still recognize buttons, lace, and other features that make this a dress.

In some ways, then, interpretation of historical events and objects, including written texts, is enhanced by historical distance. You can understand the Gettysburg Address because the essential meaning of the words lives on. Gadamer would agree that understanding a text involves looking at the enduring meanings of that text within a tradition and apart from the original communicators' intentions. Texts therefore become contemporaneous and speak to us in our own time.

The Gettysburg Address was originally a piece of spoken discourse designed to achieve a certain effect during the Civil War. Once spoken, however, the text lived on as an object of its own, rife with internal meaning. Unessential details—that it was written on the back of an envelope on the train by a tall, lanky president—drop away as the text itself reveals its meanings to us in our own time.

The meaning we get from a text, then, is a result of a dialogue between our own present-day meanings and those embedded in the language of the text. You do recognize and understand an old dress because of its features that still have meaning, but, at the same time, you also apply your own current ideas about the dress—that it is silly, stodgy, inconvenient, heavy, hot, oppressive, or whatever. You understand the terms of the Gettysburg Address because those words live on, but at the same time, your interpretation is influenced by your own background and experience of today.

This interpretive process is paradoxical: We let the text speak to us, yet we cannot understand it apart from our own prejudices and presuppositions. Because change results from the dialogue between the prejudices of the present and the meanings of the text, prejudice is a positive force, to be acknowledged and used productively in our lives. As one observer has noted, "The problem for the study of communication is not the existence of prejudices but the unawareness of their presence and subsequent

---

21   Gadamer's major work is *Truth and Method* (New York: Seabury, 1975). An excellent secondary treatment can be found in Richard J. Bernstein, *Beyond Objectivism and Relativism: Science, Hermeneutics, and Praxis* (Philadelphia: University of Pennsylvania Press, 1983), pp. 107–169. See also Palmer, *Hermeneutics*, pp. 162–222; Tracy, "Interpretation."

inability to separate appropriate from inappropriate ones."[22]

Hermeneutics is not only a process of questioning the meaning of the text but also of allowing it to question us. What questions does the text itself suggest, and when we ask those questions, what answers does the text offer? What, for example, can we learn about ourselves from the Gettysburg Address?

Like Heidegger, Gadamer believes that experience is inherently linguistic. We cannot separate our experience from language. The perspectives of tradition, from which we always view the world, are in the words. Note how this conception differs from the structural view of language summarized in Chapter 4, in which language is seen as an arbitrary tool for expressing and referring to an objective reality. Gadamer's view is also different from the interactionist notion (even Fish's), which suggests that language and meaning are created through social interaction. Gadamer's point is that language itself prefigures all experience. The world is presented to us through language. Thus, in communication, two people are not using language to interact with each other; rather, communication involves a triad of two individuals and a language.[23]

To get this idea across, Gadamer uses the analogy of the game. A game has its own existence apart from individual players. The basic structure of the game will be the same whether it is being played or not and regardless of who is playing. Poker is poker, whether played in 1920 by four old Italian men or in 1994 by a young college student and her roommates. The game lives on, only the players change.

Language and life are like games: We play them, just as we experience life, but they come to us preformed and remain intact after our particular playing is finished. One commentator explains it this way: "The world is already meaningful. That is, the world which comes to us in the only way that the human world can come to us, through language, is an already meaningful world."[24]

Gadamer brings phenomenology and hermeneutics together in one process. Phenomenol-ogy, or understanding through experience, and hermeneutics, or interpretation, are inseparable processes.

CULTURAL INTERPRETATION

Cultural interpretation involves trying to understand the actions of a group or culture such as the Zulu, residents of the Castro in San Francisco, or New York City high school students.[25] This kind of hermeneutics requires observing and describing the actions of a group, just as one might examine a written text, and trying to figure out what they mean.[26] Another term for cultural interpretation is *ethnography.*

One of the leading cultural interpreters of our day is Clifford Geertz.[27] Geertz describes cultural interpretation as *thick description,* in which interpreters describe cultural practices "from the native's point of view." This level of interpretation is contrasted with *thin description,* in which people merely describe the behavioral pattern with little sense of what it means to the participants themselves.

Like all hermeneutics, cultural interpretation uses a hermeneutic circle. Geertz's version of the circle involves a movement from experience-near concepts to experience-distant ones. *Experience-near concepts* are those that have meaning to the members of the culture, and *experience-distant concepts* have meaning to outsiders. The cultural interpreter essentially translates between the

22   Stanley Deetz, "Conceptualizing Human Understanding: Gadamer's Hermeneutics and American Communication Studies," *Communication Quarterly* 26 (1978): 14.
23   John Angus Campbell, "Hans-Georg Gadamer's Truth and Method," *Quarterly Journal of Speech* 64 (1978): 101–122.
24   Campbell, "Hans-Georg Gadamer's Truth and Method," p. 107.
25   For a discussion of the role of culture in the communication field, see John H. Powers, "On the Intellectual Structure of the Human Communication Discipline," *Communication Education* 44 (1995): 191–222.
26   See Michael Agar, *Speaking of Ethnography* (Beverly Hills, CA: Sage, 1986); Paul Atkinson, *Understanding Ethnographic Texts* (Newbury Park, CA: Sage, 1992).
27   See especially *The Interpretation of Cultures* (New York: Basic, 1973) and *Local Knowledge: Further Essays in Interpretive Anthropology* (New York: Basic, 1983).

two, so that observers outside can have an understanding of the insider's feelings and meanings in a situation. The interpretation process, then, is one of going back and forth in a circle between what appears to be happening from outside to what insiders define as happening. Slowly, a suitable vocabulary can be developed to explain the natives' point of view to outsiders without forsaking natives' own experience-near concepts.[28]

For example, an ethnographer might wonder about the meaning of wearing oversized pants. From an experience-distant perspective, it might appear to be a form of group conformity. If you ask several young people what it means, they would answer in a more experience-near way with something like, "Oh, it's cool, man." The ethnographer would need to investigate what it means for something to be "cool" and perhaps relate this response to statements made by others. Eventually, a vocabulary acceptable to informants and understandable to those who are not members of this group would be created.

Ethnographic problems arise when an interpreter has a lack of adequate understanding. The researcher witnesses something that cannot be understood from his or her concepts, such as wearing pants so large that you can hardly walk, and seeks to resolve the difficulty by creating an explanation. Ethnography attempts to understand things that are otherwise foreign.

How would you make sense of a cult's ceremony involving the fondling of rattlesnakes? Most of us have no frame for understanding such actions, but the ethnographer would—through careful examination, interviews, inference, and experience—create an explanation that would make such behavior understandable.

The interpreter, of course, does not begin an ethnography empty-handed. Previous experience always provides some kind of schema for understanding an event, but ethnography is a process in which one's understandings become increasingly more refined and accurate.

You can see that as a hermeneutic activity, ethnography is a very personal process, a process in which the researcher experiences a culture and interprets its various forms. Although ethnographers take different approaches to this process, many believe that the best approach is to live the culture firsthand. On this point, Lyall Crawford writes: "As an ethnographer, I am an expert about what only I verify—a state of affairs subject to emotional vulnerabilities, intellectual instabilities, and academic suspicion. Thought of in these terms, taking the ethnographic turn, living and writing the ethnographic life, is essentially a self-report of personal experiences."[29]

Donal Carbaugh and Sally Hastings describe ethnographic theorizing as a four-part process.[30] The first is to develop a basic orientation to the subject. Here the ethnographer assesses his or her own assumptions about culture and its manifestations. Communication ethnographers, for instance, define communication as central to culture and worthy of ethnographic study and decide to focus on various aspects of communication. They may assume further that clothing is an important expression of meaning and a form of communication.

The second phase of ethnographic theorizing defines the classes or kinds of activity that will be observed. A communication ethnographer, for example, might decide to look at the ways clothing is worn.

Next, the ethnographer theorizes about the specific culture under investigation. Here certain activities will be interpreted within the context of the culture itself. So, for example, when young people wear baggy pants, this could be taken as a sign of group conformity and acceptance.

Finally, in the fourth phase, the ethnographer moves back out to look again at the general theory of culture he or she is operating with and tests it with the specific case. The ethnographer might, for example, conclude that baggy pants are yet another instance of how clothing is used by members of a culture to establish communal bonds.

28   Geertz, *Local Knowledge,* p. 57.
29   Lyall Crawford, "Personal Ethnography," *Communication Monographs* 63 (1996): 158.
30   Donal Carbaugh and Sally Hastings, "A Role for Communication Theory in Ethnography and Cultural Analysis," *Communication Theory* 2 (1992): 156–165.

In this section we will look at four forms of cultural interpretation prominent in the communication field—the ethnography of communication, performance ethnography, organizational culture, and interpretive media studies.

Ethnography of Communication

The ethnography of communication is simply the application of ethnographic methods to the communication patterns of a group. Here, the interpreter attempts to make sense of the forms of communication employed by the members of a community or culture.

Gerry Philipsen isolates four assumptions of the ethnography of communication.[31] The first is that participants in a local cultural community create shared meaning. They use codes that have some degree of common understanding. Second, communicators in any cultural group must coordinate their actions. There must be some order or system to what is done in communication. Third, meanings and actions are particular to individual groups. In other words, they differ from culture to culture. Fourth, not only are patterns of behavior and codes different from group to group, but each group also has its own ways of understanding certain codes and actions.

The originator of this research tradition is anthropologist Dell Hymes.[32] Hymes suggests that formal linguistics is not sufficient by itself to uncover a complete understanding of language because it ignores the highly variable ways in which language is used in everyday communication.

Cultures communicate in different ways, but all forms of communication require a shared code, communicators who know and use the code, a channel, a setting, a message form, a topic, and an event created by transmission of the message. Anything may qualify as communication as long as it is construed as such by the natives. Is snake handling communication? How about baggy pants? Perhaps these are shared codes for expressing something among the members of the group. We cannot know until further ethnographic study is undertaken.

In short, culture is a powerful influence on human life in general and human lives in particular. Recognizing that cultures are richly different from one another makes generalization difficult. To meet this challenge, comparative ethnography creates categories with which one can compare cultures. Within the ethnography of communication, Hymes suggests a set of nine categories that can be used to compare different cultures:[33]

1. *Ways of speaking*, or patterns of communication familiar to the members of the group
2. *Ideal of the fluent speaker*, or what constitutes an exemplary communicator
3. *Speech community*, or the group itself and its boundaries
4. *Speech situation*, or those times when communication is considered appropriate in the community
5. *Speech event*, or what episodes are considered to be communication for the members of the group
6. *Speech act*, or a specific set of behaviors taken as an instance of communication within a speech event
7. *Components of speech acts*, or what the group considers to be the elements of a communicative act
8. *The rules of speaking in the community*, or the guidelines or standards by which communicative behavior is judged
9. *The functions of speech in the community*, or what communication is believed to accomplish

This set of concepts is nothing more than a list of categories by which various cultures can be compared. Two cultures—the Apache and the Ilongot, for example—would have many different events that count as communication, varying

---

31   Gerry Philipsen, "An Ethnographic Approach to Communication Studies," in *Rethinking Communication: Paradigm Exemplars,* eds. Brenda Dervin, Lawrence Grossberg, Barbara J. O'Keefe, and Ellen Wartella (Newbury Park, CA: Sage, 1989), pp. 258–269.
32   Dell Hymes, *Foundations in Sociolinguistics: An Ethnographic Approach* (Philadelphia: University of Pennsylvania Press, 1974).
33   Hymes, *Foundations*, pp. 29–66.

behaviors that would be considered appropriate within those speaking events, and perhaps some distinct rules for how to communicate. On the other hand, they might have some similar types and functions of communication as well.

According to Donal Carbaugh, communication ethnography addresses at least three types of problems.[34] The first is to discover the type of *shared identity* created by communication in the cultural community, be it African Americans, cheerleaders, Rotarians, Japanese businessmen, or John's Autobody Bowlers. This identity is the members' sense of who they are as a group. It is a common set of qualities with which most members of the community would identify.

The second problem is to uncover the *shared meanings of public performances* seen in the group. What constitutes communication within the culture, and what meanings do the various displays evoke? What does "playing the dozens" mean in the Black youth culture? What is communicated by cheerleaders at a high school basketball game? What meaning is assigned to the "fines" at a Rotary meeting?

The third is to explore *contradictions,* or paradoxes, of the group. How are these handled through communication? How, for example, might a culture treat its members as individuals while also providing a sense of community? How might autonomy be granted while maintaining authority? How might roles be taught while instilling ideals of freedom?

In attacking these ethnographic problems, three types of questions are pursued. *Questions of norms* look for the ways communication is used to establish a set of standards and the ways notions of right and wrong affect communication patterns. *Questions of forms* look at the types of communication used within the society. What behaviors count as communication, and how are they organized? *Questions of cultural codes* draw attention to the meanings of the symbols and behaviors used as communication in the cultural community.

Although ethnography highlights aspects of group life, it can also reveal how persons see themselves as persons. In other words, our group identities give rise to our individual identities. Who you are, your identity as a person, is determined in large measure by how you communicate, with whom, and in what settings. From his own studies—of a college basketball audience, workers in a television station, married person's names, a television talk show, and a community land-use controversy—Carbaugh concludes:

> I could not understand very well what people were saying, or communicating to me, until I explored the deeper particulars of their "sayings" in their specific social scenes. . . . I could not hear (or know) the individuals I met along the way very well until I listened within (or understood) their particular social and cultural scenes. . . . Individuals, social identities (or social classes), and cultural agents are not isolates. They are thought of and acted together in the specific scenes of particular communities.[35]

As an example of an ethnography of communication, consider Tamar Katriel's study on Israeli "griping."[36] Based on her own experience as a "native griper" and about fifty interviews with middle-class Israelis, Katriel explains the common communication form *kiturim.* This form of communication takes place throughout adult Israeli society, but it is most often seen among the middle class and commonly takes place at Friday night social gatherings called *mesibot kiturim,* or griping parties.

This communication form is so common that it is widely recognized by Israelis as part of their national character. Griping does not deal with personal problems but national (and sometimes local) public ones. It seems to affirm the Israeli identity as having important common national concerns. These are concerns that society could do something about theoretically but that the individual has little power to change. Thus, griping

34 Donal Carbaugh, ed., "Culture Talking About Itself," in *Cultural Communication and Intercultural Contact* (Hillsdale, NJ: Erlbaum, 1990), pp. 1–9.
35 Donal Carbaugh, *Situating Selves: The Communication of Social Identities in American Scenes* (Albany: SUNY Press, 1996), p. 197.
36 Tamar Katriel, "'Griping' as a Verbal Ritual in Some Israeli Discourse," in *Cultural Communication and Intercultural Contact,* ed. Donal Carbaugh (Hillsdale, NJ: Erlbaum, 1990), pp. 99–114.

is a kind of shared venting of frustration. It is more than this, however, since Katriel's informants told her that it provides a sense of solidarity and is fun. In fact, griping and joke telling are often viewed together as the primary means of establishing cohesiveness in a social group.

Griping is ritualistic, and the content of the communication does not seem to be important. One must not mistake griping for serious problem solving on topics of concern. In fact, there is a strict prohibition against griping in the presence of non-Israelis, like tourists, because outsiders do not understand the nature of griping and may take it literally, which would be embarrassing to the Israelis.

Griping follows a predictable pattern. It usually begins with an initial gripe, followed by an acknowledgment and a gripe by another person. The pattern of a griping session can go from general societal problems to local ones, or the other way around. Katriel found two interesting variants on the griping theme. *Metagriping* is griping about griping, or complaining that Israelis gripe too much. The other form is the *antigripe:* "Stop griping, and start doing something."

This study illustrates Hymes' categories of comparative ethnography very well. The griping session is a communication event, which consists of particular types of speech acts. It has rules and meets particular functions. The example also illustrates the ethnographic problems of identity, meaning, and tension. Griping reflects a certain national identity in Israel. It is understood among Israelis according to particular meanings, and griping is a mechanism for managing the tension between such opposites as serious concern and pleasant company.

Griping is a form of communication understood within a larger speech code. Gerry Philipsen has written extensively about such codes.[37] A *speech code* is a distinctive set of understandings within a culture about what counts as communication, the significance of communication forms within the culture, how those forms are to be understood, and how they are to be performed. The speech code is a culture's unwritten and often subconscious "guidebook" for how to communicate within the culture. How does a teenager in the United States know how to communicate at school—what to say, how to understand what others say, and how to talk? Their group's speech code enables them to do this. Philipsen makes several claims about speech codes.

First, such codes are distinctive. They vary from one culture to another. The manner and meaning of griping in Israel are entirely different from communication found in other cultures.

Second, speech codes constitute a culture's distinctive sense of how to be a person, how to connect with other people, and how to act or communicate within the social group. The code is more than a list of semantic meanings; it establishes the actual forms of communication in which competent members of the culture must act.

Third, the code guides what communicators actually experience when they interact with one another. It tells them what certain actions should count as. It defines the meaning of speech acts (Chapter 5). When people engage in a particular communication act such as "griping," they know what they are doing. They have meaning for the act itself.

Fourth, speech codes are not separate entities, but are embedded in daily speech. You can "see" the code in the patterns of communication commonly used, the terms communicators use to describe what they are doing when they speak, and how they explain, justify, or evaluate the communication being used. You can detect speech codes also in how members of the culture change their behavior and vocabulary in different forms of communication.

Fifth, speech codes are powerful. They form the basis on which the culture will evaluate and conduct its communication. The skill or quality of performance in communication is noticed and evaluated based on the requirements of the speech code. Moral judgments are made about whether individuals and groups communicate properly and make appropriate use of cultural communication forms.

37   See, for example, Gerry Philipsen, "A Theory of Speech Codes," in *Developing Communication Theories*, eds. Gerry Philipsen and Terrance L. Albrecht (Albany: SUNY Press, 1997), pp. 119–156.

Visit any American high school, and you will see speech codes at work. Listen to how students talk to one another, notice when they do so, and observe the different forms of communication they use. Notice that they know what they are doing and that their communication patterns have meaning to them. Our communication is always constrained by the codes in use. We are able to switch codes as we move from one cultural setting to another, but we are never free from them.

Performance Ethnography

If you were to do fieldwork in a foreign culture, you would experience many things through your senses. Most important, however, would be "seeing" what the people of the culture actually do. You would watch them and see what they do with their bodies.

The anthropologist Victor Turner is best known for bringing our attention to the fact that culture is performed.[38] So much of ethnography focuses on what members of the culture say and not enough on what they do. Of course, saying is a kind of doing, but it needs to be put into a larger frame similar to a play in the theatre. In fact, Turner sees much in common between theatre and everyday cultural life. Like actors, we say our lines as we perform with our bodies.

Cultural performance involves the manipulation of various media that may be experienced by eyes, ears, nose, tongue, and touch. And how these media are used both makes and reflects the meanings of the culture:

> Different types of incense burned at different times in a performance communicate different meanings, gestures and facial expressions are assigned meanings with reference to emotions and ideas to be communicated. . . . Thus certain sensory codes are associated with each medium. The master-of-ceremonies, priest, producer, or director creates art from the ensemble of media and codes, just as a conductor in the single genre of classical music blends and opposes the sounds of the different instruments to produce an often unrepeatable effect.[39]

The public performances in a culture are like *social dramas,* in which the group works out their relationships and ideas. Such dramas are *liminal,*

meaning that they mark a transition from one state to another or a border between one thing and another. A *limin* is like a threshold, or door between two places. Rites of passage are a good example, as they depict movement from one stage of life to another. Often rituals are liminal in the sense that they connect the sacred with the secular or symbolize the change of seasons.

Turner notes that social dramas tend to follow a certain process. The first stage is a *breach,* or some kind of violation or threat to community order. This is followed by a *crisis,* as members of the community become agitated and take various sides on the issues raised by the breach. In the third phase, *redressive or remedial procedures,* members of the culture make performances that mend the breach or in some way return to a state of acceptance. This stage of the social drama often involves the most self-examination and is the place where new meanings are created or old ones reproduced. There is a fourth stage, *reintegration,* or restoration of peace.

The way a community responds to a threat such as an attack or a natural disaster constitutes a kind of social drama. Or, on a smaller scale, certain groups might perform rituals that symbolize its understanding of threat and response.

Not all members of a group or culture participate in these social dramas and performances. Often certain members take the lead, and others may be selected to participate. Cultural performances, like presidential elections, are ways that "stars" show an audience its own culture. By seeing how the performers work things out through breach, crisis, redressive action, and reintegration, the culture is both formed and learned.

Sporting events are a good example of social dramas. The teams come together in competition, which creates a breach, or threat to order. As the teams play and make gains against one another, a spirit of crisis arises, and fans take sides, cheer, boo, feel elated, and then disappointed. Rules, officials, time-outs, halftime, huddles, and coaching offer moments of redressive action, as the

---

38   Victor Turner, *The Anthropology of Performance* (New York: PAJ, 1987).
39   Turner, *Anthropology of Performance,* p. 23.

teams and fans deal with the crisis in a variety of ways. And at the end of the game, reintegration occurs, as teams shake hands, fans tear down goalposts, people leave and turn on their car radios, or even tune in to another game.

A major sporting event reproduces many aspects of the culture. It teaches us about competition, collaboration, loyalty, and a host of other values. It shows teamwork and expert coaching and play.

Performance ethnography is significant because it broadens the field beyond its traditional fixation on language and text to include *embodied practice*.[40] The performance ethnography movement is significant for the field of communication because communication itself is easily understood as performance, and indeed many communication scholars are primarily interested in performance.[41] This move—from text to performance—raises a number of interesting questions:[42]

1. Is *culture* better understood as a verb rather than a noun?
2. Is ethnographic fieldwork a joint performance between the researcher and the subject?
3. How does performance impact interpretation, and can performance be considered a kind of hermeneutics?
4. How should the results of performance ethnography be published, and how should scholarly representation itself make use of performance?
5. What is the relationship between performance and power?

One of the places in which social drama is especially important is organizations. Studying organizations as cultures is a fascinating endeavor, and we turn to this subject now.

Organizational Culture

Organizations, viewed as cultures, present opportunities for cultural interpretation.[43] An organization, which can be a way of life for its members, creates a shared reality that distinguishes it from other cultures. Gareth Morgan explains:

Shared meaning, shared understanding, and shared sense making are all different ways of describing culture. In talking about culture we are really talking about a process of reality construction that allows people to see and understand particular events, actions, objects, utterances, or situations in distinctive ways. These patterns of understanding also provide a basis for making one's own behavior sensible and meaningful.[44]

Organizational culture is produced by interactions of the members. Task-oriented actions not only achieve immediate objectives but also create or reinforce certain ways of understanding experience. But culture is created in other ways besides the official task behaviors of employees, since the most mundane everyday activities contribute to the organization's culture.

Michael Pacanowsky and Nick O'Donnell-Trujillo, leaders in the organizational culture movement, ask particular kinds of questions designed to uncover cultural patterns in an organization. Following the lead of Victor Turner, these authors note that "performances are those very actions by which members constitute and reveal their culture to themselves and others."[45] These scholars explain the difference between this approach and traditional methods in these terms:

We believe that an intriguing thing about communication is the way in which it creates and constitutes the taken-for-granted reality of the world. Social activity, as we see it, is primarily the communicative accomplishment of interrelated actions. So whereas the underlying motive of traditional research is coming to an understanding of how to make organizations work

40   Dwight Conquergood, "Rethinking Ethnography: Toward a Critical Cultural Politics," *Communication Monographs* 58 (1991): 179–194; "Ethnography, Rhetoric, and Performance," *Quarterly Journal of Speech* 78 (1992): 80–97.
41   See, for example, the journal *Text and Performance Studies.*
42   Conquergood, "Rethinking Ethnography."
43   For a brief description of this approach, see Michael Pacanowsky, "Creating and Narrating Organizational Realities," in *Rethinking Communication: Paradigm Exemplars,* eds. Brenda Dervin, Lawrence Grossberg, Barbara J. O'Keefe, and Ellen Wartella (Newbury Park, CA: Sage, 1989), pp. 250–257.
44   Gareth Morgan, *Images of Organization* (Beverly Hills, CA: Sage, 1986), p. 128.
45   Michael E. Pacanowsky and Nick O'Donnell-Trujillo, "Organizational Communication as Cultural Performance," *Communication Monographs* 50 (1983): 131. See also Victor Turner, *Dramas, Fields, and Metaphors* (Ithaca, NY: Cornell University Press, 1974).

better, the underlying motive of the organizational culture approach is coming to understand how organizational life is accomplished communicatively. To understand how organizational life is brought into being, we cannot let ourselves be limited to asking questions that require some implicit or explicit link to organizational productivity for their legitimacy.[46]

What do organizational members use to create and display their understanding of events within the organization? There are many indicators, including relevant constructs and related vocabulary, perceived facts, practices or activities, metaphors, stories, and rites and rituals. All these are performances because they display the lived experience of the group. However, performances, like stage plays, are also accomplishments; they bring something about—the reality of the culture: ". . . performance brings the significance or meaning of some structural form— be it symbol, story, metaphor, ideology, or saga— into being."[47]

Pacanowsky and O'Donnell-Trujillo outline four characteristics of communication performances. First, they are interactional, more like dialogues than soliloquies. They are social actions, not solitary ones. Organizational performances are something people participate in together. Second, performances are contextual. They cannot be viewed as independent acts but are always embedded in a larger frame of activity. Context consists of the who, where, and when of the action. The performance both reflects and produces its context. Third, performances are episodes. They are events with a beginning and an end, and the performers can identify the episode and distinguish it from others. Finally, performances are improvised. There is flexibility in how a communication episode is played out, and although the same performances may be given again and again, they are never repeated exactly the same way.

The authors present a suggestive list of organizational communication performances. The first is ritual. A *ritual* is repeated regularly. It is familiar and routine, such as staff meetings or company picnics. Rituals are especially important because they constantly renew our under-

standings of our common experience, and they lend legitimacy to what we are thinking, feeling, and doing. Here is an example:

> Each and every day, Lou Polito, owner and general manager of Lou Polito Dodge, opens all the company mail. On those occasions when he is "free," he personally delivers this mail to the appropriate divisions in the company. This is just his way of letting his people know that he is keeping in touch with what they are doing.[48]

This is an example of a *personal ritual.* Another type is a *task ritual*, which is a repeated activity that helps members do their jobs:

> When a Valley View patrolman stops a driver for some traffic violation, he launches into a conversational routine that involves a question-answer sequence. "May I see your driver's license please?" "Is this your correct address?" "May I see your registration please?" "Do you know why I stopped you?" "Do you know what the speed limit is on this street?" "Do you know how fast you were going?" "Do you want to see the reading on the radar gun?" Although the officer has been taught this routine at the Police Academy as a way of being polite and professional, the Valley View police use it in order to see how the driver responds, to "size him up," and decide whether or not to give him any "breaks" in issuing a citation or warning.[49]

Social rituals are not task-related, yet they are important performances within organizations. The after-work drink is a good example: "Every Friday afternoon, the foremen from Steele Manufacturing go to the 'Pub,' one of the few places in their part of town that serves beer. The conversations are often filled with 'shop talk' but can range from sports . . . to politics."[50]

Finally, *organizational rituals* are those in which an entire work group participates with

46 Michael E. Pacanowsky and Nick O'Donnell-Trujillo, "Communication and Organizational Cultures," *Western Journal of Speech Communication* 46 (1982): 121.
47 Pacanowsky and O'Donnell-Trujillo, "Organizational Communication," p. 129.
48 Pacanowsky and O'Donnell-Trujillo, "Organizational Communication," p. 135.
49 Pacanowsky and O'Donnell-Trujillo, "Organizational Communication," p. 136.
50 Pacanowsky and O'Donnell-Trujillo, "Organizational Communication," p. 137.

some regularity: "Each year, the department of communication has its annual picnic, highlighted by the traditional softball game which pits the graduate students against the faculty. Competition is typically fierce; but alas for the graduate nine, they have had but one win in the last five years."[51]

The second category of performances is what the authors call *passion*. Here, workers put on performances that make otherwise dull and routine duties interesting or passionate. Perhaps the most common way this is done is by *storytelling*. Almost everybody tells stories about their work, and the telling is often lively and dramatic. Further, these stories are told over and over, and people often enjoy telling one another the same stories again and again. We tell stories about ourselves (personal stories), about other people (collegial stories), or about the organization (corporate stories).

Another way drama is created on the job is *passionate repartee*, which consists of dramatic interactions and the use of lively language: "The Valley View police, for example, do not deal with 'civilians,' but rather with 'assholes,' 'dirtbags,' 'creeps,' and 'maggots'—labels which serve as reminders that the 'negative element' is so much a part of the everyday experience of being a police officer."[52]

A third category of performance involves *sociality*, which reinforces a common sense of propriety and makes use of social rules within the organization. Courtesies and pleasantries are examples. *Sociabilities* are performances that create a group sense of identification and include things like joking, "bitching," and "talking shop." *Privacies* are sociality performances that communicate sensitivity and privacy. They include such things as confessing, consoling, and criticizing.

A fourth category of performance involves *organizational politics*. These performances, which create and reinforce notions of power and influence, may include showing personal strength, cementing allies, and bargaining.

A fifth category is *enculturation*, or processes of "teaching" the culture to organizational members. Enculturation is ongoing, but certain performances are especially vital to this process. Orientation of newcomers is an example. On a less formal scale, "learning the ropes" consists of a series of performances in which individuals teach others how things are done. Although this can be accomplished by direct instruction ("That's how we do it here"), most often this kind of learning occurs when people talk about things that happened in a way that helps other individuals learn how to interpret events.

In a police department, for example, officer Davis tells rookie Benson how to handle a rowdy drunk. Benson says he heard that Davis almost got in a fight with a drunk, and Davis replies, "Not really. I didn't give the guy a chance to get mad at me." Pacanowsky and O'Donnell-Trujillo present the following interpretation of this exchange:

> We take Davis' interaction with Benson as a unique enculturation performance, a metacommunicative commentary that instructs Benson in how he should interpret the prior performance. This metacommunication informs the rookie that the prior exchange was not an endorsement of fighting but was backstage "play." And, as the rookie observes more instances of this backstage "tough" talk, he comes to understand it as "not real," but serious nonetheless.[53]

Coming to understand the cultural meanings of organizational performances such as this exchange between the officers proceeds like any ethnography. The researcher first describes the actions of the organizational members and then constructs an interpretation of them in terms that are not only faithful from the native's point of view but are also understandable by people outside the organization. This is in every way a hermeneutic process.

Interpretive Media Studies

Traditional media studies view media as channels for transmitting information to an audience (see Chapter 15). A different, and increasingly

---

51   Pacanowsky and O'Donnell-Trujillo, "Organizational Communication," p. 137.
52   Pacanowsky and O'Donnell-Trujillo, "Organizational Communication," p. 139.
53   Pacanowsky and O'Donnell-Trujillo, "Organizational Communication," p. 145.

popular, way of approaching media is to think of the audience as numerous interpretive communities, each with its own meanings for what is read, viewed, or heard.[54]

We already discussed interpretive communities earlier in this chapter in the section on Stanley Fish, who had a significant impact on interpretive media studies.[55] For Fish, interpretive communities come into being around specific media and content. A community develops around a shared pattern of consumption: common understandings of the content of what is read, heard, or viewed, and shared outcomes. For example, a television audience consists of a number of "cultures," or communities of viewers, who use and perceive the medium—even individual programs—differently. Thus, if you want to discover how television affects the audience, you have to understand the cultures of these various communities.

Because the outcomes of media consumption depend on the cultural constructions of the community, this approach requires cultural interpretation.[56] James Lull refers to this type of work as the "ethnography of mass communication."[57]

For example, a program like *Sesame Street* appeals to a variety of interpretive communities. One such community might be middle-class children whose parents encourage them to watch and discuss it with them. Another community might be children who view the program on their own to kill time before dinner every evening.

Another example of an interpretive community would be people who get their news by listening to National Public Radio's *All Things Considered* in the car on the way home from work. Still another might consist of people who watch a lot of weekend football for relaxation, entertainment, and social life.

Any person may be a member of a variety of interpretive communities, and particular social groups, such as the family, may be a crossing point for a number of such communities. For example, various members of a family may enjoy television news, top-40 radio programming, sitcoms, children's programs, and biographies and are therefore members of a variety of communities.

Thomas Lindlof outlines three dimensions of an interpretive community.[58] Because interpretive communities define their own meanings for media, Lindlof refers to these elements as *genres,* or general types of media outcomes created by interaction within the interpretive community. This idea is consistent with the social phenomenology of Schutz discussed earlier in this chapter and with social constructionism discussed in Chapter 9.

The first genre that characterizes an interpretive community is *content,* which consists of the types of programs and other media consumed by the community. One group shares an interest in televised football, another in mystery novels, and still another in music videos. It is not enough that a community share an interest in one type of medium content; it must also share some common meanings for that content. A mother who thinks *Sesame Street* is a cute and harmless pastime for her children, the children who become intimately involved with the characters day after day, the teenage son who thinks it is silly, and the grandfather who loves the Muppets do not constitute an interpretive community because they see very different things in the content of that program.

Genres of *interpretation,* then, revolve around shared meaning. Members of a community interpret the content of programs and other media in similar ways. The impact on their behavior, especially what they say about the media and

---

54   This work is part of social action media studies. See Chapter 15 and Gerard T. Schoening and James A. Anderson, "Social Action Media Studies: Foundational Arguments and Common Premises," *Communication Theory* 5 (1995): 93–116.
55   Fish, *Is There a Text in This Class?*
56   See, for example, Thomas R. Lindlof and Timothy P. Meyer, "Mediated Communication as Ways of Seeing, Acting, and Constructing Culture: The Tools and Foundations of Qualitative Research," in *Natural Audiences: Qualitative Research of Media Uses and Effects,* ed. T. R. Lindlof (Norwood, NJ: Ablex, 1987), pp. 1–32; Thomas R. Lindlof, "Media Audiences as Interpretive Communities," in *Communication Yearbook 11,* ed. J. A. Anderson (Newbury Park, CA: Sage, 1988), pp. 81–107; Kevin M. Carragee, "Interpretive Media Study and Interpretive Social Science," *Critical Studies in Mass Communication* 7 (1990): 81–96; Klaus Bruhn Jensen, "When Is Meaning? Communication Theory, Pragmatism, and Mass Media Reception," in *Communication Yearbook 14,* ed. J. A. Anderson (Newbury Park, CA: Sage, 1991), pp. 3–32.
57   James Lull, "The Social Uses of Television," *Human Communication Research* 6 (1980): 197–209; see also Shaun Moores, *Interpreting Audiences: The Ethnography of Media Consumption* (London: Sage, 1993).
58   Lindlof, "Media Audiences."

the language used to describe it, is similar. The Tuesday morning quarterback is a good example. Members of the Monday night football club spend a good deal of time on Tuesday morning analyzing the game.

Finally, genres of *social action* are shared sets of behaviors toward the media in question, including not only how the media content is consumed (when and where it is viewed or read) but also the ways it affects the conduct of the members of the community. How are members' relationships among themselves affected by the media? Does a particular type of content facilitate the relationship in some way? Do people talk to one another about what they have seen or heard? Do they use relationships viewed on television as models for their own relationships?

An example of a cultural analysis of media is Linda Steiner's investigation of the "No Comment" section of *Ms.* magazine.[59] *Ms.* has regularly published a page titled "No Comment," featuring quotations and entries from other sources, sent in by readers, to illustrate the oppression of women in media. The title of the section implies that the quotation stands by itself without comment.

Items from other magazines (especially print ads), journals, newspapers, and even textbooks and manuals have found their way onto the "No Comment" page. All items were originally published with a particular meaning in mind, but the readers of *Ms.* interpret them differently. The fact that readers choose similar items again and again to make a point at odds with the original publisher's intent makes these readers an interpretive community, sharing attitudes and perceptions about the media's treatment of women.

In her analysis Steiner isolates a number of meanings for various items. For example, many depict women as the property of men. Some mock feminism as offensive. Others make use of women's bodies in ways that are exploitative. Still others promote sexual abuse and violence

against women. In each case, the deliberate reading opposes that intended by the originator of the quoted item. Steiner shows how contributing to and reading the "No Comment" section solidifies a set of values and views shared by the interpretive community of *Ms.* readers.

◖ COMMENTARY AND CRITIQUE

The theories presented in this chapter are members of an extended family. Like any family, they have important differences but share a common relationship. These approaches privilege conscious human perception and experience in one form or another. In phenomenology the conscious experience of the individual provides an eye to truth. In hermeneutics the interpretation of a culture or text is a disciplined and conscious human task. We have seen several varieties of these two traditions, including classical, social, and hermeneutic phenomenology, and we have also examined theories of cultural and textual hermeneutics.

Many important theoretical questions about experience and interpretation remain. Is human experience primarily individual or social? Can reality be ascertained by careful bracketing of experience, or is reality constructed by human action? Is meaning in the text or in the reader? Or does it arise from interaction between text and reader? What is the role of history and tradition in establishing meaning?

Setting these questions aside for the moment, three serious debates surround phenomenology and hermeneutics. First, these approaches conflict with traditional structural and cognitive perspectives summarized in Chapters 6 and 7. Second, they clash also with poststructuralism and critical theory (see Chapter 11). Third, there is a tension between textual and cultural interpretation. We will now consider each of these controversies in turn.

The structuralist critique is easily anticipated from ideas presented earlier in this book. We

---

59   Linda Steiner, "Oppositional Decoding as an Act of Resistance," *Critical Studies in Mass Communication* 5 (1988): 1–15.

have encountered it before in the discussions of philosophical issues in communication theory and in the critiques of structuralism, cognitivism, and constructionism. The critique begins with the opposing assumption that structures are real apart from the human experience of them and that these realities impact human experience in ways neither anticipated nor understood by communicators themselves. For the structural or cognitive theorist, these powerful outside influences must be discovered by controlled observation, and hermeneutic interpretation is inadequate for this task.[60]

Traditional critics believe that interpretive approaches ignore important psychological and social structures that influence human behavior. By concentrating on conscious experience, they miss the ways outside factors affect human life. Interpretive media studies are an example. As Kevin Carragee points out,

> In their desire to examine audience interpretations and uses of media content, interpretive studies largely have ignored the organizational and economic factors that influence the media texts. . . . The interpretive project's failure to incorporate research examining encoding processes reduces media texts to autonomous signifying systems; they are cut off from their origin in organizational routines and procedures.[61]

According to the structural-cognitive critique, the structures that affect human life are largely unintentional and out of awareness. Cognition is a complex set of processes, many of which are hidden from the individual.[62] Although much of what we do is indeed conscious, many important structures governing social life are beyond awareness.[63]

Social structures, too, exist apart from any design or intention as people live their lives. Anthony Giddens calls these the "unintended consequences" of purposeful actions. As individuals go about their daily activities, according to Giddens, certain outcomes that may not be intended nor even conscious come about, and these have a serious impact on subsequent actions. Giddens notes the importance of such structures:

History is not an intentional project, and all intentional activity takes place in the context of institutions sedimented over long-term periods of time. The unintended consequences of action are of fundamental importance to social theory, especially insofar as they are systematically incorporated within the processes of the reproduction of institutions.[64]

This thesis flies in the face of phenomenology, which gives conscious experience great power to apprehend the structures of reality. Early phenomenologists like Husserl would probably agree that the essence of reality is not normally within the awareness of the individual when in the natural attitude, but they would suggest that what becomes conscious in reduction is that which is essential and real about an experience.

Later phenomenologists of the social and hermeneutic traditions would find the structuralist objection unacceptable in any version. For these theorists, reality is always experience as lived.

Hermeneutics is a method that grants individuals the ability to interpret actions and texts. For theorists of this tradition, there is no structural reality outside of actions or texts, and ambiguity demands interpretation. Interpretation is a necessary conscious human experience.

To the structuralist, on the other hand, people may not accurately understand, nor can they reliably report, their experience. If your intentions are elusive and important processes are hidden, what is really going on in social life is not something a perceiver can tap into experientially. Instead, scientific methods of discovery are necessary. Research on attribution theory (Chapter 7)

---

60   D. W. Hamlyn, "The Concept of Social Reality," in *Explaining Human Behavior: Consciousness, Human Action, and Social Structure*, ed. Paul F. Secord (Beverly Hills, CA: Sage, 1982), p. 194.
61   Carragee, "Interpretive Media Study."
62   See, for example, Michael T. Motley, "Consciousness and Intentionality in Communication: A Preliminary Model and Methodological Approaches," *Western Journal of Speech Communication* 50 (1986): 3–23.
63   William Bailey, "Consciousness and Action/Motion Theories of Communication," *Western Journal of Speech Communication* 50 (1986): 74.
64   Anthony Giddens, "On the Relation of Sociology to Philosophy," in *Explaining Human Behavior: Consciousness, Human Action, and Social Structure*, ed. Paul F. Secord (Beverly Hills, CA: Sage, 1982), p. 180.

illustrates the difficulty of explaining one's own actions.[65]

Another objection of traditional social science is that interpretive methods tend to be case-oriented and do not lend themselves to generalization and theory building. In phenomenology each thing must be understood in and of itself by careful bracketing of experience. In hermeneutics one interprets a set of group actions or a text, but generalizations beyond the individual case are discouraged. Even comparative ethnography, though it may look for commonalities, is equally interested in cultural difference. What, then, can be known from this method other than the facts of the case? For some, like Schutz, the facts of the case are good enough. These thinkers eschew theory as misleading because theories espouse generalizations that are not there. For others, like Hymes, generalizations can be made after examination of several cases.

The culture approach to organizations illustrates the difficulty of generalization. If you assume that the social reality of an organization comes from the interactions among members of the organization and that organizational cultures thereby differ, you put yourself into the difficult theoretical position of being unable to make generalizations or predictions about organizational life. Each organization must be studied independently, and generalizations become difficult.

An answer, of course, is that theories should not attempt to be predictive but should capture general categories of action, which we expect to be played out differently in various cultures. For example, although every organization is different, there are categories such as rituals and stories that all organizations can be expected to have. Such middle-range theories, like that of Pacanowsky and O'Donnell-Trujillo and of Hymes, enable us to observe cultures with a sensitivity to their rich individuality and their commonalities as well.

The structural-cognitive critique can be thought of as conservative because it argues from the tradition of Western thought and social science in the twentieth century. In a sense, then, this first set of concerns is a critique from the

right. There is also a critique from the left. It comes from a movement that is by definition critical of traditional social science, a movement that aims to transform the work of social science. If the critique from the right accuses interpretive theories of ignoring, bending, or breaking traditional notions of reality and structure, the critique from the left accuses them of being overly conservative and insensitive to the need for change.

As we will see in the following chapter, interpretive and critical approaches to communication theory have certain common principles. There is, however, a substantial difference between the two, which has become the source of a debate.[66] Critical theory is transformative: It not only presents a picture of society but also aims to change social structure by raising consciousness about power in society.

Critical theory accuses interpretive approaches of being conservative and of failing to recognize their own ideological character. In other words, understanding human action by itself does not go far enough. Scholars must study the ways individuals are oppressed so that people can change the circumstances of their lives. The failure of interpretive scholarship to do so merely legitimizes repressive power structures and perpetuates oppression in society. The most significant problem of phenomenology, from this vantage point, is that it denies the political nature of everyday experience.[67]

In fact, many critical scholars accuse interpretive theory of bolstering the dominant ideology.

65 R. E. Nisbett and T. D. Wilson, "Telling More Than We Can Know: Verbal Reports on Mental Processes," *Psychological Review* 84 (1977): 231–259. See also Pamela J. Benoit and William L. Benoit, "Consciousness: The Mindlessness/Mindfulness and Verbal Report of Controversies," *Western Journal of Speech Communication* 50 (1986): 41–63. Critics of attribution theory are quick to point out that the findings in this line of research do not accurately reflect the everyday experience of people acting in context. Indeed, this criticism has been leveled against all positivistic social science research. See, for example, John Shotter, *Social Accountability and Selfhood* (New York: Blackwell, 1984), pp. 167–172; Kenneth Gergen, *Toward Transformation in Social Knowledge* (New York: Springer-Verlag, 1982), pp. 126–133.
66 This debate is summarized in Brian Fay, *Social Theory and Political Practice* (London: Allen & Unwin, 1975); and Ricoeur, *Hermeneutics.*
67 This argument is made by Stanley Deetz, *Democracy in an Age of Corporate Colonization* (Albany: SUNY Press, 1992), pp. 113–144.

The cultural approach to organizational theory is an example. The downside to the organizational culture movement is that the empirically minded manager may come to think of culture as just another variable to be manipulated in the management of the organization. This idea can lead to the negative consequence of ideological control.[68]

The critique from the left points out that any interpreter brings an orientation, an ideology, and a set of values to the subject under investigation. This state of affairs is not merely an obstacle to the validity of observation, because there is no one cultural form to be validly observed in any situation. Rather, a cultural description is always a product of a perspective, because the orientation of the ethnographer determines to some degree what the interpretation will be.

Even more, the interaction between researcher and subject is fraught with power relations. This eventuality affects not only the outcome of the investigation, the interpretation presented, and the way it represents persons and cultures, but also the way research subjects are treated.[69]

There have been at least four responses to this criticism. The first is to acknowledge the power of writing in the construction of an interpretation and to pay careful attention to *how* one writes up the interpretation. Here the goal is to use writing as a way to capture and express the ideology of the ethnographer.[70]

The second response, somewhat at odds with the first, is to account for the power relationship between the subject and the researcher, to acknowledge that the researcher has a source of power in defining the subject and a special responsibility to empower the subject. Interview methods, for example, can affect the political relationship between the investigator and the participant, and ethnographers need to acknowledge and describe the ways this happens.[71]

The third response is for the ethnographer to get as close as possible to the embodied performances of the native culture, to experience that culture as the natives do, to get out of one's own way of seeing things as much as possible.[72] This is precisely one of the most important objectives

of the performance ethnography movement discussed in this chapter.

A fourth response is to adopt the critical stance outright and use ethnography as a means to uncover oppressive power structures within a culture. Often called critical ethnography, this approach uses cultural interpretation as a form of social critique.[73]

This critique from the left is not as unified as might be implied in the above discussion. Indeed, on the question of how much power individuals and groups have to determine their fate, the voice of the left is equivocal. There are two schools of thought on this point.

The first is poststructuralism.[74] Poststructuralism denies the reality of universal structures of language and discourse, while also denying the certainty of meaning in action or text. Poststructuralists see interpretive approaches as essentially foundationalist in that they seek some sort of essential meaning in practices and texts. Phenomenologists seek the essence of experience; poststructuralists deny essence. Hermeneutic scholars are devoted to finding the center or central meaning of texts; poststructuralists deny that there is any central meaning in texts.

The version of poststructuralism most opposed to interpretation is *deconstructionism,* or the movement to obliterate meaning.[75] Interpretation reconstructs meaning; deconstruction shows that whatever meaning is derived is wrong. Since

---

68   This problem is explored by Sonja A. Sackmann, "Managing Organizational Culture: Dreams and Possibilities," *Communication Yearbook 13,* ed. James A. Anderson (Newbury Park, CA: Sage, 1990), pp. 114–148.
69   This controversy is summarized by James T. West, "Ethnography and Ideology: The Politics of Cultural Representation," *Western Journal of Communication* 57 (1993): 209–220.
70   See, for example, Atkinson, *Understanding Ethnographic Texts.* See also, Conquergood, "Rethinking Ethnography."
71   Bette J. Kauffman, "Feminist Facts: Interview Strategies and Political Subjects in Ethnography," *Communication Theory* 2 (1992): 187–206.
72   Dwight Conquergood, "Rethinking Ethnography."
73   Jim Thomas, *Doing Critical Ethnography* (Newbury Park, CA: Sage, 1993).
74   For an excellent summary of poststructuralism, see Art Berman, *From the New Criticism to Deconstruction* (Urbana, IL: University of Chicago Press, 1988).
75   The scholar most associated with deconstruction is Jacques Derrida. See *Of Grammatology,* trans. G. Spivak (Baltimore: Johns Hopkins University Press, 1976).

there is an unending set of possible meanings in any text, there can be no central or true meaning at all.

This postmodern critique is countered by the second school of thought, which ironically resembles the conservative structuralist objection discussed earlier. This group believes that there is certain meaning, and this is to be found in hidden oppressive social structures, expressed in discourse. These deep structural meanings determine power relations among classes and groups of people, and individuals have little or no freedom to act in the world. These structuralists believe that interpretive theories are naive in assuming that groups and individuals influence their worlds in any way.[76]

The above discussion implies that experiential and interpretive theories are a unified and cohesive block of ideas under attack from the outside. This is a misleading impression. In fact, substantial differences exist among the theories in this chapter. One of the most important is the difference between textual and cultural interpretation, which is a dispute about the locus of meaning.[77]

For most cultural interpretivists, meaning is found in the practices of a culture. For most textual interpretivists, meaning is found in language and text. Indeed, Ricoeur's concept of distanciation is designed to capture the separation of text from cultural practice. The culture-interpretive view is that texts are a product of social interaction, whereas the text-interpretation view holds that texts prefigure culture in important ways.

Actually, cultural interpretation and social constructionism are closely related and could easily have been put in the same chapter of this book. Both are children of social phenomenology, and both see meaning as inherent in social practice. Thus, the tension between text and practice mirrors the debate between traditional text hermeneutics and social constructionism.

This controversy can be seen in debates on media. The idea of interpretive communities assigns great power to the practices of social groups in constructing the meaning of media in their own lives. Media text theorists, on the other hand, assign great power to the content of media in the creation of culture. Carragee continues his critique of interpretive studies in this way:

> Interpretive researchers need to devote far more attention to the properties and structures of media messages, to the symbolic power of texts. Characterizations of texts or indeed media as empty vessels deny the ways in which texts and media help to constitute meanings and realities for their audiences by highlighting certain meanings and values while excluding others.[78]

An important question at this juncture is whether the text-practice dispute is a true disjunction. Some important commentators believe it is not. It may be entirely possible—indeed desirable—to grant power both to text and cultural practice.

Gadamer's work is especially important because he does precisely this. For Gadamer, readers cannot be separated from their interpretive communities in the way suggested by Ricoeur. At the same time, the text itself does have inherent meaning, and readers must be open to a dialogue between the reader and the text. The text has rich meaning to convey, and the reader always approaches that text from within an interpretive tradition. The interpretive frame informs the reading of the text, whereas the text helps shape the interpretive frame itself.

In the following chapter, we continue the discussion of meaning and social power. The emphasis now switches from interpretation of text and action to their transformation.

---

76   This objection is discussed in some detail by Michael Huspek, "Dueling Structures: The Theory of Resistance in Discourse," *Communication Theory* 3 (1993): 1–25.
77   This controversy is discussed by Berman, *From the New Criticism*, pp. 281–292.
78   Carragee, "Interpretive Media Study," p. 89.

CHAPTER

11

CRITICAL
THEORIES

Criticism has a long history in the field of communication. Rhetorical criticism, for example, carefully examines and judges the quality of discourse and other communication forms.[1] Our subject in this chapter is another kind of critique—critical social science.[2]

Although there are several varieties of critical social science, all share three essential features.[3] First, critical social scientists believe it necessary to understand the lived experience of real people in context. As such, critical theories share some of the ideas and methodologies of the interpretive theories discussed in Chapter 10. What makes critical scholarship different from much of the work discussed in that chapter is that it focuses on oppression.

Second, critical approaches examine social conditions and uncover oppressive power arrangements. For this reason critical theories also borrow from structuralism (Chapter 4). Most critical theories teach that knowledge is power, for understanding the ways you are oppressed enables you to take action and overcome oppressive forces.

In the field of communication, critical scholars are particularly interested in how messages reinforce oppression in society. Although critical scholars are interested in social action, they also focus on discourse and the texts that promote particular ideologies, establish and maintain power, and subvert the interests of certain groups and classes. Critical discourse analysis looks at actual features of texts that manifest these oppressive arrangements.[4]

Third, critical social science makes a conscious attempt to fuse theory and action. Such theories are clearly normative and act to accomplish

1   This chapter does not cover rhetorical criticism. For more information on this topic, see, for example, Sonja K. Foss, *Rhetorical Criticism: Exploration and Practice* (Prospect Heights, IL: Waveland, 1989).
2   This is not to imply that rhetorical criticism and critical social theory are necessarily separate fields. An argument for connecting them is made by Omar Swartz, *Conducting Socially Responsible Research* (Thousand Oaks, CA: Sage, 1997).
3   Brian Fay, *Social Theory and Political Practice* (London: Allen & Unwin, 1975), p. 94.
4   See, for example, Teun van Dijk, "Discourse Semantics and Ideology," *Discourse and Society* 6 (1995): 243–289; Teun van Dijk, "Principles of Critical Discourse Analysis," *Discourse and Society* 4 (1993): 249–283.

change in the conditions that affect our lives, or as Della Pollock and Robert Cox put it, "to *read* the world with an eye towards *shaping* it."[5] Critical research aims to reveal the ways in which competing interests clash and the manner in which conflicts are resolved in favor of particular groups over other ones. Processes of domination are often hidden from view, and critical theory aims to uncover these processes.[6] Critical theories therefore frequently ally themselves with the interests of marginalized groups.

Although critical theories have traditionally focused on clashing interests within societies, they can also feature the domination of one society over another. *Postcolonial theory* is a movement that looks at the ways in which certain societies dominate others intellectually, focusing especially on the role of discourse and media in such domination. The way in which First World peoples, including scholars, write and talk about the world maintains self-serving power structures. This tendency is propelled by the domination of Western media in the world.[7]

Whether it centers on the domination of interests within a society or imperialism by one society against another, critical social science is usually economic and political in nature, and communication is usually an important ingredient. In practice, critical theorists are usually reluctant to separate communication from other factors in the overall system of oppressive forces.[8]

Critical theories as a group are nearly impossible to characterize validly. At the beginning of this chapter, it is important for us to take a closer look at the various types of critical theory.

● SORTING OUT CRITICAL THEORIES

Because critical theories are so broad and cast such a wide net, they are often hard to place and categorize within the overall body of communication theory. Dennis Mumby provides a simple and clear scheme that will be helpful to us at this point.[9]

Mumby classifies communication scholarship into two broad groups—modern and postmodern. Rather than think of this distinction as a simple dichotomy, however, he presents four "discursive positions" along a continuum from the radical modern to the radical postmodern. As we are using the term here, the first two types are not considered critical, and the second two are.

The first kind of scholarship is the *discourse of representation,* or the positivist version of modernism. Here scholars make a sharp distinction between the observer and the world. Persons can perceive reality outside themselves and represent that reality with language. Many of the theories we have already covered in this book, including some brands of semiotics and theories of message production and reception, are examples of this kind of discourse.

The second category is the *discourse of understanding,* or interpretive modernism. Here the line between the observer and observed is less distinct. Reality is defined by an interaction between the knower and the known, and the observer structures observation in ways that can influence what is seen. We looked at many examples of this kind of discourse in previous

5   Della Pollock and J. Robert Cox, "Historicizing 'Reason': Critical Theory, Practice, and Postmodernity," *Communication Monographs* 58 (1991): 171.
6   This characteristic of critical theory is discussed by Nancy Fraser, *Unruly Practices: Power, Discourse, and Gender in Contemporary Social Theory* (Minneapolis: University of Minnesota Press, 1989), p. 113.
7   Raka Shome, "Postcolonial Interventions in the Rhetorical Canon: An 'Other' View," *Communication Theory* 6 (1996): 40–59; Saba Mahmood, "Cultural Studies and Ethnic Absolutism: Comments on Stuart Hall's 'Culture, Community, and Nation,'" *Cultural Studies* 10 (1996): 1–11. See also Anandam P. Kavoori, "Getting Past the Latest 'Post': Assessing the Term 'Post-Colonial,'" *Critical Studies in Mass Communication* 15 (1998): 195–202; Raka Shome, "Caught in the Term 'Post-Colonial': Why the 'Post-Colonial' Still Matters," *Critical Studies in Mass Communication* 15 (1998): 203–212.
8   For a discussion of the problems associated with separating communication as a focus, see Milton Mueller, "Why Communications Policy Is Passing 'Mass Communication' By: Political Economy as the Missing Link," *Critical Studies in Mass Communication* 12 (1995): 455–472.
9   Dennis K. Mumby, "Modernism, Postmodernism, and Communication Studies: A Rereading of an Ongoing Debate," *Communication Theory* 7 (1997): 1–28.

chapters on symbolic interaction, social construction, interpretation, and culture.

The third and fourth categories are what we are calling "critical" in this text and are primarily the subject of the current chapter. These are the discourses of *suspicion,* or critical modernism, and *vulnerability,* or postmodernism. Critical modernism is in the "structural" tradition, because it is a critique of an imagined structure of social arrangements that truly exist outside human perception and endure over time. Postmodernism is "poststructural" because it denies the existence of any true enduring social arrangements.

This distinction between modern and postmodern versions marks a significant fault line within the critical tradition.[10] The modern version—often referred to as "structural"—centers on oppressive social structures, which are considered real and enduring, though they may be hidden from the consciousness of most people. Critical scholars in this group attempt to name and expose these oppressive arrangements.

In contrast, the postmodern version teaches that there is no objectively real structure or central meaning and that oppressive "structures" are ephemeral. There is a struggle, but it is not a struggle between monolithic ideologies. It is a struggle between fluid interests and ideas.[11]

The structural tradition in critical social science is highly "theoretical" in the sense that it presents a standing version of social life to explain how oppressive structures work. The postmodern tradition is rather "antitheoretical" because it denies the existence of any particular structure over time.

Now, labels become confusing here. Many critical approaches are marxist, but because Marx the modernist was highly structural and theoretical, postmodernists sometimes object to being called "marxist." Also, because they generally deny the validity of "theory," postmodernists sometimes are excluded from the label "critical theory."

We are treating both modernist and postmodernist approaches in this chapter as "critical" be-cause of their shared position of opposition to traditional social science. Pollock and Cox write that although these two schools of thought have important differences, they share "a sense of failed hope and the difficulty, if not impossibility, of effecting social change. Conditioned by the atrocities of dogma and the advancing commercialization of every aspect of social life, they also similarly distrust 'centristic' thinking or 'totalizing' modes of discourse."[12]

In the remainder of the chapter, we will look at three broad traditions of critical studies—structuralism, poststructuralism, and feminism. Structuralist theories show us what the modernist tradition of critical theory looks like, and poststructuralist theories illustrate the postmodern. Both kinds of theory are present in feminist scholarship.

◖ STRUCTURAL APPROACHES

Marxist Foundations

Although critical theory has come a long way since Marx, much of it is still basically marxist. In fact, one of the most important intellectual strands of the twentieth century is marxist-based social theory. Originating with the ideas of Karl Marx and Friedrich Engels, this movement consists of a number of loosely related theories challenging the dominant order of society. Virtually

---

10   For more detailed discussions of these schools of thought see Mats Alvesson and Stanley Deetz, "Critical Theory and Postmodernism Approaches to Organizational Studies," in *Handbook of Organizational Studies,* eds. S. Clegg, C. Harding, and W. Nord (London: Sage, 1996), pp. 173–202; Douglas Kellner, *Media Culture: Cultural Studies, Identity and Politics Between the Modern and the Postmodern* (London: Routledge, 1995); Thomas McCarthy, *Ideals and Illusions: On Reconstruction and Deconstruction in Contemporary Critical Theory* (Cambridge, MA: MIT Press, 1993); Pollock and Cox, "Historicizing"; Donald G. Ellis, "Poststructuralism and Language: Non-Sense," *Communication Monographs* 58 (1991): 213–224; and Michael Huspek, "Taking Aim on Habermas's Critical Theory: On the Road Toward a Critical Hermeneutics," *Communication Monographs* 58 (1991): 225–233.
11   For a good description and critique of postmodern media studies, see John B. Harms and David R. Dickens, "Postmodern Media Studies: Analysis or Symptom," *Critical Studies in Mass Communication* 13 (1996): 210–227.
12   Pollock and Cox, "Historicizing," p. 175.

all branches of social science, including communication, have been influenced by this line of thought.[13]

Marx taught that the means of production in society determines the nature of society.[14] This is the basic linear idea of Marxism, the *base-superstructure* relationship: The economy is the base of all social structure. In capitalistic systems, profit drives production and therefore dominates labor.

Working-class groups are oppressed by more powerful groups that benefit from profit. All institutions that perpetuate domination within a capitalistic society are made possible by this economic system.[15] Only when the working class rises up against dominant groups can the means of production be changed and the liberation of the worker be achieved. Such liberation furthers the natural progress of history in which forces in opposition clash in a dialectic that results in a higher social order. This classical Marxist theory is called the *critique of political economy.*

Today, marxist critical theory is thriving, although it has become diffused and multitheoretical. Not all adherents to critical theory are "Marxist," in the classical sense of Marx's teachings, but there is no question that Marx had an immense influence on this school of thought. Although few critical theorists today adopt Marx's ideas on political economy, the basic concerns of dialectical conflict, domination, and oppression remain important. For this reason critical theory today is frequently labeled "neo-marxist" or "marxist" (with a lowercase *m*).

In contrast to the simple base-superstructure model of Marxism, most contemporary critical theories view social processes as *overdetermined,* or caused by multiple sources. They see social structure as a system in which many things interact and affect one another (Chapter 3).

Critical theorists view their task as uncovering oppressive forces through *dialectical analysis,* which is designed to expose an underlying struggle between opposing forces.[16] Although the population generally perceives a kind of surface order to things, the critical theorist's job is to point out the contradictions that exist. Only by

becoming aware of the dialectic of opposing forces in a struggle for power can individuals be liberated and free to change the existing order. Otherwise, they will remain alienated from one another and co-opted into their own oppression.

Marxism places great emphasis on the means of communication in society. Communication practices are an outcome of the tension between individual creativity and the social constraints on that creativity. Only when individuals are truly free to express themselves with clarity and reason will liberation occur, and that condition cannot come about in a class-based society.

On the other hand, many critical theorists believe that contradiction, tension, and conflict are inevitable aspects of the social order and can never be eliminated. The ideal state is a social environment in which all voices can be heard so that no force dominates any other.

Language is an important constraint on individual expression, for the language of the dominant class makes it difficult for working-class groups to understand their situation and to get out of it. In other words, the dominant language defines and perpetuates the oppression of marginalized groups. It is the job of the critical

---

13   For a brief overview of the movement, see Everett M. Rogers, *A History of Communication Study: A Biographical Approach* (New York: Free Press, 1994), pp. 102–128; Tom Bottomore and Armand Mattelart, "Marxist Theories of Communication," in *International Encyclopedia of Communications,* vol. 2, ed. E. Barnouw (New York: Oxford University Press, 1989), pp. 476–483. For coverage of a variety of marxist-based ideas, see Cary Nelson and Lawrence Grossberg, eds., *Marxism and the Interpretation of Culture* (Urbana: University of Illinois Press, 1988).

14   Karl Marx's best-known works are *The Communist Manifesto* (London: Reeves, 1888) and *Capital* (Chicago: Kerr, 1909).

15   For a discussion of capitalist oppression as the basis for critical theory, see Graham Murdock, "Across the Great Divide: Cultural Analysis and the Condition of Democracy," *Critical Studies in Mass Communication* 12 (1995): 89–95.

16   See, for example, Robert Pryor, "On the Method of Critical Theory and Its Implications for a Critical Theory of Communication," in *Phenomenology in Rhetoric and Communication,* ed. S. Deetz (Washington, DC: Center for Advanced Research in Phenomenology/University Press of America, 1981), pp. 25–35; Jennifer Daryl Slack and Martin Allor, "The Political and Epistemological Constituents of Critical Communication Research," *Journal of Communication* 33 (1983): 128–218; Dallas W. Smythe and Tran Van Dinh, "On Critical and Administrative Research: A New Critical Analysis," *Journal of Communication* 33 (1983): 117–127; Everett M. Rogers, "The Empirical and the Critical Schools of Communication Research," in *Communication Yearbook 5,* ed. M. Burgoon (New Brunswick, NJ: Transaction, 1982), pp. 125–144.

theorist to create new forms of language that will enable the predominant ideology to be exposed and competing ideologies to be heard.

The term *ideology* is important in most critical theories. An ideology is a set of ideas that structure a group's reality, a system of representations or a code of meanings governing how individuals and groups see the world.[17] In classical Marxism an ideology is a false set of ideas perpetuated by the dominant political force. For the classical Marxist, science must be used to discover truth and to overcome the *false consciousness* of ideology.

More recent critical theorists tend to assert that there is no single dominant ideology but that the dominant classes in society are themselves constituted by a struggle among several. Many current thinkers reject the idea that an ideology is an isolated element in the social system; rather, it is deeply embedded in language and all other social and cultural processes.

Perhaps the best-known ideology theorist is the French Marxist Louis Althusser.[18] For Althusser, ideology is present in the structure of society itself and arises from the actual practices undertaken by institutions within society. As such, ideology actually forms the individual's consciousness and creates the person's subjective understanding of experience. In this model the superstructure (social organization) creates ideology, which in turn affects individuals' notions of reality.

For Althusser, this superstructure consists of *repressive state apparatuses*, such as the police and the military, and *ideological state apparatuses*, such as education, religion, and mass media. The repressive mechanisms enforce an ideology when it is threatened by deviant action, and the ideological apparatuses reproduce it more subtly in everyday activities of communication by making an ideology seem normal.

We live within a real set of conditions, but we normally do not understand our relationship to actual conditions except through an ideology. The real conditions of existence can only be discovered through science, which Althusser poses in opposition to ideology. This idea has been

highly controversial because it is based on a realist notion of truth, which much critical theory now opposes.

Marxist theories tend to see society as the grounds for a struggle among interests through the domination of one ideology over another. *Hegemony* is the process of domination, in which one set of ideas subverts or co-opts another. It is a process by which one group in society exerts leadership over all others. The concept was perhaps best elaborated by the Italian Marxist Antonio Gramsci.[19]

The process of hegemony can occur in many ways and in many settings. In essence, it happens when events or texts are interpreted in a way that promotes the interests of one group over those of another. This can be a subtle process of co-opting the interests of a subordinate group into supporting those of a dominant one. For example, advertisers often play into the "women's liberation" theme, making it look as though the corporation supports women's rights. What is happening here is that women's interests are being reinterpreted to promote the interests of the capital economy. Ideology plays a central role in this process because it structures the way people understand their experience, and it is therefore powerful in shaping how they interpret events.

Dennis Mumby has presented a persuasive theory of hegemony within organizations that illustrates this process very well.[20] Mumby shows how organizations are sites in which hegemonic struggles occur. Power is established within an

---

17 For a brief discussion of theories of ideology, see Stuart Hall, "Ideology," in *International Encyclopedia of Communications*, vol. 2, ed. E. Barnouw (New York: Oxford University Press, 1989), pp. 307–311.
18 Louis Althusser, *For Marx*, trans. B. Brewster (New York: Vintage, 1970); *Lenin and Philosophy*, trans. B. Brewster (New York: Monthly Review Press, 1971). Althusser's work is summarized by Stuart Hall, "Signification, Representation, Ideology: Althusser and the Post-Structuralist Debates," *Critical Studies in Mass Communication* 2 (1985): 91–114; Dennis K. Mumby, *Communication and Power in Organizations: Discourse, Ideology, and Domination* (Norwood, NJ: Ablex, 1988), pp. 1–78.
19 Antonio Gramsci, *Selections from the Prison Notebooks*, trans. Q. Hoare and G. Nowell Smith (New York: International, 1971). For a brief summary, see Joseph P. Zompetti, "Toward a Gramscian Critical Rhetoric," *Western Journal of Communication* 61 (1997): 66–86.
20 Dennis K. Mumby, "The Political Function of Narrative in Organizations," *Communication Monographs* 54 (1987): 113–127; Mumby, *Communication and Power.*

organization by the domination of one ideology over others. We saw in the previous chapter that communication in organizations functions in part to create an organizational culture. This occurs through rituals, stories, and the like, and Mumby shows how the culture of an organization involves an inherently political process. Communication within the organization serves not only to establish meaning but also to create power and domination.

One way this happens is through storytelling, or the use of narrative. Narratives are certain kinds of texts that create and perpetuate ideologies. For example, there is a story that has been repeatedly retold at IBM. As the story goes, the chairman of the board was stopped by a 22-year-old female security guard because he did not have the appropriate badge to enter the area she was guarding. Although you might think that the boss would pull rank, he quietly secured the proper badge and got entry.[21] One reading of this story is that the chairman was a nice guy who wanted to follow the rules. But the story would not be noteworthy at all if power relations were not important. Consequently, the story reinforces the idea of power relations in this company.

More recently, Mumby has made clear his interpretation of hegemony as a pragmatic, interactive, and dialectical process of assertion and resistence. Hegemony is not so much a question of an active and powerful group dominating a passive and less powerful one, but a process of power arrangements emerging as an active process of multigroup social construction. Hegemony is a necessary result—neither always bad, nor always good—that results from struggle among stakeholder groups in everyday situated action.[22]

The Frankfurt School and Universal Pragmatics

One of the longest and best-known Marxist traditions is the Frankfurt School. The *Frankfurt School* is such an important tradition in critical studies that it is often known simply as *Critical*

Theory. These theorists originally based their ideas on Marxist thought, although it has gone far afield from that origin in the past fifty years. Communication takes a central place in this movement, and the study of mass communication has been especially important.[23]

This brand of critical theory began with the work of Max Horkheimer, Theodor Adorno, Herbert Marcuse, and their colleagues at the Frankfurt Institute for Social Research in 1923.[24] The group was originally guided by Marxist principles, although they were never members of any political party, and their work was distinctly scholarly rather than activist. With the rise of the National Socialist Party in Germany in the 1930s, the Frankfurt scholars immigrated to the United States and there became intensely interested in mass communication and the media as structures of oppression in capitalistic societies.

The early Frankfurt scholars reacted strongly to the classical ideals of Marxism and the success of the Russian revolution. They saw capitalism as an evolutionary stage in the development, first, of socialism and then of communism. Their ideas at that time formed a harsh critique of capitalism and liberal democracy.

Since the early years of the Frankfurt School, however, no agreed-on unified theory characterizes its members. The best-known contemporary Frankfurt scholar is Jürgen Habermas, whose theory of universal pragmatics and the transformation of society has had considerable influence in Europe and an increasing influence in the United States. Habermas is clearly the most im-

21   Mumby, "Political Function," pp. 120–125; *Communication and Power*, pp. 115–124.
22   Dennis K. Mumby, "The Problem of Hegemony: Rereading Gramsci for Organizational Communication Studies," *Western Journal of Communication* 61 (1997): 343–375.
23   Michael Huspek, "Toward Normative Theories of Communication with Reference to the Frankfurt School: An Introduction," *Communication Theory* 7 (1997): 265–276. See also Douglas Kellner, "Media Communications vs. Cultural Studies: Overcoming the Divide," *Communication Theory* 5 (1995): 162–177.
24   For a brief historical perspective, see Thomas B. Farrell and James A. Aune, "Critical Theory and Communication: A Selective Literature Review," *Quarterly Journal of Speech* 65 (1979): 93–120. See also Andrew Arato and Eike Gebhardt, eds., *The Essential Frankfurt School Reader* (New York: Continuum, 1982).

Three Interests of Society

Type	Nature of Interest	Rationality	Associated Scholarship
Work	Technical	Instrumental	Empirical sciences
Interaction	Practical	Practical	History/hermeneutics
Power	Emancipatory	Self-reflection	Critical theory

portant spokesperson for the Frankfurt School today.[25] His theory draws from a wide range of thought and presents a coherent critical view of communication and society. We turn now to a closer look at his contribution.

Habermas teaches that society must be understood as a mix of three major interests: work, interaction, and power. All three interests are necessary. *Work,* the first major interest, consists of the efforts to create material resources. Because of its highly instrumental nature—achieving tangible tasks and accomplishing concrete objectives—work is basically a "technical interest." It involves an instrumental rationality and is represented by the empirical-analytical sciences. In other words, technology is used as an instrument to accomplish practical results and is based on scientific research. It designs computers, builds bridges, puts satellites in orbit, administers organizations, and enables wondrous medical treatments.

The second major interest is *interaction,* or the use of language and other symbol systems of communication. Because social cooperation is necessary for survival, Habermas names this second item the "practical interest." It involves practical reasoning and is represented in historical scholarship and hermeneutics. The interaction interest can be seen in speeches, conferences, psychotherapy, family relations, and a host of other cooperative endeavors.

The third major interest is *power.* Social order naturally leads to the distribution of power, yet we are also interested in being freed from domination. Power leads to distorted communication,

but by becoming aware of the ideologies that dominate in society, groups can themselves be empowered to transform society. Consequently, power is an "emancipatory interest." The rationality of power is self-reflection, and the branch of scholarship that deals with it is critical theory. For Habermas, the kind of work done by the critical theorists discussed thus far in this chapter is emancipatory because it can empower otherwise powerless groups. Table 11.1 summarizes the basic interests of work, interaction, and power.

As an example of these interests at work, consider the study by Steven Ealy of a Georgia State job-classification survey in the 1970s.[26] At that time Georgia was strapped with the responsibility of reclassifying 45,000 state job positions, a monumental task; according to Ealy, the result was a serious communication breakdown. The state employed a consulting firm to conduct the

25 The important works of Habermas include *Postmetaphysical Thinking: Philosophical Essays,* trans. William Mark Hohengarten (Cambridge, MA: MIT Press, 1992); *Knowledge and Human Interests,* trans. J. J. Shapiro (Boston: Beacon, 1971); *Legitimation Crisis,* trans. T. McCarthy (Boston: Beacon, 1975); *The Theory of Communicative Action, Volume 1: Reason and the Rationalization of Society,* trans. T. McCarthy (Boston: Beacon, 1984). For critical commentary, see the special issue of *Communication Theory* 7 (November 1997). Excellent secondary summaries can be found in Thomas B. Farrell, *Norms of Rhetorical Culture* (New Haven, CT: Yale University Press, 1993); Sonja K. Foss, Karen A. Foss, and Robert Trapp, *Contemporary Perspectives on Rhetoric* (Prospect Heights, IL: Waveland, 1991), pp. 241–272; see also Sue Curry Jansen, "Power and Knowledge: Toward a New Critical Synthesis," *Journal of Communication* 33 (1983): 342–354; Mumby, *Communication and Power,* pp. 23–54; Richard L. Lanigan, *Phenomenology of Communication: Merleau-Ponty's Thematics in Communicology and Semiology* (Pittsburgh: Duquesne University Press, 1988), pp. 75–99.
26 Steven D. Ealy, *Communication, Speech, and Politics: Habermas and Political Analysis* (Washington, DC: University Press of America, 1981).

necessary survey, and a plan was drafted to collect information about each position, develop job specifications, classify the positions, and then determine pay.

A strong technical interest guided the reclassification study. There was a job to be done, and the consultants developed a method to achieve this goal. They proceeded as if the task could be solved by the use of "objective" or scientific procedures—gathering data, classifying jobs, and the like.

The employees and the departments, however, did not think of the study this way. They saw the study as a practical problem, one that affected their daily work and pay. For the departments, collecting data and implementing the results should have involved a good deal of interaction and consensus building, but it did not. Immediately, then, there was a clash of interests.

Because they held the power, the organizational decision makers' technical interests prevailed, the consultants' methods were imposed, and all practical interests were eliminated. In other words, the employees were expected simply to comply with the survey without much discussion about their needs and the practical problems like operational difficulties, management problems, and moral questions that reclassification might create.

In short, the participants were unequal in power and knowledge, and the interests of workers were subverted by those of management. The study lacked the kind of open communication that Habermas says is necessary in a free society. As a result the new classification system was not accepted by employees and was implemented only partially after many delays, new studies, lawsuits, and appeals.

As this case illustrates, human life cannot be properly conducted from the perspective of only one interest—work, interaction, or power. Any activity is likely to span all three categories. Thus, all are necessary.

For example, the development of a new drug is a clear reflection of a technical interest, but it cannot be done without cooperation and communication, requiring an interaction interest as

well. In a market economy, the drug is developed by a corporation to gain a competitive advantage, which is clearly a power interest too.

No aspect of life is interest free, even science. An emancipated society is free from unnecessary domination of any one interest, and everybody has equal opportunity to participate in decision making. Habermas believes that a strong public sphere, apart from private interests, is necessary to ensure this state of affairs.

Habermas is especially concerned with the domination of the technical interest in contemporary capitalistic societies.[27] In such societies, the public and private are intertwined to the point that the public sector cannot guard against the oppression of private, technical interests. Ideally, the public and private should be balanced, and the public sector should be strong enough to provide a climate for free expression of ideas and debate. In modern society, however, that climate is stifled.

It is clear from the foregoing discussion that Habermas values communication as essential to emancipation, because language is the means by which the emancipatory interest is fulfilled. Communicative competence is therefore necessary for effective participation in decision making. Competence involves knowing how to use speech appropriately to accomplish goals, which requires compelling argument.[28]

Habermas' approach to communication is based largely on speech-act theory, which is summarized in Chapter 5. Habermas refers to his theory of speech acts as *universal pragmatics*, which includes the universal principles of language. He outlines three types of speech acts. *Constatives*, or assertions, are designed to get across a proposition as true. For example, if you were involved in a labor–management dispute,

27   See especially Habermas, *Legitimation Crisis*.
28   This emphasis on communication competence takes a major step away from the earlier Frankfurt scholars, who emphasized social and economic structure as the root of oppression. For a good discussion of the differences between Habermas and other members of the Frankfurt School in this regard, see William Fusfield, "Communication Without Constellation? Habermas's Argumentative Turn in (and Away from) Critical Theory," *Communication Theory* 7 (1997): 301–320.

you might accuse the union of engaging in unfair labor practices.

Regulatives are intended to affect one's relationship with another person or party through influence. Examples are commands and promises. In the labor–management example, your statement about unfair labor practices would be regulative if it were intended to bring the union to the bargaining table. Here, your purpose is to influence the other party in some way, to regulate their behavior—specifically, to initiate negotiations.

Finally, *avowals* are designed to express the speaker's internal condition, to affirm something about oneself. In labor–management negotiations, for example, participants often express anger over the other party's activities.

Notice that a message you might present could include any combination of these speech acts because you can achieve a number of intentions at once. So, for example, you might make an angry statement about unfair union practices, which is an "avowal" because it expresses your internal condition (anger), a "regulative" because it is designed to get negotiations underway, and a "constative" because you are trying to prove the truth of your statement.

Further, the type of speech act determines the kind of validity that one must meet in a statement. In a constative speech act, one must demonstrate the truth of the claim. In a regulative speech act, one must meet standards of appropriateness. And an avowal must be sincere or truthful.

Because a single speech act may fulfill any of the three types, various combinations of validity forms may also have to be met. For example, to meet all three validity requirements, your statement about union practices must be taken as true (that the union is indeed engaged in certain practices), as appropriate (that under the circumstances, bargaining is proper), and as sincere (that you are truly angry over the situation).

These validity claims are not always easy to secure, since people do not always believe that one's statements are valid. In the labor–management case, you might have some difficulty proving your case, as happened in the Georgia reclassification situation. Here, the management's validity claims about the new system were severely challenged in the form of objections, lawsuits, and individual appeals.

Habermas uses the term *discourse* to describe the special kind of communication required when a speaker's statements are challenged. Unlike normal communication, "discourse" is a systematic argument that makes special appeals to demonstrate the validity of a claim.

Again, there are different kinds of discourse, depending on the type of speech act being defended. Truth claims are argued with *theoretic discourse,* which emphasizes evidence. If the union denied your allegations of improper conduct, you would be pressed to make a case by expanding your argument to include evidence showing that the union did, indeed, participate in certain activities.

When appropriateness is being argued, *practical discourse* is used. This emphasizes norms. If the union resisted your attempts to begin bargaining, you would have to create practical discourse to demonstrate the appropriateness of negotiations. Challenges to one's sincerity also require special action to demonstrate genuine concern, but this is usually direct action rather than discourse.

Of course, there is no guarantee that the union would agree with your evidence or the norms used to appeal for bargaining. Where communicators do not share the same standards or concepts for evaluating the strength of an argument, they must move to a higher level of discourse, which Habermas calls *metatheoretical discourse.* Here, communicators argue about what constitutes good evidence for a claim or what norms are indeed appropriate in the given situation. This is the kind of thing the Supreme Court does.

An even higher level of discourse is sometimes necessary—*metaethical discourse.* Here, the very nature of knowledge itself is under contention and must be argued. Such discourse is a philosophical argument about what constitutes proper knowledge, which is precisely what critical theory does, for it challenges the assumed procedures for generating knowledge in society.

Habermas believes that free speech is necessary for productive normal communication and higher levels of discourse to take place. Although impossible to achieve, Habermas describes an *ideal speech situation* on which society should be modeled. First, the ideal speech situation requires freedom of speech; there must be no constraints on what can be expressed. Second, all individuals must have equal access to speaking. In other words, all speakers and positions must be recognized as legitimate. Finally, the norms and obligations of society are not one-sided but distribute power equally to all strata in society. Only when these requirements are met can completely emancipatory communication take place.

Emancipatory communication in the form of higher levels of discourse is essential to transform society so that the needs of the individual can be met. Habermas believes that people normally live in an unquestioned *life-world*—the ordinary, daily activities of people. The life-world, however, is constrained by certain aspects of the social system such as money, bureaucracy, and corporate power. We see here shades of Althusserian ideology in Habermas' theory: the idea that the superstructure creates an ideology that affects the ordinary understanding of citizens in their everyday lives.

Habermas frames this problem as *colonization*, or the power of the system over individuals. When the life-world is colonized by the system, there is less opportunity to use language to achieve positive goals for individuals.

Here is where critical theory comes in. The primary function of critical theory is to raise questions and call attention to problems about the life-world that make critical reflection and resolution necessary. Only when we are aware of the problems of our life-world and the ways the system influences our view of life can we become emancipated from the entanglements of the system.

There is more opportunity to accomplish emancipation in modern society than in traditional society because of the relatively greater amount of conflict in modernity. In modern society we have the opportunity to hear a variety of

viewpoints, but only if the system will allow free expression. Modern capitalistic societies have not yet achieved emancipation, and critical theorists have a responsibility to work toward making this possible.

◖● THE POSTSTRUCTURALIST TRADITION

In this section we will look at two theories normally considered poststructural in orientation. These are cultural studies and the work of Michel Foucault. Actually, these are quite different from each other and take the poststructural tradition in quite different directions.

Cultural Studies

Cultural studies involves investigations of the ways culture is produced through a struggle among ideologies.[29] The most notable group of cultural scholars, British Cultural Studies, is associated with the Centre for Contemporary Cultural Studies at the University of Birmingham. The origins of this tradition are usually traced to the writings of Richard Hoggart and Raymond Williams in the 1950s, which examined the British working class after World War II.[30] Today, the leader of the movement is Stuart Hall.[31]

---

29   For a readable overview, see Ben Agger, *Cultural Studies as Critical Theory* (London: Falmer, 1992). See also the review essay by Thomas Rosteck, "Cultural Studies and Rhetorical Studies," *Quarterly Journal of Speech* 81 (1995): 386–421; Kellner, "Media Communications vs. Cultural Studies."

30   Richard Hoggart, *Uses of Literacy* (London: Chatto & Windus, 1957); Raymond Williams, *The Long Revolution* (New York: Columbia University Press, 1961).

31   For a good survey of the work of Hall and others at the Centre, see Stuart Hall, Dorothy Hobson, Andrew Lowe, and Paul Willis, eds., *Culture, Media, Language* (London: Hutchinson, 1981). See also Stuart Hall, "Cultural Studies: Two Paradigms," in *Media, Culture, and Society: A Critical Reader*, ed. R. Collins (London: Sage, 1986); and Hall, "Signification." Four secondary treatments are especially helpful: Anne Makus, "Stuart Hall's Theory of Ideology: A Frame for Rhetorical Criticism," *Western Journal of Speech Communication* 54 (1990): 495–514; Ronald Lembo and Kenneth H. Tucker, "Culture, Television, and Opposition: Rethinking Cultural Studies," *Critical Studies in Mass Communication* 7 (1990): 97–116; Samuel L. Becker, "Marxist Approaches to Media Studies: The British Experience," *Critical Studies in Mass Communication* 1 (1984): 66–80; Robert White, "Mass Communication and Culture: Transition to a New Paradigm," *Journal of Communication* 33 (1983): 279–301.

The cultural studies tradition is distinctly reformist in orientation. These scholars want to see changes in Western society, and they view their scholarship as an instrument of socialist cultural struggle.[32] They believe that such change will occur in two ways: (1) by identifying contradictions in society, the resolution of which will lead to positive, as opposed to oppressive, change; and (2) by providing interpretations that will help people understand domination and the kinds of change that would be desirable. Samuel Becker describes their goal as "jarring both the audience and the workers in the media back from becoming too accepting of their illusions or existing practices so they will question them and their conditions."[33]

The study of mass communication is central to this work, for the media are perceived as powerful tools of the dominant ideology. In addition, media have the potential of raising the consciousness of the population about issues of class, power, and domination. We must be cautious in interpreting cultural studies in this light, however, because media are part of a much larger set of institutional forces. Media are important, but they are not the sole concern of these scholars, which is why they refer to their field as "cultural studies" rather than "media studies."

What is meant by *culture* in "cultural studies"? Two definitions have been employed. The first is the common ideas on which a society or group rests, its ideology, or the collective ways by which a group understands its experience. The second is the practices or the entire way of life of a group—what individuals do materially from day to day. These two senses of culture cannot really be separated, for the ideology of a group is produced and reproduced in its practices. In fact, the general concern of cultural theorists is the link between the actions of society's institutions such as the media and the culture. Practices and ideas always occur together within a historical context.

For example, people watch television every day. The entire television industry is a cultural production because it is a means for creating, disputing, reproducing, and changing culture.

The concrete or material practices involved in producing and consuming television are a crucial mechanism in the establishment of ideology, as are standing in line, eating breakfast, or driving a car.

We share a common sense about how things are. This shared understanding is an ideology determined by numerous, often subtle, influences that come together and make common experience seem real to us. In cultural studies, this process of having our realities reinforced from many sources is called *articulation*. Our shared understandings seem real because of the connection, or articulation, among several sources of verification.[34]

For example, it may seem absolutely essential to you to get a college degree. You think that a college education is good and leads to success in life. You think that you will get a good career by attending college and that you will be able to have a more meaningful life from what you learn in college. You think that a college education will make you more literate and able to participate more critically in our democratic society. These beliefs are commonly accepted by many people in our culture, but they are socially constructed ideas reinforced seemingly from every direction—from family, media, and school itself. Our acceptance of the superiority of higher education is a product of a very strong articulation.

Because of articulation, not all ideologies exist on an equal footing in society. Cultural theory posits that capitalistic societies are dominated by a particular ideology of the elite. For the workers of society, the dominant ideology is false because it does not reflect their interests. Instead, the dominant ideology is involved in a hegemony against powerless groups.

Hegemony, however, is always a fluid process, what Hall calls a temporary state in a "theatre of struggle." We must therefore "think of

---

32   Murdock, "Across the Great Divide."
33   Becker, "Marxist," p. 67.
34   This point is explained in greater detail by Ian Angus, "The Politics of Common Sense: Articulation Theory and Critical Communication Studies," in *Communication Yearbook 15*, ed. Stanley Deetz (Newbury Park, CA: Sage, 1992), pp. 535–570.

societies as complex formations, necessarily contradictory, always historically specific."[35] In other words, the struggle between contradictory ideologies is constantly changing.

Social institutions like education, religion, and government are interlinked in ways that support the dominant ideology, making resistance difficult. Especially important is the link between infrastructure and superstructure. *Infrastructure* is sometimes referred to as the "base," or basic economic arrangements of a society, including buildings, monetary system, capital, machinery, and so on. The *superstructure* consists of societal institutions. The exact relationship between infrastructure and superstructure is in dispute.

Early Marxist theory taught that the infrastructure (economic resource base) determined superstructure.[36] In cultural studies, however, the relationship is believed to be more complex. The forces of society are considered to be *overdetermined,* or caused by multiple sources. Infrastructure and superstructure may therefore be mutually interdependent. Because of the complexity of causation in society, no one set of conditions is required for a particular outcome to occur.

The same is true of ideology. Multiple ideologies exist next to one another in dynamic tension. Hall puts the matter this way:

> The important thing about systems of representation is that they are not singular. . . . As you enter an ideological field and pick out any one nodal representation or idea, you immediately trigger off a whole chain of connotative associations. Ideological representations connote—summon—one another.[37]

Communication, especially through the media, has a special role in affecting popular culture through the dissemination of information. The media are extremely important because they directly present a way of viewing reality. Even though the media portray ideology explicitly and directly, opposing voices will always be present as part of the dialectical struggle between groups in a society.

Still the media are dominated by the prevailing ideology, and they therefore treat opposing views from within the frame of the dominant ideology, which has the effect of defining opposing groups as "fringe." The irony of media, especially television, is that they present the illusion of diversity and objectivity, when in fact they are clear instruments of the dominant order.[38]

Producers control the content of media by particular ways of encoding messages. As Becker describes the process,

> Events do not signify . . . to be intelligible events must be put into symbolic form . . . the communicator has a choice of codes or sets of symbols. The one chosen affects the meaning of the events for receivers. Since every language—every symbol—coincides with an ideology, the choice of a set of symbols is, whether conscious or not, the choice of an ideology.[39]

For example, advertisers carefully design television commercials to create a certain image and thereby sell the product. Other kinds of programming such as news and comedy may seem less ideological, but they are every bit as much so.

At the same time, however, audiences may use their own categories to decode the message, and they often reinterpret media messages in ways never intended by the source.[40] As a result of alternative meanings, oppositional ideologies can and do arise in society. The intended meaning of a commercial may be completely lost on certain parts of the audience that interpret it in different ways. For example, an advertiser may use sex appeal for men, but feminist viewers may see the image as demeaning to women.

For Hall and his colleagues, the interpretation of media texts always occurs within a struggle of ideological control. Ronald Lembo and Kenneth

35 Hall, "Cultural Studies," p. 36.
36 This problem and other issues facing the cultural studies program are discussed in Stuart Hall, "Cultural Studies and the Centre: Some Problematics and Problems," in *Culture, Media, Language,* eds. S. Hall, D. Hobson, A. Lowe, and P. Willis (London: Hutchinson, 1981), pp. 15–47.
37 Hall, "Signification," p. 104.
38 This point is explored and challenged by Kevin M. Carragee, "A Critical Evaluation of the Media Hegemony Thesis," *Western Journal of Communication* 57 (1993): 330–348.
39 Becker, "Marxist," p. 72.
40 This idea is explored in more detail by Poonam Pillai, "Rereading Stuart Hall's Encoding/Decoding Model," *Communication Theory* 2 (1992): 221–233.

Tucker describe the process as "a competitive arena where individuals or groups express opposing interests and battle for cultural power."[41] Rap music is a good example of this struggle. Does it reflect the genuine values and interests of the black youth culture, or is it a sign of the degeneration of society? The answer depends on which interpretive community is asked.

The chief aim of cultural studies, then, is to expose the ways ideologies of powerful groups are unwittingly perpetuated and the ways they can be resisted to disrupt the system of power that disfranchises certain groups.

Lawrence Grossberg's study of rock music is an especially interesting illustration of how cultural scholars work. In his essay on the subject, he discusses a sweeping range of issues related to the meaning of rock and roll in contemporary culture, the role of punk, and the place of youths in society.[42]

For Grossberg, rock and roll is an "apparatus" of culture, a movement unified by the feeling it engenders among its fans. Like any cultural text, there should be no privileged reading of it. Rock and roll of all types elicits a plethora of meanings in its various audiences and can be used for a variety of purposes. Rock music therefore has a strong potential for becoming oppositional. Grossberg points to the following evidence of rock and roll's oppositional nature:

> Rock and roll has, repeatedly and continuously, been attacked, banned, ridiculed and relegated to an insignificant cultural status. The fact that so much effort has been brought to bear in the attempt to silence it, makes it reasonable to assume that some struggle is going on, some opposition is being voiced.[43]

Three characteristics demarcate rock and roll. First, it is associated with a particular group of fans, marking these individuals as somehow different from all other people. Second, the music is involved in the everyday lives of its listeners and is part of the larger context of their lives. Third, the entire rock apparatus provides intense pleasure to its fans, a pleasure of bodily sensation and emotional feeling. In short, it transforms the everyday lives of its fans: "The rock and roll ap-

paratus is a kind of machine which, like a cookie cutter constantly changing its shape, produces or imprints a structure on the fans' desires and relations by organizing the material pieces of their lives."[44]

Rock is oppositional because it defines the youth culture as being different from "straight" and "boring." By concentrating on surface, style, and artifice, rock music opposes the predominant post–World War II hegemonic ideology of serious depth, purpose, and order. "The rock and roll apparatus not only energizes new possibilities within everyday life, it places that energy at the center of a life without meaning."[45] Grossberg identifies this primary oppositional character as the "attitude" of rock and roll.

Grossberg believes that the advent of punk had a profound effect on the role of rock music as an oppositional force. Punk itself seems to say that anything goes and that nothing matters. Punk "deconstructed" all forms, including traditional rock and roll. As such, punk itself became an oppositional force. Punk, along with a host of other social and cultural factors, has led to a deconstruction of the youth culture, which had been the chief source of meaning for rock and roll among its fans: "Punk attacked rock and roll for having grown old and fat, for having lost that which puts it in touch with its audience and outside of the hegemonic reality."[46] Grossberg is confident that youth is currently under reconstruction, but he is uncertain how.

Most of the work in critical studies has been applied to mass media of communication. The reason is clear: Media are powerful instruments of ideology in society. However, as the rock and roll case illustrates, the marxist approach need not be limited to applications in media. Indeed, any aspect of social structure can be examined in this way.

41 Lembo and Tucker, "Culture, Television, and Opposition," p. 100.
42 Lawrence Grossberg, "Is There Rock After Punk?" *Critical Studies in Mass Communication* 3 (1986): 50–73.
43 Grossberg, "Is There Rock After Punk?" p. 53.
44 Grossberg, "Is There Rock After Punk?" p. 55.
45 Grossberg, "Is There Rock After Punk?" p. 57.
46 Grossberg, "Is There Rock After Punk?" p. 62.

Michel Foucault

Foucault is normally thought of as a poststructuralist but is, in fact, impossible to classify neatly.[47] Although he denies a structuralist bias in his work, his writings bridge poststructural and structural traditions in critical theory.

Foucault says that each period has a distinct worldview, or conceptual structure, that determines the nature of knowledge in that period. The character of knowledge in a given epoch Foucault calls the *episteme,* or *discursive formation.* The vision of each age is exclusive and incompatible with visions from other ages, making it impossible for people in one period to think like those of another. The episteme, or way of thinking, is determined not by people but by the predominant discursive structures of the day. These discursive structures are deeply embedded ways of practicing or expressing ideas, and you cannot separate what people know from the structure of discourse used to express that knowledge. For Foucault, discourse includes written texts, but it also includes spoken language and nonverbal forms such as architecture, institutional practices, even charts and graphs.

An example of how discourse shapes knowledge is Richard Nixon's famous "Checkers" speech. Martha Cooper applied Foucault's ideas to this speech to show how the discourse made use of, indeed created, standards for responding to an accusation.[48] In the presidential campaign of 1952, vice-presidential candidate Richard Nixon was accused of harboring a secret campaign fund. He responded to this accusation by denying the charge, opening his private finances to public scrutiny, and claiming that the only possible illegitimate contribution he had received was a dog named Checkers.

This speech has been analyzed by several scholars of rhetoric, each looking at the ways this particular speaker used strategies to appeal to the national audience at that time. For Foucault, this kind of analysis is irrelevant. Cooper shows how this speech was an event that served to create and reinforce knowledge structures in our culture. In particular, the speech defined what it meant to respond to an accusation, reinforcing the rule that when accused, people should respond.

The structure of discourse is a set of inherent rules that determines the form and substance of discursive practice. Foucault's use of rules is not entirely like that of the other theories in this chapter, because for him, rules apply across the culture in a variety of types of discourse and function on a deep and powerful level. These are not merely rules for how to talk but rules that determine the very nature of our knowledge, power, and ethics. These rules control what can be talked or written about and who may talk or write (or whose talk is to be taken seriously). Such rules also prescribe the form that discourse must take. In our day, for example, "scientific authorities" are given great credibility, and in matters of "fact," most people prefer the form of "objective studies" over the form of conjecture or myth.

So in the "Checkers" speech, for instance, we see what counts as good evidence for a claim that a politician is corrupt (or not corrupt). We learn from this discourse that politicians must speak out when accused of wrongdoing, and the model of the honest, average American is created here as well.

Contrary to popular belief, according to Foucault, people are not responsible for establishing the conditions of discourse. Inversely, it is discourse that determines the place of the person in

---

47   Foucault's primary works on this subject include *The Archaeology of Knowledge,* trans. A. M. Sheridan Smith (New York: Pantheon, 1972); *The Order of Things: An Archaeology of the Human Sciences* (New York: Pantheon, 1970); and *Power/Knowledge: Selected Interviews and Other Writings 1927–1977,* trans. Colin Gordon and others, ed. Colin Gordon (New York: Pantheon, 1980). For an excellent short summary, see Foss, Foss, and Trapp, *Contemporary Perspectives on Rhetoric.* See also Carole Blair, "The Statement: Foundation of Foucault's Historical Criticism," *Western Journal of Speech Communication* 51 (1987): 364–383; Sonja K. Foss and Ann Gill, "Michel Foucault's Theory of Rhetoric as Epistemic," *Western Journal of Speech Communication* 51 (1987): 384–402; Fraser, *Unruly Practices.*
48   Martha Cooper, "Rhetorical Criticism and Foucault's Philosophy of Discursive Events," *Central States Speech Journal* 39 (1988): 1–17.

the scheme of the world. Our present discursive structure defines humans as the foundation and origin of knowledge, but people have never before achieved this status in any other period and will soon lose it. Foucault believes that the episteme will again shift, and humans will once again disappear from their central place in the world: "It is comforting . . . and a source of profound relief to think that man is only a recent invention, a figure not yet two centuries old, a new wrinkle in our knowledge, and that he will disappear again as soon as that knowledge has discovered a new form."[49]

This radical idea does not mean that humans do not produce discourse. Indeed, they do; but any number of individuals could have produced a given statement, and any speaker or writer is merely fulfilling a role in making a statement. That Nixon was the speaker of the "Checkers" address is unimportant. Nixon took the role of agent in this case, and since then any number of other politicians have done essentially the same thing. Discourse, then, does not require a knowing subject—a person who creates it, consumes it, understands it, and uses it. Rather, language itself prefigures personhood: Language creates the person. A Nixon type was created by the language in the "Checkers" speech.

In our era, persons are believed to obtain knowledge and have power, but this idea is a creation of the predominant discursive formation of our day, and the rules of expression with which we communicate establish this notion. In other times, entirely different ideas about knowledge and power emerged from the discourse in use.

Foucault's research on the penal system is a good example of this.[50] He found a dramatic shift in the eightteenth and nineteenth centuries away from torture and public punishment to incarceration and protection of the criminal from bodily harm. Prior to this period, convicts were publicly tortured or executed in a kind of spectacle. In the discursive formation of that day, the body was seen as the central object of political relations. It was very natural that power should be exerted against the body and that punishment should involve bodily pain. In the latter discursive formation, however, the body lost this status, as power became more a matter of the individual human psyche or soul. Thus locking people up came to be viewed as a more appropriate punishment than flogging them in public.

Foucault's work centers on analyzing discourse in a way that reveals its rules and structure. This he calls *archaeology*. Archaeology seeks to uncover, through careful description, the regularities of discourse. It displays disparities or contradictions, rather than coherence, and reveals a succession of one form of discourse after another. For this reason, Foucault places emphasis on comparative descriptions of more than one piece of discourse.

Interpretation, or establishing the meaning of a text, cannot be avoided in text analysis, but it should be minimized because interpretation does not reveal discursive structure and, in fact, may obscure it. Foucault thinks that analysts should avoid associating discourse with authors because authors are merely fulfilling the discourse's function and are not instrumental in any fundamental way in establishing the structure of the texts they produce. This is why Nixon as the speaker in the "Checkers" event is unimportant. We look to what the discourse says about knowledge, power, and ethics rather than viewing it as an instrument of one particular author.

Foucault's writings center on the subject of power. He believes that power is an inherent part of all discursive formation. As such, it is a function of discourse or knowledge and not a human or institutional property. The episteme, as expressed in language, grants power. Thus, power and knowledge cannot be divided. Power, however, is a good, creative force that finds its zenith in "disciplinary power" or the prescription of standards of correct behavior.

---

49   Foucault, *The Order of Things*, p. xxii.
50   Michel Foucault, *Discipline and Punish: The Birth of the Prison*, trans. A. Sheridan (New York: Vintage, 1979).

◖ FEMINIST STUDIES

"Feminist studies" is a generic label for a perspective that explores the meaning of gender in society.[51] Feminist theorists have observed that many aspects of life are "gendered," meaning that they are experienced in terms of the masculine and the feminine. This includes not only biological sex but also virtually every facet of human life—including language, work, family roles, education, and socialization.

Feminist theory begins with the assumption that gender is a pervasive category of experience. Gender is a social construction that, although useful, has been dominated by a male bias and is particularly oppressive to women. Feminist theory aims to challenge the prevailing gender assumptions of society and to achieve more liberating ways for women and men to exist in the world.

Feminist criticism has become increasingly popular in the study of communication. Feminist communication scholars examine the ways the male language bias affects the relations between the sexes, the ways male domination has constrained communication for females, the ways women have both accommodated and resisted male patterns of speech and language, the powers of women's communication forms, and other similar concerns.

Feminist scholars point out that research and theory building, like all aspects of life, are dominated by gender biases. For the feminist scholar, traditional methods of research and male-biased theories are not only misleading but also dangerous because they mute the experience of women and hide the values of women's experience. For this reason, feminist scholarship usually focuses on women's experience as central, legitimizing the value of women's experience itself.

Approaches that focus on the experiences of women in society as a muted group have been labeled *feminist standpoint theories*. In general, this view holds that women's experiences lead them to have certain understandings. These experiences enable them to see privilege and power in ways that men cannot.[52]

Feminist theorists acknowledge that the world can be understood in a variety of productive ways, and they resist the search for positive truth. They also see the feminine as a way of knowing that is distinct from the masculine, a view reflected, for example, in Carol Gilligan's well-known book, *In a Different Voice*, in which she outlines the powers of the feminine values of intimacy, caring, and relationship.[53]

Although few would claim that there is an essential or monolithic female experience, a set of perspectives have been characterized as feminist in much of the literature. These include, for example, a sense of interdependence and relationship, the legitimacy of emotionality, fusion of public and private realms of experience, egalitarian values, concern for process over product, and openness to multiple ways of seeing and doing.

As a movement in which a variety of voices can be heard, feminism is not a single theory or a simple system of thought.[54] Feminist thinking has been diversified and enriched in many ways. One source of renewal has been the contribution of feminists of color. Marsha Houston, for example, has written about the different perspec-

---

51   Feminist theory is discussed in numerous sources. See, for example, Karen A. Foss, Sonja K. Foss, and Cindy L. Griffin, *Feminist Rhetorical Theories* (Thousand Oaks, CA: Sage, 1999); Ramona R. Rush and Autumn Grubb-Swetman, "Feminist Approaches," in *An Integrated Approach to Communication Theory and Research*, eds. Michael B. Salwen and Don W. Stacks (Mahwah, NJ: Erlbaum, 1996), pp. 497–518; Lisa McLaughlin, "Feminist Communication Scholarship and 'The Woman Question' in the Academy," *Communication Theory* 5 (1995): 144–161; Karen A. Foss and Sonja K. Foss, "Personal Experience as Evidence in Feminist Scholarship," *Western Journal of Communication* 58 (1994): 39–43; Lana F. Rakow, ed., *Women Making Meaning: New Feminist Directions in Communication* (New York: Routledge, 1992); Cheris Kramarae, "Feminist Theories of Communication," in *International Encyclopedia of Communications*, vol. 2, eds. E. Barnouw and others (New York: Oxford University Press, 1989), pp. 157–160; Brenda Dervin, "The Potential Contribution of Feminist Scholarship to the Field of Communication," *Journal of Communication* 37 (1987): 107–120.
52   See, for example, Lynn O'Brien Hallstein, "A Postmodern Caring: Feminist Standpoint Theories, Revisioning Caring, and Communication Ethics," *Western Journal of Communication* 63 (1999): 32–56.
53   Carol Gilligan, *In a Different Voice* (Cambridge, MA: Harvard University Press, 1982).
54   See, for example, Celeste Condit, "In Praise of Eloquent Diversity: Gender and Rhetoric as Public Persuasion," *Women's Studies in Communication* 20 (1997): 91–116; and Sonja K. Foss, Cindy L. Griffin, and Karen A. Foss, "Transforming Rhetoric Through Feminist Reconstruction: A Response to the Gender-Diversity Perspective," *Women's Studies in Communication* 20 (1997): 117–136.

tives of African American and White women,[55] and Lisa Flores has developed a Chicana feminist view.[56]

One useful distinction is between liberal and radical feminism. *Liberal feminism,* the foundation of the women's movement of the 1960s and 1970s, is based in liberal democracy, the idea that justice involves the assurance of equal rights for all individuals. Liberal feminists say that women have been oppressed as a group and that they have not had equal rights with men, as evidenced by women's lower average income, women's exclusion from centers of power and decision making, and women's lack of opportunity to advance in careers of their choice. In short, liberal feminism deals primarily with the public image and rights of women.

In contrast to the liberal school of thought, *radical feminism* believes that the oppression of women runs far deeper than public rights. For radical feminists, the problem is not a question of equal rights. The problem goes to the heart of our social structure, which is patriarchal. The patriarchy perpetuates a set of gender-laden meanings that promote masculine interests and subordinate feminine ones. Women are oppressed because the very fabric of society is based on a constructed reality that devalues and marginalizes women's experience. If gender is a social construction, then in our present order of things it is a man-made construction. The term *radical* is appropriate for this movement because it goes to the root of social structure and demands *basic redefinitions* of all facets of society.

Whereas liberal feminists want women to be able to have what men already have, radical feminists do not see this as an answer. In fact, to emulate the status of men in society only perpetuates the patriarchal definition of what is important and what is not. So, for example, instead of thinking merely that there should be more women physicians, society itself must redefine the whole nature of medicine, especially in regard to how it treats the experience of women. Instead of limiting the struggle to overcoming the glass ceiling, women must strive to change the very definition of commerce and economy in

society at large so that it no longer damages the welfare of women and children.

Today, many radical feminists call for women to define their own reality and their own social order, to rely on their own instincts and experience as a guide to self-definition and interpersonal relationships. In other words, the answer can only be a complete restructuring of how our society defines human experience and a remaking of the world.

Feminism presents an increasingly popular challenge to mainstream communication scholarship. Sonja Foss, Karen Foss, and Robert Trapp discuss this challenge in terms roughly equivalent to the liberal and radical schools of feminism.[57] The first type of challenge, which these authors call the *inclusion stage,* is an attempt to get more public recognition for the contributions of women.[58] It includes research on sexist language, including the ways language creates inequality between the sexes and sex differences in communication, including investigations into differences between the communication behavior of men and women.[59] This stage also includes studies of great women speakers, including research into the contributions of women to the history of public address. Studies of women's culture, including the differences between the ways men and women think and act, are also included here. In general, the inclusion stage highlights the legitimation of women's ways of knowing and being in the world.

The *revisionist stage* is consistent with radical feminism in that it challenges the very definitions used to characterize communication in society. These writings aim to revise such definitions to

---

55 Marsha Houston, "What Makes Scholarship About Black Women and Communication Feminist Communication Scholarship?" *Women's Studies in Communication* 10 (1988): 78–88.
56 Lisa A. Flores, "Creating Discursive Space Through a Rhetoric of Difference: Chicana Feminists Craft a Homeland," *Quarterly Journal of Speech* 82 (1996): 142–156.
57 Foss, Foss, and Trapp, *Contemporary Perspectives on Rhetoric.*
58 For example, see Foss, Foss, and Griffin, *Feminist Rhetorical Theories,* chap. 1.
59 For a recent example, see Marianne LaFrance and Nancy M. Henley, "An Oppressing Hypothesis: Or Differences in Nonverbal Sensitivity Revisited," in *Power/Gender: Social Relations in Theory and Practice,* eds. H. Lorraine Radtke and Henderikus J. Stam (London: Sage, 1994), pp. 287–311.

include women's experience. Issues such as the definition of rhetoric, what constitutes effective speech, the eloquence of ordinary women's forms of expression, the importance of communication in private settings, the nature of social movements, and the character of persuasion and influence are questioned and reformulated in this kind of work.

The number of feminist theorists recognized in the communication field is growing. For example, in their recent book, *Feminist Rhetorical Theories*, Karen Foss, Sonja Foss, and Cindy Griffin present detailed summaries of the work of Gloria Anzaldúa, Paula Gunn Allen, bell hooks, Sonia Johnson, Sally Miller Gearhart, Starhawk, Mary Daly, Trinh T. Min-ha, and Cheris Kramarae.[60] Space limits our ability to include this rich body of theory. Instead, we focus here on two well-known feminist theories of communication.

Language and Power

One of the most well-developed areas in feminist studies is the exploration of sexism in language and the relationship between language and power. Julia Penelope has been a leading thinker in this area.[61] For Penelope, a linguist, language is central to all human experience and society. Our experience is always prefigured by our culture's language. It comes as no surprise, then, that language is an instrument of oppression. Those who accept the language essentially accept its categories of truth, and the vast majority of language users do so without question.

Cheris Kramarae has continued this line of work and developed a strong and coherent theory of gender and power in language.[62] Like Penelope, she has shown that language is instrumental in constructing the world in which we live and that social power arrangements are largely embedded in language. Because language is patriarchal, it often creates an unsafe and uncomfortable world for women. Indeed, language makes a world that often silences women in profound ways.

On the latter point, Kramarae incorporates the work of anthropologists Edwin Ardener and

Shirley Ardener on muted-group theory.[63] Edwin Ardener observed that anthropologists tend to characterize a culture in terms of the masculine, since ethnography seems biased toward observation of males in a culture. On closer examination, however, it appeared to Ardener that the actual language of a culture has an inherent male bias, that men created the meanings for a group, and that the feminine voice is suppressed, or "muted." This silencing of women, in Ardener's observation, leads to the inability of women to express themselves eloquently in the male parlance.

Shirley Ardener added to the theory by suggesting that the silence of women has several manifestations and is especially evident in public discourse. Women are less comfortable and less expressive in public situations than are men, and they are less comfortable in public situations than they are in private. Consequently, women monitor their own communications more intensely than do men. Women watch what they say and translate what they are feeling and thinking into male terms. When masculine and feminine meanings and expressions conflict, the masculine tends to win out because of the dominance of males in society, and the result is that women are muted.

Kramarae expands the Ardeners' work by incorporating it with the results of research on women and communication. She states that because men and women have different experiences based on the division of labor in society, they perceive the world differently. Men are po-

60   Foss, Foss, and Griffin, *Feminist Rhetorical Theories*.
61   Julia Penelope, *Speaking Freely: Unlearning the Lies of the Fathers' Tongues* (New York: Pergamon, 1990).
62   See, for example, Cheris Kramarae, *Women and Men Speaking: Frameworks for Analysis* (Rowley, MA: Newbury House, 1981), pp. 1–63; For an excellent secondary treatment, see Foss, Foss, and Griffin, *Feminist Rhetorical Theories*. For a complete list of Kramarae's works, see the bibliography in Foss, Foss, and Griffin, *Feminist Rhetorical Theories*.
63   Edwin Ardener, "Some Outstanding Problems in the Analysis of Events" (paper delivered at the Association of Social Anthropologists' Decennial Conference, 1973); "The 'Problem' Revisited," in *Perceiving Women*, ed. Shirley Ardener (London: Malaby, 1975); Shirley Ardener, *Defining Females: The Nature of Women in Society* (New York: Wiley, 1978). This theory is explored in some detail by Dale Spender, *Man Made Language* (London: Routledge & Kegan Paul, 1980), pp. 76–105.

litically dominant in society, and their systems of perception are therefore dominant, which prevents women's perceptions from being publicly adopted. Further, women must translate their own ways of understanding into the terms of the male worldview in order to participate in public life. Kramarae shows the many ways that the resulting silencing of women comes out.

For one, women sometimes express themselves with more difficulty than do men. A common female experience is to lack a word for a feminine experience, apparently because men, who do not share that experience, have not developed a term for it. At the same time, however, women understand men's meanings more easily than men understand women's. This may be the case because when men fail to understand what women are talking about, they may distance themselves from it. Further, women are subjected to language experiences that men have not had, such as lacking a word for something, and men may suppress women and rationalize it on the grounds that women are not as rational or clear. Because of the power inequities in communication, women are forced to learn the male system of communication, but men in contrast do not need to learn the language of women.

And, indeed, women do have their own forms of expression, as they have created their own ways of saying things that lie outside the dominant male system. Letters, diaries, consciousness-raising groups, and alternative art forms are examples. Foss and Foss interviewed a number of women and examined their forms of communication. Their book, *Women Speak: The Eloquence of Women's Lives*, challenges a number of assumptions about what constitutes eloquent communication, showing that many of the forms of communication used by women have value in their own right, despite the fact that they are not viewed as significant in the masculine, public world.[64] The book makes this kind of work more public in an attempt to give voice to women normally muted in society.

Kramarae notes that because they are verbally muted, women rely more on nonverbal expression and use different nonverbal forms than do men. Some research has shown, for example, that facial expressions, vocal pauses, and bodily gestures are more important in women's discussions than they are in men's. Women also seem to display a wider variability of expression in their speech.

As a consequence of being silenced, women often make efforts to change the dominant rules of communication in order to get around or resist conventional rules. Advocates for women's liberation, for example, have created new words such as *Ms.* and *herstory* and have developed different communication forms that incorporate women's experiences. Consciousness-raising groups are a good example of this.

Kramarae is very interested in technology and its impact on gender relations in society. For example, the Internet seems to reproduce the same patterns of gender inequity found in society at large. As another example, she believes that female faculty and students for the most part have been excluded from technology policymaking on campuses. She points to video games as yet another example of how masculine values are perpetuated in the new technologies.

Conversation is another area in which gender power relations are enacted. Kramarae says that men tend to control conversations in a variety of ways. They often dominate, interrupt, and respond only minimally to women. Men tend to withhold feelings and personal information, which gives them further control within a conversation. These patterns occur both in live conversations and on the Internet.

The ultimate exercise of power over women occurs through violence. Rape is an example of direct physical violence, but women have been the victims of communication violence as well, through electronic harassment, street harassment, and sexual harassment on the job.

Kramarae is a strong advocate of having women take control of their worlds by making communication forms that are more comfortable and hospitable. She would like to see women

64   Karen A. Foss and Sonja K. Foss, *Women Speak: The Eloquence of Women's Lives* (Prospect Heights, IL: Waveland, 1991).

make a world that is safe for the free and critical exploration of ideas. This can happen when people reject all forms of oppression, including arrogant language forms. She wants to see a world that makes connections rather than separations and a world that respects, rather than rejects, differences. She wants a world in which information is freely accessible to everyone. Along these lines, she wants cyberspace to be both accessible and comfortable to women and girls, as to all people.

How can women move toward achieving these goals? For Kramarae, this means taking control of language and becoming emancipated from patriarchal domination. She sees three ways of doing this. First, we must analyze and better understand the sometimes subtle forms of linguistic domination. Second, we must study women's communication to learn more about alternative forms. Finally, new forms must be created and used.

One thing women can do is to create new words to express their own experience. For example, a group of students was asked to create new words for aspects of their experience, which they did easily. Some of the words they created are as follows:

soul rinse—feeling after a big cry

solo wholo—describing a person not in a relationship with a significant other, not actively searching, yet not eliminating the possibility, and perfectly satisfied with the way he or she is

femipotent—female virility

silonuts—no reaction from a male; domination by silence[65]

Along the same lines, linguist Suzette Elgin has created an entire language, Láadan, to reflect women's experience.[66] Kramarae herself, along with colleagues Paula Treichler and Ann Russo, has written *A Feminist Dictionary*.[67] This work attempts to capture the features of a *feminist universe of discourse* by including words with special meaning for women as well as definitions that

are consistent, not with men's, but with women's experience. For example, *birth name* is "a term used by feminists as a more accurate label for the name received at birth than the older term *maiden name,* which has sexual double standard implications."[68] *Birthing* is "another of the archetypal experiences exclusive to the female."[69] A *foremother* is "an ancestor."[70]

Another thing women can do is redefine terms previously used by men to perpetuate their power. This can take the form of making a negative term positive, such as referring to oneself proudly as a "hag." It can also take the form of making explicit the normally hidden power meanings of a word. For example, *tipping* might be defined as a means of paying less than minimum wages to women.

Women can also take control by interacting with others in new ways that break the cycle of male domination. For example, women can pay more attention and respond more to other women in conversations.

The work on language and power illustrates one way that feminist scholars work—to raise consciousness about power relations and suggest strategies for increasing the power of women. Another, and somewhat different, kind of feminist work involves the reconstruction or revision of traditional forms of communication—not so much to grant power to women but to change the way in which human beings interact. We turn now to a theory of this type.

Invitational Rhetoric

A group of communication scholars has offered an alternative view of communication that embodies feminist values. Most frequently associ-

65 Personal communication from Karen Foss, 1991. See also Cheris Kramarae, Paula A. Treichler, and Ann Russo, *A Feminist Dictionary* (Boston: Pandora, 1985).
66 Suzette Elgin, *A First Dictionary and Grammar of Láadan,* 2nd ed. (Madison, WI: Society for the Furtherance and Study of Fantasy and Science Fiction, 1988). See also Elgin's novel, *Native Tongue* (New York: Daw, 1984).
67 Kramarae, Treichler, and Russo, *Feminist.*
68 Kramarae, Treichler, and Russo, *Feminist,* p. 72.
69 Kramarae, Treichler, and Russo, *Feminist,* p. 70.
70 Kramarae, Treichler, and Russo, *Feminist,* p. 166.

ated with the work of Sonja Foss and her colleagues, this approach is best described as *invitational rhetoric*.[71] This theory proposes a shift in how we define rhetoric—from persuasion or influence to invitation.

Traditional views of persuasion and rhetoric are based on a patriarchal worldview that projects the values of change, competition, and domination. Any attempt to influence, even by persuasion, assumes that one has the right to pressure or sway others, implying that one's own view is superior to that of one's audience. In place of this, Sonja Foss and her colleagues propose a rhetoric based on the feminist values of equality, immanent value, and self-determination. An attitude of *equality* places each perspective on an equal plane and engenders relationships of respect and nondomination. An attitude of *immanent value* places worth and dignity on all life. One's worth does not rest upon reputation or earned credibility but inherent value. Finally, an attitude of *self-determination* affords everyone the right to decide for themselves what they want to do.

Instead of taking the stance of changing others, invitational communicators invite others into their world to create understanding. Indeed, the communicator herself tries to respect and understand the view of the other in the dialogue. Any change that results from this process comes from insight, not influence. Such insight and change can be painful, as communicators discover the powers and limits of their own views and change as a result.

Sonja Foss and Cindy Griffin suggest that this form of communication happens by *offering perspectives*. In an offering, the communicator does not hold up his or her own position as superior, but presents it as a conversation starter, a way of looking, an opening. The grammar, or manner, in which the offering is made is important. For example, rather than say, "You should call your mother tonight," you might ask, "When did you last call your mother?" or, "I'm worried that your mother hasn't heard from you lately." The tone of an offering sounds like putting an idea out for consideration rather than promoting or pressuring. We make offers in a variety of ways,

both direct and indirect. We can offer a perspective in how we dress, how we act, and how we respond to others.

One way of making an offering suggested by Sally Miller Gearhart is *re-sourcement*. This strategy is especially helpful in tense conflict situations, where others are exerting power. The idea is that you do not engage the resources of power in that situation, but go to a new source, a different place. Re-sourcement enables the communicator to disengage from the conflict and suggest a new, creative perspective. If someone started arguing with you, for example, you might just acknowledge their point of view and then offer them a cookie. Important about re-sourcement is that the communicator refuses to engage in the struggle.

If an offering is to be accepted as the opening of a new conversation, three *external conditions* must be met, or, better, created by the communicators. The first is *safety*, or a feeling of security. This means that communicators should avoid attempts to hurt, degrade, or belittle; they should express an openness to explore ideas other than their own. The second condition is *value*, or respect. People will not generally engage in a true dialogue if they do not feel that what they have to offer will be valued. This condition is probably best expressed in the quality of the communicators' listening. Third, communicators can work to create an atmosphere of *freedom*. In other words, they can allow others the power to make their own choices.

Invitational rhetoric has been greatly influenced by the work of Gearhart.[72] For Gearhart, all attempts to persuade or influence are a form of violence because they aim to undo or change

71 This theory is perhaps best codified in Sonja K. Foss and Cindy L. Griffin, "Beyond Persuasion: A Proposal for an Invitational Rhetoric," *Communication Monographs* 62 (1995): 2–18. See also Sonja K. Foss and Karen A. Foss, *Inviting Transformation: Presentational Speaking for a Changing World* (Prospect Heights, IL: Waveland, 1994).
72 See, for example, Sally Miller Gearhart, "Womanpower: Energy Re-Sourcement," in *The Politics of Women's Spirituality: Essays on the Rise of Spiritual Power Within the Feminist Movement*, ed. Charlene Spretnak (Garden City, NY: Doubleday, 1982), pp. 194–206. Gearhart's work is summarized in Foss, Foss, and Griffin, *Feminist Rhetorical Theories*, pp. 257–292.

what is important to someone else. Change itself is not the problem; that is a natural condition. We can and should want change, but to *want to change* another person assumes superiority and violates the values of the other. Instead of *changing the other*, we should aim to *enfold the other*. Indeed, the term *enfoldment* nicely describes the manner in which people should communicate with one another.

To enfold is to make oneself available. It is to invite, to offer, to listen. Enfoldment is a process of trying to understand the other person. It acknowledges that change can only happen when one is ready to change and chooses to change. Change occurs when people are ready and the external conditions are right. Change, then, is never something that you can do to someone else. You cannot force societal change. Societal change happens as a result of persons choosing to change themselves.

In practical terms, then, how should one communicate? Gearhart suggests six components of enfoldment. First is *acknowledgement*. This means listening and stating what you hear to be important to the other person. Second is *searching for common ground*. This means looking for a meeting place, a ground on which communicators can join one another. It means talking about the positive resources you have in common, finding common beliefs and values on which to build. Third is *mutual sharing of perspectives*. This means listening with true curiosity, asking open questions to learn more, and offering one's own ideas as a perspective, not superior truth. Fourth is *willingness to yield*. This means being open to change. Fifth is *witnessing*. This means being observationally present and recording what you see and hear. It is a way of showing that you take seriously and honor the presentations of others. Sixth is *asking permission to share*. This means inquiring as to whether the other person is interested in hearing one's opinions or ideas.

Imagine being in a situation in which you end up in opposition to a group of people. If you were to use traditional methods, you would probably prepare to engage in conflict. You would garner your best arguments and attempt to change the group's opinion. As an alternative, however, you could take a different approach, that of invitational rhetoric, and communicate with an attitude of enfoldment. Here you would listen carefully for the wisdom of the others and acknowledge their point of view. You would look for common ground and invite the others into a discussion of what you share. You would ask the others' permission to share your perspective and offer it as an alternative. You would open yourself up to possible change and allow that to happen if it felt appropriate. You would feel good about the communication if you felt that you understood the other group better, you sensed that they understood you better, and you gained insights that you may not have had previously.

COMMENTARY AND CRITIQUE

We have looked at three important areas of critical theory in this chapter—all explicitly displaying a set of values to raise consciousness and thereby empower people to resist dominant and oppressive ideological forces.

Feminist theory places the blame for the oppression of women on the patriarchy. Masculine values are believed to permeate society and govern all power centers, thus marginalizing the experience of women. This reasoning is not unlike that of the original Frankfurt School, which viewed capitalistic society as dominated by a singular hegemonic interest: the political economy. Although the reasoning used by the Frankfurt scholars and feminists is similar, their explanatory variables are different, as the marxists would say that class, not gender, is the genesis of oppression.

The cultural studies tradition takes a more complex view. These scholars do not see any single set of ideas as perpetually dominant. Although various interests may dominate at any particular time and certain classes of people are almost always marginalized in this process, the field of ideological struggle is constantly in flux.

This thesis is essentially a rejection of feminism's gender base. For the cultural scholar, gender would be just one of many elements of society in dynamic tension with all others.

Feminist theory revolves around the conceptual division of masculine and feminine, but critics question the very utility of this dualism.[73] Although the masculine–feminine distinction has been useful for critical purposes, it may have oversimplified the situation and created a conceptualization that does not accurately reflect reality. Such labeling may, in fact, reify or reinforce distinctions that feminists themselves are trying to overcome. Linda Putnam states the point in these terms: "The problem of reification, the use of feminist labels, has the double-edged effect of recognizing women while simultaneously isolating them."[74] And again, "Efforts to degenderize behaviors have the potential to liberate us from sex-role classifications that emanate from dualism."[75] The answer, according to Putnam, is not to abandon feminist theory or feminist ideals but to look at the process of communication differently. Instead of simply assuming that gender is the cause of other effects, we should also examine the ways communication patterns have led to gender distinctions themselves. If the cultural studies scholars are right, gender itself may be a construction of an ideology into which feminists themselves have been co-opted.[76]

Almost all versions of feminist and contemporary marxist theory see the answer to domination and oppression as consciousness raising and empowerment. For the feminists, when women become conscious of their own oppression, they are empowered to create a reality of their own that gives voice to their interests. For marxists, consciousness leads to the ability to create oppositional understandings that change the field of conflict in ways that promote a different, hopefully healthier, set of values in society. A common theme that seems to run through all critical theories, then, is giving voice to oppressed groups. The thesis of Habermas' work, for example, is precisely this: to create an ideal speech community in which all interests have an equal chance of being heard.

In Chapter 2 we discussed the value dimension of theory. The value issue can be stated in two ways, depending on whose perspective you take. From the perspective of traditional science, the issue is whether the theory contains value statements. From the perspective of critical theory, the issue is whether the theorist is conscious of inevitable values present in all theories.

The theories discussed in this chapter are unabashedly value laden. Critical theorists would say that all forms of research contain values, and values are only dangerous when they are not recognized or acknowledged. This belief is the basis of a critique of traditional social science. Although critical theories borrow liberally from relevant concepts of other traditions—such as system theory, structuralism, interpretation, and social construction—they also constitute an oppositional critique of many of these other traditions.

Critical theories represent a double critique, of society and of traditional social science. In a way, this is really the same critique because traditional social science is an institution within society that perpetuates its own dominant interests.

Political scientist Paul Lazarsfeld was perhaps the first to label these two theoretical camps as "administrative" and "critical."[77] *Administrative research* is designed to aid the administration of public and private programs, and *critical research* is designed to oppose and resist the administration of power in society. For critical theorists

73 Celeste Condit, "Gender Diversity: A Theory of Communication for the Postmodern Era," in *Communication: Views from the Helm for the 21st Century,* ed. Judith S. Trent (Boston: Allyn & Bacon, 1998), pp. 177–183; Linda L. Putnam, "In Search of Gender: A Critique of Communication and Sex-Roles Research," *Women's Studies in Communication* 5 (1982): 1–9; see also Julia T. Wood and W. Barnett Pearce, "Sexists, Racists, and Other Classes of Classifiers: Form and Function of 'ist' Accusations," *Quarterly Journal of Speech* 66 (1980): 239–250.
74 Putnam, "Search," p. 4.
75 Putnam, "Search," p. 7.
76 Deborah Kerfoot and David Knights, "Into the Realm of the Fearful: Power, Identity, and the Gender Problematic," in *Power/Gender: Social Relations in Theory and Practice,* eds. H. Lorraine Radtke and Henderikus J. Stam (London: Sage, 1994), pp. 67–88.
77 Paul Lazarsfeld, "Remarks on Administrative and Critical Communications Research," *Studies in Philosophy and Social Science* 9 (1941): 2–16.

today, all research that is not critical is administrative because it automatically serves administrative interests.[78]

It is not surprising, then, to find a sharp line, even animosity, between theorists of traditional social science and those of the critical theory tradition.[79] Critical theorists accuse traditionalists of conserving centers of power, of being naively oblivious to the ways in which their work perpetuates hegemony, and of possessing a stubborn adherence to the belief in a realist epistemology.[80]

Traditional social scientists are no less harsh in their criticisms of critical theories. They accuse their critical colleagues of rationalizing ideas without data, of pushing a narrow and ill-informed agenda, and of operating on the basis of a head-in-the-clouds utopianism. Television researcher James Lull comments: "Marxist and neo-Marxist criticism in particular now sound more like an echo in the hallway than a leading theoretical perspective."[81]

Jay Blumler summarizes the chief objections against critical theory.[82] First, even if media institutions should become more egalitarian, the critical approach does not provide sufficient guidance on how this is to be done: "But the critical paradigm, as so far enunciated, lacks a clarity of ethic and realism of political diagnosis that, when drawn on and applied, could help communication institutions to realize a vision of human beings as active, choosing, purposeful subjects."[83]

Second, the movement has a "self-defeating tendency to utopianism."[84] In other words, these theories downplay the realities of political life that require democracy, and they ignore the fact that media are required for democracy to work. Indeed, contemporary marxist approaches are inherently antidemocratic: "The critical perspective tends to slam shut, instead of prying open, doors of possible improvement in the contributions of journalism to democracy."[85]

Finally, administrative researchers deplore marxist antipathy toward behavioral and social research. The marxist claims are suspect because they are not supported by the kind of data traditional researchers find credible.

There are, of course, many differences among the various versions of feminist and contemporary marxist theory. In a way this suits critical theory because of the common belief in the existence of contradiction. Society itself is filled with contradiction, so why should critical studies be any different? In fact, one of the chief claims of critical theory is that we must be willing to acknowledge the presence of contradiction and learn to deal with it productively.

The problem for critical theory is determining where it stands in the absence of a unifying thesis. Feminism is an excellent case in point. On the one hand, feminists seem to be asking for equal rights for women, a public acknowledgment that women have the same qualities and powers as men and can perform as well in all walks of life. On the other hand, they also seem to be saying that women are different from men and that their powers and forms of expression should be valued in their own right. On one level of analysis, it may be that these are merely different brands of feminist theory. On another level these two theses, both of which seem to have validity, form a true paradox. For women to be valued and to have equal rights, the powers of the feminine must be acknowledged, but highlighting the powers of the feminine reinforces the patriarchal view that women have their place.

78   This division is amply discussed in the special edition of *Journal of Communication* entitled "Ferment in the Field," 33 (Summer 1983).
79   Mike Allen, "Critical and Traditional Science: Implications for Communication Research," *Western Journal of Communication* 57 (1993): 200–208; Joseph F. Hanna, "Critical Theory and the Politicization of Science," *Communication Monographs* 58 (1991): 202–212.
80   See, for example, John W. Lannamann, "Interpersonal Communication Research as Ideological Practice," *Communication Theory* 1 (1991): 179–203.
81   James Lull, "The Audience as Nuisance," *Critical Studies in Mass Communication* 5 (1988): 239.
82   Jay Blumler, "Communication and Democracy: The Crisis Beyond and the Ferment Within," *Journal of Communication* 33 (1983): 166–173. See also Michael Real, "The Debate on Critical Theory and the Study of Communications," *Journal of Communication* 34 (autumn 1984): 72–80.
83   Blumler, "Communication," p. 168.
84   Blumler, "Communication," p. 168.
85   Blumler, "Communication," p. 169.

This is precisely the problem that radical feminists are trying to overcome. Instead of pitting men against women, they are involved in a project of redefining the feminine and creating a world in which disjunction is not central. The work of invitational rhetoric illustrates this move very well. This is not considered a rhetoric by and for women, but a form of communication that embodies traditional feminine values to reconstruct the nature of communication for everyone.

There is in cultural studies, as in all critical theory, confusion about the power of groups and individuals to accomplish opposition. At times cultural studies seem to view society as a complex machine in which ideologies are constantly in conflict. At other times these theorists seem to want to give power to individuals to create oppositional readings to media texts, to take action to overcome hegemonic forces.

This is the old issue of the power of the subject. How much power do individuals have to assign meaning to messages? Are the minds of individuals shaped by social structure and language, or can individuals create their own structures and languages to meet their own ends?[86] Feminist language theories such as that of Penelope waffle on this issue. If women are oppressed by patriarchal language, how can they find the power to overcome it?

An important split in critical theory is that between the structuralists and the poststructuralists, discussed earlier in the chapter. These two schools of thought oppose each other in significant ways. For example, Habermas, representing the structural tradition, has created a rather elaborate theory of society and uses it as a template for uncovering oppression. But this theory has been criticized as being heavy-handed and ignoring the constantly changing construction of meaning that occurs in the everyday lives of individuals.[87]

This conflict is not unlike that between interpretive and critical theory. Critical theorists like Habermas accuse interpretive theorists such as Hans-Georg Gadamer (Chapter 10) of being too conservative. Indeed, the goal of interpretation is to describe meaning structures in texts and in social relations. Critical theory, on the other hand, is inherently radical. It aims to change the basis of society and is impatient with the conservative moves commonly found in phenomenology.

Interpretivists like Gadamer revere tradition and accuse critical theory of trying to tear down the very history from which it can never escape. Interpretivists seek ways to uncover meanings and to overcome misunderstandings so that traditions can speak to us in positive ways, and they object to critical theorists' claims that such misunderstandings are systematic distortions by powerful groups. Finally, from their position of dialogue, interpretivists object to critical theorists' call for ideal communication designed to rescue society from its iniquities.[88] Instead, they believe, language and communication as naturally given in everyday life constitute a positive voice that should be heard. Gadamer says that you cannot remove yourself from tradition, that any intellectual project is always a part of a tradition that shapes its perspectives and values.

Two related issues are suggested by Gadamer's point. First, what is the cultural tradition from which critical theory arises, and how does this influence the truth claims being made by this movement? If critical theory is a soundly Eurocentric enterprise, how relevant is it to the dynamics of cultures other than Western societies? Second, how do critical theorists get out of an ideology long enough to make judgments about ideology?

Early Marxists had an easy answer; they deferred to science as nonideological. Latter-day marxists, however, are skeptical of this solution because they do not see science as interest free.

---

86   Sara Cobb, "A Critique of Critical Discourse Analysis: Deconstructing and Reconstructing the Role of Intention," *Communication Theory* 4 (1994): 132–152.

87   Kenneth Baynes, "Communicative Ethics, the Public Sphere and Communication Media," *Critical Studies in Mass Communication* 11 (1994): 315–326; Huspek, "Taking Aim."

88   The primary opponents in this debate have been Gadamer and Habermas. The debate is summarized by Paul Ricoeur, *Hermeneutics and the Human Sciences: Essays on Language, Action, and Interpretation,* trans. and ed. J. B. Thompson (Cambridge: Cambridge University Press, 1981), pp. 64–80.

Science itself promotes particular ideologies. The most promising resolution of this dilemma is that of Hall and his colleagues, who claim that there will always be competing ideas, and the aim of cultural studies is to expose the struggle, not to suggest a permanent solution. Cultural studies seems more interested in promoting oppositional readings of texts rather than pointing to any one ideology that should be overcome.

Ricoeur crystallizes the perspectives of interpretive theory and critical theory in these terms:

> What is at stake can be expressed in terms of an alternative: either a hermeneutical consciousness or a critical consciousness. . . . In contrast to the positive assessment of hermeneutics, the theory of ideology adopts a suspicious approach, seeing tradition as merely the systematically distorted expression of communication under unacknowledged conditions of violence.[89]

Ricoeur himself argues for a "zone of intersection which . . . ought to become the point of departure for a new phase of hermeneutics."[90] Ricoeur believes that through distanciation (Chapter 10), one can understand texts in a way that reveals the limits of context. Once it is freed from situation and author, text provides insights into the problems of historical circumstances. In addition, when disembodied texts speak to us, they reveal our own limits and the limits of our own times. Such textual interpretation also opens up possibilities for new ways of being in the future. For Ricoeur then, interpretive theory and critical theory are not very far apart.

A movement that attempts to fuse the interpretive and critical traditions is critical ethnography. Critical ethnographers value the insights of both traditions. They see the need for ethnographic description, but they want to go beyond mere description to make value statements about oppressive structures observed in a culture.[91]

In many ways the answers to these questions depend on the site of meaning. How is meaning established? If meaning comes prepackaged in language, as many feminists and contemporary marxists suggest, then the individual is left powerless to struggle against it. On the other hand, if meaning is constructed in social interaction, as other feminists and marxists suggest, then individuals do have some power to create new realities. This issue brings us full circle back to the question of a structural versus constructional epistemology. The interest of critical theory in creating social change requires a constructionist version of society, but the need for critical theory to prove conditions requiring change requires a structuralist one. This may be the ultimate contradiction of critical theory.[92]

---

89   Ricoeur, *Hermeneutics,* p. 64.
90   Ricoeur, *Hermeneutics,* p. 79.
91   See, for example, Jim Thomas, *Doing Critical Ethnography* (Newbury Park, CA: Sage, 1993); Huspek, "Taking Aim."
92   This conflict is discussed especially well by Michael Huspek, "Dueling Structures: The Theory of Resistance in Discourse," *Communication Theory* 3 (1993): 1–25.

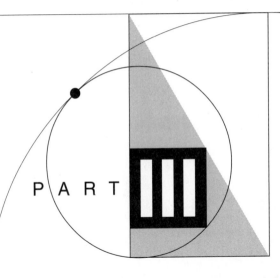

PART **III**

CONTEXTUAL THEMES

CHAPTER

12

COMMUNICATION
IN
RELATIONSHIPS

With this chapter, we begin Part III of the book. Here we explore a set of important contextual themes found in communication theory—relationships, decision making, networks, and media. Chapter 12 deals with relationships, which are central to the study of interpersonal communication.[1] A *relationship* is a set of expectations two people have for their behavior based on the pattern of interaction between them. This idea lies at the hub of interpersonal communication theories, and we explore it here.

The recognition that relationships are significant in interpersonal communication goes back at least to the 1960s. Although research on relationships has been done from a diversity of perspectives, most of what is referred to as "relational communication" theory is based on a core of common assumptions.[2] First, relationships are always connected to communication and cannot be separated from it. Second, the nature of the relationship is defined by the communication between its members. Third, relationships are usually defined implicitly rather than explicitly.

Fourth, relationships develop over time through a negotiation process between those involved. Consequently, relationships are dynamic.[3] These assumptions are further explored and elaborated by the theories in this chapter.[4]

1   For an overview of interpersonal communication, see Mark L. Knapp and Gerald R. Miller, eds., *Handbook of Interpersonal Communication* (Thousand Oaks, CA: Sage, 1994). For a brief history, see Charles R. Berger, "Interpersonal Communication," in *An Integrated Approach to Communication Theory and Research*, eds. Michael B. Salwen and Don W. Stacks (Mahwah, NJ: Erlbaum, 1996), pp. 277–296; Mark L. Knapp, Gerald R. Miller, and Kelly Fudge, "Background and Current Trends in the Study of Interpersonal Communication," in *Handbook of Interpersonal Communication*, eds. Mark L. Knapp and Gerald R. Miller (Thousand Oaks, CA: Sage, 1994), pp. 3–20.
2   Barbara M. Montgomery, "Communication as the Interface Between Couples and Culture," in *Communication Yearbook 15*, ed. Stanley Deetz (Newbury Park, CA: Sage, 1992), pp. 475–507.
3   Carol M. Werner and Leslie A. Baxter, "Temporal Qualities of Relationships: Organismic, Transactional, and Dialectical Views," in *Handbook of Interpersonal Communication*, eds. Mark L. Knapp and Gerald R. Miller (Thousand Oaks, CA: Sage, 1994), pp. 323–379.
4   For a discussion of the way in which relationships are made in communication, see Steve Duck and Garth Pittman, "Social and Personal Relationships," in *Handbook of Interpersonal Communication*, eds. Mark L. Knapp and Gerald R. Miller (Thousand Oaks, CA: Sage, 1994), pp. 676–695. See also Steve Duck, *Meaningful Relationships: Talking, Sense, and Relating* (Thousands Oaks, CA: Sage, 1994).

THE NATURE OF RELATIONSHIPS

In this section we look at two lines of theory that give impetus to the study of communication in relationships, beginning with the classic work of the Palo Alto Group.

Basic Axioms of Relational Communication

Most relationship theorists acknowledge the importance of the work of Gregory Bateson, Paul Watzlawick, and their colleagues in the early years of the study of interpersonal communication. Bateson was briefly covered in Chapter 3, where we saw that his ideas about metacommunication have been highly formative in our field.

Bateson's early followers were known as the Palo Alto Group because they founded and worked at the Mental Research Institute based in Palo Alto, California. Their ideas are most clearly laid out in *Pragmatics of Human Communication*, now a classic.[5] In the book Paul Watzlawick, Janet Beavin, and Don Jackson present a well-known analysis of communication based on system principles (Chapter 3).

Relationships are an important part of a system. Two people communicating with each other—in addition to whatever else they may be doing—are also defining their relationship.[6] People in a relationship are always creating a set of expectations, reinforcing old ones, or changing an existing pattern of interaction.

Relationships are created through interaction. For example, if one spouse consistently exerts control over the other, a dominant-submissive relationship will result. Communication between workers in an organization might result in a status relationship in which one person is more highly esteemed than the other. The interaction between neighbors might turn out to be an equal-and-polite relationship. Implicit rules are numerous in any ongoing relationship, be it a friendship, business partnership, love affair, family, or any other type.

Watzlawick, Beavin, and Jackson present five basic axioms about communication.[7] The first is, "one cannot not communicate." This axiom has been quoted again and again in textbooks on communication. Its point is important, because it emphasizes that we are always affecting others' perceptions, whether we want to or not. This axiom also emphasizes that any perceivable behavior is potentially communicative.[8] It does not mean that every behavior always communicates, but it does mean that when in the presence of another person, you are always communicating something about your relationship with the other person. Even if you don't want a relationship, you will signal this to the other person, which itself is information about the "noncommunicating" relationship.[9] For example, if you are not in the mood to have a conversation on a plane, you might open a book and begin reading. This signals to the person next to you: "I am not available to talk."

The second axiom is that every conversation, no matter how brief, involves two messages—a content message and a relationship message. When two people are interacting, each is relating information to the other, and simultaneously each is also "commenting" on the information at a higher level. This simultaneous

5   Paul Watzlawick, Janet Beavin, and Don Jackson, *Pragmatics of Human Communication: A Study of Interactional Patterns, Pathologies, and Paradoxes* (New York: Norton, 1967).
6   Watzlawick, Beavin, and Jackson, *Pragmatics*, pp. 120–121.
7   Watzlawick, Beavin, and Jackson, *Pragmatics*.
8   This axiom has been challenged by Michael Motley, "On Whether One Can(not) Not Communicate: An Examination via Traditional Communication Postulates," *Western Journal of Speech Communication* 54 (1990): 1–20. See also "Forum: Can One Not Communicate?" *Western Journal of Speech Communication* 54 (1990): 593–623; Peter A. Andersen, "When One Cannot Not Communicate: A Challenge to Motley's Traditional Communication Postulates," *Communication Studies* 42 (1991): 309–325; Michael T. Motley, "How One May Not Communicate: A Reply to Andersen," *Communication Studies* 42 (1991): 326–339; Theodore Clevenger, Jr., "Can One Not Communicate? A Conflict of Models," *Communication Studies* 42 (1991): 351.
9   Janet Beavin Bavelas, "Behaving and Communicating: A Reply to Motley," *Western Journal of Speech Communication* 54 (1990): 593–602.

relationship talk, which often is nonverbal, is called *metacommunication.*

For example, when your professor announces an upcoming test, many possible relationship messages might be communicated at the same time. She could be saying, I am the authority in this classroom; I teach, you learn; what I have lectured about is important; I need feedback on your progress; I have a need to judge you; I want you to think I am fulfilling my role as professor; or any number of other relationship messages. Of course, the students' responses also include a relationship dimension, which might express compliance, defiance, respect, fear, equality, or other messages. In communicating about tests and all other topics, the teacher and student constantly define and redefine the nature of their relationship.

Judee Burgoon and her colleagues have conducted a huge survey of the interpersonal communication literature to find possible elements of relational communication and isolated twelve common aspects of relationships that seem to be communicated, labeling them the *fundamental topoi of relational communication.*[10] These include varying levels of dominance, intimacy, affection, involvement, inclusion, trust, superficiality, emotional arousal, composure, similarity, formality, and task-social orientation. These topics were further narrowed into four basic, independent dimensions of relational communication:

1. Emotional arousal, composure, and formality
2. Intimacy and similarity
3. Immediacy (liking, or attraction)
4. Dominance-submission

In announcing an examination, the professor might communicate a sense of formality (dimension 1), distance from the student (dimension 2), neutrality toward individual students (dimension 3), and dominance (dimension 4).

10   Judee K. Burgoon and Jerold L. Hale, "The Fundamental Topoi of Relational Communication," *Communication Monographs* 51 (1984): 193–214; Judee K. Burgoon, David B. Buller, Jerold L. Hale, and Mark A. deTurck, "Relational Messages Associated with Nonverbal Behaviors," *Human Communication Research* 10 (1984): 351–378.

A student's questions about the exam could reflect anxiety (dimension 1), distance from the professor (dimension 2), dislike of the professor (dimension 3), and acceptance of her right to administer the exam (dimension 4). Another professor and student might have a very different relationship, which would be reflected in a different set of metamessages on the same four dimensions.

Burgoon and her associates further studied the question of how nonverbal behaviors specifically affect these perceptions, and some interesting results emerged. Four behaviors seem especially important in metacommunication. *Proximity* can be significant in communicating intimacy, attraction, trust, caring, dominance, persuasiveness, and aggressiveness. *Smiling* seems especially important in communicating emotional arousal, composure, and formality, as well as intimacy and liking. *Touching,* too, communicates intimacy. *Eye contact* is like an exclamation point in intensifying the effect of other nonverbal behaviors.

Watzlawick, Beavin, and Jackson's third axiom says that interaction is always organized by the communicators into meaningful patterns, called *punctuation.* Interaction sequences, like sentences, cannot be understood as a string of isolated elements. To make sense they must be punctuated.

An interaction may look like a string of verbal and nonverbal behaviors. Like the series of sounds in a sentence, communication is never a simple chain. Certain behaviors are perceived to be a response to other ones. Behaviors are thus grouped or punctuated into larger units, which help define the meaning of the entire set of actions. This grouping is largely a matter of personal perception, and there is no guarantee that the participants will punctuate their interaction the same way.

Any given string of behaviors might be punctuated in various ways. For example, consider a marriage involving nagging by the husband and withdrawing by the wife. This sequence can be punctuated in at least two ways. The wife's withdrawing could be seen as a response to the husband's nagging: nag-withdraw, nag-withdraw. Alternatively, the husband's nagging could be viewed as a response to the wife's withdrawal: withdraw-nag, withdraw-nag. In the first case, the punctuation of "nag-withdraw" implies an attack-retreat relationship, but the punctuation of "withdraw-nag" implies ignoring-imploring. The meaning of the interaction, then, depends on the punctuation, and in this example the husband and wife have different meanings for what is going on, a common problem in relationships.

Watzlawick, Beavin, and Jackson's fourth axiom is that people use both digital and analogic codes. *Coding* was discussed in some detail in Chapter 4. As we learned there, digital coding is arbitrary, for the sign and the referent, though associated, have no intrinsic relation to each other. The relationship between the sign and the referent is strictly arbitrary. Using *bear* to designate a large black animal with claws wandering around the woods is entirely arbitrary. Further, digital signs are discrete; they are "on" or "off," uttered or not uttered. You either say *bear,* or you do not; you can't say it partially. The most common digital code in human communication is language. Sounds, words, and phrases are digital signs arranged to communicate meanings. Certain nonverbal signs, especially gestures like the victory sign or obscene gestures, are also digital.

The *analogic code* is quite different. Analogic signs are not arbitrary like digital ones. Analogic signs can actually resemble the object, as in the case of drawing a picture in the air with your hands, or they can be part of the object or condition being signified, as in the case of crying. Further, an analogue is continuous rather than discrete; it has degrees of intensity or longevity and is not just "on" or "off."

Most nonverbal signs are analogic. For example, a facial expression of surprise is not only a sign of a feeling or condition but is also actually part of the surprise itself. Its meaning is intrinsic, and the facial expression is not an either/or sign but a continuous variable between no expression and extreme facial distortion. Emotion in the voice is another analogic code with the same properties.

Although the digital and analogic codes are different from each other, they are used together and cannot be separated in ongoing communication. For instance, a word, which is digital, can be uttered in a variety of analogic ways (loud, soft; high, low; and so on). Similarly, a written message consisting of digital letters and words is presented on paper using various layouts, styles of handwriting or print, and other analogic codes.

Within the stream of behaviors in interaction, both digital and analogic codes blend, and theorists believe that they serve different functions. Digital signs, having relatively precise meanings, communicate the content dimension, whereas the analogic code, rich in feeling and connotation, is the vehicle for relationship messages. So while people are communicating content digitally, they are commenting about their relationship analogically.

Suppose a father at a playground sees his daughter fall and scrape her knee. Immediately, he says, "Don't cry. Daddy is coming." The content meaning is clear, but what is the relationship message? It depends on how the message is delivered. The father might communicate his own fear, worry, anger, boredom, or dominance. At the same time, he might communicate a number of possible perceptions, including, "You are careless," "You are an attention getter," "I was paying enough attention," and so on. When it comes to relationships, then, actions do speak louder than words.

The final axiom of communication deals with the matching or meshing of messages in an interaction. The axiom states that communicators may respond similarly to or differently from one another. When two communicators in a relationship behave similarly and differences are minimized, the relationship is said to be *symmetrical.* When communicator response differences are maximized, however, a *complementary* relationship is said to exist.

In a marriage when two partners both vie for power, they are involved in a symmetrical relationship. Similarly, co-workers are communicating symmetrically when each wants the other to tell him or her what to do. A complementary marital relationship would exist when the wife is domineering and the husband responds submissively. In the work setting, a complementary relationship would exist when the boss gives orders, and the employee is happy to follow them.

The variable most often examined in regard to this axiom is *control.* To explore this idea, let us look at the work of Edna Rogers and Frank Millar. Their work remains one of the most cogent and valuable statements about relational communication, and it provides a concrete extension of the work of the Palo Alto Group.[11] Although Millar and Rogers have discussed various dimensions of relationships, including trust and intimacy, most of their research has centered on control.

Like all aspects of relational communication, control cannot be defined by one person's behavior. You have to look at the pattern of behavior between partners over time. Let's see how this works in the control dimension.

When one person makes an assertion, the other person can respond in one of three ways. He or she can accept the assertion, which is a *one-down* move. He or she can make a counter-assertion, or reject the first person's move. This is called *one-up.* The third kind of response is *one-across,* which neither accepts nor rejects the first persons bid for control.

A complementary exchange occurs when one partner asserts a one-up message and the other responds one-down. When this kind of interaction predominates in a relationship, we can say that the relationship itself is complementary. The individual whose one-up message predominates at a given time is said to be *dominant.* Notice the difference here between "dominance" and "domineeringness." A one-up move is domineering, but it is not dominant unless the other person accepts it. A symmetrical exchange involves both partners responding the same way. Table 12.1 illustrates nine control states generated by combinations of these types of control messages.[12]

The Dialectics of Relationships

Thinking Dialectically About Relationships.
A *dialectic* is a tension between two or more contradictory elements of a system, and dialectical

analysis looks at the ways the system develops or changes, how it moves, in response to these tensions. Looked at dialectically, relationships are defined and shaped over time by the ways in which partners manage contradictions.

This section summarizes the work of Leslie Baxter, Barbara Montgomery, and their colleagues to explore this popular idea in the realm of relationships.[13] This section is organized around the four dimensions of dialectic outlined in their theory—contradiction, change, praxis, and totality.[14]

Contradiction is tension among opposites. These are not a finite list of objective forces, but arise in the give-and-take of interaction within a relationship. Although frequently discussed as bipolar opposites such as dependence-independence or stability-change, Baxter and Montgomery feel that this oversimplifies a much more complex process in which various forces tug at one another. At any moment, certain dominant, or *centripetal*, forces work in opposition to countervailing, or *centrifugal*, ones. You can think of these as forces that tend to pull us toward a center (centripetal) and those that tend to pull us away from a center (centrifugal). Baxter and Montgomery see these as a cluster of forces, or a "knot of contradiction."[15]

11   Although this work is explained in several sources, perhaps the most complete theoretical treatment is Frank E. Millar and L. Edna Rogers, "A Relational Approach to Interpersonal Communication," in *Explorations in Interpersonal Communication,* ed. G. R. Miller (Beverly Hills, CA: Sage, 1976), pp. 87–105. See also Millar and Rogers, "Power Dynamics in Marital Relationships," in *Perspectives on Marital Interaction,* eds. P. Noller and M. Fitzpatrick (Clevedon, England: Multilingual Matters, 1988), pp. 78–97; "Relational Dimensions of Interpersonal Dynamics," in *Interpersonal Processes: New Directions in Communication Research,* eds. M. E. Roloff and G. R. Miller (Newbury Park, CA: Sage, 1987), pp. 117–139.
12   Millar and Rogers, "Relational Approach," p. 97.
13   See, for example, Barbara M. Montgomery and Leslie A. Baxter, eds., *Dialectical Approaches to Studying Personal Relationships* (Mahwah, NJ: Erlbaum, 1998); "A Dialectical Perspective on Communication Strategies in Relationship Development," in *Handbook of Personal Relationships,* ed. S. Duck (New York: Wiley, 1988), pp. 257–273.
14   Leslie A. Baxter and Barbara M. Montgomery, "A Guide to Dialectical Approaches to Studying Personal Relationships," in *Dialectical Approaches to Studying Personal Relationships,* eds. Barbara Montgomery and Leslie Baxter (Mahwah, NJ: Erlbaum, 1998), pp. 1–15.
15   Barbara M. Montgomery and Leslie A. Baxter, "Dialogism and Relational Dialectics," in *Dialectical Approaches to Studying Personal Relationships,* eds. Barbara Montgomery and Leslie Baxter (Mahwah, NJ: Erlbaum, 1998), p. 160.

TABLE **12.1**

Control Configurations

Control direction of speaker A's message	Control direction of speaker B's message		
	One-up (↑)	One-down (↓)	One-across (→)
One-up (↑)	1.(↑↑) Competitive symmetry	4. (↑↓) Complementarity	7. (↑→) Transition
One-down (↓)	2. (↓↑) Complementarity	5. (↓↓) Submissive symmetry	8. (↓→) Transition
One-across (→)	3. (→↑) Transition	6. (→↓) Transition	9. (→→) Neutralized symmetry

Control Pattern Examples

1. Competitive symmetry (one-up/one-up):
   A: You know I want you to keep the house picked up during the day.
   B: I want you to help sometimes.

2. Complementarity (one-down/one-up):
   A: Please help. I need you.
   B: Sure, I know how.

3. Transition (one-across/one-up):
   A: Let's compromise.
   B: No, my way is best.

4. Complementarity (one-up/one-down):
   A: Let's get out of town this weekend.
   B: Okay.

5. Submissive symmetry (one-down/one-down):
   A: I'm so tired. What should we do?
   B: I can't decide. You decide.

6. Transition (one-across/one-down):
   A: My Dad was pretty talkative tonight.
   B: You're right; he sure was.

7. Transition (one-up/one-across):
   A: I definitely think we should have more kids.
   B: Lots of people seem to be having kids these days.

8. Transition (one-down/one-across):
   A: Please help me. What can I do?
   B: I don't know.

9. Neutralized symmetry (one-across/one-across):
   A: The neighbor's house needs paint.
   B: The windows are dirty too.

Each cluster consists of a variety of related contradictions that can occur in relationships.[16] One cluster, for example, is *integration and separation,* or the tension between coming together and moving apart. This can be a tension between meeting the demands of one's partner versus interacting with others outside the relationship. It could also include a struggle between individuality and mutuality. Whenever you struggle with decisions about whether to support another person or strike out on your own, you are facing this contradiction.

A second cluster is *expression-nonexpression.* This is the tension between whether to reveal information or keep it secret. When you are trying to decide whether to tell your partner something and feel reluctant to do so, you are probably experiencing this tension.

A third cluster is *stability-change,* or the tension between being predictable and consistent versus being spontaneous and different. Often couples experience a quandary about whether to keep doing the same old thing or to try new things, and when this happens, they are feeling this particular tension.

16 Leslie Baxter, "The Social Side of Personal Relationships: A Dialectical Perspective," in *Social Context and Relationships: Understanding Relationship Processes,* vol. 3, ed. Steve Duck (Newbury Park, CA: Sage, 1993), pp. 139–169; Werner and Baxter, "Temporal Qualities."

Contradiction is a crucial part of the dialectical process, but contradiction itself is not the whole of dialectic. Indeed, the dynamic interplay among opposing forces leads to *change*, which is the second element of dialectical analysis. The struggle with contradictions within a relationship almost always involve attempts to manage the ongoing tension between change and stability. How do you interact in a way that keeps things somewhat predictable and stable while allowing the relationship to change and grow?

In general, we can say that the management of contradiction is the primary force leading to relationship development. Development naturally implies change over time, and relationships do change in a variety of ways. Carol Werner and Leslie Baxter write about five qualities that change as relationships develop.[17] These are amplitude, salience, scale, sequence, and pace/rhythm. These qualities can be defined briefly as follows:

- *Amplitude*—the strength of feelings, behaviors, or both. For example, at certain points in a relationship, you may be very active and have strong feelings about what is going on. At other times, you may be more laid back or calm.
- *Salience*—focus on past, present, or future. At some moments in a relationship, you may find yourself concentrating a lot on what happened between you in the past. At other times you may be very centered on what is going on right now; and at other times, you may think mostly about the future, or where the relationship seems to be headed, or where you would like it to be going.
- *Scale*—how long patterns last. You and your partner may have some rituals that stick for a very long time, or perhaps you find yourselves doing things a certain way for a much shorter period of time.
- *Sequence*—the order of events in the relationship. As a relationship changes, a variety of things may be undertaken, but they are not always organized the same way for the entire length of the relationship. It is interesting to reflect back on the history of your relationship. Look at how the two of you have organized your time and the actions you do around and with each other. You will probably find that these sequences are different from one moment to another. Some sequences are rather stable and last a long time, while others are short-lived and easily replaced by new patterns of behavior in the relationship.
- *Pace/Rhythm*—the rapidity of events in the relationship and the interval between events. During certain periods in a relationship, events may occur in a rapid-fire way, with everything seeming to happen quickly. At other times, the pace may be much slower.

At a given time, a relationship will be characterized by some combination of these variables. Tracking the development of a relationship means watching the ways in which the profile changes over time. According to Werner and Baxter, we can look at such changes in three different ways. The *linear* view draws attention to the pattern of change over time as the relationship moves from one state to another. The *cyclical/spiraling* view focuses on the ways in which patterns return and repeat themselves over time. Using the linear perspective is like tracing the development of the relationship along a course or line. Using the cyclical perspective is like following the movement of the relationship around the turns in a spiral.

Any of the temporal qualities outlined above can be viewed in either of these ways (except rhythm, which is strictly cyclical). So, for example, using a linear view, we would notice the order, or sequence, of events and how one leads to another over time. Using a cyclical approach, we would notice how events are repeated in patterns and how those patterns repeat themselves at various points in the history of the relationship.

Having some idea of how change results from dialectical tension, let us move now to the third element of dialectical analysis—praxis. *Praxis* is a

---

17 Werner and Baxter, "Temporal Qualities."

Latin term for "practice." It means doing, action, behavior—what people actually do. Praxis includes how people act and how they are acted on. In relationship theory, this idea is very important because it means that some sort of relational pattern and definition arises in the give-and-take of material action. Relationships are not something you work out cognitively in your head, but something that you "make" through communication. In the dialectical, relational tradition, things are worked out incrementally and defined as the relationship evolves.

Finally, dialectical analysis rests on assumptions about *totality*. Totality means wholeness or inseparability (see Chapter 3). Contradictions cannot be separated from one another. Each entails others, correlates with others, and leads to others. Totality is the "knot" of contradictions.

Much work in the dialectic of relationships aims to discover some of the ways that relational partners manage tensions. C. Arthur Van Lear, for example, outlines four common patterns used in dialectical management.[18] The first is *redefinition*. Here you redefine one of the opposing elements so that it does not appear to contradict others. For example, if you are struggling between doing what your partner wants to do and doing what you want to do, you might reason that what you really want is for your partner to be happy.

Another approach is *balancing*, or behaving in a moderate way on both options. You might, for example, do some things you want to do and some things your partner wants to do. The third strategy is *contingent selection*, or doing one thing in one situation and another thing in a different situation. Here, for example, you might decide what to do based on how strongly you or your partner feels about it. When your partner wants to do something very passionately, you will go along with it, but when you want to do something very much, you will take that course of action. Finally, there is *cyclical alternation*, a pattern in which the couple goes back and forth between one action and another in a kind of periodic trade-off. So one week you might do what your partner wants, and the next week you do what you want.

To explore the management of dialectical tension in greater detail, we look now at a fascinating study of contradiction in friendships.

Dialectics in Friendships. William Rawlins' *dialectical theory of friendships* is an intriguing and sophisticated approach to this subject.[19] Rawlins believes that friendship at any stage of life presents an interesting and often complex set of challenges. The challenges of friendship arise chiefly from the need to manage a variety of dialectical contradictions. As you will see, Rawlins' dialectics are not unlike those of Baxter reviewed in the previous section.

Rawlins has done extensive research on friendships. He has surveyed the social science literature, examined reported case studies, read fictional accounts, conducted over a hundred personal interviews, and explored in-depth case studies of his own. In his book he discusses the changing texture of friendships over the life span, including those in childhood, adolescence, young adulthood, middle adulthood, and late adulthood. Although the challenges of friendship change over the life course, all people of all ages must manage dialectical tension in one way or another. Rawlins' work applies primarily to middle-class White U.S. culture.

Rawlins suggests that two general classes of dialectics operate in friendships. The first, contextual dialectics, deals with the meaning of friendship within the broader culture. The second, interactional dialectics, deals with the ambiguities of everyday communication in any friendship.

Contextual dialectics relate to the question of the place of friendship in society at large. You

18   C. Arthur Van Lear, "Dialectical Empiricism: Science and Relationship Metaphors," in *Dialectical Approaches to Studying Personal Relationships*, eds. Barbara Montgomery and Leslie Baxter (Mahwah, NJ: Erlbaum, 1998), pp. 109–136.
19   William K. Rawlins, *Friendship Matters: Communication, Dialectics, and the Life Course* (Hawthorne, NY: Aldine, 1992); see also William K. Rawlins, "A Dialectical Analysis of the Tensions, Functions, and Strategic Challenges of Communication in Young Adult Friendships," in *Communication Yearbook 12*, ed. J. A. Anderson (Newbury Park, CA: Sage, 1989), pp. 157–189; "Writing About *Friendship Matters*: A Case Study in Dialectical and Dialogical Inquiry," in *Dialectical Approaches to Studying Personal Relationships*, eds. Barbara Montgomery and Leslie Baxter (Mahwah, NJ: Erlbaum, 1998), pp. 63–81.

cannot really characterize friendship in simple terms. Any definition must mediate two contradictions. The first contradiction is between *the public and the private*. Friendship is inherently private. By definition it is something two people work out between themselves, and yet it is simultaneously governed by social and cultural expectations. The conflict here is between what society says a friendship should be (the public realm) and what the friends themselves have worked out between themselves (the private realm). This dialectic usually involves representing one's friendship to the world at large in a way that is socially acceptable.[20]

An example of this tension occurs in cross-sex friendships. Because society more or less reserves such relationships for romance, love, and sex, a platonic relationship between a man and woman often has to be explained to others, and there may be a good deal of pressure by outsiders to move the relationship from a friendship to something more intimate.

The second contextual dialectic is that between *the ideal and the real.* Our culture gives us a set of ideals to achieve, and yet very few friendships meet this set of values. Friends must act in a way that accommodates this tension. For example, friends are supposed to be loyal and available to each other, yet total loyalty may diminish one's own self-integrity, individuality, and freedom.

You can see that the two contextual dialectics are related to each other because the public view of friendship is laden with ideals, whereas the private actuality is governed by real relations negotiated by the friends themselves.

The second type of tensions that affect friendships is *interactional dialectics*, involving the ambiguities and ambivalence within individual friendships. They include all conflicts that friends must endure and manage in order to sustain the friendship. Because these tensions govern communication in a friendship, Rawlins concentrates primarily on this area. He believes that four dia-

lectical principles are used to manage the communication in friendships.

The first is to establish *the freedom to be independent and the freedom to be dependent*. People are supposed to let their friends lead their own lives, and yet they are also supposed to be available to help, counsel, and guide one another. Every time you make a decision to back off or to engage a friend, you are dealing with this contradiction. There are various ways of achieving temporary resolution of the contradiction, one of the most common being to let the other person make his or her own choices, including the choice to ask for help.

One of Rawlins' cases is that of Lana and Darlene, 26-year-old women who have been friends since their freshman year in high school. Dependence and independence are important issues for Lana and Darlene. Over the years they have gone through several stages, and the friendship can accommodate both dependence and independence. At times either or both women desire independence, especially when their relationships with spouses and boyfriends are going well. At other times when help and support are needed, such as during Darlene's divorce, dependency is permitted.

The second principle is the dialectic of *affection and instrumentality*. Friendships often have a tension between valuing the friend as an end in itself versus using the friend as a means to some other end. This is a tension between affection and utility. Do you call a friend to help you move? You might think twice about it. Do you let a friend borrow your car? Probably so, because that's what friends are for, or are they? How do people call on a friend to help them do something without the risk of having the friend feel used? Again, people work this out in different ways. Often, for example, friends have developed particular ways of asking for help or have become particularly sensitive to the timing of such requests. Friends may work hard to ensure genuine expressions of affection as well as the willingness to be of assistance.

Friendships during middle adulthood, especially between men, often arise from career contacts, entangling friendship with career advance-

20 This dialectic is also explored by Montgomery, "Communication."

ment. Because the affection side of the tension is often unfulfilled in middle-aged men, they may feel they have no best friend other than their wife. Women during this period seem to balance the two sides of the dialectic more effectively and usually say they have a best friend other than their husband.

The third principle is the dialectic of *judgment and acceptance.* Friends are supposed to accept us as we are, but they are also called on to make judgments and give advice. Sometimes we criticize friends, and other times we try hard to refrain from doing so. When we criticize, we usually choose our words carefully, and we often equivocate between expressing a judgment and accepting friends as they are. Again, each set of friends works out a pattern that manages this dialectic more or less effectively.

One of Rawlins' cases is that of Carol and Brent, who by their early 20s had been close friends for seven years. The tension between judgment and acceptance is a real issue in this friendship. In their interviews they both expressed how important acceptance has been in the friendship, and for this reason they have come to be cautious about making judgments about each other. Carol, for example, most dislikes Brent when he comes off like a brother and criticizes her boyfriends.

The fourth dialectic is that between *expressiveness and protectiveness.* To what extent can you express your feelings openly with a friend? Should you protect a friend from hurtful or difficult information? In many ways this is a tension between spontaneity and strategy. It is a tension between honesty and rhetorical adaptation. You want to feel that your friends are honest with you, but at the same time you do not want to hurt your friends. A frequent response to this dialectic is to try to accomplish both horns of the dilemma at the same time—to be honest but to be careful in how that honesty is expressed. For most friends, this is a rhetorical feat.

Friendships constitute a unique and interesting context in which relationships are developed, and Rawlins' work helps us see more clearly what dialectical analysis of relationships involves.

● MANAGING RELATIONSHIPS

A distinguishing characteristic of relational communication theory is that it focuses on the ways in which people together manage various aspects of their relationships. In this section, we look at several theories that illustrate this feature.

Managing Uncertainty and Anxiety

The brainchild of Charles Berger, William Gudykunst, and their colleagues, this line of theory deals with the ways we gather information about other people, why we do so, and what results when we do so. It deals with the ways individuals monitor their social environments and come to know more about themselves and others. Berger's theory is referred to as *uncertainty reduction theory* (URT) and Gudykunst's extension on Berger's work as *anxiety-uncertainty management* (AUM).[21] Let us begin with URT.

Uncertainty Reduction Theory. This theory has two concerns—self-awareness and knowledge of others. From research in social psychology, Berger observes that *self-awareness* varies from person to person and from situation to situation.[22] In *objective self-awareness,* the person centers on the self rather than other objects in the environment. *Subjective self-awareness,* on the other hand, puts the self in a peripheral position so that it blends into the momentary stream of experience.

When you give a speech, for example, you are conscious that the audience is watching you and you become aware of yourself as an object, which is the main reason you are nervous. On the other hand, when you are involved in a nonthreatening

---

21   For an excellent summary of the two theories together, see William Gudykunst, "The Uncertainty Reduction and Anxiety-Uncertainty Reduction Theories of Berger, Gudykunst, and Associates," in *Watershed Research Traditions in Human Communication Theory,* eds. Donald P. Cushman and Branislav Kovačić (Albany: SUNY Press, 1995), pp. 67–100.

22   For more information on self-awareness, see, for example, S. Duval and R. A. Wicklund, *A Theory of Objective Self-Awareness* (New York: Academic, 1972).

conversation with a good friend, your self-awareness is much more subjective and natural.

Research indicates objective self-awareness is common because we are often required to concentrate on ourselves in various situations, but it tends to be an uncomfortable state. Although an individual's self-awareness will vary from moment to moment, each person has a relatively enduring norm of self-awareness. Some individuals are often or always self-aware, whereas others are rarely or never so.

The enduring trait of being objectively self-aware is *self-consciousness*, and this characteristic is dominated by a tendency to *self-monitor*, or "watch yourself." High self-monitors are guarded and careful about the impression they give to others. They are highly sensitive to others' feedback and try to adapt their behaviors to suit other people. Low self-monitors tend to be less sensitive to themselves or to others and are less concerned with making impressions. Whereas high self-monitors tend to be actors, low self-monitors tend to "tell it like it is." In these ways, then, we develop knowledge about ourselves.

We also have a need in interpersonal communication to get information about the other person, which is really the focal point of URT.[23] When we encounter a stranger, we may have a strong desire to reduce uncertainty about that person by gaining information about him or her. We tend to be uncertain about other people's ability to communicate, their goals and plans,

their feelings at the moment, and other information about them. Berger proposes that people have a difficult time with uncertainty, that they want to be able to predict behavior, and that they are therefore motivated to seek information about others. Indeed, this kind of uncertainty reduction is one of the primary dimensions of a developing relationship.

As we communicate, according to Berger, we are making plans to accomplish our goals. We formulate plans for our communications with others based on our goals as well as the information we have about the others involved. The more uncertain we are, the more vigilant we must become, and the more we must rely on data available to us in the situation. At highly uncertain moments, we will become more conscious or mindful of the planning we are doing. When we are very uncertain about another person, we will tend to be less confident in our plans and make more contingency plans, or alternative ways of responding.

Attraction or affiliation seems to correlate positively with uncertainty reduction. For example, nonverbal expressiveness seems to reduce uncertainty, and reduction in uncertainty seems to increase nonverbal expressiveness. Higher levels of uncertainty seem to create distance, but reduced uncertainty tends to bring people together. As communicators discover similarities between them, their attraction to one another goes up, and their apparent need for more information goes down.

Often, the behavior of the other person immediately reduces your uncertainty, greatly lessening the desire to get additional information. This is especially true when your involvement with the other person is limited to a particular situation and you have all the information you need to understand their behavior in this situation. However, under certain circumstances, your need to know more about a person is heightened. Such circumstances include abnormal behavior on the part of the other person, the expectation that you will be communicating with the other person in the future, or the prospect that the encounter will be especially rewarding or

23   Uncertainty reduction theory is summarized in various versions in Charles R. Berger, "Producing Messages Under Uncertainty," in *Message Production: Advances in Communication Theory*, ed. John O. Greene (Mahwah, NJ: Erlbaum, 1997), pp. 221–244; Charles R. Berger and James J. Bradac, *Language and Social Knowledge: Uncertainty in Interpersonal Relations* (London: Arnold, 1982). See also Charles R. Berger and R. J. Calabrese, "Some Explorations in Initial Interaction and Beyond: Toward a Developmental Theory of Interpersonal Communication," *Human Communication Research* 1 (1975): 99–112; Charles R. Berger, R. R. Gardner, M. R. Parks, L. Schulman, and G. R. Miller, "Interpersonal Epistemology and Interpersonal Communication," in *Explorations in Interpersonal Communication*, ed. G. R. Miller (Beverly Hills, CA: Sage, 1976), pp. 149–171; and Charles R. Berger and William Douglas, "Thought and Talk: 'Excuse Me, But Have I Been Talking to Myself?'" in *Human Communication Theory*, ed. F. E. X. Dance (New York: Harper & Row, 1982), pp. 42–60. For a good, comprehensive secondary treatment, see John F. Cragan and Donald C. Shields, *Understanding Communication Theory: The Communicative Forces for Human Action* (Boston: Allyn & Bacon, 1998), pp. 122–148.

costly. Under these conditions, you will probably take action to get more information about the other person.

For example, if you hired a plumber to fix a leak in your house, you would probably not have a very great need to learn more about this contractor. On the other hand, if the plumber noticed that you had a "Room for Rent" sign in your window and expressed an interest in finding a new place to live, you would suddenly be motivated to get more information about this person. In particular, you would be interested in reducing *predictive uncertainty* about this individual so that you would have a better idea of *what* you expect in his or her behavior, and you would want to reduce *explanatory uncertainty*, so that you could better *understand* your possible tenant's behavior.

Berger believes that uncertainty is an extremely important variable in the development of relationships. So in initial interactions, people will talk a lot to get more information, and as uncertainty is eliminated, questioning and other information-seeking strategies will decline.

How, then, do you go about getting such information about others? Berger suggests a variety of ways. *Passive strategies* are observational, whereas *active* ones require the observer to do something to get the information. *Interactive strategies* rely directly on communication with the other person.

The first passive strategy is *reactivity searching.* Here the individual is observed actually doing something—reacting in some situation. For example, if you were interested in getting to know a classmate, you might observe this person discreetly for a period of time. You might watch the way he or she reacted to events in the class—questions from the instructor, class discussions, and so forth. Observers generally prefer to see how a person reacts when communicating with another person, so you might listen in on conversations this person was having with other people in class.

Disinhibition searching is another passive strategy in which people are observed in informal situations where they are less likely to be self-

monitoring and are behaving in a more natural way. You might therefore be especially interested in observing your classmate outside of class in settings such as the cafeteria or residence hall.

Active strategies of information involve asking others about the target person and manipulating the environment in ways that set up the target person for observation. You might, for example, try to get assigned to a project group with this classmate.

Interactive strategies include interrogation and self-disclosure. Self-disclosure, which is discussed in more detail later, is a significant strategy for obtaining information because if you disclose something about yourself, the other person is likely to disclose in return. Once in the project group, for instance, you would probably talk to this other person, and you might ask questions and make disclosures.

To discover the ways strangers get information about one another, Charles Berger and Katherine Kellermann videotaped about fifty conversations in their laboratory.[24] The couples varied in terms of how much information they were told to get. Some participants were told to get as much information about the other person as possible, others were told to get as little as possible, and a third group was not given any instructions along these lines. Also, the dyads themselves were mixed, so that some consisted of couples in which both had been asked to get a great deal of information, some consisted of couples in which both had been asked to get little information, and some included one person from each category.

The videotaped conversations were coded by judges in a variety of ways. The researchers were interested chiefly in finding out what the communicators actually did to get or to resist getting information. Predictably, the most common strategy for getting information was to ask questions, but some other strategies were also used, such as putting the other person at ease and using

---

24   Charles R. Berger and Katherine Ann Kellermann, "To Ask or Not to Ask: Is That a Question?" in *Communication Yearbook 7,* ed. R. Bostrom (Beverly Hills, CA: Sage, 1983), pp. 342–368.

self-disclosure. Even the low-information seekers used questions, but their questions tended to be innocuous inquiries into the weather and other noninformative topics.

Individuals who were trying to get a great deal of information asked significantly more questions than the low-information subjects. Those who were not given any instructions asked about the same number of questions as those who were told to get a great deal of information, which suggests that we normally tend to ask many questions when talking with strangers. This hypothesis was supported because the low-information seekers in this experiment had a harder time than did the high-information seekers and normal subjects. As expected, high-information seekers asked more open-ended questions, requiring explanation, than did low-information seekers.

Michael Sunnafrank suggests that the chief reason we seek information is not to reduce uncertainty per se but to assess the potential outcome of the communication. His *predicted-outcome value theory* suggests that people are motivated to reduce uncertainty because they want to know whether continued communication will be positive or negative.[25] The main reason you would want to know more about your plumber, for example, is not just to reduce uncertainty but to decide whether to rent a room to this person. When you receive information that leads you to predict a rewarding outcome, you will probably be more attracted to the other person, and you will probably want to continue the association. On the other hand, if your initial information leads to a negative prediction, you will probably do all you can to decrease information and cut off the relationship.

Anxiety-Uncertainty Management. William Gudykunst and his colleagues have extended Berger's work in important ways, especially by looking at uncertainty and anxiety in intercultural situations. They have found that all cultures seek to reduce uncertainty in the initial stages of a relationship, but they do so in different ways.[26] The difference can be explained by whether one is a member of a high-context culture or a low-context culture.[27] *High-context cultures* rely heavily on the overall situation to interpret events, and *low-context cultures* rely more on the explicit verbal content of messages. Members of high-context cultures such as the Japanese rely on nonverbal cues and information about a person's background to reduce uncertainty, but members of low-context cultures such as the British ask direct questions related to experience, attitudes, and beliefs.

The process of uncertainty reduction between people from different cultures is affected by additional variables as well. When you strongly identify with your own cultural group and you think the other person is typical of a different group, you will probably feel a certain amount of anxiety, and your uncertainty will be great. On the other hand, your confidence in getting to know the other person will be higher and your anxiety about doing so will be lower if you expect the results to be positive. Experience and friendships with other people from different cultures may also increase your confidence when meeting a stranger from another group. In addition, knowing the other person's language will help, as will a certain amount of tolerance for ambiguity. Also, when you are more confident and less anxious about meeting someone from a different group, you will probably do a better job of getting information and reducing uncertainty.

Uncertainty and anxiety in intercultural situations seem to be underlying causes of ineffectiveness and lack of adaptation. The less you know and the more anxious you are, the less effective

25 Michael Sunnafrank, "Predicted Outcome Value During Initial Interactions," *Human Communication Research* 13 (1986): 3–33; "Predicted Outcome Value and Uncertainty Reduction Theories: A Test of Competing Perspectives," *Human Communication Research* 17 (1990): 76–103.

26 This work is summarized in Gudykunst, "The Uncertainty Reduction and Anxiety-Uncertainty Reduction Theories"; William B. Gudykunst, "Uncertainty and Anxiety," in *Theories in Intercultural Communication*, ed. Y. Y. Kim and W. B. Gudykunst (Newbury Park, CA: Sage, 1988), pp. 123–156; and "Culture and the Development of Interpersonal Relationships," in *Communication Yearbook 12*, ed. J. A. Anderson (Newbury Park, CA: Sage, 1989), pp. 315–354.

27 This concept is developed by Edward T. Hall, *Beyond Culture* (New York: Doubleday, 1976).

you will probably be in intercultural situations. This makes the reduction, or management of uncertainty anxiety, especially important.

There is no clear line that marks the point at which difficult or problematic communication will result. Instead, different individuals have different thresholds for uncertainty and anxiety. If your level of uncertainty exceeds your upper threshold, you will not feel very confident, and if the level of anxiety is too high for you, you might avoid communication altogether. There are also low-end thresholds, below which your motivations to communicate would disappear. If you met a stranger from another culture and you were too uncertain about this person, you might avoid communicating with her because you felt that you didn't know how. At the same time, if you did not feel enough uncertainty, you would not be motivated to communicate because you felt you already knew enough. If you are too anxious, you will be nervous and avoid communicating, but if you are not anxious enough, you will not care enough to try. The ideal in intergroup situations, then, is for uncertainty and anxiety to be between your upper and lower thresholds, which would lead to motivation and uncertainty reduction strategies.

Gudykunst in recent years has elaborated this theory in great detail, to the point that it now includes about fifty propositions related to self-concept, motivation, reactions to strangers, social categorization, situational processes, connection with strangers, and a host of other concerns dealing with anxiety and effectiveness.[28]

Managing Face

We looked at the topic of facework earlier in this book as an issue of politeness in Chapter 6 and self-presentation in Chapter 8. We return now to this subject by looking at facework in the context of relationships. *Face-negotiation theory* has been developed by Stella Ting-Toomey as a way of predicting how people will accomplish facework in different cultures.[29]

Face refers to one's self-image in the presence of others. It involves feelings of respect, honor, status, connection, loyalty, and other similar values. In other words, face means feeling good about yourself in whatever ways your culture prescibes. For some, it means being a good member of the family; for others, it may mean being an effective professional practitioner. *Facework* is the communication behaviors people use to build and protect their own face and to protect, build, or threaten the face of another person.

When you observe facework in action, you can see various things going on. For example, you might notice the *locus of facework*, or whether it is directed at self or others. You might notice people bragging about an accomplishment or praising another person for a job well done. As you observe people communicating, you might also notice *face valence*, or whether a person's actions are positive, as in the case of defending, maintaining, or honoring one's face, or whether the actions are negative, or attacking. Next, you might notice *temporality*, or whether the communication is designed to prevent loss of face in the future or restore loss of face that has already happened.

Face is a universal concern, but how face is defined and the ways in which facework is accomplished varies significantly from person to person and culture to culture. All cultures have ways to accomplish both preventive and restorative facework. *Preventive facework* involves communication designed to protect a person from feelings of threat to personal or group face. If you needed to discuss a problem with your boss, for example, you begin by saying, "I know you are very busy, and I'm sorry to intrude, but . . ." *Restorative facework* is designed to rebuild one's face after loss has already occurred. If you made an insulting comment to a friend in a moment of

28 Gudykunst, "The Uncertainty Reduction and Anxiety-Uncertainty Reduction Theories."
29 Stella Ting-Toomey, "Toward a Theory of Conflict and Culture," in *Communication, Culture, and Organizational Processes*, eds. William Gudykunst, Lea Stewart, and Stella Ting-Toomey (Beverly Hills, CA: Sage, 1985), pp. 71–86; Stella Ting-Toomey, "Intercultural Conflict Styles: Face-Negotiation Theory," in *Theories in Intercultural Communication*, eds. Yung Y. Kim and William Gudykunst (Newbury Park, CA: Sage, 1988), pp. 213–235; Stella Ting-Toomey and Atsuko Kurogi, "Facework Competence in Intercultural Conflict: An Updated Face-Negotiation Theory," *International Journal of Intercultural Relations* 22 (1998): 187–225.

anger, you might later apologize and say, "You are really a great friend, and I'm sorry I said that, 'cause I didn't really mean it."

Two primary cultural variables seem to affect facework. The first is *individualism-collectivism*. Many cultures honor the individual above the community or group. These cultures promote autonomy, individual responsibility, and individual achievement. Governed by an "I-identity," these cultures are considered *individualist*. Other cultures, in contrast, tend to honor the community or collective above the individual person. Important for these cultures is the connection among people, and promoting the interests of any one person would feel odd or inappropriate. These cultures, defined as *collectivist*, are governed by a "we-identity."

Cultures are never purely one or the other. Most people have feelings of both individuality and collectivism, but within a given culture, one of these will usually predominate. Northern and western European and North American cultures tend to be individualist, while collectivism is common in Asia, Africa, the Middle East, and Latin America.

The second cultural variable affecting facework is *power distance*. In many cultures of the world, there is a strong hierarchy, or sense of status, in which certain members or groups exert great influence and control over others. Members of these cultures accept the unequal distribution of power as normal. In different cultures, however, the felt distance among groups and individuals is less. Again, power distance is a variable, with some cultures having a great deal and other cultures having less. High power-distance cultures can be found in such regions as Malaysia, certain Latin American cultures, the Philippines, and Arab countries. Lower power-distance cultures can be found in such places as New Zealand and Scandinavia.

Because honor means different things in different cultures, facework will vary significantly across cultures. We would expect that members of individualist cultures would do more work to honor people as autonomous individuals. They would see themselves as important apart from others and work to build their own esteem as well as that of other individuals. When a person in an individualist culture is attacked or threatened in some way, it would be considered appropriate to help build that individual's face, to repair the damage or honor the person to compensate for the face threat. In collectivist cultures, by contrast, honor is defined in terms of how one defers to the values of the group, and facework is not normally self-oriented. Instead, one acknowledges the group or community. Members of collectivist cultures tend to be somewhat self-effacing and deferential. They accept face loss and rebuild it by acknowledging the need to work harder on behalf of the group.

In an individualist culture, you might be expected to make excuses for yourself, explaining why you were unable to live up to someone's expectations. You would probably compliment other people for a job well done, or restore their face by reminding them of something they were good at. In a collectivist culture, on the other hand, you would accept criticism, talk about the effectiveness of others, and promise to do a better job of living up to the group's standards in the future. In restoring another person's face in such cultures, you would compliment a group with which the person affiliates or perhaps tell the person what a good member of the group he or she is.

Face is usually an issue in conflict situations. When you are having a conflict with another person, respect and honor are often compromised. Face threats can happen because of a competition or desire to win, as a result of anger or feeling disconfirmed in some way, or due to conflicting values, opinions, or attitudes. In any case, face threats are common in conflict, so that facework is a regular part of conflict communication. Often the facework is negative and takes the form of an attack on the other person. Other times, we try hard to work through the conflict using positive facework to accomplish our own goals while helping the other person feel good about him- or herself in the process.

Because of culture, people have different styles in conflict. Individualists, for example, tend to use more direct personal attack, and they may try to protect or rebuild their own face or that of others by showing personal respect. Collectivists, on the other hand, will use less personal attack and be more indirect in conflicts. They may avoid the issue at hand, talk around it, discuss side issues, take more time to get to the point, and generally talk in ways that build the group over themselves. Individualists in a conflict tend to want to get through it by solving the problem or settling the dispute. Collectivists, in contrast, are more interested in affirming the relationship. Collaboration and compromise mean different things in these different cultures. For individualists, collaboration and compromise are ways of solving the problem, but for collectivists, they are a means for building a relationship.

Of course, facework and conflict management become even more complex when we factor in power distance. In low power-distance situations, consultation and participation are key. Everyone wants to be involved. As a result, people communicate more directly and personally. In high power-distance settings, decisions will tend to be made by higher-status individuals, which is accepted by everyone. People behave differently depending upon their status, so that their facework varies. High-status members already have the power, so they do not need to be very direct. They can communicate indirectly, avoid threatening the face of lower-status members, and still get their way. Lower-status individuals, on the other hand, will be more self-effacing and deferential. They will acknowledge the high-status person's right to make the decision. In these situations, the aims of the communication are to maintain the power distance by using more formality. Conflict is often resolved by a mediator in such cultures— someone who is respected by both high-power and low-power individuals.

According to Ting-Toomey, culture largely determines how facework and conflict are enacted, but culture is not the only factor. There are important individual differences that must be entered into the equation. The individual characteristic that seems to matter most is *self-construal*, or one's sense of independence or interdependence

with other people. This variable is simply how you see yourself in relation to others. "Independents" tend to use more direct, problem-solving communication, while "interdependents" are more relationally oriented in their conflicts. People who see themselves as both independent and interdependent tend to have a larger repertoire of strategies for facework and conflict than the other types. People who are ambivalent may use more third-party (mediator) interventions.

Clearly, intercultural communication presents many challenges. It is hard enough with friends and colleagues who share our cultural views, but in an increasingly intercultural and international world, conflict can be even more difficult. We must be vigilant and develop the ability to communicate with members of other cultures by knowing more about them, observing carefully, and developing skills in listening, facework, and dialogue.

Managing Boundaries

Self-disclosure was an important theme in communication theory in the 1960s and 1970s. Largely as a consequence of the humanistic school in psychology, an ideology of "honest communication" arose, and much of our thinking about what makes good interpersonal communication was affected by this movement.[30] Spurred by the work of Carl Rogers, the so-called Third Force in psychology taught that the goal of communication is accurate understanding of self and others and that understanding can only happen with genuine self-disclosure.[31]

---

30   For a review of early research on self-disclosure, see Shirley J. Gilbert, "Empirical and Theoretical Extensions of Self-Disclosure," in *Explorations in Interpersonal Communication,* ed. G. R. Miller (Beverly Hills, CA: Sage, 1976), pp. 197–216. A leader in this movement was Sidney Jourard. See Sidney Jourard, *Disclosing Man to Himself* (New York: Van Nostrand, 1968); *Self-Disclosure: An Experimental Analysis of the Transparent Self* (New York: Wiley, 1971); *The Transparent Self* (New York: Van Nostrand Reinhold, 1971). See also P. W. Cozby, "Self-Disclosure: A Literature Review," *Psychological Bulletin* 79 (1973): 73–91. For a good summary of self-disclosure theories, see the second edition of this book, *Theories of Human Communication* (Belmont, CA: Wadsworth, 1983), pp. 193–199.
31   The work of Carl Rogers is summarized and interpreted by Kenneth J. Cissna and Rob Anderson, "The Contributions of Carl R. Rogers to Philosophical Praxis of Dialogue," *Western Journal of Speech Communication* 54 (1990): 125–147.

Today, we understand relationship development as a more complex process than we did in earlier times.[32] Instead of reducing relationships to increasing intimacy and self-disclosure, we think of it as a process of managing information about the self. This is a process of making decisions about where to place the boundary between the private and the public. We look now at some of the most influential and important theories in this area.

Social Penetration Theory. One of the most widely studied processes of relational development is social penetration, or the idea that relationships become more intimate over time when partners disclose more and more information about themselves. *Social penetration*, then, is the process of increasing disclosure and intimacy in a relationship.

The best-known theory of social penetration is that of Irwin Altman and Dalmas Taylor. In fact, Altman and Taylor coined the term *social penetration*.[33] This theory imagines that a person can be represented by a sphere with layers with both breadth and depth. Breadth is the variety of experiences that have been incorporated into the person's life. Depth is the amount of information available on each aspect of experience. On the outermost shell are highly visible levels of information, like dress and speech. Inside are increasingly private details about the individual's life, feelings, and thoughts. As the relationship between two individuals develops, the partners share more aspects of the self, adding both depth and breadth to what they know about one another.

Altman and Taylor's original theory was based on one of the most popular ideas in social science: Relationships are sustained when they are relatively rewarding and decline when they are relatively costly. This process is known as *social exchange*.[34] According to Altman and Taylor, relational partners not only assess the rewards and costs of the relationship at a given moment but also use the information they have gathered to predict the rewards and costs in the future.

The theorists posited four stages of relational development. *Orientation* consists of impersonal communication, in which one discloses only very public information about oneself. If this stage is rewarding to the participants, they will move to the next stage, the *exploratory affective exchange*, in which initial expansion of information and movement to a deeper level of disclosure take place. The third stage, *affective exchange*, centers on evaluative and critical feelings at a deeper level. This stage will not be entered unless the partners perceive substantial rewards relative to costs in earlier stages. Finally, *stable exchange* is highly intimate and allows the partners to predict each other's actions and responses very well.

Original social penetration theory was important in focusing our attention on relationship development as a communication process. However, it did not hold up very well to the actual experience of relationships in daily life. Many students of relationship development now believe that social penetration is a cyclical, dialectical process.[35] It is cyclical because it proceeds in back-and-forth cycles, and it is dialectical because it involves the management of the tension between opposites. This is certainly a view consistent with the dialectical approach explained earlier in this chapter.

In their later writings, Altman and his colleagues have revised social penetration theory to

---

32   Duck and Pittman, "Social and Personal Relationships."
33   Irwin Altman and Dalmas Taylor, *Social Penetration: The Development of Interpersonal Relationships* (New York: Holt, Rinehart & Winston, 1973). For an update and summary, see Dalmas A. Taylor and Irwin Altman, "Communication in Interpersonal Relationships: Social Penetration Theory," in *Interpersonal Processes: New Directions in Communication Research*, eds. M. E. Roloff and G. R. Miller (Newbury Park, CA: Sage, 1987), pp. 257–277.
34   An excellent summary of this entire line of work is Michael E. Roloff, *Interpersonal Communication: The Social Exchange Approach* (Beverly Hills, CA: Sage, 1981). The best-known social exchange theory is that of John W. Thibaut and Harold H. Kelley, *The Social Psychology of Groups* (New York: Wiley, 1959); see also Harold H. Kelley and John W. Thibaut, *Interpersonal Relations: A Theory of Interdependence* (New York: Wiley, 1978). For a brief summary of the theory, see the third edition of this book, *Theories of Human Communication*, 1989, pp. 185–186.
35   This work is briefly summarized by C. Arthur Van Lear, "Testing a Cyclical Model of Communicative Openness in Relationship Development: Two Longitudinal Studies," *Communication Monographs* 58 (1991): 337–361.

incorporate this idea. They point out that relationships generally do not move in a single line toward greater openness. Rather, couples go back and forth between sharing and distance as they manage the tension between the need for privacy and the need for connection.[36] Relationships go back and forth between stability and change as the couple manages its contradictory needs for predictability and flexibility.

Altman and his associates now say that these dialectics are usually managed in a long-term relationship by a kind of predictability of cycles. In other words, as the relationship develops, the couple's cycle of openness and closedness possesses a certain regularity or predictable rhythm. At the same time, in more developed relationships, the cycle is larger than in a less developed one. This is because, consistent with the basic tenet of social penetration theory, developed relationships have more disclosure on the average.

Something else happens as relationships develop. Partners become more able to coordinate the cycle of disclosure. Their timing and extent of disclosure are synchronized, at least in theory. The research evidence is somewhat mixed but basically supports the general idea of cycles and dialectics.

To test this idea, Arthur Van Lear paired up a number of students into dyads.[37] Each couple met one-half hour per week for five weeks to talk, and their conversations were tape-recorded for analysis. The conversations were later analyzed for the amount and type of self-disclosure, and these disclosures were then examined statistically for cyclical patterns. The analysis indicated that cycles of openness did occur in these conversations and some synchronization did occur.

To compare these results with real, ongoing relationships, another group of students was asked to monitor their conversations with another person with whom they were having a relationship (such as a spouse, friend, or romantic partner) for ten weeks. After each conversation of at least fifteen minutes, they filled out a "conversation monitoring form" that asked about satisfaction and perceived openness/closedness. The

results of this study mirrored those of the first study. Both studies indicated that cycles do occur, that these are complex, that the partners recognized their cycles, and that matching and synchronization often occur. Important to note, however, is the finding that the amount of synchrony is not the same for each couple, which means that there are differences between couples in their ability to coordinate self-disclosure cycles.

Boundary Management Theory. A recent theory that further elaborates the disclosure-development process is that of Sandra Petronio.[38] Entitled *communication boundary management theory* (CBM), this work is based on Petronio's own research and a survey of other studies on the topic of relationship development and disclosure.

According to Petronio, individuals involved in relationships are constantly managing boundaries between the public and private, between those feelings and thoughts they are willing to share with others and those they are not. The boundary is the line between what is private and what is not private. Sometimes the boundary is permeable, meaning that certain information can be revealed. Other times, it is impermeable and never shared. Of course, the permeability of a boundary will change, and situations may lead to opening or closing the boundaries. Maintaining a closed boundary can lead to greater autonomy and safety, whereas opening the boundary can promote greater intimacy and sharing, at the cost of personal vulnerability.

This play between the need to share and the need to protect oneself is constant and requires couples to negotiate and coordinate their boundaries. When do you disclose and when do you not? And when your partner discloses personal

36 Irwin Altman, "Dialectics, Physical Environments, and Personal Relationships," *Communication Monographs* 60 (1993): 26–34; Irwin Altman, A. Vinsel, and B. Brown, "Dialectic Conceptions in Social Psychology: An Application to Social Penetration and Privacy Regulation," in *Advances in Experimental Social Psychology*, vol. 14, ed. L. Berkowitz (New York: Academic, 1981), pp. 76–100.
37 Van Lear, "Testing a Cyclical Model."
38 Sandra Petronio, *Boundaries of Private Disclosure* (Albany: SUNY Press, 2001).

information, how do you respond? We all have a sense of ownership of information about ourselves, and we feel we have the right to control that information. We are constantly making decisions about what to reveal, who should have this information, and when and how to reveal it. Petronio sees this decision-making process as a dialectic—an interplay between pressures to reveal and pressures to conceal.

Once we reveal private information to another person, that person becomes a co-owner of the information, and co-ownership has its own set of negotiated rights and responsibilities. For example, your family probably has an implicit rule that certain things are not to be discussed with others outside the family. The family co-owns the information, but there is a boundary between what is private to the family and what is not, and each family member understands this.

When a person discloses something, he or she is making a demand on the other to respond appropriately. Demands and responses need to be coordinated. When you disclose something to your partner, he or she can respond in a way that promotes relationship quality and happiness or in a way that does not.

Boundary management, then, requires consideration and thought. People make decisions about how and when to disclose, and they make decisions about how to respond to the demands of others.

Petronio sees boundary management as a rule-based process. It is not merely an individual decision—Do I tell or not? Rather, it is a negotiation of the rules by which the information will be kept and managed. When a married woman thinks that she might be pregnant, she will almost always consider when and how to reveal it. Some women will tell their husbands immediately. Others will wait a while to see what happens. Eventually, when the woman tells her husband, the information becomes co-owned and then the couple will discuss when and how to make it known to others. Do they tell other family members first? Do they announce it to all of their friends and family at the same time? When and how do they reveal that they are expecting? Some couples wait

until "it shows." Others may call all their friends and relatives as soon as "the rabbit dies."

Family boundary rules are interesting because they are so important to family's identify. Notice the different ways in which families manage information about health, finances, work, children, and other important issues.

The rules for boundary management are developed on the basis of criteria and risk assessment. *Criteria* include certain cultural expectations, gender differences, personal motivations, and situational demands. When you become pregnant, you will probably decide who and when to tell based on your sense of privacy as a woman, how pregnancy has been handled traditionally in your family, how you are personally feeling about it, and even how many children you already have.

Risk assessment means thinking about the costs and rewards of revealing the information. For example, if you have had a series of miscarriages, you may find that revealing a new pregnancy is very risky. On the other hand, if you have been trying to get pregnant and this is your first pregnancy, you may want to share your joy with your friends and family and receive their congratulations and support in return.

Boundary rules do change as circumstances change. Some rules are persistent, routine, and dependable, but others may be highly dynamic. There may be a long-standing rule between a married couple, for example, not to discuss family finances with others. This rule could last for years and years, and yet at some point, maybe in retirement, it changes as the benefits of discussing money with friends become obvious.

Negotiating the rules for co-ownership of information can be tricky. The various parties who share private information must coordinate and synchronize their behavior. Explicit and implicit agreements must be forged about how to manage shared information. Partners must negotiate rules about *boundary permeability*, or how open or closed the boundary is supposed to be. This is why a married couple will discuss how and when to reveal that they are expecting a baby. Partners also need to negotiate rules about *boundary linkage*, which involves an agreement about who is in and who is out. In other words, who is included within our boundary, and who is not. So, for example, the couple may agree that their parents can be told about the pregnancy, but no one else. Third, partners must negotiate *boundary ownership*, or the rights and responsibilities of the co-owners. This is a clear concern when you tell someone something and then swear him to secrecy.

Often boundary rules are clear. Other times, however, partners may not have shared rules, or the rules are ambiguous. Sometimes, too, partners deliberately violate the rules. Gossiping about something you know is private is a good example of this type of violation. When this occurs, sanctions may be invoked. For example, you may be reluctant to reveal future private information to a person who violated your rules of privacy. Petronio refers to these moments of fuzzy, unshared, or violated boundary rules as *boundary turbulence*. Such turbulence is frequently the source of conflict and presents the need for stronger or more careful action in establishing or changing the rules.

Boundary Management in the Family.   Mary Anne Fitzpatrick is a well-recognized researcher on family communication. Her extensive studies have led to a theory of marriage types and family communication.[39] Fitzpatrick's research is based on the work of David Kantor and William Lehr, who argue that marriages can be characterized by how the partners use their space, time, and energy and the extent to which they express feelings, exert power, and share a common philosophy of marriage.[40]

Fitzpatrick administered a large number of questionnaires on these topics to almost 1,500

married persons. Fitzpatrick discovered that these items measured three basic factors—ideology, interdependence, and conflict. *Ideology* is a variable involving conventional versus nonconventional notions of family. *Interdependence* is a variable reflecting dependence versus autonomy in a marriage. *Conflict* deals with the amount of disagreement or clash in the marriage. Although she did not frame her work in these terms, Fitzpatrick's findings cast light on the various ways in which families manage their boundaries.

Fitzpatrick discovered that married couples tend to cluster into three distinct groups along the above dimensions. Specifically, she found three types of marriages—the traditionals, the independents, and the separates. The *traditionals* tend to be conventional in their views of marriage and place more value on stability and certainty in role relations than on variety and spontaneity. They have strong interdependence and share much companionship. Although they are not assertive about disagreement, they do not avoid conflict.

A traditional wife, for example, would take her husband's name. Traditional couples would probably oppose infidelity, and they would share much time and space. They would try to work out a standard time schedule and spend as much time together as possible, and they probably would not have separate rooms for their own activities.

There is not too much conflict in a traditional marriage because power and decision making are distributed according to customary norms. Husbands, for example, may be in charge of certain kinds of decisions and wives in charge of others. Consequently, there is little need to negotiate and resolve conflict in these marriages. At the same time, there is little impetus for change and growth in the relationship. A traditional couple can be assertive with each other when necessary, but each person tends to support his or her requests with appeals to the relationship rather than by refuting each other's arguments.

Traditional couples are highly expressive and disclose both joy and frustration. The communication in this kind of family seems to encourage

---

39   Mary Anne Fitzpatrick, *Between Husbands and Wives: Communication in Marriage* (Newbury Park, CA: Sage, 1988). For updates on the theory, see Mary Anne Fitzpatrick, "Interpersonal Communication on the Starship Enterprise: Resilience, Stability, and Change in Relationships in the Twenty-First Century," in *Communication: Views from the Helm in the 21st Century*, ed. Judith S. Trent (Boston: Allyn & Bacon, 1998), pp. 41–46.
40   David Kantor and William Lehr, *Inside the Family* (New York: Harper & Row, 1975).

expression of feelings, even from men. They send many positive nonverbal cues and seem supportive of each other.

The second type of marriage is *independent*. These individuals tend to be unconventional in their views of marriage and do not rely on each other much. Although they may spend time together and share a great deal, they value their own autonomy and often have separate rooms in the house. They may also have separate interests and friends outside the family.

Because they do not rely on conventional roles, the relationship is constantly renegotiated. Because of their individuality, there is much conflict in a typical independent marriage, and partners often vie for power, use a variety of persuasive techniques, and are not reluctant to refute each other's arguments. Like the traditionals, the independents are also expressive. They respond to each other's nonverbal cues, and they usually understand each other well.

The third type of marriage is the *separates*. These individuals seem to be ambivalent about their roles and relationship. They may have a fairly conventional view of marriage, but they are not very interdependent and do not share much. For this reason, Fitzpatrick refers to separates as "emotionally divorced." They have their opinions and can be contentious, but conflicts never last long because separates are quick to retreat from conflict. Actually, they do not seem able to coordinate their actions long enough to sustain a conflict. Their attempts to gain compliance rarely use relationship appeals and often mention the bad things that will happen if the spouse does not comply.

Separates have a watchful attitude. They ask many questions but offer little advice. Predictably, then, they are not very expressive, and they do not understand their partners' emotions very well.

About 60 percent of the couples Fitzpatrick has tested fall into one of these categories. In these cases the husband and wife agreed sufficiently in their questionnaire answers to classify themselves as purely traditional, independent, or separate. Obviously, spouses will not always agree, how-

ever, and a substantial number of Fitzpatrick's subjects did not. These couples are considered to be mixed, including the combinations of separate-traditional, traditional-independent, or independent-separate. The characterization of mixed types is naturally more complex.

This typology usefully classifies marriages into the pure and mixed types. Couples in different types of marriages have different patterns of interaction, and the categories reflect the way individuals in our culture think about marriage.[41] Thus, besides being marriage types, the categories of traditional, independent, and separate are cognitive schemas with which individuals understand marriage and all that it includes. When both partners have the same schema, they share a way of understanding, and they clearly fit one of the types. When the partners do not have the same schema, they are obviously mixed in type. These schemas are used to understand your relationship with your spouse; they are used to guide your actions in relating and interacting with your husband or wife and guide how you understand your entire family system.

Fitzpatrick and her colleagues have found various ways in which these types of families orient to communication and boundary management. The first is *conformity*, a set of way of thinking that encourages similarity of belief. Some families are high in conformity orientation, and other families are lower in this dimension. The second orientation is *conversation*, which encourages all family members to participate freely in spontaneous discussions. Again, this dimension is a variable with some families being high in conversation and others being lower.

If you put the two dimensions of conformity and conversation together, you come up with four modes of communication within families. The first is *consensual*, or high in both confor-

---

41   This point is developed in Fitzpatrick, *Husbands and Wives*, pp. 255–256; Nancy A. Burrell and Mary Anne Fitzpatrick, "The Psychological Reality of Marital Conflict," in *Intimates in Conflict: A Communication Perspective*, ed. D. D. Cahn (Hillsdale, NJ: Erlbaum, 1990), pp. 167–186; and Mary Anne Fitzpatrick and L. David Ritchie, "Communication Schemata Within the Family: Multiple Perspectives on Family Interaction," *Human Communication Research* 20 (1994): 275–301.

mity and conversation. This form of communication is characterized by exploration of new ideas in a way that does not disturb the family's consensual patterns of decision making. Husbands and wives in these families tend to be traditionals. The second type of communication is *pluralistic*, implying that family members communicate openly in a way that fosters independent ideas. The parents in such families tend to be independents. The third mode of communication is *protective*, which emphasizes obedience with little exploration of ideas. The children in protective families tend to be easily influenced by authorities, and their parents tend to be of the separate type. Finally, there is *laissez-faire* communication, marked by lack of involvement and detachment among family members. Children in these families are apt to identify more with external social groups, and the mother and father are probably of a mixed type, most likely separate/independent.

Are all of these forms of communication and marriage types equally positive? Fitzpatrick now believes that they are not. Although different family patterns work well for different people, mixed and laissez-faire families probably tend to be dysfunctional.

Managing Conflict

Virtually all of the theories presented in this chapter deal with conflict in one form or another. Indeed, relational communication itself is largely a process managing difference, and conflict has been a popular topic in the literature.[42] If we take a relational perspective, we can gain a rich and complex view of the nature of conflict. Conflict may involve issues of control, managing dialectical tensions, facework, culture, and boundary management. It may also involve competing goals. In this section we look at two theories that address how people respond or act in conflict situations.

Game Theory. Game theory was developed many years ago by John von Neumann and Oskar Morgenstern as a tool to study economic

behavior and has since provided a base for popular research tools in a variety of disciplines.[43] For researchers studying the processes of decision making and goal competition, game theory provides a useful approach, and it has been used extensively to study conflict. Although not prevalent in the communication field today, it is historically important and is included in this book because of its impact and perspective.

Game theory itself is not a relational communication theory, although it has implications for relationships. Because game research involves the moves and countermoves of individuals, it is potentially useful in this area, as we will see.

Games consist of structured situations where players take turns making choices that lead to payoffs. In all games the rational decision-making process is stressed. The question is how players behave in order to gain rewards. Types of games vary in several ways, including the amount of information provided to players, the amount of communication permitted between them, and the extent of cooperation versus competition built into the payoff matrix.

Because game theory stresses rational decision making, it involves games of strategy. In such games a player makes moves (choices) that lead to rewards or punishments based on the moves of others. The object is to maximize gains and minimize losses.

For example, suppose that you and your spouse were having a disagreement about where to take your vacation; you would probably try to get your way. You might make a variety of moves, such as calling the travel agent, talking

42   A number of reviews are available. See, for example, Dudley D. Cahn, ed., *Intimates in Conflict: A Communication Perspective* (Hillsdale, NJ: Erlbaum, 1990); Michael E. Roloff, "Communication and Conflict," in *Handbook of Communication Science*, eds. C. E. Berger and S. H. Chaffee (Newbury Park, CA: Sage, 1987), pp. 484–536; Alan Sillars and Judith Weisberg, "Conflict as a Social Skill," in *Interpersonal Processes: New Directions in Communication Research*, eds. M. E. Roloff and G. R. Miller (Newbury Park, CA: Sage, 1987), pp. 140–171; Joyce Frost and William Wilmot, *Interpersonal Conflict* (Dubuque, IA: Brown, 1978).
43   John von Neumann and Oskar Morgenstern, *The Theory of Games and Economic Behavior* (Princeton, NJ: Princeton University Press, 1944). Numerous secondary sources are also available. See, for example, Morton Davis, *Game Theory: A Non-technical Introduction* (New York: Basic, 1970).

with friends, buying clothes, and discussing your preference with your partner. Each move is designed to win, to get the vacation you want. If you do, you have won, and your partner has lost.

One of the most commonly used games is the *prisoner's dilemma*.[44] This simple game is useful because it illustrates a number of salient features of games in general. Also, it is interesting as a *mixed-motive game* because players can cooperate or compete, and genuine reasons are present for doing either.

Here is the prisoner's dilemma: You and an accomplice are arrested for a crime. After being separated, each of you must choose whether to confess or not. If you confess and your accomplice does not, you will be allowed to go free, and your testimony will send the other person to prison for twenty years. If you both confess, both will be sent to prison for five years. If neither confesses, both of you will go to prison for one year on a lesser charge. Figure 12.1 illustrates the choices.

With no communication between you and your accomplice, the two of you will not know the choice of the other. Each is in a dilemma about whether to trust and cooperate with the other prisoner by remaining silent or to compete with the other prisoner by confessing. If both of you are willing to cooperate by not confessing, the long-term payoff is maximized for both. But if one does not cooperate, the other cannot cooperate. Over several trials, most people will move ultimately toward the noncooperative strategy.

Although our earlier vacation example appears to be a win-win conflict, this kind of situation is usually not so simple; it is most often a mixed-motive conflict such as the prisoner's dilemma. You can either compete to get your way, or you can cooperate and come up with a vacation spot that suits both of you. If you compete and win, you will presumably enjoy your vacation more (although your partner will enjoy it less). If you cooperate and compromise, you will

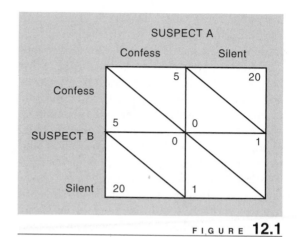

FIGURE 12.1

Prisoner's Dilemma

still have a good time. Will you cooperate or compete? That is the question of a mixed-motive game.

Thomas Steinfatt and Gerald Miller reviewed the literature in which games were used to investigate the process of communication in conflict. Using games as an analogue, they list three ways parties in conflict come to assess each other's strategies. The first way is to observe the opponent's moves over several trials. In games such as the prisoner's dilemma, subjects play through a number of trials of the game. Typically, a player will observe the opponent's moves and decide what to do next. So, for example, if your partner goes out and buys beach clothes, you know that he is serious about going to the coast. So you go out and buy hiking boots to show that you are serious about going into the mountain wilderness.

The second way of assessing strategy is to observe the total conflict situation. In so doing a player makes inferences from the situation to the opponent's strategy. The player would study the game matrix and try to guess what the opponent's strategy is likely to be. Having gone on many vacations with your spouse, you try to figure out what he likes and what he will do to get to go where he wants.

The third approach is direct communication. The authors point out,

44   This game is explained in Davis, *Game Theory*, pp. 93–107. This book is an excellent source of real-world analogues for many types of games.

Ideally, communication makes it possible to conduct the entire conflict at the symbolic level, with each player stating how he would respond to the stated, rather than the actual, moves of the other. . . . Besides avoiding the hostility, disruption, and subsequent losses resulting from actual moves, negotiations allow the parties to move away from a winner-take-all position toward a solution that provides some rewards for everyone.[45]

If the players in the prisoner's dilemma game could communicate and agree to cooperate, both would receive lesser sentences. Similarly, if you just sat down and talked about your vacation, you would probably realize that there is a spot that both of you would like to visit. Diplomacy in international relations is considered superior to war because the parties can try to work out their differences by talking rather than killing.

Direct communication has three advantages. The first point is that communication is symbolic and does not have the actual consequence of the real move. Thus, communication is a way to try out an idea rather than doing something that you may later regret. Second, communication changes the probability of moves and may reduce the amount of competitiveness on the part of the conflicting parties. So, for example, if your husband tells you why he wants to go to the beach, you may be more understanding and less inclined to block his decision. Third, communication may result in changing the other person's orientations toward the problem. In other words, you may directly persuade him or her and change what he or she wants to do.

By communicating, then, the parties may reduce their own tendencies to behave chauvinistically. In fact, studies have shown that this is what tends to happen. Pregame discussions increase cooperation. The greatest effect occurs when communication exists from the beginning of the conflict. Studies also show that the fuller the communication, the more open the channels, and the greater the resultant cooperation.

Mixed-motive games are designed to study competitive and cooperative behavior. Since the original game-oriented work was done, scholars have taken a more discriminating look at the various ways that people orient to conflict, as the following theory illustrates.

An Attribution Theory of Conflict. Recall from Chapter 7 that attribution theory deals with the ways people infer the causes of behavior. The premise of this approach to conflict is that people develop their own theories to explain the conflicts they are involved with, and these theories are largely a product of their attributions. In other words, how you deal with a conflict depends on how you place blame. Alan Sillars has developed a theory of conflict based on this idea.[46] Sillars' theory is included here because it integrates a great deal of mainstream work in conflict communication, codifies many types of conflict behavior, and provides a level of explanation rarely found in conflict theories.

According to Sillars, three general strategies of conflict resolution are seen in interpersonal relationships. These include strategies designed to avoid or minimize conflict, those that aim to win in a conflict, and those that attempt to achieve mutual positive outcomes for both parties. Sillars has refined his scheme over the years and refers to these categories simply as avoidance behaviors, competitive behaviors, and cooperative behaviors.

Avoidance behaviors employ no communication or, at best, indirect communication. *Competitive behaviors* involve negative messages, and *cooperative behaviors* entail more open and positive communication. Table 12.2 illustrates a variety of strategies found by Sillars in his research.[47]

45 Thomas Steinfatt and Gerald Miller, "Communication in Game Theoretic Models of Conflict," in *Perspectives on Communication in Conflict*, eds. G. R. Miller and H. Simons (Englewood Cliffs, NJ: Prentice-Hall, 1974), pp. 14–75.
46 Alan L. Sillars, Stephen F. Coletti, Doug Parry, and Mark A. Rogers, "Coding Verbal Conflict Tactics: Nonverbal and Perceptual Correlates of the 'Avoidance-Distributive-Integrative' Distinction," *Human Communication Research* 9 (1982): 83–95; Alan L. Sillars, "Attributions and Communication in Roommate Conflicts," *Communication Monographs* 47 (1980): 180–200; "The Sequential and Distributional Structure of Conflict Interaction as a Function of Attributions Concerning the Locus of Responsibility and Stability of Conflict," in *Communication Yearbook 4*, ed. D. Nimmo (New Brunswick, NJ: Transaction, 1980), pp. 217–236.
47 Alan L. Sillars, *Manual for Coding Interpersonal Conflict* (unpublished manuscript, Department of Communication, University of Montana, 1986).

Conflict Management Coding Scheme

Avoidance Behaviors

Denial and Equivocation

1. *Direct denial.* Person explicitly denies a conflict is present.
2. *Implicit denial.* Statements that imply denial by providing a rationale for a denial statement, although the denial is not explicit.
3. *Evasive remark.* Failure to acknowledge or deny the presence of a conflict following a statement or inquiry about the conflict by the partner.

Topic Management

4. *Topic shifts.* A break in the natural flow of discussion that directs the topic focus away from discussion of the issue as it applies to the immediate parties. Do not count topic shifts that occur after the discussion appears to have reached a natural culmination.
5. *Topic avoidance.* Statements that explicitly terminate the discussion of a conflict issue before it has been fully discussed.

Noncommittal Remarks

6. *Abstract remarks.* Abstract principles, generalizations, or hypothetical statements. Speaking about the issue on a high level of abstraction. No reference is made to the actual state of affairs between the immediate parties.
7. *Noncommittal statements.* Statements that neither affirm nor deny the presence of a conflict and that are not evasive replies or topic shifts.
8. *Noncommittal questions.* Unfocused questions or those that rephrase the questions given by the researcher.
9. *Procedural remarks.* Procedural statements that supplant discussion of the conflict.

Irreverent Remarks

10. *Joking.* Nonhostile joking that interrupts or supplements serious consideration of the issue.

Cooperative Behaviors

Analytic Remarks

1. *Description.* Nonevaluative, nonblaming, factual description of the nature and extent of the problem.
2. *Qualification.* Discussion explicitly limits the nature and extent of the problem by tying the issue to specific behavioral events.

3. *Disclosure.* Providing "nonobservable" information: i.e., information about thoughts, feelings, intentions, causes of behavior, or past experience relevant to the issue that the partner would not have the opportunity to observe.
4. *Soliciting disclosure.* Asking specifically for information concerning the other that the person himself or herself would not have the opportunity to observe (i.e., thoughts, feelings, intentions, causes of behavior, experiences).
5. *Soliciting criticism.* Nonhostile questions soliciting criticism of oneself.

Conciliatory Remarks

6. *Empathy or support.* Expressing understanding, support, or acceptance of the other person or commenting on the other's positive characteristics or shared interests, goals, and compatibilities.
7. *Concessions.* Statements that express a willingness to change, show flexibility, make concessions, or consider mutually acceptable solutions to conflict.
8. *Accepting responsibility.* Statements that attribute some causality for the problem to oneself.

Competitive Behaviors

Confrontative Remarks

1. *Personal criticism.* Stating or implying a negative evaluation of the partner.
2. *Rejection.* Rejecting the partner's opinions in a way that implies personal rejecting as well as disagreement.
3. *Hostile imperatives.* Threats, demands, arguments, or other prescriptive statements that implicitly blame the partner and seek change in the partner's behavior.
4. *Hostile questioning.* Questions that fault or blame the other person.
5. *Hostile joking or sarcasm.* Joking or teasing that is used to fault the other person.
6. *Presumptive attribution.* Attributing thoughts, feelings, intentions, and causes to the partner that the partner does not acknowledge. This code is the opposite of "soliciting disclosure."
7. *Denial of responsibility.* Statements that deny or minimize personal responsibility for the conflict.

As an example of how people use these different strategies in interpersonal conflicts, consider a study by Sillars and his colleagues on conflict in marriage.[48] In this study the researchers solicited the cooperation of forty married couples. Each couple was given a kit to take home, consisting of a set of questionnaires for each spouse, a list of ten potential conflict areas, and an audiotape. Each couple was told to answer the questions separately and to seal them in an envelope before proceeding with the rest of the protocol. Then, the couple was to discuss each of the ten topics and to tape their discussions. The topics included such things as work pressures, lack of affection, how to spend leisure time, and child discipline.

The couples also completed a marital adjustment scale and Fitzpatrick's measure of marital types (discussed above). One objective of the study was to see how well-adjusted couples in each of Fitzpatrick's categories differed from less well-adjusted couples in their conflict communication. The tape recordings were analyzed in terms of the amount of apparent conflict and the various types of strategies used by the couple in their discussion.

The investigators discovered that in all marriage types, more satisfied couples used a more positive tone of voice than less satisfied couples. Separates tended to be avoiders: They maintained a fairly neutral tone and kept their discussions of conflict areas to a minimum. The satisfied separates tended to be even more extreme in this regard. The independents, whether satisfied with their marriage or not, tended to express negative feelings. The more satisfied members of the independent category tended to use more description and self-disclosure than did the less satisfied members of this group. Finally, there was little difference between the satisfied and nonsatisfied traditionals in the sample.

Perhaps Sillars' most important contribution is his use of attribution theory to explain conflict

behavior. Recall from Chapter 7 that attributions are inferences made about the causes of behavior. One may make inferences about the causes of some effect, a disposition or trait of another person or oneself, or a predicted outcome of a situation. Whenever people try to explain an event by making inferences, attribution is involved.

Sillars believes that in at least three ways attributions are important determinants of the definition and outcome of conflicts. First, individuals' attributions in a conflict determine what sorts of strategies they will choose to deal with the conflict. This is true not only because one's reactions and feelings are colored by their attributions but also because future expectations are formed largely as a result of what has gone on in the past. If, for example, you were to see a partner as cooperative, you would probably choose a cooperative strategy, but if you saw this person as competitive, you would probably use a competitive one.

Your assessment of responsibility is also important: If you thought you were to blame, you would probably be more cooperative, but if you thought the other communicator were responsible, you would probably be more competitive. Also if you thought your partner had certain negative personality traits, you would be less likely to cooperate.

Second, biases in the attribution process discourage the use of integrative strategies. These include a tendency to see others as personally responsible for negative events and to see oneself as merely responding to circumstances. People tend to believe that others cause conflict because of bad intentions, lack of consideration, competitiveness, or inadequacy, but people tend to see their own behavior as merely responding to the provocations of others.

Third, the strategy chosen affects the outcome of the conflict. Cooperative strategies encourage integrative solutions and information exchange. Competitive strategies escalate the conflict and may lead to less satisfying solutions.

We have just touched on the work related to communication and conflict, and you can see that it is an important part of the literature of

48   Alan L. Sillars, Gary R. Pike, Tricia S. Jones, and Kathleen Redmon, "Communication and Conflict in Marriage," in *Communication Yearbook 7*, ed. R. Bostrom (Beverly Hills, CA: Sage, 1983), pp. 414–429.

relationships. Most important from the standpoint of communication theory is that communication is an integral part of the creation and management of interpersonal conflict.

● COMMENTARY AND CRITIQUE

In this chapter we have taken a brief look at some of the most significant theorizing in interpersonal communication. Many of the theories discussed here have been immensely popular and influential. Most focus on the interactive and relational nature of interpersonal communication. De-emphasizing individual traits and personal behavior distinguishes this body of theory from the more cognitive theories of message presentation and reception covered in Chapters 6 and 7. Cognitive theories are psychological in orientation, explaining communication differences in terms of individual variables such as traits, behaviors, or cognitive structures. Relational theories are more interactional in looking at what goes on between communicators rather than within them.

Not all theories in this chapter are strictly relational in this sense, however. There is still a presumption among many researchers in this field that interpersonal communication is primarily psychological, or individual. Leslie Baxter calls this the "hegemonic status [of] psychologically oriented work."[49] For example, uncertainty reduction theory is basically psychological because it concentrates on what individuals do, albeit in response to other individuals. Even Fitzpatrick's theory of marriage types, although it appears to be relational on the surface, is based mostly on the individual perceptions of marriage partners. So, too, for face-negotiation theory. In many ways, this is merely a typology of cultural and individual traits and their associated face behaviors with little, if any, attention to the relational dynamics in which facework is actually done.

There is a tendency in many individualistic theories to be overly rational. Social exchange theory and game theory, for example, see rela-

tionships as a sequence of moves motivated by personal gain. Research in game theory and social exchange theory examines the choices people make in response to different reward and cost contingencies, using points or tokens as game outcomes, but we are not at all sure whether social rewards work in this way.[50] These theories assume that people behave rationally in making decisions and that they always want to maximize positive outcomes. However, establishing exactly what outcomes people are seeking in social life is not always simple. How people behave in real social conflict depends in part on their self-concept, motives, mental health, individual life goals, and an array of other complex factors. Steinfatt and Miller crystallize this objection: "In the daily political, economic, and social conflicts we all face, mutually advantageous solutions are seldom this sharply defined, and in seeking an acceptable solution, communication serves a myriad of cognitive and affective functions."[51]

Nothing is inherently wrong with individualistic analysis, but it fails to capture important interactional dimensions of the relationship, such as conflict, control, power, mutual definition, and social meaning. Baxter expresses the difficulty of psychological theorizing in these terms:

> [Psychological] theories share the assumption that relationship dynamics can be explained adequately by understanding the individuals who comprise the relationship. Theoretical frustration with this atomistic orientation is a frequently expressed complaint in the relationship communication literature; however, the relationships field still displays a paucity of genuine relationship-level theories.[52]

---

49   Leslie A. Baxter, "Locating the Social in Interpersonal Communication," in *Communication: Views from the Helm for the 21st Century*, ed. Judith S. Trent (Boston: Allyn & Bacon, 1998), p. 60.

50   John L. LaGaipa, "Interpersonal Attraction and Social Exchange," in *Theory and Practice in Interpersonal Attraction*, ed. S. Duck (New York: Academic, 1971), pp. 129–164.

51   Steinfatt and Miller, "Communication," p. 70. For an excellent debate on the value of game theory in communication research, see Robert Bostrom, "Game Theory in Communication Research," *Journal of Communication* 18 (1968): 369–388; and Thomas Beisecker, "Game Theory in Communication Research: A Rejoinder and a Re-orientation," *Journal of Communication* 20 (1970): 107–120.

52   Leslie A. Baxter, "A Dialectical Perspective on Communication Strategies in Relationship Development," in *Handbook of Personal Relationships*, ed. S. Duck (New York: Wiley, 1988), p. 258.

The original work of the Palo Alto Group is an example of the interactionist thinking that relational theory strives to accomplish. The notion that communication patterns define relationships has been and remains its central idea. This idea is what makes the research of Millar and Rogers so interesting and important; it examines not individual messages but pairs of messages in response to each other.

Most relational theories focus on face-to-face interaction patterns and the ways the relationship is shaped by these patterns. On the surface much relational communication theory may imply that interaction leads to simple and clear patterns, which in turn create discernible relationship types. Relationships are seen as complementary or symmetrical, control patterns are well defined, and marriages can be typed.

But such clarity is not always found. In her interviews, for example, Baxter found "contradictions, contingencies, nonrationalities, and multiple realities to which people gave voice in their narrative sense-making of their relational lives."[53] Relationships are, in fact, complicated, and relational partners have difficult issues to work through and balance in their lives.[54] Rather than trying to discover types or patterns, then, perhaps it would be more productive to seek the processes by which contradictions and complexities are worked out. This is one of the advantages of the dialectical approach, followed by Baxter, Rawlins, Burgoon, Petronio, and others.

Another problem with a strict focus on interactionist patterns is that it distracts us from the interpretations and understandings that partners construct in their interaction. Despite all their talk about how communication is used to define the nature of a relationship within a system, original relational theorists from the Palo Alto Group and disciples like Millar and Rogers essentially ignore the definitions of the relationship held by the participants themselves, making much of this theory ironically behavioristic.[55]

The research in this tradition often deals with observable behavior, and the coding is done from the perspective of the outside observer, not from within the relationship. Although interaction analysis is powerful in detecting patterns of

behavior, it tells us little about what those patterns mean to the participants themselves. Here is where the later work by researchers like Fitzpatrick, Rawlins, Baxter, and Sillars fills the gap.

Even these researchers, however, ignore yet another aspect of relationships that could and, according to some recent thinkers, should be addressed in this literature. It is one thing to concentrate on observable behavioral patterns, as most of the theories in this chapter do, or meanings, as other theories do. It is quite another to look at the unintended and largely unconscious social outcomes of relational patterns.

A recent critique of this literature calls for a critical investigation of the power arrangements that relational patterns establish, including ideological domination.[56] The problem here is really twofold: It involves the failure to acknowledge the ideology of interpersonal relationships and that of the methods used to study them.

Like most investigators not affiliated with the critical tradition, interpersonal researchers tend to assume they are studying processes of some universality. But critics point out that the kinds of social arrangements studied by relationship theorists have not always existed and do not always appear. They are historical products, and the methods employed in the study of relationships themselves contribute to the construction of these historically based arrangements.[57] This outcome is inevitable but needs to be

53   Leslie A. Baxter, "Interpersonal Communication as Dialogue: A Response to the 'Social Approaches' Forum," *Communication Theory* 2 (1992): 330.
54   Baxter, "Locating the Social"; Judith K. Burgoon, "It Takes Two to Tango: Interpersonal Adaptation and Implications for Relational Communication, " in *Communication: Views from the Helm for the 21st Century,* ed. Judith S. Trent (Boston: Allyn & Bacon, 1998), pp. 53–59.
55   Edna Rogers herself discusses this problem in "Analyzing Relational Communication: Implications of a Pragmatic Approach" (paper delivered at the annual conference of the Speech Communication Association, Washington, DC, November 1983).
56   John W. Lannamann, "Interpersonal Communication Research as Ideological Practice," *Communication Theory* 1 (1991): 179–203; John W. Lannamann, "Deconstructing the Person and Changing the Subject of Interpersonal Studies," *Communication Theory* 2 (1992): 139–148.
57   Kristine L. Fitch, "Culture, Ideology, and Interpersonal Communication Research," *Communication Yearbook 17,* ed. Stanley A. Deetz (Thousand Oaks, CA: Sage, 1994), pp. 104–135; Lannamann, "Interpersonal Communication"; Timothy Stephen and Teresa M. Harrison, "Interpersonal Communication, Theory, and History," *Communication Theory* 3 (1993): 163–171.

acknowledged, especially the power arrangements that accrue from it. This idea was explored in some detail in Chapter 11, and we will not belabor it here, except to note that the critique of communication now extends beyond media and organizational structures to interpersonal relationships.

Another aspect of relationships that is deemphasized by certain theories involves the mechanisms that provide relational continuity—processes that do not always involve face-to-face interaction. In addition to observable interaction behavior, there seems to be a kind of interaction-in-imagination that allows relationships to continue, even when the partners are absent from one another. Stuart Sigman suggests a number of ways this continuity occurs and proposes more investigation into this issue.[58]

Another difficulty in relational communication theory is conceptual confusion. The very term *communication,* for example, is fuzzy in much of this literature. Watzlawick, Beavin, and Jackson's first axiom—that you cannot not communicate—has been widely confusing.[59] There is confusion too about the report and command functions, or metacommunication.[60] One critical treatment calls the concept "muddled and confusing."[61] The problem is that the Palo Alto Group, at different points in their writing, imply as many as three different meanings for *metacommunication.* (The use of other terms, such as *command message* and *relational message,* does not help in this regard.) At points *metacommunication* refers to a verbal or nonverbal classification of the content message, in which one's partner guides the coding of the content. At other times *metacommunication* refers to nonverbal statements about the relationship itself, such as control. Or, the term sometimes refers to explicit discussion by individuals about the nature of their relationship. To make matters worse, metacommunication has been treated alternatively as

strictly analogic, analogic and digital, nonverbal, and both verbal and nonverbal.

An important contribution of most of the theories in this chapter is their process-oriented, developmental focus. Development is difficult to study, and it is tempting to oversimplify the process of relational definition and development. Theories therefore often assume a single trajectory or a single set of processes without discriminating among types of relationships or variability among relationships. For example, social penetration theory's originally assumed linear trajectory is really too orderly, as several more recent theorists have pointed out.[62] Different relationships may have different processes operating, and we cannot assume that cost-reward operates in each phase of a relationship.[63]

Relational communication theory is an immensely interesting, important, and challenging field of study. We see in the theories established to date noble efforts to advance our understanding of one of the most difficult aspects of human life, and although any single theory leaves many questions unanswered, as a group they provide a great deal of insight.

---

58   Stuart J. Sigman, "Handling the Discontinuous Aspects of Continuous Social Relationships: Toward Research on the Persistence of Social Forms," *Communication Theory* 1 (1991): 106–127.
59   See Motley, "On Whether."
60   This problem is discussed by William Wilmot, "Metacommunication: A Re-examination and Extension," in *Communication Yearbook 4,* ed. D. Nimmo (New Brunswick, NJ: Transaction, 1980), pp. 61–69.
61   Arthur Bochner and Dorothy Krueger, "Interpersonal Communication Theory and Research: An Overview of Inscrutable Epistemologies and Muddled Concepts," in *Communication Yearbook 3,* ed. D. Nimmo (New Brunswick, NJ: Transaction, 1979), p. 203.
62   In addition to the earlier citations in this chapter, see James L. Applegate and Gregory B. Leichty, "Managing Interpersonal Relationships: Social Cognitive and Strategic Determinants of Competence," in *Competence in Communication: A Multi-Disciplinary Approach,* ed. R. N. Bostrom (Beverly Hills, CA: Sage, 1984), p. 39.
63   Arthur P. Bochner, "The Functions of Human Communicating in Interpersonal Bonding," in *Handbook of Rhetorical and Communicating Theory,* eds. Carroll C. Arnold and John Waite Bowers (Boston: Allyn & Bacon, 1984), p. 579.

C H A P T E R **13**

COMMUNICATION IN GROUP DECISION MAKING

Small-group communication has long been an important topic in the communication field.[1] By far, the most important theme associated with this subject in communication research and theory has been decision making. In this chapter we look at some of the most interesting and insightful theories related to this central motif.

Contemporary research and theory in group communication stem from a variety of early twentieth-century sources.[2] One such source was the work of Mary Parker Follett on integrative thinking.[3] Follett wrote in 1924 that group, organizational, and community problem solving is a creative threefold process of (1) gathering information from experts, (2) testing that information in everyday experience, and (3) developing integrative solutions that meet a variety of interests rather than competing among interests. Dealing with problems and conflicts through discussion gained general acceptance in twentieth-century American thought.

Another major influence on current theories was the group-discussion movement in the field

of speech.[4] Here, students were taught how to converse productively with others, a concern still popular in high school and college speech

---

1   A number of sources on small groups reflect the breadth of work in this area. See, for example, Lawrence R. Frey, ed., *The Handbook of Group Communication Theory and Research* (Thousand Oaks, CA: Sage, 1999); Randy Hirokawa, Abran J. Salazar, Larry Erbert, and Richard J. Ice, "Small Group Communication," in *An Integrated Approach to Communication Theory and Research*, eds. Michael B. Salwen and Don W. Stacks (Mahwah, NJ: Erlbaum, 1996), pp. 359–382; John F. Cragan and David W. Wright, "Small Group Communication Research of the 1980s: A Synthesis and Critique," *Communication Studies* 41 (1990): 212–236; Marshall Scott Poole, "Do We Have Any Theories of Group Communication?" *Communication Studies* 41 (1990): 237–247.
2   For historical overviews of theory development, see Dennis S. Gouran, "Communication in Groups: The Emergence and Evolution of a Field of Study," in *The Handbook of Group Communication Theory and Research*, ed. Lawrence R. Frey (Thousand Oaks, CA: Sage, 1999), pp. 3–36; and Dennis S. Gouran, Randy Y. Hirokawa, Michael Calvin McGee, and Laurie L. Miller, "Communication in Groups: Research Trends and Theoretical Perspectives," in *Building Communication Theories: A Socio/Cultural Approach*, ed. Fred L. Casmir (Hillsdale, NJ: Erlbaum, 1994), pp. 241–268.
3   Mary Parker Follett, *Creative Experience* (New York: Longmans, Green, 1924).
4   For a brief summary of this work, see Dennis S. Gouran, "The Paradigm of Unfulfilled Promise: A Critical Examination of the History of Research on Small Groups in Speech Communication," in *Speech Communication in the 20th Century*, ed. T. W. Benson (Carbondale: Southern Illinois University Press, 1985), p. 90.

communication curricula. A third source of current group-communication theory has been the tremendous body of group dynamics research in social psychology.

Most of the research over the years has followed an input-process-output model.[5] This model segments the group experience into the factors that affect the group (input), the happenings within the group (process), and the results (output). For example, a study might examine the effects of heterogeneity of group members (input variable) on the amount of talking in a group and the effect of interaction patterns (process variables) on member satisfaction (output variable).

THE INPUT-PROCESS-OUTPUT MODEL

A General Organizing Model

Figure 13.1 is the model of Barry Collins and Harold Guetzkow.[6] This simple model captures the major themes of research on task groups, and it illustrates the input-process-output approach very well.

This model shows that a task group is confronted with two types of problems—task and interpersonal obstacles. *Task obstacles* are the difficulties encountered by the group in tackling its assignment, such as planning an event or approving a policy. Group members deal directly with the problem. They analyze the situation, suggest possible solutions, and weigh alternatives.

Decision making in a group is different from individual problem solving because of interpersonal relations. Whenever two or more people come together to handle a problem, *interpersonal obstacles* also arise. Such obstacles include the need to make your ideas clear to others, handle conflict, manage differences, and so forth. Thus, in any group discussion, members will be dealing simultaneously with task and interpersonal obstacles.

The basic distinction between task work and interpersonal relations has been an overriding

concern in the research and theory on small-group communication. Both types of behavior are important in being productive, and any analysis of group problem solving must deal with both.[7]

When task and interpersonal work is integrated effectively, an *assembly effect* occurs in which the group solution or product is superior to the individual work of even the best member. So, for example, if a club meets to plan a picnic and handles its interpersonal relations and task work well, the event should turn out to be better than if it were planned by just one person.

Group rewards can be positive or negative. Successful goal achievement is usually positively rewarding to group members. In addition, the resolution of conflict and successful communication often reap interpersonal rewards. Negative "rewards" will influence the group adversely.

A successfully planned picnic, for instance, is a task reward, and the fun involved in planning it is an interpersonal reward. If the job is well done and enjoyed by the members, their future decision making will be affected in a positive way. If the task was not well done or the members did not handle their differences well, negative feedback may make it more difficult next time.

Groups expend energy. Some of the effort goes to solve task obstacles, and some goes to deal with interpersonal ones. Raymond Cattell uses the term *synergy* for this group effort. The amount of energy devoted to interpersonal hassles is called *intrinsic synergy,* and the remaining energy available for the task is *effective synergy.* If effective synergy is high, the task will

5 This model is discussed by Marshall Scott Poole, David R. Seibold, and Robert D. McPhee, "A Structural Approach to Theory-Building in Group Decision-Making Research," in *Communication and Group Decision-Making,* eds. R. Y. Hirokawa and M. S. Poole (Beverly Hills, CA: Sage, 1986), pp. 238–240. See also Susan Jarboe, "A Comparison of Input-Output, Process-Output, and Input-Process-Output Models of Small Group Problem-Solving Effectiveness," *Communication Monographs* 55 (1988): 121–142.
6 Barry Collins and Harold Guetzkow, *A Social Psychology of Group Processes for Decision-Making* (New York: Wiley, 1964), p. 81.
7 One proposed theory that explains leadership competence in terms of task and interpersonal variables is published in J. Kevin Barge and Randy Y. Hirokawa, "Toward a Communication Competency Model of Group Leadership," *Small Group Behavior* 20 (1989): 167–189.

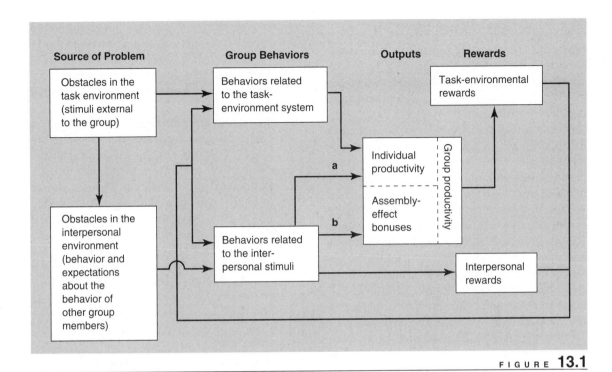

FIGURE **13.1**

A Simple Working Model of Decision-Making Groups

From *A Social Psychology of Group Processes for Decision-Making* by Barry Collins and Harold Guetzkow; John Wiley & Sons, publisher. Used by permission.

be accomplished effectively. If not, it will be done poorly.[8]

The level of synergy in a group results from the attitudes of the members toward one another. Conflict requires that a great deal of energy be devoted to group maintenance, leaving little for task accomplishment. On the other hand, if individuals possess similar attitudes, there is less need for an interpersonal investment, and the effective synergy will be greater.

Suppose that you form a study group for your communication theory class. You discover that the members have varying attitudes toward the subject matter, different levels of motivation, and different styles of studying. In your meetings you waste a lot of time arguing about how to organize your efforts and learn the material. You are frus-

trated by the fact that not everyone is contributing equally to the group effort. All of the hassles around these interpersonal issues constitute its intrinsic synergy. Now assume that after getting your test grade back, you sense that the study group failed to achieve the goal of mutual benefit, and you decide to join another group or study alone. In this case the effective synergy of the group was so low that it did not accomplish more than you could have done by yourself.

But suppose that you join another group that agrees immediately on how to proceed and gets down to work. Because the interpersonal barriers are few, the group is cohesive. The effective synergy is high, and group members do better on the exam than they would have done had they studied alone. Experience in these two groups shows the importance of interpersonal energy (intrinsic synergy) and its relationship to outcome (effective synergy).

---

8   Raymond Cattell, "Concepts and Methods in the Measurement of Group Syntality," *Psychological Review* 55 (1948): 48–63.

The Functional Tradition

Functional theories of group communication view the process as an instrument by which groups make decisions, emphasizing the connection between the quality of communication and the quality of the group's output.[9] Communication does a number of things, or *functions* in a number of ways, in determining group outcome: It is a means of sharing information, it is the way group members explore and identify errors in thinking, and it is a tool of persuasion.

This work has been strongly influenced by the pragmatics of teaching small-group discussion. It is based in large measure on the work of philosopher John Dewey, which, since the publication of *How We Think* in 1910, has greatly influenced twentieth-century pragmatic thought.[10]

Dewey's version of the problem-solving process has six steps: (1) expressing a difficulty, (2) defining the problem, (3) analyzing the problem, (4) suggesting solutions, (5) comparing alternatives and testing them against a set of objectives or criteria, and (6) implementing the best solution. The theories of the functional tradition address the ways communication affects each of these elements.

A General Functional Theory. Randy Hirokawa and his colleagues have been leaders in the functional tradition. Their work looks at a variety of mistakes that groups can make, aiming to identify the kinds of things groups need to take into consideration to become more effective.[11] His description of the group decision-making process essentially mirrors that of Dewey's problem-solving sequence.

Groups normally begin by *identifying and assessing a problem,* and here they deal with a variety of questions: What happened? Why? Who was involved? What harm resulted? Who was hurt? Next, the group *gathers and evaluates information* about the problem. As the group discusses possible solutions, information continues to be gathered.

Next, the group generates a variety of *alternative proposals* for handling the problem and dis-

cusses the *objectives* it wishes to accomplish in solving it. These objectives and alternative proposals are *evaluated*, with the ultimate goal of reaching consensus on a course of action. This general sequence of problem solving is depicted in Figure 13.2.[12]

The factors contributing to faulty decisions are easily inferred from this decision-making process. The first is *improper assessment* of the problem, which stems from inadequate or inaccurate analysis of the situation. The group may fail to see the problem, or it may not accurately identify the causes of the problem. The second source of error in decision making is *inappropriate goals and objectives*. The group may neglect important objectives that ought to be achieved, or it may work toward unnecessary ones. The third problem is *improper assessment of positive and negative qualities,* ignoring certain advantages, disadvantages, or both of various proposals. Or it may overestimate the positive or negative outcomes expected. Fourth, the group may develop an *inadequate information base,* which can happen in several ways. Valid information may be rejected, or invalid information may be accepted. Too little information may be collected, or too much information may cause overload and confusion. Finally, the group may be guilty of *faulty reasoning* from the information base.

---

9   This tradition is discussed by Dennis S. Gouran, Randy Y. Hirokawa, Kelly M. Julian, and Geoff B. Leatham, "The Evolution and Current Status of the Functional Perspective on Communication in Decision-Making and Problem-Solving Groups," in *Communication Yearbook 16,* ed. Stanley A. Deetz (Newbury Park, CA: Sage, 1993), pp. 573–600.
10   John Dewey, *How We Think* (Boston: Heath, 1910).
11   Randy Y. Hirokawa and Dirk R. Scheerhorn, "Communication in Faulty Group Decision-Making," in *Communication and Group Decision-Making,* eds. R. Y. Hirokawa and M. S. Poole (Beverly Hills, CA: Sage, 1986), pp. 63–80; Dennis S. Gouran and Randy Y. Hirokawa, "Counteractive Functions of Communication in Effective Group Decision-Making," in *Communication and Group Decision-Making,* eds. R. Y. Hirokawa and M. S. Poole (Beverly Hills, CA: Sage, 1986), pp. 81–92; Randy Y. Hirokawa, "Group Communication and Problem-Solving Effectiveness I: A Critical Review of Inconsistent Findings," *Communication Quarterly* 30 (1982): 134–141; Randy Y. Hirokawa, "Group Communication and Problem-Solving Effectiveness II," *Western Journal of Speech Communication* 47 (1983): 59–74; Randy Y. Hirokawa, "Group Communication and Problem-Solving Effectiveness: An Investigation of Group Phases," *Human Communication Research* 9 (1983): 291–305.
12   Hirokawa and Scheerhorn, "Faulty Group," p. 66.

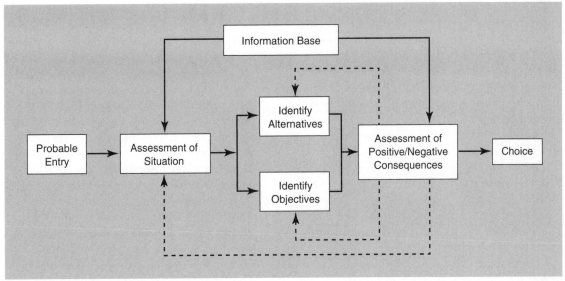

FIGURE **13.2**

General Model of the Group Decision-Making Process

Why do groups fall into these traps? Hirokawa believes that the errors most often arise from the communication in the group. The group is swayed by certain members who unwittingly mislead the group in some way, an outcome that requires someone to counteract it by exerting a positive influence on the group.

As part of his investigations, Hirokawa conducted a study of four aspects of decision quality: appropriate understanding of the problem, appropriate understanding of the objectives and standards of a good decision, appropriate assessment of the positive qualities of alternatives, and appropriate assessment of the negative qualities of alternatives.[13] In his laboratory Hirokawa formed about forty three-person groups and had them discuss what to do about a certain plagiarism case at the university. The discussions were from 17 to 47 minutes in length, and each was videotaped. Two professors experienced in student ethics cases judged the groups' decisions in terms of overall quality, and a panel of judges rated the extent to which each of the four critical elements listed above was fulfilled. Statistical analysis showed that the quality of a group's de-

cision is definitely related to these four elements, and when the very best groups were compared to the very worst, there was a significant difference in the extent to which each was accomplished by the group. Clearly, groups that were more effective in meeting the four functions made better decisions.

Janis' Theory of Groupthink.   The work of Irving Janis and his colleagues has been immensely influential within the functional tradition.[14] Here we will look at one of his theories, most often referred to as the *groupthink hypothesis*.[15]

Janis examines in some detail the adequacy of group decisions. Emphasizing critical thinking, he shows how certain conditions can lead to high group satisfaction but ineffective output.

13   Randy Y. Hirokawa, "Group Communication and Decision Making Performance: A Continued Test of the Functional Perspective," *Human Communication Research* 14 (1988): 487–515.
14   See, for example, Irving Janis and Leon Mann, *Decision Making: A Psychological Analysis of Conflict, Choice, and Commitment* (New York: Free Press, 1977); Irving Janis, *Crucial Decisions: Leadership in Policy Making and Crisis Management* (New York: Free Press, 1989).
15   Irving Janis, *Groupthink: Psychological Studies of Policy Decisions and Fiascoes* (Boston: Houghton Mifflin, 1982).

Groupthink is a direct result of cohesiveness in groups, which was first discussed in some depth by Kurt Lewin in the 1930s and has since come to be seen as a crucial variable in group effectiveness.[16] *Cohesiveness* is the degree of mutual interest among members. In a highly cohesive group, a strong mutual identification keeps a group together.

Cohesiveness is a result of the degree to which all members perceive that their goals can be met within the group. This does not require that the members have similar attitudes but that members are interdependent and rely on one another to achieve certain mutually desired goals. The more cohesive a group, the more pressure it exerts on the members.

Cohesiveness can be a good thing because it brings the members together and enhances the group's interpersonal relationships. Although Janis does not deny the potential value of cohesiveness, he also recognizes its dangers. For one, highly cohesive groups may invest too much energy in maintaining goodwill in the group to the detriment of decision making. Members invest much intrinsic energy in groups because of the potential rewards for doing so: friendship, prestige, and confirmation of one's self-worth. Because our self-esteem needs are high, we will sometimes devote too much energy to establishing positive bonds, and this can lead to groupthink.

Under conditions of low cohesiveness, certain factors may prevent the illusion of unanimity. The natural conflict in noncohesive groups leads to much debate and consideration of all sides of an issue. Janis found in his research that groupthink can have six negative outcomes:

1. The group limits its discussion to only a few alternatives without considering a full range of creative possibilities. The solution may seem obvious and simple to the group, and there is little exploration of other ideas.

2. The position initially favored by most members is never restudied to seek out less obvious pitfalls. In other words, the group is not very critical in examining the ramifications of the preferred solution.

3. The group fails to reexamine those alternatives originally disfavored by the majority. Minority opinions are quickly dismissed and ignored, not only by the majority but also by those who originally favored them.

4. Expert opinion is not sought. The group is satisfied with itself and may feel threatened by outsiders.

5. The group is highly selective in gathering and attending to available information. The members tend to concentrate only on the information that supports the favored plan.

6. The group is so confident in its ideas that it does not consider contingency plans. It does not foresee the possibility of failure and does not plan for failure.

All these things result from a lack of critical thinking and overconfidence in the group. Janis maintains that groupthink is marked by a number of symptoms. The first symptom is an *illusion of invulnerability*, which creates an undue air of optimism. There is a strong sense that, "We know what we are doing, so don't rock the boat." Second, the group creates collective efforts to *rationalize* the course of action decided on. It creates a story that makes its decision seem absolutely right and literally talks itself into thinking it did the right thing.

Third, the group maintains an unquestioned belief in its inherent *morality*, seeing itself as being well motivated and working for the best outcome. That leads the group to soft-pedal ethical and moral consequences. Fourth, out-group leaders are *stereotyped* as evil, weak, or stupid.

Fifth, *direct pressure* is exerted on members not to express counteropinions. Dissent is quickly squelched, which leads to the sixth symptom: the *self-censorship* of disagreement. Individual members are reluctant to state opposing opinions and silently suppress their reservations. Thus, seventh, there is a shared *illusion of unanimity* within

---

16   Kurt Lewin, *Resolving Social Conflicts: Selected Papers on Group Dynamics* (New York: Harper & Row, 1948). For information on Lewin's theory of group dynamics, see Everett M. Rogers, *A History of Communication Study: A Biographical Approach* (New York: Free Press, 1994), pp. 316–355.

the group. Even if the decision is not unanimous, the group rallies outwardly around a position of solidarity.

Finally, eighth, groupthink involves the emergence of self-appointed *mindguards* to protect the group and its leader from adverse opinions and unwanted information. The mindguard typically suppresses negative information by counseling participants not to make things difficult.

What is the answer to the problem of groupthink? Janis believes that decision-making groups need to recognize the dangers of groupthink and suggests steps to prevent it:

1. Encourage everyone to be a critical evaluator and express reservations whenever they come up.
2. Do not have the leader state a preference up front.
3. Set up several independent and separate policymaking groups.
4. Divide into subgroups.
5. Discuss what is happening with others outside the group.
6. Invite outsiders into the group to bring fresh ideas.
7. Assign an individual at each meeting to be devil's advocate.
8. Spend considerable time surveying warning signals.
9. Hold a second-chance meeting to reconsider decisions before making them final.

Janis' approach is intriguing. He uses historical data to support his theory by analyzing six national political decision-making episodes in which outcomes were either good or bad, depending on the extent of groupthink. The negative examples include the Bay of Pigs invasion, the Korean War, Pearl Harbor, and the escalation of the Vietnam War. Positive examples include the Cuban missile crisis and the Marshall Plan.[17]

One of Janis' cases of successful decision making is the Kennedy administration's response to the Cuban missile crisis. In October 1962, Cuba was caught building offensive nuclear weapon stations and arming them with Soviet missiles. President Kennedy had already suffered through one instance of groupthink in the Bay of Pigs invasion the year before, and he seemed to have learned what not to do in these kinds of international crises. In the missile crisis, Kennedy constantly encouraged his advisors to challenge and debate one another. He refrained from leading the group too early with his own opinion, and he set up subgroups to discuss the problem independently so as not to reinforce members' opinions. Various members, including Kennedy, talked with outsiders and experts about the problem to make sure that fresh opinions were heard. In the end Kennedy successfully invoked a military blockade and stopped the Cuban-Soviet development.

The Interactional Tradition

As we have learned, a group's outcome depends largely on the nature of interaction in the group. Theories of group interaction are especially important in this book because of their concern with communication as the core of group productivity. Here, we look at two theories of group interaction. The first, an old standard, is Robert Bales' interaction process analysis. The second modifies Bales' notion of interaction and takes it in a different direction.

Interaction Process Analysis.   One of the most prominent small-group theories is Robert Bales' *interaction process analysis.*[18] Using his many years of research as a foundation, Bales created a unified and well-developed theory of small-group interaction, aiming to explain the pattern of responses in the small task group.

Figure 13.3 illustrates the categories of interactions in Bales' scheme.[19] Each is a type of statement that someone could make in a group. These

---

17   For a laboratory test of the groupthink hypothesis, see John A. Courtright, "A Laboratory Investigation of Groupthink," *Communication Monographs* 45 (1978): 229–246.

18   Robert F. Bales, *Interaction Process Analysis: A Method for the Study of Small Groups* (Reading, MA: Addison-Wesley, 1950); *Personality and Interpersonal Behavior* (New York: Holt, Rinehart & Winston, 1970); Robert F. Bales, Stephen P. Cohen, and Stephen A. Williamson, *SYMLOG: A System for the Multiple Level Observation of Groups* (London: Collier, 1979).

19   Adapted from Bales, *Personality,* p. 92.

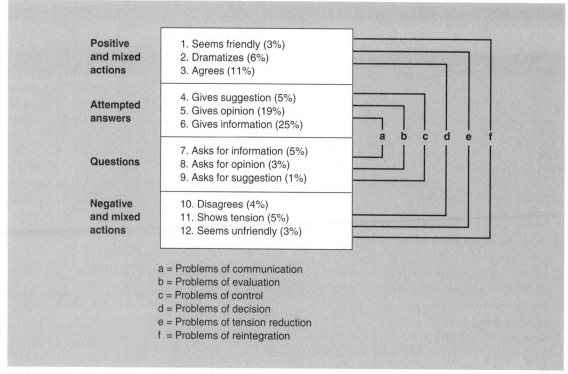

Positive
and mixed
actions

1. Seems friendly (3%)
2. Dramatizes (6%)
3. Agrees (11%)

Attempted
answers

4. Gives suggestion (5%)
5. Gives opinion (19%)
6. Gives information (25%)

Questions

7. Asks for information (5%)
8. Asks for opinion (3%)
9. Asks for suggestion (1%)

Negative
and mixed
actions

10. Disagrees (4%)
11. Shows tension (5%)
12. Seems unfriendly (3%)

a b c d e f

a = Problems of communication
b = Problems of evaluation
c = Problems of control
d = Problems of decision
e = Problems of tension reduction
f = Problems of reintegration

FIGURE **13.3**

Categories for Interaction Process Analysis

twelve categories are grouped into four broader sets, as outlined at the left of the figure. In addition, the behavior types are paired, and each pair implies a particular problem area for groups, as labeled in the figure. *Gives information* is paired with *asks for information, gives opinion* is paired with *asks for opinion,* and *gives suggestion* is paired with *asks for suggestion.*

Bales found that one of the ways groups release tension is by telling stories, or *dramatizing.* In Chapter 8 we looked at Ernest Bormann's development of this idea in symbolic convergence theory, which has special application in small groups.[20] Bormann believes that this form of communication is crucial not only in reducing

tension but also in affecting the quality of group discussion in general. Stories are often told and retold within a group. They consist of *fantasy themes,* or shared knowledge, that build a common identity in the group. Fantasy themes constitute the mechanism by which cohesiveness is developed in a group. As we know, cohesiveness can have both positive and negative effects on decision making.

There are two general classes of communication behavior. The first is *socioemotional,* represented by positive and negative actions like *seeming friendly, showing tension,* and *dramatizing,* and the second is *task behavior,* represented by *suggestions, opinions,* and *information.* (These classes are consistent with the categories of tasks and interpersonal functions found throughout the small-group literature and encountered earlier in this chapter.)

20   Ernest Bormann, "Symbolic Convergence and Communication in Group Decision Making," in *Communication and Group Decision-Making,* eds. R. Y. Hirokawa and M. S. Poole (Beverly Hills, CA: Sage, 1986), pp. 219–236.

In investigating leadership, Bales has found that the same group will have two different kinds of leaders. The *task leader*, who facilitates and coordinates the task-related comments, directs energy toward getting the job done. Equally important is the *socioemotional leader*, who works for improved relations in the group, concentrating on interactions in the positive and negative sectors. Usually the task and socioemotional leaders are different people.

Bales has shown how the perception of an individual's position in a group is a function of three dimensions. These include (1) dominant versus submissive, (2) friendly versus unfriendly, and (3) instrumental versus emotional. These factors can be visualized in a three-dimensional space, with the axes of the space labeled "positive-negative," "upward-downward," and "forward-backward."

Within a particular group, any member's behavior can be placed in this three-dimensional space. An individual's position depends on the quadrant in which that individual appears (for instance, upward-positive-forward, or UPF). One's position within the quadrant is determined by the degree of each dimension represented. Thus, for example, a UPF could appear at various points in the space, depending on the degree of U, P, and F. When all group members' behavior types are plotted on the spatial graph, their relationships and networks can be seen. The larger the group, the greater the tendency for subgroups of coalitions to develop. These subgroups consist of individuals with similar value dimensions. Obviously, affinity exists among individuals who are close in value dimension and direction, whereas distant individuals are not connected.

Not only can we predict the coalitions and networks of a group from the distribution of types, but Bales also has shown that behavior type is related to the kinds of statements a person makes. The interaction that a person initiates and receives depends in part on his or her behavior type.

Fisher's Interaction Analysis.   Although Bales' theory is called "interactional," it really deals

with individual acts. Aubrey Fisher and Leonard Hawes refer to this as a *human system model*. These authors believe that a more sensible approach for the study of group communication is the *interact system model*, which emphasizes associated acts, called "interacts."[21] An *interact* is the act of one person followed by the act of another. Examples are question-answer, statement-statement, and greeting-greeting. Here, the unit for analysis is not an individual behavior, like making a suggestion, but a contiguous pair of acts, like making a suggestion and responding to it. Interacts can be classified along the *content dimension* and the *relationship dimension*. For example, if someone were to ask you a question, you would probably answer it, but the manner in which you stated the answer might tip off the group that you thought it was a dumb question. Here, your answer is the content dimension and your nonverbal manner the relationship dimension.

Despite the potential utility of analyzing the relational dimension in a group discussion, Fisher has concentrated on the content dimension. Because almost all comments in a task group are related in one way or another to a decision proposal, Fisher classifies statements in terms of how they respond to a decision proposal.[22] Statements might agree or disagree with a proposal, for example.

Two essential differences exist between the theories of Bales and Fisher. First, Bales classifies a given act strictly in terms of its task or socioemotional function. Fisher assumes that any given act may fulfill either or both functions simultaneously. Second, Bales classifies only single acts, whereas Fisher classifies interacts, two acts at a time. In other words, the observer will classify each act *and* its following act, a favorable comment followed by an unfavorable one, perhaps. In this way the researcher can actually see the character and frequency of act pairs in a group discussion.

21   B. Aubrey Fisher and Leonard Hawes, "An Interact System Model: Generating a Grounded Theory of Small Groups," *Quarterly Journal of Speech* 57 (1971): 444–453.
22   B. Aubrey Fisher, *Small Group Decision Making: Communication and the Group Process* (New York: McGraw-Hill, 1980), p. 117.

In his "theory of decision emergence," Fisher outlines four phases through which task groups tend to proceed: orientation, conflict, emergence, and reinforcement.[23] In observing the distribution of interacts across these phases, Fisher notes the ways interaction changes as the group decision formulates and solidifies.

The *orientation phase* involves getting acquainted, clarifying, and beginning to express points of view. A high level of agreement characterizes this stage, and comments are often designed to test the group. Thus, positions are both qualified and tentative. In this phase people grope for direction and understanding.

The *conflict phase* includes a great deal of dissent. People in this second phase begin to solidify their attitudes, and much polarization results. Here the interacts include more disagreement and unfavorable evaluation. Members argue and attempt to persuade, and they may form coalitions.

These coalitions tend to disappear in the third, *emergence,* phase. Here the first inklings of cooperation begin to show. People are less tenacious in defending their viewpoints. As they soften their positions and undergo attitude change, their comments become more ambiguous. The number of favorable comments increases until a group decision begins to emerge.

In the final phase, *reinforcement,* the group decision solidifies and receives reinforcement from group members. The group unifies and stands behind its solution. Comments are almost uniformly positive and favorable. The ambiguity that marked the third phase tends to disappear.

To illustrate the phases of group development, Fisher presents an analysis of a mock jury deliberation in a lawsuit over an automobile-pedestrian accident.[24] In the first phase, the jury explores its responsibility. What is it supposed to do, and how is it supposed to do it? What are the possible verdicts? Much uncertainty is expressed until clarification emerges. Considerable disagreement arises in the conflict phase as the jury argues over whether the defendant is negligent and the criteria by which they should decide.

Here, the interaction tends to be somewhat emotional and heated at times.

In the emergence phase, the jury begins to agree that the defendant is not negligent and that the pedestrian could have avoided the accident. This agreement is somewhat tentative, and the jurors go back and forth on the issue, but the emotionality and debate definitely subside during this period. In the final reinforcement phase, the jury is convinced, and everybody affirms their agreement in this verdict.

The phases of group decision making characterize the interaction as it changes over time. An important related topic is that of *decision modification.*[25] Fisher finds that groups typically do not introduce only one idea at a time, nor do they introduce a single proposal and continue to modify it until consensus is reached. Instead, decision modification is cyclical. Several proposals are made, each discussed briefly, and some of them reintroduced at a later time. Discussion of proposals seems to proceed in spurts of energy. Proposal A will be introduced and discussed. The group will suddenly drop this idea and move to proposal B. After discussion of this, the group may introduce and discuss other proposals. Then someone will revive proposal A, perhaps in modified form. The group finally will settle on a modified plan that was introduced earlier in the discussion in a different form.

Why does discussion usually proceed in such an erratic fashion? Probably because the interpersonal demands of discussion require "breaks" from task work. In effect, the group attention span is short because of the intense nature of group work, and "flight" behavior helps manage tension and conflict.

Fisher finds that in modifying proposals, groups tend to follow one of two patterns. If conflict is low, the group will reintroduce proposals

23   B. Aubrey Fisher, "Decision Emergence: Phases in Group Decision Making," *Speech Monographs* 37 (1970): 53–60; Fisher, *Decision Making.*
24   Fisher, *Decision Making*, pp. 298–306.
25   Fisher, *Decision Making;* also B. Aubrey Fisher, "The Process of Decision Modification in Small Discussion Groups," *Journal of Communication* 20 (1970): 51–64.

in less abstract, more specific language. For example, in a discussion of a public health nursing conference, an original idea to begin "with a nonthreatening something" was modified to "begin with a history of the contributions which public health has made to the field of nursing."[26] A group, as it successively returns to a proposal, seems to follow the pattern of stating the problem, discussing criteria for solution, introducing an abstract solution, and moving finally to a concrete solution. Keep in mind, however, that the group most likely will not move through these four steps smoothly, but will probably do so sporadically as members depart from and return to the proposal in a stop-and-start fashion.

Another pattern is common when conflict is higher. Here, the group does not attempt to make a proposal more specific. Because disagreement exists on the basic idea, the group introduces substitute proposals of the same level of abstraction as the original. In the first pattern, which involves making proposals more specific, the group task seems to be one of mutual discovery of the best specific implementation of a general idea.

Fisher's theory is an example of a phase model of group development. Phase models predict that groups go through a series of stages in dealing with a problem or set of tasks. Because there have been many such models in the history of small-group theory, the phase approach constitutes the dominant view of group development.[27] Recently, however, phase models have been criticized for being overly simple.[28] In the next section, we examine a theory that views group action and development in a more complex and potentially more useful way than have the preceding approaches.

◖● THE STRUCTURATIONAL PERSPECTIVE

The input-process-output model has contributed much to our understanding of small-group decision making, but it is limited in its approach. Recently, a fresh perspective—the structurational approach—has been proposed.

Recall from our previous discussion of this theory in Chapter 8 that structuration is a process in which individuals create unintended consequences that later constrain their own future action. For example, a group member who tries to be creative in inventing new options for the group may inadvertently create an expectation or role for himself that he must live up to in the future. As group members, then, we are free to act in ways that help achieve personal and group goals, but we are not totally free. We are always constrained by the social structures created in the structuration process.[29]

Marshall Scott Poole and his colleagues have been working for several years on a structurational theory of group decision making.[30] This theory teaches that group decision making is a process in which group members attempt to achieve *convergence*, or agreement, on a final decision and in so doing structure their social system. Individuals express their opinions and preferences and thereby produce and reproduce certain rules by which convergence can be achieved or blocked.

Three elements of action—interpretation, morality, and power—affect how groups work

26   Fisher, *Decision Making,* p. 155.
27   Some of the most prominent phase models are discussed in R. F. Bales and F. L. Strodbeck, "Phases in Group Problem-Solving," *Journal of Abnormal and Social Psychology* 46 (1951): 485–495; M. A. Bell, "Phases in Group Problem-Solving," *Small Group Behavior* 13 (1982): 475–495; W. G. Bennis and H. A. Shepard, "The Theory of Group Development," *Human Relations* 9 (1956): 415–437; R. Lacoursiere, *The Life Cycle of Groups* (New York: Human Sciences, 1980); Bruce Tuckman, "Developmental Sequence in Small Groups," *Psychological Bulletin* 63 (1965): 384–399.
28   These arguments are summarized in Marshall Scott Poole, "Decision Development in Small Groups III: A Multiple Sequence Model of Group Decision Development," *Communication Monographs* 50 (1983): 321–342.
29   See, for example, Anthony Giddens, *New Rules of Sociological Method* (New York: Basic, 1976); *Studies in Social and Political Theory* (New York: Basic, 1977).
30   Marshall Scott Poole, David R. Seibold, and Robert D. McPhee, "Group Decision-Making as a Structurational Process," *Quarterly Journal of Speech* 71 (1985): 74; Poole, Seibold, and McPhee, "Structurational Approach." See also Julie M. Billingsley, "An Evaluation of the Functional Perspective in Small Group Communication," in *Communication Yearbook 16,* ed. Stanley Deetz (Newbury Park, CA: Sage, 1993), pp. 615–622.

(see Chapter 8). *Interpretation* is made possible through language, *morality* is established through group norms, and *power* is achieved through the interpersonal power structures that have emerged in the group.

Suppose, for example, that you are interested in persuading other members of a group to endorse a particular plan. You might share an interpretation of the plan by using the terms commonly employed and understood by group members. (Some of these words might even be rather specialized and specific to the group.) By employing a particular style of speaking, then, you would be acting in a manner that is condoned by the group according to its norms. To be effective as a speaker, you would also make use of a variety of sources of power, like leadership ability or status. Your comments in the meeting may or may not accomplish your objective, but they will certainly have the unintended consequence of contributing to the shared understandings and language, norms, and power structures of the group.

Outside factors always influence the group's actions. However, these outside factors can only have meaning insofar as they are understood and interpreted by the group, and these interpretations are negotiated through interaction within the group. One of the most important outside factors is task type—what the group has been given to do—for the task makes certain rules appropriate and others inappropriate. For example, a study group will behave in one way when preparing for an exam and in an entirely different way when researching a group report, but the group itself will need to work through what each of these means in practical terms.

Further, we act toward others in ways that reflect our views of their place in the group, and in time a "group" definition of each person and of the group as a whole emerges. This group definition subsequently affects the interaction among the members of the group and is thereby reproduced again and again. Some members, for example, might become task leaders, others socioemotional leaders, others information providers, and still others conflict managers.

The process of structuration usually leads to contradictions, and task groups are often confronted with these. Group actions both cause and resolve these inherent tensions. For example, the group must make a good decision before a deadline, but the time pressure of the deadline is inconsistent with the need for adequate time to do a good job. A group must attend to the requirements of the task, but in so doing they must also take care of their socioemotional needs. The problem, as we saw earlier in the chapter, is that meeting socioemotional needs can detract from the quality of task work. Further, members join a group to meet individual objectives, but they can only do so by paying attention to group objectives, which may undercut their own individual needs. Convergence can only come about through agreement, yet the group is told it must disagree in order to test ideas.

One of the most interesting contributions of this theory is its version of the processes followed by groups as they make decisions. Poole and his colleagues propose that groups can follow a variety of paths in the development of a decision, depending on the *contingencies* with which they are faced. Groups sometimes follow a predictable procedure such as the one Hirokawa recommends, sometimes they are unsystematic, and sometimes they develop their own pathway in response to unique needs.

How a group operates depends on three sets of variables. The first is *objective task characteristics*, which are the standard attributes of the task such as the degree to which the problem comes with preestablished solutions, the clarity of the problem, the kind of expertise it requires, the extent of the impact of the problem, the number and nature of values implicit in the problem, and whether the solution is a one-shot action or will have broader policy implications.

For example, you might be involved in a club that has to decide whether and how to participate in a town festival, a difficult decision involving many possible options. The potential number of values entering into the decision is fairly high, and what you decide to do this year may affect what you can do in other years. This decision may take some time, and the decision path may be complex.

On the other hand, if your group merely has to decide whether to have a taco booth, the decision is simple. The range of options is limited, the values involved in the decision are few, and the decision will have little impact outside the club. This decision will probably be made quickly and simply.

The second set of variables that affects the group's decision path is *group task characteristics,* and these will vary from group to group. They include the extent to which the group has previous experience with the problem, the extent to which an innovative solution is required as opposed to adoption of a standard course of action, and the urgency of the decision.

The third group of factors affecting the path of a group is *group structural characteristics,* including cohesiveness, power distribution, history of conflict, and group size. If your club has many members, gives the officers most of the power, and has a history of conflict, one kind of process will be used, but if it is small, cohesive, and has shared power, quite another would be predicted.

These three sets of factors will operate to influence the process adopted by the group, including whether it uses a standard or a unique path, the complexity of the decision path, the amount of organization or disorganization with which the task is handled, and the amount of time devoted to various activities.

To continue our example, your club might use a standard method of solving problems, such as Hirokawa's pattern, or it might develop a different method. The club's procedure may turn out to be simple and brief, but it could become complex and contorted; similarly, it could turn out to be organized, even though complex, or it may be completely unsystematic.

To discover various decision paths adopted by different groups, Poole and Jonelle Roth studied forty-seven decisions made by twenty-nine different groups.[31] The groups differed in their size, task complexity, urgency, cohesiveness, and conflict history. They included a medical school teaching team, an energy conservation–planning

group, student term-project groups, a dormitory management committee, and a number of others. Each discussion was tape-recorded and analyzed. Each task statement in a discussion was classified by judges according to type, and these were combined into interacts similar to those of Fisher discussed earlier. Also, every 30-second segment was classified according to a set of relationship categories. With a sophisticated method of analysis, the researchers could see the various decision paths that emerged in these interactions on both the task and relationship tracks.

Three general types of paths were discovered. Some groups followed a *standard unitary sequence,* although not always exactly the same way. Several groups followed what Poole and Roth call a *complex cyclic sequence.* Most of these were problem-solution cycles, in which the group would go back and forth in concentrated work between defining the problem and generating solution ideas, much as Fisher imagined. The third type of sequence was *solution-oriented,* in which almost no problem analysis occurred.

The decision paths taken by a group consist of three interwoven *activity tracks,* or courses along which the group develops or moves. A group may develop in different ways on each track, and the course of action taken on each track is affected in part by the three contingency variables discussed above—objective task characteristics, group task characteristics, and group structural characteristics.

There are probably many possible tracks, but three are elaborated in this theory—the task-process track, the relational track, and the topic-focus track. The *task-process track* consists of activities that directly deal with the problem or task, including, for example, problem analysis, designing solutions, evaluating solutions, and getting off on tangents. The *relational track* involves activities that affect interpersonal relationships in the group, such as disagreeing and

31 Marshall Scott Poole and Jonelle Roth, "Decision Development in Small Groups IV: A Typology of Group Decision Paths," *Human Communication Research* 15 (1989): 323–356; "Decision Development in Small Groups V: Test of a Contingency Model," *Human Communication Research* 15 (1989): 549–589.

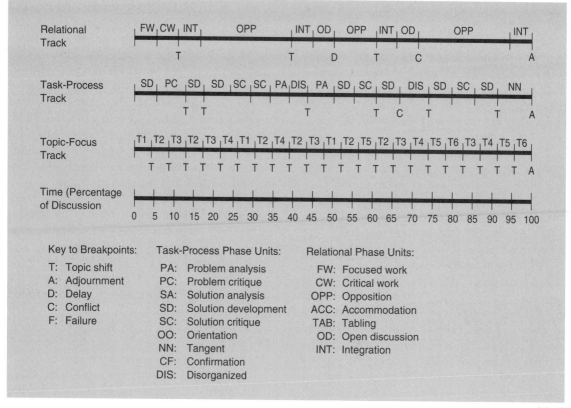

Key to Breakpoints:

T: Topic shift
A: Adjournment
D: Delay
C: Conflict
F: Failure

Task-Process Phase Units:

PA: Problem analysis
PC: Problem critique
SA: Solution analysis
SD: Solution development
SC: Solution critique
OO: Orientation
NN: Tangent
CF: Confirmation
DIS: Disorganized

Relational Phase Units:

FW: Focused work
CW: Critical work
OPP: Opposition
ACC: Accommodation
TAB: Tabling
OD: Open discussion
INT: Integration

FIGURE **13.4**

Sample Discussion with Activity Tracks

making accommodations. These two correspond neatly with the task-maintenance duality encountered in several other theories presented in this chapter. The third track, the *topic-focus track,* is a series of issues, topics, or concerns of the group over time. Figure 13.4 illustrates the activity tracks and how they work together.[32]

The multiple-sequence model imagines that the group moves along the various tracks over time, as illustrated by the time scale at the bottom of the graph. At a given moment, the group may be at a particular spot in the development of each track. The figure shows the three tracks divided into various activity segments. The activity segments are identified by code letters above the line. (The letters below the line are breakpoints, which will be explained later.)

In the discussion depicted in Figure 13.4, the group begins with topic 1 (T1). In discussing this topic, the group is involved in focused work (FW) in the relational track and solution development (SD) in the task-process track. As they move to another topic, the group enters problem critique (PC) on the task-process track while they are engaged in critical work (CW) on the relational track. The discussion goes on for some time through a number of phases until the end, when they go off on a tangent (NN) on the task-process track but accomplish integration (INT) on the relational track. Notice that the activity segments or phases on the different tracks in the

32   Adapted from Poole, "Decision Development III," pp. 327, 329; Poole and Roth, "Decision Development IV," pp. 334–335.

discussion depicted in this graph do not necessarily correspond to one another, which adds to the complexity of the path.

During the discussion, points of transition occur from time to time. These are *breakpoints,* or interruptions, designated by a code letter below the lines in Figure 13.4. Sometimes a breakpoint will mark a change in a single track, but often it will mark changes in several tracks. Breakpoints are important because they signal key points in the development of the group's decision-making activity.

Three types of breakpoints are apparent. *Normal breakpoints* are the expected, natural points of termination or transition. They include such things as adjournment, caucusing, or topic shifts. *Delays* are unexpected problems that cause a pause in normal group functioning. Delays often consist of rediscussion of issues necessary for the group to resolve conflicts or establish understanding. Delays may be a sign of impending difficulty, or they may be a more positive sign of careful thought or creative activity. *Disruptions* are more serious. These consist of major disagreements and group failures.

Although this is a somewhat complex and sophisticated theory, it expresses the structurational character of group decision making very well. It shows that groups do adopt particular courses of action to meet their needs but that in so doing they create structures that limit future action.

COMMENTARY AND CRITIQUE

Groups are important to individuals and society. As a person moves about in the world, cooperation becomes essential in achieving goals. People use communication to share resources in the solution of problems, and group communication thereby becomes not only an instrument for accomplishing tasks but also a means of group maintenance and cohesion.

Group communication can be viewed as a system of inputs, internal processes, and outputs. In decision making the inputs include information, group resources, and task characteristics. The process includes group interaction and decision development, and the outputs include completed tasks and decisions.

Group communication is also a form of structuration. The practices of the group create structures that limit future practices. Input-process-output models and structuration theories are not necessarily incompatible but provide two different ways of looking at group functioning. In many ways the theory of Poole and his associates is an input-process-output model because it posits a set of factors that affect processing, which in turn shapes outcomes. The difference is that this structurational model acknowledges the power of groups to shape the course of their own process to a certain extent.

Theories of small-group decision making form a distinct tradition. Their common threads and lines of influence are clear and provide a kind of coherence that binds this work. Certain basic ideas run through this history, as subsequent theories extend and develop earlier ideas.

The first basic idea is *the division of group effort into task and socioemotional factors.* It appears in almost all theories discussed in this chapter. Task energy is directed at problem solving, and socioemotional energy is directed at group maintenance and interpersonal relationships. Group effectiveness seems to depend on the balance between these two kinds of communication. Inadequate attention to these two factors can lead to dissatisfaction and poor decision making.

Perhaps the most influential theory to make the task–relationship distinction is Bales' foundational work. Bales' theory is an excellent beginning for understanding interaction in groups. His approach is highly parsimonious and internally consistent. It is built on a sensible and intuitively appealing conceptual base, from which a number of propositions about group interaction are derived.

Bales envisions the group as a body that swings between discussion of task matters and discussion of social matters, back and forth. Careful examination of groups in action, however, shows that task and socioemotional functions are thoroughly mixed. One can fulfill both task and social functions in a single statement, and in classifying group behavior, validly separating these functions is difficult. True, a given statement may be mostly task or mostly social, but to separate them completely would be a mistake.

This theory is strictly act-oriented and fails to describe true interaction. It presumes that any statement will stand on its own apart from contiguous statements by other persons. Fisher, as the second generation of interaction, looks at contiguous acts as the basic unit of analysis. Although Fisher's theory admits to the existence of the relational dimension of interaction, it makes no attempt to correlate the content and relational aspects of group discussion.

In general, Bales' and Fisher's theories share a common strength and a common weakness. The strength is that interaction analysis, of either type, allows us to look carefully at the communication behavior of groups, correlating messages with other group factors. In other words, interaction analysis provides a way to analyze group communication. Thus, these theories are both appropriate and heuristic. These advantages, however, have been gained at the price of a trade-off, which leads to their common weakness. When individual acts (or interacts) are analyzed according to a classification scheme, rich idiosyncratic meanings are glossed over. The value of understanding general group trends is bought at the price of thorough understanding of particular events in groups.

The third generation of work on task and relationship communication is represented by the research of Poole and his colleagues. It is an advance on Fisher's theory because it accounts for both tracks at the same time. It also takes a step toward capturing the idiosyncratic nature of the group experience by showing how groups can create very different patterns of decision making.

A second theme of group decision making is *group structure.* Group structure occurs in a variety of ways. Individuals differ in the kinds of statements they make in a group. Bales' research in the early 1950s classifies statements according

to various categories and relates individual actions to roles. He shows how the group interaction is shaped by the types of statements made and the roles assigned to individuals from their statements. He also shows how subgroups form according to the personalities of the individuals in the group.

Fisher uses somewhat different categories, and he is interested in how statements respond to one another in interacts. Even Poole's sophisticated work begins with the classification of statements and interacts. Poole, however, goes far beyond any of his predecessors in showing how interacts combine into activity segments and how these segments combine into phases. Poole's notion of group structure is sophisticated and complex because he shows how several structures may be present in a group.

A third long-term theme in small-group research is *decision development.* Interaction differs from one time period within a discussion to another, and most theorists see this movement as a linear process of development. The precise nature of this development is unclear and in dispute, but the theorists are still looking for it. Poole's theory has great potential for revealing the complexity and individuality of group-decision development. This has been an intriguing theme: How do groups come to agree on a decision? Several theories in this chapter address this concern, and it seems clear that careful, critical consideration is an important ingredient. For several years, Renée Meyers, Dale Brashers, and their colleagues have studied the process of argumentation in groups and have established the importance of back-and-forth arguing as a form of critical thinking that can lead to convergence and agreement in the end.[33]

The fourth trend in small-group theory is its *interest in effectiveness,* as the functionalist tradition so well illustrates. Janis' theory is especially appealing because it is a highly focused and intuitively attractive explanation of effectiveness.

33   This work is summarized and codified in Renée A. Meyers and Dale E. Brashers, "Argument in Group Decision Making: Explicating a Process Model and Investigating the Argument-Outcome Link," *Communication Monographs* 65 (1998): 262–281.

It stems not only from laboratory research but also from field application and historical case study. It is a theory that demonstrates the utility of ideas about group dynamics for understanding actual groups at work.

As we have seen repeatedly in this book, one of the failings of most communication theories is that they are based on limited perspectives or on limited types of research. Theories such as Janis' are like a breath of fresh air in this regard. In fact, if you look at the kind of data used throughout small-group research, you see a wide spectrum of variety and real-world application. Poole's use of real decision-making groups in the field is another example.

Janis' theory is different also because of its applied nature. It is a normative, or prescriptive, theory, providing guidelines for improved group functioning. However, this aspect of the theory leads to one of its weaknesses, namely, that it does not take us far in understanding or explaining how groups function. It suggests a way of guarding against one particular danger in groups, but it does not help us understand the nature of cohesiveness, conflict, roles, or communication. For this reason some scholars would be reluctant to call Janis' work a theory at all. Janis himself refers to this application merely as an "hypothesis."

Hirokawa's theory is also highly normative. It is consistent with the everyday experience of groups in our society, and it seems to have practical potential in helping groups become more effective. Hirokawa's theory also limits group functioning to a kind of rational task-only process. It fails to acknowledge the ways group successes and failures are a result of socioemotional, relational, or structurational activity. In addition, the theory does not adequately integrate problems that are out of the control of the group, such as the vagaries of the situation or the pragmatic obstacles to information gathering.[34]

Small-group theory is an interesting and important part of the overall study of communication, but it does not seem very popular now. Actually, however, if you look at the work being done in several fields, there is more activity than

there may appear. Poole refers to this problem as a "diaspora" and calls for greater community and interaction among group researchers in many fields.[35]

Group communication has been characterized over the years by a great deal of research on specific variables. As illustrated in this chapter, some insightful theory has emerged, but group communication has been commonly criticized for being under-theorized. In other words, we have a plethora of research findings without sufficient theory to explain and connect these findings. As a case in point, Joseph Bonito and Andrea Hollingshead completed a large survey of literature on the variable of participation, one of the most researched topics in the field. Their conclusion was precisely this: We have much information about participation, but we lack theories to help us understand what this information means.[36] In fairness, however, a good deal of theory has been produced in this field in the past twenty or thirty years, and some coherent directions have been established.[37] Certainly, one area for future theory involves relationships between group communication and other contexts.

For the most part, group communication studies have remained somewhat disconnected from other related areas such as interpersonal communication and organizational studies. When you think about it, group communication is the ideal interface between microstructures such as conversation and interaction and macrostructures such as organizations and communities.[38] Yet, researchers in this area have not put a great deal of energy into making these connections. A noted exception is the work of Bormann

---

34   These problems are discussed in some detail by Cynthia Stohl and Michael E. Holmes, "A Functional Perspective for Bona Fide Groups," in *Communication Yearbook 16*, ed. Stanley Deetz (Newbury Park, CA: Sage, 1993), pp. 601–614.

35   Marshall Scott Poole, "The Small Group Should Be *the* Fundamental Unit of Communication Research," in *Communication: Views from the Helm for the 21st Century*, ed. Judith S. Trent (Boston: Allyn & Bacon, 1998), pp. 94–97.

36   Joseph A. Bonito and Andrea B. Hollingshead, "Participation in Small Groups," in *Communication Yearbook 20*, ed. Brant R. Burleson (Thousand Oaks, CA: Sage, 1997), pp. 227–261.

37   For a theoretical defense of this area, see Gouran, Hirokawa, McGee, and Miller, "Communication in Groups."

38   This argument is made by Poole, "The Small Group."

and his colleagues on convergence theory (Chapter 8.) These theorists began with the work of Bales on fantasy themes in groups and expanded this notion in ways that are relevant to many contexts.[39]

David Seibold makes a special case for connecting group and organizational theory. He believes that organizational and group researchers have conducted their work in ways that tend to separate these contexts, when in fact they are so closely associated that they should not be divided.[40] In an extended critique of traditional group studies, Linda Putnam, Cynthia Stohl, and their colleagues have called for more careful study of *bona fide groups*.[41] The problem, they say,

is that by studying groups in isolation, you cannot get a very good idea of how groups are connected to one another and larger systems, nor can you ascertain important interaction effects among groups and systems.

Putnam and Stohl notice that most group theories use a "container metaphor," which probably distracts observers from some very important dynamics within and between groups. All groups are bona fide, but we do not always study them in ways that show how they work in everyday life. The key characteristics of groups, as bona fide, is that they are embedded in larger systems and have permeable boundaries. Members span from one group to another. People are members of multiple groups, and they communicate from one group to another. Often groups and their members must negotiate identities and borders within larger systems, and group energy must somehow be coordinated within larger contexts. Conflict among groups is common as groups frequently stand in opposition to one another. When you look at groups in conflict, they appear to have stable but permeable boundaries. Yet because of the constant and dynamic shifting that occurs within the system, they also have unstable and ambiguous borders.

Each of these concerns are thought-provoking and should challenge not only small-group theorists but also scholars in all areas of the field.

39   See, for example, John F. Cragan and Donald Shields, *Understanding Communication Theory: The Communicative Forces for Human Action* (Boston: Allyn & Bacon, 1998), pp. 93–121
40   David R. Seibold, "Groups and Organizations: Premises and Perspectives," in *Communication: Views from the Helm for the 21st Century,* ed. Judith S. Trent (Boston: Allyn & Bacon, 1998), pp. 162–168.
41   See, for example, Linda L. Putnam and Cynthia Stohl, "Bona Fide Groups: A Reconceptualization of Groups in Context," *Communication Studies* 41 (1990): 248–265; Cynthia Stohl and Linda L. Putnam, "Group Communication in Context: Implications for the Study of Bona Fide Groups," in *Group Communication in Context: Studies of Natural Groups,* ed. L. R. Frey (Hillsdale, NJ: Erlbaum, 1994), pp. 285–292; Linda L. Putnam and Cynthia Stohl, "Bona Fide Groups: An Alternative Perspective for Communication and Small Group Decision Making," in *Communication and Group Decision Making,* eds. R. Y. Hirokawa and M. S. Poole (Thousand Oaks, CA: Sage, 1996), pp. 247–278.

C H A P T E R **14**

COMMUNICATION AND ORGANIZATIONAL NETWORKS

According to sociologist Amatai Etzioni,

> Our society is an organizational society. We are born in organizations, educated in organizations, and most of us spend much of our lives working for organizations. We spend much of our leisure time playing and praying in organizations. Most of us will die in an organization, and when the time comes for burial, the largest organization of all—the state—must grant official permission.[1]

A large body of literature has been written about organizational communication.[2] Organizations can be viewed from a variety of perspectives. Gareth Morgan outlines a number of metaphors capturing their various aspects.[3] The first metaphor is the *machine.* Organizations, like machines, have parts that produce products and services. Another metaphor is the *organism.* Like a plant or animal, the organization is born, grows, functions, and adapts to changes in the environment, and eventually it dies. Third, organizations are like *brains:* They process information, they have intelligence, they conceptualize,

and they make plans. Fourth, organizations are like *cultures* because they create meaning, have values and norms, and are perpetuated by shared stories and rituals.

Next, organizations are like a *political system* in which power is distributed, influence is exerted, and decisions are made. Morgan shows also that organizations are *psychic prisons* because they can shape and limit the lives of their members, and she asserts that organizations can be understood as *flux and transformation,* because

---

1 Amatai Etzioni, *Modern Organizations* (Englewood Cliffs, NJ: Prentice-Hall, 1964), p. 1.
2 See, for example, Myria Watkins Allen, M. Michael Gotcher, and Joy Hart Seibert, "A Decade of Organizational Communication Research: Journal Articles 1980–1991," in *Communication Yearbook 16,* ed. Stanley Deetz (Newbury Park, CA: Sage, 1993), pp. 252–330; Stacia Wert-Gray, Candy Center, Dale E. Brashers, and Renée A. Meyers, "Research Topics and Methodological Orientations in Organizational Communication: A Decade in Review," *Communication Studies* 42 (1991): 141–154.
3 Gareth Morgan, *Images of Organization* (Beverly Hills, CA: Sage, 1986). See also Linda L. Putnam, "Metaphors of Communication and Organization," in *Communication: Views from the Helm for the 21st Century,* ed. Judith S. Trent (Boston: Allyn & Bacon, 1998), pp.145–152.

they adjust, change, and grow on the basis of information, feedback, and logical force. Finally, Morgan says that organizations are like *instruments of domination,* for they possess competing interests, some of which dominate others.

We can add another metaphor to Morgan's list—the network—and this is the metaphor chosen to organize this chapter. *Networks* are social structures created by communication among individuals and groups.[4] As people communicate with others, contacts and links are made, and these channels become instrumental in all forms of social functioning—in organizations and in society at large. Networks, then, can touch upon virtually all aspects of organizational communication in one way or another.

Network theory tells us about the structures and functions of an organization. It addresses the means by which social reality is constructed within the organization, illustrating that networks are not only instrumental but also cultural. In addition, networks are the channels through which influence and power are exerted, not only by management in a formal way but also informally among organizational members.

ORGANIZATIONAL NETWORKS

Many theorists have helped to elaborate the network concept.[5] In this section, we rely on the summary of Cynthia Stohl, whose book integrates an eclectic set of ideas in an internally consistent fashion that provides a synthesis of the network theory.[6]

Network theory begins with the idea that the structure of an organization consists of patterns of interaction among its members. Who talks to whom? What is the flow of information? Stohl defines organizational communication as "the collective and interactive process of generating and interpreting messages."[7] The basic structural idea of network theory is *connectedness*: the idea that there are relatively stable pathways of communication among individuals. Individuals who communicate together are linked together into

groups that are in turn linked together into the overall network.

Let's begin by looking at the *individual.* Every person has a unique set of connections with others in the organization. These are *personal networks.* Because individuals tend to communicate more frequently with certain other organizational members, they cluster together into more tightly connected groups, so that the *group network* becomes an important part of the overall organization. In many ways, organizations consist of many smaller groups, but these groups are not isolated. Since their members communicate with others outside the group, they are linked—again, connected—in such a way that *organizational networks* can be seen.

Although some organizational networks are *formally prescribed* by the organization chart, probably the real character of the organization is determined by the informal structure, or *emergent networks,* that show the true connections that people make everyday. Of course there are *inter-organization networks* as well, since no organization is every isolated from others. Whether group, organizational, or inter-organizational, the links that tie people together are made from person to person.

The basic unit of organization, then, is the *link* between two persons, and the organizational system consists of innumerable links that cluster people into groups and connect them to the organization. A link can be defined by its purpose or purposes, how much it is shared, and its functions within the organization. Most links have more than one purpose. You might, for example, use a link for both information sharing and

---

4   This metaphor is suggested by Cynthia Stohl, *Organizational Communication: Connectedness in Action* (Thousand Oaks, CA: Sage, 1995). See also Peter R. Monge, "The Network Level of Analysis," in *Handbook of Communication Science,* eds. C. R. Berger and S. H. Chaffee (Newbury Park, CA: Sage, 1987), pp. 239–270.
5   These have been organized and codified by Peter Monge and Eric Eisenberg, "Emergent Communication Networks,"in *Handbook of Organizational Communication: An Interdisciplinary Perspective,* eds. F. M. Jablin and others (Newbury Park, CA: Sage, 1987), pp. 304–342; Richard V. Farace, Peter R. Monge, and Hamish Russell, *Communicating and Organizing* (Reading, MA: Addison-Wesley, 1977).
6   Stohl, *Organizational Communication.*
7   Stohl, *Organizational Communication,* p. 4.

friendship. Occasionally, a link may be exclusive, but usually it is shared with many others.

A link can also define a particular *network role*, meaning that it serves to connect groups in particular ways. As the members of an organization communicate with one another, they fulfill a variety of roles vis-à-vis the network. For example, a *bridge* is a member of a group who is also a member of another group. A *liaison* connects two groups, but is a member of neither.

An organization never consists of a single network but is shaped by numerous overlapping ones. Although most networks are multifunctional, they may concentrate more on one function than another. For example, you may find networks that exert power or influence, often called *authority or instrumental networks*. Others include friendship or affiliation, information, production, and innovation.

A network can be characterized by a number of qualities. One is *size,* or the sheer number of people. Another is *inter-connectedness,* the ratio of actual links to possible links. A highly connected network is strong and close. Such networks can exert much influence by establishing norms for thought and behavior. You will feel closer and be more influenced by a group of students you see and interact with every day in the residence hall than students you only see occasionally in various classes.

Another characteristic of a network is it *centrality,* or the degree to which it is connected to other networks. A highly centralized organization has a high degree of connection among a few groups or individuals, with most individuals and groups remaining less connected. A *decentralized* system has more connectedness among everyone overall. If you have to go through the same small group of individuals every time you need something, you will not be very connected to other members of the organization. On the other hand, if you have freedom to contact just about anyone, you will be more connected generally throughout the organization.

Network theory is a good master metaphor for our purposes because it is able to integrate a wide spectrum of perspectives. Peter Monge and

Eric Eisenberg see network theory as a way of pulling together three traditions of organizational studies.[8] The first is the *positional tradition,* which is concerned with formal structure and roles in organizations. The organization in this tradition is viewed as a set of positions like administrator, teacher, and student. Each position has certain functions.

The second tradition related to networks is the *relational.* This tradition deals with the ways relationships naturally develop among participants in an organization and the manner in which networks emerge from these relationships. Here, the organization is seen as a living, changing system constantly shaped and given meaning by the interactions among members.

The third tradition is *cultural.* Here, symbols and meaning are central. The world of the organization is created by the members in stories, rituals, and task work. The real structure of the organization is not predesigned but emerges from the actions of the members informally in their daily work.

THE POSITIONAL TRADITION

The positional tradition consists of a number of theories of formal communication networks. These theories tend to examine the ways management uses formal networks to achieve its objectives. A foundational theory of this genre is Max Weber's theory of bureaucracy. The positional tradition is not much in favor in the communication field these days, but it does represent the classical approach to organizing and provides historical background. In this book, we include two quite different exemplars representing work on bureaucracy and human relations.

Classical Foundations: Weber

Certainly, Max Weber was one of the most prominent social theorists of all time. In his lifetime,

8   Monge and Eisenberg, "Emergent Communication Networks."

from 1864 to 1920, he produced a great quantity of work on the nature of human institutions. One area for which he is best known is his theory of bureaucracy.[9] Weber's ideas, developed at the beginning of the century, are part of what we now refer to as "classical organizational theory."[10]

Weber defines an organization as a system of purposeful, interpersonal activity designed to coordinate tasks.[11] *Power*—the ability of a person to influence others and overcome resistance—is fundamental to most social relationships. When power is "legitimate," or authorized formally by the organization, compliance is effective and complete. Whether communications will be accepted in an organization, then, hinges on the degree to which the superior has *legitimate authority*. You tend to do what your boss says because the organization grants this person the legitimate authority to give orders.

Where does this authority come from? The most common form of authority stems from the organization's rules and regulations, which leads to *bureaucratic,* or *rational-legal, authority*. This is the kind of authority vested in supervisors and managers.

Weber sees bureaucracy as the most efficient pattern for mass administration, and it is governed by a number of well-known principles. First, bureaucracy is based on rules. Such rules allow the solution of problems, standardization, and equality in the organization. Second, bureaucracies are based on sphere of competence, in which a systematic division of labor exists. Within the sphere, each role has clearly defined rights and powers. Third, the essence of bureaucracy is hierarchy, which is seen in the formal organizational chart. Fourth, administrators are appointed on the basis of their knowledge and training. They are not usually elected, nor do they inherit their positions, but gain them through training, experience, and selection. Fifth, the members of the bureaucracy must not share in the ownership of the organization. Sixth, bureaucrats must be free to allocate resources within their realms of influence without fear of outside infringement. Seventh, a bureaucracy requires carefully maintained records—a principle that has led to the strong rule in most organizations to document all important transactions.

Another feature of a bureaucracy is that it is usually headed by a nonbureaucrat. Nonbureaucratic heads are often elected or inherit their positions. They include presidents, cabinets, boards of trustees, and monarchs. Bureaucrats are dispensable; they may be replaced by similarly trained individuals, but the succession of the nonbureaucratic head may well be a crisis, precipitating innovation and change.

Weber's theory is included here primarily as a general background for the theories to come and to illustrate the positional tradition. In this regard the theory serves two functions. First, it provides a "classical," or standard, picture with which the other theories can be contrasted. Second, it presents the traditional view of organizations. The theory has implicit ideas of what communication is like in organizations, but communication is not treated as an explanatory variable, nor is it seen as important. As such this is not really a communication theory. As the upcoming sections show, this failure is significant.

Likert's Four Systems

Rensis Likert is a theorist in the human relations school. Human relations, in reaction to classical theories such as Weber's, focused on the workers—their feelings and needs. It was an especially popular movement from the 1940s through the 1960s. Human relations really has a foot in both the positional and relational traditions, but most

---

9   Max Weber, *The Theory of Social and Economic Organizations,* trans. A. M. Henderson and T. Parsons (New York: Oxford University Press, 1947). A lengthy interpretation and discussion of Weber's theory can be found in Parsons' introduction to the above book. For a more complete bibliography of primary and secondary sources on Weber, see S. N. Eisenstadt, *Max Weber on Charisma and Institution Building* (Chicago: University of Chicago Press, 1968).
10   The most important classical theories are those of Henri Fayol and Frederick Taylor. See Henri Fayol, *General and Industrial Management* (New York: Pitman, 1949), originally published in 1925; and Frederick W. Taylor, *Principles of Scientific Management* (New York: Harper Brothers, 1947), originally published in 1912.
11   Weber, *Social and Economic Organizations,* p. 151.

of these theories, Likert's included, look at human relations from a production, management-oriented perspective. They teach that if you care for and nurture workers, the organization's operations will improve.[12] Likert's theory illustrates the positional nature of human relations.[13]

According to Likert, an organization can function at any point along a continuum of four systems. Under system 1, the *exploitative-authoritative system,* the executive manages with an iron hand. Decisions are made by the boss, with no use of feedback. One step away is system 2, *benevolent-authoritative leadership.* Here, the manager is sensitive to the needs of the worker. Moving farther along the continuum, we come to system 3, the *consultative system,* in which authority figures still maintain control but seek consultation from below. At the far extreme of the spectrum, system 4, or *participative management,* allows the worker to participate fully in decision making.

The system chosen by management will cause certain outcomes to occur. In Likert's scheme, then, the system of management is a *causal* variable. In addition, certain *intervening* variables also affect the outcome, as outlined in Figure 14.1.[14]

For Likert, system 4 is clearly the best because it leads to high performance and an increased sense of responsibility and motivation. If management is authoritative, there is less group loyalty, more conflict, and consequently less mutual support. Workers have a lower attitude toward management and not much motivation to produce. The predictable result is lower sales, higher costs, and lower earnings. Consultative and participative management, on the other hand, leads to greater loyalty, higher performance goals, more mutual support, and more positive attitudes. The motivation to produce is higher, so that sales are greater, costs are less, and earnings are increased.

How does communication figure in all of this? Likert treats communication as one of several intervening variables. Exploitative management does not think about communication very much

except to express its desires clearly and forcefully to the workers. There is little upward communication, and what information that does go up the line tends to be distorted. Supervisors and subordinates are not very close to one another, and there is little accurate understanding between them. On the other hand, participative management includes strong upward and downward communication. This communication tends to be accurate and clear. Managers and workers tend to be close and understand one another well. Although Likert's theory and the human relations movement have been criticized for being simplistic and mechanistic, there does seem to be some truth to Likert's notion that in some organizations exploitative systems have negative results, whereas participative ones have positive ones.

Virginia Richmond and James McCroskey conducted a study of employee satisfaction among 183 teachers in 39 school districts.[15] The teachers were given a battery of tests related to, among other things, management style, manager's tolerance for disagreement, and satisfaction. Four styles—called "tells," "sells," "consults," and "joins"—were measured in the study. These are essentially identical to Likert's systems 1, 2, 3, and 4.

The data showed a clear relationship between the perceived style of the manager and employee satisfaction. Employees who thought that their manager used a consulting or joining style were more satisfied than those who thought that a telling or selling style was used. The same relationship held for tolerance for disagreement.

12   For a more detailed discussion and critique of the human relations movement, see Charles Perrow, *Complex Organizations: A Critical Essay* (Glenview, IL: Scott, Foresman, 1972).
13   Rensis Likert, *New Patterns of Management* (New York: McGraw-Hill, 1961); *The Human Organization* (New York: McGraw-Hill, 1967).
14   Rensis Likert, "New Patterns in Sales Management," in *Changing Perspectives in Marketing Management,* ed. Martin Warshaw (Ann Arbor: Bureau of Business Research, University of Michigan, 1972), p. 24.
15   Virginia P. Richmond and James C. McCroskey, "Management Communication Style, Tolerance for Disagreement, and Innovativeness as Predictors of Employee Satisfaction: A Comparison of Single-Factor, Two-Factor, and Multiple-Factor Approaches," in *Communication Yearbook 3,* ed. D. Nimmo (New Brunswick, NJ: Transaction, 1979), pp. 359–373.

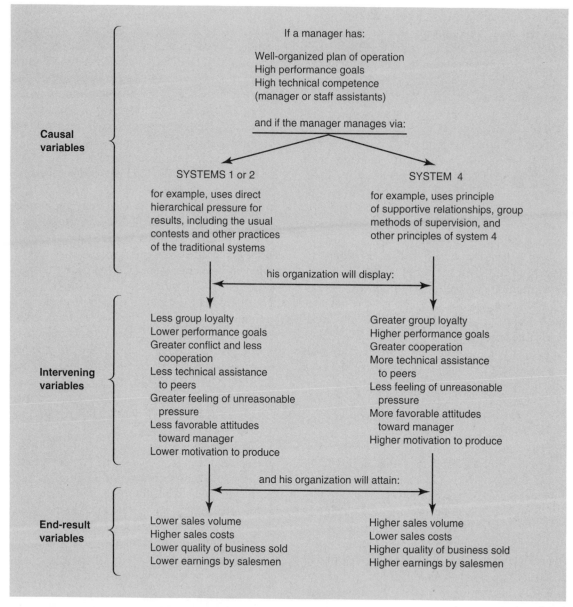

Sequence of Developments in a Well-Organized Enterprise, as Affected by Use of System 1 or 2 or System 4

From "New Patterns in Sales Management," in *Changing Perspectives in Marketing Management,* ed. Martin Warshaw.

Employees who thought that their managers had less tolerance for disagreement were less satisfied than those who thought their managers had a higher level of disagreement tolerance.

One function of formal communication in an organization is to elicit cooperation on the part of employees. Likert suggests that this can be done by participative management. The following theory explores some of the less obvious ways in which cooperation is gained in organizations.

◖ THE RELATIONAL TRADITION

Theories in the relational tradition are concerned with the ways organization is accomplished by interaction among individuals. These theories are less concerned with the lines of communication running through the organization and more concerned with how people accomplish things through interaction.

We looked at relational communication theory in Chapter 12. Recall that these theories are less interested in the messages that one person sends to another than they are with the effect of mutual interaction among people. This tradition has had a significant impact on the work in organizational communication as well. The chief proponent of the interactional view in organization studies is Carl Weick, and we look at his theory first.

The Process of Organizing

One of the most influential theories of the relational genre is that of Carl Weick.[16] Weick's theory of organizing is significant in the communication field because it uses communication as a basis for human organizing and provides a rationale for understanding how people organize.

The feature that distinguishes this theory from those of the positional school is that organizations are not structures made of positions and roles, but communication activities. It is more proper to speak of "organizing" than of "organizations" because organizations are something that people accomplish through a continuing process of communication. When people go through their daily interactions, their activities *create* organization. Behaviors are interlocked, since one person's behavior is contingent on another's.

In this analysis, an *act* is a statement or behavior of one individual, an *interact* involves an act followed by a response, and a *double interact* consists of an act followed by a response and then an adjustment or follow-up by the first person. Weick believes that all organizing activities are double interacts.

Consider an executive and an administrative assistant as an example. The executive asks the assistant to undertake an activity (act); the assistant then asks for clarification (interact); and the executive explains (double interact). Or the executive asks the administrative assistant a favor (act), and the administrative assistant follows through (interact), after which the executive responds with a thank you (double interact). Simple? Yes, but these activities are exactly the kind of which Weick believes organizations are made.

Organizing activities fulfill the function of reducing the uncertainty of information received from the *environment*, or surroundings. Weick uses the term *equivocality* to mean uncertainty, or complication, ambiguity, and lack of predictability. All information from the environment, according to Weick, is equivocal to some degree, and organizing activities are designed to reduce this uncertainty.

Let's return to the example of the executive again. Suppose the executive receives a directive from the firm's president to solve a problem of plant safety. What is the nature of this problem, and how should the executive go about solving it? The answers to these questions are not clear, inasmuch as the problem can be defined and

---

16   Carl Weick, *The Social Psychology of Organizing*, 2nd ed. (Reading, MA: Addison-Wesley, 1979). For a more recent secondary source, see James L. Everett, "Communication and Sociocultural Evolution in Organizations and Organizational Populations," *Communication Theory* 4 (1994): 93–110. See also the special section in *Communication Studies* 40 (Winter 1989): 231–265.

solved in a number of ways. In other words, the executive is faced with equivocal information.

Weick is saying that organizing activities, which consist of double interacts, or interlocked behaviors, are designed to make such situations clearer. Of course, the importance of information and the degree of equivocality in the information vary. Asking an administrative assistant a favor may be an insignificant act whose equivocality is low, but the example of solving safety hazards illustrates a more significant problem that has a great deal of equivocality.

This difference is not important to Weick. What is important is that organizing is accomplished through processes developed to deal with equivocal information, mild or great. The exact nature of that information is irrelevant to the fact that organizational members engage in it. Interaction serves to achieve common meanings among group members, and the meanings that individuals together assign to information provide the mechanism by which equivocality is reduced. In other words, as we interact we come to some amount of common understanding, which reduces uncertainty.

To test the relationship between equivocality and interaction, Gary Kreps studied the discussions of the faculty senate at the University of Southern California for a year.[17] He asked a sample of senate members to evaluate each of the twenty-four motions considered that year in terms of their equivocality. They filled out scales to test how complicated or uncomplicated, how predictable or unpredictable, and how ambiguous or unambiguous each motion was. Kreps then chose the five most equivocal and five least equivocal motions and counted the number of double interacts in the discussions of each of these. The difference is clear: Highly equivocal motions required much more discussion than did less equivocal ones. The average number of double interacts for less equivocal motions was

seven, whereas that for highly equivocal ones was seventy-four.

We have discussed how individuals interact to deal with equivocal information from the environment, but what is the environment? Organizers are always surrounded by a mix of stimuli to which they must respond, but the "environment" has no meaning apart from what the individual makes of it. In other words, the environment is a product of the person, not something outside the person. What makes the environment salient for the individual is the person's attention to particular aspects of the stimuli. People are selective in what they attend to in any situation and what is attended to becomes the environment. Hence, like every other aspect of the organizational reality, the environment is enacted by the people in the organization. People are continually reenacting their environments, depending on their attitudes, values, and experiences of the moment.

For example, the executive of our safety example is faced with a situation in which interpretation is necessary. Immediately, he or she will attend to certain aspects of the "safety problem." In enlisting the aid of others such as the administrative assistant, the executive is beginning processes that will enable the group to treat the safety problem as its environment of the moment. To deal with this equivocal environment, group members make proposals (acts) to which others respond (interacts) so that the proposers can refine their initial proposals (double interacts).

The executive may ask the administrative assistant to check the files for accident records. This constitutes a proposal, an attempt to reduce the equivocality. The administrative assistant may comply, pulling the appropriate file, so that the executive can be assured that the company knows the extent of the safety problem. Here, the sequence of the double interact would be as follows: request file (act), provide file (interact), take file and review it (double interact).

Weick views organizing as an evolutionary process that relies on a series of three major pro-

17   Gary L. Kreps, "A Field Experimental Test and Revaluation of Weick's Model of Organizing," in *Communication Yearbook 4*, ed. D. Nimmo (New Brunswick, NJ: Transaction, 1980), pp. 389–398.

cesses: enactment, selection, and retention. *Enactment* is the definition of the situation, or registering equivocal information from outside. It is attention to stimuli and acknowledgment that equivocality exists. The mere acceptance of certain aspects of the environment removes some equivocality. Accepting the task of dealing with safety problems narrows the field for the executive, so that some uncertainty already is removed from the field of all possible problems that could be addressed.

The second process is *selection*, which enables the group to admit certain aspects and reject other aspects of information. It narrows the field, eliminating alternatives with which the organization does not wish to deal. This process therefore removes even more equivocality from the initial information. For example, in dealing with the safety problem, the organization may decide to consider only the aspects of safety that management can control, eliminating everything they cannot control.

The third process of organizing is *retention*, in which certain aspects of the information will be saved for future use. Retained information is integrated into the existing body of information on which the organization operates. The safety group may decide to deal with safety problems that are caused strictly by machinery, rejecting all other kinds of problems. As you can see, the problem has become much less ambiguous; it has moved from equivocality toward clarity.

After retention occurs, organization members face a *choice point*. They must decide first whether to reenact the environment in some way. Here, they address the question, "Should we (or I) attend to some aspect of the environment that was rejected before?" The executive may decide, for example, to have the group review the rate of accidents that are not related to machinery. Then members must choose whether to modify their behavior. Here the question is, "Should I take a different action than I did before?" For instance, the executive may decide that solutions for both machinery and nonmachinery accidents should be developed.

So far this summary may lead you to believe that organizations move from one process of organizing to another in lockstep fashion: enactment, selection, retention, choice. Such is not the case. Individual subgroups in the organization are continually working on activities in all these processes for different aspects of the environment. Although certain segments of the organization may specialize in one or more of the organizing processes, nearly everybody engages in each part at one time or another.

Behavior cycles are sets of interlocked behaviors that enable the group to come to an understanding about which meanings should be included and which rejected. Thus, the safety meeting called by the executive would enable interested individuals to discuss the safety problem and decide how to proceed. Behavior cycles are a natural part of each of the three processes of organizing.

Within a behavior cycle, members' actions are governed by *assembly rules* that guide the choice of routines used to accomplish the process being conducted (enactment, selection, or retention). Rules are sets of criteria on which organizers decide what to do to reduce equivocality. The question answered by assembly rules is this: Out of all possible behavior cycles in this organization, which will we use now? For example, in the selection process the executive might invoke the assembly rule that "two heads are better than one" and on this basis call a meeting of plant engineers.

Now we have completed the basic elements of Weick's model. They are environment, equivocality, enactment, selection, retention, choice points, behavior cycles, and assembly rules, all of which contribute to the reduction of equivocality. Weick envisions these elements working together in a system, each element related to the others.

Weick's most significant contribution is the idea that organizations are made in a process of interaction among people. This idea has been expanded by James Taylor and his colleagues in the following theory.

Conversation and Text in the Process of Organizing

As does Weick, James Taylor and his colleagues see organizing as a process of interaction.[18] This group of theorists has developed a wide-ranging theory drawn from many literatures in linguistics, discourse, and organizational theory, to create a picture of how organizations are made in conversation.[19] This outcome depends on the dual processes of conversation and text. The process begins when members interact and come to interpret, or understand, the texts they produce in language.

Organizing is a circular process, with interaction and interpretation each entailing the other. Taylor refers to the interaction as *conversation* and the linguistic production of conversation as *text*. *Conversation* is the action itself, or how participants behave toward one another—what words they use, their demeanor, their gestures. *Text* is what is said—the content and ideas embedded in language.

Think of it this way: When you are talking to another person, the two of you behave in a variety of ways, back and forth, but these behaviors mean something; they have content, purpose, and effect. When you are concentrating on what is happening, you are focusing on the conversation; when you are concentrating on what is being said, you are focusing on text. The language of the text—be it an employee manual or a comment made by someone just seconds ago—provide a structure of words and grammar on which we rely when we interpret the meaning of what was written or said.

But these two processes—conversation and text—cannot really be separated. The conversation is understood in terms of the text, and the text is understood in terms of the conversation. This is a process the authors call *double translation*. Here's how it works: First, behavior is translated into meaning. The language and gestures used determine what is being said. This is the first translation—from text to conversation, or from how something should be said to the actual saying of it. At the same time, however, you assign meaning to the behavior, you bracket it, or you focus on connections and make decisions about what the behavior should stand for. This is the second translation—from conversation to text. These two translations are happening simultaneously and are closely tied to each other.

Although we do have freedom to communicate in a variety of ways, we are more or less constrained in how to say things because of the conventions of the language and the forms of communication already established in the organization and society at large. The same is true of interpretation. We do interpret texts differently, but within a range of possibilities determined largely by the structure of the language and pre-established forms of discourse. Let's say, for example, that a manager wants to tell employees about a new policy. Although the manager can say this in a variety of ways, he or she cannot use any combination of words willy-nilly. The language structure would not permit it, nor would the employees be able to understand what the manager wished to say. The manager also has lots of ways or forms in which to communicate this information, but, again, the organization has established certain acceptable types of discourse for this sort of communication, and the discourse form selected has certain embedded meanings. So, for example, the manager might send out a memo with the subject line, "Change of policy," which will carry a certain force of authority.

One of the resources that make human communication possible are certain models, or frames, for understanding what communication entails. In communication, the idea that communication involves "transfer" from one agent to

18   James R. Taylor, Francois Cooren, Nicole Giroux, and Daniel Robichaud, "The Communicational Basis of Organization: Between the Conversation and the Text," *Communication Theory* 6 (1996): 1–39. See also James R. Taylor, "Shifting from a Heteronomous to an Autonomous Worldview of Organizational Communication: Communication Theory on the Cusp," *Communication Theory* 5 (1995): 1–35; James R. Taylor, *Rethinking the Theory of Organizational Communication: How to Read an Organization* (Norwood, NJ: Ablex, 1993).
19   For a thorough discussion of the details of the theory and its antecedents, see James R. Taylor and Elizabeth J. Van Every, *The Emergent Organization: Communication as its Site and Surface* (Mahwah, NJ: Erlbaum, 2000).

another seems to be a critical component of the frame for understanding communication. Who is transferring, what is being transferred, and who is receiving the transfer will vary from moment to moment, but communication is understood in part by this notion of transfer. For example, we sometimes see that information is being transferred, aimed at developing a shared image of the world. However, the idea of transfer from one agent to another is never sufficient for conversation to take place. To be complete, communication must include *interaction* in which the ultimate meaning of the interaction is determined not only by the act initiated but also by the response to that act.

Taylor and his associates call this process *co-orientation*. This is the idea that two people both orient to a common object (a topic, issue, concern, situation, idea, goal, person, group, and so on), and the communicators work at negotiating a coherent meaning toward that object. Sometimes they are successful in doing so, and sometimes they are not, and it can take considerable interaction to achieve some sort of common meaning. The manager, for example, may feel that a policy change is vital, while a certain employee feels that it is minor. Here their co-orientation toward the policy is unbalanced, and there may be many interactions designed to establish a coherent, or workable, co-orientation. Taylor uses the analogy of interlinked tiles to get across this idea of organization. Each tile is like an interaction, and each interaction in turn is connected to others, just as one tile is connected to others in tilework.

This idea of an organization as being built up through a series of connected tiles is what Taylor calls a "flatland" view. It contrasts with the more traditional, top-down view, which suggests that the organization is "made" by those in command who direct the activities below. Although there is some truth to the management model, in fact the actual structure of the organization is constantly reproduced or reinvented by interactions at every level. Managerial interactions are just one type of many, and all interactions contribute to the organization. The macro (overall large view of the organization) and micro (minute daily interactions) entail one another, each affecting the other so that you cannot really separate overall structure from daily interaction.

Our constant interpretations of conversations give form and life to the organization. Organizations are made in this process of interaction in co-orientational triads. Each interaction is always linked to others, so that they become an intertwined net of interactions that bring the organization into being, sustain it, and change it over time.

Let's say that you are a firefighter and work about 40 hours a week for the city fire department. What do you do every day? You talk, give and take directions, maintain the station and equipment, give fire permits, visit schools, respond to emergency calls, and engage in many other often mundane activities. Each of these activities is done in a series of conversations, but the fire department as an organization is more than just a bunch of actions. Something results from all of this that defines and structures the organization itself. Something bigger is happening.

How do you know, then, exactly what characterizes the fire department as an organization? This question shows why text is so important. It is the texts, that which is written and spoken, that represent symbolically how members are defining the organization. Theoretically, you could "listen in" to what people are saying to get a sense of the way they understand their structures and functions. (Actually, this is what some researchers do.)

A better way would be to look at organizational *maps*. Certain individuals will take the role of *agent* for the organization and codify aspects of the organization in a more or less formal text that is taken as a sort of map of some aspect of the organization. For example, Human Resources may write an employee manual, the executive committee may draft an organization chart, the CEO might give a speech to a community group, a department might write an annual report, a hiring committee might write up a description as part of a job announcement, a work group might keep a log of what they do, or an outside researcher may write a book about the organization. These texts are especially important as maps because they provide a generally accepted picture of the organization's boundaries, activities, and the roles of members.

If you observe people actually communicating and see their patterns of interaction and their relationships, you are noticing the *surface structure* of the organization—the daily activities of the members. But these are not random or unconnected interactions. Rather, they are generated from the *deep structure* of the organization. The deep structure is like a grammar or structural arrangement that gives the organization its character and guides its actions. This deep structure is a complex network of rules about the patterns of interaction that are permissible in the organization, obligations of members, and expected duties and responsibilities. It is a moral order or a sense of how things should be done. A map as an organizational text will provide some clues as to the deep structure of the organization.

There is a recursive relationship between the deep structure and the actual conversations of an organization. The deep structure is made by people communicating with one another, and that deep structure in turn guides the communication itself. This is a circle of influence, a reciprocal back and forth between the deep structure and the surface structure. At times this relationship is highly stable, which makes organizational life very predictable. Other times it is less stable, as the texts and conversations of the organization go through changes.

Of course all of this is not rationally planned by some master designer. Indeed, it happens incrementally and over time as real people interact with one another in their daily organizational lives. The structures that are created in the process are largely unintended, and we look more closely at how this happens in the following section.

Structuration in Organizations

Recall that the theory of structuration, attributable to sociologist Anthony Giddens, deals with the ways actions bring about unintended consequences, which in turn form social systems that affect future actions. The circle of actions and consequences is the mechanism by which sociocultural resources are produced and reproduced in all social systems.[20] People act intentionally to accomplish their goals, but they are not totally free to act any way they wish. Instead, actions are constrained by structures created throughout a history of interaction within the social system.[21]

Organizations, like any other social structure, are produced through actions and interactions among individuals. As people rely on organizational resources such as roles, norms, and rules to guide their actions, they not only accomplish individual and organizational goals but also reproduce the organizational system itself, or what Weick calls enactment.

Scott Poole and Robert McPhee have applied this idea to two aspects of organizational communication—structure and climate.[22] In an essay on the subject, McPhee recognizes the importance of organizational structure: "I would say that structure is a defining characteristic of an organization—it is what brings about or makes possible that quality of atmosphere, that sustained, routine purposiveness that distinguishes work in an organization from activities in a group, a mob, a society, and so forth."[23] Organizational structure provides the form necessary to accomplish a variety of functions. Structure is both a manifestation and a product of communication in the organization.

20   Anthony Giddens, *Central Problems in Social Theory* (Berkeley: University of California Press, 1979); *Profiles and Critiques in Social Theory* (Berkeley: University of California Press, 1982).
21   For a summary of this idea, see Craig R. Scott, Steven R. Corman, and George Cheney, "Development of a Structurational Model of Identification in the Organization," *Communication Theory* 8 (1998): 298–336.
22   Marshall Scott Poole and Robert D. McPhee, "A Structurational Analysis of Organizational Climate," in *Communication and Organizations: An Interpretive Approach*, eds. L. L. Putnam and M. E. Pacanowsky (Beverly Hills, CA: Sage, 1983), pp. 195–220; Marshall Scott Poole, "Communication and Organizational Climates: Review, Critique, and a New Perspective," in *Organizational Communication: Traditional Themes and New Directions*, eds. R. D. McPhee and P. K. Tompkins (Beverly Hills, CA: Sage, 1985), pp. 79–108; Robert D. McPhee, "Formal Structure and Organizational Communication," in *Organizational Communication: Traditional Themes and New Directions*, eds. R. D. McPhee and P. K. Tompkins (Beverly Hills, CA: Sage, 1985), pp. 149–178. For additional commentary on structuration theory, see Stephen P. Banks and Patricia Riley, "Structuration Theory as an Ontology for Communication Research," *Communication Yearbook 16*, ed. Stanley A. Deetz (Newbury Park, CA: Sage, 1993), pp. 167–196.
23   McPhee, "Formal Structure," p. 150.

The formal structure of an organization as announced in employee manuals, organizational charts, and policies is really two types of communication. First, it is an indirect way of telling employees about the organization—its values, procedures, and methods. Second, it is a form of metacommunication (Chapter 12) in which the organization addresses its own communication patterns directly.

Organizational structure is created when individuals communicate with others in three metaphorical "sites," or *centers of structuration.*[24] The first includes all those episodes of organizational life in which people make decisions and choices that limit what can happen within the organization. This is the site of *conception.* A university's decision to establish a new college of creative arts, for example, will affect the lines of communication within the organization.

The second site of organizational structuration is the formal codification and announcement of decisions and choices, the site of *implementation.* Once the decision is made to establish the new college, the provost may send out a formal memorandum to the faculty and staff announcing the change. That formal announcement itself will be instrumental in shaping the structure of the organization in the future.

Finally, structuration occurs as organizational members act in accordance with the organizational decisions, which is the site of *reception.* To continue the example, after the decision is made to establish a college of arts, a dean will be recruited, certain department heads will meet with the new dean, and faculty lines of communication will change.

Although anyone in an organization may from time to time participate in communication at any or all three sites, structuration tends to be specialized. Top management usually is involved in conceptual communication, various staff personnel perform the job of implementation, and the general workforce itself participates in reception.

The communication activities at these three sites are often difficult and conflict laden. Indeed, rarely is a new college established at a university without considerable disagreement and resistance at all three stages, which is the case with major changes in any kind of organization. The communication patterns at the three sites may be complex and time-consuming, and the outcome is very much affected by the skill of the people involved.

The second area in which Poole and McPhee have applied structurational thinking is organizational climate,[25] which is one of the most heavily researched topics in organizational communication.[26] Traditionally, climate has been viewed as one of the key variables affecting communication and the subsequent productivity and satisfaction of employees. For Poole and McPhee, climate is the general collective description of the organization or a part of the organization that shapes members' expectations and feelings and therefore the organization's performance. Climates are enacted by the members of the organization as they go through their daily activities, and any organization may actually have a variety of climates for different groups of people.

Poole and McPhee define climate structurationally as "a collective attitude, continually produced and reproduced by members' interaction."[27] In other words, a climate is not an objective "variable" that affects the organization, nor is it an individual's perception of the organization. Rather, climate arises out of the interaction among those who affiliate with the organization. Climate is a product of structuration: It is both a medium and an outcome of interaction.[28]

Poole sees climate as a hierarchy of three strata. The first is a set of terms that members use to define and describe the organization: the *concept pool.* The second is a basic, highly abstract shared conception of the atmosphere of the organization: the *kernel climate.* Finally, the groups'

24   Robert D. McPhee, "Organizational Communication: A Structurational Exemplar," in *Rethinking Communication: Paradigm Exemplars,* eds. Brenda Dervin, Lawrence Grossberg, Barbara J. O'Keefe, and Ellen Wartella (Beverly Hills, CA: Sage, 1989), pp. 199–212.
25   Poole, "Communication and Organizational Climates"; Poole and McPhee, "Structurational Analysis."
26   This work is summarized in Poole, "Communication and Organizational Climates," pp. 79–97.
27   Poole and McPhee, "Structurational Analysis," p. 213.
28   For a contrast of the structurational approach to climate with traditional approaches, see Poole and McPhee, "Structurational Analysis."

Concept pool	Kernel climate	Particular climates	Behavorial/affective reactions
Profit	"The firm has a rigid formal structure that is often constraining"	[For First-Generation Employees:]	[For First-Generation Employees:]
First generation–second generation		"Pressure is manageable"	"High commitment"
Specialist-generalist	"Contribution to profits is very important"	"There is room for growth"	"High evaluation of own performance"
Commitment			"High satisfaction"
Creative-routine	"Creative work is valued over routine work"	[For Second-Generation Employees:]	[For Second-Generation Employees:]
Structure		"Pressure hinders performance"	"High commitment"
Bureaucracy	"Commitment of employees is important"	"Little room for growth"	"Uneven evaluation of own performance"
Renaissance man			"Low satisfaction"

FIGURE   **14.2**

Schematic of Climate Structure

translations of the kernel climate into more concrete terms affecting their particular part of an organization constitutes the third element: the *particular climate*. The kernel climate permeates the entire organization, but particular climates may vary from one segment of the organization to another.

The three layers in the hierarchy are related in a linear way: (1) The concepts create an understanding of what is going on in the organization; (2) from these basic understandings, the kernel climate arises; then (3) subgroups translate these general principles into specific elements of climate that in turn affect the thinking, feeling, and behavior of the individuals.

An example of this process is found in a study of a consulting firm.[29] The firm consisted of two generations of employees—a group that had been with the firm a relatively long time and a group of more recent employees. Though the two groups shared a common set of concepts, they seemed to experience different climates.

From these core concepts, four key elements of a kernel climate emerged in this organization:

1. "The firm has a rigid formal structure that is often constraining."
2. "Contribution to profits is very important."
3. "Creative work is valued over routine work."
4. "Commitment of employees is important."

These four elements of the kernel climate were translated differently into the particular climates of the two groups.

The first-generation employees believed that "pressure is manageable, and that there is room for growth." The second-generation employees, however, believed that "pressure hinders performance and that there is little room for growth." Figure 14.2 illustrates this example.[30]

---

29   This model of climate is based on a reinterpretation of a case study by H. Johnson in "A New Conceptualization of Source of Organizational Climate," *Administrative Science Quarterly* 3 (1976): 275–292.
30   Poole, "Communication and Organizational Climates," p. 98.

How do the elements of climate develop in an organization? We know already from a structurational perspective that the climate is produced by the practices of organizational members; and, in turn, climate affects and constrains those practices. Thus, climate is not static but constantly in the process of development. Three interacting factors enter into this developmental process.

The first is the *structure of the organization* itself. Because structure limits the kinds of interactions and practices that can be engaged in, it limits the kind of climate that can result from these interactions and practices. For example, if the organization is highly segmented with strong differentiation among employees and departments, individuals will have a limited pool of co-workers with whom they can communicate, which increases the chance of a "restrained" climate.

The second factor affecting climate is various *climate-producing apparatuses*, or mechanisms designed to affect employee perceptions and performance, such as newsletters, training programs, and the like.

The third factor is *member characteristics*, their skills and knowledge. For example, if employees are sufficiently intelligent and reflective, they may challenge existing authority and "see through" apparatuses. Member characteristics also include the degree of agreement or coordination within work groups.

Structuration in Organizational Control and Identity

Phillip Tompkins, George Cheney, and their colleagues have developed a useful and fresh approach to organizational communication.[31] They see that control is exerted in organizations in four ways.[32] The first is *simple control,* or use of direct, open power. This is much like Likert's system 1 management, in which supervisors simply force workers to comply.

The second is *technical control,* or use of machinery. For example, if employees are given a computer and told to use it for their work, the computer itself limits what they can do and how they can do it.

The third form of control is *bureaucratic,* which involves the use of organizational procedures and formal rules, much as Weber envisioned. Employees may be given a manual that includes policies to be followed, and memos and reports are used to communicate additional expectations.

The fourth, and most interesting to Cheney and Tompkins, is *concertive control*—the use of interpersonal relationships and teamwork. This is the most subtle form of control because it relies on a shared reality and shared values:

> In the concertive organization, the explicitly written rules and regulations are largely replaced by the common understanding of values, objectives, and means of achievement, along with a deep appreciation for the organization's "mission." This we call . . . the "soul of the new organization."[33]

With its emphasis on concertive control, this theory is really in both the positional and relational traditions. Because the premises on which concertive control is based are managerial and because control is accomplished at least in part through formal channels, it is included among the positional theories in this chapter.

Although the four types of control are normally found in various combinations, there is a trend away from simple, direct control toward this more subtle and complex form. The theory of unobtrusive control deals primarily with the

31   George Cheney and Phillip K. Tompkins, "Coming to Terms with Organizational Identification and Commitment," *Central States Speech Journal* 38 (1987): 1–15; Phillip K. Tompkins and George Cheney, "Account Analysis of Organizations: Decision Making and Identification," in *Communication and Organizations: An Interpretive Approach,* eds. L. L. Putnam and M. E. Pacanowsky (Beverly Hills, CA: Sage, 1983), pp. 123–146; Phillip K. Tompkins and George Cheney, "Communication and Unobtrusive Control in Contemporary Organizations," in *Organizational Communication: Traditional Themes and New Directions,* eds. R. D. McPhee and P. K. Tompkins (Beverly Hills, CA: Sage, 1985), pp. 179–210. For a summary and extension see James S. Sass and Daniel J. Canary, "Organizational Commitment and Identification: An Examination of Conceptual and Operational Convergence," *Western Journal of Speech Communication* 55 (1991): 275–293.
32   Tompkins and Cheney base this conceptualization on the work of R. Edwards, "The Social Relations of Production at the Point of Production," in *Complex Organizations: Critical Perspectives,* eds. M. Zey-Ferrell and M. Aiken (Glenview, IL: Scott, Foresman, 1981).
33   Tompkins and Cheney, "Communication and Unobtrusive Control," p. 184.

ways control is managed within the concertive system.

Organizational control is a kind of "discipline," or force that maintains order and consistency, and power is the means by which this kind of discipline is accomplished.[34] Power can never be avoided and is always in the system. At the same time, power is not an external force but is always created by various forms of interaction within the organization. Power, then, accomplishes control, but by submitting to control, the organization itself reinforces the very sources of power.

In concertive control, discipline is accomplished by "normalizing" behaviors, making certain ways of operating normal and natural, something organizational members want to do. Many things become normalized in organizations, including power relations. So again we see that discipline reinforces the very power relations that makes discipline possible. In contemporary organizations, disciplinary control is best accomplished in four ways.

First, it involves unobtrusive methods. Discipline is not necessarily obvious or conscious but is part of the ongoing daily activity of the organization. For example, something as simple as normal work hours is a form of control, and to the extent that employees accept these hours, they are participating in their own control.

Second, discipline is collaboratively produced. Organizational members work together to make a set of practices normal, to establish a set of standards, a discipline. Meetings are a good example. In many organizations, meetings tend to start on the hour and end on the hour. Whether one, two, or three hours in length, this pattern is common. People collaborate in making this a normal state of affairs. They come on time and when the hour is up, they—following their expectations—pack up and head for the door.

Third, discipline is a part of social relations. What people say and do to one another is both governed by and produces normalized practices. The unacknowledged rules in an organization tell you what topics you can and cannot talk about on the job, when and where interaction can take place, what nonverbal behaviors are appropriate or inappropriate, and who can initiate conversations.

Finally, the most effective means of control are based on the values that motivate organizational members—the very things for which they strive. This may include money, time, accomplishment, sense of teamwork, and so forth.

Following the classical work of Herbert Simon,[35] Tompkins and Cheney show how control is accomplished by shaping the decisions made by organizational members. Simon believes that organizational decision making follows a syllogistic pattern, in which decision makers reason deductively from general premises and in which choices are based on those premises. Control is exerted when workers, who accept certain general premises, reason to the conclusions desired by management.

The premises are accepted because of incentives like wages and the authority of people with legitimate power (see Weber). This acceptance does not come automatically, however, because conflict often results from differences between employees' personal beliefs and the premises of the organization. Indeed, a substantial amount of industrial strife results from such differences. How, then, do organizations achieve concertive control in the face of potential conflict? The answer lies in the process of constructing personal identity.[36]

Among many things created through interaction in organizations is personal identity. Naturally, we have complex personal identities, and much of who we are is based in the relationships we establish with others within groups and organizations. One's identity is tightly connected to identification. *Identification* is a process of linking oneself with others. You might identify with a relative or friend, with a group, or with an entire organization. In organizational life, we identify,

---

34 James R. Barker and George Cheney, "The Concept and the Practices of Discipline in Contemporary Organizational Life," *Communication Monographs* 61 (1994): 19–43.
35 Herbert Simon, *Administrative Behavior* (New York: Free Press, 1976). See also Perrow, *Complex Organizations*.
36 This process is detailed in Scott, Corman, and Cheney, "Development of a Structurational Model."

or link ourselves, with many different sources. Here, the theorists rely largely on the work of Kenneth Burke (Chapter 8). *Identification* occurs when individuals become aware of their common ground. We identify with individuals with whom we share something in common; and the more we share with one another, the more the potential identification between us. When employees identify with the organization, they are more likely to accept the organization's premises and make decisions consistent with organizational objectives.

Who we are in the organization, our identities, determine to a certain extent the identifications we forge. At the same time, our identifications shape who we are, our identities. This two-way street is referred to in the theory as the *identity-identification duality*. The theorists believe that the identity-identification process is structurational. In other words, in the process of actively seeking affiliations with others, we unwittingly create structures that in turn affect our identities. Many a professor has been made this way. A student finds a professor he or she really likes, identifies with this person, establishes a relationship with the professor, starts to take on academic values, and helps the professor. The effect of all of this is a set of expectations between the student, the professor, and perhaps others that lead to the development of an academic identity leading to the decision to go to graduate school and then on to university teaching, where the pattern is continued.

What will begin to happen within an organization over time is that members create a mutual identification with the organization. Because their personal identity is shaped in part by this identification, they begin to take on the values, ideas, and ideals of the organization. This identification shapes members' assumptions and behaviors, and this is the essence of concertive control, in which members come to "reason" jointly with shared premises. The acceptance of organizational premises is part of a process of organizational identification.[37]

Once a certain amount of identification is achieved, organizational enthymemes make con-

certive control possible. Described by Aristotle over two thousand years ago, the *enthymeme* is a rhetorical device used to involve audiences in the advocate's reasoning process.[38] In an enthymeme, one or more premises in a reasoning chain are left out, to be supplied by the audience. In organizations, members are a kind of audience that reaches particular conclusions based on shared implicit premises. Sometimes the suppressed premises are widely accepted cultural values; other times they are inculcated through persuasion.

For example, a speaker advocating the prohibition of offshore drilling might reason that (1) offshore drilling endangers the fragile coastal ecology; (2) coastal ecology is valuable and should be protected; (3) therefore, offshore drilling should be prohibited. In addressing fellow members of an environmental organization, this speaker would not need to be explicit about this argument and could rely on members' acceptance of these premises, leading to an almost automatic acceptance of the claim. They would readily work against offshore drilling because of their identification with the environmental organization.

Tompkins and Cheney are especially interested in how enthymemes are used in organizations for unobtrusive control of decision making. These authors point out that when members display loyalty and behave "organizationally," they are essentially accepting key organizational premises. Often organizations directly sell their premises to employees through company newsletters, training programs, and the like. Other times, organizations employ a variety of incentives to induce employees to become loyal. In any case, once employees accept certain premises, their conclusions and decisions are controlled.

For example, one premise of many industrial firms is that obsolescence is positive because it

---

37   George Cheney, "The Rhetoric of Identification and the Study of Organizational Communication," *Quarterly Journal of Speech* 69 (1983): 143–158.
38   Lane Cooper, *The Rhetoric of Aristotle* (New York: Meredith, 1932). See also Lloyd Bitzer, "Aristotle's Enthymeme Revisited," *Quarterly Journal of Speech* 45 (1959): 399–408; Jesse Delia, "The Logic Fallacy, Cognitive Theory, and the Enthymeme: A Search for the Foundations of Reasoned Discourse," *Quarterly Journal of Speech* 56 (1970): 140–148.

maintains progress, sustains the market, and protects jobs. Once engineers buy this idea, they opt automatically for designs that include planned obsolescence because they accept the basic organizational premise.

To explore organizational identification, Michael Papa, Mohammad Auwal, and Arvind Singhal studied the Grameen Bank in Bangladesh.[39] Grameen (meaning "rural bank") was founded in 1976 as an experiment in rural development and empowerment. It was designed to extend banking services to the poor, eliminate exploitation, create an employment base, and establish small, local banking institutions run by the people themselves.

From the beginning, participants, including loan applicants, were recruited to support the mission of the bank. Through such means as inspirational talks, new employees were induced to establish identification and buy into the values and goals of the organization. They were invited into a team concept, in which all employees, and even clients, were to be working together to achieve the permanent elimination of poverty. The bank has been very successful and has received international acclaim, an honor that is shared with employees at every level. The workers are the strongest advocates for the mission and values of the organization, and they enforce very high standards (not mandated by management) on themselves and other employees.

The organization represents the epitome of concertive control through identification. Members work long hours and do whatever they need to do to ensure that loan recipients make their payments. Because employees' identities are so wrapped up in the bank, they exert tremendous peer pressure to work hard on behalf of the organization.

Employees identify both with the bank mission of uplifting the poor and with other employees at their local branch office. This very strong level of concertive control is paradoxical. It seems to empower employees to establish their own standards, but in the process, their procedures and work ethic have become institutionalized, which ironically disempowers employees, who might otherwise want to establish new ways of working. Employees are emancipated from oppression, but they are oppressed anew by the very forms they themselves have created.

Concertive control is one of several mechanisms used by organizations to manage multiple identities. The complex organization today does not have a single image with a single set of consistent interests. Rather, it is a complex system of interacting, sometimes contradictory, identities, and organizational communication must manage this multiple state of affairs. George Cheney explains the difficulty:

> To speak of collective identity is to speak of collective or shared interests—or at least of how the interests of a collective are represented and understood. This is a fundamental concern of contemporary organizations. Large bureaucratic organizations are in the business of identity management; their controlling members must be concerned about how to (re)present the organization as a whole *and* how to connect the individual identities of many members to that embracing collective identity.[40]

Thus the organization must have a way of inducing individuals, with all their variable interests, into a common identification with the organization. A diversity of identities, even conflicting ones, can be handled if there is at least some level of overall identification with the organization as a whole. Sometimes organizations must change, which means altering an identity, but to survive, the organization must create a new identity based in part on the interests of a substantial portion of its membership.

For these reasons, unbridled pluralism and diversity cannot be tolerated by an organization, and concertive control through identification is therefore essential.

39   Michael J. Papa, Mohammad A. Auwal, and Arvind Singhal, "Organizing for Social Change Within Concertive Control Systems: Member Identification, Empowerment, and the Masking of Discipline," *Communication Monographs* 64 (1997): 219–249.
40   George Cheney et al., *Rhetoric in an Organizational Society: Managing Multiple Identities* (Columbia: University of South Carolina Press, 1991), p. 14.

THE CULTURAL TRADITION

The cultural tradition in organizational studies emphasizes the ways people construct an organizational reality. As the study of an organization's way of life, this approach looks at the meanings and values of the members. It examines the way individuals use stories, rituals, symbols, and other types of activity to produce and reproduce a set of understandings.[41]

John Van Maanen and Stephen Barley outline four "domains" of organizational culture.[42] The first domain, the *ecological context,* is the physical world, including the location, the time and history, and the social context within which the organization operates. The second domain of culture consists of networks, or *differential interaction.* Then there are the common ways of interpreting events, or *collective understanding.* It is the "content" of the culture—its ideas, ideals, values, and practices. Finally, there are the practices or actions of individuals, which constitutes the *individual* domain.

Few large organizations comprise a single culture. In most cases, subcultures identified with particular groups will emerge. You can imagine an organization as a set of Venn diagrams or overlapping cultural circles.

We encountered the cultural tradition in organizational studies in Chapter 10, where we looked at Michael Pacanowsky and Nick O'Donnell-Trujillo's interpretive theory, which examines the ways the members of an organization create and perpetuate an understanding of their experience through stories, rituals, symbols, and other means.[43] For more information about organizational cultures, you may want to refer back to that chapter.

The cultural traditions in organizational communication theory mark an important shift in this field—a shift from functionalism to interpretation, from the assumption that the organization has preexisting elements that act on one another in predictable ways to the assumption that it is a constantly changing set of meanings constructed through communication.

This distinction is not limited to organizational communication but is now seen in virtually every area of the field. It was discussed in some detail earlier in the book, especially in Chapters 1, 9, and 10. Dennis Mumby believes that the increasing popularity of the interpretive approach is not trivial:

> Beginning roughly in the 70s, researchers have become increasingly concerned with examining the various ways in which communication functions dynamically, processually, and constitutively to create the collective meaning systems to which we give the name "organization." . . . This move toward a more "meaning-centered" approach to organizations has been successful in problematizing many of the terms associated with mainstream functionalist organizational research—terms such as hierarchy, message, effectiveness, and most importantly, the term "organization" itself. In effect, the shift to interpretive theory and research has created a fruitful and productive "crisis of representation" . . . in organizational communication studies. This crisis has resulted in fundamental challenges.[44]

Mumby identifies two schools of thought in this tradition. The first, "a descriptive hermeneutic," depicts the process by which communication creates organization and presents useful interpretations of organizational events. Another branch of this work is the "hermeneutic of suspicion," in which a more critical approach is taken. Consistent with the critical theories discussed in Chapter 11, this version of hermeneutics looks at the organization as a site of domination, a place

---

41   See James A. Anderson, ed., *Communication Yearbook 11* (Newbury Park, CA: Sage, 1988), pp. 310–405; Michael Pacanowsky, "Creating and Narrating Organizational Realities," in *Rethinking Communication: Paradigm Exemplars,* eds. Brenda Dervin, Lawrence Grossberg, Barbara J. O'Keefe, and Ellen Wartella (Newbury Park, CA: Sage, 1989), pp. 250–257.
42   John Van Maanen and Stephen R. Barley, "Cultural Organization: Fragments of a Theory," in *Organizational Culture,* eds. P. J. Frost and others (Beverly Hills, CA: Sage, 1985), pp. 31–54.
43   Michael E. Pacanowsky and Nick O'Donnell-Trujillo, "Communication and Organizational Cultures," *Western Journal of Speech Communication* 46 (1982): 115–130. See also Michael E. Pacanowsky and Nick O'Donnell-Trujillo, "Organizational Communication as Cultural Performance," *Communication Monographs* 50 (1983): 126–147.
44   Dennis K. Mumby, "Critical Organizational Communication Studies: The Next 10 Years," *Communication Monographs* 60 (1993): 18–25.

where ideology is taught and the hegemony of interests promoted.[45]

The critical tradition in organizational communication is growing in popularity and visibility. Dennis Mumby shows that organizational cultures are not neutral, spontaneous creations but are products of ideology that promote the interests of certain groups over those of others.[46] Cultures are political, or power laden, and the language and other symbols used within the organization are products of dominant cultures and reinforce dominant interests.

Stanley Deetz adds to this analysis by writing that in contemporary democracies, the public voice is being replaced by corporate interests that dominate virtually all other aspects of society, and our lives are determined in large measure by the decisions made in the interest of managing corporate organizations, a movement called "managerialism."[47] One of the profound effects of managerialism is the privileging of managerial interests over those of other stakeholders. Deetz calls for a stakeholder/multiple-interest model in which dialogue becomes the privileged form of communication and conflict is worked through rather than covered up.[48]

◐ COMMENTARY AND CRITIQUE

We learn from the theories in this chapter that organizations are created through communication as people interact to accomplish their individual and joint goals. The process of communication also results in a variety of structural outcomes such as authority relations, roles, communication networks, and climate. All these structural elements are results of the interaction among individuals and groups within the organization, and all in turn affect future interactions within the organization.

The theme of networks was chosen to organize the material in this chapter because this term captures the interactive nature of organizational structure and function. Network theory is

based on individual interactions among people, which build up into a macrostructure. The idea of multiple networks accommodates most of the ideas presented in this chapter, including bureaucracy, control, managerial style, culture, and structuration.

In this chapter we have looked at three traditions related to organizational networks—the positional, the relational, and the cultural. Strictly positional theories express a common structuralist mythology, but for the communication scholar, they omit a great deal. Classical theories such as Weber's reflect and may have contributed to a powerful cultural norm about how organizing should occur. These theories, however, do not provide a sense of how the interaction among members results in meaningful outcome. Indeed, one contribution of communication theory has been to provide additional insights into the importance of communication in organizations.

Likert's theory is somewhat better than earlier theories in showing the importance of communication, but even this theory fails to recognize the pervasiveness of communication as the very means by which organizing occurs. The theory is appealing because of its formalistic explanatory style. This is a strictly linear theory, however, which leaves little to the imagination of indi-

45   For summaries of this work, see David Carlone and Bryan Taylor, "Organizational Communication and Cultural Studies: A Review Essay," *Communication Theory* 8 (1998): 337–367; and Branislav Kovačić, "The Democracy and Organizational Communication Theories of Deetz, Mumby, and Associates," *Watershed Research Traditions in Human Communication Theory*, eds. Donald P. Cushman and Branislav Kovačić (Albany: SUNY Press, 1995): 211–238.
46   Dennis K. Mumby, *Communication and Power in Organizations: Discourse, Ideology, and Domination* (Norwood, NJ: Ablex, 1988). See also Dennis K. Mumby, "The Problem of Hegemony: Rereading Gramsci for Organizational Communication Studies," *Western Journal of Communication* 61 (1997): 343–375.
47   Stanley Deetz, *Democracy in an Age of Corporate Colonization: Developments in Communication and the Politics of Everyday Life* (Albany: SUNY Press, 1992). See also Mats Alvesson and Stanley Deetz, "Critical Theory and Postmodernism Approaches to Organization Studies," in *Handbook of Organizational Studies*, eds. S. Clegg, C. Harding, and W. Nord (London: Sage, 1996), pp. 173–202.
48   Stanley A. Deetz, "Stakeholders and Negotiating the New Social Contracts: A Communication Theory Perspective," in *Communication: Views from the Helm for the 21 Century*, st ed. Judith S. Trent (Boston: Allyn & Bacon, 1998), pp. 153–161.

viduals other than those who establish the managerial system of the company.

Likert's theory is part of the human relations movement. The movement helped practitioners and scholars understand that people have needs and values related to organizational functioning and that communication is an important aspect of organizational life. Likert's version, like several others, though, is simplistic in its linear, causal reasoning.

Human relations was criticized almost from its beginning.[49] Its problems are primarily attributable to its extreme position and simplistic view that high morale improves productivity. The correlations that are claimed to exist between human relations factors and organizational effectiveness have, for the most part, failed the test of empirical study. We reviewed one study in which a positive correlation was found between managerial style and satisfaction, but this study does not address productivity. In many cases the correlations have not been found in research, and where they do appear, serious methodological objections have been raised.

In some ways what the human relations movement was trying to do has been more successfully accomplished by the organizational culture movement—namely, to recognize and characterize the human needs within the organization. Indeed, apart from achieving task-oriented goals, organizations are also human cultures, rich with tradition, shared meaning, and ritual. What people do in organizations creates and reflects the underlying culture of the organization.

The cultural approach to organizational theory is a major advance. It refocuses our attention on a set of processes that are not examined carefully in traditional management-oriented, variable-analytical studies. Traditionally, management is seen as a rational process of manipulating "things" for the benefit of the organization. The culture approach shows us that this is only partly true. In fact, a culture that is out of the conscious control of management is a major part of what characterizes an organization. The cultural approach refutes the idea that managers

can somehow manipulate "objects" (like materials and machines) that are independent from the organization itself. The objects are only known through the meanings of the organizational culture, and those meanings will change from one organization, or even suborganization, to another. Organizations are not adapted to environments; rather, organizations in a real way create their own environments based on shared conceptions and interpretations.

The whole notion of boundary is fuzzy and controversial. Where, exactly, does an organization begin and end? David Seibold has written that groups and organizations so entail one another that any separation is false.[50] In a similar argument, Linda Putnam, Cynthia Stohl, and their colleagues have written that groups are never containers but always part of a larger environment rich with intergroup and organizational connections.[51]

Not realizing this, the empirically minded manager may think of culture as just another variable to be manipulated and that the culture can be managed.[52] This idea can lead to the negative consequence of attempted ideological control. The answer to this criticism is that all forms of management exert some kind of ideological control, even if it is concertive. Let us therefore create the most humane and productive cultures possible.

Once you acknowledge that all interactions contribute to a cascading construction of culture

49   For a comprehensive critique, see Perrow, *Complex Organizations*.
50   David R. Seibold, "Groups and Organizations: Premises and Perspectives," in *Communication: Views from the Helm for the 21st Century*, ed. Judith S. Trent (Boston: Allyn & Bacon, 1998), pp. 162–168.
51   See, for example, Linda L. Putnam and Cynthia Stohl, "Bona Fide Groups: A Reconceptualization of Groups in Context," *Communication Studies* 41 (1990): 248–265; Cynthia Stohl and Linda L. Putnam, "Group Communication in Context: Implications for the Study of Bona Fide Groups," in *Group Communication in Context: Studies of Natural Groups*, ed. L. R. Frey (Hillsdale, NJ: Erlbaum, 1994), pp. 285–292; Linda L. Putnam and Cynthia Stohl, "Bona Fide Groups: An Alternative Perspective for Communication and Small Group Decision Making," in *Communication and Group Decision Making*, eds. R. Y. Hirokawa and M. S. Poole (Thousand Oaks, CA: Sage, 1996), pp. 247–278.
52   A discussion of this possibility is presented by Sonja A. Sackmann, "Managing Organizational Culture: Dreams and Possibilities," in *Communication Yearbook 13*, ed. James Anderson (Newbury Park, CA: Sage, 1990), pp. 114–148.

within the organization, it is a small step to begin wondering about how the network of associations within an organization might be made more humane and inclusive. This question has led to the workplace democracy movement, in which the voices of multiple stakeholder groups, including all employees and important groups "outside" the organization, are recognized as important in organizational decision making.[53] The various theories of organizational democracy constitute a deep critique of structural and positional approaches to the organization. Instead of a top-down, managerial approach to control in which conflict is suppressed, democratic theories call for dialogue, participation, and valuing conflict as a way of enhancing the organizational life of everyone involved.

There is a kinship between much of the work in workplace democracy and that of critical theory. Although not as well developed in this field as in media studies, critical approaches to organizational communication do appear to be on the rise. Mumby alerts us to the need to address three issues in critical studies.[54] First, because the act of research is itself political, the researcher must become more aware of his or her own power over those studied and the ways research studies shape organizational relations. Second, organizational communication scholars must look at how the field itself has constructed a view of organizations that promotes certain interests over others. Finally, organizational communication has been seemingly oblivious to developments in feminist theory and should incorporate feminist insights into the critique of organization.[55]

Communication theory has made a tremendous contribution to our understanding of organizations. By showing the importance of communication patterns in the construction of network connections, power structures, and culture, this work has greatly enhanced the field of organizational studies.

---

53   George Cheney et al., "Democracy, Participation, and Communication at Work: A Multidisciplinary Review," in *Communication Yearbook 21*, ed. Michael E. Roloff (Thousand Oaks, CA: Sage, 1998), pp. 35–91.
54   Mumby, "Critical."
55   See, for example, Judi Marshall, "Viewing Organizational Communication from a Feminist Perspective: A Critique and Some Offerings," in *Communication Yearbook 16*, ed. Stanley Deetz (Newbury Park, CA: Sage, 1993), pp. 122–143.

CHAPTER

15

COMMUNICATION
AND MEDIA

We are living in what Marshall McLuhan calls the "global village." Modern communication media make it possible for millions of people throughout the world to be in touch with nearly any spot on the globe. George Gerbner points to the importance of the media in society:

> This broad "public-making" significance of mass media of communications—the ability to create publics, define issues, provide common terms of reference, and thus to allocate attention and power—has evoked a large number of theoretical contributions.[1]

Mass communication is the process whereby media organizations produce and transmit messages to large publics and the process by which those messages are sought, used, understood, and influenced by audiences.

Central to any study of mass communication are the media.[2] Media organizations distribute messages that affect and reflect the cultures of society, and they provide information simultaneously to large heterogeneous audiences, making media part of society's institutional forces.

"Media," of course, imply "mediation" because they come between the audience and the world. Denis McQuail suggests several metaphors to capture this idea: Media are *windows* that enable us to see beyond our immediate surroundings, *interpreters* that help us make sense of experience, *platforms* or *carriers* that convey information, *interactive communication* that includes audience feedback, *signposts* that provide us with instructions and directions, *filters* that screen out parts of experience and focus on others, *mirrors*

---

1   George Gerbner, "Mass Media and Human Communication Theory," in *Human Communication Theory,* ed. F. E. X. Dance (New York: Holt, Rinehart & Winston, 1967), p. 45.

2   For recent overviews and histories of mass communication theory, see Bradley S. Greenberg and Michael B. Salwen, "Mass Communication Theory and Research: Concepts and Models," in *An Integrated Approach to Communication Theory and Research,* eds. Michael B. Salwen and Don W. Stacks (Mahwah, NJ: Erlbaum, 1996), pp. 63–78; and Robert S. Fortner, "Mediated Communication Theory," in *Building Communication Theories: A Socio/Cultural Approach,* ed. Fred L. Casmir (Hillsdale, NJ: Erlbaum, 1994), pp. 209–240. Definitions of *mass communication* are discussed in Sandra J. Ball-Rokeach and Muriel G. Cantor, eds., *Media, Audience, and Social Structure* (Beverly Hills, CA: Sage, 1986), pp. 10–11; and Denis McQuail, *Mass Communication Theory: An Introduction* (London: Sage, 1987), pp. 29–47.

FIGURE **15.1**

An Organizing Model

that reflect ourselves back to us, and *barriers* that block the truth.[3] Joshua Meyrowitz adds three additional metaphors—media as *conduits,* media as *languages,* and media as *environments.*[4] What are media, then? There is no single or simple definition.

◖ AN ORGANIZING MODEL

Media scholars recognize two faces of mass communication.[5] One face looks from the media to the larger society and its institutions. Theorists interested in the media–society link are concerned with the ways media are embedded in society and the mutual influence between larger social structures and the media. This is the *macro* side of mass communication theory.

The second face looks toward people, as groups and individuals. This face reflects the link between the media and audiences. Theorists interested in the media–audience link focus on group and individual effects and outcomes of the media transaction. This is the *micro* side of mass communication theory.[6]

Figure 15.1 illustrates the two faces of mass communication. The model may imply that these two sides are different things, but in truth they are the same thing looked at from different perspectives. The relationship between media and institutions is possible only through the media's transaction with audiences, and the audience–media relationship is impossible to separate from the institutions of the society in which those audiences reside. Thus, the model is not a map of the mass communication process but depicts the areas of media research and theory.

The chapter is divided into five sections corresponding to the parts of the model: (1) media content and structure, (2) the media–institution link, (3) the media–audience link, (4) cultural outcomes, and (5) individual outcomes.

3   McQuail, *Mass Communication,* pp. 52–53.
4   Joshua Meyrowitz, "Images of Media: Hidden Ferment—and Harmony—in the Field," *Journal of Communication* 43 (1993): 55–67.
5   For an excellent exploration of the links between the media and larger sociocultural structures and smaller personal and individual effects, see Karl Erik Rosengren, "Culture, Media, and Society: Agency and Structure, Continuity and Change," in *Media Effects and Beyond: Culture, Socializations, and Lifestyles,* ed. Karl Erik Rosengren (London: Routledge, 1994), pp. 3–28. See also Veikko Pietilä, "Perspectives on Our Past: Charting the Histories of Mass Communication Studies," *Critical Studies in Mass Communication* 11 (1994): 346–361.
6   This conceptualization is adapted from a discussion of mass communication theory by McQuail, *Mass Communication,* pp. 53–57.

◖ MEDIA CONTENT AND STRUCTURE

Certain theories have emphasized intrinsic structural properties of media and media messages. Of particular concern here is the "sending" side of the mass communication process, or what media producers actually produce. A useful term for this general process is *encoding*.[7] There are two aspects of production considered important. The first is the medium in which communication takes place, and the second is the content of mediated messages. In the following two sections, we look at each of these.

Medium Theory

Perhaps Marshall McLuhan is most responsible for calling our attention to the importance of media as media. He is a well-known figure in the study of popular culture, receiving attention because of his interesting and bizarre style and his startling and thought-provoking ideas.[8] Although the specifics of McLuhan's theory are often rejected today, his general thesis has received widespread acceptance: Media, apart from whatever content is transmitted, impact individuals and society. This idea in its various forms is what we mean by "medium theory."

McLuhan was not the first to write about this idea. Indeed, his ideas were profoundly affected by the work of his mentor Harold Adams Innis, who taught that communication media are the essence of civilization and that history is directed by the predominant media of each age.[9]

For McLuhan and Innis, media are extensions of the human mind, so that the primary interest of any historical period is biased by the predominant media in use. In other words, what happens and what seems significant in a historical period are determined by the media. Heavy media such as parchment, clay, or stone are lasting and therefore *time binding*. Because they facilitate communication from one generation to another, these media are biased toward tradition. In contrast, *space-binding* media such as paper are light and

easy to transport, so they facilitate communication from one location to another, fostering empire building, large bureaucracy, and the military.

Speech as a medium, because it is produced one sound at a time, encourages people to organize their experience chronologically. Speech also requires knowledge and tradition and therefore supports community and relationship. Written media, which are spatially arranged, produce a different kind of culture. The space-binding effect of writing produces interests in political authority and the growth of empires across the land.

McLuhan's thesis is that people adapt to their environment through a certain balance or ratio of the senses, and the primary medium of the age brings out a particular sense ratio, thereby affecting perception.[10] McLuhan sees every medium as an extension of some human faculty, exaggerating the sense. "The wheel . . . is an extension of the foot. The book is an extension of the eye. . . . Clothing, an extension of the skin. . . . Electric circuitry, an extension of the central nervous system."[11]

Before printing was invented, tribal people were primarily hearing-oriented communicators, emotionally and interpersonally close. For the tribal person, "hearing was believing." But the invention of the printing press changed all that.

---

7   An excellent summary of the vast amount of work in this area is provided by David Barker and Bernard M. Timberg, "Encounters with the Television Image: Thirty Years of Encoding Research," in *Communication Yearbook 15*, ed. Stanley Deetz (Newbury Park, CA: Sage, 1992), pp. 209–238.

8   McLuhan's best-known works are *The Gutenberg Galaxy: The Making of Typographic Man* (Toronto: University of Toronto Press, 1962); *The Mechanical Bride* (New York: Vanguard, 1951); *Understanding Media* (New York: McGraw-Hill, 1964); Marshall McLuhan and Quentin Fiore, *The Medium Is the Massage* (New York: Bantam, 1967). I have relied on the synthesis of Bruce Gronbeck, "McLuhan as Rhetorical Theorist," *Journal of Communication* 31 (1981): 117–128.

9   J. W. Carey, "Harold Adams Innis and Marshall McLuhan," *Antioch Review* 27 (1967): 5–39. Innis' works include *The Bias of Communication* (Toronto: University of Toronto Press, 1951); and *Empire and Communications*, 2nd ed. (Toronto: University of Toronto Press, 1972).

10   Good brief summaries of McLuhan's theory can be found in the following: Kenneth Boulding, "The Medium Is the Massage," in *McLuhan: Hot and Cool*, ed. G. E. Stearn (New York: Dial, 1967), pp. 56–64; Tom Wolfe, "The New Life Out There," in *McLuhan: Hot and Cool*, ed. G. E. Stearn (New York: Dial, 1967), pp. 34–56; Carey, "Innis and McLuhan."

11   McLuhan and Fiore, *Massage.*

The Gutenberg age brought a new sense ratio into being, in which sight predominated. The rise of print in Western culture forced people into a linear, logical, and categorical kind of perception.

Electronic technology has brought back an aural, or hearing, predominance. The Gutenberg technology of printing created an explosion in society, separating and segmenting individual from individual, but the electronic age has created an implosion, bringing the world back together in a "global village." As a result, "it is forcing us to reconsider and reevaluate practically every thought, every action, and every institution formerly taken for granted."[12] If McLuhan had lived long enough, what would he have said about the Internet?

McLuhan is perhaps best known for his saying "The medium is the message."[13] This curious and thought-provoking catchphrase highlights the general influence that a medium has apart from its content. Tom Wolfe puts the matter this way: "It doesn't matter if the networks show twenty hours a day of sadistic cowboys caving in people's teeth or twenty hours of Pablo Casals droning away on his cello in a pure-culture white Spanish drawing room. It doesn't matter about the content."[14] And here, of course, McLuhan parts company from most contemporary mass communication researchers, who believe that the content matters a great deal. Today, most media theorists would agree that both content and medium matter.

Donald Ellis summarized the literature on medium theory and presented a well-codified set of propositions representing a contemporary perspective on this subject.[15] Following Innis and McLuhan, Ellis notes that the predominant media at any given time will shape behavior and thought. As media change, so do the ways in which we think, manage information, and relate to one another. There are sharp differences among oral, written, and electronic media.

Oral communication is highly malleable and organic. Oral messages are immediate and ephemeral, so that individuals and groups must keep information in their minds and pass it on through speech. Because everyday experience cannot really be separated from the oral medium of transmission, life and knowledge cannot be separated. The telling and retelling of stories over time privilege narrative as a form of communication and require group memory as the "holder" of society's knowledge. This can lead to a collective consciousness in which little distinction is made between self and group. Group identification and cohesiveness are high when oral media predominate.

Writing, and especially the advent of printing, led to profound changes in society. When you can write something down, you can separate it from the moment. You can manipulate it, change it, edit, and recast. In other words, you can "act on" information and knowledge in a way that is not evident in the oral tradition. This leads to a separation of knowledge (what is known) from the knower (who knows it). Those who can read and write have special status, so that formal education takes on an important role. What can be known (that which is written down) can become known by reading. Knowledge, then, becomes objectified and can assume the status of truth, and individuals and groups can be divided among those who "have" the truth and those who do not. Further, information can be stored, or saved, which makes literacy a tool of conservation. Importance is assigned to that which is "stored" in written language.

The third major shift occurs when electronic media come to the fore. Electronic media are something like orality in that they can be immediate and ephemeral, but they are not tied down to a particular place because they can be broadcast. Electronic media extend your perception beyond where you are at any given moment, creating the "global village." At the same time, like print, electronic media allow information to be stored. Because they are more readily available than print, electronic media create an informa-

12   McLuhan and Fiore, *Massage*.
13   McLuhan, *Understanding Media*, p. 7.
14   Wolfe, "New Life," p. 19.
15   Donald G. Ellis, *Crafting Society: Ethnicity, Class, and Communication Theory* (Mahwah, NJ: Erlbaum, 1999).

tion explosion, and a great competition occurs among various media to be heard and seen. Information in electronic media is sold like a commodity, which creates pressure for information to be attractive. Knowledge in the electronic age changes rapidly, and we become aware of different versions of truth. The constant change created by electronic media can make us feel confused and perhaps unsettled.

If orality creates a culture of community and literacy creates a culture of class, then electronic communication creates a culture of "cells," or groups pitted against one another to promote their special interests. A new kind of public not bound to place is created. The politics of interest prevails, and democracy, along with its attendant value of civility, assumes importance as a way to manage differences. Yet, ironically the competition and commodity-based economy that accompanies electronic media fight against the very values most needed in this environment—civility and collegiality. So, electronic communication creates the paradox of separation through difference and the importance of participatory democracy.

If you were a member of a primarily oral culture, difference would be minimal, and decisions would be made collectively based on the wisdom of tradition as it has been passed down generation to generation. If you were a member of a primarily print-oriented culture, decisions would rely on "truth" stored in documents, and those who had access to information would have great influence as a class in society's decision making. But today, you are likely a member of a primarily electronic culture in which you identify with interest groups that vie against one another. You experience many voices, and societal decisions must be made by hearing all the voices, integrating these in some way, and creating forms that accommodate as many interests as possible.

Ellis' compilation of ideas about media give us a good sense of medium theory and how it places media qua media at the center of social structure and change. To continue this analysis, we turn now to the work of Jean Baudrillard.

Jean Baudrillard and the Semiotics of Media

Semiotics has provided a powerful tool for examining the impact of mass media. For the semiotician, content is important, but content is a product of the use of signs. This approach focuses on the ways producers create signs and the ways audiences understand them.

Semiotics has a long history of development in the twentieth century (see Chapter 4).[16] This field helps us see how signs are used to interpret events and can be an especially good tool for analyzing the content of media messages.[17] Most would agree that signs take on special significance in the media, and the media shape in many ways how signs function for us. To pursue this idea in greater detail, we will take a closer look at the work of the French social critic Jean Baudrillard.[18]

Baudrillard believes that signs have become increasingly separated from the objects they represent and that the media have propelled this process to the point where nothing is real. The media did not suddenly create this condition but exacerbated a tendency that has been going on throughout modern history.

Sign use has gone through an evolution in society. At first, a sign was a simple representation of an object or condition. The sign had a clear connection with the signified. This Baudrillard calls the stage of the *symbolic order*, common in feudal society. In the second stage, *counterfeits*,

16   See, for example, Wendy Leeds-Hurwitz, *Semiotics and Communication: Signs, Codes, Cultures* (Hillsdale, NJ: Erlbaum, 1993).
17   Especially good summaries of this field are provided by Donald L. Fry and Virginia H. Fry, "A Semiotic Model for the Study of Mass Communication," in *Communication Yearbook 9*, ed. M. L. McLaughlin (Beverly Hills, CA: Sage, 1986), pp. 443–462; and Klaus Bruhn Jensen, "When Is Meaning? Communication Theory, Pragmatism, and Mass Media Reception," in *Communication Yearbook 14*, ed. James A. Anderson (Newbury Park, CA: Sage, 1991), pp. 3–32.
18   Among Baudrillard's many works are *Simulations*, trans. Paul Foss, Paul Patton, and Philip Beitchman (New York: Semiotext(e), 1983); *The Illusion of the End*, trans. Chris Turner (Cambridge: Polity, 1994); *Symbolic Exchange and Death*, trans. Iain Hamilton Grant (Thousand Oaks, CA: Sage, 1993). For a good summary of his work, see Sonja K. Foss, Karen A. Foss, and Robert Trapp, *Contemporary Perspectives on Rhetoric*, 3rd ed. (Prospect Heights, IL: Waveland), in press.

common from the Renaissance to the Industrial Revolution, signs assumed a less direct relationship to the things of life. Signs actually produced new meanings not necessarily a natural part of the experience of that which was signified. For example, status, wealth, and prestige were connected to things because of how they were signified. The next stage, that of the Industrial Revolution, is that of *production*, in which machines were invented to take the place of humans, making objects independent of any human use of signifiers.

Today we are in an era of *simulation*, in which signs no longer represent—but create—our reality. Simulation determines who we are and what we do. No longer tools to represent our experience, signs establish it. Disneyland epitomizes the era of simulation. Theme parks are fantasies constructed from signs. The real thing—pirates, frontier, fantasyland, and so on—can be reproduced any time anywhere. Because they dominate our lives, the new media bombard us with simulation, literally creating our worlds. Rather than have genuine communication involving interaction among people, the media dominate our lives with information that forms what we perceive to be genuine experience, but it is far removed from the natural order of things. This leads us to obscenely exaggerated forms of life. We feel that these are real experiences, but in fact they are experiences within the simulations created by the media.

Our commodity culture is one aspect of the simulation in which we live. The simulated environment tells us what we want. It forms our tastes, choices, preferences, and needs. Consumption takes on value in and of itself. Most important is that we are consuming, not that we desire real things that have actual functions. We think we are different, but in fact most people's values and behaviors are highly constrained by the "reality" simulated in the media. We think that our individual needs are being met, but those are homogenized needs shaped by the use of signs in the media.

Because objects are separated from their original natural state, they take on bizarre meanings

for us. Possession is more important than use. Where once we needed farm animals to do work for us, we now value pets as a matter of ownership. Our lives are full of gizmos that have no real use, but sit on shelves for us to possess and look at and make a life of pure "symbolicity." We buy a watch, not really to tell time, but to wear as a form of apparel.

As a result of this process of simulation, we make fewer and fewer distinctions. Meanings collapse, or implode, into a huge mass, which Baudrillard refers to as *hypertelia*. This is a process of exaggeration in which we thrive on hype. Rather than distinguish between good and bad, beautiful and ugly, we mash everything together into the hyperreal, leading to a life of excess in which nuance is unimportant.

The line of thinking begun by Innis and continued today by scholars like Baudrillard may resonate with your experience. You probably have a sense that the ubiquitous media of mass communication do affect our lives in profound ways, but this approach may also feel overly simple and reductionistic. We begin this chapter with this line of work because it brings out the importance of media, but much more work has been done to isolate other factors and effects, as we will see below.

MEDIA AS SOCIAL INSTITUTION

Media are more than simple mechanisms for disseminating information: They are complex organizations and an important social institution of society. Perhaps the most important line of theory to address the institutional aspect of media is marxist critical theory. Because critical theory is discussed in Chapter 11, we will not cover it in great detail here.[19] Recall that critical

19   See the Chapter 11 section of the Selected Bibliography for readings in this area. McQuail's *Mass Communication* (1987) discusses marxist theories of media in some detail. See also Lawrence Grossberg, "Strategies of Marxist Cultural Interpretation," *Critical Studies in Mass Communication* 1 (1984): 392–421.

theories are concerned with the distribution of power in society and the domination of certain interests over others. Clearly, the media are a major player in this ideological struggle. Dominant ideologies can be perpetuated by the media. Most critical communication theories are concerned with mass media primarily because of the media's potential for disseminating dominant ideologies and their potential for expressing alternative and oppositional ones. For some critical theorists, media are part of a culture industry that literally creates symbols and images that can oppress marginalized groups.

According to McQuail there are five major branches of marxist media theory.[20] The first is *classical Marxism.* Here, the media are seen as instruments of the dominant class and a means by which capitalists promote their profit-making interests. Media disseminate the ideology of the ruling classes in society and thereby oppress certain classes.

The second is *political-economic media theory,* which, like classical Marxism, blames media ownership for society's ills. In this school of thought, media content is a commodity to be sold in the marketplace, and the information disseminated is controlled by what the market will bear. This system leads to a conservative, non-risk-taking operation, making certain kinds of programming and certain media outlets dominant and others marginalized.

The third line of theory is the *Frankfurt School.* This school of thought, seeing media as a means of constructing culture, places more emphasis on ideas than on material goods. In this way of thinking, media lead to the domination of the ideology of the elite. This outcome is accomplished by media manipulation of images and symbols to benefit the interests of the dominant class.

The fourth school is the *hegemonic theory.* Hegemony is the domination of a false ideology or way of thinking over true conditions. Ideology is not caused by the economic system alone but is deeply embedded in all activities of society. Thus, ideology is not forced by one group on another but is pervasive and unconscious. The dominant ideology perpetuates the interests of certain classes over others, and the media obviously take a major role in this process.

The final approach to marxist media studies is the *sociocultural approach,* usually called simply "cultural studies." Relying largely on semiotics, this group of scholars is interested in the cultural meanings of media products, looking at the ways media content is interpreted, including both dominant and oppositional interpretations. Cultural studies sees society as a field of competing ideas in a struggle among meanings. What, for example, is the meaning of a music video? In cultural studies, various competing meanings are viewed as cultural productions. Cultural studies is becoming an increasingly popular and useful approach, and it can be used to integrate insights from a variety of schools of thought.[21]

Although critical communication theories have gained presence in North America, their real development and strength occurred in Europe and Latin America. European critical theory is perhaps more widely known, because of the larger number of sources translated into English and the greater attention paid to European traditions. In contrast, Latin American communication theory, which remains largely untranslated, has received relatively little attention in the United States. Robert Huesca and Brenda Dervin have written a good summary of this work.[22]

According to Huesca and Dervin, Latin American communication scholarship challenges the predominant North American approach on many fronts. In general, this work honors horizontal, artistic, democratic, and participatory communication over vertical, industrial, authoritarian, and elite forms. It tends to look more at grass-roots efforts rather than top-down ones, and self-managed communication systems rather than centralized systems. Latin American

---

20   McQuail, *Mass Communication,* pp. 63–68.
21   Dennis K. Davis and Thomas F. N. Puckett, "Mass Entertainment and Community: Toward a Culture-Centered Paradigm for Mass Communication Research," in *Communication Yearbook 15,* ed. Stanley Deetz (Newbury Park, CA: Sage, 1992), pp. 3–34.
22   Robert Huesca and Brenda Dervin, "Theory and Practice in Latin American Alternative Communication Research," *Journal of Communication* 44 (1994): 53–73.

communication research also concentrates on human liberation rather than information transfer, conscience building rather than domination, unity rather than fragmentation, and antiauthoritarian rather than authoritarian content.

Although these trends tend to be as dualistic as is most North American scholarship, pitting one point against another, many Latin American scholars have attempted to overcome dualism altogether. They have done this in a number of ways. For example, they have refused to dichotomize the communication source from the audience and have shown that the audience itself participates in the creation of meaning. These scholars have also emphasized global over national trends and have called for coalitions, networks, and dialogue among groups and ideas.

◖ MEDIA AND AUDIENCE

No area in media theory has presented such quandaries and debates as studies of the audience. Media theorists are far from consensus on how to conceptualize the audience and audience effects. Disputes on the nature of the audience seem to involve two related dialectics. The first is a tension between the idea that the audience is a mass public versus the idea that it is a small community. The second is a tension between the idea that the audience is passive versus the belief that it is active. Let us consider each of these debates in turn.

Mass Society Versus Community

This controversy involves different opinions about the audience. Some see the audience as an undifferentiated mass, and some see it as a variegated set of small groups or communities. In the case of the former, audiences are viewed as a large population that can be molded by the media. In the case of the latter, audiences are viewed as discriminating members of small groups who are influenced mostly by their peers.

The theory of mass society is a concept growing out of the large, complex, bureaucratic nature of the modern state.[23] The theory envisions a malleable mass of people in which small groupings, community life, and ethnic identity are replaced by societywide depersonalized relations. This conception of society has led to widespread criticism of modern life and of the media. We already got a taste of mass society theory in the work of Baudrillard above.

Critics of the mass society have suggested several propositions. First, rapid developments in transportation and communication have increased human contact, and economic considerations have made people more and more interdependent. Thus, like a giant system, imbalance in one part affects everybody. Ironically, we are all more interdependent while becoming increasingly estranged from one another. Community and family ties are broken, and old values are questioned.

Second, because society is no longer believed to be led by the elite, morals, tastes, and values decline.[24] Rapid changes in society hurl men and women into multiple-role situations, causing a loss of the sense of self.[25] People become more anxious, and a charismatic leader ultimately may be required to lift society out of the abyss.

The dismal view of the theory of mass society has several implications for the mass media of communication. Critics of mass society fear that minds will be pounded and altered by propaganda through the media. As Paul Lazarsfeld and Robert Merton state: "There is the danger that these technically advanced instruments of mass communication constitute a major avenue for deterioration of aesthetic tastes and popular cultural standards."[26]

---

23   The most prominent critics of mass society are Ortega y Gasset, Karl Mannheim, Karl Jaspers, Paul Tillich, Gabriel Marcel, and Emil Lederer. Syntheses can be found in a variety of sources. See, for example, Patrick Brantlinger, *Bread and Circuses: Theories of Mass Culture as Social Decay* (Ithaca, NY: Cornell University Press, 1983).
24   See, for example, E. D. Hirsch, *Cultural Literacy: What Every American Needs to Know* (Boston: Houghton Mifflin, 1987); Allan Bloom, *The Closing of the American Mind* (New York: Simon & Schuster, 1987).
25   See, for example, Kenneth J. Gergen, *The Saturated Self: Dilemmas of Identity in Contemporary Life* (New York: HarperCollins, 1991).
26   Paul Lazarsfeld and Robert K. Merton, "Mass Communication, Popular Taste, and Organized Social Action," in *The Process and Effects of Mass Communication*, eds. W. Schramm and D. Roberts (Urbana: University of Illinois Press, 1971), p. 557.

Add to this the thesis that the media are blurring social boundaries and community divisions that previously gave stability and meaning to the lives of citizens. Joshua Meyrowitz writes in his book *No Sense of Place* that television has caused us to lose our sense of boundaries—between the private and public, between the physical and social, and between social groups. People are essentially losing their "place" in the world.[27]

The theory of mass society is still popular among the general population. Although this theory is not as prevalent among scholars today as it was a few decades ago, it still has an influence. McLuhan's theory is certainly a mass society theory, as are some of the marxist theories. Certain "powerful-effects" theories, including the well-known cultivation theory discussed later in the chapter, are strongly influenced by mass society thinking.

In contrast to mass society thinking is the position that the audience cannot be characterized as an amorphous mass, that it consists of numerous highly differentiated communities, each with its own values, ideas, and interests. Media content is interpreted within the community according to meanings that are worked out socially within the group, and individuals are influenced more by their peers than by the media.[28] We explored the idea of media-interpretive communities in Chapter 10, where we saw that the meanings of media messages are worked out interactively within groups of people who use a medium in a similar way.

Gerard Schoening and James Anderson call the community-based approach *social action media studies*, and they outline six premises of this work.[29] First, meaning is not in the message itself but is produced by an interpretive process in the audience. Different audiences will interpret or understand what they read and view in different ways. For example, talk radio programs may be taken to mean many things, depending on who is listening.

The second premise of social action media studies is that the meaning of media messages and programs is not determined passively, but produced actively. This means that audiences actually do something with what they view and read. They act as they view. Some listeners, for example, may turn on talk radio to combat boredom while driving, others may turn it on late in the evening as a sleep aid, and still others may listen to it actively during the day as a means of getting information about current events. What a particular talk radio program means, therefore, is a product of how listeners treat it, what they do with it.

The third premise is that the meanings of media shift constantly as the members approach the media in different ways. Sometimes the talk radio program may be strictly entertainment, sometimes serious information, and sometimes just background noise, depending on when and how it is listened to.

Fourth, the meaning of a program or message is never individually established, but communal. It is part of the tradition of a group, community, or culture. The implication of this is that when you join a community (by birth or membership), you accept the ongoing activities and meanings of that community or group. Your own behavior may influence the group or change the activities and meanings in some way, but the outcome at any given time is always sitting in the community or group.

Fifth, the actions that determine a group's meanings for media content are done in interaction among members of the group. In other words, how we act toward the media and what meanings emerge from those actions are social interactions. This does not mean that you never watch TV by yourself, but it does mean that how you watch TV and what you do with the television set are part of an ongoing interaction between yourself and others. If you listen to talk

27   Joshua Meyrowitz, *No Sense of Place: The Impact of Electronic Media on Social Behavior* (New York: Oxford University Press, 1985).
28   For an excellent statement of this position, see Thomas R. Lindlof, "Media Audiences as Interpretive Communities," in *Communication Yearbook 11*, ed. J. A. Anderson (Newbury Park, CA: Sage, 1988), pp. 81–107. Supportive of this position, too, is reader reception theory, which is most notably developed by John Fiske, *Introduction to Communication Studies* (New York: Methuen, 1982); *Television Culture* (New York: Methuen, 1987); *Reading the Popular* (Winchester, MA: Unwin Hyman, 1989); and *Understanding Popular Culture* (Winchester, MA: Unwin Hyman, 1989).
29   Gerard T. Schoening and James A. Anderson, "Social Action Media Studies: Foundational Arguments and Common Premises," *Communication Theory* 5 (1995): 93–116.

radio in the car while you commute to work, this pattern is part of a larger web of interactions with people at home and at work. It is a routine that is made possible by a huge network of interactions involving work, home, radio, boredom, cars, highways, and so on.

Finally, the sixth premise of social action media studies is that researchers join the communities they study, if only temporarily, and therefore have an ethical obligation to be open about what they are studying and share what they learn with those studied.

Active Audience Versus Passive Audience

Another controversy is the passive versus active audience. The passive-audience view suggests that people are easily influenced in a direct way by the media, whereas the active-audience view suggests that people make more active decisions about how to use the media. For the most part, mass society theories tend to subscribe to a passive conception of audience, although not all passive-audience theories can legitimately be called mass society theories. Similarly, most community theories subscribe to an active notion of audience.

These ideas about audiences are associated with various theories of media effects discussed later in the chapter. The "powerful-effects" theories tend to be based on the passive audience, whereas the "minimal-effects" theories are based more on an active one.

Frank Biocca discusses five characteristics of the active audience implied by the theories of this genre.[30] The first is *selectivity*. Active audiences are considered to be selective in the media they choose to use. The second characteristic is *utilitarianism*. Active audiences are said to use media to meet particular needs and goals. The third characteristic is *intentionality*, which implies the purposeful use of media content. The fourth characteristic is *involvement*, or effort. Here, audiences are actively attending, thinking about, and using the media. Finally, active audi-

ences are believed to be *impervious to influence,* or not very easily persuaded by the media alone.

Many media scholars believe that the mass community and active-passive dichotomies are too simple, that they do not capture the true complexity of audiences. It may be that audiences have some elements of mass society and other elements of local communities. Audiences may be active in some ways and passive in others or active at some times and passive at other times. Rather than ask whether audiences are easily influenced by the media, it might be better to ask when and under what conditions they are influenced and when they are not. This view changes the debate from one over what the audience really is to its meaning for people at different times and in different places.[31]

▶ THEORIES OF CULTURAL OUTCOMES

We turn now to a study of the outcomes of media communication. Of all areas of mass communication research, outcome studies are the most prevalent, especially in the United States. An overriding question throughout the history of media theory has been the effects of media on society and individuals.[32]

Karl Erik Rosengren shows that media outcomes are complex and wide-ranging.[33] Various theories concentrate on different outcomes—short term and long term, narrow and individual, broad and cultural. He lists five examples of such differences:

30 Frank A. Biocca, "Opposing Conceptions of the Audience: The Active and Passive Hemispheres of Mass Communication Theory," in *Communication Yearbook 11,* ed. J. A. Anderson (Newbury Park, CA: Sage, 1988), pp. 51–80. This article is an excellent discussion of the active-passive distinction and provides a review of the various theories on each side.
31 This view is espoused by Martin Allor, "Relocating the Site of the Audience," *Critical Studies in Mass Communication* 5 (1988): 217–233.
32 See, for example, Pietilä, "Perspectives"; Jennings Bryant and Dolf Zillmann, eds., *Perspectives on Media Effects* (Hillsdale, NJ: Erlbaum, 1986).
33 Rosengren, "Culture, Media, and Society."

- News diffusion research (hours and days)
- Agenda setting (weeks and months)
- Spiral of silence (months and years)
- Cultivation (years and decades)
- Research on public sphere (decades and centuries)

The theories included here are divided into two sections: those focusing on general cultural outcomes and those focusing on individual effects. This section deals with the former and the next section with the latter.

The Functions of Mass Communication

For many years, media theory concentrated on how media work and their effects on audiences. This was essentially a functionalist approach (see Chapter 1) that concentrated on the system of mass communication, how it works, and what it does.[34]

One of the earliest and best-known theorists in this tradition was Harold Lasswell. In his classic 1948 article, he presented the simple and often quoted model of communication:[35]

Who

Says what

In which channel

To whom

With what effect

This model outlines the basic elements of communication, the last element of which directs us to the entire outcome-research literature.

Lasswell identifies three functions of the media of communication. These are providing information about the environment, which he terms *surveillance;* presenting options for solving problems, or *correlation;* and socializing and education, referred to as *transmission*.[36]

The Lasswell model is a classic. Notice that it essentially lists the parts of the mass communication system and the things that mass communication accomplishes. Since this early work,

many other functions have been explored. We will look at several in this chapter, beginning in the following section with the diffusion of information and influence.

The Diffusion of Information and Influence

The community view of audience discussed above was given impetus by a now-classic voting study in 1940 conducted by Lazarsfeld and his colleagues in Elmira, New York.[37] The researchers unexpectedly found that the effect of media was influenced by interpersonal communication. This effect, which came to be known as the *two-step flow hypothesis,* was startling, and it had a major impact on our understanding of the role of mass media.

This study was the beginning of a line of research on how information and influence are distributed in society. Lazarsfeld hypothesized that information flows from the mass media to certain opinion leaders in the community, who pass information on by talking to peers. He found that voters seem to be more influenced by their friends during a campaign than by the media. Since the original Elmira study, much additional data have come in, and this hypothesis has received substantial support.[38]

The two-step flow theory is best summarized in Elihu Katz and Paul Lazarsfeld's classic work *Personal Influence*.[39] These authors confirm that

34 For a brief history of this tradition, see Carl Patrick Burrowes, "From Functionalism to Cultural Studies: Manifest Ruptures and Latent Continuities," *Communication Theory* 6 (1996): 88–103.
35 Harold Lasswell, "The Structure and Function of Communication in Society," in *The Communication of Ideas,* ed. L. Bryson (New York: Institute for Religious and Social Studies, 1948), p. 37. For information regarding Lasswell's contribution to communication, see Everett M. Rogers, *A History of Communication Study: A Biographical Approach* (New York: Free Press, 1994), pp. 203–243.
36 Lasswell, "Structure and Function."
37 Paul Lazarsfeld, Bernard Berelson, and H. Gaudet, *The People's Choice* (New York: Columbia University Press, 1948). See also Rogers, *A History,* pp. 244–315.
38 An excellent summary of this hypothesis is Elihu Katz, "The Two-Step Flow of Communication," *Public Opinion Quarterly* 21 (1957): 61–78.
39 Elihu Katz and Paul Lazarsfeld, *Personal Influence: The Part Played by People in the Flow of Mass Communications* (New York: Free Press, 1955).

certain individuals known as *opinion leaders* receive information from the media and pass it to their peers.[40] Opinion leaders are in all groups: occupational, social, community, and others. These individuals are difficult to distinguish from other group members because opinion leadership is not a trait but a role taken by some individuals in certain circumstances. Opinion leadership changes from time to time and from issue to issue.

Opinion leaders may be of two kinds: those influential on one topic, or *monomorphism*, and those influential on a variety of topics, or *polymorphism*. Monomorphism becomes more predominant as systems become more modern.

Research more recent than the Lazarsfeld study has shown that the dissemination of ideas is not a simple two-step process. A *multiple-step model* is now more generally accepted.[41] This model is similar to the two-step hypothesis but admits to more possibilities. Research has shown that the ultimate number of relays between the media and final receivers is variable. In the adoption of an innovation, for example, certain individuals will hear about it directly from media sources, whereas others will be many steps removed.

The diffusion of information and innovations is now part of the interactional and network tradition discussed in some detail in Chapters 13 and 14. We saw in those chapters that interaction in networks plays an important role in relationships, small groups, and organizations. Here, we see that it plays an important role in mass communication too. The diffusion of information is one of the most significant outcomes of communication. Often distributed information promotes the adoption of innovations.

The diffusion of an innovation occurs when the adoption of an idea, practice, or object spreads by communication through a social system. Several prominent American and foreign researchers in fields such as agriculture and rural studies, national development, and organizational communication have been responsible for this line of research.

The broadest and most communication-oriented theory of diffusion is that of Everett Rogers and his colleagues.[42] Rogers relates dissemination to the process of social change, which consists of invention, diffusion (or communication), and consequences. Such change can occur internally from within a group or externally through contact with outside change agents. Contact may occur spontaneously or accidentally, or it may result from planning on the part of outside agencies.

In the diffusion of innovations, many years may be required for an idea to spread. Rogers states, in fact, that one purpose of diffusion research is to discover the means to shorten this lag. Once established, an innovation will have consequences—be they functional or dysfunctional, direct or indirect, manifest or latent. Change agents normally expect their impact to be functional, direct, and manifest, although this positive result does not always occur.

The diffusion of innovations is well illustrated by the family-planning program instituted in South Korea in 1968. Mothers' clubs were established in about 12,000 villages throughout Korea for the purpose of disseminating information about family planning. Overall, the program was successful, and Korea saw a major decline in birthrate during this period. This program was built on the idea that interpersonal channels of communication would be crucial to the adoption of birth control methods. In 1973 Rogers and his colleagues studied the Korean case by interviewing about a thousand women in twenty-four villages to gather information about the networks the women used for family planning.[43]

---

40   Research on opinion leadership is summarized in Everett M. Rogers, *Diffusion of Innovations* (New York: Free Press, 1995), pp. 290–304.

41   Rogers, *Diffusion of Innovations*, pp. 281–334.

42   Rogers, *Diffusion of Innovations*. For a summary of this theory, see John F. Cragan and Donald C. Shields, *Understanding Communication Theory: The Communicative Forces for Human Action* (Boston: Allyn & Bacon, 1998), pp. 175–207.

43   Everett M. Rogers and D. Lawrence Kincaid, *Communication Networks: Toward a New Paradigm for Research* (New York: Free Press, 1981). The Korean case is discussed throughout the book. See especially pages 258–285.

They found that the village leaders initially received their information about family planning from the mass media and family-planning worker visits, but interpersonal networks turned out to be most important in the dissemination-adoption process. Two network variables were especially important. The first was the degree to which the mothers' club leader was connected with others in the village network. The second variable was the amount of overlap between the family-planning network and the general village network. Birth control adoption was greatest in the villages in which the leader talked to many people personally, and the village women talked about it among themselves. Rogers has found that people do talk about ideas, and that is how change happens.

When innovations such as the cell phone, DSL lines, a new HIV therapy, or Internet shopping are introduced, it takes a while for them to catch on. Some innovations never catch on, but others spread with varying amounts of speed. Interpersonal influence is very important in this process. People raise awareness of the innovation as they talk with one another about it. They share opinions, discuss their experience with the innovation, sometimes advocate its use, and sometimes resist it. The rate of adoption is determined by perceptions of the innovation's relative advantage and its compatibility with existing values and experiences. The complexity of the innovation matters, and potential adopters will more readily accept an innovation with which they can experiment, or try out, without making a huge commitment. They may also want to observe others' adoption before taking the plunge.

People do vary in their levels of resistance and the social support needed to adopt the idea, practice, or object. There are always individuals who will adopt an innovation early, before most others consider doing so. These early adopters will set the stage, and they usually have an influence on others. As more and more people adopt, a critical mass of adoption occurs that gives rise to a rapid increase in general adoption.[44] A few people may be very slow to adopt and must see the innovation all around them before they will consider it. These are the late adopters. Of course, some may never adopt the new practice. In general, Rogers and his colleagues have found that adoption approximates an S-curve. On a time scale, the rise of adoption is slow at first, a critical mass is hit after which a sudden rise in adoption occurs, and then it levels out.

In some circumstances, however, people do not talk, and now we will look at a theory that explains why.

Public Opinion and the Spiral of Silence

As the research on Korean family planning discussed above illustrates, communication has much to do with public opinion. The topic of public opinion has been of great concern in political science, in which the concept represents opinions publicly expressed, opinions regarding public affairs, and opinions of the general public as a group rather than of smaller groups of individuals. Elisabeth Noelle-Neumann's theory of the "spiral of silence" continues this analysis by demonstrating how interpersonal communication and media operate together in the development of public opinion.[45]

As a political researcher in Germany, Noelle-Neumann observed that in elections certain views seem to get more play than others. Sometimes people mute their opinions rather than talk about them. Noelle-Neumann calls this the *spiral*

---

44 The idea of critical mass is discussed in Alwin Mahler and Everett M. Rogers, "The Diffusion of Interactive Communication Innovations and the Critical Mass: The Adoption of Telecommunications Services by German Banks," *Telecommunications Policy* 23 (1999): 719–740; and Everett M. Rogers, "Diffusion Theory: A Theoretical Approach to Promote Community-Level Change," in *Handbook of HIV Prevention*, eds. John L. Peterson and Ralph J. DiClemente (New York: Kluwer Academic, 2000), pp. 57–65.
45 Elisabeth Noelle-Neumann, *The Spiral of Silence: Public Opinion—Our Social Skin* (Chicago: University of Chicago Press, 1984). See also "The Theory of Public Opinion: The Concept of the Spiral of Silence," in *Communication Yearbook 14*, ed. J. A. Anderson (Newbury Park, CA: Sage, 1991), pp. 256–287. For a brief summary, see Charles T. Salmon and Carroll J. Glynn, "Spiral of Silence: Communication and Public Opinion as Social Control," in *An Integrated Approach to Communication Theory and Research*, eds. Michael B. Salwen and Don W. Stacks (Mahwah, NJ: Erlbaum, 1996), pp. 165–180.

of silence. The spiral of silence occurs when individuals who perceive that their opinion is popular express it, whereas those who do not think their opinion is popular remain quiet. This process occurs in a spiral, so that one side of an issue ends up with much publicity and the other side with little.

In everyday life we express our opinions in a variety of ways: We talk about them, we wear buttons, and we put bumper stickers on our cars. According to this theory, people are more apt to do these kinds of things when they perceive that others share their opinion and less apt to do so when they do not.

This thesis rests on two premises. The first is that people know which opinions are prevalent and which are not. This is called the *quasi-statistical sense* because people are not reluctant to make educated guesses about public opinion and have a sense of the percentages of the population for and against certain positions. The second assumption is that people adjust their expressions of opinion to these perceptions.

Noelle-Neumann presents much research evidence to support these assumptions. In political elections, for example, people usually perceive quite accurately the prevailing opinion about the candidates and issues, and they are likely to express their preferences when these are shared by others.

An interesting test of the tendency to remain silent on unpopular positions is the "train test."[46] Here, respondents are asked to imagine that they were in a train compartment with a stranger for five hours and to decide whether they would be willing to discuss certain topics with this person. Respondents were told that they were to imagine that the other person mentioned his or her opinion on the subject and were then asked whether they would prefer to talk to the other person about this topic or not. Topics ranged from spanking children to the government of Germany.

Interviewers presented this problem to 3,500 respondents covering numerous topics over several years. The overwhelming tendency was to freely discuss the topic when one agrees with the

majority but to let it slide when one does not. People seem to not want to "make waves."

Of course, other factors enter into the decision to express one's opinion: Young people are more expressive than older people; educated individuals will speak up more than uneducated ones; men are generally more willing to disclose their opinions than women. However, the spiral of silence is also a factor, and according to this research, a powerful one.

The spiral of silence seems to be caused by the fear of isolation. The spiral of silence is not just a matter of wanting to be on the winning side but is an attempt to avoid being isolated from one's social group. Threats of criticism from others were found to be powerful forces in silencing individuals. For example, smokers who are repeatedly criticized for advocating smokers' rights were found to remain silent rather than state their views on this subject in the presence of vocal nonsmokers.

In some cases the threat of expressing an opinion is extreme:

> Slashed tires, defaced or torn posters, help refused to a lost stranger—questions of this kind demonstrate that people can be on uncomfortable or even dangerous ground when the climate of opinion runs counter to their views. When people attempt to avoid isolation, they are not responding hypersensitively to trivialities; these are existential issues that can involve real hazards.[47]

One can easily see how this process affects public opinion. There are, of course, exceptions to the spiral of silence. There are groups and individuals who do not fear isolation and who will express their opinions no matter what the consequences—a characteristic of innovators, change agents, and the avant-garde.

When polled, individuals usually state that they feel powerless in the face of media. Two kinds of experience accentuate this feeling of helplessness. The first is the difficulty of getting publicity for a cause or point of view. The second

---

46   Noelle-Neumann, *Spiral*, pp. 16–22.
47   Noelle-Neumann, *Spiral*, p. 56.

is being scapegoated by the media in what Noelle-Neumann calls the *pillory function* of media. In each case the individual feels powerless against the media, making the media an important part of the spiral of silence. The media publicize which opinions are prevalent and which are not.

Although public opinion is formed by both personal observation and media, individuals mix the two and confuse what is learned through the media with what is learned through interpersonal channels. This tendency is especially true for television, with which so many people have a personal relationship:

> The longer one has studied the question, the clearer it becomes that fathoming the effects of the mass media is very hard. These effects do not come into being as a result of a single stimulus; they are as a rule cumulative, following the principle that "water dripping constantly wears away stone." Further discussions among people spread the media's messages further, and before long no difference can be perceived between the point of media reception and points far removed from it. The media's effects are predominantly unconscious; people cannot provide an account of what has happened. Rather, they mix their own direct perceptions and the perceptions filtered through the eyes of the media into an indivisible whole that seems to derive from their own thoughts and experiences.[48]

It sometimes happens that journalists' opinions differ from those of the general public, so that media depictions contradict the prevailing expressions of individuals. When this occurs, a dual climate of opinion results. Here, two versions of reality operate: that of the media and that of the public. Noelle-Neumann likens this event to an unusual weather situation—interesting and seemingly bizarre.

The spiral of silence, then, is a phenomenon involving personal and media channels of communication. The media publicize public opinion, making evident which opinions predominate. Individuals express their opinions or not, depending on the predominant points of view; the media, in turn, attend to the expressed opinion, and the spiral continues.

Cultivation Analysis

Another theoretical program dealing with the sociocultural outcomes of mass communication is that of George Gerbner and his colleagues.[49] These researchers believe that because television is the great common experience of almost everyone, it has the effect of providing a shared way of viewing the world:

> Television is a centralized system of storytelling. It is part and parcel of our daily lives. Its drama, commercials, news, and other programs bring a relatively coherent world of common images and messages into every home. Television cultivates from infancy the very predispositions and preferences that used to be acquired from other primary sources. Transcending historic barriers of literacy and mobility, television has become the primary common source of socialization and everyday information (mostly in the form of entertainment) of an otherwise heterogeneous population. The repetitive pattern of television's mass-produced messages and images forms the mainstream of a common symbolic environment.[50]

Gerbner calls this effect *cultivation*, since television is believed to be a homogenizing agent in culture. Cultivation analysis is concerned with the totality of the pattern communicated cumulatively by television over a long period of exposure rather than by any particular content or specific effect. In other words, this is not a theory of individual media "effects" but instead makes a statement about the culture as a whole. It is not

48 Noelle-Neumann, *Spiral*, p. 169.
49 George Gerbner, "Living with Television: The Dynamics of the Cultivation Process," in *Perspectives on Media Effects*, ed. Jennings Bryant and Dolf Zillmann (Hillsdale, NJ: Erlbaum, 1986), pp. 17–40; Michael Morgan and James Shanahan, "Two Decades of Cultivation Research: An Appraisal and Meta-Analysis," *Communication Yearbook 20*, ed. Brant R. Burleson (Thousand Oaks, CA: Sage, 1997), pp. 1–45; Nancy Signorielli and Michael Morgan, "Cultivation Analysis: Research and Practice," in *An Integrated Approach to Communication Theory and Research*, eds. Michael B. Salwen and Don W. Stacks (Mahwah, NJ: Erlbaum, 1996), pp. 111–126; Nancy Signorielli and Michael Morgan, eds., *Cultivation Analysis: New Directions in Media Effects Research* (Newbury Park, CA: Sage, 1990).
50 George Gerbner, Larry Gross, Michael Morgan, and Nancy Signorielli, "Living with Television," in *Perspectives on Media Effects*, eds. J. Bryant and D. Zillmann (Hillsdale, NJ: Erlbaum, 1986), p. 18.

concerned with what any strategy or campaign can do but with the total impact of numerous strategies and campaigns over time. Total immersion in television, not selective viewing, is important in cultivation of ways of knowing and images of reality. Indeed, subcultures may retain their separate values, but general overriding images depicted on television will cut across individual social groups and subcultures, affecting them all.

As you might imagine, the theory predicts a difference in the social reality of heavy television viewers as opposed to light viewers. Heavy viewers will believe in a reality that is consistent with that shown on television, even though television does not necessarily reflect the actual world. Gerbner's research on prime-time television, for example, has shown that there are three men to every woman on television, there are few Hispanics and those shown are typically minor characters, there are almost entirely middle-class characters, and there are three times as many law enforcement officers as blue-collar workers.

One of the most interesting aspects of cultivation is the "mean-world syndrome." Although less than 1 percent of the population are victims of violent crimes in any one-year period, heavy exposure can lead you to believe that no one can be trusted in what appears to be a violent world.

Nancy Signorielli reports a study of the mean-world syndrome, in which violent acts in children's television programming were analyzed.[51] Over 2,000 programs, including 6,000 main characters, during prime time and weekends from 1967 to 1985 were analyzed with interesting results. About 71 percent of prime-time and 94 percent of weekend programs included acts of violence. Prime-time programs averaged almost five acts of violence each, and weekend programs averaged six. That amounts to over five acts per hour during prime time and about twenty per hour on weekends.

As part of this study, people were surveyed on five occasions between 1980 and 1986 regarding their views of the state of the world. To measure feelings of alienation and gloom, they were asked whether they agreed with three statements: (1) "Despite what some people say, the lot of the average man is getting worse, not better." (2) "It's hardly fair to bring a child into the world with the way things look for the future." (3) "Most public officials are not interested in the problems of the average man."

In addition, they were asked three questions to measure feelings about a mean world: (1) "Would you say that most of the time people try to be helpful, or are they mostly just looking out for themselves?" (2) "Do you think that most people would try to take advantage of you if they got a chance, or would they try to be fair?" (3) "Generally speaking, would you say that most people can be trusted, or you can't be too careful in dealing with people?" The findings indicate that heavy viewers tend to see the world as gloomier and meaner than do light viewers, and heavy viewers tend to mistrust people more than light viewers do.

Cultivation analysis has also found that there is a general fallout effect from television to the entire culture so that culture becomes homogenized, or *mainstreamed,* through TV. Television is not a force for change as much as it is a force for stability.

Mainstreaming can be seen in the mean-world data reviewed above. Even though heavy viewers scored higher on the mean-world index than did light viewers, a substantial number of light viewers also scored high. In fact, if you remove people with a college education from the sample, heavy and light viewers scored about the same.

Although cultivation is a general outcome of television viewing, it is not a universal phenomenon, despite the mainstreaming effect. In fact, different groups are affected differently by cultivation. Your interaction with others affects your tendency to accept TV reality. For example, adolescents who interact with their parents about television viewing are less likely to be affected by television images than are adolescents who do

51   Nancy Signorielli, "Television's Mean and Dangerous World: A Continuation of the Cultural Indicators Perspective," in *Cultivation Analysis: New Directions in Media Effects Research,* eds. N. Signorielli and M. Morgan (Newbury Park, CA: Sage, 1990), pp. 85–106.

not talk with their parents about television. Interestingly, people who watch more cable television tend to manifest more mainstreaming than do people who watch less.

The Agenda-Setting Function

Scholars have long known that media have the potential for structuring issues for the public.[52] One of the first writers to formalize this idea was Walter Lippmann, a prominent American journalist. Lippmann is known for his journalistic writing, speeches, and social commentary.[53] Lippman took the view that the public responds not to actual events in the environment but to "the pictures in our heads," which he calls the *pseudoenvironment:*

> For the real environment is altogether too big, too complex, and too fleeting for direct acquaintance. We are not equipped to deal with so much subtlety, so much variety, so many permutations and combinations. And altogether we have to act in that environment, we have to reconstruct it on a simpler model before we can manage with it.[54]

The agenda-setting function has been described best by Donald Shaw, Maxwell McCombs, and their colleagues.[55] These authors write:

> Considerable evidence has accumulated that editors and broadcasters play an important part in shaping our social reality as they go about their day-to-day task of choosing and displaying news. . . . This impact of the mass media— the ability to effect cognitive change among individuals, to structure their thinking—has been labeled the agenda-setting function of mass communication. Here may lie the most important effect of mass communication, its ability to mentally order and organize our world for us. In short, the mass media may not be successful in telling us what to think, but they are stunningly successful in telling us what to think about.[56]

In other words, agenda setting establishes the salient issues or images in the minds of the public.

Agenda setting occurs because the press must be selective in reporting the news. The news outlets, as gatekeepers of information, make choices about what to report and how to report it. What the public knows about the state of affairs at any given time is largely a product of media gatekeeping.[57] Further, we know that how a person votes is determined mainly by what issues the individual believes to be important. For this reason some researchers have come to believe that the issues reported during a candidate's term in office may have more effect on the election than the campaign itself.

There are two levels of agenda setting. The first establishes the general issues that are important, and the second determines the parts or aspects of those issues that are important. In many ways the second level is as important as the first, because it gives us a way to frame the issues that constitute the public and media agendas. For example, the media may tell us that deregulation of the electric industry is an important issue (first level), but they may also focus on differences between the states, framing this issue as a question of *how* deregulation is accomplished (second level).[58]

52   For an overview, see Maxwell McCombs and Tamara Bell, "The Agenda Setting Role of Mass Communication," in *An Integrated Approach to Communication Theory and Research,* eds. Michael B. Salwen and Don W. Stacks (Mahwah, NJ: Erlbaum, 1996), pp. 93–110.

53   See, for example, M. Childs and J. Reston, eds., *Walter Lippmann and His Times* (New York: Harcourt Brace, 1959).

54   Walter Lippmann, *Public Opinion* (New York: Macmillan, 1921), p. 16.

55   Donald L. Shaw and Maxwell E. McCombs, *The Emergence of American Political Issues* (St. Paul, MN: West, 1977). For a very good summary of this whole line of work, see Jian-Hua Zhu and Deborah Blood, "Media Agenda-Setting Theory: Telling the Public What to Think About," in *Emerging Theories of Human Communication,* ed. Branislav Kovačić (Albany: SUNY Press, 1997): pp. 88–114. See also Maxwell McCombs, "New Frontiers in Agenda Setting: Agendas of Attributes and Frames," *Mass Communication Review* 24 (1997): 4–24; Everett M. Rogers and James W. Dearing, "Agenda-Setting Research: Where Has It Been, Where Is It Going?" in *Communication Yearbook 11,* ed. J. A. Anderson (Newbury Park, CA: Sage, 1988), pp. 555–593; Stephen D. Reese, "Setting the Media's Agenda: A Power Balance Perspective," in *Communication Yearbook 14,* ed. J. A. Anderson (Newbury Park, CA: Sage, 1991), pp. 309–340. See also David Protess and Maxwell McCombs, *Agenda Setting: Readings on Media, Public Opinion, and Policymaking* (Hillsdale, NJ: Erlbaum, 1991).

56   Shaw and McCombs, *Emergence,* p. 5.

57   Pamela J. Shoemaker, "Media Gatekeeping," in *An Integrated Approach to Communication Theory and Research,* eds. Michael B. Salwen and Don W. Stacks (Mahwah, NJ: Erlbaum, 1996), pp. 79–91.

58   The idea of framing as a media effect is explored by Dietram A. Scheufele, "Framing as a Theory of Media Effects," *Journal of Communication* 49 (1999): 103–122. See also McCombs, "New Frontiers."

The agenda-setting function is a three-part linear process.[59] First, the priority of issues to be discussed in the media, *or media agenda,* must be set. Second, the media agenda in some way affects or interacts with what the public thinks, or the *public agenda.* Finally, the public agenda affects or interacts in some way with what policymakers consider important, or the *policy agenda.* In the theory's simplest and most direct version, then, the media agenda affects the public agenda, and the public agenda affects the policy agenda.

Although a number of studies show that the media can be powerful in affecting the public agenda, it is still not clear whether the public agenda does not itself affect the media agenda. The relationship may be one of mutual causation rather than linear causation. Further, it appears that actual events have some impact on both the media agenda and the public agenda.

The prevailing opinion among media researchers seems to be that the media can have a powerful effect on the public agenda, but not always. The power of media depends on such factors as media credibility on particular issues at particular times, the extent of conflicting evidence as perceived by individual members of the public, the extent to which individuals share media values at certain times, and the public's need for guidance. Media most often will be powerful when media credibility is high, conflicting evidence is low, individuals share media values, and the audience has a high need for guidance.

Karen Siune and Ole Borre studied some of the complexities of agenda setting in a Danish election.[60] Because in Denmark the election campaigns last only three weeks and the number of political broadcasts are more limited than in the United States, the researchers had an excellent opportunity to study the agenda-setting process.

Three kinds of political broadcasts on radio and television were aired in this election. These included programs made by the political parties, programs in which the candidates were asked questions by a panel of journalists and citizens, and debates. All these programs were recorded and analyzed by counting the number of statements made about each issue in the campaign. In addition, about 1,300 voters were interviewed at various points in the campaign to establish the public agenda. From this data the researchers could determine the media agendas of the politicians, the press, and voters.

This study suggests three kinds of agenda-setting effects. The first is the degree to which the media reflect the public agenda, called *representation.* In a representational agenda, the public influences the media. The second is the maintenance of the same agenda by the public the entire time, which is called *persistence.* In a persistent public agenda, the media may have little effect. The third occurs when the media agenda influences the public agenda, referred to as *persuasion.* This third kind of effect—media influencing the public—is exactly what classic agenda-setting theory predicts.

If you determine agendas at three points in a campaign—at the beginning (time 1), at the middle (time 2), and at the end (time 3)—you can get a sense of these three effects. A correlation between the public agenda at time 1 and the media agenda at time 2 suggests representation, or audience influencing media. A correlation between the public agenda at time 1 and at time 3 suggests persistence, or stability of the public agenda. Finally, a correlation between the media agenda at time 2 and the public agenda at time 3 suggests persuasion, or media influencing the public agenda. It is possible for any combination of these three to occur at the same time.

In their Danish study, Siune and Borre found much persistence in the public agenda, but there was also some persuasion in the sense that the broadcasts seemed to affect the public agenda somewhat. The most persuasive effects seemed to come from programs in which citizens set the media agenda. There was also a fair agenda-setting effect from the reporters and from the politicians themselves. The researchers did not find a representation effect in which the public affected the media.

59   This idea is developed by Rogers and Dearing, "Agenda-Setting Research."
60   Karen Siune and Ole Borre, "Setting the Agenda for a Danish Election," *Journal of Communication* 25 (1975): 65–73.

A natural question is, Who affects the media agenda in the first place? This is a complex and difficult question. It appears that media agendas result from pressures both within media organizations and from outside sources.[61] In other words, the media agenda is established by some combination of internal programming, editorial and managerial decisions, and external influences from nonmedia sources such as socially influential individuals, government officials, commercial sponsors, and the like.

The power of media in establishing a public agenda depends in part on their relations with power centers. If the media have close relationships with the elite class in society, that class will probably affect the media agenda and the public agenda in turn. Many critical theorists believe that media can be an instrument of the dominant ideology in society, and when this happens, that dominant ideology will permeate the public agenda.

Four types of power relations between the media and outside sources can be found. The first is a high-power source and high-power media. In this kind of arrangement, if the two see eye to eye, a positive symbiotic relationship will exert great power over the public agenda. This would be the case, for example, with a powerful public official who has especially good relations with the press. On the other hand, if the powerful media and the powerful sources do not agree, a struggle may take place between them.

The second kind of arrangement is a high-power source and low-power media. Here, the external source will probably co-opt the media and use them to accomplish its own ends. This is what happens, for example, when politicians buy airtime or when a popular president such as Ronald Reagan gives the press the "privilege" of interviewing him.

In the third type of relation, a lower-power source and high-power media, the media organizations themselves will be largely responsible for their own agenda. This happens when the media marginalize certain news sources such as the student radicals in the 1960s.

The fourth type of relation is where both media and external sources are low in power, and the public agenda will probably be established by the events themselves rather than the media or the leaders.

As you can see, agenda setting is no simple matter, and our understanding of its complexity has come a long way since the early days of simplistic agenda-setting theory.

◖ THEORIES OF INDIVIDUAL OUTCOMES

The theories summarized in the previous section emphasize societal and cultural outcomes of mass communication. Other research has dealt with the *individual effects* of mass communication. In this section we discuss several of the theories of this individual-effects tradition.

The Effects Tradition

The theory of mass communication effects has undergone a curious evolution in this century.[62] Early on, researchers believed in the "magic bullet" theory of communication effects. Individuals were believed to be directly and heavily influenced by media messages, since media were considered to be extremely powerful in shaping public opinion.[63] According to this model, if you heard on the radio that you should try Pepsodent, you would.

Then, during the 1950s when the two-step flow hypothesis was becoming popular, media

61   Reese, "Setting the Media's Agenda."
62   This chronology is discussed by McQuail, *Mass Communication,* 1987, pp. 252–256. For a recent survey of a portion of this literature, see Tara M. Emmers-Sommer and Mike Allen, "Surveying the Effect of Media Effects: A Meta-Analytic Summary of the Media Effects Research," *Human Communication Research* 25 (1999): 478–497. For an especially good overview of theories of media violence, see W. James Potter, *On Media Violence* (Thousand Oaks, CA: Sage, 1999), pp. 11–24.
63   For explorations of the history of the magic bullet or hypodermic needle theory, see J. Michael Sproule, "Progressive Propaganda Critics and the Magic Bullet Myth," *Critical Studies in Mass Communication* 6 (1989): 225–246; Jeffery L. Bineham, "A Historical Account of the Hypodermic Model in Mass Communication," *Communication Monographs* 55 (1988): 230–246.

effects were considered to be minimal. It was believed that a commercial for Pepsodent would not directly influence very many people to try it. Later, in the 1960s, we came to think that the media effects were mediated by other variables and were therefore only moderate in strength. A Pepsodent commercial might or might not influence you, depending on other variables.

Now, after research in the 1970s and the 1980s, many scholars have returned to the powerful-effects model, in which the public is considered to be heavily influenced by media. This later research centers on television as the powerful medium.

Limited or Powerful Effects?

Perhaps the best-known early work on limited effects was the reinforcement approach most notably articulated by Joseph Klapper.[64] Klapper, in surveying the literature on mass communication effects, developed the thesis that mass communication is not a necessary and sufficient cause of audience effects but that it is mediated by other variables. Thus, media are only a contributing cause.

Raymond Bauer observes that audiences are difficult to persuade, and he calls them *obstinate*.[65] Bauer denies the idea that a direct hypodermic-needle effect operates between communicator and audience. Instead, many variables involved in the audience interact to shape effects in various ways.[66] Audience effects are mediated by group and interpersonal factors and by selectivity, among others. Studies have shown that audience members are selective in their exposure to information.[67] In its simplest form, the hypothesis of selective exposure predicts that people in most circumstances will select information consistent with their attitudes.

The reinforcement approach was a definite step in the right direction at the time it was in vogue. Compared with the bullet theory, the reinforcement approach viewed mass communication as more complicated than had previously been imagined. It envisioned situations ripe with

mediating variables that would inhibit media effects. The research in this tradition did identify some important mediating variables, completing a more elaborate puzzle than had previously been constructed.

The problem of the limited-effects model is that it maintained a linear, cause-to-effect pattern.[68] It failed to take into account the social forces on the media or the ways that individuals might affect the media. In addition, the limited-effects model concentrated almost exclusively on attitude and opinion effects, ignoring other kinds of effects and functions such as cultivation or diffusion. Finally, true to tradition, such research focused on short-term effects of mass communication without questioning whether repeated exposure or time might affect the audience.

The work of Klapper and others on limited effects resulted in two general types of response. The first was a rejection of limited effects in favor of powerful effects, and the second was an attempt to explain limited effects in terms of the powers of audience members rather than media.

Perhaps the most vocal contemporary spokesperson in favor of powerful effects is Noelle-Neumann.[69] She believes that limited-effects theory has "distorted the interpretation of research findings over the years," and "that the 'dogma of media powerlessness' is no longer tenable."[70] Noelle-Neumann claims that the pen-

64   Joseph T. Klapper, *The Effects of Mass Communication* (Glencoe, IL: Free Press, 1960).
65   Raymond Bauer, "The Obstinate Audience: The Influence Process from the Point of View of Social Communication," *American Psychologist* 19 (1964): 319–328.
66   Raymond Bauer, "The Audience," in *Handbook of Communication,* eds. I. de sola Pool and others (Chicago: Rand McNally, 1973), pp. 141–152.
67   Studies on selectivity are well summarized in David O. Sears and Jonathan I. Freedman, "Selective Exposure to Information: A Critical Review," in *The Process and Effects of Mass Communication,* eds. W. Schramm and D. F. Roberts (Urbana: University of Illinois Press, 1971), pp. 209–234.
68   Criticism of the limited-effects approach can be found in Werner J. Severin and James W. Tankard, *Communication Theories: Origins, Methods, Uses* (New York: Hastings House, 1979), p. 249.
69   Elisabeth Noelle-Neumann, "Return to the Concept of Powerful Mass Media," in *Studies of Broadcasting,* eds. H. Eguchi and K. Sata (Tokyo: Nippon Hoso Kyokii, 1973), pp. 67–112; "The Effect of Media on Media Effects Research," *Journal of Communication* 33 (1983): 157–165.
70   Noelle-Neumann, "Effect of Media," p. 157.

dulum, which began swinging in the other direction after Klapper's famous work, has now reached its full extension and that most researchers believe that the media indeed have powerful effects.

Noelle-Neumann says that most limited-effects researchers were either academic journalists or people who held the media in a free society in high regard. They were interested in painting a picture of the media as disseminators of information, but not of influence. If viewed as important but not controlling, the media would continue to have the freedom to investigate and report whatever they felt to be important at a particular time, and journalists liked that. This interest led to the tendency to "see" limited rather than powerful effects in media-research results, which Noelle-Neumann calls "the media's effect on media research."

In summarizing the research literature on the effects of media violence, James Potter reports several clear effects.[71] For example, viewing violent portrayals can lead to increased aggressiveness, fear, and desensitization in the short term. Long-term exposure to violence can create increased aggression, which in turn can lead to more viewing of violence. It can also lead to an increased feeling of being potentially victimized and to the greater acceptance of violence. Potter is careful to point out, however, that these results do not necessarily support a powerful-effects model because effects are mediated by individual, situational, institutional, and message variables, all of which complicate the effects picture. Indeed, Potter himself says that the powerful-effects model has been discredited for fifty years![72] He calls for a systemic approach that looks at a host of factors along with methods that admit to more complete definitions of violence and effects.

It is clear, then, that neither the limited-effects nor powerful-effects models have a great deal of credibility at this time. In the following sections, we review theories that paint a more moderate and complex picture than either the limited- or powerful-effects models portray.

Uses, Gratifications, and Dependency

One of the most popular theories of mass communication is the uses-and-gratifications approach.[73] Here, we examine the original idea of uses and gratifications and then look at some interesting extensions.

The Original Idea. The uses-and-gratifications approach focuses on the consumer—the audience member—rather than the message.[74] Unlike the powerful-effects tradition, this approach imagines the audience member to be a discriminating user of media. The basic stance is summarized as follows:

> Compared with classical effects studies, the uses and gratifications approach takes the media consumer rather than the media message as its starting point, and explores his communication behavior in terms of his direct experience with the media. It views the members of the audience as actively utilizing media contents, rather than being passively acted upon by the media. Thus, it does not assume a direct relationship between messages and effects, but postulates instead that members of the audience put messages to use, and that such usages act as intervening variables in the process of effect.[75]

Here the audience is assumed to be active and goal-directed. The audience member is largely responsible for choosing media to meet needs and knows his or her own needs and how to meet them. Media are considered to be only one way of meeting personal needs, and individuals

71   Potter, *On Media Violence*, pp. 25–42.
72   Potter, *On Media Violence*, p. 211.
73   For historical overviews, J. D. Rayburn, II, "Uses and Gratifications," in *An Integrated Approach to Communication Theory and Research*, eds. Michael B. Salwen and Don W. Stacks (Mahwah, NJ: Erlbaum, 1996), pp. 145–163; Alan M. Rubin, "Audience Activity and Media Use," *Communication Monographs* 60 (1993): 98–105.
74   Elihu Katz, Jay Blumler, and Michael Gurevitch, "Uses of Mass Communication by the Individual," in *Mass Communication Research: Major Issues and Future Directions*, eds. W. P. Davidson and F. Yu (New York: Praeger, 1974), pp. 11–35. See also Jay Blumler and Elihu Katz, eds., *The Uses of Mass Communication* (Beverly Hills, CA: Sage, 1974). See also the entire issue of *Communication Research* 6 (January 1979).
75   Katz, Blumler, and Gurevitch, "Uses," p. 12.

may meet their needs through the media or in some other way. In other words, out of the options that media present, the individual chooses ways to gratify needs.

As you can see, this is an interesting idea, but it really does not tell us very much. Let's look now at some extensions that add detail.

Expectancy-Value Theory.   Acknowledging the lack of theoretical coherence in early uses-and-gratifications work, Philip Palmgreen created a theory based on his own work, that of Karl Rosengren, and others.[76] The theory is based on *expectancy-value theory,* which you read about in Chapter 7.

According to this theory, you orient yourself by your own attitudes. In Chapter 7 you learned that an attitude consists of a cluster of beliefs and evaluations, and this theory of media uses and gratifications is just an extension of this basic idea. Here your attitude toward some segment of the media is determined by your beliefs about and evaluations of it.

The gratifications you seek from media are determined by your attitudes toward the media—your beliefs about what a medium can give you and your evaluations of this material. For example, if you believe that sitcoms provide entertainment and you like to be entertained, you will seek gratification of your entertainment needs by watching sitcoms. If, on the other hand, you believe that sitcoms provide an unrealistic view of life and you don't like this kind of thing, you will avoid viewing them.

Of course, your opinion of sitcoms consists of several beliefs and evaluations, and whether you actually watch them will be determined by several things. Your orientation to any type of program will be determined by your entire cluster of beliefs and evaluations. Palmgreen's formula for this, which mirrors the general expectancy-value formula presented in Chapter 7, is as follows:

$$GS_i = \sum_i^n b_i e_i$$

where

GS = gratification sought
b_i = belief
e_i = evaluation

The extent to which you seek gratifications in any segment of the media (a program, a program type, a particular kind of content, or an entire medium) would be determined by the same formula. As you gain experience with a part of the media, the gratifications you obtain will in turn affect your beliefs, reinforcing the viewing pattern.

To test the connection between expectancy values and media gratifications, David Swanson and Austin Babrow conducted a study of the television news-viewing habits of students.[77] About three hundred students at the University of Illinois were asked to fill out a questionnaire on their news viewing. To find out whether they watched the news and how they felt about it, the students were asked how many times a week they viewed network and local news, how likely they were to view news in an average week, and whether other people thought they should watch the news. The questionnaire also tested the students' attitudes toward the news.

To find out the extent to which the news gratified various media needs, the questionnaire asked whether each of a number of gratifications were met by watching the news. These included such items as keeping up on current events, getting entertained, and giving them things to talk about. In all, fourteen possible gratifications were included. The researchers found that the students' expectancy values (their attitudes) toward the news did relate to how much they used the news to gratify certain media needs.

---

76   Philip Palmgreen, "Uses and Gratifications: A Theoretical Perspective," in *Communication Yearbook 8,* ed. R. N. Bostrom (Beverly Hills, CA: Sage, 1984), pp. 20–55. See also K. Rosengren, L. Wenner, and P. Palmgreen, eds., *Media Gratifications Research: Current Perspectives* (Beverly Hills, CA: Sage, 1985).
77   David L. Swanson and Austin S. Babrow, "Uses and Gratifications: The Influence of Gratification-Seeking and Expectancy-Value Judgments on the Viewing of Television News," in *Rethinking Communication: Paradigm Exemplars,* eds. Brenda Dervin, Lawrence Grossberg, Barbara J. O'Keefe, and Ellen Wartella (Newbury Park, CA: Sage, 1989), pp. 361–375.

Dependency Theory. The uses-and-gratifications approach is a limited-effects theory. In other words, it grants individuals much control over how they employ media in their lives. Although media scholars are divided on just how powerful the media are, some scholars have argued that the limited-effects and powerful-effects models are not necessarily incompatible. Dependency theory takes a step toward showing how both may explain media effects.

Dependency theory was originally proposed by Sandra Ball-Rokeach and Melvin DeFleur.[78] Like uses-and-gratifications theory, this approach also rejects the causal assumptions of the early reinforcement hypothesis. To overcome this weakness, these authors take a broad system approach. In their model they propose an integral relationship among audiences, media, and the larger social system.

Consistent with uses-and-gratifications theory, this theory predicts that you depend on media information to meet certain needs and achieve certain goals. But you do not depend on all media equally. What determines how dependent you will become? There seem to be two factors.

First, you will become more dependent on media that meet a number of your needs than on media that provide just a few. Media can serve a number of functions such as monitoring government activities and providing entertainment. For any given group of people, some of these functions are more important than others, and your dependence on information from a medium increases when it supplies information that is more central to you. If you follow sports carefully, you will probably become dependent on ESPN or *Sports Illustrated.* A person who is not interested in sports will probably not even know where ESPN is on the dial, may never have looked at *Sports Illustrated,* and typically skips the entire sports section of the newspaper.

The second source of dependency is social stability. When social change and conflict are high, established institutions, beliefs, and practices are challenged, forcing you to reevaluate and make new choices. At such times your reliance on the media for information will increase. At other, more stable times your dependency on media may go way down. During times of war, for example, people become incredibly dependent on news programming.

This model shows that social institutions and media systems interact with audiences so as to create needs, interests, and motives. These in turn influence the audience to select various media and nonmedia sources that can subsequently lead to various dependencies. Individuals who grow dependent on a particular segment of the media will be affected cognitively, affectively, and behaviorally by that segment. Consequently, people are affected in different ways and to different degrees by the media.

Of course, one's needs are not always strictly personal but may be shaped by the culture or by various social conditions. In other words, individuals' needs, motives, and uses of media are contingent on outside factors that may not be in the individuals' control. These outside factors act as constraints on what and how media can be used and on the availability of other nonmedia alternatives.

For example, an elderly person who does not drive and has few friends may come to depend on television in a way that other individuals, whose life situations are different, will not. A commuter may come to rely on radio for information and news. A teenager may become dependent on music videos because of certain norms in the social group. In general, "the more readily available, the greater the perceived instrumentality, and the more socially and culturally acceptable the use of a medium is, the more probable that media use will be regarded as the most appropriate functional alternative."[79]

78   Sandra J. Ball-Rokeach and Melvin L. DeFleur, "A Dependency Model of Mass-Media Effects," *Communication Research* 3 (1976): 3–21. See also Melvin L. DeFleur and Sandra J. Ball-Rokeach, *Theories of Mass Communication* (New York: Longman, 1982), pp. 240–251.
79   Alan M. Rubin and Sven Windahl, "The Uses and Dependency Model of Mass Communication," *Critical Studies in Mass Communication* 3 (1986): 193.

Furthermore, the more alternatives an individual has for gratifying needs, the less dependent he or she will become on any single medium. The number of functional alternatives, however, is not just a matter of individual choice or even of psychological traits but is limited also by factors such as availability of certain media.

◖ COMMENTARY AND CRITIQUE

Mass communication involves the dissemination of information and influence in society through media and interpersonal channels. It is an integral part of culture and is inseparable from other large-scale social institutions. Media forms like television, film, and print—as well as media content—affect our ways of thinking and seeing the world. Indeed, media participate in the very creation of culture itself, and many believe that media are instrumental in the dissemination of power and domination in society and are thereby instruments of ideology and hegemony.

Early mass communication theories concentrated on the structure and function of media. For example, Harold Lasswell's models outlined such functions as information, entertainment, and interpretation. Other functionalist theories presented additional ones such as shaping public opinion, diffusing innovations, cultivating common values, perpetuating majority views, and setting the public agenda. By the 1980s at least, this functionalist tradition was challenged vigorously by other perspectives.[80]

The extent and power of media influence is a matter of dispute. Mass communication is believed by some to reinforce attitudes and opinions, but evidence suggests that sometimes media effects are more profound than simple reinforcement. At the same time, however, people make active use of media to gratify their own needs. In fact, as people become dependent on certain types of media and content, the impact of those outlets may increase.[81]

The controversies about media functions reflect a persistent conflict in the study of mass communication. How powerful are media in the control of culture? Some, like McLuhan, Meyrowitz, and Gerbner, argue that media are powerful forces in determining the character of culture and individual life. Other theorists claim that individuals have much control over the outcomes of media transactions in their lives. Yet a third group believes that mass media are important but that they are only part of a complex of factors involved in social domination and that individuals are influenced by the entire system of dominating forces.

The outcome of the media-influence process is complex. In the final analysis, the outcome of mass communication may be a product of the interaction among various societal structures and individual needs, desires, and dependencies, and it seems unlikely that this system will ever be reduced to an identifiable calculus. The theories in this chapter emphasize different aspects of this complex relationship.

McLuhan's theory is not much in favor anymore, but few would deny that his basic idea—that media forms in and of themselves do have an impact on culture—has had a major effect on our thinking about media. Media scholars today are just less glib about what those specific effects are than was McLuhan.

McLuhan's ideas are useful for stimulating a fresh look at the subject matter, but they provide little guidance on how to understand the process of mass communication. They are valuable in that they point to the importance of media forms in society, but they do not give a realistic picture of the variables involved in the effects of media forms. In sum, Kenneth Boulding points out, "It is perhaps typical of very creative minds that they hit very large nails not quite on the head."[82]

More popular today is semiotics. This field has had a major impact throughout communica-

80   Burrowes, "From Functionalism to Cultural Studies."
81   This issue is explored in some detail by Roger Desmond and Rod Carveth, "Illuminating the Black Box: The Psychological Tradition in Media Studies," in *Watershed Research Traditions in Human Communication Theory*, eds. Donald P. Cushman and Branislav Kovačić (Albany: SUNY Press, 1995), pp. 241–265.
82   Boulding, "The Medium," p. 68.

tion studies, and it has been especially popular in media scholarship. The reasons are obvious. Semiotics provides a clear idea of what to look at when analyzing the meaning of media messages. In semiotics you look at visual, auditory, and verbal signs. Semiotics has also been useful to help explain why the media have differential effects. It is valuable, too, because it enables the observer to analyze the structure of media messages without ignoring the interpretive processes of the audience.

One of the most important lines of research on the cultural impact of media is critical theory, which maintains that media are powerful forces for dominant interests in society. The so-called media hegemony thesis maintains that media are instruments of the dominant ideology and by representing the interests of those already in power subvert the interests of marginalized groups. This thesis is hotly debated, as Kevin Carragee points out in a review.[83] Scholars opposing media hegemony claim that the media actually represent a diversity of values and often speak out in opposition to the ideology of the powerful in society.

One of the obvious issues in media studies is the role of groups and interpersonal communication in the mass communication process. A whole line of research on diffusion of ideas and innovation supports the idea that interpersonal communication is a powerful part of this process. Beginning with the work of Paul Lazarsfeld, the research and theory of diffusion has been immensely successful. Dennis Davis and Stanley Baran remark of Lazarsfeld: "If one person deserves the title of founder of the field of mass communication research, that person is Paul Lazarsfeld. No one has done more to determine the way in which theory and research methods would be developed to aid our understanding of mass communication."[84]

The parsimony of diffusion theories has enabled observers to deal with a huge and complex phenomenon with relative ease. Additionally, these theories have been highly heuristic and have produced a large body of research. For many years the idea of the two-step flow (and later multiple-step flow) in the diffusion of information and innovation has been a mainstay of mass communication theory.

Traditional diffusion theory uses a linear pattern in which messages flow from person to person along a network. Some contemporary diffusion theorists now believe that this logic does not explain enough. Research has not consistently supported this notion of how diffusion occurs. At times the media appear to inform the public directly, with little interpersonal involvement; at other times different forms of diffusion are revealed. Further, the strict dichotomy between opinion leaders and followers is overly simple. In the give-and-take of everyday conversation, people exchange information, question it, argue about it, and come to a shared understanding.

Another problem with the linear model of diffusion is that it downplays context; the actual circumstances under which diffusion occurs may have a great deal to do with the pattern of dissemination used by individuals in sharing information and innovations. Dissemination is more a matter of convergence or the achievement of shared meaning than of strict linear influence.

One of the problems of diffusion theory is to explain why information sometimes does not flow in the network. An interesting explanation is the spiral of silence. The spiral of silence exemplifies careful theory development through research. Beginning with a simple hypothesis in the early 1970s, Noelle-Neumann undertook numerous studies designed to test the basic hypothesis, its assumptions, and ramifications.

At the same time, however, the spiral of silence does not seem to apply in all societies. Hernando González, for example, in a study of public opinion in the Philippine revolution, says that the Philippine experience is not consistent with the spiral of silence. Indeed, alternative media were heard, and no spiral of silence

83   Kevin Carragee, "A Critical Evaluation of Debates Examining the Media Hegemony Thesis," *Western Journal of Communication* 57 (summer 1993): 330–348.

84   Dennis K. Davis and Stanley J. Baran, *Mass Communication and Everyday Life: A Perspective on Theory and Effects* (Belmont, CA: Wadsworth, 1981), p. 27.

appeared to be in favor of a dominant opinion in this society.[85]

From another corner, cultural scholars and marxists would point to this line of research as an example of the kind of work they most distrust. First, they believe that it is false to assume that one can find an underlying structure to public opinion through surveys. Social science methods cannot be trusted to reveal any kind of reality beyond the meanings assigned by observers. Second, the failure to acknowledge the ideological nature of the public opinion is a major oversight. Third, critical scholars would point out that the spiral of silence is one possible factor in a general hegemony, in which the interests of dominant groups in society are perpetuated. Fourth, these critics would object to the suggestion that the spiral of silence is a universal phenomenon. All social life must be viewed in the context of history, and the spiral of silence, like most traditional social science findings, abstracts beyond the material world. Finally, this kind of research is truly "administrative" in the sense that it becomes a tool in which the dominant ideology can be managed or promulgated.

Another theory of cultural media outcomes is cultivation analysis. Cultivation analysis, which is bolstered by two decades of research on cultural indicators, calls our attention to the power of television; however, the cultivation hypothesis has not been without critique.[86] In fact, television researcher Paul Hirsch has spoken out harshly against the cultivation effect. He reanalyzed Gerbner's data and failed to find evidence for cultivation. Hirsch concluded that "acceptance of the cultivation hypothesis as anything more than an interesting but unsupported speculation is premature and unwarranted at this time."[87] Gerbner and his colleagues have responded to this critique by reaffirming the validity of their findings and concluding that "Hirsch's analysis is flawed, incomplete, and tendentious."[88]

The more common tendency is to look on the cultivation effect as a possible and significant finding but to be suspicious of the authors' precise explanation.[89] Cultivation theory is based on a simple premise: Television viewing causes in-

dividuals to accept the TV view of reality, and the more one watches television, the greater that acceptance. Critics question several things about this prediction. First, the effect may not be constant over all groups and all levels of viewing. Second, the causation may not be in the direction predicted; people may use TV to reinforce previously held beliefs. Third, there is some question about the strength or power of the cultivation effect among all of the other factors, such as education, that may affect our cultural beliefs. There is probably a grain of truth in cultivation theory, perhaps a very large grain, but some observers suspect that it does not tell the whole story.

Another important cultural outcome of media communication is agenda setting. Agenda-setting theory is appealing for two reasons. It returns a degree of power to the media after an era in which media effects were thought to be minimal, and its focus on cognitive effects rather than attitude and opinion change adds a badly needed dimension to effects research. The idea of issue salience as a media effect is intriguing and important.

The basic problem with this line of work is that although the theory is clear in positing a causal link between media and issue salience, the research evidence on this point is not convincing.[90] Research has uncovered a strong correla-

85   Hernando González, "Mass Media and the Spiral of Silence: The Philippines from Marcos to Aquino," *Journal of Communication* 34 (1988): 33–48. For a summary of the failure of international research to confirm the theory, see Salmon and Glynn, "Spiral of Silence."
86   Morgan and Shanahan, "Two Decades of Cultivation Research."
87   Paul M. Hirsch, "The 'Scary World' of the Nonviewer and Other Anomalies: A Reanalysis of Gerbner et al.'s Findings on Cultivation Analysis," *Communication Research* 7 (1980): 404. See also Paul M. Hirsch, "On Not Learning from One's Own Mistakes: A Reanalysis of Gerbner et al.'s Findings on Cultivation Analysis, Part II," *Communication Research* 8 (1981): 3–38.
88   George Gerbner, Larry Gross, Michael Morgan, and Nancy Signorielli, "A Curious Journey into the Scary World of Paul Hirsch," *Communication Research* 8 (1981): 39.
89   A critique of this type is W. James Potter, "Cultivation Theory and Research: A Conceptual Critique," *Human Communication Research* 19 (1993): 564–601. See also John Tapper, "The Ecology of Cultivation: A Conceptual Model for Cultivation Research," *Communication Theory* 5 (1995): 36–57.
90   Criticism of this work can be found in Severin and Tankard, *Communication Theories*, pp. 253–254.

tion between audience and media views on the importance of issues, but it does not always demonstrate that media choices cause audience salience. In fact, as we saw previously, some theorists argue that the emphasis given to issues in the media can be a reflection, not a cause, of audience agendas. This is a chicken-egg issue. Sometimes there may be an interaction between media and public in terms of the issue agenda, and situational factors probably always enter into how powerful the media are at any time in establishing the public agenda.

That certain studies do not support a direct causal link between media activity and audience attention does not mean that a relationship is not there. It may simply be a more complicated one. For example, there may be intervening variables or a nonlinear relationship. For example, W. R. Neuman explores the possibility that public response to an issue is aroused rather quickly at first and then levels off as a saturation point is reached.[91]

The uses-and-gratifications approach was like a breath of fresh air in media research. For the first time scholars in this tradition focused on receivers as active participants in the communication process, rather than the traditional viewpoint of the passive, unthinking audience. This approach is certainly one of the most popular frameworks for the study of mass communication, but a good deal of criticism has been leveled against it.[92]

The criticism of the uses-and-gratifications approach can be divided into three major strands.[93] The first set of objections deals with the lack of coherence and theory in the tradition. Although this objection had merit until recently, we have seen that more unified versions in the form of value-expectancy and value-dependency theories are emerging.

The second line of criticism focuses on social and political objections, which come primarily from critical theory. The problem is that uses and gratifications is so functional in orientation that it ignores the dysfunctions of media in society and culture. It is conservative at heart and sees media primarily as positive ways in which indi-

viduals meet their needs, without any attention to the overall negative cultural effects of media in society.

Finally, some critics have objected to the instrumental philosophy of uses and gratifications. Uses and gratifications makes media consumption extremely rational, behavioristic, and individualistic. Individuals are believed to control their media-consuming behavior according to conscious goals. No attention is paid to the ways media may be consumed mindlessly or ritualistically. The theory does not study the ways media content forms and reflects cultural values or patterns of action. In other words, much of our consumption of mass media may not be easily traced to individual needs but rather to habits of the culture. Also, individuals may not be aware of many of the factors that enter into their consumption choices. Attribution theory, which was covered in greater detail in Chapter 7, suggests that people often misjudge the causes of their own behavior; some research indicates that this principle holds true for media consumption as well.[94]

McQuail, a noted researcher of uses and gratifications, takes this third point seriously and proposes that the traditional gratifications model is only part of what happens in media use.[95] He suggests that although individuals do use media for guidance, surveillance, and information, they also have a generalized arousal need that comes from and is informed by the culture.

Dependency theory makes an attempt to reconcile some of the problems of uses and gratifications with other powerful-effects models. This

---

91   W. R. Neuman, "The Threshold of Public Opinion," *Public Opinion Quarterly* 54 (1990): 159–176.
92   See especially Philip Elliott, "Uses and Gratifications Research: A Critique and Sociological Alternative," in *The Uses of Mass Communication*, eds. J. Blumler and E. Katz (Beverly Hills, CA: Sage, 1974), pp. 249–268; and David L. Swanson, "Political Communication Research and the Uses and Gratifications Model: A Critique," *Communication Research* 6 (1979): 36–53.
93   Denis McQuail, "With the Benefits of Hindsight: Reflections on Uses and Gratifications Research," *Critical Studies in Mass Communication* 1 (1984): 177–193.
94   See, for example, Dolf Zillmann, "Attribution and Misattribution of Excitatory Reactions," in *New Directions in Attribution Research*, vol. 2, eds. J. H. Harvey, W. Ickes, and R. F. Kidd (Hillsdale, NJ: Erlbaum, 1978), pp. 335–368.
95   McQuail, "Hindsight."

theory accounts for both individual differences in responses to media and general media effects. As a system theory, it shows the complexity of the interactions among the various aspects of the media transaction. The fusion of uses-and-gratifications and dependency theories provides an even more complete integration.

Like most of the theories in this chapter, however, both dependency theory and uses-and-gratifications theory clash with the critical theory school. This clash points out a number of stasis points in media theory: Are media powerful in influencing culture, or are effects and cultural realities the accomplishments of individuals and interpretive communities? Do individuals make real choices, and how extensive are the cultural limits on individual media choice? To what extent should theory describe and explain, and to what extent should it reform? There will always be answers to these questions, but consensus will probably never be achieved.

CAPSTONE

C H A P T E R **16**

MAKING COMMUNICATION THEORY

By now you have a good idea of what communication theories look like. Given our tendency as human beings to seek clear and useful explanations, it is not surprising that scientists and scholars formalize theories. Before taking this communication theory course, you may have thought that a theory is an educated guess about how something works. To a certain extent, this is accurate, but in this book, you have learned to understand theory in a more sophisticated way. A theory is a way of packaging reality, a way of understanding it. Since our experience can be represented in a variety of ways, a number of theories could be useful. Human beings always represent reality symbolically, and they are always operating in the realm of theory. A theory is a system of thought, a way of looking. We can never "view" reality purely. Instead, we must use a set of concepts and symbols to define what we see, and our theories provide the lenses with which we observe and experience the world.

Theories, then, are made. Scholars label the concepts in the theory, they decide what connections or relationships to feature, they determine

how to organize the theory, and they give the theory a name. They then use the theory to talk about what they experience. There is no standard against which all theory must be measured. The creation and development of theory is a *human social activity* that is subjectively determined. Human beings create it, test it, and evaluate it. As a *social* activity, theory making is done within communities of scholarship that share a way of knowing and a set of common practices. In the end, the community of scholars or practitioners decides what works for them and what theories prevail. Because the communities of practice vary tremendously, they will differ in what they consider to be valid and valuable. A theory widely adopted by one community may be rejected entirely by another. So creating a theory is largely a question of persuading some community that the theory has fit and utility for their purposes.

Students often do not realize exactly how theory is made. If you are an undergraduate student, you may have found all of the footnotes in the book to be a bit odd, but actually they are

very important because they show the importance of research and publication in the development of theory. If you are a graduate student, you
may appreciate the same footnotes because they
can help you get started in your own research.

The formal presentations of scholarship reflected in the footnotes provide the means by
which scholarly work is "tested." There is no
scale that can be applied objectively to scholarship, so it must be judged subjectively by peers.
Although scholars apply well-worked standards
in the evaluation of one another's work, evaluation is always a matter of judgment, and consensus about the value of a piece of scholarship is
rare. Just as a group of students might disagree
as to why their professor is a good or bad
teacher, scholars also disagree about the merits
of particular research and theory.

Although standards vary from one academic
community to another, scholars follow a fairly
predictable pattern of production. First, a scholar
or group of scholars becomes curious about a
topic. Sometimes the topic relates to something
personal in the scholar's own life. Sometimes it is
an extension of what he or she has been reading
in the literature. Often a conversation with men-
tors or colleagues will provoke an interest in a
particular subject. Also, professors are often challenged by questions that come up when they are
preparing lectures or having class discussions.

Scholars are usually motivated to investigate
interesting subjects because their professional
advancement may depend on it. They cannot get
a Ph.D. without developing scholarly curiosity
that leads to research on a topic of their choice.
They often will not be able to get pay raises, ten-
ure, or promotion without doing this kind of
work. There are many other incentives as well,
including the ability to get grant money, travel,
be recognized as a leader, get awards, and so
forth. So the process begins with curiosity about
a topic, but it can never end there.

To develop their work, scholars begin to do
some kind of research on the topic, which almost
always includes a survey of literature to see what
others have done on this subject. The research
will also include some kind of systematic obser-

vation. What the scholar observes and how he or
she collects data depend upon the tradition of research and theory being used. There is tremendous variation in research practice from one
community to another. Some focus on texts and
interpret meaning. Some apply critical standards. Some do experiments and use sophisticated statistics. Some conduct interviews. Some
observe behavior in natural settings.

Since scholarship is never a solitary activity,
the results of reading, observing, and thinking
must be shared with others. On the most informal level, scholars often share their work with
students. They may bring some of their latest
work into the classroom as a lecture or basis for
discussion, which can be helpful in refining
ideas. Graduate students are aware of this, but
undergraduates often do not realize that their
professors "test" their theoretical ideas in classes.
When you have to lecture on a topic, you can see
the holes that need to be filled, the weaknesses of
the line of argument, and the strengths of the
conceptualization as well.

Ultimately, a scholar's work must go out for
peer review. One of the first formal "tests" a
scholar may use is the convention paper. The researcher writes a paper and submits it to a professional association to be presented at a regional
or national meeting. Most of these are reviewed
by a panel of peers. This review itself is a level of
evaluation that can help a scholar determine if he
or she is on the right track. Universities usually
encourage professors to submit papers by agreeing to pay their travel expenses if they have a paper accepted.

Whether a paper is reviewed for acceptance
before the convention or not, the presentation
permits at least two other forms of peer assessment. One—more informal—consists of the comments that colleagues make after hearing the
presentation. This kind of feedback may come in
the bar, hallway, or airport. Colleagues may even
enjoy a phone call or email exchange about one
another's work. More formally, there is often a
designated critic who delivers comments about
several papers to the audience right after they
are presented.

Conventions are very valuable for scholars as an initial testing ground for ideas. Not only do the convention-goers have the opportunity to hear the most recent research, but the presenters can refine their work based on the reactions they receive. Often a group of researchers will present various iterations of their work several times at conventions before they go to publication.

There are two forms of publication most valued in the academic community. The first is a journal article, and the second is a monograph, or book. There are literally thousands of academic journals around the world, and every field, no matter how small, will have at least one—and usually several—journals. A glance through the Selected Bibliography of this book will reveal several of the most important journals in the communication field. One of the most important of these in communication theory is a journal by the same name, *Communication Theory*. This outlet is one of the most important for introducing theories to our field. Indeed, if you scan the footnotes of each chapter of this book, you will see just how important this journal has become. But there are many other journals that are also highly recognized in the field, including, for example, *Human Communication Research, Critical Studies in Mass Communication,* and *Communication Monographs*.

The members of the field subscribe to these journals, use their contents as background for their own research, and learn about the latest and best developments in the field. Usually, the articles in a journal are refereed, meaning that they are formally reviewed and judged by a panel of peers for quality. Since only the best articles are published, the majority of papers submitted to journals do not end up appearing in print. This rigorous form of review is the primary force establishing what is taken seriously within an academic community.

Many research and theory projects find their way to another level of publication—the scholarly monograph or book. After a group of scholars develop a line of research and theory in some detail—usually after a number of convention presentations and journal articles—they may write it all up in a book manuscript. These books are not the same as textbooks. Textbooks are written primarily to help students learn the content of certain courses. Scholarly treatises are published for the benefit of other scholars, as a convenient way to "house" the results of a major research program. Mostly graduate students and other scholars use these books, and many professors use scholarly books as a basis for their lectures in classes. Again, peers review manuscripts submitted for publication as a book, and only a few manuscripts are deemed good enough for publication. Having a scholarly book is considered a great honor in most fields.

Through this process of convention presentation and journal publication, the scholarship considered most interesting, profound, useful, or progressive will "bubble up" and form the corpus of recognized work within the community of scholars. As this work develops, those responsible, along with their colleagues, begin to develop more formal explanations that tie the work together. Initially, these explanations may be mere interpretations of research findings, but as they give more convention papers and publish more articles on their work, the scholars' explanations become more formal and codified, and that is where we see theory emerging. Once a theory, or emerging theory, is identified, other scholars may use it to guide additional research, which adds in turn to the body of research and theory taken as standard within the community.

Once a group of scholars have established a name for themselves, they are often invited to write about and summarize their work in edited volumes, or books of essays, consisting of the work of a number of theorists around a topic. This form of publication is very common in the communication field, and it is useful because it helps students and professors see what the current state of theory is in a particular area of the field.

Now you can begin to see how theory development is a social activity. Once you live through several years of producing research, positing theory, being reviewed, revising your work, publishing, and using the published work of others, you cannot deny that theories are social constructions that are only as valuable as the collective wisdom of the scholarly community establishes.

Reading the chapters of this book will give you a glimpse of this world. The authors cited in these chapters are all established scholars in the communication field. All of them have given numerous convention papers, published many journal articles, and many have produced books. Keep in mind that the theories selected for this book have been judged to be important ways of understanding communication by at least one of the academic communities within the field of communication.

Notice that the theories here vary in terms of how they were generated, the kind of research used, the style in which they are presented, and the aspect of communication they address. These theories are different because they come from various academic communities within the field, each of which has its own standards of excellence. What is judged valuable within one community may not be considered very interesting or rigorous within another. That's just the way it is in the world of scholarship. Indeed, huge debates rage about which community's methods and standards should prevail, but these debates will never be settled. In the end we need to realize two things: (1) Theory is the product of human judgment and social interaction; and (2) we live in a multi-valued world in which different people prefer different ways of knowing. Do not take this state of affairs as a problem. Instead, treat it as a rich resource for developing a more thorough and complex understanding of your communication experience.

The communication discipline consists of many subfields, and each of these has its own body of theory available to the members of a scholarly community. Although the boundaries between the communities of scholarship are fuzzy and bodies of theory overlap, most scholars can name the theories they most trust and use. They may not agree on which theories are most important or useful, but they will agree that theories are available to guide their work.

A body of theory is really just a snapshot in time. It provides a brief glance at a moment in the evolving history of ideas within a community of scholars. The metaphor of "body" is good because it captures the qualities of growth, change, development, aging, and renewal. A community of scholars, like any community, changes over time, and one way to see this change is to note what happens to its theories during particular periods.

Over time, then, in almost every field, you will see the body of theory change. What a scholar came to respect and use in graduate school will not be the same set of theories he or she uses in mid-career, and that will probably not resemble very closely what is most valued within the community late in one's career. Scholars are often bemused by these changes at moments when they read old journal articles, cull their library, or prepare to teach new courses.

Still, some body of theory will always exist at any point in time, and this is always a vital force. The body of theory provides shape and meaning to the discipline. It offers a set of tools for research, practice, and teaching. The body of theory helps members of the community identify their primary areas of interest and work, it pulls them together as a community, and provides a set of standards for how scholarly work should proceed.

What, then, makes a leading theory? Although leading theories change over time, they share certain important characteristics. First, leading theories provide insights we would not ordinarily have. When you read a really good theory, you have an "aha" reaction. You realize that this makes sense, yet it is not something you would otherwise consider. In other words, the theory introduces you to new things and helps you see things in new ways.

Second, a leading theory is conceptually interesting. It does not belabor the obvious or repeat what most of us already know from the perspective of our culture. Instead, leading theories can be fascinating precisely because their concepts are intriguing and helpful.

Third, leading theories are constantly evolving. They change. They morph into new forms. The leading theory of today is an evolution of earlier theoretical ideas that have grown, combined, and expanded through research and careful thinking. One of the hallmarks of a leading theory is that it has a history. It started small and was developed over time, and you realize that it is open-ended and will continue to evolve into the future.

Fourth, leading theories have staying power. They may change, but they stick around for a while. They are so useful, insightful, or interesting that they are not easily abandoned. True, leading theories do pass, but the best theories of the present time are not new to the scene. Certain theories are leaders because they have been known in one form or another for a number of years. Indeed, some theories continue to be taught, not because they are necessarily in vogue today, but because they had such an influence in earlier times. Such theories are classics.

Fifth, leading theories are the product of teams of several people. Rarely is a single person responsible for a major theory. Indeed, there may be one scholar whose name is most often associated with the theory, but if you look at the publications related to the theory, you will see many contributors. This is an important sign because it means that the work has attracted a number of curious scholars, that these individuals have introduced their students to the work, and that the original team of researchers are now "grandparents," sometimes even "great-grandparents," to generations of scholars who continue the line of work and carry the theorizing further and further.

The business captured in this book is not trivial. It could not be more important to the intellectual character of the human mind. Theory making has been throughout history and remains today one of the most significant human endeavors.

SELECTED BIBLIOGRAPHY

Chapter 1
Communication Theory and Scholarship

Andersen, Peter A. "When One Cannot Not Communicate: A Challenge to Motley's Traditional Communication Postulates." *Communication Studies* 42 (1991): 309–325.

Anderson, James A. *Communication Theory: Epistemological Foundations.* New York: Guilford, 1996.

Atwater, Tony. "Communication Theory and Research: The Quest for Credibility in the Social Sciences." In *An Integrated Approach to Communication Theory.* Edited by M. B. Salwen and D. W. Stacks. Mahwah, NJ: Erlbaum, 1996, pp. 539–549.

Barnlund, Dean C. *Interpersonal Communication: Survey and Studies.* New York: Houghton Mifflin, 1968.

Bavelas, Janet Beavin. "Behaving and Communicating: A Reply to Motley." *Western Journal of Speech Communication* 54 (1990): 593–602.

Beach, Wayne A. "On (Not) Observing Behavior Interactionally." *Western Journal of Speech Communication* 54 (1990): 603–612.

Berger, Charles R., and Chaffee, Steven H. "The Study of Communication as a Science." In *Handbook of Communication Science.* Edited by Charles R. Berger and Steven H. Chaffee. Newbury Park, CA: Sage, 1987, pp. 15–19.

Blalock, Hubert M. *Basic Dilemmas in the Social Sciences.* Beverly Hills, CA: Sage, 1984.

Bormann, Ernest G. *Theory and Research in the Communicative Arts.* New York: Holt, Rinehart & Winston, 1965.

Bowers, John Waite, and Bradac, James J. "Issues in Communication Theory: A Metatheoretical Analysis." In *Communication Yearbook 5.* Edited by Michael Burgoon. New Brunswick, NJ: Transaction, 1982, pp. 1–28.

Burrell, G., and Morgan, G. *Sociological Paradigms and Organizational Analysis.* London: Heinemann, 1979.

Cappella, Joseph N., ed. "Symposium on Mass and Interpersonal Communication." *Human Communication Research* 15 (1988): 236–318.

Clevenger, Theodore, Jr., "Can One Not Communicate? A Conflict of Models." *Communication Studies* 42 (1991): 340–353.

Cohen, Jonathan, and Metzger, Miriam. "Social Affiliation and the Achievement of Ontological Security Through Interpersonal and Mass Communication." *Critical Studies in Mass Communication* 15 (1998): 41–60.

Craig, Robert T. "Communication Theory as a Field." *Communication Theory* 9 (1999): 119–161.

———. "Why Are There So *Many* Communication Theories?" *Journal of Communication* 43 (1993): 26–33.

Dallmayr, Fred R. *Language and Politics.* Notre Dame, IN: University of Notre Dame Press, 1984.

Dance, Frank E. X. "The 'Concept' of Communication." *Journal of Communication* 20 (1970): 201–210.

Dance, Frank E. X., and Larson, Carl E. *The Functions of Human Communication: A Theoretical Approach.* New York: Holt, Rinehart & Winston, 1976.

Deetz, Stanley A. "Describing Differences in Approaches to Organization Science." *Organization Science* 7 (1996): 191–207.

———. "Future of the Discipline: The Challenges, the Research, and the Social Contribution." In *Communication Yearbook 17.* Edited by Stanley A. Deetz. Thousand Oaks, CA: Sage, 1994, pp. 565–600.

Delia, Jesse G. "Communication Research: A History." In *Handbook of Communication Science.* Edited by Charles R. Berger and Steven H. Chaffee. Newbury Park, CA: Sage, 1987, pp. 20–98.

de Saussure, Ferdinand. *Course in General Linguistics.* London: Peter Owen, 1960.

Diefenbeck, James A. *A Celebration of Subjective Thought.* Carbondale: Southern Illinois University Press, 1984.

Dissanayake, Wimal. *Communication Theory: The Asian Perspective.* Singapore: Asian Mass Communication Research and Information Center, 1988.

———. "The Need for the Study of Asian Approaches to Communication." *Media Asia* 13 (1986): 6–13.

Durkheim, Emile. *The Division of Labor in Society.* London: Collier-Macmillan, 1964.

Ellis, Donald G. *Crafting Society: Ethnicity, Class, and Communication Theory.* Mahwah, NJ: Erlbaum, 1999.

Farrell, Thomas B. "Beyond Science: Humanities Contributions to Communication Theory." In *Handbook of Communication Science.* Edited by Charles R. Berger and Steven H. Chaffee. Newbury Park, CA: Sage, 1987, pp. 123–139.

Fiske, Donald W., and Shweder, Richard A. "Introduction: Uneasy Social Science." In *Metatheory in Social Science:*

Pluralisms and Subjectivities. Edited by Donald W. Fiske and Richard A. Shweder. Chicago: University of Chicago Press, 1986, pp. 1–18.

Friedrich, Gustav W., and Boileau, Don M. "The Communication Discipline." In *Teaching Communication.* Edited by Anita L. Vangelisti, John A. Daly, and Gustav Friedrich. Mahwah, NJ: Erlbaum, 1999, pp. 3–13.

Gergen, Kenneth J. *Toward Transformation in Social Knowledge.* New York: Springer-Verlag, 1982.

Giddens, Anthony. *Central Problems in Social Theory.* Berkeley: University of California Press, 1979.

——. *Profiles and Critiques in Social Theory.* Berkeley: University of California Press, 1983.

Grossberg, Lawrence. "Does Communication Theory Need Intersubjectivity? Toward an Immanent Philosophy of Interpersonal Relations." In *Communication Yearbook 6.* Edited by Michael Burgoon. Beverly Hills, CA: Sage, 1984, pp. 171–205.

Hanson, N. R. *Patterns of Discovery.* Cambridge: Cambridge University Press, 1961.

Harper, Nancy. *Human Communication Theory: The History of a Paradigm.* Rochelle Park, NJ: Hayden, 1979.

Hawkins, Robert P., Wiemann, John M., and Pingree, Suzanne, eds. *Advancing Communication Science.* Newbury Park, CA: Sage, 1988.

Holton, Gerald. "Science, Science Teaching, and Rationality." In *The Philosophy of the Curriculum.* Edited by Sidney Hook. Buffalo, NY: Prometheus, 1975, pp. 101–108.

Jarrett, James L. *The Humanities and Humanistic Education.* Reading, MA: Addison-Wesley, 1973.

Kincaid, D. Lawrence. *Communication Theory: Eastern and Western Perspectives.* San Diego: Academic, 1987.

Krippendorff, Klaus. "Conversation or Intellectual Imperialism in Comparing Communication (Theories)." *Communication Theory* 3 (1993): 252–266.

Kuhn, Thomas S. *The Structure of Scientific Revolutions,* 2nd ed. Chicago: University of Chicago Press, 1970.

Lakoff, George, and Johnson, Mark. *Metaphors We Live By.* Chicago: University of Chicago Press, 1980.

Littlejohn, Stephen W. "An Overview of the Contributions to Human Communication Theory from Other Disciplines." In *Human Communication Theory: Comparative Essays.* Edited by Frank E. X. Dance. New York: Harper & Row, 1982, pp. 243–285.

McKeon, Richard. "Gibson Winter's Elements for a Social Ethic: A Review." *Journal of Religion* 49 (1969): 77–84.

Miller, Gerald R. "On Defining Communication: Another Stab." *Journal of Communication* 16 (1966): 92.

Miller, Gerald R., and Nicholson, Henry. *Communication Inquiry.* Reading, MA: Addison-Wesley, 1976.

Monge, Peter R. "Communication Theory for a Globalizing World." In *Communication: Views from the Helm for the 21st Century.* Edited by Judith S. Trent. Boston: Allyn & Bacon, 1998, pp. 3–7.

Motley, Michael T. "Communication as Interaction: A Reply to Beach and Bavelas." *Western Journal of Speech Communication* 54 (1990): 613–623.

——. "How One May Not Communicate: A Reply to Andersen." *Communication Studies* 42 (1991): 326–339.

——. "On Whether One Can(not) (Not) Communicate: An Examination Via Traditional Communication Postulates." *Western Journal of Speech Communication* 54 (1990): 1–20.

O'Sullivan, Patrick B. "Bridging the Mass-Interpersonal Divide." *Human Communication Research* 25 (1999): 569–588.

Pearce, W. Barnett. *Communication and the Human Condition.* Carbondale: Southern Illinois University Press, 1989.

——. "Scientific Research Methods in Communication Studies and Their Implications for Theory and Research." In *Speech Communication in the 20th Century.* Edited by Thomas W. Benson. Carbondale: Southern Illinois University Press, 1985, pp. 255–281.

Pearce, W. Barnett, and Foss, Karen A. "The Historical Context of Communication as a Science." In *Human Communication: Theory and Research.* Edited by Gordon L. Dahnke and Glen W. Clatterbuck. Belmont, CA: Wadsworth, 1990, pp. 1–20.

Peters, John Durham. "The Gaps of Which Communication Is Made." *Critical Studies in Mass Communication* 11 (1994): 117–140.

——. "Tangled Legacies." *Journal of Communication* 46 (1996): 85–147.

Powers, John H. "On the Intellectual Structure of the Human Communication Discipline." *Communication Education* 44 (1995): 191–222.

Reardon, Kathleen K., and dePillis, Emmeline G. "Multichannel Leadership: Revisiting the False Dichotomy." In *An Integrated Approach to Communication Theory and Research.* Edited by M. B. Salwen and D. W. Stacks. Mahwah, NJ: Erlbaum, 1996, pp. 399–407.

Rogers, Everett M. "Anatomy of the Two Subdisciplines of Communication Study." *Human Communication Research* 25 (1999): 618–631.

——. *A History of Communication Study: A Biographical Approach.* New York: Free Press, 1994.

Rosengren, Karl Erik. "Culture, Media, and Society: Agency and Structure, Continuity and Change." In *Media Effects and Beyond.* Edited by Karl Erik Rosengren. London: Routledge, 1994, pp. 3–28.

——. "From Field to Frog Ponds." *Journal of Communication* 43 (1993): 6–17.

Ruesch, Jurgen. "Technology and Social Communication." In *Communication Theory and Research.* Edited by L. Thayer. Springfield, IL: Thomas, 1957, p. 462.

Sholle, David. "Resisting Disciplines: Repositioning Media Studies in the University." *Communication Theory* 5 (1995): 130–143.

Smith, Ted J., III. "Diversity and Order in Communication Theory: The Uses of Philosophical Analysis." *Communication Quarterly* 36 (1988): 28–40.

Snow, C. P. *The Two Cultures and a Second Look.* Cambridge: Cambridge University Press, 1964.

Sparks, Glen G., Potter, W. James, Cooper, Roger, and Dupagne, Michel. "Is Media Research Prescientific?" *Communication Theory* 5 (1995): 273–289.

Stacks, Don W., and Salwen, Michael B. "Integrating Theory and Research: Starting with Questions." In *An Integrated Approach to Communication Theory and Research.* Edited by M. B. Salwen and D. W. Stacks. Mahwah, NJ: Erlbaum, 1996, pp. 3–14.

Stewart, John. *Language as Articulate Contact.* Albany: SUNY Press, 1995.

——. "Speech and Human Being." *Quarterly Journal of Speech* 72 (1986): 55–73.

Streeter, Thomas. "Introduction: For the Study of Communication and Against the Discipline of Communication." *Communication Theory* 5 (1995): 117–129.

Winch, Peter. *The Idea of a Social Science and Its Relation to Philosophy.* London: Routledge & Kegan Paul, 1958.

Winter, Gibson. *Elements for a Social Ethic: Scientific and Ethical Perspectives on Social Process.* New York: Macmillan, 1966.

Chapter 2
Theory in the Process of Inquiry

Achinstein, P. *Laws and Explanation.* New York: Oxford University Press, 1971.

Andersen, Peter A. "The Trait Debate: A Critical Examination of the Individual Differences Paradigm in the Communication Sciences." In *Progress in Communication Sciences.* Edited by B. Dervin and M. J. Voight. Norwood, NJ: Ablex, 1986.

Anderson, James A. *Communication Theory: Epistemological Foundations.* New York: Guilford, 1996.

Beatty, Michael J. "Thinking Quantitatively." In *An Integrated Approach to Communication Theory and Research.* Edited by M. B. Salwen and D. W. Stacks. Mahwah, NJ: Erlbaum, 1996, pp. 33–44.

Berger, Charles R. "Evidence? For What?" *Western Journal of Communication* 58 (1994): 11–19.

Berger, Peter, and Luckmann, Thomas. *The Social Construction of Reality.* Garden City, NY: Doubleday, 1966.

Bostrom, Robert, and Donohew, Lewis. "The Case for Empiricism: Clarifying Fundamental Issues in Communication Theory." *Communication Monographs* 59 (1992): 109–129.

Bowers, John Waite, and Bradac, James J. "Issues in Communication Theory: A Metatheoretical Analysis." In *Communication Yearbook 5.* Edited by Michael Burgoon. New Brunswick, NJ: Transaction, 1982, pp. 1–28.

Brinberg, David, and McGrath, Joseph E. *Validity and the Research Process.* Beverly Hills, CA: Sage, 1985.

Brummett, Barry. "Some Implications of 'Process' or 'Intersubjectivity': Postmodern Rhetoric." *Philosophy and Rhetoric* 9 (1976): 21–51.

Casmir, Fred L. "The Role of Theory and Theory Building." In *Building Communication Theories: A Socio/Cultural Approach.* Edited by Fred L. Casmir. Hillsdale, NJ: Erlbaum, 1994, pp. 7–45.

Chaffee, Steven H. "Thinking About Theory." In *An Integrated Approach to Communication Theory and Research.* Edited by M. B. Salwen and D. W. Stacks. Mahwah, NJ: Erlbaum, 1996, pp. 15–32.

Cragan, John F., and Shields, Donald C. *Understanding Communication Theory: The Communicative Forces for Human Action.* Boston: Allyn & Bacon, 1998, pp. 1–31.

Craig, Robert T. "Communication Theory as a Field." *Communication Theory* 9 (1999): 119–161.

Craig, Robert T., and Tracy, Karen. "Grounded Practical Theory: The Case of Intellectual Discussion." *Communication Theory* 5 (1995): 248–272.

Cushman, Donald P., and Pearce, W. Barnett. "Generality and Necessity in Three Types of Theory About Human Communication, with Special Attention to Rules Theory." *Human Communication Research* 3 (1977): 344–353.

Deetz, Stanley A. *Democracy in an Age of Corporate Colonization: Developments in Communication and the Politics of Everyday Life.* Albany: SUNY Press, 1992.

DePaulo, Bella M., Ansfield, Matthew E., and Bell, Kathy L. "Theories About Deception and Paradigms for Studying It: A Critical Appraisal of Buller and Burgoon's Deception Theory and Research." *Communication Theory* 6 (1996): 297–311.

Dervin, Brenda, Grossberg, Lawrence, O'Keefe, Barbara, and Wartella, Ellen, eds. *Rethinking Communication: Paradigm Issues.* Newbury Park, CA: Sage, 1989.

Deutsch, Karl W. "On Communication Models in the Social Sciences." *Public Opinion Quarterly* 16 (1952): 356–380.

Fay, Brian. *Social Theory and Political Practice.* London: Allen & Unwin, 1975.

Fisher, B. Aubrey. *Perspectives on Human Communication.* New York: Macmillan, 1978.

Fiske, Donald W., and Shweder, Richard A., eds. *Metatheory in Social Science: Pluralisms and Subjectivities.* Chicago: University of Chicago Press, 1986.

Gergen, Kenneth J. "The Social Constructionist Movement in Modern Psychology." *American Psychologist* 40 (1985): 266–275.

———. *Toward Transformation in Social Knowledge.* New York: Springer-Verlag, 1982.

Hall, Calvin S., and Lindzey, Gardner. *Theories of Personality.* New York: Wiley, 1970.

Hamelink, Cees J. "Emancipation or Domestication: Toward a Utopian Science of Communication." *Journal of Communication* 33 (1983): 74–79.

Hanson, N. R. *Patterns of Discovery.* Cambridge, MA: Cambridge University Press, 1961.

Harré, Rom, and Secord, Paul F. *The Explanation of Social Behavior.* Totowa, NJ: Littlefield, Adams, 1979.

Houna, Joseph. "Two Ideals of Scientific Theorizing." In *Communication Yearbook 5.* Edited by Michael Burgoon. New Brunswick, NJ: Transaction, 1982, pp. 29–48.

Jacobsen, Thomas L. "Theories as Communications." *Communication Theory* 2 (1991): 145–150.

Jensen, Joli. "The Consequences of Vocabularies." *Journal of Communication* 43 (1993): 67–74.

Kaplan, Abraham. *The Conduct of Inquiry.* San Francisco: Chandler, 1964.

Krippendorff, Klaus. "Conversation or Intellectual Imperialism in Comparing Communication (Theories)." *Communication Theory* 3 (1993): 252–266.

Kuhn, Thomas S. *The Structure of Scientific Revolutions*, 2nd ed. Chicago: University of Chicago Press, 1970.

Levy, Mark R., ed. *The Future of the Field.* Special issue of *Journal of Communication* 43 (Summer 1993).

Littlejohn, Stephen W. "Communication Theory." In *Encyclopedia of Rhetoric and Composition: Communication from Ancient Times to the Information Age.* Edited by Teresa Enos. New York: Garland, 1996, pp. 117–121.

———. "An Overview of Contributions to Human Communication Theory from Other Disciplines." In *Human Communication Theory: Comparative Essays.* Edited by Frank E. X. Dance. New York: Harper & Row, 1982, pp. 243–285.

Lustig, Myron W. "Theorizing About Human Communication." *Communication Quarterly* 34 (1986): 451–459.

MacIntyre, Alasdair. "Ontology." In *The Encyclopedia of Philosophy*, vol. 5. Edited by Paul Edwards. New York: Macmillan, 1967, pp. 542–543.

Macy, Joanna. *Mutual Causality in Buddhism and General System Theory*. Albany: SUNY Press, 1991, pp. 117–137.

McNamee, Sheila. "Research as Social Intervention: A Research Methodology for the New Epistemology." Paper delivered at the Fifth International Conference on Culture and Communication, Philadelphia, October 1988.

Miller, Gerald. "The Current Status of Theory and Research in Interpersonal Communication." *Human Communication Research* 4 (1978): 175.

Pavitt, Charles. "The Third Way: Scientific Realism and Communication Theory." *Communication Theory* 9 (1999): 162–188.

Pearce, W. Barnett. "Metatheoretical Concerns in Communication." *Communication Quarterly* 25 (1977): 3–6.

———. "On Comparing Theories: Treating Theories as Commensurate or Incommensurate." *Communication Theory* 2 (1991): 159–164

Penman, Robyn. "Good Theory and Good Practice: An Argument in Progress." *Communication Theory* 3 (1992): 234–250.

Pepper, Stephen. *World Hypotheses*. Berkeley: University of California Press, 1942.

Polanyi, Michael. *Personal Knowledge*. London: Routledge & Kegan Paul, 1958.

Rorty, Richard. *Philosophy and the Mirror of Nature*. Princeton, NJ: Princeton University Press, 1979.

Rosengren, Karl Erik. "Substantive Theories and Formal Models—Bourdieu Confronted." *European Journal of Communication* 10 (1995): 7–39.

Secord, Paul F., ed. *Explaining Human Behavior: Consciousness, Human Action, and Social Structure*. Beverly Hills, CA: Sage, 1982.

Sigman, Stuart. "Do Social Approaches to Interpersonal Communication Constitute a Contribution to Communication Theory?" *Communication Theory* 2 (1992): 347–356.

Stiff, James B. "Theoretical Approaches to the Study of Deceptive Communication: Comments on Interpersonal Deception Theory." *Communication Theory* 6 (1996): 289–296.

Taylor, John R. *Linguistic Categorization: Prototypes in Linguistic Theory*. London: Clarendon, 1995.

Van Lear, Arthur. "Dialectical Empiricism: Science and Relationship Metaphors." In *Dialectical Approaches to Studying Personal Relationships*. Edited by Barbara M. Montgomery and Leslie A. Baxter. Mahwah, NJ: Erlbaum, 1998, pp. 109–136.

von Wright, Georg H. *Explanation and Understanding*. Ithaca, NY: Cornell University Press, 1971.

Wallace, Walter L. *Sociological Theory: An Introduction*. Chicago: Aldine, 1969.

Williams, Kenneth R. "Reflections on a Human Science of Communication." *Journal of Communication* 23 (1973): 239–250.

Chapter 3
System Theory

Allport, Gordon W. "The Open System in Personality Theory." In *Modern Systems Research for the Behavioral Scientist*. Edited by Walter Buckley. Chicago: Aldine, 1968, pp. 343–350.

Ashby, W. Ross. "Principles of the Self-Organizing System." In *Principles of Self-Organization*. Edited by Heinz von Foerster and George Zopf. New York: Pergamon, 1962, pp. 255–278.

Bahg, Chang-Gen. "Major Systems Theories Throughout the World." *Behavioral Science* 35 (1990): 79–107.

Bar-Hillel, Yehoshua. "Concluding Review." In *Information Theory in Psychology*. Edited by Henry Quastler. Glencoe, IL: Free Press, 1955, p. 3.

Bateson, Gregory. *Naven*. Stanford, CA: Stanford University Press, 1958.

———. *Steps to an Ecology of Mind*. New York: Ballantine, 1972.

Beach, Wayne. "Stocktaking Open-Systems Research and Theory: A Critique and Proposals for Action." Paper delivered at the annual conference of the Western Speech Communication Association, Phoenix, November 1977.

Berger, Charles. "The Covering Law Perspective as a Theoretical Basis for the Study of Human Communication." *Communication Quarterly* 75 (1977): 7–18.

Bertalanffy, Ludwig von. "General Systems Theory: A Critical Review." *General Systems* 7 (1962): 1–20.

———. *General Systems Theory: Foundations, Development, Applications*. New York: Braziller, 1968.

Bochner, Arthur P., and Eisenberg, Eric M. "Family Process: System Perspectives." In *Handbook of Communication Science*. Edited by Charles R. Berger and Steven H. Chaffee. Newbury Park, CA: Sage, 1987, pp. 540–563.

Boulding, Kenneth. "General Systems Theory—The Skeleton of Science." In *Modern Systems Research for the Behavioral Scientist*. Edited by Walter Buckley. Chicago: Aldine, 1968, pp. 3–10.

Brier, Søren. "Forward." *Cybernetics and Human Knowing: A Journal of Second Order Cybernetics and Cyber-Semantics* 1 (1992). *http://www.db.dk/dbaa/sbr/vol1/v1-1for.htm*

Broadhurst, Allan R., and Darnell, Donald K. "An Introduction to Cybernetics and Information Theory." *Quarterly Journal of Speech* 51 (1965): 442–453.

Buckley, Walter. "Society as a Complex Adaptive System." In *Modern Systems Research for the Behavioral Scientist*. Edited by Walter Buckley. Chicago: Aldine, 1968, pp. 490–513.

———. *Sociology and Modern Systems Theory*. Englewood Cliffs, NJ: Prentice-Hall, 1967.

Buckley, Walter, ed. *Modern Systems Research for the Behavioral Scientist*. Chicago: Aldine, 1968.

Caley, Michael T., and Sawada, Daiyo, eds. *Mindscapes: The Epistemology of Magoroh Maruyama*. Amsterdam: Gordon and Breach, 1994.

Cherry, Colin. *On Human Communication*, 3rd ed. Cambridge, MA: MIT Press, 1978.

Conant, Roger C. "A Vector Theory of Information." In *Communication Yearbook 3*. Edited by Dan Nimmo. New Brunswick, NJ: Transaction, 1979, pp. 177–196.

Crowley, D. J. *Understanding Communication: The Signifying Web*. New York: Gordon and Breach, 1982.

Cushman, Donald. "The Rules Perspective as a Theoretical Basis for the Study of Human Communication." *Communication Quarterly* 25 (1977): 30–45.

Delia, Jesse. "Alternative Perspectives for the Study of Human Communication: Critique and Response." *Communication Quarterly* 25 (1977): 51–52.

Deutsch, Karl. "Toward a Cybernetic Model of Man and Society." In *Modern Systems Research for the Behavioral Sci-*

entist. Edited by Walter Buckley. Chicago: Aldine, 1968, pp. 387–400.

Dissanayake, Wimal. "The Communication Significance of the Buddhist Concept of Dependent Co-Origination." *Communication* 8 (1983): 29–45.

Donaldson, Rodney E. "Cybernetics and Human Knowing: One Possible Prolegomenon." *Cybernetics and Human Knowing* 1 (1992): 1–4.

Fink, Edward L. "Dynamic Social Impact Theory and the Study of Human Communication." *Journal of Communication* 46 (1996): 4–77.

Fisher, B. Aubrey. *Perspectives on Human Communication.* New York: Macmillan, 1978.

———. *Small Group Decision Making: Communication and the Group Process.* New York: McGraw-Hill, 1980.

Fisher, B. Aubrey, and Hawes, Leonard C. "An Interact System Model: Generating a Grounded Theory of Small Groups." *Quarterly Journal of Speech* 57 (1971): 444–453.

Foerster, Heinz von. "Ethics and Second-Order Cybernetics," *SEHR* 4 (2): 4. *http://shr.stanford.edu/shreview/4-2/text/foerster.html*

———. *Observing Systems: Selected Papers of Heinz von Foerster.* Seaside, CA: Intersystems, 1981.

Giddens, Anthony. *Profiles and Critiques in Social Theory.* Berkeley: University of California Press, 1982.

Grene, Marjorie. *The Knower and the Known.* Berkeley: University of California Press, 1974.

Guilbaud, G. T. *What Is Cybernetics?* New York: Grove, 1959.

Hall, A. D., and Fagen, R. E. "Definition of System." In *Modern Systems Research for the Behavioral Scientist.* Edited by Walter Buckley. Chicago: Aldine, 1968, pp. 81–92.

Handy, Rollo, and Kurtz, Paul. "A Current Appraisal of the Behavioral Sciences: Information Theory." *American Behavioral Scientist* 7 (6, 1964): 99–104.

Koestler, Arthur. *The Ghost in the Machine.* New York: Macmillan, 1967.

Krippendorff, Klaus. "Cybernetics." In *International Encyclopedia of Communications,* vol. 1. Edited by Erik Barnouw et al. New York: Oxford University Press, 1989, pp. 443–446.

———. "Information Theory." In *Communication and Behavior.* Edited by Gerhard Hanneman and William McEwen. Reading, MA: Addison-Wesley, 1975, pp. 351–389.

Latané, Bibb. "Dynamic Social Impact: Robust Predictions from Simple Theory." In *Modeling and Simulation in the Social Sciences from the Philosophy of Science Point of View.* Edited by R. Hegselmann, U. Mueller, and K. G. Troitzsch. Dordrecht, Netherlands: Kluwer Theory and Decision Library, 1996, pp. 287–310.

"Ludwig von Bertalanffy." *General Systems* 17 (1972): 219–228.

Macy, Joanna. *Mutual Causality in Buddhism and General System Theory.* Albany: SUNY Press, 1991.

Maruyama, Magoroh. "The Second Cybernetics: Deviation-Amplifying Mutual Causal Processes." *American Scientist* 51 (1963): 164–179. (Reprinted in *Modern Systems Research for the Behavioral Scientist.* Edited by Walter Buckley. Chicago: Aldine, 1968, pp. 304–316.)

Mattelart, Armand, and Mattelart, Michèle. *Theories of Communication: A Short Introduction.* London: Sage, 1998, pp. 43–55.

Maturana, Humberto, and Varella, Francisco. *The Tree of Knowledge: The Biological Roots of Human Understanding.* Boston: Shambhala, 1992.

Miller, Gerald R. "The Pervasiveness and Marvelous Complexity of Human Communication: A Note of Skepticism." Keynote address, Fourth Annual Conference on Communication, California State University, Fresno, May 1977.

Monge, Peter. "The Systems Perspective as a Theoretical Basis for the Study of Human Communication." *Communication Quarterly* 25 (1977): 19–29.

Pask, Gordon. *An Approach to Cybernetics.* New York: Harper & Row, 1961.

Pressman, Todd Evan. "A Synthesis of Systems Inquiry and the Eastern Mode of Inquiry." *System Research* 9 (1992): 46–63.

Rapoport, Anatol. "The Promises and Pitfalls of Information Theory." *Behavioral Science* 1 (1956): 303–309. (Reprinted in *Modern Systems Research for the Behavioral Scientist.* Edited by Walter Buckley. Chicago: Aldine, 1968, pp. 137–142.)

Rogers, Everett M. *A History of Communication Study: A Biographical Approach.* New York: Free Press, 1994, pp. 41–64.

Rosenbleuth, Arturo, Weiner, Norbert, and Bigelow, Julian. "Behavior, Purpose, and Teleology." *Philosophy of Science* 10 (1943): 18–24. (Reprinted in *Modern Systems Research for the Behavioral Scientist.* Edited by Walter Buckley. Chicago: Aldine, 1968, pp. 221–225.)

Searight, H. Russell, and Merkel, William T. "Systems Theory and Its Discontents: Clinical and Ethical Issues." *The American Journal of Family Therapy* 19 (1991): 19–31.

Shannon, Claude, and Weaver, Warren. *The Mathematical Theory of Communication.* Urbana: University of Illinois Press, 1949.

Toda, Masanao, and Shuford, Emir H. "Logic of Systems: Introduction to a Formal Theory of Structure." *General Systems* 10 (1965): 3–27.

Varela, Francisco. "Heinz von Foerster, the Scientist, the Man: Prologue to the Interview." *SEHR* 4(2). *http://shr.stanford.edu/shreview/4-2/text/varella.html*

Wheatley, Margaret. *Leadership and the New Science: Learning About Organization from an Orderly Universe.* San Francisco: Berrett-Kochler, 1992.

Whitaker, Randall. "Overview of Autopoietic Theory." *http://www.acm.org/signois/auto/ATReview.html#Background*

Wiener, Norbert. *Cybernetics or Control and Communication in the Animal and the Machine.* Cambridge, MA: MIT Press, 1961.

———. *The Human Use of Human Beings: Cybernetics and Society.* Boston: Houghton Mifflin, 1954.

Yerby, Janet. "Family Systems Theory Reconsidered: Integrating Social Construction Theory and Dialectical Process." *Communication Theory* 5 (1995): 339–365.

Chapter 4
Theories of Signs and Language

Akmajian, Adrian, Demers, Richard A., Farmer, Ann K., and Harnish, Robert M. *An Introduction to Language and Communication.* Cambridge, MA: MIT Press, 1994, pp. 123–192.

Baudrillard, Jean. *The Illusion of the End*. Translated by Chris Turner. Cambridge: Polity, 1994.

Berger, Arthur Asa. *Signs in Contemporary Culture: An Introduction to Semiotics*. Salem, WI: Sheffield, 1989.

Berman, Art. *From the New Criticism to Deconstruction*. Urbana: University of Illinois Press, 1988.

Birdwhistell, Ray. *Introduction to Kinesics*. Louisville, KY: University of Louisville Press, 1952.

———. *Kinesics and Context*. Philadelphia: University of Pennsylvania Press, 1970.

———. "A System for the Notation of Proxemic Behavior." *American Anthropologist* 65 (1963): 1003–1026.

Bloomfield, Leonard. *Language*. New York: Holt, Rinehart & Winston, 1933.

Bourdieu, Pierre. *Language and Symbol Power*. Cambridge, MA: Harvard University Press, 1991.

Burgoon, Judee K. "Nonverbal Signals." In *Handbook of Interpersonal Communication*. Edited by Mark L. Knapp and Gerald R. Miller. Thousand Oaks, CA: Sage, 1994, pp. 229–285.

Burgoon, Judee K., and Saine, Thomas. *The Unspoken Dialogue: An Introduction to Nonverbal Communication*. Boston: Houghton Mifflin, 1978.

Chomsky, Noam. *Aspects of the Theory of Syntax*. Cambridge, MA: MIT Press, 1965.

———. *Cartesian Linguistics: A Chapter in the History of Rationalist Thought*. New York: Harper & Row, 1966.

———. *Current Issues in Linguistic Theory*. The Hague: Mouton, 1970.

———. *Essays on Form and Interpretation*. New York: North Holland, 1977.

———. *Language and Mind*. New York: Harcourt Brace Jovanovich, 1972.

———. *The Logical Structure of Linguistic Theory*. New York: Plenum, 1975.

———. *Problems of Knowledge and Freedom*. New York: Pantheon, 1971.

———. *Reflections on Language*. New York: Pantheon, 1975.

———. *Rules and Representations*. New York: Columbia University Press, 1980.

———. *The Sound Pattern of English*. New York: Harper & Row, 1968.

———. *Studies on Semantics in Generative Grammar*. The Hague: Mouton, 1972.

———. *Syntactic Structures*. The Hague: Mouton, 1957.

———. "Three Models for the Description of Language." *Transactions on Information Theory* IT-2 (1956): 113–124.

———. *Topics in the Theory of Generative Grammar*. The Hague: Mouton, 1966.

Dallmayr, Fred. *Language and Politics*. Notre Dame, IN: University of Notre Dame Press, 1984.

Descartes, René. *Meditations on First Philosophy*. Translated by Lawrence J. LaFleur. Indianapolis: Bobbs-Merrill, 1960.

Eco, Umberto. *A Theory of Semiotics*. Bloomington: Indiana University Press, 1976.

Ekman, Paul, and Friesen, Wallace. *Emotion in the Human Face: Guidelines for Research and an Integration of Findings*. New York: Pergamon, 1972.

———. "Hand Movements." *Journal of Communication* 22 (1972): 353–374.

———. "Nonverbal Behavior in Psychotherapy Research." In *Research in Psychotherapy*, vol. 3. Edited by J. Shlien.

Washington, DC: American Psychological Association, 1968, pp. 179–216.

———. "The Repertoire of Nonverbal Behavior: Categories, Origins, Usage, and Coding." *Semiotica* 1 (1969): 49–98.

———. *Unmasking the Face*. Englewood Cliffs, NJ: Prentice-Hall, 1975.

Ellis, Donald G. *Crafting Society: Ethnicity, Class, and Communication Theory*. Mahwah, NJ: Erlbaum, 1999.

———. "Fixing Communicative Meaning: A Coherentist Theory." *Communication Research* 22 (1995): 515–544.

———. *From Language to Communication*. Mahwah, NJ: Erlbaum, 1999.

———. "Syntactic and Pragmatic Codes in Communication." *Communication Theory* 2 (1992): 1–23.

Fisch, Max H. *Peirce, Semiotic, and Pragmatism*. Bloomington: Indiana University Press, 1986.

Fodor, J. A., Bever, T. G., and Garrett, M. F. *The Psychology of Language: An Introduction to Psycholinguistics and Generative Grammar*. New York: McGraw-Hill, 1974.

Fodor, Jerry, Jenkins, James, and Saporta, Sol. "Psycholinguistics and Communication Theory." In *Human Communication Theory*. Edited by Frank E. X. Dance. New York: Holt, Rinehart & Winston, 1967, pp. 160–201.

Foss, Sonja K., Foss, Karen A., and Trapp, Robert. *Contemporary Perspectives on Rhetoric*, 3rd ed. Prospect Heights, IL: Waveland, in press.

Fries, Charles. *The Structure of English*. New York: Harcourt, Brace & World, 1952.

Giddens, Anthony. *Central Problems in Social Theory: Action, Structure, and Contradiction in Social Analysis*. Berkeley: University of California Press, 1979.

Goudge, Thomas A. *The Thought of Peirce*. Toronto: University of Toronto Press, 1950.

Graddol, David, Cheshire, Jenny, and Swann, Joan. *Descriptive Language*. Buckingham, England: Open University Press, 1994, pp. 65–101.

Hall, Edward T. *The Hidden Dimension*. New York: Random House, 1966.

———. *The Silent Language*. Greenwich, CT: Fawcett, 1959.

Harmon, Gilbert. *On Noam Chomsky: Critical Essays*. Garden City, NY: Anchor, 1974.

Harper, Robert G., Weiss, Arthur, and Motarozzo, Joseph. *Nonverbal Communication: The State of the Art*. New York: Wiley, 1978.

Harris, Zellig. *Structural Linguistics*. Chicago: University of Chicago Press, 1951.

Harrison, Randall. *Beyond Words: An Introduction to Nonverbal Communication*. Englewood Cliffs, NJ: Prentice-Hall, 1974.

———. "Nonverbal Communication." In *Handbook of Communication*. Edited by Ithiel de sola Pool and others. Chicago: Rand McNally, 1973.

Hirsch, E. D. *Validity in Interpretation*. New Haven, CT: Yale University Press, 1967.

Hodge, Robert, and Kress, Gunther. *Social Semiotics*. Ithaca, NY: Cornell University Press, 1988.

Hookway, Christopher. *Peirce*. London: Routledge & Kegan Paul, 1985.

Jacobs, Scott. "Language and Interpersonal Communication." In *Handbook of Interpersonal Communication*. Edited by Mark L. Knapp and Gerald R. Miller. Thousand Oaks, CA: Sage, 1994, pp. 199–228.

Knapp, Mark, and Hall, Judith. *Nonverbal Communication in Human Interaction*. New York: Holt, Rinehart & Winston, 1992.

Knapp, Mark, Wiemann, John, and Daly, John. "Nonverbal Communication: Issues and Appraisal." *Human Communication Research* 4 (1978): 271–280.

Langer, Susanne. *Mind: An Essay on Human Feeling*. 3 vols. Baltimore: Johns Hopkins University Press, 1967, 1972, 1982.

————. *Philosophy in a New Key*. Cambridge, MA: Harvard University Press, 1942.

Leeds-Hurwitz, Wendy. *Semiotics and Communication: Signs, Codes, Cultures*. Hillsdale, NJ: Erlbaum, 1993.

Lyne, John R. "Rhetoric and Semiotic in C. S. Peirce." *Quarterly Journal of Speech* 66 (1980): 155–168.

Martyna, Wendy. "What Does 'He' Mean?" *Journal of Communication* 28 (1978): 131–138.

Mead, George H. *Mind, Self, and Society*. Chicago: University of Chicago Press, 1934.

Mertz, Elizabeth, and Parmentier, Richard J., eds. *Semiotic Mediation: Sociocultural and Psychological Perpsectives*. Orlando: Academic, 1985.

Moriarty, Sandra E. "Abduction: A Theory of Visual Interpretation." *Communication Theory* 6 (1996): 167–187.

Morris, Charles. "Foundations in the Theory of Signs." In *International Encyclopedia of Unified Science*, vol. 1, part 1. Chicago: University of Chicago Press, 1955, p. 84.

————. *Signification and Significance*. Cambridge, MA: MIT Press, 1964.

————. *Signs, Language, and Behavior*. New York: Braziller, 1946.

Motley, Michael T. "Facial Affect and Verbal Context in Conversation." *Human Communication Research* 20 (1993): 3–40

Motley, Michael T., and Camden, Carl T. "Facial Expression of Emotion: A Comparison of Posed Expressions Versus Spontaneous Expressions in an Interpersonal Communication Setting." *Western Journal of Speech Communication* 52 (1988): 1–22.

Ogden, C. K., and Richards, I. A. *The Meaning of Meaning*. London: Kegan, Paul, Trench, Trubner, 1923.

Parmentier, Richard J. "Signs' Place in Medias Res: Peirce's Concept of Semiotic Mediation." In *Semiotic Mediation: Sociocultural and Psychological Perspectives*. Edited by Elizabeth Mertz and Richard Parmentier. Orlando: Academic, 1985, pp. 23–48.

Peirce, Charles Saunders. *Charles S. Peirce: Selected Writings*. Edited by P. O. Wiener. New York: Dover, 1958.

Powers, John H. "On the Intellectual Structure of the Human Communication Discipline." *Communication Education* 4 (1995): 191–222.

Redner, Harry. *A New Science of Representation: Towards an Integrated Theory of Representation in Science, Politics, and Art*. Boulder, CO: Westview, 1994.

Roskill, Mark. "'Public' and 'Private' Meanings: The Paintings of Van Gogh." *Journal of Communication* 29 (1979): 157–169.

Saussure, Ferdinand de. *Course in General Linguistics*. London: Peter Owen, 1960.

Sebeok, Thomas. "The Doctrine of Sign." In *Frontiers in Semiotics*. Edited by J. Deely, B. Williams, and F. E. Kruse. Bloomington: Indiana University Press, 1986.

Silverman, Kaja. *The Subject of Semiotics*. New York: Oxford University Press, 1983.

Stewart, John. *Language as Articulate Contact: Toward a Post-Semiotic Philosophy of Communication*. Albany: SUNY Press, 1995, pp. 76–81.

————. "The Symbol Model vs. Language as Constitutive Articulate Contact." In *Beyond the Symbol Model: Reflections on the Representational Nature of Language*. Edited by John Stewart. Albany: SUNY Press, 1996, pp. 9–63.

Wasow, Thomas. "Grammar." In *International Encyclopedia of Communications*, vol. 2. Edited by Erik Barnouw et al. New York: Oxford University Press, 1989, pp. 234–238.

Weiser, Irwin. "Linguistics." In *Encyclopedia of Rhetoric and Composition*. Edited by Theresa Enos. New York: Garland, 1996, pp. 386–391.

Chapter 5
Theories of Discourse

Austin, J. L. *How to Do Things with Words*. Cambridge, MA: Harvard University Press, 1962.

————. *Philosophy of Language*. Englewood Cliffs, NJ: Prentice-Hall, 1964.

Beach, Wayne. "Orienting to the Phenomenon." In *Communication Yearbook 13*. Edited by James A. Anderson. Newbury Park, CA: Sage, 1990, pp. 216–244.

Berger, Charles R. "The Covering Law Perspective as a Theoretical Basis for the Study of Human Communication." *Communication Quarterly* 25 (1977): 12.

Berman, Art. *From the New Criticism to Deconstruction: The Reception of Structuralism and Post-Structuralism*. Urbana: University of Illinois Press, 1988.

Blair, Carole. "The Statement: Foundation of Foucault's Historical Criticism." *Western Journal of Speech Communication* 51 (1987): 364–383.

Buller, David B., and Burgoon, Judee K. "Another Look at Information Management: A Rejoinder to McCornack, Levine, Morrison, & Lapinski." *Communication Monographs* 63 (1996): 92–98.

Buttny, Richard. "The Ascription of Meaning: A Wittgensteinian Perspective." *Quarterly Journal of Speech* 72 (1986): 261–273.

Button, Graham, ed. *Ethnomethodology and the Human Sciences*. Cambridge: Cambridge University Press, 1991.

Campbell, Paul N. "A Rhetorical View of Locutionary, Illocutionary, and Perlocutionary Acts." *Quarterly Journal of Speech* 59 (1973): 284–296.

Cappella, Joseph N. "The Management of Conversations." In *Handbook of Interpersonal Communication*. Edited by Mark L. Knapp and Gerald R. Miller. Beverly Hills, CA: Sage, 1985, pp. 393–439.

Chimombo, Moira, and Roseberry, Robert L. *The Power of Discourse: An Introduction to Discourse Analysis*. Mahwah, NJ: Erlbaum, 1998.

Cooper, Martha. "Rhetorical Criticism and Foucault's Philosophy of Discursive Events." *Central States Speech Journal* 39 (1988): 1–17.

Craig, Robert T., and Tracy, Karen, eds. *Conversational Coherence: Form, Structure, and Strategy*. Beverly Hills, CA: Sage, 1983.

Cushman, Donald P. "The Rules Approach to Communication Theory: A Philosophical and Operational Perspective." In *Communication Theory: Eastern and Western Perspectives*. Edited by D. Lawrence Kincaid. San Diego: Academic, 1987, pp. 223–234.

———. "The Rules Perspective as a Theoretical Basis for the Study of Human Communication." *Communication Quarterly* 25 (1977): 30–45.

Delia, Jesse. "Alternative Perspectives for the Study of Human Communication: Critique and Response." *Communication Quarterly* 25 (1977): 54.

Derrida, Jacques. *Of Grammatology*. Translated by Gayatri Spivak. Baltimore: Johns Hopkins University Press, 1976.

Ellis, Donald. "Fixing Communicative Meaning: A Coherentist Theory." *Communication Research* 22 (1995): 515–544.

———. *From Language to Communication*. Mahwah, NJ: Erlbaum, 1999.

———. "Post-Structuralism and Language: Non-Sense." *Communication Monographs* 58 (1991): 213–224.

Ellis, Donald G., and Donohue, William A., eds. *Contemporary Issues in Language and Discourse Processes*. Hillsdale, NJ: Erlbaum, 1986.

Foss, Sonja K., Foss, Karen A., and Trapp, Robert. *Contemporary Perspectives on Rhetoric*. Prospect Heights, IL: Waveland, 1991.

Foss, Sonja K., and Gill, Ann. "Michel Foucault's Theory of Rhetoric as Epistemic." *Western Journal of Speech Communication* 51 (1987): 384–402.

Foucault, Michel. *The Archaeology of Knowledge*. Translated by A. M. Sheridan Smith. New York: Pantheon, 1972.

———. *The Order of Things: An Archaeology of the Human Sciences*. New York: Pantheon, 1970.

———. *Power/Knowledge: Selected Interviews and Other Writings 1927–1977*. Translated by Colin Gordon and others and edited by Colin Gordon. New York: Pantheon, 1980.

Fraser, Nancy. *Unruly Practices: Power, Discourse, and Gender in Contemporary Social Theory*. Minneapolis: University of Minnesota Press, 1989.

Gaines, Robert. "Doing by Saying: Toward a Theory of Perlocution." *Quarterly Journal of Speech* 65 (1979): 207–217.

Garfinkel, Harold. *Studies in Ethnomethodology*. Englewood Cliffs, NJ: Prentice-Hall, 1967.

Giddens, Anthony. *Central Problems in Social Theory: Action, Structure, and Contradiction in Social Analysis*. Berkeley: University of California Press, 1979.

Grice, H. Paul. "Logic and Conversation." In *Syntax and Semantics*, vol. 3. Edited by P. Cole and J. Morgan. New York: Academic, 1975, pp. 41–58.

Hopper, Robert, Koch, Susan, and Mandelbaum, Jennifer. "Conversation Analysis Methods." In *Contemporary Issues in Language and Discourse Processes*. Edited by Donald G. Ellis and William A. Donohue. Hillsdale, NJ: Erlbaum, 1986, pp. 169–186.

Jackson, Sally, and Jacobs, Scott. "Characterizing Ordinary Argument: Substantive and Methodological Issues." *Journal of the American Forensic Association* 22 (1986): 42–57.

———. "The Collaborative Production of Proposals in Conversational Argument and Persuasion: A Study of Disagreement Regulation." *Journal of the American Forensic Association* 18 (1981): 77–90.

———. "Conversational Relevance: Three Experiments on Pragmatic Connectedness in Conversation." In *Communication Yearbook 10*. Edited by Margaret L. McLaughlin. Newbury Park, CA: Sage, 1987, pp. 323–347.

———. "Structure of Conversational Argument: Pragmatic Bases for the Enthymeme." *Quarterly Journal of Speech* 66 (1980): 251–265.

Jacobs, Scott. "Language and Interpersonal Communication." In *Handbook of Interpersonal Communication*. Edited by Mark L. Knapp and Gerald R. Miller. Thousand Oaks, CA: Sage, 1994, pp. 199–228.

———. "Recent Advances in Discourse Analysis." *Quarterly Journal of Speech* 66 (1980): 450–472.

Jacobs, Scott, Dawson, Edwin J., and Brashers, Dale. "Information Manipulation Theory: A Replication and Assessment." *Communication Monographs* 63 (1996): 70–82.

Jacobs, Scott, and Jackson, Sally. "Argument as a Natural Category: The Routine Grounds for Arguing in Conversation." *Western Journal of Speech Communication* 45 (1981): 118–132.

———. "Building a Model of Conversational Argument." In *Rethinking Communication: Paradigm Exemplars*, vol. 2. Edited by Brenda Dervin, Lawrence Grossberg, Barbara O'Keefe, and Ellen Wartella. Newbury Park, CA: Sage, 1989, pp. 153–171.

———. "Speech Act Structure in Conversation: Rational Aspects of Pragmatic Coherence." In *Conversational Coherence: Form, Structure, and Strategy*. Edited by Robert T. Craig and Karen Tracy. Beverly Hills, CA: Sage, 1983, pp. 47–66.

———. "Strategy and Structure in Conversational Influence Attempts." *Communication Monographs* 50 (1983): 285–304.

Janik, Allan, and Toulmin, Stephen. *Wittgenstein's Vienna*. New York: Simon & Schuster, 1973.

Kellermann, Kathy, and Sleight, Carra. "Coherence: A Meaningful Adhesive for Discourse." In *Communication Yearbook 12*. Edited by James A. Anderson. Newbury Park, CA: Sage, 1989, pp. 95–129.

Lacan, Jacques. *The Four Fundamental Concepts of Psycho-Analysis*. Translated by A. Sheridan. New York: Norton, 1981.

Lyne, John. "Speech Acts in a Semiotic Frame." *Communication Quarterly* 29 (1981): 202–208.

Mandelbaum, Jenny. "Interpersonal Activities in Conversational Storytelling." *Western Journal of Speech Communication* 53 (1989): 114–126.

McCornack, Steven A. "Information Manipulation Theory." *Communication Monographs* 59 (1992): 1–17.

McCornack, Steven A., et. al. "When the Alteration of Information Is Viewed as Deception: An Empirical Test of Information Manipulation Theory." *Communication Monographs* 59 (1992): 17–29.

McCornack, Steven A., Levine, Timothy R., Morrison, Kelly, and Lapinski, Maria. "Speaking of Information Manipulation: A Critical Rejoinder." *Communication Monographs* 63 (1996): 83–92.

McLaughlin, Margaret L. *Conversation: How Talk Is Organized*. Beverly Hills, CA: Sage, 1984.

Mura, Susan Swan. "Licensing Violations: Legitimate Violations of Grice's Conversational Principle." In *Conversational Coherence: Form, Structure, and Strategy*. Edited by

Robert T. Craig and Karen Tracy. Beverly Hills, CA: Sage, 1983, pp. 101–115.

Nofsinger, Robert. *Everyday Conversation*. Newbury Park, CA: Sage, 1991.

O'Keefe, Barbara J., and Lambert, Bruce L. "Managing the Flow of Ideas: A Local Management Approach to Message Design." In *Communication Yearbook 18*. Edited by Brant R. Burleson. Thousand Oaks, CA: Sage, 1995, pp. 54–82.

O'Keefe, Daniel J. "Two Concepts of Argument." *Journal of the American Forensic Association* 13 (1977): 121–128.

Pearce, W. Barnett. "Rules Theories of Communication: Varieties, Limitations, and Potentials." Paper delivered at the annual meeting of the Speech Communication Association, New York, 1980.

Pomerantz, Anita, and Fehr, B. J. "Conversation Analysis: An Approach to the Study of Social Action as Sense Making Practices." In *Discourse as Social Interaction*. Edited by Teun A. van Dijk. Thousand Oaks, CA: Sage, 1997, pp. 64–91.

Potter, Jonathan, and Wetherell, Margaret. *Discourse and Social Psychology: Beyond Attitudes and Behavior*. London: Sage, 1987.

Powers, John. "On the Intellectual Structure of the Human Communication Discipline." *Communication Education* 44 (1995): 191–222.

Psathas, George. *Conversation Analysis: The Study of Talk-in-Interaction*. Thousand Oaks, CA: Sage, 1995.

Sacks, Harvey, Schegloff, Emanuel, and Jefferson, Gail. "A Simplest Systematics for the Organization of Turn Taking for Conversation." *Language* 50 (1974): 696–735.

Searle, John. *Speech Acts: An Essay in the Philosophy of Language*. Cambridge: Cambridge University Press, 1969.

Shimanoff, Susan B. *Communication Rules: Theory and Research*. Beverly Hills, CA: Sage, 1980.

Sigman, Stuart J. "On Communication Rules from a Social Perspective." *Human Communication Research* 7 (1980): 37–51.

Silverman, David, and Torode, Brian. *The Material Word: Some Theories of Language and Its Limits*. London: Routledge & Kegan Paul, 1980.

Stenström, Anna-Brita. *An Introduction to Spoken Interaction*. London: Longman, 1994.

Stewart, John. "Concepts of Language and Meaning: A Comparative Study." *Quarterly Journal of Speech* 58 (1972): 123–133.

Stillar, Glenn F. *Analyzing Everyday Texts: Discourse, Rhetoric, and Social Processes*. Thousand Oaks, CA: Sage, 1998).

Tracy, Karen. "Discourse Analysis in Communication." In *Handbook of Discourse Analysis*. Edited by D. Schiffrin, D. Tannen, and H. Hamilton. Oxford: Blackwell, in press.

Trapp, Robert. "The Role of Disagreement in Interactional Argument." *Journal of the American Forensic Association* 23 (1986): 23–41.

van Dijk, Teun A. *Communicating Racism: Ethnic Prejudice in Thought and Talk*. Newbury Park, CA: Sage, 1987.

——. "Discourse Semantics and Ideology." *Discourse and Society* 6 (1995): 243–289

——. *Macrostructures: An Interdisciplinary Study of Global Structures in Discourse, Interaction, and Cognition*. Hillsdale, NJ: Erlbaum, 1980.

——. *News as Discourse*. Hillsdale, NJ: Erlbaum, 1988.

——. "Principles of Critical Discourse Analysis." *Discourse and Society* 4 (1993): 249–283.

——. *Studies in the Pragmatics of Discourse*. The Hague: Mouton, 1981.

van Eemeren, Frans H., and Grootendorst, Rob. *Argumentation, Communication, and Fallacies: A Pragma-Dialectical Perspective*. Hillsdale, NJ: Erlbaum, 1992.

van Eemeren, Frans H., Grootendorst, Rob, Jackson, Sally, and Jacobs, Scott. *Reconstructing Argumentative Discourse*. Tuscaloosa: University of Alabama Press, 1993.

Walton, Douglas N. *Plausible Argument in Everyday Conversation*. Albany: SUNY Press, 1992.

Wittgenstein, Ludwig. *Philosophical Investigations*. Oxford: Blackwell, 1953.

——. *Tractatus Logico-Philosophicus*. London: Routledge & Kegan Paul, 1922.

Young, Robert, ed. "Post-Structuralism: An Introduction." In *Untying the Text: A Post-Structuralist Reader*. Boston: Routledge & Kegan Paul, 1981, pp. 1–28.

Chapter 6
Theories of Message Production

Andersen, Peter A. "The Trait Debate: A Critical Examination of the Individual Differences Paradigm in the Communication Sciences." In *Progress in Communication Sciences*. Edited by B. Dervin and M. J. Voigt. Norwood, NJ: Ablex, 1986.

Applegate, James L. "The Impact of Construct System Development on Communication and Impression Formation in Persuasive Messages." *Communication Monographs* 49 (1982): 277–289.

Applegate, James L., and Sypher, Howard E. "A Constructivist Theory of Communication and Culture." In *Theories in Intercultural Communication*. Edited by Young Y. Kim and William B. Gudykunst. Newbury Park, CA: Sage, 1988, pp. 41–65.

Babrow, Austin. "The Advent of Multiple-Process Theories of Communication." *Journal of Communication* 43 (1993): 110–118.

Beatty, Michael J., and McCroskey, James C. "Interpersonal Communication as Temperamental Expression." In *Personality and Communication: Trait Perspectives*. New York: Hampton, 1998.

Beatty, Michael J., McCroskey, James C., and Heisel, Alan D. "Communication Apprehension as Temperamental Expression: A Communibiological Paradigm." *Communication Monographs* 65 (1998): 197–219.

Bellah, Robert N., and others. *Habits of the Heart*. Berkeley: University of California Press, 1985.

Berger, Charles R. "Goal Detection and Efficiency: Neglected Aspects of Message Production." *Communication Theory* 10 (2000): 156–166.

——. *Planning Strategic Interaction: Attaining Goals Through Communicative Action*. Mahwah, NJ: Erlbaum, 1997.

Berger, Charles R., Karol, Susan H., and Jordan, Jerry M. "When a Lot of Knowledge Is a Dangerous Thing: The Debilitating Effects of Plan Complexity on Verbal Fluency." *Human Communication Research* 16 (1989): 91–119.

Brown, Penelope, and Levinson, Stephen. *Politeness: Some Universals in Language Usage.* Cambridge: Cambridge University Press, 1987.

Brown, Roger. "Politeness Theory: Exemplar and Exemplary." In *The Legacy of Solomon Asch: Essays in Cognition and Social Psychology.* Edited by Irvin Rock. Hillsdale, NJ: Erlbaum, 1990, pp. 23–38.

Buck, Ross. "From DNA to MTV: The Spontaneous Communication of Emotional Messages." In *Message Production: Advances in Communication Theory.* Edited by John O. Greene. Mahwah, NJ: Erlbaum, 1997, pp. 313–340.

Burgoon, Judee K. "It Takes Two to Tango: Interpersonal Adaptation and Implications for Relational Communication." In *Communication from the Helm for the 21st Century.* Edited by Judith S. Trent. Boston: Allyn & Bacon, 1998, pp. 53–59.

Burgoon, Judee K., Dillman, Leesa, and Stern, Lesa A. "Adaptation in Dyadic Interaction: Defining and Operationalizing Patterns of Reciprocity and Compensation." *Communication Theory* 3 (1993): 295–316.

Burgoon, Judee K., Stern, Lesa A., and Dillmann, Leesa. *Interpersonal Adaptation: Dyadic Interaction Patterns.* New York: Cambridge University Press, 1995.

Burgoon, Judee K., and White, Cindy H. "Researching Nonverbal Message Production: A View from Interaction Adaptation Theory." In *Message Production: Advances in Communication Theory.* Edited by John O. Greene. Mahwah, NJ: Erlbaum, 1997, pp. 279–312.

Burleson, Brant R. "The Constructivist Approach to Person-Centered Communication: Analysis of a Research Exemplar." In *Rethinking Communication: Paradigm Exemplars.* Edited by Brenda Dervin, Lawrence Grossberg, Barbara O'Keefe, and Ellen Wartella. Newbury Park, CA: Sage, 1989, pp. 29–46.

Burleson, Brant R., Albrecht, Terrance L., and Sarason, Irwin C., eds. *Communication of Social Support: Messages, Interactions, Relationships, and Community.* Thousand Oaks, CA: Sage, 1994.

Burleson, Brant R., and Planalp, Sally. "Producing Emotion(al) Messages." *Communication Theory* 10 (2000): 221–250.

Crockett, Walter H. "Cognitive Complexity and Impression Formation." In *Progress in Experimental Personality Research,* vol. 2. Edited by Brendon A. Maher. New York: Academic, 1965, pp. 47–90.

Cronen, Vernon E. "Communication Theory for the Twenty-First Century: Cleaning Up the Wreckage of the Psychology Project." In *Communication: Views from the Helm for the 21st Century.* Edited by Judith S. Trent. Boston: Allyn & Bacon, 1998, pp. 18–38.

Darnell, Donald, and Brockriede, Wayne. *Persons Communicating.* Englewood Cliffs, NJ: Prentice-Hall, 1976.

Delia, Jesse G. "Interpersonal Cognition, Message Goals, and Organization of Communication: Recent Constructivist Research." In *Communication Theory: Eastern and Western Perspectives.* Edited by D. Lawrence Kincaid. San Diego: Academic, 1987, pp. 255–274.

Delia, Jesse G., Kline, Susan L., and Burleson, Brant R. "The Development of Persuasive Communication Strategies in Kindergartners Through Twelfth-Graders." *Communication Monographs* 46 (1979): 241–256.

Delia, Jesse G., O'Keefe, Barbara J., and O'Keefe, Daniel J. "The Constructivist Approach to Communication." In *Human Communication Theory: Comparative Essays.* Edited by Frank E. X. Dance. New York: Harper & Row, 1982, pp. 147–191.

Devine, Patricia G., Hamilton, David L., and Ostrom, Thomas M. *Social Cognition: Impact on Social Psychology.* San Diego: Academic, 1994.

Dillard, James Price. "Explicating the Goal Construct: Tools for Theorists." In *Message Production: Advances in Communication Theory.* Edited by John O. Greene. Mahwah, NJ: Erlbaum, 1997, pp. 47–70.

Eisenberg, Eric. "Equivocal Communication." *Communication Theory* 1 (1991): 351–354.

Eysenck, H. J. "Biological Dimensions of Personality." In *Handbook of Personality.* Edited by L. A. Pervin. New York: Guilford, 1991, pp. 244–276.

Garko, Michael G. "Perspectives on and Conceptualizations of Compliance and Compliance-Gaining." *Communication Quarterly* 38 (1990): 138–157.

Gastil, John. "An Appraisal and Revision of the Constructivist Research Program." In *Communication Yearbook 18.* Edited by Brant Burleson. Thousand Oaks, CA: Sage, 1995, pp. 83–104.

Giles, Howard, Coupland, Justine, and Coupland, Nikolas. "Accommodation Theory: Communication, Context, and Consequence." In *Contexts of Accommodation: Developments in Applied Sociolinguistics.* Edited by Howard Giles, Justine Coupland, and Nikolas Coupland. Cambridge: Cambridge University Press, 1991, pp. 1–68.

Giles, Howard, Mulac, Anthony, Bradac, James J., and Johnson, Patricia. "Speech Accommodation Theory: The First Decade and Beyond." In *Communication Yearbook 10.* Edited by Margaret L. McLaughlin. Newbury Park, CA: Sage, 1987, pp. 13–48.

Giles, Howard, and Street, Richard L., Jr. "Communicator Characteristics and Behavior." In *Handbook of Interpersonal Communication.* Edited by Mark L. Knapp and Gerald R. Miller. Thousand Oaks, CA: Sage, 1994, pp. 103–161.

Goldsmith, Daena J. "The Role of Facework in Supportive Communication." In *Communication of Social Support.* Edited by Brant R. Burleson, Terrance L. Albrecht, and Irwin G. Sarason. Thousand Oaks, CA: Sage, 1994, pp. 29–49.

Greene, John O. "Action Assembly Theory: Metatheoretical Commitments, Theoretical Propositions, and Empirical Applications." In *Rethinking Communication: Paradigm Exemplars.* Edited by Brenda Dervin, Lawrence Grossberg, Barbara O'Keefe, and Ellen Wartella. Newbury Park, CA: Sage, 1989, pp. 117–128.

———. "A Cognitive Approach to Human Communication: An Action Assembly Theory." *Communication Monographs* 51 (1984): 289–306.

———. "Evaluating Cognitive Explanations of Communication Phenomena." *Quarterly Journal of Speech* 70 (1984): 241–254.

———. "Evanescent Mentation: An Ameliorative Conceptual Foundation for Research and Theory on Message Production." *Communication Theory* 10 (2000): 139–155.

Greene, John O., ed. *Message Production: Advances in Communication Theory.* Mahwah, NJ: Erlbaum, 1997.

Greene, John O., and Geddes, Deanna. "An Action Assembly Perspective on Social Skill." *Communication Theory* 3 (1993): 26–49.

Hale, Claudia. "Cognitive Complexity-Simplicity as a Determinant of Communication Effectiveness." *Communication Monographs* 47 (1980): 304–311.

Harré, Rom. "Language Games and Texts of Identity." In *Texts of Identity.* Edited by John Shotter and Kenneth J. Gergen. London: Sage, 1989, pp. 20–35.

Hewes, Dean E., and Planalp, Sally. "The Individual's Place in Communication Science." In *Handbook of Communication Science.* Edited by Charles R. Berger and Steven H. Chaffee. Newbury Park, CA: Sage, 1987, pp. 146–183.

Infante, Dominic A., and Rancer, Andrew S. "A Conceptualization and Measure of Argumentativeness." *Journal of Personality Assessment* 46 (1982): 72–80.

Infante, Dominic A., Rancer, Andrew S., and Womack, Deanna F. *Building Communication Theory.* Prospect Heights, IL: Waveland, 1990.

Kellermann, Kathy, and Cole, Tim. "Classifying Compliance Gaining Messages: Taxonomic Disorder and Strategic Confusion." *Communication Theory* 4 (1994): 3–60.

Kelly, George. *The Psychology of Personal Constructs.* New York: North, 1955.

Kim, Min-Sun. "Cross-Cultural Perspectives on Motivations of Verbal Communication: Review, Critique, and a Theoretical Framework." In *Communication Yearbook 22.* Edited by Michael E. Roloff. Thousand Oaks, CA: Sage, 1999, pp. 51–89.

Kline, Susan L., and Ceropski, Janet M. "Person-Centered Communication in Medical Practice." In *Emergent Issues in Human Decision Making.* Edited by Gerald M. Phillips and Julia T. Wood. Carbondale: Southern Illinois University Press, 1984, pp. 120–141.

Lannamann, John W. "Deconstructing the Person and Changing the Subject of Interpersonal Studies." *Communication Theory* 2 (1992): 139–148.

———. "Interpersonal Communication Research as Ideological Practice." *Communication Theory* 1 (1991): 179–203.

MacIntyre, Alistair. *After Virtue.* Notre Dame, IN: University of Notre Dame Press, 1984.

Marwell, Gerald, and Schmitt, David R. "Dimensions of Compliance-Gaining Strategies: A Dimensional Analysis." *Sociometry* 30 (1967): 350–364.

Matson, Floyd W. *The Idea of Man.* New York: Delacorte, 1976.

McCroskey, James C. "The Communication Apprehension Perspective." In *Avoiding Communication: Shyness, Reticence, and Communication Apprehension.* Edited by John A. Daly and James C. McCroskey. Beverly Hills, CA: Sage, 1984, pp. 13–38.

McCroskey, James C., ed. *Personality and Communication: Trait Perspectives.* New York: Hampton, 1998.

McCroskey, James C., and Beatty, Michael J. "Communication Apprehension." In *Personality and Communication: Trait Perspectives.* Edited by James C. McCroskey. New York: Hampton, 1998.

Meyer, Janet R. "Cognitive Influences on the Ability to Address Interaction Goals." In *Message Production: Advances in Communication Theory.* Edited by John O. Greene. Mahwah, NJ: Erlbaum, 1997, pp. 71–90.

Miller, Gerald R. "Persuasion." In *Handbook of Communication Science.* Edited by Charles R. Berger and Steven H. Chaffee. Newbury Park, CA: Sage, 1987, pp. 446–483.

———. "Some (Moderately) Apprehensive Thoughts on Avoiding Communication." In *Avoiding Communication: Shyness, Reticence, and Communication Apprehension.* Edited by John A. Daly and James C. McCroskey. Beverly Hills, CA: Sage, 1984, pp. 237–246.

Miller, Lynn C., Cody, Michael J., and McLaughlin, Margaret L. "Situations and Goals as Fundamental Constructs in Interpersonal Communication Research." In *Handbook of Interpersonal Communication,* 2nd ed. Edited by Mark L. Knapp and Gerald R. Miller. Thousand Oaks, CA: Sage, 1994, pp. 162–197.

Nicotera, Anne Maydan. "The Constructivist Theory of Delia, Clark, and Associates." In *Watershed Research Traditions in Human Communication Theory.* Edited by Donald P. Cushman and Branislav Kovačić. Albany: SUNY Press, 1995, pp. 45–66.

O'Keefe, Barbara J. "Variation, Adaptation, and Functional Explanation in the Study of Message Design." In *Developing Communication Theories.* Edited by Gerry Philipsen. Albany: SUNY Press, 1997, pp. 85–118.

O'Keefe, Barbara J., and Lambert, Bruce L. "Managing the Flow of Ideas: A Local Management Approach to Message Design." In *Communication Yearbook 18.* Edited by Brant R. Burleson. Thousand Oaks, CA: Sage, 1995, pp. 54–82.

O'Keefe, Barbara J., and Shepherd, Gregory J. "The Pursuit of Multiple Objectives in Face-to-Face Persuasive Interactions: Effects of Construct Differentiation on Message Organization." *Communication Monographs* 54 (1987): 396–419.

O'Keefe, Daniel J. "From Strategy-Based to Feature-Based Analyses of Compliance Gaining Message Classification and Production." *Communication Theory* 4 (1994): 61–69.

———. *Persuasion: Theory and Research.* Newbury Park, CA: Sage, 1990.

Patterson, Miles L., McCroskey, James C., and Heisel, Alan D. "Communication Apprehension as Temperamental Expression: A Communibiological Paradigm." *Communication Monographs* 65 (1998): 197–219.

Planalp, Sally. "Communication, Cognition, and Emotion." *Communication Monographs* 60 (1993): 3–4.

Powers, John H. "On the Intellectual Structure of the Human Communication Discipline." *Communication Education* 44 (1995): 191–222.

Seibold, David R., Cantrill, James G., and Meyers, Renée A. "Communication and Interpersonal Influence." In *Handbook of Interpersonal Communication,* 2nd ed. Edited by Mark L. Knapp and Gerald R. Miller. Thousand Oaks, CA: Sage, 1994, pp. 542–588.

Semin, Gün R. "Everyday Assumptions, Language, and Personality." In *Everyday Understanding: Social and Scientific Implications.* Edited by Gün R. Semin and Kenneth J. Gergen. London: Sage, 1990, pp. 151–175.

Shotter, John, and Gergen, Kenneth J. "Social Construction: Knowledge, Self, Others, and Continuing the Conversation." In *Communication Yearbook 17.* Edited by Stanley Deetz. Thousand Oaks, CA: Sage, 1994, pp. 3–33.

Stiff, James B. *Persuasive Communication.* New York: Guilford, 1994.

Waldron, Vincent R., and Cegala, Donald J. "Assessing Conversational Cognition: Levels of Cognitive Theory and Associated Methodological Requirements." *Human Communication Research* 18 (1992): 606.

Werner, H. "The Concept of Development from a Comparative and Organismic Point of View." In *The Concept of Development.* Edited by D. B. Harris. Minneapolis: University of Minnesota Press, 1957.

Wheeless, Lawrence R., Barraclough, Robert, and Stewart, Robert. "Compliance-Gaining and Power in Persuasion." In *Communication Yearbook 7.* Edited by Robert N. Bostrom. Beverly Hills, CA: Sage, 1983, pp. 105–145.

Wilson, Steven R. "Developing Theories of Persuasive Message Production: The Next Generation." In *Message Production: Advances in Communication Theory.* Edited by John O. Greene. Mahwah, NJ: Erlbaum, 1997, pp. 15–46.

Chapter 7
Theories of Message Reception and Processing

Ajzen, Icek, and Fishbein, Martin. *Understanding Attitudes and Predicting Social Behavior.* Englewood Cliffs, NJ: Prentice-Hall, 1980.

Allen, Mike, and Reynolds, Rodney. "The Elaboration Likelihood Model and the Sleeper Effect: An Assessment of Attitude Change over Time." *Communication Theory* 8 (1993): 73–82.

Andersen, Peter A. "Nonverbal Immediacy in Interpersonal Communication." In *Multichannel Integrations of Nonverbal Behavior.* Edited by A. W. Siegman and S. Feldstein. Hillsdale, NJ: Erlbaum, 1985, pp. 1–36.

Andersen, Peter A., Guerrero, Laura K., Buller, David, and Jorgensen, Peter F. "An Empirical Comparison of Three Theories of Nonverbal Immediacy Exchange." *Human Communication Research* 24 (1998): 501–535.

Anderson, Norman H. "Integration Theory and Attitude Change." *Psychological Review* 78 (1971): 171–206.

Aronson, Elliot. *The Social Animal.* New York: Viking, 1972.

Babrow, Austin. "Communication and Problematic Integration: Understanding Diverging Probability and Value, Ambiguity, Ambivalence, and Impossibility." *Communication Theory* 2 (1992): 95–130.

Buller, David B., and Burgoon, Judee K. "Interpersonal Deception Theory." *Communication Theory* 6 (1996): 203–242.

Burgoon, Judee K. "Communicative Effects of Gaze Behavior: A Test of Two Contrasting Explanations." *Human Communication Research* 12 (1986): 495–524.

———. "Nonverbal Signals." In *Handbook of Interpersonal Communication.* Edited by Mark L. Knapp and Gerald R. Miller. Thousand Oaks, CA: Sage, 1994, pp. 253–255.

Burgoon, Judee K., et. al. "Interpersonal Deception: XII. Information Management Dimensions Underlying Deceptive and Truthful Messages." *Communication Monographs* 63 (1996): 50–69.

Burgoon, Judee K., Dillman, Leesa, and Stern, Lesa A. "Adaptation in Dyadic Interaction: Defining and Operationalizing Patterns of Reciprocity and Compensation." *Communication Theory* 3 (1993): 295–316.

Burgoon, Judee K., and Hale, Jerold L. "Nonverbal Expectancy Violations: Model Elaboration and Application." *Communication Monographs* 55 (1988): 58–79.

Burgoon, Judee K., Stern, Lesa A, and Dillman, Leesa. *Interpersonal Adaptation: Dyadic Interaction Patterns.* New York: Cambridge University Press, 1995.

Burgoon, Judee K., and White, Cindy H. "Researching Nonverbal Message Production: A View from Interaction Adaptation Theory." In *Message Production: Advances in Communication Theory.* Edited by John O. Greene. Mahwah, NJ: Erlbaum, 1997, pp. 279–312.

Burgoon, Michael, Newton, Deborah A., and Birk, Thomas S. "A Theory of Belief, Attitude, Intention, and Behavior Extended to the Domain of Corrective Advertising." In *Communication Yearbook 15.* Edited by Stanley A. Deetz. Newbury Park, CA: Sage, 1992, pp. 263–286.

Burhans, David T. "The Attitude-Behavior Discrepancy Problem: Revisited." *Quarterly Journal of Speech* 57 (1971): 418–428.

Burleson, Brant R. "Attribution Schemes and Causal Inference in Natural Conversations." In *Contemporary Issues in Language and Discourse Processes.* Edited by Donald G. Ellis and William A. Donohue. Hillsdale, NJ: Erlbaum, 1986, pp. 63–86.

Cappella, Joseph N. "The Management of Conversational Interaction in Adults and Infants." In *Handbook of Interpersonal Communication.* Edited by Mark L. Knapp and Gerald R. Miller. Thousand Oaks, CA: Sage, 1994, pp. 406–407.

Cappella, Joseph N., and Greene, John O. "A Discrepancy-Arousal Explanation of Mutual Influence in Expressive Behavior for Adult-Adult and Infant-Adult Interaction." *Communication Monographs* 49 (1982): 89–114.

Chapanis, Natalia P., and Chapanis, Alphonse. "Cognitive Dissonance: Five Years Later." *Psychological Bulletin* 61 (1964): 21.

Dillard, James Price. "Persuasion Past and Present: Attitudes Aren't What They Used to Be." *Communication Monographs* 60 (1993): 90–97.

Dillard, James Price, Kinney, Terry A., and Cruz, Michael G. "Influence, Appraisals, and Emotions in Close Relationships." *Communication Monographs* 63 (1996): 105–131.

Donnelly, J. H., and Ivancevich, J. M. "Post-Purchase Reinforcement and Back-Out Behavior." *Journal of Marketing Research* 7 (1970): 399–400.

Festinger, Leon. *A Theory of Cognitive Dissonance.* Stanford, CA: Stanford University Press, 1957.

Festinger, Leon, and Carlsmith, James M. "Cognitive Consequences of Forced Compliance." *Journal of Abnormal and Social Psychology* 58 (1959): 203–210.

Fishbein, Martin. "A Behavior Theory Approach to the Relations Between Beliefs About an Object and the Attitude Toward the Object." In *Readings in Attitude Theory and Measurement.* Edited by Martin Fishbein. New York: Wiley, 1967, pp. 389–400.

Fishbein, Martin, and Ajzen, Icek. *Belief, Attitude, Intention, and Behavior.* Reading, MA: Addison-Wesley, 1975.

Gergen, Kenneth J., and Semin, Gün R. "Everyday Understanding in Science and Daily Life." In *Everyday Understanding: Social and Scientific Implications.* Edited by Gün R. Semin and Kenneth J. Gergen. London: Sage, 1990, pp. 1–18.

Hamilton, Mark A., Hunter, John E., and Boster, Franklin J. "The Elaboration Likelihood Model as a Theory of Attitude Formation: A Mathematical Analysis." *Communication Theory* 8 (1993): 50–64.

Heider, Fritz. *The Psychology of Interpersonal Relations.* New York: Wiley, 1958.

Hovland, Carl I., Harvey, O. J., and Sherif, Muzafer. "Assimilation and Contrast Effects in Reactions to Communication and Attitude Change." *Journal of Abnormal and Social Psychology* 55 (1957): 244–252.

Krippendorff, Klaus. "The Past of Communication's Hoped-For Future." *Journal of Communication* 43 (1993): 34–44.

Lannamann, John W. "Deconstructing the Person and Changing the Subject of Interpersonal Studies." *Communication Theory* 2 (1992): 139–148.

———. "Interpersonal Communication: Research as Ideological Practice." *Communication Theory* 1 (1991): 179–203.

LePoire, Beth A. "Two Contrasting Explanations of Involvement Violations: Expectancy Violations Theory Versus Discrepancy Arousal Theory." *Human Communication Research* 20 (1994): 560–591.

Martin, Leonard, and Tesser, Abraham, eds. *The Construction of Social Judgments.* Hillsdale, NJ: Erlbaum, 1992.

Mongeau, Paul, and Stiff, James B. "Specifying Causal Relationships in the Elaboration Likelihood Model." *Communication Theory* 8 (1993): 65–72.

O'Keefe, Daniel J. *Persuasion: Theory and Research.* Newbury Park, CA: Sage, 1990.

Osgood, Charles. *Cross Cultural Universals of Affective Meaning.* Urbana: University of Illinois Press, 1975.

———. "The Nature and Measurement of Meaning." In *The Semantic Differential Technique.* Edited by James Snider and Charles Osgood. Chicago: Aldine, 1969, pp. 9–10.

———. "On Understanding and Creating Sentences." *American Psychologist* 18 (1963): 735–751.

———. "Semantic Differential Technique in the Comparative Study of Cultures." In *The Semantic Differential Technique.* Edited by James Snider and Charles Osgood. Chicago: Aldine, 1969, pp. 303–334.

Osgood, Charles, and Richards, Meredith. "From *Yang* and *Yin* to *and* or *but.*" *Language* 49 (1973): 380–412.

Ostrom, Thomas M., Skowronski, John J., and Nowak, Andrzej. "The Cognitive Foundation of Attitudes: It's a Wonderful Construct." In *Social Cognition: Impact on Social Psychology.* Edited by Patricia G. Devine, David L. Hamilton, and Thomas M. Ostrom. San Diego: Academic, 1994, pp. 196–258.

Patterson, M. L. *Nonverbal Behavior: A Functional Perspective.* New York: Springer-Verlag, 1983.

Petty, Richard E., and Cacioppo, John T. *Communication and Persuasion: Central and Peripheral Routes to Attitude Change.* New York: Springer-Verlag, 1986.

Petty, Richard E., Cacioppo, John T., and Goldman, R. "Personal Involvement as a Determinant of Argument-Based Persuasion." *Journal of Personality and Social Psychology* 41 (1981): 847–855.

Petty, Richard E., and others. "Conceptual and Methodological Issues in the Elaboration Likelihood Model of Persuasion: A Reply to the Michigan State Critics." *Communication Theory* 3 (1993): 336–362.

Rokeach, Milton. *Beliefs, Attitudes, and Values: A Theory of Organization and Change.* San Francisco: Jossey-Bass, 1969.

———. *The Nature of Human Values.* New York: Free Press, 1973.

Roskos-Ewoldsen, David R. "Attitude Accessibility and Persuasion: Review and a Transactive Model." In *Com-*

munication Yearbook 20. Edited by Brant Burleson. Thousand Oaks, CA: Sage, 1997, pp. 185–225.

Seibold, David R., and Spitzberg, Brian H. "Attribution Theory and Research: Formalization, Review, and Implications for Communication." In *Progress in Communication Sciences,* vol. 3. Edited by B. Dervin and M. J. Voigt. Norwood, NJ: Ablex, 1981, pp. 85–125.

Sherif, Muzafer. *Social Interaction—Process and Products.* Chicago: Aldine, 1967.

Sherif, Muzafer, and Hovland, Carl I. *Social Judgment.* New Haven, CT: Yale University Press, 1961.

Sherif, Muzafer, Sherif, Carolyn, and Nebergall, Roger. *Attitude and Attitude Change: The Social Judgment-Involvement Approach.* Philadelphia: Saunders, 1965.

Sillars, Alan L. "Attribution and Communication." In *Social Cognition and Communication.* Edited by Michael E. Roloff and Charles R. Berger. Beverly Hills, CA: Sage, 1982, pp. 73–106.

———. "Attributions and Communication in Roommate Conflicts." *Communication Monographs* 47 (1980): 180–200.

———. "The Sequential and Distributional Structure of Conflict Interaction as a Function of Attributions Concerning the Locus of Responsibility and Stability of Conflict." In *Communication Yearbook 4.* Edited by Dan Nimmo. New Brunswick, NJ: Transaction, 1980, pp. 217–236.

Smith, Eliot R. "Social Cognition Contributions to Attribution Theory and Research." In *Social Cognition: Impact on Social Psychology.* Edited by Patricia G. Devine, David L. Hamilton, and Thomas M. Ostrom. San Diego: Academic, 1994, pp. 77–108.

Smith, Mary John. *Persuasion and Human Action: A Review and Critique of Social Influence Theories.* Belmont, CA: Wadsworth, 1982.

Snider, James, and Osgood, Charles, eds. *The Semantic Differential Technique.* Chicago: Aldine, 1969.

Stiff, James B. *Persuasive Communication.* New York: Guilford, 1994.

Wyer, Robert S. *Cognitive Organization and Change.* Hillsdale, NJ: Erlbaum, 1974.

Wyer, Robert S., and Goldberg, Lee. "A Probabilistic Analysis of the Relationship Between Beliefs and Attitudes." *Psychological Review* 77 (1970): 100–120.

Chapter 8
Theories of Symbolic Interaction, Structuration, and Convergence

Bales, Robert F. *Personality and Interpersonal Behavior.* New York: Holt, Rinehart & Winston, 1970.

Banks, Stephen P, and Riley, Patricia. "Structuration Theory as an Ontology for Communication Research," *Communication Yearbook 16.* Edited by Stanley Deetz. Newbury Park, CA: Sage, 1993, pp. 167–196.

Becker, Howard. "Becoming a Marihuana User." *American Journal of Sociology* 59 (1953): 235–242.

Blumer, Herbert. *Symbolic Interactionism: Perspective and Method.* Englewood Cliffs, NJ: Prentice-Hall, 1969.

Bormann, Ernest G. *Communication Theory.* New York: Holt, Rinehart & Winston, 1980.

———. "Fantasy and Rhetorical Vision: The Rhetorical Criticism of Social Reality." *Quarterly Journal of Speech* 58 (1972): 396–407.

———. "Fantasy and Rhetorical Vision: Ten Years Later." *Quarterly Journal of Speech* 68 (1982): 288–305.

———. *The Force of Fantasy: Restoring the American Dream.* Carbondale: Southern Illinois University Press, 1985.

Bormann, Ernest G., Cragan, John F., and Shields, Donald C. "An Expansion of the Rhetorical Vision Component of the Symbolic Convergence Theory: The Cold War Paradigm Case." *Communication Monographs* 63 (1996): 1–28.

———. "In Defense of Symbolic Convergence Theory: A Look at the Theory and Its Criticisms After Two Decades." *Communication Theory* 4 (1994): 259–294.

Brock, Bernard L. "Evolution of Kenneth Burke's Criticism and Philosophy of Language." In *Kenneth Burke and Contemporary European Thought: Rhetoric in Transition.* Edited by Bernard L. Brock. Tuscaloosa: University of Alabama Press, 1995, pp. 1–33.

Burke, Kenneth. *Attitudes Toward History.* New York: New Republic, 1937.

———. *Counter-Statement.* New York: Harcourt, Brace, 1931.

———. *A Grammar of Motives.* Englewood Cliffs, NJ: Prentice-Hall, 1945.

———. *Language as Symbolic Action.* Berkeley: University of California Press, 1966.

———. *Permanence and Change.* New York: New Republic, 1935.

———. *The Philosophy of Literary Form.* Baton Rouge: Louisiana State University Press, 1941.

———. *A Rhetoric of Motives.* Englewood Cliffs, NJ: Prentice-Hall, 1950.

———. *A Rhetoric of Religion.* Boston: Beacon, 1961.

Cahill, Spencer. "Erving Goffman." In *Symbolic Interactionism: An Introduction, an Interpretation, an Integration.* Edited by Joel M. Charon. Englewood Cliffs, NJ: Prentice-Hall, 1992, pp. 185–200.

Charon, Joel M. *Symbolic Interactionism: An Introduction, an Interpretation, an Integration.* Englewood Cliffs, NJ: Prentice-Hall, 1992.

Chesebro, James. "Extending the Burkeian System: A Response to Tompkins and Cheney." *Quarterly Journal of Speech* 80 (1994): 83–90.

Cragan, John F., and Shields, Donald C. *Applied Communication Research: A Dramatistic Approach.* Prospect Heights, IL: Waveland, 1981.

———. *Symbolic Theories in Applied Communication Research: Bormann, Burke, and Fisher.* Cresskill, NJ: Hampton, 1995.

———. *Understanding Communication Theory: The Communicative Forces for Human Action.* Boston: Allyn & Bacon, 1998, pp. 93–121.

Delia, Jesse G. "Communication Research: A History." In *Handbook of Communication Science.* Edited by Charles R. Berger and Steven H. Chaffee. Newbury Park, CA: Sage, 1987, pp. 30–37.

Denzin, Norman K. *Symbolic Interactionism and Cultural Studies: The Politics of Interpretation.* Oxford: Blackwell, 1992.

Fine, Gary Alan. "The Sad Demise, Mysterious Disappearance, and Glorious Triumph of Symbolic Interactionism." *Annual Review of Sociology* 19 (1993): 61–87.

Foss, Karen A., and Littlejohn, Stephen W. "*The Day After*: Rhetorical Vision in an Ironic Frame." *Critical Studies in Mass Communication* 3 (1986): 317–336.

Foss, Sonja K., Foss, Karen A., and Trapp, Robert. *Contemporary Perspectives on Rhetoric.* Prospect Heights, IL: Waveland, 1991.

Giddens, Anthony. *New Rules of Sociological Method.* New York: Basic Books, 1976.

———. *Profiles and Critiques in Social Theory.* Berkeley: University of California Press, 1982, pp. 8–11.

———. *Studies in Social and Political Theory.* New York: Basic, 1977.

Goffman, Erving. *Behavior in Public Places.* New York: Free Press, 1963.

———. *Encounters: Two Studies in the Sociology of Interaction.* Indianapolis: Bobbs-Merrill, 1961.

———. *Frame Analysis: An Essay on the Organization of Experience.* Cambridge, MA: Harvard University Press, 1974.

———. *Interaction Ritual: Essays on Face-to-Face Behavior.* Garden City, NY: Doubleday, 1967.

———. *The Presentation of Self in Everyday Life.* Garden City, NY: Doubleday, 1959.

———. *Relations in Public.* New York: Basic, 1971.

Gronbeck, Bruce E. "Dramaturgical Theory and Criticism: The State of the Art (or Science?)." *Western Journal of Speech Communication* 44 (1980): 315–330.

Hall, Peter M. "Structuring Symbolic Interaction: Communication and Power." In *Communication Yearbook 4.* Edited by Dan Nimmo. New Brunswick, NJ: Transaction, 1980, pp. 49–60.

Hickman, C. A., and Kuhn, Manford. *Individuals, Groups, and Economic Behavior.* New York: Holt, Rinehart & Winston, 1956.

Johnson, C. David, and Picou, J. Stephen. "The Foundations of Symbolic Interactionism Reconsidered." In *Micro-Sociological Theory: Perspectives on Sociological Theory,* vol. 2. Edited by H. J. Helle and S. N. Eisenstadt. Beverly Hills, CA: Sage, 1985, pp. 54–70.

Katovich, Michael A., and Reese, William A., III. "Postmodern Thought in Symbolic Interaction: Reconstructing Social Inquiry in Light of Late-Modern Concerns." *The Sociological Quarterly* 34 (1993): 391–411.

Kuhn, Manford H. "Major Trends in Symbolic Interaction Theory in the Past Twenty-Five Years." *Sociological Quarterly* 5 (1964): 61–84.

Kuhn, Manford H., and McPartland, Thomas S. "An Empirical Investigation of Self-Attitudes." *American Sociological Review* 19 (1954): 68–76.

Lal, Barbara Ballis. "Symbolic Interaction Theories." *American Behavioral Scientist* 38 (1995): 421–441.

Leeds-Hurwitz, Wendy. "A Social Account of Symbols." In *Beyond the Symbol Model: Reflections on the Representational Nature of Language.* Edited by John Stewart. Albany: SUNY Press, 1996, pp. 257–278.

———. "Social Approaches to Interpersonal Communication." *Communication Theory* 2 (1992): 131–139.

Leeds-Hurwitz, Wendy, ed. *Social Approaches to Communication.* New York: Guilford, 1995.

Ling, David A. "A Pentadic Analysis of Senator Edward Kennedy's Address to the People of Massachusetts July 25, 1969." *Central States Speech Journal* 21 (1970): 81–86.

Lofland, John. "Interactionist Imagery and Analytic Interruptus." In *Human Nature and Collective Behavior.* Edited by Tamotsu Shibutani. Englewood Cliffs, NJ: Prentice-Hall, 1970.

Manis, Jerome G., and Meltzer, Bernard N. "Appraisals of Symbolic Interactionism." In *Symbolic Interaction*. Edited by Jerome G. Manis and Bernard N. Meltzer. Boston: Allyn & Bacon, 1978, pp. 393–440.

Manis, Jerome G., and Meltzer, Bernard N, eds. *Symbolic Interaction*. Boston: Allyn & Bacon, 1978.

McCall, Michal M., and Becker, Howard S. *Symbolic Interaction and Cultural Studies*. Chicago: University of Chicago Press, 1990.

Mead, George H. *Mind, Self, and Society*. Chicago: University of Chicago Press, 1934.

Meltzer, Bernard N. "Mead's Social Psychology." In *Symbolic Interaction*. Edited by Jerome G. Manis and Bernard N. Meltzer. Boston: Allyn & Bacon, 1972, pp. 4–22.

Meltzer, Bernard N., and Petras, John W. "The Chicago and Iowa Schools of Symbolic Interactionism." In *Human Nature and Collective Behavior*. Edited by Tamotsu Shibutani. Englewood Cliffs, NJ: Prentice-Hall, 1970.

Meltzer, Bernard N., Petras, John, and Reynolds, Larry. *Symbolic Interactionism: Genesis, Varieties, and Criticism*. London: Routledge & Kegan Paul, 1975.

Mohrmann, G. P. "An Essay on Fantasy Theme Criticism." *Quarterly Journal of Speech* 68 (1982): 109–132.

Morris, Charles. "George H. Mead as Social Psychologist and Social Philosopher." In *Mind, Self, and Society* (Introduction). Chicago: University of Chicago Press, 1934, pp. ix–xxxv.

Musolf, Gil Richard. "Structure, Institutions, Power, and Ideology: New Directions Within Symbolic Interactionism." *The Sociological Quarterly* 33 (1992): 171–189.

Reynolds, Larry T. *Interactionism: Exposition and Critique*. Dix Hills, NY: General Hall, 1990.

Rogers, Everett M. *A History of Communication Study: A Biographical Approach*. New York: Free Press, 1994.

Rueckert, William, ed. *Critical Responses to Kenneth Burke*. Minneapolis: University of Minnesota Press, 1969.

Scheff, Thomas J. *Microsociology: Discourse, Emotion, and Social Structure*. Chicago: University of Chicago Press, 1990.

Sigman, Stuart J. *A Perspective on Social Communication*. Lexington, MA: Lexington, 1987.

Simons, Herbert W., and Melia, Trevor, eds. *The Legacy of Kenneth Burke*. Madison: University of Wisconsin Press, 1989.

Stewart, John. *Language as Articulate Contact*. Albany: SUNY Press, 1995.

Swartz, Omar. *Conducting Socially Responsible Research*. Thousand Oaks, CA: Sage, 1997, pp. 68–90.

Tedeschi, J. T., and Reiss, M. "Verbal Strategies in Impression Management." In *The Psychology of Ordinary Explanations of Social Behavior*. Edited by Charles Antaki. New York: Academic, 1981, pp. 271–309.

Tucker, Charles W. "Some Methodological Problems of Kuhn's Self-Theory." *Sociological Quarterly* 7 (1966): 345–358.

Verhoeven, Jef. "Goffman's Frame Analysis and Modern Micro-Sociological Paradigms." In *Micro-Sociological Theory: Perspectives on Sociological Theory*, vol. 2. Edited by H. J. Helle and S. N. Eisenstadt. Beverly Hills, CA: Sage, 1985, pp. 71–100.

Wiley, Norbert. *The Semiotic Self*. Chicago: University of Chicago Press, 1994.

Woodward, Wayne. "Triadic Communication as Transactional Participation." *Critical Studies in Mass Communication* 13 (1996): 155–174.

Chapter 9
Theories of Social and Cultural Reality

Alvy, K. T. "The Development of Listener Adapted Communication in Grade-School Children from Different Social Class Backgrounds." *Genetic Psychology Monographs* 87 (1973): 33–104.

Averill, James. "The Acquisition of Emotions During Adulthood." In *The Social Construction of Emotions*. Edited by Rom Harré. New York: Blackwell, 1986, pp. 98–119.

———. *Anger and Aggression: An Essay on Emotion*. New York: Springer-Verlag, 1982.

———. "A Constructivist View of Emotion." In *Theories of Emotion*. Edited by K. Plutchik and H. Kellerman. New York: Academic, 1980, pp. 305–339.

———. "On the Paucity of Positive Emotions." In *Assessment and Modification of Emotional Behavior*. Edited by K. R. Blankstein, P. Pliner, and J. Polivy. New York: Plenum, 1980, pp. 7–45.

Berger, Peter L., and Luckmann, Thomas. *The Social Construction of Reality: A Treatise in the Sociology of Knowledge*. New York: Doubleday, 1966.

Bernstein, Basil. *Class, Codes, and Control: Theoretical Studies Toward a Sociology of Language*. London: Routledge & Kegan Paul, 1971.

Bostrom, Robert, and Donohew, Lewis. "The Case for Empiricism: Clarifying Fundamental Issues in Communication Theory." *Communication Monographs* 59 (1992): 109–129.

Branham, Robert J., and Pearce, W. Barnett. "Between Text and Context: Toward a Rhetoric of Contextual Reconstruction." *Quarterly Journal of Speech* 71 (1985): 19–36.

Brenders, David A. "Fallacies in the Coordinated Management of Meaning: A Philosophy of Language Critique of the Hierarchical Organization of Coherent Conversation and Related Theory." *Quarterly Journal of Speech* 73 (1987): 329–348.

Burr, Vivien. *Introduction to Social Constructionism*. London: Routledge, 1995.

Buttny, Richard. "Accounts as a Reconstruction of an Event's Context." *Communication Monographs* 52 (1985): 57–77.

Cappella, Joseph. "Remaking Communication Inquiry." In *Rethinking Communication: Paradigm Issues*. Edited by Brenda Dervin, Lawrence Grossberg, Barbara O'Keefe, and Ellen Wartella. Newbury Park, CA: Sage, 1989, p. 142.

Carroll, John B. "Introduction." In *Language, Thought, and Reality*. Edited by Benjamin L. Whorf. New York: Wiley, 1956, pp. 1–34.

Cherwitz, Richard A., and Hikins, James W. *Communication and Knowledge: An Investigation in Rhetorical Epistemology*. Columbia: University of South Carolina Press, 1986.

Cronen, Vernon E., Chen, Victoria, and Pearce, W. Barnett. "Coordinated Management of Meaning: A Critical Theory." In *Theories in Intercultural Communication*. Edited by Young Yun Kim and William B. Gudykunst. Newbury Park, CA: Sage, 1988, pp. 66–98.

Cronen, Vernon E., Johnson, Kenneth M., and Lanna-mann, John W. "Paradoxes, Double Binds, and Reflexive Loops: An Alternative Theoretical Perspective." *Family Process* 20 (1982): 91–112.

Cronen, Vernon, and Lang, Peter. "Language and Action: Wittgenstein and Dewey in the Practice of Therapy and Consultation." *Human Systems: The Journal of Systemic Consultation and Management* 5 (1994): 5–43.

Cronen, Vernon E., Pearce, W. Barnett, and Changsheng, Xi. "The Meaning of 'Meaning' in the CMM Analysis of Communication: A Comparison of Two Traditions." *Research on Language and Social Interaction* 23 (1989–1990): 1–40.

Cronen, Vernon, Pearce, W. Barnett, and Harris, Linda. "The Coordinated Management of Meaning." In *Comparative Human Communication Theory.* Edited by Frank E. X. Dance. New York: Harper & Row, 1982.

———. "The Logic of the Coordinated Management of Meaning." *Communication Education* 28 (1979): 22–38.

Deetz, Stanley. "Future of the Discipline: The Challenges, the Research, and the Social Contribution." In *Communication Yearbook 17.* Edited by Stanley Deetz. Thousand Oaks, CA: Sage, 1994, pp. 565–600.

Ellis, Donald G. *Crafting Society: Ethnicity, Class, and Communication Theory.* Mahwah, NJ: Erlbaum, 1999.

———. "Fixing Communicative Meaning: A Coherentist Theory." *Communication Research* 22 (1995): 515–544.

Geertz, Clifford. *Local Knowledge: Further Essays in Interpretive Anthropology.* New York: Basic, 1983.

Gergen, Kenneth J. "The Social Constructionist Movement in Modern Psychology." *American Psychologist* 40 (1985): 266–275.

———. *Toward Transformation in Social Knowledge.* New York: Springer-Verlag, 1982.

Giddens, Anthony. *Profiles and Critiques in Social Theory.* Berkeley: University of California Press, 1982.

Harré, Rom. "Is There Still a Problem About the Self?" In *Communication Yearbook 17.* Edited by Stanley Deetz. Thousand Oaks, CA: Sage, 1994.

———. "An Outline of the Social Constructionist Viewpoint." In *The Social Construction of Emotions.* Edited by Rom Harré. New York: Blackwell, 1986, pp. 2–14.

———. *Personal Being: A Theory for Individual Psychology.* Cambridge, MA: Harvard University Press, 1984.

———. *Social Being: A Theory for Social Behavior.* Totowa, NJ: Littlefield, Adams, 1979.

Harré, Rom, and Secord, Paul. *The Explanation of Social Behavior.* Totowa, NJ: Rowman & Littlefield, 1972.

Krippendorff, Klaus. "The Past of Communication's Hoped-For Future." *Journal of Communication* 43 (1993): 34–44.

Leeds-Hurwitz, Wendy, ed. *Social Approaches to Communication.* New York: Guilford, 1995.

Lutz, Catherine. "Morality, Domination, and Understandings of 'Justifiable Anger' Among the Ifaluk." In *Everyday Understanding: Social and Scientific Implications.* Edited by Gün R. Semin and Kenneth J. Gergen. London: Sage, 1990, pp. 204–226.

McLaughlin, Margaret L., Cody, Michael J., and O'Hair, H. Dan. "The Management of Failure Events: Some Contextual Determinants of Accounting Behavior." *Human Communication Research* 9 (1983): 208–224.

McLaughlin, Margaret L., Cody, Michael J., and Read, Stephen, eds. *Explaining One's Self to Others: Reason-Giving in a Social Context.* Hillsdale, NJ: Erlbaum, 1992.

McLaughlin, Margaret L., Cody, Michael J., and Rosenstein, Nancy E. "Account Sequences in Conversations Between Strangers." *Communication Monographs* 50 (1983): 102–125.

Narula, Uma, and Pearce, W. Barnett. *Development as Communication: A Perspective on India.* Carbondale: Southern Illinois University Press, 1986.

Pearce, W. Barnett. "A 'Camper's Guide' to Constructionisms." *Human Systems: The Journal of Systemic Consultation and Management* 3 (1992): 139–161.

———. *Communication and the Human Condition.* Carbondale: Southern Illinois University Press, 1989.

———. "The Coordinated Management of Meaning: A Rules Based Theory of Interpersonal Communication." In *Explorations in Interpersonal Communication.* Edited by Gerald R. Miller. Beverly Hills, CA: Sage, 1976, pp. 17–36.

———. "A Sailing Guide for Social Constructionists." In *Social Approaches to Communication.* Edited by Wendy Leeds-Hurwitz. New York: Guilford, 1995, pp. 88–113.

Pearce, W. Barnett, and Cronen, Vernon. *Communication, Action, and Meaning.* New York: Praeger, 1980.

Pearce, W. Barnett, and Pearce, Kimberly A. "Extending the Theory of the Coordinated Management of Meaning (CMM) Through a Community Dialogue Process." *Communication Theory* 10 (2000): 405–423.

Penman, Robyn. "Good Theory and Good Practice: An Argument in Progress." *Communication Theory* 2 (1992): 234–250.

Philipsen, Gerry. "The Coordinated Management of Meaning Theory of Pearce, Cronen, and Associates." In *Watershed Research Traditions in Human Communication Theory.* Edited by Donald P. Cushman and Branislav Kovačić. Albany: SUNY Press, 1995, pp. 13–43.

Powers, John H. "On the Intellectual Structure of the Human Communication Discipline." *Communication Education* 44 (1995): 191–222.

Sankoff, Gillian. *The Social Life of Language.* Philadelphia: University of Pennsylvania Press, 1980.

Sapir, Edward. *Language: An Introduction to the Study of Speech.* New York: Harcourt, Brace & World, 1921.

Schonbach, P. A. "A Category System for Account Phases." *European Journal of Social Psychology* 10 (1980): 195–200.

Schutz, Alfred. *On Phenomenology and Social Relations.* Chicago: University of Chicago Press, 1970.

Shotter, John. "Before Theory and After Representationalism: Understanding Meaning 'From Within' a Dialogue Process." In *Beyond the Symbol Model: Reflections on the Representational Nature of Language.* Edited by John Stewart. Albany: SUNY Press, 1996, pp. 103–134.

———. *Social Accountability and Selfhood.* Oxford: Blackwell, 1984.

———. "Social Accountability and the Social Construction of 'You.'" In *Texts of Identity.* Edited by John Shotter and Kenneth J. Gergen. London: Sage, 1989, pp. 133–151.

Shotter, John, and Gergen, Kenneth J. "Social Construction: Knowledge, Self, Others, and Continuing the Conversation." In *Communication Yearbook 17.* Edited by Stanley Deetz. Thousand Oaks, CA: Sage, 1994, pp. 3–33.

Sigman, Stuart J. "Do Social Approaches to Interpersonal Communication Constitute a Contribution to Communication Theory?" *Communication Theory* 2 (1992): 347–356.

Steinfatt, Thomas M. "Linguistic Relativity." In *Language, Communication, and Culture: Current Directions*. Edited by Stella Ting-Toomey and Felipe Korzenny. Newbury Park, CA: Sage, 1989, pp. 35–75.

Stewart, John. *Language as Articulate Contact: Toward a Post-Semiotic Philosophy of Communication*. Albany: SUNY Press, 1995.

———. "The Symbol Model vs. Language as Constitutive Articulate Contact." In *Beyond the Symbol Model: Reflections on the Representational Nature of Language*. Edited by John Stewart. Albany: SUNY Press, 1996, pp. 9–68.

Taylor, James R., Cooren, Francois, Giroux, Nicole, and Robichaud, Daniel. "The Communicational Basis of Organization: Between the Conversation and the Text." *Communication Theory* 6 (1996): 1–39.

Whorf, Benjamin L. "Language, Mind, and Reality." In *Language, Thought, and Reality*. Edited by John B. Carroll. New York: Wiley, 1956, pp. 246–270.

———. *Language, Thought, and Reality*. Edited by John B. Carroll. New York: Wiley, 1956.

Chapter 10
Theories of Experience and Interpretation

Agar, Michael. *Speaking of Ethnography*. Beverly Hills, CA: Sage, 1986.

Anderson, James A. *Communication Theory: Epistemological Foundations*. New York: Guilford, 1996.

Atkinson, Paul. *Understanding Ethnographic Texts*. New York: Basic, 1973.

Bailey, William. "Consciousness and Action/Motion Theories of Communication." *Western Journal of Speech Communication* 50 (1986): 74.

Bauman, Zygmunt. *Hermeneutics and Social Science*. New York: Columbia University Press, 1978.

Benoit, Pamela J., and Benoit, William L. "Consciousness: The Mindlessness/Mindfulness and Verbal Report of Controversies." *Western Journal of Speech Communication* 50 (1986): 41–63.

Berman, Art. *From the New Criticism to Deconstruction*. Urbana, IL: University of Chicago Press, 1988.

Bernstein, Richard J. *Beyond Objectivism and Relativism: Science, Hermeneutics, and Praxis*. Philadelphia: University of Pennsylvania Press, 1983.

Campbell, John Angus. "Hans-Georg Gadamer's Truth and Method." *Quarterly Journal of Speech* 64 (1978): 101–122.

Carbaugh, Donal, ed. "Culture Talking About Itself." In *Cultural Communication and Intercultural Contact*. Hillsdale, NJ: Erlbaum, 1990, pp. 1–9.

———. *Situating Selves: The Communication of Social Identities in American Scenes*. Albany: SUNY Press, 1996.

Carbaugh, Donal, and Hastings, Sally. "A Role for Communication Theory in Ethnography and Cultural Analysis." *Communication Theory* 2 (1992): 156–165.

Carragee, Kevin M. "Interpretive Media Study and Interpretive Social Science." *Critical Studies in Mass Communication* 7 (1990): 81–96.

Cheney, George, and Tompkins, Phillip K. "On the Facts of the Text as the Basis of Human Communication Research." In *Communication Yearbook 11*. Edited by James A. Anderson. Newbury Park, CA: Sage, 1988, pp. 455–501.

Conquergood, Dwight. "Ethnography, Rhetoric, and Performance." *Quarterly Journal of Speech* 78 (1992): 80–97.

———. "Rethinking Ethnography: Toward a Critical Cultural Politics." *Communication Monographs* 58 (1991): 179–194.

Crawford, Lyall. "Personal Ethnography." *Communication Monographs* 63 (1996): 158.

Deetz, Stanley. "Conceptualizing Human Understanding: Gadamer's Hermeneutics and American Communication Studies." *Communication Quarterly* 26 (1978): 14.

———. *Democracy in an Age of Corporate Colonization*. Albany: SUNY Press, 1992, pp. 113–144.

———. "Words Without Things: Toward a Social Phenomenology of Language." *Quarterly Journal of Speech* 59 (1973): 40–51.

Derrida, Jacques. *Of Grammatology*. Translated by Gayatri Spivak. Baltimore: Johns Hopkins University Press, 1976.

Dilthey, Wilhelm. "The Rise of Hermeneutics." Translated by Fredric Jameson. *New Literary History* 3 (1972): 229–244.

Fay, Brian. *Social Theory and Political Practice*. London: Allen & Unwin, 1975.

Fish, Stanley. *Is There a Text in This Class?* Cambridge, MA: Harvard University Press, 1980.

Froman, Wayne. *Merleau-Ponty: Language and the Act of Speech*. Lewisburg, PA: Bucknell University Press, 1982.

Gadamer, Hans-Georg. *Truth and Method*. New York: Seabury, 1975.

Geertz, Clifford. *The Interpretation of Cultures*. New York: Basic, 1973.

———. *Local Knowledge: Further Essays in Interpretive Anthropology*. New York: Basic, 1983.

Gergen, Kenneth. *Toward Transformation in Social Knowledge*. New York: Springer-Verlag, 1982, pp. 126–133.

Giddens, Anthony. "On the Relation of Sociology to Philosophy." In *Explaining Human Behavior: Consciousness, Human Action, and Social Structure*. Edited by Paul F. Secord. Beverly Hills, CA: Sage, 1982, pp. 175–188.

Gorman, Robert A. *The Dual Vision: Alfred Schutz and the Myth of Phenomenological Social Science*. London: Routledge & Kegan Paul, 1977.

Hamlyn, D. W. "The Concept of Social Reality." In *Explaining Human Behavior: Consciousness, Human Action, and Social Structure*. Edited by Paul F. Secord. Beverly Hills, CA: Sage, 1982, pp. 189–210.

Heidegger, Martin. *Being and Time*. Translated by John Macquarrie and Edward Robinson. New York: Harper & Row, 1962.

———. *An Introduction to Metaphysics*. Translated by Ralph Manheim. New Haven, CT: Yale University Press, 1959.

———. *On the Way to Language*. Translated by Peter Hertz. New York: Harper & Row, 1971.

Huspek, Michael. "Dueling Structures: The Theory of Resistance in Discourse." *Communication Theory* 3 (1993): 1–25.

Husserl, Edmund. *Ideas: General Introduction to Pure Phenomenology.* Translated by W. R. Boyce Gibson. New York: Collier, 1962.

———. *Phenomenology and the Crisis of Philosophy.* Translated by Quentin Lauer. New York: Harper & Row, 1965.

Hyde, Michael J. "Transcendental Philosophy and Human Communication." In *Interpersonal Communication.* Edited by Joseph J. Pilotta. Washington, DC: Center for Advanced Research in Phenomenology, 1982, pp. 15–34.

Hymes, Dell. *Foundations in Sociolinguistics: An Ethnographic Approach.* Philadelphia: University of Pennsylvania Press, 1974.

Ihde, Don, ed. *The Conflict of Interpretations: Essays on Hermeneutics* [by Paul Ricoeur]. Evanston, IL: Northwestern University Press, 1974.

Jensen, Klaus Bruhn. "When Is Meaning? Communication Theory, Pragmatism, and Mass Media Reception." In *Communication Yearbook 14.* Edited by James A. Anderson. Newbury Park, CA: Sage, 1991, pp. 3–32.

Kauffman, Bette J. "Feminist Facts: Interview Strategies and Political Subjects in Ethnography." *Communication Theory* 2 (1992): 187–206.

Kwant, Remy C. *The Phenomenological Philosophy of Merleau-Ponty.* Pittsburgh: Duquesne University Press, 1963.

Lanigan, Richard L. *Phenomenology of Communication: Merleau-Ponty's Thematics in Communicology and Semiology.* Pittsburgh: Duquesne University Press, 1988.

———. "A Treasure House of Preconstituted Types: Alfred Schutz on Communicology." In *Phenomenology of Communication: Merleau-Ponty's Thematics in Communicology and Semiology.* Pittsburgh: Duquesne University Press, 1988, pp. 203–222.

Lindlof, Thomas R. "Media Audiences as Interpretive Communities." In *Communication Yearbook 11.* Edited by James A. Anderson. Newbury Park, CA: Sage, 1988, pp. 81–107.

Lindlof, Thomas R., and Meyer, Timothy P. "Mediated Communication as Ways of Seeing, Acting, and Constructing Culture: The Tools and Foundations of Qualitative Research." In *Natural Audiences: Qualitative Research of Media Uses and Effects.* Edited by Thomas R. Lindlof. Norwood, NJ: Ablex, 1987, pp. 1–32.

Lull, James. "The Social Uses of Television." *Human Communication Research* 6 (1980): 197–209.

Mallin, Samuel B. *Merleau-Ponty's Philosophy.* New Haven, CT: Yale University Press, 1979.

Merleau-Ponty, Maurice. *Phenomenology of Perception.* New York: Humanities, 1962 (original published in Paris, 1945).

———. *The Phenomenology of Perception.* Translated by Colin Smith. London: Routledge & Kegan Paul, 1974.

Moores, Shaun. *Interpreting Audiences: The Ethnography of Media Consumption.* London: Sage, 1993.

Morgan, Gareth. *Images of Organization.* Beverly Hills, CA: Sage, 1986.

Motley, Michael T. "Consciousness and Intentionality in Communication: A Preliminary Model and Methodological Approaches." *Western Journal of Speech Communication* 50 (1986): 3–23.

Nisbett, R. E., and Wilson, T. D. "Telling More than We Can Know: Verbal Reports on Mental Processes." *Psychological Review* 84 (1977): 231–259.

Pacanowsky, Michael. "Creating and Narrating Organizational Realities." In *Rethinking Communication: Paradigm Exemplars.* Edited by Brenda Dervin, Lawrence Grossberg, Barbara O'Keefe, and Ellen Wartella. Newbury Park, CA: Sage, 1989, pp. 250–257.

Pacanowsky, Michael, and O'Donnell-Trujillo, Nick. "Communication and Organizational Cultures." *Western Journal of Speech Communication* 46 (1982): 121.

———. "Organizational Communication as Cultural Performance." *Communication Monographs* 50 (1983): 129–145.

Palmer, Richard E. *Hermeneutics: Interpretation Theory in Schleiermacher, Dilthey, Heidegger, and Gadamer.* Evanston, IL: Northwestern University Press, 1969.

Philipsen, Gerry. "An Ethnographic Approach to Communication Studies." In *Rethinking Communication: Paradigm Exemplars.* Edited by Brenda Dervin, Lawrence Grossberg, Barbara O'Keefe, and Ellen Wartella. Newbury Park, CA: Sage, 1989, pp. 258–269.

———. "A Theory of Speech Codes." In *Developing Communication Theories.* Edited by Gerry Philipsen and Terrance L. Albrecht. Albany: SUNY Press, 1997, pp. 119–156.

Powers, John H. "On the Intellectual Structure of the Human Communication Discipline." *Communication Education* 44 (1995): 191–222.

Ricoeur, Paul. *Hermeneutics and the Human Sciences: Essays on Language, Action and Interpretation.* Translated and edited by John B. Thompson. Cambridge: Cambridge University Press, 1981.

———. *Interpretation Theory: Discourse and the Surplus of Meaning.* Fort Worth: Texas University Press, 1976.

Sackmann, Sonja A. "Managing Organizational Culture: Dreams and Possibilities." *Communication Yearbook 13.* Edited by James A. Anderson. Newbury Park, CA: Sage, 1990, pp. 114–148.

Schleiermacher, Friedrich. *Hermeneutik.* Edited by Heinz Kimmerle. Heidelberg, Germany: Carl Winter, Universitaetsverlag, 1959.

Schoening, Gerard T., and Anderson, James A. "Social Action Media Studies: Foundational Arguments and Common Premises." *Communication Theory* 5 (1995): 93–116.

Schutz, Alfred. *The Phenomenology of the Social World.* Translated by George Walsh and Frederick Lehnert. Evanston, IL: Northwestern University Press, 1967 (original published in 1932).

Shotter, John. *Social Accountability and Selfhood.* New York: Blackwell, 1984, pp. 167–172.

Steiner, Linda. "Oppositional Decoding as an Act of Resistance." *Critical Studies in Mass Communication* 5 (1988): 1–15.

Stewart, John. "One Philosophical Dimension of Social Approaches to Interpersonal Communication." *Communication Theory* 2 (1992): 337–347.

Thomas, Jim. *Doing Critical Ethnography.* Newbury Park, CA: Sage, 1993.

Tracy, David. "Interpretation (Hermeneutics)." In *International Encyclopedia of Communications.* Edited by Erik Barnouw. New York: Oxford University Press, 1989, pp. 343–348.

Turner, Victor. *The Anthropology of Performance.* New York: PAJ, 1987.

———. *Dramas, Fields, and Metaphors.* Ithaca, NY: Cornell University Press, 1974.

Warnick, Barbara. "A Ricoeurian Approach to Rhetorical Criticism." *Western Journal of Speech Communication* 51 (1987): 227–244.

West, James T. "Ethnography and Ideology: The Politics of Cultural Representation." *Western Journal of Communication* 57 (1993): 209–220.

Chapter 11
Critical Theories

Agger, Ben. *Cultural Studies as Critical Theory.* London: Falmer, 1992.

Allen, Mike. "Critical and Traditional Science: Implications for Communication Research." *Western Journal of Communication* 57 (1993): 200–208.

Althusser, Louis. *Lenin and Philosophy.* Translated by B. Brewster. New York: Monthly Review, 1971.

———. *For Marx.* Translated by B. Brewster. New York: Vintage, 1970.

Alvesson, Mats, and Deetz, Stanley. "Critical Theory and Postmodernism Approaches to Organizational Studies." In *Handbook of Organizational Studies.* Edited by S. Clegg, C. Harding, and W. Nord. London: Sage, 1996, pp. 173–202.

Angus, Ian. "The Politics of Common Sense: Articulation Theory and Critical Communication Studies." In *Communication Yearbook 15.* Edited by Stanley Deetz. Newbury Park, CA: Sage, 1992, pp. 535–570.

Arato, Andrew, and Gebhardt, Eike, eds. *The Essential Frankfurt School Reader.* New York: Continuum, 1982.

Ardener, Edwin. "The 'Problem' Revisited." In *Perceiving Women.* Edited by Shirley Ardener. London: Malaby, 1975.

Ardener, Shirley. *Defining Females: The Nature of Women in Society.* New York: Wiley, 1978.

Baynes, Kenneth. "Communicative Ethics, the Public Sphere and Communication Media." *Critical Studies in Mass Communication* 11 (1994): 315–326.

Becker, Samuel L. "Marxist Approaches to Media Studies: The British Experience." *Critical Studies in Mass Communication* 1 (1984): 66–80.

Blair, Carole. "The Statement: Foundation of Foucault's Historical Criticism." *Western Journal of Speech Communication* 51 (1987): 364–383.

Blumler, Jay. "Communication and Democracy: The Crisis Beyond and the Ferment Within." *Journal of Communication* 33 (1983): 166–173.

Bottomore, Tom, and Mattelart, Armand. "Marxist Theories of Communication." In *International Encyclopedia of Communications*, vol. 2. Edited by Erik Barnouw and others. New York: Oxford University Press, 1989, pp. 476–483.

Carragee, Kevin M. "A Critical Evaluation of the Media Hegemony Thesis." *Western Journal of Communication* 57 (1993): 330–348.

Cobb, Sara. "A Critique of Critical Discourse Analysis: Deconstructing and Reconstructing the Role of Intention." *Communication Theory* 4 (1994): 132–152.

Condit, Celeste. "Gender Diversity: A Theory of Communication for the Postmodern Era." In *Communication:*

Views from the Helm for the 21st Century. Edited by Judith S. Trent. Boston: Allyn & Bacon, 1998, pp. 177–183.

———. "In Praise of Eloquent Diversity: Gender and Rhetoric as Public Persuasion." *Women's Studies in Communication* 20 (1997).

Cooper, Martha. "Rhetorical Criticism and Foucault's Philosophy of Discursive Events." *Central States Speech Journal* 39 (1988): 1–17.

Dervin, Brenda. "The Potential Contribution of Feminist Scholarship to the Field of Communication." *Journal of Communication* 37 (1987): 107–120.

Ealy, Steven D. *Communication, Speech, and Politics: Habermas and Political Analysis.* Washington, DC: University Press of America, 1981.

Elgin, Suzette. *A First Dictionary and Grammar of Láadan,* 2nd ed. Madison, WI: Society for the Furtherance and Study of Fantasy and Science Fiction, 1988.

Ellis, Donald G. "Poststructuralism and Language: Non-Sense." *Communication Monographs* 58 (1991): 213–224.

Farrell, Thomas B. *Norms of Rhetorical Culture.* New Haven CT: Yale University Press, 1993.

Farrell, Thomas B., and Aune, James A. "Critical Theory and Communication: A Selective Literature Review." *Quarterly Journal of Speech* 65 (1979): 93–120.

Fay, Brian. *Social Theory and Political Practice.* London: Allen & Unwin, 1975.

Flores, Lisa A. "Creating Discursive Space Through a Rhetoric of Difference: Chicana Feminists Craft a Homeland." *Quarterly Journal of Speech* 82 (1996): 142–156.

Foss, Karen A., and Foss, Sonja K. "Personal Experience as Evidence in Feminist Scholarship." *Western Journal of Communication* 58 (1994): 39–43.

———. *Women Speak: The Eloquence of Women's Lives.* Prospect Heights, IL: Waveland, 1991.

Foss, Karen A., Foss, Sonja, and Griffin, Cindy L. *Feminist Rhetorical Theories.* Thousand Oaks, CA: Sage, 1999.

Foss, Sonja K. *Rhetorical Criticism: Exploration and Practice.* Prospect Heights, IL: Waveland, 1989.

Foss, Sonja K., Foss, Karen A., and Trapp, Robert. *Contemporary Perspectives on Rhetoric.* Prospect Heights, IL: Waveland, 1991.

Foss, Sonja K., and Gill, Ann. "Michel Foucault's Theory of Rhetoric as Epistemic." *Western Journal of Speech Communication* 51 (1987): 384–402.

Foss, Sonja K., Griffin, Cindy L., and Foss, Karen A. "Transforming Rhetoric Through Feminist Reconstruction: A Response to the Gender-Diversity Perspective." *Women's Studies in Communication* 20 (1997): 117–136.

Foucault, Michel. *The Archaeology of Knowledge.* Translated by A. M. Sheridan Smith. New York: Pantheon, 1972.

———. *Discipline and Punish: The Birth of the Prison.* Translated by A. Sheridan. New York: Vintage, 1979.

———. *The Order of Things: An Archaeology of the Human Sciences.* New York: Pantheon, 1970.

———. *Power/Knowledge: Selected Interviews and Other Writings 1927–1977.* Translated by Colin Gordon and others. Edited by Colin Gordon. New York: Pantheon, 1980.

Fraser, Nancy. *Unruly Practices: Power, Discourse, and Gender in Contemporary Social Theory.* Minneapolis: University of Minnesota Press, 1989.

Fusfield, William. "Communication Without Constellation? Habermas's Argumentative Turn in (and Away from) Critical Theory." *Communication Theory* 7 (1997): 301–320.

Gearhart, Sally Miller. "Womanpower: Energy Re-Sourcement." In *The Politics of Women's Spirituality: Essays on the Rise of Spiritual Power Within the Feminist Movement.* Edited by Charlene Spretnak. Garden City, NY: Doubleday, 1982, pp. 194–206.

Gilligan, Carol. *In a Different Voice.* Cambridge, MA: Harvard University Press, 1982.

Gramsci, Antonio. *Selections from the Prison Notebooks.* Translated by Q. Hoare and G. Nowell Smith. New York: International, 1971.

Grossberg, Lawrence. "Is There Rock After Punk?" *Critical Studies in Mass Communication* 3 (1986): 50–73.

———. "Strategies of Marxist Cultural Interpretation." *Critical Studies in Mass Communication* 1 (1984): 392–421.

Habermas, Jürgen. *Knowledge and Human Interests.* Translated by Jeremy J. Shapiro. Boston: Beacon, 1971.

———. *Legitimation Crisis.* Translated by Thomas McCarthy. Boston: Beacon, 1975.

———. *Postmetaphysical Thinking: Philosophical Essays.* Translated by William Mark Hohengarten. Cambridge, MA: MIT Press, 1992.

———. *The Theory of Communicative Action, Volume 1: Reason and the Rationalization of Society.* Translated by Thomas McCarthy. Boston: Beacon, 1984.

Hall, Stuart. "Cultural Studies and the Centre: Some Problematics and Problems." In *Culture, Media, Language.* Edited by Stuart Hall, Dorothy Hobson, Andrew Lowe, and Paul Willis. London: Hutchinson, 1981, pp. 15–47.

———. "Cultural Studies: Two Paradigms." In *Media, Culture, and Society: A Critical Reader.* Edited by R. Collins. London: Sage, 1986.

———. "Ideology." In *International Encyclopedia of Communications,* vol. 2. Edited by Erik Barnouw and others. New York: Oxford University Press, 1989, pp. 307–311.

———. "Signification, Representation, Ideology: Althusser and the Post-Structuralist Debates." *Critical Studies in Mass Communication* 2 (1985): 91–114.

Hall, Stuart, Hobson, Dorothy, Lowe, Andrew, and Willis, Paul, eds. *Culture, Media, Language.* London: Hutchinson, 1981.

Hallstein, Lynn O'Brien. "A Postmodern Caring: Feminist Standpoint Theories, Revisioning Caring, and Communication Ethics." *Western Journal of Communication* 63 (1999): 32–56.

Hanna, Joseph F. "Critical Theory and the Politicization of Science." *Communication Monographs* 58 (1991): 202–212.

Harms, John B., and Dickens, David R. "Postmodern Media Studies: Analysis or Symptom." *Critical Studies in Mass Communication* 13 (1996): 210–227.

Hoggart, Richard. *Uses of Literacy.* London: Chatto & Windus, 1957.

Houston, Marsha. "What Makes Scholarship About Black Women and Communication Feminist Communication Scholarship?" *Women's Studies in Communication* 10 (1988): 78–88.

Huspek, Michael. "Dueling Structures: The Theory of Resistance in Discourse." *Communication Theory* 3 (1993): 1–25.

———. "Taking Aim on Habermas's Critical Theory: On the Road Toward a Critical Hermeneutics." *Communication Monographs* 58 (1991): 225–233.

———. "Toward Normative Theories of Communication with Reference to the Frankfurt School: An Introduction." *Communication Theory* 7 (1997): 265–276.

Jansen, Sue Curry. "Power and Knowledge: Toward a New Critical Synthesis." *Journal of Communication* 33 (1983): 342–354.

Kavoori, Anandam P. "Getting Past the Latest 'Post': Assessing the Term 'Post-Colonial.'" *Critical Studies in Mass Communication* 15 (1998): 195–202.

Kellner, Douglas. "Media Communications vs. Cultural Studies: Overcoming the Divide." *Communication Theory* 5 (1995): 162–177.

Kerfoot, Deborah, and Knights, David. "Into the Realm of the Fearful: Power, Identity, and the Gender Problematic." In *Power/Gender: Social Relations in Theory and Practice.* Edited by H. Lorraine Radtke and Henderikus J. Stam. London: Sage, 1994, pp. 67–88.

———. *Media Culture: Cultural Studies, Identity and Politics Between the Modern and the Postmodern.* London: Routledge, 1995.

Kramarae, Cheris. "Feminist Theories of Communication." In *International Encyclopedia of Communications,* vol. 2. Edited by Erik Barnouw and others. New York: Oxford University Press, 1989, pp. 157–160.

———. *Women and Men Speaking: Frameworks for Analysis.* Rowley, MA: Newbury House, 1981.

Kramarae, Cheris, Treichler, Paula A., and Russo, Ann. *A Feminist Dictionary.* Boston: Pandora, 1985.

LaFrance, Marianne, and Henley, Nancy M. "An Oppressing Hypothesis: Or Differences in Nonverbal Sensitivity Revisited." In *Power/Gender: Social Relations in Theory and Practice.* Edited by H. Lorraine Radtke and Henderikus J. Stam. London: Sage, 1994, pp. 287–311.

Lanigan, Richard L. *Phenomenology of Communication: Merleau-Ponty's Thematics in Communicology and Semiology.* Pittsburgh: Duquesne University Press, 1988.

Lannamann, John W. "Interpersonal Communication Research as Ideological Practice." *Communication Theory* 1 (1991): 179–203.

Lazarsfeld, Paul. "Remarks on Administrative and Critical Communications Research." *Studies in Philosophy and Social Science* 9 (1941): 2–16.

Lembo, Ronald, and Tucker, Kenneth H. "Culture, Television, and Opposition: Rethinking Cultural Studies." *Critical Studies in Mass Communication* 7 (1990): 97–116.

Lull, James. "The Audience as Nuisance." *Critical Studies in Mass Communication* 5 (1988): 239.

Mahmood, Saba. "Cultural Studies and Ethnic Absolutism: Comments on Stuart Hall's 'Culture, Community, and Nation.'" *Cultural Studies* 10 (1996): 1–11.

Makus, Anne. "Stuart Hall's Theory of Ideology: A Frame for Rhetorical Criticism." *Western Journal of Speech Communication* 54 (1990): 495–514.

Marx, Karl. *Capital.* Chicago: Kerr, 1909.

———. *The Communist Manifesto.* London: Reeves, 1888.

McCarthy, Thomas. *Ideals and Illusions: On Reconstruction and Deconstruction in Contemporary Critical Theory.* Cambridge, MA: MIT Press, 1993.

McLaughlin, Lisa. "Feminist Communication Scholarship and 'The Woman Question' in the Academy." *Communication Theory* 5 (1995): 144–161.

Mueller, Milton. "Why Communications Policy Is Passing 'Mass Communication' By: Political Economy as the

Missing Link." *Critical Studies in Mass Communication* 12 (1995): 455–472.

Mumby, Dennis K. *Communication and Power in Organizations: Discourse, Ideology, and Domination.* Norwood, NJ: Ablex, 1988.

———. "Modernism, Postmodernism, and Communication Studies: A Rereading of an Ongoing Debate." *Communication Theory* 7 (1997): 1–28.

———. "The Political Function of Narrative in Organizations." *Communication Monographs* 54 (1987): 113–127.

Murdock, Graham. "Across the Great Divide: Cultural Analysis and the Condition of Democracy." *Critical Studies in Mass Communication* 12 (1995): 89–95.

Nelson, Cary, and Grossberg, Lawrence, eds. *Marxism and the Interpretation of Culture.* Urbana: University of Illinois Press, 1988.

Penelope, Julia. *Speaking Freely: Unlearning the Lies of the Fathers' Tongues.* New York: Pergamon, 1990.

Pillai, Poonam. "Rereading Stuart Hall's Encoding/Decoding Model." *Communication Theory* 2 (1992): 221–233.

Pollock, Della, and Cox, J. Robert. "Historicizing 'Reason': Critical Theory, Practice, and Postmodernity." *Communication Monographs* 58 (1991): 170–178.

Pryor, Robert. "On the Method of Critical Theory and Its Implications for a Critical Theory of Communication." In *Phenomenology in Rhetoric and Communication.* Edited by Stanley Deetz. Washington, DC: Center for Advanced Research in Phenomenology/University Press of America, 1981, pp. 25–35.

Putnam, Linda L. "In Search of Gender: A Critique of Communication and Sex-Roles Research." *Women's Studies in Communication* 5 (1982): 1–9.

Rakow, Lana F., ed. *Women Making Meaning: New Feminist Directions in Communication.* New York: Routledge, 1992.

Real, Michael. "The Debate on Critical Theory and the Study of Communications." *Journal of Communication* 34 (autumn 1984): 72–80.

Ricoeur, Paul. *Hermeneutics and the Human Sciences: Essays on Language, Action, and Interpretation.* Translated and edited by John B. Thompson. Cambridge: Cambridge University Press, 1981.

Rogers, Everett M. "The Empirical and the Critical Schools of Communication Research." In *Communication Yearbook 5.* Edited by Michael Burgoon. New Brunswick, NJ: Transaction, 1982, pp. 125–144.

———. *A History of Communication Study: A Biographical Approach.* New York: Free Press, 1994, pp. 102–128.

Rosteck, Thomas. "Cultural Studies and Rhetorical Studies," *Quarterly Journal of Speech* 81 (1995): 386–421.

Rush, Ramona R., and Grubb-Swetman, Autumn. "Feminist Approaches." In *An Integrated Approach to Communication Theory and Research.* Edited by Michael B. Salwen and Don W. Stacks. Mahwah, NJ: Erlbaum, 1996, pp. 497–518.

Shome, Raka. "Caught in the Term 'Post-Colonial': Why the 'Post-Colonial' Still Matters." *Critical Studies in Mass Communication* 15 (1998): 203–212.

———. "Postcolonial Interventions in the Rhetorical Canon: An 'Other' View." *Communication Theory* 6 (1996): 40–59.

Slack, Jennifer Daryl, and Allor, Martin. "The Political and Epistemological Constituents of Critical Communication Research." *Journal of Communication* 33 (1983): 128–218.

Smythe, Dallas W., and Dinh, Tran Van. "On Critical and Administrative Research: A New Critical Analysis." *Journal of Communication* 33 (1983): 117–127.

Swartz, Omar. *Conducting Socially Responsible Research.* Thousand Oaks, CA: Sage, 1997.

Thomas, Jim. *Doing Critical Ethnography.* Newbury Park, CA: Sage, 1993.

van Dijk, Teun. "Discourse Semantics and Ideology." *Discourse and Society* 6 (1995): 243–289.

———. "Principles of Critical Discourse Analysis." *Discourse and Society* 4 (1993): 249–283.

White, Robert. "Mass Communication and Culture: Transition to a New Paradigm." *Journal of Communication* 33 (1983): 279–301.

Williams, Raymond. *The Long Revolution.* New York: Columbia University Press, 1961.

Wood, Julia T., and Pearce, W. Barnett. "Sexists, Racists, and Other Classes of Classifiers: Form and Function of 'ist' Accusations." *Quarterly Journal of Speech* 66 (1980): 239–250.

Zompetti, Joseph P. "Toward a Gramscian Critical Rhetoric." *Western Journal of Communication* 61 (1997): 66–86.

Chapter 12
Communication in Relationships

Altman, Irwin. "Dialectics, Physical Environments, and Personal Relationships." *Communication Monographs* 60 (1993): 26–34.

Altman, Irwin, and Taylor, Dalmas. *Social Penetration: The Development of Interpersonal Relationships.* New York: Holt, Rinehart & Winston, 1973.

Altman, Irwin, Vinsel, A., and Brown, B. "Dialectic Conceptions in Social Psychology: An Application to Social Penetration and Privacy Regulation." In *Advances in Experimental Social Psychology,* vol. 14. Edited by L. Berkowitz. New York: Academic, 1981, pp. 76–100.

Andersen, Peter J. "When One Cannot Not Communicate: A Challenge to Motley's Traditional Communication Postulates." *Communication Studies* 42 (1991): 326–339.

Applegate, James L., and Leichty, Gregory B. "Managing Interpersonal Relationships: Social Cognitive and Strategic Determinants of Competence." In *Competence in Communication: A Multi-Disciplinary Approach.* Edited by Robert N. Bostrom. Beverly Hills, CA: Sage, 1984.

Bavelas, Janet Beavin. "Behaving and Communicating: A Reply to Motley." *Western Journal of Speech Communication* 54 (1990): 593–602.

Baxter, Leslie A. "A Dialectical Perspective on Communication Strategies in Relationship Development." In *Handbook of Personal Relationships.* Edited by Steve Duck. New York: Wiley, 1988, pp. 257–273.

———. "Interpersonal Communication as Dialogue: A Response to the 'Social Approaches' Forum." *Communication Theory* 2 (1992): 330.

———. "The Social Side of Personal Relationships: A Dialectical Perspective." In *Social Context and Relationships: Understanding Relationship Processes,* vol. 3. Edited by Steve Duck. Newbury Park, CA: Sage, 1993, pp. 139–169.

———. "Strategies for Ending Relationships: Two Studies." *Western Journal of Speech Communication* 46 (1982): 223–241.

————. "Trajectories of Relationship Disengagement." *Journal of Social and Personal Relationships* 1 (1984): 29–48.

Baxter, Leslie A., and Montgomery, Barbara M. "A Guide to Dialectical Approaches to Studying Personal Relationships." In *Dialectical Approaches to Studying Personal Relationships.* Edited by Barbara Montgomery and Leslie Baxter. Mahwah, NJ: Erlbaum, 1998, pp. 1–15.

Beisecker, Thomas. "Game Theory in Communication Research: A Rejoinder and a Re-orientation." *Journal of Communication* 20 (1970): 107–120.

Berger, Charles R. "Interpersonal Communication." In *An Integrated Approach to Communication Theory and Research.* Edited by Michael B. Salwen and Don W. Stacks. Mahwah, NJ: Erlbaum, 1996, pp. 277–296.

Berger, Charles R., and Bradac, James J. *Language and Social Knowledge: Uncertainty in Interpersonal Relations.* London: Arnold, 1982.

Berger, Charles R., and Calabrese, R. J. "Some Explorations in Initial Interaction and Beyond: Toward a Developmental Theory of Interpersonal Communication." *Human Communication Research* 1 (1975): 99–112.

Berger, Charles R., and Douglas, William. "Thought and Talk: 'Excuse Me, But Have I Been Talking to Myself?'" In *Human Communication Theory.* Edited by Frank E. X. Dance. New York: Harper & Row, 1982, pp. 42–60.

Berger, Charles R., Gardner, R. R., Parks, M. R., Schulman, L., and Miller, G. R. "Interpersonal Epistemology and Interpersonal Communication." In *Explorations in Interpersonal Communication.* Edited by Gerald R. Miller. Beverly Hills, CA: Sage, 1976, pp. 149–171.

Berger, Charles R., and Kellermann, Katherine Ann. "To Ask or Not to Ask: Is That a Question?" In *Communication Yearbook 7.* Edited by Robert Bostrom. Beverly Hills, CA: Sage, 1983, pp. 342–368.

Bochner, Arthur, and Krueger, Dorothy. "Interpersonal Communication Theory and Research: An Overview of Inscrutable Epistemologies and Muddled Concepts." In *Communication Yearbook 3.* Edited by Dan Nimmo. New Brunswick, NJ: Transaction, 1979, pp. 197–211.

Bostrom, Robert. "Game Theory in Communication Research." *Journal of Communication* 18 (1968): 369–388.

Burgoon, Judee K., Buller, David B., Hale, Jerold L., and deTurck, Mark A. "Relational Messages Associated with Nonverbal Behaviors." *Human Communication Research* 10 (1984): 351–378.

Burgoon, Judee K., and Hale, Jerold L. "The Fundamental Topoi of Relational Communication." *Communication Monographs* 51 (1984): 193–214.

Burrell, Nancy A., and Fitzpatrick, Mary Anne. "The Psychological Reality of Marital Conflict." In *Intimates in Conflict: A Communication Perspective.* Edited by Dudley D. Cahn. Hillsdale, NJ: Erlbaum, 1990, pp. 167–186.

Cahn, Dudley D., ed. *Intimates in Conflict: A Communication Perspective.* Hillsdale, NJ: Erlbaum, 1990.

Cissna, Kenneth J., and Anderson, Rob. "The Contributions of Carl R. Rogers to Philosophical Praxis of Dialogue." *Western Journal of Speech Communication* 54 (1990): 125–147.

Cozby, P. W. "Self-Disclosure: A Literature Review." *Psychological Bulletin* 79 (1973): 73–91.

Cragan, John F., and Shields, Donald C. *Understanding Communication Theory: The Communicative Forces for Human Action.* Boston: Allyn & Bacon, 1998, pp. 122–148.

Cupach, William R., and Metts, Sandra. *Facework.* Thousand Oaks, CA: Sage, 1994.

Davis, Morton. *Game Theory: A Non-technical Introduction.* New York: Basic, 1970.

Duck, Steve. *Meaningful Relationships: Talking, Sense, and Relating.* Thousand Oaks, CA: Sage, 1994.

Duck, Steve, and Pittman, Garth. "Social and Personal Relationships." In *Handbook of Interpersonal Communication,* 2nd ed. Edited by Mark L. Knapp and Gerald R. Miller. Thousand Oaks, CA: Sage, 1994, pp. 676–695.

Duval, S., and Wicklund, R. A. *A Theory of Objective Self-Awareness.* New York: Academic, 1972.

Fitch, Christine L. "Culture, Ideology, and Interpersonal Communication Research." In *Communication Yearbook 17.* Edited by Stanley A. Deetz. Thousand Oaks, CA: Sage, 1994, pp. 104–135.

Fitzpatrick, Mary Anne. *Between Husbands and Wives: Communication in Marriage.* Newbury Park, CA: Sage, 1988.

Fitzpatrick, Mary Anne, and Ritchie, L. David. "Communication Schemata Within the Family: Multiple Perspectives on Family Interaction." *Human Communication Research* 20 (1994): 275–301.

Frost, Joyce, and Wilmot, William. *Interpersonal Conflict.* Dubuque, IA: Brown, 1978.

Gilbert, Shirley J. "Empirical and Theoretical Extensions of Self-Disclosure." In *Explorations in Interpersonal Communication.* Edited by Gerald R. Miller. Beverly Hills, CA: Sage, 1976, pp. 197–216.

Gudykunst, William B. "Culture and the Development of Interpersonal Relationships." In *Communication Yearbook 12.* Edited by James A. Anderson. Newbury Park, CA: Sage, 1989, pp. 315–354.

————. "Uncertainty and Anxiety." In *Theories in Intercultural Communication.* Edited by Young Yun Kim and William B. Gudykunst. Newbury Park, CA: Sage, 1988, pp. 123–156.

Hall, Edward T. *Beyond Culture.* New York: Doubleday, 1976.

Hofstede, G. *Cultures Consequences.* Beverly Hills, CA: Sage, 1980.

Jourard, Sidney. *Disclosing Man to Himself.* New York: Van Nostrand, 1968.

————. *Self-Disclosure: An Experimental Analysis of the Transparent Self.* New York: Wiley, 1971.

————. *The Transparent Self.* New York: Van Nostrand Reinhold, 1971.

Kantor, David, and Lehr, William. *Inside the Family.* New York: Harper & Row, 1975.

Kelley, Harold H., and Thibaut, John W. *Interpersonal Relations: A Theory of Interdependence.* New York: Wiley, 1978.

Knapp, Mark L., and Miller, Gerald R., eds. *Handbook of Interpersonal Communication.* Thousand Oaks, CA: Sage, 1994.

Knapp, Mark L., Miller, Gerald R., and Fudge, Kelly. "Background and Current Trends in the Study of Interpersonal Communication." In *Handbook of Interpersonal Communication.* Edited by Mark L. Knapp and Gerald R. Miller. Thousand Oaks, CA: Sage, 1994, pp. 3–20.

LaGaipa, John L. "Interpersonal Attraction and Social Exchange." In *Theory and Practice in Interpersonal Attraction.* Edited by Steve Duck. New York: Academic, 1971, pp. 129–164.

Lannamann, John W. "Deconstructing the Person and Changing the Subject of Interpersonal Studies." *Communication Theory* 2 (1992): 139–148.

———. "Interpersonal Communication Research as Ideological Practice." *Communication Theory* 1 (1991): 179–203.

Millar, Frank E., and Rogers, L. Edna. "Power Dynamics in Marital Relationships." In *Perspectives on Marital Interaction*. Edited by P. Noller and M. Fitzpatrick. Clevedon, England: Multilingual Matters, 1988, pp. 78–97.

———. "A Relational Approach to Interpersonal Communication." In *Explorations in Interpersonal Communication*. Edited by Gerald R. Miller. Beverly Hills, CA: Sage, 1976, pp. 87–203.

———. "Relational Dimensions of Interpersonal Dynamics." In *Interpersonal Processes: New Directions in Communication Research*. Edited by Michael E. Roloff and Gerald R. Miller. Newbury Park, CA: Sage, 1987, pp. 117–139.

Montgomery, Barbara M. "Communication as the Interface Between Couples and Culture." In *Communication Yearbook 15*. Edited by Stanley Deetz. Newbury Park, CA: Sage, 1992, pp. 475–507.

Montgomery, Barbara M., and Baxter, Leslie A., eds. *Dialectical Approaches to Studying Personal Relationships*. Mahwah, NJ: Erlbaum, 1998.

———. "A Dialectical Perspective on Communication Strategies in Relationship Development." In *Handbook of Personal Relationships*. Edited by Steve Duck. New York: Wiley, 1988, pp. 257–273.

———. "Dialogism and Relational Dialectics." In *Dialectical Approaches to Studying Personal Relationships*. Edited by Barbara Montgomery and Leslie Baxter. Mahwah, NJ: Erlbaum, 1998, p. 160.

Morton, Teru L., and Douglas, Mary Ann. "Growth of Relationships." In *Personal Relationships 2: Developing Personal Relationships*. Edited by Steve Duck and Robin Gilmour. London: Academic, 1981, pp. 3–26.

Motley, Michael. "On Whether One Can(not) Not Communicate: An Examination via Traditional Communication Postulates." *Western Journal of Speech Communication* 54 (1990): 1–20.

Neumann, John von, and Morgenstern, Oskar. *The Theory of Games and Economic Behavior*. Princeton, NJ: Princeton University Press, 1944.

Parks, Malcolm R. "Ideology in Interpersonal Communication: Off the Couch and into the World." In *Communication Yearbook 5*. Edited by Michael Burgoon. New Brunswick, NJ: Transaction, 1982, pp. 79–108.

Petronio, Sandra. *Boundaries of Private Disclosure*. Albany: SUNY Press, 2001.

———. "Communication Boundary Management: A Theoretical Model of Managing Disclosure of Private Information Between Marital Couples." *Communication Theory* 1 (1991): 311–335.

Rawlins, William K. "A Dialectical Analysis of the Tensions, Functions, and Strategic Challenges of Communication in Young Adult Friendships." In *Communication Yearbook 12*. Edited by James A. Anderson. Newbury Park, CA: Sage, 1989, pp. 157–189.

———. *Friendship Matters: Communication, Dialectics, and the Life Course*. Hawthorne, NY: Aldine, 1992.

———. "Writing About *Friendship Matters*: A Case Study in Dialectical and Dialogical Inquiry." In *Dialectical Approaches to Studying Personal Relationships*. Edited by Barbara Montgomery and Leslie Baxter. Mahwah, NJ: Erlbaum, 1998, pp. 63–81.

Rogers, Carl. *Client-Centered Therapy*. Boston: Houghton Mifflin, 1951.

Rogers-Millar, L. Edna, and Millar, Frank E. "Domineeringness and Dominance: A Transactional View." *Human Communication Research* 5 (1979): 238–246.

Roloff, Michael E. "Communication and Conflict." In *Handbook of Communication Science*. Edited by Charles R. Berger and Steven H. Chaffee. Newbury Park, CA: Sage, 1987, pp. 484–536.

———. *Interpersonal Communication: The Social Exchange Approach*. Beverly Hills, CA: Sage, 1981.

Royce, Joseph R., and Mos, Leendert P., eds. *Humanistic Psychology: Concepts and Criticisms*. New York: Plenum, 1981.

Sigman, Stuart J. "Handling the Discontinuous Aspects of Continuous Social Relationships: Toward Research on the Persistence of Social Forms." *Communication Theory* 1 (1991): 106–127.

Sillars, Alan L. "Attributions and Communication in Roommate Conflicts." *Communication Monographs* 47 (1980): 180–200.

———. *Manual for Coding Interpersonal Conflict*. Unpublished manuscript, Department of Communication, University of Montana, 1986.

———. "The Sequential and Distributional Structure of Conflict Interaction as a Function of Attributions Concerning the Locus of Responsibility and Stability of Conflict." In *Communication Yearbook 4*. Edited by Dan Nimmo. New Brunswick, NJ: Transaction, 1980, pp. 217–236.

Sillars, Alan L., Coletti, Stephen F., Parry, Doug, and Rogers, Mark A. "Coding Verbal Conflict Tactics: Nonverbal and Perceptual Correlates of the 'Avoidance-Distributive-Integrative' Distinction." *Human Communication Research* 9 (1982): 83–95.

Sillars, Alan L., Pike, Gary R., Jones, Tricia S., and Redmon, Kathleen. "Communication and Conflict in Marriage." In *Communication Yearbook 7*. Edited by Robert Bostrom. Beverly Hills, CA: Sage, 1983, pp. 414–429.

Sillars, Alan, and Weisberg, Judith. "Conflict as a Social Skill." In *Interpersonal Processes: New Directions in Communication Research*. Edited by Michael E. Roloff and Gerald R. Miller. Newbury Park, CA: Sage, 1987, pp. 140–171.

Steinfatt, Thomas, and Miller, Gerald. "Communication in Game Theoretic Models of Conflict." In *Perspectives on Communication in Conflict*. Edited by Gerald R. Miller and Herbert Simons. Englewood Cliffs, NJ: Prentice-Hall, 1974, pp. 14–75.

Stephen, Timothy, and Harrison, Teresa M. "Interpersonal Communication, Theory, and History." *Communication Theory* 3 (1993): 163–171.

Stewart, John. *Language as Articulate Contact*. Albany: SUNY Press, 1995.

Sunnafrank, Michael. "Predicted Outcome Value During Initial Interactions." *Human Communication Research* 13 (1986): 3–33.

———. "Predicted Outcome Value and Uncertainty Reduction Theories: A Test of Competing Perspectives." *Human Communication Research* 17 (1990): 76–103.

Taylor, Dalmas A., and Altman, Irwin. "Communication in Interpersonal Relationships: Social Penetration Theory." In *Interpersonal Processes: New Directions in Communication Research*. Edited by Michael E. Roloff and Gerald R. Miller. Newbury Park, CA: Sage, 1987, pp. 257–277.

Thibaut, John W., and Kelley, Harold H. *The Social Psychology of Groups*. New York: Wiley, 1959.

Ting-Toomey, Stella. "Intercultural Conflict Styles: Face-Negotiation Theory." In *Theories in Intercultural Communication*. Edited by Yung Y. Kim and William Gudykunst. Newbury Park, CA: Sage, 1988, pp. 213–235.

———. "Toward a Theory of Conflict and Culture." In *Communication, Culture, and Organizational Processes*. Edited by William Gudykunst, Leah Stewart, and Stella Ting-Toomey. Beverly Hills, CA: Sage, 1985, pp. 71–86.

Ting-Toomey, Stella, and Kurogi, Atsuko. "Facework Competence in Intercultural Conflict: An Updated Face-Negotiation Theory." *International Journal of Intercultural Relations* 22 (1998): 187–225.

Van Lear, C. Arthur. "Dialectical Empiricism: Science and Relationship Metaphors." In *Dialectical Approaches to Studying Personal Relationships*. Edited by Barbara Montgomery and Leslie Baxter. Mahwah, NJ: Erlbaum, 1998, pp. 109–136.

———. "Testing a Cyclical Model of Communicative Openness in Relationship Development: Two Longitudinal Studies." *Communication Monographs* 58 (1991): 337–361.

Watzlawick, Paul, Beavin, Janet, and Jackson, Don. *Pragmatics of Human Communication: A Study of Interactional Patterns, Pathologies, and Paradoxes*. New York: Norton, 1967.

Werner, Carol M., and Baxter, Leslie A. "Temporal Qualities of Relationships: Organismic, Transactional, and Dialectical Views." In *Handbook of Interpersonal Communication*. Edited by Mark L. Knapp and Gerald R. Miller. Thousand Oaks, CA: Sage, 1994, pp. 323–379.

Wilmot, William. "Meta-communication: A Re-examination and Extension." In *Communication Yearbook 4*. Edited by Dan Nimmo. New Brunswick, NJ: Transaction, 1980, pp. 61–69.

Chapter 13
Communication in Group Decision Making

Bales, Robert F. *Interaction Process Analysis: A Method for the Study of Small Groups*. Reading, MA: Addison-Wesley, 1950.

———. *Personality and Interpersonal Behavior*. New York: Holt, Rinehart & Winston, 1970.

Bales, Robert F., Cohen, Stephen P., and Williamson, Stephen A. *SYMLOG: A System for the Multiple Level Observation of Groups*. London: Collier, 1979.

Bales, Robert F., and Strodbeck, F. L. "Phases in Group Problem-Solving." *Journal of Abnormal and Social Psychology* 46 (1951): 485–495.

Barge, J. Kevin, and Hirokawa, Randy Y. "Toward a Communication Competency Model of Group Leadership." *Small Group Behavior* 20 (1989): 167–189.

Bell, M. A. "Phases in Group Problem-Solving." *Small Group Behavior* 13 (1982): 475–495.

Bennis, W. G., and Shepard, H. A. "The Theory of Group Development." *Human Relations* 9 (1956): 415–437.

Billingsley, Julie M. "An Evaluation of the Functional Perspective in Small Group Communication." In *Communication Yearbook 16*. Edited by Stanley Deetz. Newbury Park, CA: Sage, 1993, pp. 615–622.

Bonito, Joseph A., and Hollingshead, Andrea B. "Participation in Small Groups." In *Communication Yearbook 20*. Edited by Brant R. Burleson. Thousand Oaks, CA: Sage, 1997, pp. 227–261.

Bormann, Ernest. "Symbolic Convergence and Communication in Group Decision Making." In *Communication and Group Decision-Making*. Edited by Randy Y. Hirokawa and Marshall Scott Poole. Beverly Hills, CA: Sage, 1986, pp. 219–236.

Cattell, Raymond. "Concepts and Methods in the Measurement of Group Syntality." *Psychological Review* 55 (1948): 48–63.

Collins, Barry, and Guetzkow, Harold. *A Social Psychology of Group Processes for Decision-Making*. New York: Wiley, 1964.

Courtright, John A. "A Laboratory Investigation of Groupthink." *Communication Monographs* 45 (1978): 229–246.

Cragan, John F., and Shields, Donald. *Understanding Communication Theory: The Communicative Forces for Human Action*. Boston: Allyn & Bacon, 1998, pp. 93–121.

Cragan, John F., and Wright, David W. "Small Group Communication Research of the 1980s: A Synthesis and Critique." *Communication Studies* 41 (1990): 212–236.

Dewey, John. *How We Think*. Boston: Heath, 1910.

Fisher, B. Aubrey. "Decision Emergence: Phases in Group Decision Making." *Speech Monographs* 37 (1970): 53–60.

———. "The Process of Decision Modification in Small Discussion Groups." *Journal of Communication* 20 (1970): 51–64.

———. *Small Group Decision Making: Communication and the Group Process*. New York: McGraw-Hill, 1980.

Fisher, B. Aubrey, and Hawes, Leonard. "An Interact System Model: Generating a Grounded Theory of Small Groups." *Quarterly Journal of Speech* 57 (1971): 444–453.

Follett, Mary Parker. *Creative Experience*. New York: Longmans, Green, 1924.

Frey, Lawrence R., ed. *The Handbook of Group Communication Theory and Research*. Thousand Oaks, CA: Sage, 1999.

Giddens, Anthony. *New Rules of Sociological Method*. New York: Basic, 1976.

———. *Profiles and Critiques in Social Theory*. Berkeley: University of California Press, 1982.

———. *Studies in Social and Political Theory*. New York: Basic, 1977.

Gouran, Dennis S. "Communication in Groups: The Emergence and Evolution of a Field of Study." In *The Handbook of Group Communication Theory and Research*. Edited by Lawrence R. Frey. Thousand Oaks, CA: Sage, 1999, pp. 3–36.

———. "The Paradigm of Unfulfilled Promise: A Critical Examination of the History of Research on Small Groups in Speech Communication." In *Speech Communication in the 20th Century*. Edited by Thomas W. Benson. Carbondale: Southern Illinois University Press, 1985, pp. 90–108.

Gouran, Dennis S., and Fisher, B. Aubrey. "The Functions of Human Communication in the Formation, Maintenance, and Performance of Small Groups." In *Handbook of Rhetorical and Communication Theory.* Edited by Carroll C. Arnold and John Waite Bowers. Boston: Allyn & Bacon, 1984, pp. 622–659.

Gouran, Dennis S., and Hirokawa, Randy Y. "Counteractive Functions of Communication in Effective Group Decision-Making." In *Communication and Group Decision-Making.* Edited by Randy Y. Hirokawa and Marshall Scott Poole. Beverly Hills, CA: Sage, 1986, pp. 81–92.

Gouran, Dennis S., Hirokawa, Randy Y., Julian, Kelly M., and Leatham, Geoff B. "The Evolution and Current Status of the Functional Perspective on Communication in Decision-Making and Problem-Solving Groups." In *Communication Yearbook 16.* Edited by Stanley A. Deetz. Newbury Park, CA: Sage, 1993, pp. 573–600.

Gouran, Dennis S., Hirokawa, Randy Y., McGee, Michael Calvin, and Miller, Laurie L. "Communication in Groups: Research Trends and Theoretical Perspectives." In *Building Communication Theories: A Socio/Cultural Approach.* Edited by Fred L. Casmir. Hillsdale, NJ: Erlbaum, 1994, pp. 241–268.

Hirokawa, Randy Y. "Group Communication and Decision Making Performance: A Continued Test of the Functional Perspective." *Human Communication Research* 14 (1988): 487–515.

———. "Group Communication and Problem-Solving Effectiveness I: A Critical Review of Inconsistent Findings." *Communication Quarterly* 30 (1982): 134–141.

———. "Group Communication and Problem-Solving Effectiveness: An Investigation of Group Phases." *Human Communication Research* 9 (1983): 291–305.

———. "Group Communication and Problem-Solving Effectiveness II." *Western Journal of Speech Communication* 47 (1983): 59–74.

Hirokawa, Randy Y., and Poole, Marshall Scott, eds. *Communication and Group Decision-Making.* Beverly Hills, CA: Sage, 1986.

Hirokawa, Randy Y., and Scheerhorn, Dirk R. "Communication in Faulty Group Decision-Making." In *Communication and Group Decision-Making.* Edited by Randy Y. Hirokawa and Marshall Scott Poole. Beverly Hills, CA: Sage, 1986, pp. 63–80.

Hirokawa, Randy, Salazar, Abran J., Erbert, Larry, and Ice, Richard J. "Small Group Communication." In *An Integrated Approach to Communication Theory and Research.* Edited by Michael B. Salwen and Don W. Stacks. Mahwah, NJ: Erlbaum, 1996, pp. 359–382.

Janis, Irving. *Crucial Decisions: Leadership in Policy Making and Crisis Management.* New York: Free Press, 1989.

———. *Groupthink: Psychological Studies of Policy Decisions and Fiascoes.* Boston: Houghton Mifflin, 1982.

Janis, Irving, and Mann, Leon. *Decision Making: A Psychological Analysis of Conflict, Choice, and Commitment.* New York: Free Press, 1977.

Jarboe, Susan. "A Comparison of Input-Output, Process-Output, and Input-Process-Output Models of Small Group Problem-Solving Effectiveness." *Communication Monographs* 55 (1988): 121–142.

Lacoursiere, R. *The Life Cycle of Groups.* New York: Human Sciences, 1980.

Lewin, Kurt. *Resolving Social Conflicts: Selected Papers on Group Dynamics.* New York: Harper & Row, 1948.

Meyers, Renée A., and Brashers, Dale E. "Argument in Group Decision Making: Explicating a Process Model and Investigating the Argument-Outcome Link." *Communication Monographs* 65 (1998): 262–281.

Phillips, Gerald M., and Wood, Julia T., eds. *Emergent Issues in Human Decision Making.* Carbondale: Southern Illinois University Press, 1984.

Poole, Marshall Scott. "Decision Development in Small Groups, III: A Multiple Sequence Model of Group Decision Development." *Communication Monographs* 50 (1983): 321–342.

———. "Do We Have Any Theories of Group Communication?" *Communication Studies* 41 (1990): 237–247.

———. "The Small Group Should be *the* Fundamental Unit of Communication Research." In *Communication: Views from the Helm for the 21st Century.* Edited by Judith S. Trent. Boston: Allyn & Bacon, 1998, pp. 94–97.

Poole, Marshall Scott, and Roth, Jonelle. "Decision Development in Small Groups IV: A Typology of Group Decision Paths." *Human Communication Research* 15 (1989): 323–356.

———. "Decision Development in Small Groups V: Test of a Contingency Model." *Human Communication Research* 15 (1989): 549–589.

Poole, Marshall Scott, Seibold, David R., and McPhee, Robert D. "Group Decision-Making as a Structurational Process." *Quarterly Journal of Speech* 71 (1985): 74–102.

———. "A Structurational Approach to Theory-Building in Group Decision-Making Research." In *Communication and Group Decision-Making.* Edited by Randy Y. Hirokawa and Marshall Scott Poole. Beverly Hills, CA: Sage, 1986, pp. 238–240.

Putnam, Linda L., and Stohl, Cynthia. "Bona Fide Groups: An Alternative Perspective for Communication and Small Group Decision Making." In *Communication and Group Decision Making.* Edited by R. Y. Hirokawa and M. S. Poole. Thousand Oaks, CA: Sage, 1996, pp. 247–278.

———. "Bona Fide Groups: A Reconceptualization of Groups in Context." *Communication Studies* 41 (1990): 248–265.

Rogers, Everett M. *A History of Communication Study: A Biographical Approach.* New York: Free Press, 1994.

Stohl, Cynthia, and Holmes, Michael E. "A Functional Perspective for Bona Fide Groups." In *Communication Yearbook 16.* Edited by Stanley Deetz. Newbury Park, CA: Sage, 1993, pp. 601–614.

Stohl, Cynthia, and Putnam, Linda L. "Group Communication in Context: Implications for the Study of Bona Fide Groups." In *Group Communication in Context: Studies of Natural Groups.* Edited by L. R. Frey. Hillsdale, NJ: Erlbaum, 1994, pp. 285–292.

Tuckman, Bruce. "Developmental Sequence in Small Groups." *Psychological Bulletin* 63 (1965): 384–399.

Chapter 14
Communication and Organizational Networks

Allen, Myria Watkins, Gotcher, M. Michael, and Seibert, Joy Hart. "A Decade of Organizational Communication Research: Journal Articles 1980–1991." In *Communication*

Yearbook 16. Edited by Stanley Deetz. Newbury Park, CA: Sage, 1993, pp. 252–330.

Alvesson, Mats, and Deetz, Stanley. "Critical Theory and Postmodernism Approaches to Organizational Studies." In *Handbook of Organizational Studies.* Edited by S. Clegg, C. Harding, and W. Nord. London: Sage, 1996, pp. 173–202.

Banks, Stephen P., and Riley, Patricia. "Structuration Theory as an Ontology for Communication Research." In *Communication Yearbook 16.* Edited by Stanley A. Deetz. Newbury Park, CA: Sage, 1993, pp. 167–196.

Barker, James R., and Cheney, George. "The Concept and the Practices of Discipline in Contemporary Organizational Life." *Communication Monographs* 61 (1994): 19–43.

Carlone, David, and Taylor, Bryan. "Organizational Communication and Cultural Studies: A Review Essay." *Communication Theory* 8 (1998): 337–367.

Cheney, George. "The Rhetoric of Identification and the Study of Organizational Communication." *Quarterly Journal of Speech* 69 (1983): 143–158.

Cheney, George, et. al. "Democracy, Participation, and Communication at Work: A Multidisciplinary Review." In *Communication Yearbook 21.* Edited by Michael E. Roloff. Thousand Oaks, CA: Sage, 1998, pp. 35–91.

———. *Rhetoric in an Organizational Society: Managing Multiple Identities.* Columbia: University of South Carolina Press, 1991.

Cheney, George, and Tompkins, Phillip K. "Coming to Terms with Organizational Identification and Commitment." *Central States Speech Journal* 38 (1987): 1–15.

Deetz, Stanley. *Democracy in an Age of Corporate Colonization: Developments in Communication and the Politics of Everyday Life.* Albany: SUNY Press, 1992.

———. "Stakeholders and Negotiating the New Social Contracts: A Communication Theory Perspective." In *Communication: Views from the Helm for the 21st Century.* Edited by Judith S. Trent. Boston: Allyn & Bacon, 1998, pp. 153–161.

Delia, Jesse. "The Logic Fallacy, Cognitive Theory, and the Enthymeme: A Search for the Foundations of Reasoned Discourse." *Quarterly Journal of Speech* 56 (1970): 140–148.

Eisenstadt, S. N. *Max Weber on Charisma and Institution Building.* Chicago: University of Chicago Press, 1968.

Etzioni, Amatai. *Modern Organizations.* Englewood Cliffs, NJ: Prentice-Hall, 1964.

Everett, James L. "Communication and Sociocultural Evolution in Organizations and Organizational Populations." *Communication Theory* 4 (1994): 93–110.

Farace, Richard V., Monge, Peter R., and Russell, Hamish. *Communicating and Organizing.* Reading, MA: Addison-Wesley, 1977.

Fayol, Henri. *General and Industrial Management.* New York: Pitman, 1949.

Giddens, Anthony. *Central Problems in Social Theory.* Berkeley: University of California Press, 1979.

———. *Profiles and Critiques in Social Theory.* Berkeley: University of California Press, 1982.

Johnson, H. "A New Conceptualization of Source of Organizational Climate." *Administrative Science Quarterly* 3 (1976): 275–292.

Kovačić, Branislav. "The Democracy and Organizational Communication Theories of Deetz, Mumby, and Associates." *Watershed Research Traditions in Human Communica-*

tion Theory. Edited by Donald P. Cushman and Branislav Kovačić. Albany: SUNY Press, 1995, pp. 211–238.

Kreps, Gary L. "A Field Experimental Test and Revaluation of Weick's Model of Organizing." In *Communication Yearbook 4.* Edited by Dan Nimmo. New Brunswick, NJ: Transaction, 1980, pp. 389–398.

Likert, Rensis. *The Human Organization.* New York: McGraw-Hill, 1967.

———. *New Patterns of Management.* New York: McGraw-Hill, 1961.

Marshall, Judi. "Viewing Organizational Communication from a Feminist Perspective: A Critique and Some Offerings." In *Communication Yearbook 16.* Edited by Stanley Deetz. Newbury Park, CA: Sage, 1993, pp. 122–143.

McPhee, Robert D. "Formal Structure and Organizational Communication." In *Organizational Communication: Traditional Themes and New Directions.* Edited by Robert D. McPhee and Phillip K. Tompkins. Beverly Hills, CA: Sage, 1985, pp. 149–178.

———. "Organizational Communication: A Structurational Exemplar." In *Rethinking Communication: Paradigm Exemplars.* Edited by Brenda Dervin, Lawrence Grossberg, Barbara O'Keefe, and Ellen Wartella. Beverly Hills, CA: Sage, 1989, pp. 199–212.

Monge, Peter R. "The Network Level of Analysis." In *Handbook of Communication Science.* Edited by Charles R. Berger and Steven H. Chaffee. Newbury Park, CA: Sage, 1987, pp. 239–270.

Monge, Peter R., and Eisenberg, Eric M. "Emergent Communication Networks." In *Handbook of Organizational Communication: An Interdisciplinary Perspective.* Edited by Frederic M. Jablin, Linda L. Putnam, Karlene H. Roberts, and Lyman W. Porter. Newbury Park, CA: Sage, 1987, pp. 304–342.

Morgan, Gareth. *Images of Organization.* Beverly Hills, CA: Sage, 1986.

Mumby, Dennis K. *Communication and Power in Organizations: Discourse, Ideology, and Domination.* Norwood, NJ: Ablex, 1988.

———. "Critical Organizational Communication Studies: The Next 10 Years." *Communication Monographs* 60 (1993): 18–25.

———. "The Problem of Hegemony: Rereading Gramsci for Organizational Communication Studies." *Western Journal of Communication* 61 (1997): 343–375.

Pacanowsky, Michael. "Creating and Narrating Organizational Realities." In *Rethinking Communication: Paradigm Exemplars.* Edited by Brenda Dervin, Lawrence Grossberg, Barbara O'Keefe, and Ellen Wartella. Newbury Park, CA: Sage, 1989, pp. 250–257.

Pacanowsky, Michael, and O'Donnell-Trujillo, Nick. "Communication and Organizational Cultures." *Western Journal of Speech Communication* 46 (1982): 115–130.

———. "Organizational Communication as Cultural Performance." *Communication Monographs* 50 (1983): 126–147.

Papa, Michael J., Auwal, Mohammad, and Singhal, Arvind. "Organizing for Social Change Within Concertive Control Systems: Member Identification, Empowerment, and the Masking of Discipline." *Communication Monographs* 64 (1997): 219–249.

Perrow, Charles. *Complex Organizations: A Critical Essay.* Glenview, IL: Scott, Foresman, 1972.

Poole, Marshall Scott. "Communication and Organizational Climate: Review, Critique, and a New Perspective." In *Organizational Communication: Traditional Themes and New Directions*. Edited by Robert D. McPhee and Phillip K. Tompkins. Beverly Hills, CA: Sage, 1985, pp. 79–108.

Poole, Marshall Scott, and McPhee, Robert D. "A Structurational Analysis of Organizational Climate." In *Communication and Organizations: An Interpretive Approach*. Edited by Linda L. Putnam and Michael E. Pacanowsky. Beverly Hills, CA: Sage, 1983, pp. 195–220.

Putnam, Linda L., and Stohl, Cynthia. "Bona Fide Groups: An Alternative Perspective for Communication and Small Group Decision Making." In *Communication and Group Decision Making*. Edited by R. Y. Hirokawa and M. S. Poole. Thousand Oaks, CA: Sage, 1996, pp. 247–278.

———. "Bona Fide Groups: A Reconceptualization of Groups in Context." *Communication Studies* 41 (1990): 248–265.

Richmond, Virginia P., and McCroskey, James C. "Management Communication Style, Tolerance for Disagreement, and Innovativeness as Predictors of Employee Satisfaction: A Comparison of Single-Factor, Two-Factor, and Multiple-Factor Approaches." In *Communication Yearbook 3*. Edited by Dan Nimmo. New Brunswick, NJ: Transaction, 1979, pp. 359–373.

Sackmann, Sonja A. "Managing Organizational Culture: Dreams and Possibilities." In *Communication Yearbook 13*. Edited by James Anderson. Newbury Park, CA: Sage, 1990, pp. 114–148.

Sass, James S., and Canary, Daniel J. "Organizational Commitment and Identification: An Examination of Conceptual and Operational Convergence." *Western Journal of Speech Communication* 55 (1991): 275–293.

Scott, Craig R., Corman, Steven R., and Cheney, George. "Development of a Structurational Model of Identification in the Organization." *Communication Theory* 8 (1998): 298–336.

Siebold, David R. "Groups and Organizations: Premises and Perspectives." In *Communication: Views from the Helm for the 21st Century*. Edited by Judith S. Trent. Boston: Allyn & Bacon, 1998, pp. 162–268.

Simon, Herbert. *Administrative Behavior*. New York: Free Press, 1976.

Stohl, Cynthia. *Organizational Communication: Connectedness in Action*. Thousand Oaks, CA: Sage, 1995.

Stohl, Cynthia, and Holmes, Michael E. "A Functional Perspective for Bona Fide Groups." In *Communication Yearbook 16*. Edited by Stanley Deetz. Newbury Park, CA: Sage, 1993, pp. 601–614.

Stohl, Cynthia, and Putnam, Linda L. "Group Communication in Context: Implications for the Study of Bona Fide Groups." In *Group Communication in Context: Studies of Natural Groups*. Edited by L. R. Frey. Hillsdale, NJ: Erlbaum, 1994, pp. 285–292.

Taylor, Frederick W. *Principles of Scientific Management*. New York: Harper Brothers, 1947.

Taylor, James R. *Rethinking the Theory of Organizational Communication: How to Read an Organization*. Norwood, NJ: Ablex, 1993.

———. "Shifting from a Heteronomous to an Autonomous Worldview of Organizational Communication: Communication Theory on the Cusp." *Communication Theory* 5 (1995): 1–35.

Taylor, James R., Cooren, Francois, Giroux, Nicole, and Robichaud, Daniel. "The Communicational Basis of Organization: Between the Conversation and the Text." *Communication Theory* 6 (1996): 1–39.

Taylor, James R., and Van Every, Elizabeth J. *The Emergent Organization: Communication as its Site and Surface*. Mahwah, NJ: Erlbaum, 2000.

Tompkins, Phillip K., and Cheney, George. "Account Analysis of Organizations: Decision Making and Identification." In *Communication and Organizations: An Interpretive Approach*. Edited by Linda L. Putnam and Michael E. Pacanowsky. Beverly Hills, CA: Sage, 1983, pp. 123–146.

———. "Communication and Unobtrusive Control in Contemporary Organizations." In *Organizational Communication: Traditional Themes and New Directions*. Edited by Robert D. McPhee and Phillip K. Tompkins. Beverly Hills, CA: Sage, 1985, pp. 179–210.

Van Maanen, John, and Barley, Stephen R. "Cultural Organization: Fragments of a Theory." In *Organizational Culture*. Edited by Peter J. Frost and others. Beverly Hills, CA: Sage, 1985, pp. 31–54.

Weber, Max. *The Theory of Social and Economic Organizations*. Translated by A. M. Henderson and Talcott Parsons. New York: Oxford University Press, 1947.

Weick, Carl. *The Social Psychology of Organizing*, 2nd ed. Reading, MA: Addison-Wesley, 1979.

Wert-Gray, Stacia, Center, Candy, Brashers, Dale E., and Meyers, Renée A. "Research Topics and Methodological Orientations in Organizational Communication: A Decade in Review." *Communication Studies* 42 (1991): 141–154.

Chapter 15
Communication and Media

Allor, Martin. "Relocating the Site of the Audience." *Critical Studies in Mass Communication* 5 (1988): 217–233.

Ball-Rokeach, Sandra J., and Cantor, Muriel G., eds. *Media, Audience, and Social Structure*. Beverly Hills, CA: Sage, 1986.

Ball-Rokeach, Sandra J., and DeFleur, Melvin L. "A Dependency Model of Mass-Media Effects." *Communication Research* 3 (1976): 3–21.

Barker, David, and Timberg, Bernard M. "Encounters with the Television Image: Thirty Years of Encoding Research." In *Communication Yearbook 15*. Edited by Stanley Deetz. Newbury Park, CA: Sage, 1992, pp. 209–238.

Baudrillard, Jean. *The Illusion of the End*. Translated by Chris Turner. Cambridge, UK: Polity, 1994.

———. *Simulations*. Translated by Paul Foss, Paul Patton, and Philip Beitchman. New York: Semiotext(e), 1983.

———. *Symbolic Exchange and Death*. Translated by Iain Hamilton Grant. Thousand Oaks, CA: Sage, 1993.

Bauer, Raymond. "The Audience." In *Handbook of Communication*. Edited by Ithiel de sola Pool and others. Chicago: Rand McNally, 1973, pp. 141–152.

———. "The Obstinate Audience: The Influence Process from the Point of View of Social Communication." *American Psychologist* 19 (1964): 319–328.

Bineham, Jeffery L. "A Historical Account of the Hypodermic Model in Mass Communication." *Communication Monographs* 55 (1988): 230–246.

Biocca, Frank A. "Opposing Conceptions of the Audience: The Active and Passive Hemispheres of Mass Communication Theory." In *Communication Yearbook 11.* Edited by James A. Anderson. Newbury Park, CA: Sage, 1988, pp. 51–80.

Blumler, Jay, and Katz, Elihu, eds. *The Uses of Mass Communication.* Beverly Hills, CA: Sage, 1974.

Boulding, Kenneth. "The Medium Is the Massage." In *McLuhan: Hot and Cool.* Edited by Gerald E. Stearn. New York: Dial, 1967, pp. 56–68.

Bryant, Jennings, and Zillmann, Dolf, eds. *Perspectives on Media Effects.* Hillsdale, NJ: Erlbaum, 1986.

Burrowes, Carl Patrick. "From Functionalism to Cultural Studies: Manifest Ruptures and Latent Continuities," *Communication Theory* 6 (1996): 88–103.

Carey, J. W. "Harold Adams Innis and Marshall McLuhan." *Antioch Review* 27 (1967): 5–39.

Carragee, Kevin. "A Critical Evaluation of Debates Examining the Media Hegemony Thesis." *Western Journal of Communication* 57 (summer 1993): 330–348.

Childs, M., and Reston, J., eds. *Walter Lippmann and His Times.* New York: Harcourt Brace, 1959.

Cragan, John F., and Shields, Donald C. *Understanding Communication Theory: The Communicative Forces for Human Action.* Boston: Allyn & Bacon, 1998, pp. 175–207.

Davis, Dennis K., and Baran, Stanley J. *Mass Communication and Everyday Life: A Perspective on Theory and Effects.* Belmont, CA: Wadsworth, 1981.

Davis, Dennis K., and Puckett, Thomas F. N. "Mass Entertainment and Community: Toward a Culture-Centered Paradigm for Mass Communication Research." In *Communication Yearbook 15.* Edited by Stanley Deetz. Newbury Park, CA: Sage, 1992, pp. 3–34.

DeFleur, Melvin L., and Ball-Rokeach, Sandra J. *Theories of Mass Communication.* New York: Longman, 1982.

Elliott, Philip. "Uses and Gratifications Research: A Critique and Sociological Alternative." In *The Uses of Mass Communication.* Edited by Jay Blumler and Elihu Katz. Beverly Hills, CA: Sage, 1974, pp. 249–268.

Ellis, Donald G. *Crafting Society: Ethnicity, Class, and Communication Theory.* Mahwah, NJ: Erlbaum, 1999.

Emmers-Sommer, Tara M., and Allen, Mike. "Surveying the Effect of Media Effects: A Meta-Analytic Summary of the Media Effects Research." *Human Communication Research* 25 (1999): 478–497.

Fiske, John. *Introduction to Communication Studies.* New York: Methuen, 1982.

———. *Reading the Popular.* Winchester, MA: Unwin Hyman, 1989.

———. *Television Culture.* New York: Methuen, 1987.

———. *Understanding Popular Culture.* Winchester, MA: Unwin Hyman, 1989.

Fortner, Robert S. "Mediated Communication Theory." In *Building Communication Theories: A Socio/Cultural Approach.* Edited by Fred L. Casmir. Hillsdale, NJ: Erlbaum, 1994, pp. 209–240.

Fry, Donald L., and Fry, Virginia H. "A Semiotic Model for the Study of Mass Communication." In *Communication Yearbook 9.* Edited by Margaret L. McLaughlin. Beverly Hills, CA: Sage, 1986, pp. 443–462.

Gerbner, George. "Mass Media and Human Communication Theory." In *Human Communication Theory.* Edited by Frank E. X. Dance. New York: Holt, Rinehart & Winston, 1967.

Gerbner, George, Gross, Larry, Morgan, Michael, and Signorielli, Nancy. "A Curious Journey into the Scary World of Paul Hirsch." *Communication Research* 8 (1981): 39.

———. "Living with Television: The Dynamics of the Cultivation Process." In *Perspectives on Media Effects.* Edited by Jennings Bryant and Dolf Zillmann. Hillsdale, NJ: Erlbaum, 1986, pp. 17–40.

Gergen, Kenneth J. *The Saturated Self: Dilemmas of Identity in Contemporary Life.* New York: HarperCollins, 1991.

González, Hernando. "Mass Media and the Spiral of Silence: The Philippines from Marcos to Aquino." *Journal of Communication* 34 (1988): 33–48.

Greenberg, Bradley S., and Salwen, Michael B. "Mass Communication Theory and Research: Concepts and Models." In *An Integrated Approach to Communication Theory and Research.* Edited by Michael B. Salwen and Don W. Stacks. Mahwah, NJ: Erlbaum, 1996, pp. 63–78.

Gronbeck, Bruce. "McLuhan as Rhetorical Theorist." *Journal of Communication* 31 (1981): 117–128.

Grossberg, Lawrence. "Strategies of Marxist Cultural Interpretation." *Critical Studies in Mass Communication* 1 (1984): 392–421.

Hirsch, Paul M. "The 'Scary World' of the Nonviewer and Other Anomalies: A Reanalysis of Gerbner et al.'s Findings on Cultivation Analysis." *Communication Research* 7 (1980): 404.

Huesca, Robert, and Dervin, Brenda. "Theory and Practice in Latin American Alternative Communication Research." *Journal of Communication* 44 (1994): 53–73.

Innis, Harold Adams. *The Bias of Communication.* Toronto: University of Toronto Press, 1951.

———. *Empire and Communications,* 2nd ed. Toronto: University of Toronto Press, 1972.

Jensen, Klaus Bruhn. "When Is Meaning? Communication Theory, Pragmatism, and Mass Media Reception." In *Communication Yearbook 14.* Edited by James A. Anderson. Newbury Park, CA: Sage, 1991, pp. 3–32.

Katz, Elihu. "The Two-Step Flow of Communication." *Public Opinion Quarterly* 21 (1957): 61–78.

Katz, Elihu, Blumler, Jay, and Gurevitch, Michael. "Uses of Mass Communication by the Individual." In *Mass Communication Research: Major Issues and Future Directions.* Edited by W. Phillips Davidson and Frederick Yu. New York: Praeger, 1974, pp. 11–35.

Katz, Elihu, and Lazarsfeld, Paul. *Personal Influence: The Part Played by People in the Flow of Mass Communications.* New York: Free Press, 1955.

Klapper, Joseph T. *The Effects of Mass Communication.* Glencoe, IL: Free Press, 1960.

Lasswell, Harold. "The Structure and Function of Communication in Society." In *The Communication of Ideas.* Edited by Lyman Bryson. New York: Institute for Religious and Social Studies, 1948, pp. 37–51.

Lazarsfeld, Paul, Berelson, Bernard, and Gaudet, H. *The People's Choice.* New York: Columbia University Press, 1948.

Lazarsfeld, Paul, and Merton, Robert K. "Mass Communication, Popular Taste, and Organized Social Action." In

The Process and Effects of Mass Communication. Edited by Wilbur Schramm and Donald Roberts. Urbana: University of Illinois Press, 1971, pp. 554–578.

Leeds-Hurwitz, Wendy. *Semiotics and Communication: Signs, Codes, Cultures.* Hillsdale, NJ: Erlbaum, 1993.

Lindlof, Thomas R. "Media Audiences as Interpretive Communities." In *Communication Yearbook 11.* Edited by James A. Anderson. Newbury Park, CA: Sage, 1988, pp. 81–107.

Lippmann, Walter. *Public Opinion.* New York: Macmillan, 1921.

Mahler, Alwin, and Rogers, Everett M. "The Diffusion of Interactive Communication Innovations and the Critical Mass: The Adoption of Telecommunications Services by German Banks." *Telecommunications Policy* 23 (1999): 719–740.

McCombs, Maxwell. "New Frontiers in Agenda Setting: Agendas of Attributes and Frames." *Mass Communication Review* 24 (1997): 4–24.

McCombs, Maxwell, and Bell, Tamara. "The Agenda Setting Role of Mass Communication." In *An Integrated Approach to Communication Theory and Research.* Edited by Michael B. Salwen and Don W. Stacks. Mahwah, NJ: Erlbaum, 1996, pp. 93–110.

McLuhan, Marshall. *The Gutenberg Galaxy: The Making of Typographic Man.* Toronto: University of Toronto Press, 1962.

———. *The Mechanical Bride.* New York: Vanguard, 1951.

———. *Understanding Media.* New York: McGraw-Hill, 1964.

McLuhan, Marshall, and Fiore, Quentin. *The Medium Is the Massage.* New York: Bantam, 1967.

McQuail, Denis. *Mass Communication Theory: An Introduction.* London: Sage, 1987.

———. "With the Benefits of Hindsight: Reflections on Uses and Gratifications Research." *Critical Studies in Mass Communication* 1 (1984): 177–193.

Meyrowitz, Joshua. "Images of Media: Hidden Ferment—and Harmony—in the Field." *Journal of Communication* 43 (1993): 55–67.

———. *No Sense of Place: The Impact of Electronic Media on Social Behavior.* New York: Oxford University Press, 1985.

Morgan, Michael, and Shanahan, James. "Two Decades of Cultivation Research: An Appraisal and Meta-Analysis." In *Communication Yearbook 20.* Edited by Brant R. Burleson. Thousand Oaks, CA: Sage, 1997, pp. 1–45.

Neuman, W. R. "The Threshold of Public Opinion." *Public Opinion Quarterly* 54 (1990): 159–176.

Noelle-Neumann, Elisabeth. "The Effect of Media on Media Effects Research." *Journal of Communication* 33 (1983): 157–165.

———. "Return to the Concept of Powerful Mass Media." In *Studies of Broadcasting.* Edited by H. Eguchi and K. Sata. Tokyo: Nippon Hoso Kyokii, 1973, pp. 67–112.

———. *The Spiral of Silence: Public Opinion—Our Social Skin.* Chicago: University of Chicago Press, 1984.

———. "The Theory of Public Opinion: The Concept of the Spiral of Silence." In *Communication Yearbook 14.* Edited by James A. Anderson. Newbury Park, CA: Sage, 1991, pp. 256–287.

Palmgreen, Philip. "Uses and Gratifications: A Theoretical Perspective." In *Communication Yearbook 8.* Edited by Robert N. Bostrom. Beverly Hills, CA: Sage, 1984, pp. 20–55.

Pietilä, Veikko. "Perspectives on Our Past: Charting the Histories of Mass Communication Studies." *Critical Studies in Mass Communication* 11 (1994): 346–361.

Potter, W. James. "Cultivation Theory and Research: A Conceptual Critique." *Human Communication Research* 19 (1993): 564–601.

———. *On Media Violence.* Thousand Oaks, CA: Sage, 1999, pp. 11–24.

Protess, David, and McCombs, Maxwell. *Agenda Setting: Readings on Media, Public Opinion, and Policymaking.* Hillsdale, NJ: Erlbaum, 1991.

Rayburn, J. D., II. "Uses and Gratifications." In *An Integrated Approach to Communication Theory and Research.* Edited by Michael B. Salwen and Don W. Stacks. Mahwah, NJ: Erlbaum, 1996, pp. 145–163.

Reese, Stephen D. "Setting the Media's Agenda: A Power Balance Perspective." In *Communication Yearbook 14.* Edited by James A. Anderson. Newbury Park, CA: Sage, 1991, pp. 309–340.

Rogers, Everett M. *Diffusion of Innovations,* 4th ed. New York: Free Press, 1995.

———. *A History of Communication Study: A Biographical Approach.* New York: Free Press, 1994, chaps. 1, 6, 7, 12.

Rogers, Everett M., and Dearing, James W. "Agenda-Setting Research: Where Has It Been, Where Is It Going?" In *Communication Yearbook 11.* Edited by James A. Anderson. Newbury Park, CA: Sage, 1988, pp. 555–593.

Rogers, Everett M., and Kincaid, D. Lawrence. *Communication Networks: Toward a New Paradigm for Research.* New York: Free Press, 1981.

Rogers, Everett M., and Shoemaker, F. Floyd. *Communication of Innovations: A Cross-Cultural Approach.* New York: Free Press, 1971.

Rosengren, Karl Erik. "Culture, Media, and Society: Agency and Structure, Continuity and Change." In *Media Effects and Beyond: Culture, Socializations, and Lifestyles.* Edited by Karl Erik Rosengren. London: Routledge, 1994, pp. 3–28.

Rosengren, K., Wenner, L., and Palmgreen, P., eds. *Media Gratifications Research: Current Perspectives.* Beverly Hills, CA: Sage, 1985.

Rubin, Alan M. "Audience Activity and Media Use." *Communication Monographs* 60 (1993): 98–105.

Rubin, Alan M., and Windahl, Sven. "The Uses and Dependency Model of Mass Communication." *Critical Studies in Mass Communication* 3 (1986): 186.

Salmon, Charles T., and Glynn, Carroll J. "Spiral of Silence: Communication and Public Opinion as Social Control." In *An Integrated Approach to Communication Theory and Research.* Edited by Michael B. Salwen and Don W. Stacks. Mahwah, NJ: Erlbaum, 1996, pp. 165–180.

Scheufele, Dietram A. "Framing as a Theory of Media Effects." *Journal of Communication* 49 (1999): 103–122.

Schoening, Gerard T., and Anderson, James A. "Social Action Media Studies: Foundational Arguments and Common Premises." *Communication Theory* 5 (1995): 93–116.

Sears, David O., and Freedman, Jonathan I. "Selective Exposure to Information: A Critical Review." In *The Process and Effects of Mass Communication.* Edited by Wilbur Schramm and Donald F. Roberts. Urbana: University of Illinois Press, 1971, pp. 209–234.

Severin, Werner J., and Tankard, James W. *Communication Theories: Origins, Methods, Uses.* New York: Hastings House, 1979.

Shaw, Donald L., and McCombs, Maxwell E. *The Emergence of American Political Issues.* St. Paul, MN: West, 1977.

Shoemaker, Pamela J. "Media Gatekeeping." In *An Integrated Approach to Communication Theory and Research.* Edited by Michael B. Salwen and Don W. Stacks. Mahwah, NJ: Erlbaum, 1996, pp. 79–91.

Signorielli, Nancy. "Television's Mean and Dangerous World: A Continuation of the Cultural Indicators Perspective." In *Cultivation Analysis: New Directions in Media Effects Research.* Edited by Nancy Signorielli and Michael Morgan. Newbury Park, CA: Sage, 1990, pp. 85–106.

Signorielli, Nancy, and Morgan, Michael, eds. *Cultivation Analysis: New Directions in Media Effects Research.* Newbury Park, CA: Sage, 1990.

———. "Cultivation Analysis: Research and Practice." In *An Integrated Approach to Communication Theory and Research.* Edited by Michael B. Salwen and Don W. Stacks. Mahwah, NJ: Erlbaum, 1996, pp. 111–126.

Siune, Karen, and Borre, Ole. "Setting the Agenda for a Danish Election." *Journal of Communication* 25 (1975): 65–73.

Sproule, J. Michael. "Progressive Propaganda Critics and the Magic Bullet Myth." *Critical Studies in Mass Communication* 6 (1989): 225–246.

Swanson, David L. "Political Communication Research and the Uses and Gratifications Model: A Critique." *Communication Research* 6 (1979): 36–53.

Swanson, David L., and Babrow, Austin S. "Uses and Gratifications: The Influence of Gratification-Seeking and Expectancy-Value Judgments on the Viewing of Television News." In *Rethinking Communication: Paradigm Exemplars.* Edited by Brenda Dervin, Lawrence Grossberg, Barbara O'Keefe, and Ellen Wartella. Newbury Park, CA: Sage, 1989, pp. 361–375.

Tapper, John. "The Ecology of Cultivation: A Conceptual Model for Cultivation Research." *Communication Theory* 5 (1995): 36–57.

Wolfe, Tom. "The New Life Out There." In *McLuhan: Hot and Cool.* Edited by Gerald E. Stearn. New York: Dial, 1967, pp. 34–56.

Zhu, Jian-Hua, and Blood, Deborah. "Media Agenda-Setting Theory: Telling the Public What to Think About." In *Emerging Theories of Human Communication.* Edited by Branislav Kovačić. Albany: SUNY Press, 1997, pp. 88–114.

Zillmann, Dolf. "Attribution and Misattribution of Excitatory Reactions." In *New Directions in Attribution Research,* vol. 2. Edited by J. H. Harvey, W. J. Ickes, and R. F. Kidd. Hillsdale, NJ: Erlbaum, 1978, pp. 335–368.

CREDITS

P. 19: From *The Conduct of Inquiry* by Abraham Kaplan. Copyright © 1964. Reprinted by permission of Harper & Row Publishers. **P. 21,** Fig. 2.1: Reprinted with permission from Walter L. Wallace (ed.), *Sociological Theory: An Introduction* (New York: Aldine de Gruyter). Copyright © 1969 by Walter L. Wallace. **P. 39:** From *The Ghost in the Machine* by Arthur Koestler. Copyright © 1968 by Arthur Koestler. Reprinted by permission of Macmillan Publishing Co. and Peters, Fraser, & Dunlop, Ltd. **P. 44,** Fig. 3.2: From *Philosophy of Science*, "Behavior, Purpose, and Teleology," by Arturo Rosenbleuth, Norbert Weiner, and Julian Bigelow. Copyright © 1943 by Williams & Wilkins Co. Reprinted by permission of the publisher. **P. 48,** Fig. 3.6: From *American Scientist*, "The Second Cybernetics," by Magoroh Maruyama. Copyright © 1963. Reprinted by permission of the publisher. **Pp. 53, 89:** From *Communication Quarterly*, "Alternative Perspectives for the Study of Human Communication: Critique and Response," by Jesse Delia. Copyright © 1970 by the University of Pennsylvania Press. Reprinted by permission of the University of Pennsylvania Press. **P. 59,** Fig. 4.1: *The Meaning of Meaning* by C. K. Ogden and I. A. Richards. Copyright © 1923. Reprinted by permission of Harcourt Brace Jovanovich and Routledge & Kegan Paul. **Pp. 87, 88:** Adapted from Frans H. van Eemeren, Rob Grootendorst, Sally Jackson, and Scott Jacobs, *Reconstructing Argumentative Discourse*, p. 31. Reprinted by permission of The University of Alabama Press. **P. 111:** From *Communication Monographs*, "The Logic of Message Design: Individual Differences in Reasoning about Communication," by Barbara J. O'Keefe. Copyright © 1988. Reprinted by permission of the Speech Communication Association. **P. 134,** Fig. 7.4: From *Communication and Persuasion: Central and Peripheral Routes to Attitude Change* by Richard E. Petty and John T. Cacioppo. Copyright © 1986 by Springer-Verlag. Reprinted by permission of the publisher. **P. 137,** Fig. 7.5: From Judee K. Burgoon and Herold L. Hale, "Nonverbal Expectancy Violations: Model Elaboration and Application," *Communication Monographs 55* (1988): 64. Reprinted by permission of the Speech Communication Association and the authors. **Pp. 146–147:** From *Symbolic Interactionism: Perspective and Method* by Herbert Blumer. Copyright © 1969. Reprinted by permission of Prentice-Hall, Inc. **P. 150:** From *Frame Analysis: An Essay on the Organization of Experience* by Erving Goffman. Copyright © 1959 by Erving Goffman. Reprinted by permission of Doubleday and Company. **P. 151–152:** From *The Presentation of Self in Every-*day Life by Erving Goffman. Reprinted by permission of Doubleday and Company. **P. 159:** From *Symbolic Interactionism: An Introduction, an Interpretation, an Integration*, Fourth Edition, by Joel M. Charon, p. 49. © 1992. Reprinted by permission of Prentice Hall, Englewood Cliffs, NJ. **Pp. 170–171:** From *Social Accountability and Selfhood* by John Shotter. Copyright © 1984. Reprinted by permission of Basil Blackwell. **P. 171,** Fig. 9.1: Adapted from *Social Accountability and Selfhood* by Hohn Shotter. Copyright © 1984 by Basil Blackwell Publishers. Reprinted by permission of the publisher. **P. 172,** Fig. 9.2: From Judee K. Burgoon and Jerold L. Hale, "Nonverbal Expectancy Violations: Model Elaboration and Application," *Communication Monographs 55* (1988): 64. Reprinted by permission of the Speech Communication Association and the authors. **P. 173,** Fig. 9.3: Adapted from *Communication, Action, and Meaning* by W. Barnett Pearce and Vernon Cronen. Copyright © 1980 by Praeger Publishers. Reprinted by permission of the authors. **P. 173,** Fig. 9.4: Adapted from "Between Text and Context: Toward a Rhetoric of Contextual Reconstruction," by Robert J. Branham and W. Barnett Pearce in *Quarterly Journal of Speech 71* (1985): 23, 25. Reprinted by permission of the authors and publisher. **Pp. 174–175:** From *Communication Action and Meaning* by W. Barnett Pearce and Vernon Cronen. Copyright © 1980 by Praeger Publishers. Reprinted by permission of Praeger Publishers. **P. 175,** Fig. 9.6: From *Communication, Action, and Meaning* by W. Barnett Pearce and Vernon Cronen. Copyright © 1980 by Praeger Publishers. Reprinted by permission of the authors. **Pp. 178–180:** From *Class, Codes, and Control: Theoretical Studies Toward a Sociology of Language* by Basil Bernstein. Copyright © 1971 by Routledge and Kegan Paul. Reprinted by permission of the publisher. **Pp. 198–200:** From *Communication Monographs*, "Organizational Communication as Cultural Performance," by Michael E. Pacanowsky and Nick O'Donnel-Trujillo. Copyright © 1983 by the Speech Communication Association. Reprinted with permission. **P. 224:** From *Speaking Freely: Unlearning the Lies of the Fathers' Tongues* by Julia Penelope. Copyright © 1990 by Pergamon Press. Reprinted by permission of the publisher. **P. 238:** From *Explorations in Interpersonal Communication*, "A Relational Approach to Interpersonal Communication," by Frank E. Millar and L. Edna Rogers. Copyright © 1976 by Sage Publications. Reprinted by permission of the publisher. **P. 265,** Fig. 13.1: *A Social Psychology of Group Processes for Decision-Making* by Barry Collins and Harold

AUTHOR INDEX

Subject Index